The Protestant Crusade
1800-1860

Professor Ray Allen Billington was born in
Bay City, Michigan, and studied at the University of Wisconsin, the University of
Michigan, and Harvard University. He is
the author of *Westward Expansion, Westward Movement in the United States,* and
The Far Western Frontier. He is at present
Senior Research Associate at the Henry E.
Huntington Library, San Marino, California.

The
Protestant Crusade
1800-1860

*A Study of the Origins
of American Nativism*

by
Ray Allen Billington

Q

QUADRANGLE PAPERBACKS

Quadrangle Books / *Chicago*

Foreword

THIS book owes much of whatever merit it may possess to Professor Arthur Meier Schlesinger of Harvard University. I began my study of American nativism as a graduate student in Professor Schlesinger's course in The Social and Intellectual History of the United States. His interest in my term paper on "The Social Significance of Know-Nothingism" led me to delve further into the subject, and with his encouragement I expanded the material into a doctoral dissertation, "The Origins of American Nativism, 1800–1844," which I submitted at Harvard University in 1933. Since that time he has prodded me into gathering new material and rewriting the entire work.

In this whole process Professor Schlesinger has been both a guide and an inspiration. His genius allowed him to see the true implications of the study while it was still in its early stages. He has read the manuscript during every step in its compilation, making valuable suggestions and contributing many of the basic ideas. His encouragement has lightened the years spent in gathering material and his expert criticism has given my work whatever literary qualities and scholarly accuracy it may have. My debt to Professor Schlesinger is more than that of student to teacher, for he has been more than a teacher. His meticulous scholarship, leavened by genial humor and kindly interest, will inspire me throughout a lifetime.

Great as is my debt to Professor Schlesinger, this acknowledgment would not be complete without a due recognition of the generosity of many others who have contributed much toward this book. Professor Arthur C. Cole, of Western Reserve University, is indirectly responsible for its appearance, for it was he who first interested me in the subject of American social history. The Right Reverend Monsignor Peter Guilday, of the Catholic University of America, has read sections of the manuscript and given me constant encouragement by his helpful suggestions and scholarly interest. Professor James Blaine Hedges, of Brown University, has been kind enough to criticize the manuscript in various stages of its composition. Dr. Leften Stavrianos, formerly of Clark University, and Mr. Franklyn Palmer, of Springfield, Massachusetts, have aided me in checking footnotes and preparing the index.

I am particularly grateful to the officials of the various libraries where I have gathered material. My debt to Mr. Clarence S. Brigham, Director, to Mr. Robert W. G. Vail, Librarian, and to their staff at the American Antiquarian Society is especially great, for it was in the magnificent collections of that institution that most of my sources were found. The officials of the Harvard College Library, the Boston Public Library, the Massachusetts Historical Society, the Boston Atheneum, the Massachusetts State House Library, the Brown University Library, the Yale University Library, the New York Public Library, the Library of the Union Theological Seminary, the Library of Congress, and the Burton Historical Collection of Detroit have likewise contributed much toward the completion of this work.

The editors of the *Mississippi Valley Historical Review,* the *Catholic Historical Review,* and the *New England Quarterly* have graciously allowed me to use material first published in the columns of those journals.

Finally I am grateful to my wife, Mabel Crotty Billington, whose keen insight into the errors of my style has allowed me to smooth out a few of the literary wrinkles found herein.

RAY ALLEN BILLINGTON.

Contents

Maps

The Protestant Crusade
1800-1860

I

The Roots of Anti-Catholic Prejudice

HATRED of Catholics and foreigners had been steadily growing in the United States for more than two centuries before it took political form with the Native American outburst of the 1840's and the Know-Nothingism of the 1850's. These upheavals could never have occurred had not the American people been so steeped in antipapal prejudice that they were unable to resist the nativistic forces of their day. This prejudice had been well grounded before the first English settlement and was fostered by the events of the entire colonial period.

The England from which the American colonists came was a land newly emerged from the Reformation, and its people, like all converts to a cause, were enthusiastic about the new and bitter against the old. Both the Puritans of Massachusetts Bay and the Anglicans of Virginia, despite their many differences, shared the fear and hatred of Rome. Their grandfathers had been alive when Henry VIII led the nation away from the Church; their fathers had witnessed wars with Catholic France which threatened to restore the Pope to his former supremacy and had despaired for their faith with the ascension to the throne of Bloody Mary. The settlers themselves had been cradled in an England more bitter against Catholicism then than at any other time. They had seen the constant plot and counterplot of the reigns of Elizabeth and James I when Catholic forces threatened to engulf their land: the Irish uprising at Kerry, the projected attack of the Spanish armies under the Duke of Kent through Scotland, the intrigue of the Jesuits,

Campion and Parsons, the efforts to restore Mary Queen of Scots to the throne, the threat of the Armada, and the Gunpowder Plot. This intrigue had fastened the conviction in the minds of all loyal subjects that Catholicism was a dangerous and constantly threatening force.

The hatred with which the average Englishman of the early seventeenth century looked upon Popery was due largely to the antinational character of that religion, for Catholicism was feared not only as an antagonistic theology, but also as a force through which the English government itself was to be overthrown. From the time of Henry VIII Catholic France and Spain, constantly plotting with the papal party in England to displace the Tudor and Stuart monarchs, had found many Englishmen who were sufficiently loyal to their papal principles to sacrifice national independence as a means of restoring English allegiance to the Pope. These views were strongly resented by the majority of the people who, under the influence of the violent nationalism of that time, believed that England could save herself from Catholic aggression only by assuming the role of aggressor. Anti-Catholicism, therefore, became a patriotic as well as religious concern.

Equally vital in shaping the No-Popery sentiment in England was the quasi-historical propaganda then being widely circulated. This propaganda was sponsored by leaders of the continental Reformation, who recognized the lack of appeal of theological arguments and resorted to the popular depiction of the history of the Papacy to win converts from among the common people. If they could prove that the old order had broken down and was steeped in corruption and iniquity, they would have sufficient justification in the popular mind for the creation of a new religious system. Luther himself had endorsed this use of history, writing in an introduction to Robert Barnes' *History of the Popes* in 1536 that "all who have the spirit of Christ know well that they can bring no higher or more acceptable praise offering to God than all they can say or write against this bloodthirsty, unclean, blasphemic whore of the devil." [1]

Luther not only endorsed the writing of this form of propaganda, but actively co-operated in a collaborative history of the Church published by a group of Magdeburg scholars in 1559. While this work was of some merit, it bristled with misrepresentations designed to discredit Catholicism; in it appeared for the first time the legend of the Popess Joan and the story of the six thousand children's heads found in the nunnery fish pond in the days of Gregory I. This Magdeburg history was principally important for the imitations which it inspired, for during the seventeenth and eighteenth centuries several hundred historical works appeared in England, all based upon it and all forsaking reason and tolerance in favor of avowed propaganda. In 1757 a history of the Popes, deemed mild by comparison with other similar histories, characterized Popery as a combination of: "Avarice, ambition, sacrilege, perjury, an absolute contempt of everything sacred, the most amazing dissoluteness, every species of debauchery in excess, a total depravity and corruption of doctrine and morals." [2] Catholic historians attempted to refute these errors but the English monarchs, staunch in their defense of Protestantism, erected an effective barrier around their country to prohibit the introduction of any work upholding Catholicism.

The intense No-Popery spirit engendered by this propaganda was reflected by the English lawmakers. The Acts of Supremacy and Uniformity in 1559 began a whole series of legislative attacks on Rome which grew increasingly violent as the years passed. Catholics were excluded from the legal profession, from teaching and from the universities, priests were banished under penalty of death, poorer Catholics were afforded the same treatment, and even the well-to-do were ordered to stay within five miles of their estates and attend the services of the Church of England.[3] With the Gunpowder Plot, popular indignation was reflected in even more rigorous penal laws. The fines against those Catholics who failed to attend the established church were increased, all were required to take a new oath of allegiance to the king, and the professions which they could enter were still further narrowed. Even the sacred precincts of their homes were violated with a provision that all "married recusants" should be placed in prison and kept there until their freedom had been purchased by their mates. Had these laws been enforced, all Catholics would have been driven from England, and even the tolerant attitude of the early Stuarts did not protect them from serious persecution.

The settlers who came to America, reared in this atmosphere of intolerance, carried with them to the new land the same hatred of Popery which characterized the England of that day. In America natural conditions intensified this attitude even though there were almost no Catholics in the colonies during the seventeenth century and national security was never threatened. The isolation of the people, the introspection to which they resorted in their wilderness homes, the distance which separated the colonies from the mother country and from Europe, all fostered the bigotry which they had brought from the old world. The liberal currents that gradually diminished the intolerance of the people of those lands did not flow toward America, for the colonial clergy and governmental leaders had been trained in the intolerant England of the early seventeenth century and harbored the ideas and prejudices they had learned there long after the original counterparts had been swept away. In this sense the colonies represented a form of intellectual inbreeding, where the worst as well as the best of the original characteristics of the people were unduly magnified.

This is the only explanation that makes possible an understanding of the intense anti-Catholic feeling in seventeenth century America. Theoretically, the settlers should have been

won from their intolerance by the liberalizing influences of the
frontier; actually they continued to think of the Pope as an
"old rogue, who had a respectable pair of horns"; and the city
of Rome as "a great big lady of pleasure, patched and painted
and drunk and dressed in scarlet." [4] England encouraged this
attitude by the official pronouncements of its ministers and by
the restrictions against Catholics contained in the colonial charters.[5] The lot of the Catholic in such a setting would necessarily
be little better than in England itself.

There were two centers for the development of No-Popery
sentiment in the seventeenth century: Maryland and Massachusetts. In Maryland those who raised a cry against Rome had at
least a tangible basis for their fears, for the few Catholics who
were in the new world were concentrated in that colony, lured
by the charter which had been granted in 1632 to Sir George
Calvert, Lord Baltimore, making him a patron of all churches
to be established within his grant. Because Baltimore was a
Catholic this clearly implied toleration, although the crown
dared not make a more explicit statement for fear of offending
Massachusetts and Virginia.[6] English Catholics failed to respond in large numbers to the inducements offered by Calvert,
preferring to protect their home estates rather than follow the
will-o'-the-wisp of fortune to a new land, and Maryland, from
the point of view of population, had been a Protestant colony
from its first settlement. The proprietor's control, however,
kept the Catholic party in power there, much to the alarm of
conformists in England and America.[7]

The presence of this handful of Papists in Maryland not
only inspired almost continuous strife within the colony, but
embroiled Baltimore in several conflicts with neighboring provinces. Virginia in particular showed her open antipathy when
William Clayborne, backed by popular opinion and his official
position as secretary of the colony, sailed in a ship named *The
Reformation* to lay claim to Kent Island. While this island

was clearly within Baltimore's grant, both Clayborne and the people of Virginia obviously believed that the claims of a Catholic could be ignored without forfeiting either eternal happiness or the harmony of empire.[8]

Within Maryland the troubles confronting the proprietor were even more serious. The Protestant majority was growing so rapidly that by 1648 Baltimore, realizing that conformists must be given control of the legislature and knowing Protestant intolerance, secured the passage of the Toleration act of 1649 in an effort to protect the Catholics for whom the colony had been founded.[9] His precautions were in vain. Maryland Protestants, stimulated by the Puritan Revolution which was taking place in England just as they were securing control of the colony, began their legislative career by banishing Baltimore from his own province. In 1654 the Toleration act was repealed and in its stead a law enacted providing that "none who profess to exercise the Popish religion, commonly known by the name of Roman Catholic religion, can be protected in this province." The act did not receive Cromwell's approval, but before it could be disallowed several Catholics had been heavily fined.[10] Moreover, the home government did allow an order excluding Catholics from office holding.[11]

The Glorious Revolution in England proved the signal for a new outburst of anti-Catholic activity in the colony when Protestants seized the opportunity to rise against the political appointees of Baltimore. The rebellion which took place was headed by John Coode and was built almost entirely upon the cry of No-Popery. Stories circulated of a popish plot to kill all Protestants were so widely believed that an "Association in Arms for the Defense of the Protestant Religion and Assisting the Rights of King William and Queen Mary" was formed, making such a show of strength that Baltimore's officers turned over the colony to Coode without question. Coode made his first act as governor a proclamation against Popery and the legislature chosen under him neglected civil affairs for two years while it petitioned the crown for protection against vague Catholic threats. The new monarchs, taking these petitions seriously, finally voided the charter, deposed Baltimore and took over Maryland as a royal province. Catholics found the only bright spot in the whole series of events when the Anglican church was established in the colony, depriving the Puritans who had engineered the uprising, of the influence which they had sought.[12]

The other southern colony, Virginia, had few Catholics within its borders but it was sufficiently alarmed by the nearness of those of Maryland to provide for defense against their activities. In 1641 and 1642 the House of Burgesses provided that thereafter no "popish recusants" were to hold office in the colony and that any priest entering its borders was to leave immediately on being warned by the governor.[13] Catholics were likewise disenfranchised and threatened with other persecution.[14]

Massachusetts Bay was a center of No-Popery sentiment second only to Maryland and with far less justification, for there were few Catholics in the colony and the danger from Catholic France was not pressing until the close of the seventeenth century. This intolerance on the part of the Bay Colony's settlers grew from their Puritan religion; they were impatient of any dissent, and loyal to the dictum of John Cotton that "it was toleration that made the world anti-Christian." These beliefs presaged harsh treatment to all Catholics and other dissenters from the established order. In the first year of the colony's history Sir Christopher Gardiner was banished on the mere suspicion that he was one of the Pope's subjects and an elder of the Watertown church was removed from office for audaciously stating that the Church of Rome was a true church.[15] In 1647 the General Court decreed that any Jesuit or priest coming within the colony was to be banished and, if he should return, executed.[16] Twelve years later that body enacted a law against celebrating the popish festival Christmas, a measure made necessary by the disgraceful tendency of some of the younger colonists to flaunt the plain will of God by making merry on the birthday of His Son.[17] The Puritan fathers likewise attempted to protect their people from Romish influences by forbidding the importation of all Irish persons into the colony,[18] by administering oaths of allegiance which specifically denounced the Pope [19] and by fast days where prayers were offered that "the Protestant interest may be advanced in our English nation." [20] They objected strenuously to the proclamation of religious liberty by James II in 1687,[21] and welcomed the antipapal section of the charter of 1691 which granted "liberty of Conscience . . . in the Worship of God to all Christians [except Papists]." [22]

In New York the No-Popery sentiment led to a minor revolution. Thomas Dongan, sent out by James II as governor, was a Catholic, and his tolerant administration attracted a steady stream of members of his faith seeking a haven from persecution. This circumstance caused undue alarm among the people and the spread of rumors that a popish stronghold was to be created in the colony. When an opportunity for resistance was offered by the Glorious Revolution in England, the people of New York united against Catholicism, placed Jacob Leisler in power, and called an assembly which agreed "to suspend all Roman Catholics from Command and Places of Trust." Leisler also ordered the arrest of "reputed Papists," denied the franchise to all excepting Protestant freemen,[23] and began a vigorous campaign of harrying Romanists from the colony.[24] Although Leisler was soon deposed in favor of a regularly appointed governor, the anti-Catholic spirit still held sway, with officeholders being required to sign a declaration against the doctrine of transubstantiation and to take the sacrament according to the rites of the Church of England.[25]

In the other colonies the feeling against Popery, while no less high, was less outspoken. The first provincial assembly of

New Hampshire bestowed the franchise on "all Englishmen, being Protestants" who met the age and property qualifications. A year later, in 1681, the annual fast day proclamation called on the people to ask divine favor against the "popish party throughout the world" and in 1696, when the conspiracy against William and Mary aroused Protestant prejudice, the New Hampshire legislature required all inhabitants to take an oath against the Pope and the doctrines of the Catholic religion.[26] North Carolina extended "full liberty of conscience to all, excepting Papists" [27] and although the New Haven colony persecuted only Quakers,[28] its anti-Catholic sentiments were shown when it urged New York to pass more violent laws against "knowne Papists" than those conceived by Leisler.[29] Only in Rhode Island [30] and Pennsylvania were Catholics safe from persecution, although in the latter colony English monarchs forced the tolerant Quaker assembly to exclude Catholics from office.[31]

So general was this anti-Catholic sentiment in America that by 1700 a Catholic could enjoy full civil and religious rights only in Rhode Island, and even here it is doubtful what the interpretation of the liberal statutes might have been. This No-Popery legislation had had no legitimate basis in most colonies, for Catholics were virtually nonexistent and only the inherited bigotry of the Protestant settlers motivated their enactment of penal statutes. With the outbreak of the French and Spanish wars in 1690 the situation changed. For more than half a century England and her colonies were to be engaged in an almost continuous conflict with these Catholic powers, and every Catholic within the colonies was looked upon as a potential enemy who might let his papal allegiance supersede his loyalty to the crown by co-operating with the armies of French Canada and Spanish Florida against the settlers. Americans now felt the same Catholic threat against their national existence that the English had felt in the days of Elizabeth.

This fear was expressed by a marked stiffening of the laws against Catholics, particularly in the border colonies which were open to attack from the enemies of England. In the south, where Spain constantly threatened through Florida, every attempt was made to keep the new frontier colony of Georgia free from Catholics who might prove disloyal to the mother country. While the trustees of the colony encouraged immigration from Germany and from northern Ireland, they took pains to specify that all should be Protestants [32] and appointed an inspector who was to make sure that no followers of the Pope entered the region.[33] Catholics were granted no liberty of conscience,[34] and oaths denouncing transubstantiation were required of all officeholders after 1743.[35] Virginia, with less excuse than Georgia, showed similar alarm. Rumors that the Papists and Indians were plotting together "to cut the throats of the Protestants" [36] inspired the House of Burgesses to pass laws preventing Catholics from acting as guardians,[37] from serving as witnesses,[38] or from settling in large groups.[39] Finally, with the outbreak of the Seven Years War, Virginia disarmed all Papists within the colony and decreed that none could keep a horse valued at more than five pounds, a provision evidently intended only to annoy.[40] North Carolina and South Carolina did not go as far as Virginia, but a rigid system of oaths prevented Catholics in those two colonies from holding important offices or enjoying the free exercise of their religion,[41] and in North Carolina they were, after 1755, forbidden to serve as guardians.[42]

Maryland was even more rigorous in its treatment of Papists. Although the colony was not menaced by border attacks, the presence of a large number of Catholics [43] alarmed Protestants who believed that these Papists must be kept closely in check to prevent them from allying with the French and Indians. The first outbreak of hostilities was seized as an excuse to disarm all known Romanists, and while these arms were subsequently restored,[44] many Protestants favored a continuation of the policy long after all danger had passed.[45] Existing laws placed many obstacles in the way of the free exercise of Catholicism, but as the French danger grew more acute with the outbreak of Queen Anne's War, it was felt that the present statutes were insufficient [46] and in 1704 "An Act to Prevent the Growth of Popery" was adopted by the legislature. This prevented any "Popish Bishop Priest or Jesuit" from baptizing a child of Protestant parents, or practicing his religion, or attempting to win converts, under threat of a heavy fine and imprisonment. The same measure threatened deportation to any "Papist or Person making profession of the Popish Religion" who ventured to teach school or instruct the young,[47] while another law passed at the same time levied a heavy tax on Irish servants "to prevent the Importing of too great a number of Irish Papists." [48] It was immediately recognized that these laws were too severe and that they would, if enforced, subject Catholics to undue hardships. Before the year was out they were changed to allow priests to exercise their religious functions in private homes but in no other places.[49] In this form the laws remained in force for the balance of the colonial period.

The anti-Catholic spirit of the Maryland assembly was revived in 1716 when a measure was passed forbidding public offices to any person attending "popish assemblies" or hearing mass.[50] Two years later, at the insistence of the governor, the legislature limited the franchise to those who would take the necessary Protestant oaths.[51] Again in the 1740's Catholics were forbidden to join militia companies [52] and any priest who attempted to make converts was declared guilty of treason and subject to the usual penalties for that offense.[53] So serious had the lot of Catholics within the colony become that Charles Carroll, whose son was to sign the Declaration of Independence, was dispatched to seek a refuge for his fellow believers in French Louisiana. Probably a considerable exodus from Maryland was prevented only by the refusal of France to allow the establishment of such a settlement.

Although little actual legislation was passed to inflict disabilities on Catholics in Maryland, much was projected, and only a political division between the upper and lower branches of the assembly and the tolerant attitude of Governor Horatio Sharpe prevented the enactment of measures which might have resulted in serious persecution. The lower house, where most of the No-Popery measures were to originate, showed increasing alarm over Catholic activity between 1751 and 1753, but confined its objections to addresses to the governor pleading for his co-operation in enforcing earlier penal legislation.[54]

By this time, war with France had broken out in the back country and rumors were flying about the province of popish plots and of a combined Negro-Indian-Papal uprising against the government.[55] These reports, together with the general unrest, led the lower house to adopt several anti-Catholic laws in 1754, limiting the troops who could serve in the colonial armies to Protestants,[56] proposing a heavy tax on Catholics, [57] and providing for the confiscation of all property belonging to any "Popish Priest or Jesuit." [58] Resolutions were also sent to the governor asking him to investigate popish plots designed to aid the French, particularly in St. Mary's County where, it was rumored, Catholics "had drank the pretender's health." [59] While the governor consented to receive these petitions and promised investigations, the measures proposed by the lower house all failed to pass the upper body. This negation was due to the political situation rather than to a desire to support a popular cause, for several members of the legislature who voted against the antipapal legislation were defeated in the next election, solely on this ground.[60]

This manifestation of public favor united the 1755 legislature sufficiently to allow the passage of a measure forcing all Catholics in the colony to pay a land tax double that assessed against Protestants and although the governor opposed the bill he was afraid to block it in the face of an aroused opinion.[61] A careful investigation was also made of the conduct of Catholics in the colony, the magistrates in each county being required to submit detailed reports on their activities, a practice which was continued for several years.[62] The reluctant consent given by Governor Sharpe to this legislation so turned Protestants against him that he was repeatedly called on to defend himself before the royal officers [63] and an attempt was made on the part of the assembly to send a commission to England in the hopes of securing more support for antipapal legislation there than could be obtained from this tolerant administrator.[64] Despite his efforts Catholics had few religious or civil liberties in Maryland at the close of the colonial period.

The middle colonies were more directly concerned with the eighteenth century French wars than Virginia and Maryland, New York and Pennsylvania particularly being open to attack from Canada. Both colonies showed a marked anti-Catholic spirit in their efforts to protect their borders. In Pennsylvania the council considered several rumors of French and popish plots to overthrow the government and the possibility of checking the Catholic danger by forbidding Irish immigration,[65] but no actual steps were taken until the outbreak of the Seven Years War when French activity in the back country was so effectively portrayed by the clergy as a papal design that even the tolerant legislature with its Quaker traditions became alarmed.[66] Catholics were disarmed, forbidden to serve in the militia, burdened with additional taxation,[67] and those living in the colony were listed so that their conduct could be closely watched against any attempted uprising.[68] Although a legislative attempt to prevent Catholics from holding land was blocked by the governor,[69] the assembly did succeed in forbidding Catholic settlement in a projected western colony planned to offset French influence on the frontier.[70]

As early as 1698 New York protected herself from Catholic dangers by requiring that every Papist in the colony, under threat of imprisonment, be disarmed and give bond as security of good behavior.[71] These laws were strengthened in 1700 with the passage of an "Act Against Jesuits and Popish Priests," forbidding them to enter the colony under penalty of life imprisonment and imposing fines upon any who might harbor them.[72] In the following year the franchise was denied to all members of the papal church.[73] Although the inhabitants believed themselves so well protected that further legislation was not necessary, anti-Catholic feeling continued high. When a fort and several houses were burned down in 1741 a popish plot was immediately feared and one poor wretch who was suspected of being a priest was hanged before the excitement died down.[74] The other middle colonies were well protected from any French Catholic attack; nevertheless they showed the effect of the current No-Popery sentiment. New Jersey in 1701 ruled that only Protestants should be exempt from the penal laws relating to religion [75] and Delaware, on its separation from Pennsylvania, prevented Catholic churches and societies from receiving or holding real estate.[76]

The New England colonies in the eighteenth century continued to hold the same intolerant attitude toward Catholicism to which they had adhered since their founding. The French wars gave them a better excuse for their attitude, for the presence of French priests and emissaries promised to disrupt the entire system of defense upon which the New Englanders depended. The essence of this system lay in keeping the Iroquois and other border tribes loyal to England, for their open enmity would aid the French and bring disaster to the western outposts and even their neutrality would divert the French, unwilling to arouse the hostility of these New York Indians, from the up-country New York settlements, to attacks on the New England frontier. Any French Catholic activity among these tribes might lead them to friendship with France, thereby jeopardizing New England.

That the New England colonies recognized this situation was clearly shown by their activities following the outbreak of the French wars. Massachusetts was so well protected by previous legislation that there was no need of additional laws to curb Popery within the province, but the government was concerned with Catholic influence among the Indians. Governor Bellomont first called this to the attention of the General Court in 1700,[77] and four years later that body required the registration of all Frenchmen within the province and the immediate imprisonment of all French Catholics.[78] Their fears were given a basis in 1718 when the "Jesuite Sebastian Ralle" converted a number of Maine Indians who immediately began a series of raids against the Massachusetts settlements. His operations and insolent letters to governing officials kept the colony in a turmoil for three years; rewards for his capture and protests to the French in Canada accomplished nothing, although one expedition sent against him did succeed in destroying his house and seizing his papers.[79] Ralle's influence over the eastern Indians convinced the Massachusetts governors that vigilance was necessary to prevent similar French Catholic activity in the west.

Connecticut, which had granted toleration to Catholics from the time of its founding, denied them the right to hold office in 1724[80] and in 1743 did away with all protection which previous laws had afforded them, making its impossible for a Catholic church to exist in the colony.[81] The state of the popular mind was illustrated by the harsh treatment accorded a harmless group of Moravians when the rumor spread that they were Jesuits in disguise who intended to work among the Indians.[82] In New Hampshire an oath renouncing Rome was imposed on the legislature in 1752.[83]

The hatred of Catholicism nurtured during the long period

of French warfare was not allowed to die down after the Peace
of Paris, for between 1763 and 1774 persistent propaganda was
carried on, largely through the pulpit, which kept the people
aroused against Popery.[84] An effective lecture series was
founded at Harvard in 1750 by Paul Dudley "for the detecting
and convicting and exposing of the idolatry of the Romish
church: their tyranny, usurpations, damnable heresies, fatal
errors, abominable superstitions, and other crying wickedness
in her high places." These widely publicized speeches attracted
much attention and were normally circulated in pamphlet
form.[85] Antipapal feeling was attested even in the everyday
life of the colonies: one New England constable refused to
publish a king's letter when he suspected that it tolerated Romanism [86] and when singing was first permitted in a Connecticut service a deacon rushed from the church shouting "Popery! Popery!" [87] Even a game called "Break the Pope's Neck"
was a popular diversion around the New England firesides.[88]
School books such as the *New England Primer* were normally
anti-Catholic in sentiment and were illustrated with grotesque
pictures of the Pope, while by 1774 *A Master Key to Popery*
and similar propaganda works were being advertised in
America.[89]

The spirit engendered by these attacks on Popery played at
least a minor part in stirring up the sentiment against England
which culminated in the Revolution. Colonial resentment found
a target in the Quebec act of 1774. This measure, designed to
extend toleration to the Catholics in Quebec and to include in
that province the French settlers of the Ohio country, was
magnified by the colonists into a Rome-manipulated coup to
establish Popery on their borders. They believed that an autocratic king had sought an alliance with an equally autocratic
Pope and that the two would combine to crush the spirit of
liberty in America. The storm of protest against the measure
was an indication of the extent of this feeling. The patriotic

press deplored the act as "openly countenancing Popish con-
spiracies" designed only to array Catholic Canadians against
Protestant Americans.[90] "We may live," one journal declared,
"to see our churches converted into mass houses and our lands
plundered by tythes for the support of the Popish clergy. The
Inquisition may erect her standard in Pennsylvania and the city
of Philadelphia may yet experience the carnage of St. Bartholomew's Day." [91] Many of the pamphleteers supporting the
colonial cause touched on its ill effects, insisting that the measure actually established Romanism rather than tolerating it and
warning that:

> If Gallic Papists have a right
> To worship their own way
> Then farewell to the Liberties,
> Of poor America.[92]

The act was likewise attacked from pulpits everywhere in
the colonies. Ministers maintained that it originated in the
"Popish schemes of men who would gladly restore the race of
Stuart, and who look on Popery as a religion most favorable
to arbitrary power." [93] Petitions from individuals, from groups
and from the Continental Congress protested to the king and
people of Great Britain that England had no right to "establish a religion, fraught with sanguinary and impious tenets, or,
to erect an arbitrary form of government, in any part of the
world." [94] One clergyman in New Hampshire described the
state of the popular mind when he wrote, several years later:

We were all ready to swear, that this same George, by granting
the Quebec Bill . . . had thereby become a traitor; had broken his
coronation oath; was secretly a Papist; and whose design it was to
oblige this country to submit itself to the unconstitutional powers of
the English monarch, and, under him, and by his authority, be given
up and destroyed, soul and body, by that frightful image with seven
heads and ten horns. The real fears of Popery, in New England,
had its influence; it stimulated many timorous pious people to send

their sons to join the military ranks in the field, and jeopardize their lives in the bloody contest. The common word then was, "No King, No Popery." [95]

This feeling remained so strong through the early part of the Revolution that the president of Princeton University believed the common hatred of Popery caused by the Quebec act the only thing which cemented the divergent religious groups in the colonies together sufficiently to allow them to make war,[96] an opinion which was shared by English observers.[97]

The excitement created by the Quebec act led to the revival and spread of a popular American holiday, Pope Day. This American counterpart of the English Guy Fawkes Day, celebrated on November 5 of each year, had originated in New England when the Puritans, finding it difficult to celebrate the delivery of James I from assassination when they had themselves been responsible for the execution of his son, had begun the practice of an annual parade ending in the burning of an effigy of the Pope. The ceremony was usually participated in by the lower elements of Boston and other New England towns who marched through the streets bearing effigies of the Pope and Devil, shooting firecrackers, and demanding money from householders. In Boston a rivalry developed between the north and south ends so that each group carried its own Pope, meeting in a general combat to try to capture the rival effigies.[98]

While Pope Day had been celebrated in New England since the Restoration, the practice did not spread over the remaining colonies until the passage of the Quebec act. The enmity to Catholicism kindled by that measure led to the immediate establishment of the custom as far south as Charleston, South Carolina, where, in 1774, the Pope, Pretender, and Old Nick were burned in a bonfire of English tea.[99] Attempts of royal authorities to stamp out the practice failed [100] and even after the start of the Revolution soldiers in the army planned on staging a giant celebration of the day. Such a move would have been disastrous, for Congress was then attempting to secure the aid of Catholic Canada against England. Rumors of the plan reached Washington and he immediately issued an order deploring the "ridiculous and childish custom of burning the effigy of the Pope" and expressing surprise that there should be men in the army "so void of common sense as not to see the unpropriety of such a step at this juncture. . . ." [101] This terse warning not only prevented the soldiers' celebration, but also ended Pope Day in America. There are no records of the practice after 1775.

The anti-Catholic spirit continued strong through the early years of the Revolution, despite efforts of Washington and others who, for diplomatic reasons, tried to check its spread. Some of the colonies insisted on disarming Papists just as they had when at war with France,[102] and others exercised a rigid supervision over those serving with the militia.[103] The presence of Catholics among the British troops was often commented upon as evidence of the king's design to subject the colonies to Popery should the revolutionary movement fail [104] and public celebrations in the interest of the patriotic cause frequently included outbursts against Rome.[105] It was evident that the popular fear of Catholicism was not being neglected by the patriots and that they intended to continue to stress the close association between papal and royal tyranny as a means of stirring sentiment against England. So well grounded was this feeling that John Trumbull, writing his *McFingal,* believed that England

> Struck bargains with the Romish churches
> Infallibility to purchase ;
> Set wide for Popery the door,
> Made friends with Babel's scarlet whore.[106]

The attitude did not endure through the war, but shifted abruptly with the French alliance in 1778 which made Catholic

France no longer an enemy, but an actual friend. Enemies of
Catholicism had an opportunity to see French soldiers and officers and were forced to concede that, if these Papists had horns
at all, they were at least well concealed. The No-Popery cry
was still raised, but it was voiced now by the American Tories
who naturally sought to discredit the alliance by appealing to
the well-known prejudices of the colonists. Loyalist newspapers
such as *Rivington's Royal Gazetteer* and the *Pennsylvania
Ledger* charged that the patriots had made a grave mistake in
forsaking Protestant England for Catholic France and that the
inevitable result of the union would be the establishment of
Popery in America.[107]

The patriots refused to be duped by these arguments and for
the duration of the war remained mute, if not actually more
tolerant. Leading Catholics who had come to accept minor
persecution as part of their lot expressed amazement at the kind
treatment accorded them. Bishop Carroll, visiting Boston,
wrote:

It is wonderful to tell what great civilities have been done to me
in this town, where a few years ago a popish priest was thought to
be the greatest monster in creation. Many here, even of their principal people, have acknowledged to me that they would have crossed
to the opposite side of the street rather than meet a Roman Catholic
some time ago. The horror which was associated with the idea of a
papist is incredible; and the scandalous misrepresentations by their
ministers increased the horror every Sunday.[108]

Anti-Catholicism in America was too deeply rooted to expire
even under the influence of the French alliance and the liberal
spirit of the Declaration of Independence. Protestants might
be willing to admit that the 30,000 Catholics in the country
could do them no harm, but the state constitutions which were
adopted during the Revolution showed them still wary. The
New Jersey constitution of 1776 contained a safeguarding
clause that no Protestant could be denied enjoyment of his civil

rights because of religion and barred Catholics from state offices.[109] The North Carolina constitution of the same year contained a similar provision in respect to officeholders, as did that
of Georgia.[110] In Connecticut the colonial charter was retained
with its restrictions on Catholics. Vermont in its constitution
drafted in 1777 required an oath from officeholders in which
they owned "and professed the Protestant Religion." [111] The
New York constitution of the same year attempted to limit the
franchise to Protestants by requiring that all persons naturalized in the state must swear to give up allegiance to any foreign
power or potentate in civil or ecclesiastical matters.[112] A year
later South Carolina directly established Protestantism as the
state religion.[113] New Hampshire adopted a series of constitutions between 1779 and 1784, all of them containing anti-
Catholic clauses.[114] The Massachusetts body of laws of 1780,
justly famed for its liberalism, empowered townships to lay
taxes "for the instruction of the public worship of God,
and for the support and maintenance of public protestant
teachers of piety, religion and morality, in all cases where such
provision shall not be made voluntarily." [115] By the end of the
Revolution seven states, Massachusetts, New Hampshire, New
Jersey, Connecticut, North Carolina, South Carolina, and
Georgia, specified Protestant officeholders and other states inflicted additional liabilities on Catholics in their constitutions.

Despite this trend in the states, the federal Constitutional
Convention remained aloof from this old controversy, North
Carolina being the only state voting against the clause by which
Congress was forbidden to impose any religious test on officeholders. There was more dissension in the ratifying conventions. In Massachusetts, in North Carolina, and perhaps in
Connecticut, the fear was openly expressed that popish officials
might lead the country toward Rome and that some religious
test was necessary.[116] One delegate to the Massachusetts convention wrote that he "shuddered at the idea that Roman Catho-

lics, Papists, and Pagans might be introduced into office and that Popery and the Inquisition may be established in America." [117] These sentiments were in a distinct minority and both the framers and ratifiers showed a liberality highly commendable in view of the traditions in which they had been reared.

The tolerant spirit of the Constitution was infectious. Its first amendment, preventing Congress from making any "law respecting an establishment of religion, or prohibiting the free exercise thereof," served as a model to discourage bigotry throughout the land. At the same time other factors discredited the intolerance of the colonists. Immigration was almost at a standstill and the menace of the Catholic and foreigner seemed a thing of the past. The people, too, were so engrossed in the task of developing their country in the years of prosperity which followed the adoption of the Constitution that they had no time to reflect on the danger of Popery. This prosperity led to the rapid expansion of the frontier, especially in the north where western New York was being peopled between 1790 and 1810. Most of the settlers to this region came from the upland sections of New England, depriving the older states of many former inhabitants. Leaders of these older states, alarmed at this exodus and engaging in Puritan self-scrutiny to discover the cause, admitted that one expelling factor lay in the harsh religious laws they were inflicting on their people. This realization led to a series of changes, made easier by the activity of such prominent reformers as Thomas Jefferson and James Madison who, through their efforts to establish religious freedom and equality in Virginia, set a pattern of toleration which other states could follow.[118]

The changes in the eastern states, carried on between the adoption of the Federal Constitution and 1820, took the form of repeated recastings of the frames of government to instill into them this new spirit of liberalism. Vermont dropped the clause in its constitution inflicting liabilities on Catholics in 1786,[119] South Carolina followed in 1790 and New Hampshire attempted a similar change in 1792, although public opinion was still too strong to allow it to be carried out.[120] Before the turn of the century Delaware enfranchised every free white male inhabitant of the state regardless of creed, and Georgia did away with its religious test for officeholders.[121] Connecticut abolished her established Congregationalism in 1818.[122] Four years later New York removed her objectionable oath against Catholics.[123] Massachusetts had already abolished the religious test and in 1833 effected the complete separation of church and state.[124]

The attitude of the national government during the early years of the Republic, however, showed that while legally Catholics might be given an equal voice with Protestants, they were still viewed with suspicion. The Federalist party inherited the fear of Papists and foreigners which had been the property of the loyalists during the latter part of the Revolution, and while in power extended the probationary period for naturalization first to five years [125] and finally in the Alien act of 1798, to fourteen years. These nativistic measures were inspired partly by the French war and partly by a natural antipathy toward foreigners which was beginning to take shape within the party. Federalists not only resented the whole-hearted allegiance which aliens gave to the Jeffersonians, but were afraid that the foreign-born might plunge the country into the European arena and upset the policy of isolation which was even then taking root. Particularly were the Irish immigrants suspected of furthering such schemes. They had formed the American Society of United Irishmen to aid their countrymen during the Irish insurrections and their activity had sufficiently alarmed the English government to occasion a direct protest from the British minister.[126] The Alien and Sedition acts, adopted in the same year that the Irish insurrections broke forth, were aimed at this phase of alien activity as well as at a possible French menace.

It was no accident that Mathew Lyon, an Irish Catholic, was first to suffer under the Sedition act, nor that the alien riots in Philadelphia were staged just outside a Catholic church.[127]

The election of Thomas Jefferson to the presidency quieted these nativistic sentiments, which, after 1800, lived on only in New England where the Federalists still retained some of the power they had lost throughout the nation. There prejudice found voice when the New Englanders, goaded by economic disaster, called the Hartford Convention which proposed an amendment to the Federal Constitution barring naturalized citizens from civil office in the federal government. This proposal was inspired partly by the disappointment of the New Englanders that naturalized citizens were joining the Jeffersonian party and aiding their opponents in the war with England which was ruining the section's trade, and partly by the enthusiasm with which the New England Irish welcomed the war as a means of revenge upon England. A blow at the Jeffersonian government was a blow at these Irish, and such an opportunity was relished by the Federalists.

The point of view of the Hartford Convention was far from typical of the country as a whole. For the most part the people had been won over to the program of toleration inspired by the Declaration of Independence, the Federal Constitution and the liberal constitutions of many of the states. There were only a handful of Catholics in the country [128] and they were obviously not to be feared, so that those who still harbored nativistic sentiments were motivated more by the remembrance of a dreadful power than by the presence of instruments of that power. There was every indication in the period before 1820 that the No-Popery sentiment of colonial days had completely vanished. New forces in the next decades were to show that the same intolerant abhorrence of Rome endured beneath the surface, but it was not until those new forces were brought into play that anti-Catholic sentiment again assumed a prominent role in national life.

NOTES

[1] M. V. Hay, *A Chain of Error in Scottish History* (New York, 1927), 3–4. An excellent brief discussion of the entire Engish background for the colonial anti-Catholic sentiment is in Sister Mary Augustina, *American Opinion of Roman Catholicism in the Eighteenth Century* (New York, 1936), 11–62. This book offers a full and scholarly treatment of American No-Popery sentiment for the entire colonial period.

[2] Cited in *Ibid.*, 10. The English writings are interestingly studied by a Catholic in Herbert Thurston, *No Popery: Chapters on Anti-Papal Prejudice* (London, 1930).

[3] W. K. Jordan, *The Development of Religious Toleration in England from the Beginning of the English Reformation to the Death of Queen Elizabeth* (Cambridge, 1932).

[4] Bishop John England thus summarized the character of colonial writing on Catholicism. *Catholic Miscellany*, July 4, 1832. Quoted in Peter Guilday, *The Life and Times of John England, First Bishop of Charleston, 1786–1842* (New York, 1927), II, 424–425.

[5] Thus the Virginia charters of 1606, 1609 and 1612 stated that the colonists should be considered as Englishmen and "obliged to the duties attached to that character" which included conformity to the established church.

[6] Sanford H. Cobb, *The Rise of Religious Liberty in America* (New York, 1902), 363–365.

[7] Baltimore recognized the danger of Protestant attack so well that his first instructions to the Catholic colonists urged "all Acts of Roman Catholic Religion to be done as privately as may be" and that religious discussion be avoided. Matthew P. Andrews, *The Founding of Maryland* (Baltimore, 1933), 151.

[8] Cobb, *Rise of Religious Liberty*, 369.

[9] N. D. Mereness, *Maryland as a Proprietary Province* (New York, 1901), 430–433.

[10] H. L. Osgood, *The American Colonies in the Seventeenth Century* (New York, 197), III, 130–131.

[11] Mereness, *Maryland as a Proprietary Province*, 38.

[12] *Ibid.*, 38–42.

[13] William W. Hening (ed.), *The Statutes at Large, being a Collection of all the Laws of Virginia (1619–1792)* (Philadelphia and New York, 1823), I, 268–269. *Executive Journals of the Council of Colonial Virginia* (Richmond, 1925–1930), II, 336.

[14] Hening, *Statutes . . . of Virginia*, III, 172–238.

[15] James T. Adams, *The Founding of New England* (Boston, 1921), 149–150; Cobb, *Rise of Religious Liberty*, 173–174.

[16] *Records of the Governor and Company of the Massachusetts Bay in New England (1628–1686)* (Boston, 1853–1854), II, 193.

[17] *Ibid.*, IV, pt. i, 366.

[18] *Ibid.*, III, 291, 294.

[19] *Ibid.*, V, 193-194.

[20] N. B. Shurtleff (ed.), *Records of the Colony of New Plymouth in New England (1620-1692)* (Boston, 1855-1861), VI, 58.

[21] Cobb, *Rise of Religious Liberty*, 232-233.

[22] *Acts and Resolves, Public and Private, of the Province of The Massachusetts Bay* (Boston, 1869-1922), I, 14. Cited as *Massachusetts Province Laws.*

[23] *Documents Relating to the Colonial History of the State of New York* (Albany, 1856-1887), II, 71, III, 689; "Leisler's No Popery Revolt in New York," *American Catholic Historical Researches*, XIV (July, 1897), 123-125.

[24] *Documents Relating to the Colonial History of . . . New York*, II, 41, III, 585-586, 609, 617, 674.

[25] Cobb, *Rise of Religious Liberty*, 337.

[26] *Ibid.*, 299.

[27] Charles L. Raper, *North Carolina: A Study in English Colonial Government* (New York, 1904), 31.

[28] *Public Records of the Colony of Connecticut, 1636-1776* (Hartford, 1850-1890).

[29] *Documents Relating to the Colonial History of . . . New York*, III, 589.

[30] An alleged Rhode Island law declared "That all men professing Christianity and of competent estates and of civil conversation who acknowledge and are obedient to the civil magistrate, though of different judgment in religious affairs (Roman Catholics only excepted) shall be admitted freemen." It has been demonstrated that this law was not passed in 1664, as claimed, but was added by a committee of revisal, preparing the statutes of the colony for printing in 1744. S. S. Rider, "Inquiry Concerning the Origin of the Clause in the Laws of Rhode Island (1718-1783), Disfranchising Roman Catholics," *Rhode Island Historical Tracts,* 2nd series, No. 1. Roger Williams had no love for Catholics despite his tolerance of them. See "Letters of Roger Williams Referring to 'Romanists' and the 'Popish Leviathan,'" *American Catholic Historical Researches*, n.s., V (January, 1909), 3-4.

[31] John Gilmary Shea, *History of the Catholic Church in the United States* (New York, 1886-1892), I, 365.

[32] *Colonial Records of the State of Georgia (1732-1774)* (Atlanta, 1904-1916), I, 77-79, 119, 134-135, 137-140, 200, X, 432.

[33] *Ibid.*, II, 86.

[34] *Ibid.*, I, 21.

[35] *Ibid.*, I, 420.

[36] *Executive Journals of the Council of Colonial Virginia*, I, 104, 375-376, 519.

[37] *Ibid.*, I, 433-434, 436, 526.

[38] Hening, *Statutes . . . of Virginia*, III, 298.

[39] *Executive Journals of the Council of Colonial Virginia*, I, 139.

[40] Hening, *Statutes . . . of Virginia*, VII, 35-39; *Journals of the House of Burgesses of Virginia (1727-1776)* (Richmond, 1905-1915), VIII, 382, 385, 388, 392.

[41] *Statutes at Large of South Carolina* (Columbia, 1836-1841), II, 232;

Colonial Records of North Carolina (Raleigh, Winston and Goldsboro, 1886–1914), III, 67, 91, 110, V, 1136, VI, 525, VIII, 513–514.

[42] *Colonial Records of North Carolina*, XXV, 319, 416, XXIII, 577.

[43] A census taken in 1708 showed that there were 2,974 Catholics in a total white population of 37,743. *Archives of Maryland* (Baltimore, 1883–   ), XXV, 258–259.

[44] *Ibid.*, XIX, 36–37, XX, 224.

[45] *Ibid.*, XIX, 389–390. The council recommended a general disarming of Catholics in 1696, but the assembly refused to concur.

[46] Rumors were current of a popish plot against the colony. *Ibid.*, XXV, 178, 582–583.

[47] *Ibid.*, XXVI, 340–341.

[48] Such a measure had first been passed in 1699 levying a tax of 20 shillings. *Ibid.*, XXII, 497–500. It was re-enacted in 1704 (*Ibid.*, XXIV, 401, XXVI, 289–292) and at regular periods thereafter. In 1717 the tax was increased to 40 shillings, *Ibid.*, XXVII, 371, XXVIII, 165, 198, XXX, 326, 331, 505, 515, XXXVII, 553, XLII, 8, 14, 26, 27, 78, 143, 602, XLIV, 646, XLVI, 615–616, L, 568.

[49] This act was passed on December 9, 1704, and was to apply for only eighteen months. *Ibid.*, XXVI, 431–432. In 1706 it was extended for another twelve months (*Ibid.*, XXVI, 630–631) and in 1707 made permanent at the insistence of Queen Anne. *Ibid.*, XXVII, 147–148.

[50] *Ibid.*, XXX, 520.

[51] *Ibid.*, XXXIII, 120, 144, 149–150, 211, 224. The bill is printed in *Ibid.*, XXXIII, 287–289. Objections to this harsh treatment caused such "uneasiness and heart burnings to his Majesty's faithful subjects" that the assembly was thrown open to any complaints which Catholics might voice. When few appeared, the governor and legislature congratulated each other on exposing the pretended claims of the Papists. *Ibid.*, XXXIII, 479–485, 503, 516, 533, 620–623.

[52] *Ibid.*, XXVIII, 315, 340.

[53] *Ibid.*, XXVIII, 363–364. The proclamation was issued in 1746.

[54] *Ibid.*, XLVI, 549–550, 593–594, 602, L, 51–59, 198–205.

[55] *Ibid.*, XXXI, 47–49, 54, 72–73, 125, 208–210, VI, 501–505, 512, 518.

[56] *Ibid.*, L, 618.

[57] *Ibid.*, L, 548.

[58] *Ibid.*, L, 514–519.

[59] *Ibid.*, XXI, 487–489, 504, 506–507. Sharpe to Calvert, *Ibid.*, VI, 240.

[60] Sharpe to Calvert, October 26, 1755. *Ibid.*, VI, 302.

[61] *Ibid.*, VI, 419–420, 496.

[62] *Ibid.*, VI, 408, XXXI, 80–81, 85–89, 245–247.

[63] *Ibid.*, VI, 323, IX, 117, 315–318, 346, 400.

[64] Sharpe to Calvert, August 11, 1755. *Ibid.*, VI, 264.

[65] *Pennsylvania Colonial Records* (Philadelphia, 1852–1853), I, 299, III, 546–547; *Pennsylvania Archives* (Philadelphia and Harrisburg, 1852–   ), 4th Series, I, 455, 896.

[66] Typical sermons and expressions of views of ministers are in *American Catholic Historical Researches*, XI (April, 1894), 58–64; *Ibid.*, XVII (April, 1900), 74–77. One clergyman referred to "These dogs of Hell, *Popish* super-

stition and French tyranny" and told of how "The *slaves* of France and the
Inquisitors of Rome are approaching to crush us."

[67] *Pennsylvania Archives,* III, 131–132. The act was passed after petitions
from the inhabitants of the state had requested the measure as necessary for
their safety. *Pennsylvania Colonial Records,* VI, 503.

[68] The census showed that there were only 1,365 Catholics in the colony.
Pennsylvania Archives, III, 144–145.

[69] *Pennsylvania Colonial Records,* IX, 596.

[70] *American Catholic Historical Researches,* VI (October, 1889), 148.

[71] *Documents Relating to the Colonial History of . . . New York,* IV, 160.

[72] *Ibid.,* IV, 713.

[73] Joseph M. Flynn, *The Catholic Church in New Jersey* (Morristown,
N. J., 1904), 8.

[74] *Documents Relating to the Colonial History of . . . New York,* III, 198,
201.

[75] *Archives of the State of New Jersey* (Newark, 1880–1906), II, 407–408.

[76] *Laws of the State of Delaware* (Newcastle, 1797), I, 271–274.

[77] *Massachusetts Province Laws,* VII, 644.

[78] *Ibid.,* VIII, 54.

[79] The continued alarm of Massachusetts at Ralle's activity can be traced
in: *Ibid.,* X, 14, 28–29, 111, 125–126, 200; *Journals of the House of Representatives of Massachusetts* (Boston, 1915–   ), II, 61, 63, 270–272, 330–331,
338–339, 341, III, 89, 104, 117–118, 150, 152, 163, 188–192, IV, 54, 101–102.

[80] *Public Records of the Colony of Connecticut,* VI, 466.

[81] *Ibid.,* VIII, 522.

[82] *Ibid.,* VIII, 521.

[83] *Ibid.,* VIII, 229–230.

[84] Typical were: Thomas Foxcroft, *The Saints United Confession, in Disparagement of their own Righteousness . . . in Opposition to Popish Abuse
and Calumny* (Boston, 1750); Andrew Eliot, *A Sermon Preached October
25th, 1759. Being a Day of Public Thanksgiving Appointed by Authority for
the Success of the British Arms this year, especially in the Reduction of
Quebec, the Capital of Canada* (Boston, 1759), expressing thanks that Quebec
had fallen and that Popery might be driven from America; and Samuel
Cooper, *A Discourse on the Man of Sin* (Boston, 1774), in which an attempt
was made to show that the Catholic church was the Man of Sin referred to in
the Bible. A few early anti-Catholic books also appeared at this time, notably
*A Protestant's Resolution shewing his Reasons why he will not be a Papist
Digested* (Boston, 1746); Robert Barclay, *The Anarchy of the Ranters and
. . . the hierarchy of the Romanists . . . refuted in . . . [an] Apology for
the Quakers* (Philadelphia, 1770). See also *A Letter from a Romish Priest
in Canada to One who was taken Captive in her Infancy, and Instructed in
the Romish Faith, but some time ago returned to this her Native Country,
with an answer thereto, by a Person to whom it was Communicated* (Boston,
1729). The attitude of the clergy and the influence of colonial literature are
thoroughly discussed in Sister Mary Augustina, *American Opinion of Roman
Catholicism in the Eighteenth Century,* 63–113 and 165–214.

[85] Dudley had been an outspoken opponent of Catholicism through his life
and had published *An Essay on the Merchandize of slaves and souls of Men;*

with an Application thereof to the Church of Rome (Boston, 1731). The lectures continued without interruption until 1857 when loss of income forced their discontinuance until 1888. They were delivered every third or fourth year through the nineteenth century, despite protests from the Harvard faculty against this "indecent and unjust" attack on the "Romish church." *American Catholic Historical Researches*, n.s. I (April, 1905), 129. Typical Dudleian lectures of this period were Jonathan Mayhew, *Popish Idolatry; a Discourse . . . in the chapel of Harvard College* (Boston, 1765); Edward Wigglesworth, *Some Thoughts upon the Spirit of Infallibility, claimed by the Church of Rome . . . a Dudleian Lecture* (Boston, 1757); Edward Wigglesworth, *The Authority of Tradition Considered at the Lecture founded by the Hon. Judge Dudley in Harvard College, November 5, 1777* (Boston, 1778); John Tucker, *The Validity of Presbyterian Ordination Argued from Jesus Christ's being the Founder, the sole Legislator and Supreme Head and Ruler of the Christian Church . . . a Dudleian Lecture* (Boston, 1778). See also Sister Mary Augustina, *American Opinion of Roman Catholicism in the Eighteenth Century*, 127–138.

[86] *Records of the Governor and Company of the Massachusetts Bay in New England*, IV, pt. II, 72–73.

[87] Elias B. Sanford, *A History of Connecticut* (Hartford, 1888), 128.

[88] "Journal of Philip Fithian," *American Historical Review*, V (January, 1900), 297.

[89] *American Catholic Historical Researches*, XXI (January, 1904), 15.

[90] *Pennsylvania Journal*, October 5, 1774, quoted in *American Catholic Historical Researches*, VI (October, 1889), 157–158, 163.

[91] *Pennsylvania Packet*, October 31, 1774. Quoted in Shea, *History of the Catholic Church*, II, 137.

[92] Quoted in *American Catholic Historical Researches*, VI (October, 1889), 160–161. See also: *A Full Vindication of Measures of Congress from Calumnies of their Enemies* (New York, 1774), 26.

[93] Sermons of this nature are printed in *American Catholic Historical Researches*, VI (October, 1889), 163–169.

[94] Address to the People of Great Britain, adopted September 5, 1774. *Journal of the Continental Congress* (Washington, 1904–1931), I, 83. See also *Ibid.*, I, 88, 117. Private addresses were sent from groups in New York and Pennsylvania as well as other colonies. *Documents Relating to the Colonial History of . . . New York*, VIII, doc. XLV; *American Catholic Historical Researches*, VI (October, 1889), 163; *Ibid.*, n.s., III (July, 1907), 244; *Colonial Records of North Carolina*, X, 127, 225.

[95] Daniel Barber, *The History of My Own Times* (Washington, 1827), 17.

[96] The statement was made by President John Witherspoon in a sermon quoted in *American Catholic Historical Researches*, VI (October, 1889), 147.

[97] *The Right of Great Britain Asserted* (London, 1776), 32.

[98] Pope Day is described in John G. Shea, "Pope Day in America," *United States Catholic Historical Magazine*, II (January, 1888), 1–7, in *American Catholic Historical Researches*, n.s. III (April, 1907), 134–136, and in such contemporary documents as *South End Forever North End Forever. Extraordinary Verses on Pope Night, or, A Commemoration of the Fifth of November, giving a History of the Attempt, made by the Papishes, to*

blow up King and Parliament, A.D. 1588, together with some Account of the Pope himself, and his wife, Joan (Boston, n.d.). A brief but thorough modern discussion is in Sister Mary Augustina, *American Opinion of Roman Catholicism in the Eighteenth Century,* 256–261.

99 *Pennsylvania Journal,* November 9, 1774, quoted in *American Catholic Historical Researches,* VI (October, 1889), 159; Shea, "Pope Day in America," *loc. cit.,* 5–7.

100 "Catholic Recollections of Samuel Breck," *American Catholic Historical Researches,* XII (October, 1895), 146.

101 George Washington, *The Writings of George Washington* (New York, 1889–1893), III, 200–201.

102 Hening, *Statutes . . . of Virginia,* IX, 282. Statute of May, 1777.

103 *Pennsylvania Colonial Records,* XII, 176–177.

104 *New York Journal or General Advertiser,* November 3, 1774, *Pennsylvania Journal and Weekly Advertiser,* January 3, 1776, both quoted in *United States Catholic Historical Magazine,* II (January, 1888), 93–98.

105 A liberty pole was set up in New York in March, 1775, and patriots carried about a large flag on which was printed: "George III. Rex and the Liberties of America: No Popery." *American Catholic Historical Researches,* VI (October, 1889), 163.

106 *American Museum,* I, 313. John Adams represented the popular mind when he wrote Jefferson asking: "Can a free government possibly exist with the Roman Catholic religion?" *American Catholic Historical Researches,* VI (October, 1889), 170.

107 A number of these articles are quoted in *American Catholic Historical Researches,* VI (October, 1889), 175–177, and in the *United States Catholic Historical Magazine,* II ·(April, 1888), 202–205.

108 Quoted in Thomas O'Gorman, *History of the Roman Catholic Church in the United States* (New York, 1895), 277.

109 Isaac A. Cornelison, *The Relation of Religion to Civil Government in the United States of America* (New York, 1895), 99, 101. An excellent discussion of this whole phase of constitution making is in Sister Mary Augustina, *American Opinion of Roman Catholicism in the Eighteenth Century,* 350–393.

110 *Colonial Records of North Carolina,* X, 870; *Revolutionary Records of the State of Georgia (1769–1784)* (Atlanta, 1908), I, 285.

111 James H. Dohan, "Our State Constitutions and Religious Liberty," *American Catholic Quarterly Review,* XL (April, 1915), 295.

112 *Ibid.,* 290.

113 Cornelison, *Relation of Religion to Civil Government,* 101–103.

114 Mary P. Thompson, "Anti-Catholic Laws in New Hampshire," *Catholic World,* LI (April–May, 1890), 193–197. The New Hampshire constitution restricted office holding to Protestants and contained a clause similar to that in the Massachusetts constitution concerning Protestant teachers. The clause preventing Catholics from holding office was finally repealed in 1876.

115 Shea, *History of the Catholic Church,* II, 156.

116 Jonathan Elliot (ed.), *The Debates in the Several State Conventions, on the Adoption of the Federal Constitution* (Washington, 1836), II, 118–120, 148–151, 202, III, 191–200.

117 *Ibid.*, II, 148.

118 Richard J. Purcell, *Connecticut in Transition, 1775–1818* (Washington, 1918), 414–418.

119 Dohan, "Our State Constitutions and Religious Liberty," *loc. cit.*, 295. *Records of the State of Rhode Island and Providence Plantations in New England* (Providence, 1856–1865), IX, 674–675.

120 Cornelison, *The Relation of Religion to Civil Government*, 103–104; Dohan, "Our State Constitutions and Religious Liberty," *loc. cit.*, 228.

121 John Bach McMaster, *A History of the People of the United States* (New York, 1888–1913), V, 379.

122 Purcell, *Connecticut in Transition*, 419.

123 Dohan, "Our State Constitutions and Religious Liberty," *loc. cit.*, 292.

124 Purcell, *Connecticut in Transition*, 419–420.

125 The debate on the measure was decidedly anti-Catholic in tone. Claude G. Bowers, *Jefferson and Hamilton* (Boston, 1925), 264.

126 Edward M. Condon, "Irish Immigration to the United States Since 1790," *Journal of the American Irish Historical Society*, IV (Boston, 1904), 89.

127 Paul J. Foik, "Anti-Catholic Parties in American Politics, 1776–1860," *Records of the American Catholic Historical Society of Philadelphia*, XXXVI (March, 1925), 45.

128 Bishop Carroll estimated that there were 35,000 Roman Catholics in the United States in 1790 in a total population of about 3,000,000. Half of these lived in Maryland. The acquisition of Louisiana added a large number but members of the sect were insignificant numerically for many years. Guilday, *Life and Times of John England*, I, 7.

II

The No-Popery Cry Is Raised
1820-1829

NATIVISM had not been completely submerged by the wave of toleration which swept the country in the early years of the Republic, for there were many who still distrusted Rome. These latent fears were kept alive by a small but persistent propaganda which lasted through the postrevolutionary period. Much of this was supplied by the Dudleian lectures, which were usually extremely bitter against Catholicism and widely circulated.[1] Many newspapers and magazines adopted an anti-Catholic policy as a matter of course, and while embarking on no conscious crusade against Rome, managed to instill such hatred into their readers that as early as 1793 prominent Catholic clergymen felt called upon to complain.[2] In the same year America witnessed its first controversy between Protestant and Catholic champions when a Boston clergyman accepted a challenge from a priest of that city and the two voiced their opinions in a lengthy series of articles in the Boston *Gazette*.[3] By 1800 both native and foreign propaganda books were beginning to appear.[4]

The scarcity of these early works clearly indicated the lack of interest in the Catholic question. It was not until new forces had stimulated inherent prejudices that the No-Popery crusade took real form in America. These new forces, apparent for the first time during the decade of the 1820's, stirred ancient antipathies to the point where an anti-Catholic movement could become an important factor in the nation's life.

The advent of foreign immigration on a large scale was probably the most important causal force leading to this revival. Europe, engaged in almost constant warfare between the time of the American Revolution and the final defeat of Napoleon in 1815, had for nearly half a century been in no position to loose her natives upon American soil,[5] but with peace both the situation and the attitude of the powers changed radically. The surplus population which had found employment during the inflationary war years now hung menacingly over countries already alarmed by the enunciation of the grimly suggestive Malthusian theory. Foreign governments hastened to remove all obstacles from the paths of their nationals, who, suffering in the usual postwar depression, sought homes in the new world. This exodus was hastened by the effects of the industrial revolution. Machine methods of manufacture that had been introduced during the war years to keep pace with an artificial prosperity meant a steady decline of wages, as the productivity of each workman was increased, and of employment. The pay scale in England declined from one half to one third between 1810 and 1820 while at the same time thousands were thrown from employment and onto the relief rolls.[6] In Ireland a bad situation was made worse by the constant drain of wealth from the country under the absentee system.

These conditions forced the English government to interest itself in emigration, particularly for the Irish. There was little desire to send them to the United States, for Britain naturally did not want to increase the population strength of a country so recently its enemy in the War of 1812. Canada offered a more convenient outlet and several grants to aid emigration to this colony were made between 1823 and 1827,[7] but the bleak, sparsely settled Canadian lands were little to the liking of the Irish, and eventually nearly all of them made their way to the United States. The movement of Irish to America was fostered also by the New Brunswick lumber trade which came into being with the development of the Irish cooperage industry. Nearly every sea port along the southern and western coast of Ireland annually sent out lumber vessels that offered cheap and convenient transportation to passengers. Once in Canada, these Irish could help load the lumber ships to earn the few dollars necessary to take them to the United States on the gypsum vessels plying to the New England ports, or they could make the long trek overland to the settled communities that they sought.[8] Thousands of peasants took advantage of this opportunity and a constant stream of settlers found its way into New England from Canada.[9]

This Irish immigration, together with a steadily increasing influx from England and northern Europe, greatly alarmed Americans who, long accustomed to virtual isolation, felt unable to cope with the problem of assimilation. Many wondered if these thousands of foreigners could be absorbed or if they would engulf the native population and threaten the American institutions so cherished in that day of nationalism. Actually the United States profited by this alien flood. The manufacturing plants, fostered by the War of 1812, needed laborers; the frontier was being pushed back more rapidly than ever before; a network of internal improvements was being spread through the east. Unlimited manpower was necessary if these projects were to be carried through on the scale of which Americans dreamed—and immigration could supply that manpower.

While aliens were welcomed on these grounds by some, they aroused the antipathy and distrust of a far larger group. This hostility was particularly acute along the northeastern seaboard where the concentration of foreigners caused the full impact of the immigrant invasion to be felt in exaggerated form. New York, Philadelphia, Boston, Baltimore, and other cities became aware almost overnight of hitherto unknown problems which were directly traceable to the alien flood. Particularly alarming was the increase in pauperism which, while caused largely by the rapidly shifting industrial conditions, could be blamed entirely on the immigrants, for many of them, although not inherent paupers, had exhausted their slender resources in reaching America and needed help before they could re-establish themselves. Charitable organizations formed by their own countrymen to aid them in reaching the west proved utterly inadequate in handling the large number of newcomers,[10] who remained cooped in the eastern cities, cared for by the municipal and state authorities, and a constant burden on the taxpayers. Thus in 1835 there were 4,786 native-born paupers and 5,303 foreign paupers in the almshouses of New York, Philadelphia, Boston, and Baltimore,[11] and the Massachusetts legislature was so alarmed that it seriously considered erecting separate workhouses for aliens.[12] New York City in 1837 was spending $279,999 annually for the support of its poor, three fifths of whom were foreign born.[13] At that time there were 105,000 paupers in the United States, more than one half of whom were immigrants, and it was estimated that the annual bill for their support was more than four million dollars.[14]

American resentment at this new burden was especially great because it was generally believed that many of the paupers were deliberately sent to the United States by European powers anxious to escape the burden of their support. Although newspaper and magazine accounts of the arrival of paupers still clad in the uniforms of the European workhouses [15] were probably exaggerated, there was some justification for the complaints. The English Poor Law of 1834 empowered rate payers to raise money on the security of the poor rates to aid emigration, a law which was extended to Ireland four years later.[16] Although the law specified that paupers assisted in this way should be sent to the British colonies, the majority of those going to Canada eventually made their way to the United States. Other countries made no attempt to conceal their desire to shift their pauper load to the United States and many regularly engaged in the practice.

In the British possession of Jamaica an act of 1831 required every ship touching on the island to carry away a number of those unable to care for themselves.[17] Many towns in England openly shipped their paupers to American ports; the consul at Liverpool estimated that 90 per cent of the poor leaving that port were destined for the United States.[18] The situation in Germany was especially bad. In Hesse Cassel it was the practice to release minor criminals for transportation to America and in Leipzig a regular organization existed through which the towns could have their paupers and criminals carried to New York.[19] A congressional committee estimated in 1836 that about 41,000 paupers annually would be sent to the United States in the coming years from England alone.[20]

Many of the eastern states most affected tried to protect themselves from these European paupers, laws being passed in New York, Massachusetts, Pennsylvania, and South Carolina requiring ship captains to post bonds for all persons likely to become public charges.[21] These measures soon proved completely ineffectual. Professional bondsmen took over the task of supplying the bonds and the administration was handled so laxly that by 1828 the price had fallen as low as two dollars for bonds for a whole shipload of immigrants.[22] Moreover it was still possible for pauper aliens to enter a state which had no restrictions and immediately move into one of the states that had. In such cases the states were helpless.

Native antipathy for immigrants was to a considerable extent rationalization of previously existing prejudices. Fundamentally the aliens were opposed because they were Catholics rather than because they were paupers or criminals. The preponderant number of papal adherents among the Irish and Germans coming to the United States made Americans wonder again if their land was safe from Popery and fears were current that this immigration was a means by which Romish power could be transferred to America.

The coming of the foreigners actually did cause the Catholic church in America to go through an unprecedented period of growth. In 1807 the entire hierarchical establishment consisted of one see, with seventy priests and eighty churches caring for the needs of the 70,000 Catholics in the entire country.[23] By 1830 there were 14,000 Catholics and sixteen churches in New England alone.[24] In Ohio, where not a single church had existed fourteen years before, there were twenty-four priests and twenty-two churches, a newspaper, a college, and a seminary.[25] By this time there were ten sees in the United States, together with six seminaries, nine colleges, thirty-three monasteries and houses of religious women, and many schools and hospitals.[26]

This remarkable growth might have passed unnoticed but for a series of events occurring just at this time that attracted the attention of all Americans. The Papal Jubilee of Leo XII in 1827 was a signal for great activity and renewed interest in Catholicism the world over, and inspired priests in the United States to attempt to win new converts, an activity which centered attention upon them. The first Provincial Council of Catholicity in America which met at Baltimore in October, 1829, had even greater significance. The council had been called at the insistence of Bishop John England of the Baltimore diocese, who realized that much nativistic sentiment, inspired by the foreign nature of Catholicism, might be allayed by the creation of a more purely American church with native rather than foreign bishops.[27] Although the council's purpose was to quiet nativistic fears its effect was exactly the opposite, for the assembling of the American hierarchy in all its glory was a sight which caused grave concern among the simplicity-loving Americans. Still more alarming were the thirty-eight decrees issued by the council, warning Catholics against "corrupt translations of the Bible," urging parishes to build parochial schools to save children from "perversion" and approving the baptism of non-Catholic children when there was a prospect of their being brought up in the Catholic faith.[28] This open flaunting not only of the power but also of the ideals of Catholicism, turned many Americans against the Church. The Baltimore Council for the first time taught them something of the strength of this dreaded enemy and definitely placed them on guard.

Even more important in focusing native attention on the growth of Catholicism was the trusteeism controversy which broke out in Philadelphia during the 1820's. This conflict, which threatened for a time to cause a serious schism in the American church, revolved about the question of whether church property should be controlled by trustees representing the laymen or by the bishops of the diocese. The problem was not a new one when it assumed serious form in Philadelphia. A struggle between clergy and laymen had taken place in Baltimore in 1815 and in the same year the Bishop of New Orleans had been forced to move from his own cathedral to St. Louis to escape control by the congregation. When Bishop England took over the see of Charleston in 1820 only prompt action on his part through the co-operation of the state legislatures of North Carolina, Georgia, and South Carolina checked serious disorder.[29] These conflicts had attracted little attention, however, and it remained for the Philadelphia controversy to focus American interest on this phase of Catholicism.

This schism dated back to 1808 when St. Mary's cathedral had been erected by the congregation and control of the edifice vested in a board of trustees rather than in the bishop of the diocese. Despite efforts of the clergy, these laymen held steadfastly to their position for two decades, insisting not only on controlling the property but also on the right to name their own pastors. Affairs reached a crisis first in 1820 when the Reverend Henry Conwell, on becoming bishop of the diocese, attempted to force the trustees' hand by withdrawing the privileges of the cathedral from the Reverend William Hogan, the pastor supported by the congregation. When the trustees replied

that they were willing to defy the bishop, Conwell informed
Hogan that he must either resign or be excommunicated. Hogan
was sufficiently alarmed to be willing to withdraw, but the trustees had gone too far and forced him to continue as priest and
accept the excommunication which was pronounced in 1821. A
brief issued by the Pope against the rebellious trustees in 1824
proved the beginning of their end, for it drove Hogan into retirement and, although they found other spiritual leaders, these
were of such a poor sort that in 1826 the congregation was
forced to accept a compromise settlement with the bishop. This
was in turn rejected by the Pope, and Bishop Conwell finally
retired with the controversy still unsettled. His successor, the
Reverend Francis Patrick Kenrick, who took charge of the diocese in 1830, was of a less conciliatory nature. He immediately
announced his intention of assuming full charge of the cathedral and when the trustees objected, placed the church under an
interdict. Former worshippers there went quietly to other
churches, and the trustees, left with no financial support, were
forced to submit. Bishop Kenrick, his control undisputed, reopened the cathedral and the long controversy came to an
end.[30]

Although terminating in triumph for the Church and its hierarchy, the Philadelphia controversy did Catholicism much harm,
for the ten-year struggle and the controversial literature which
it inspired attracted hostile attention from the entire nation.[31]
American Protestants who knew nothing of the organization or
nature of the Catholic church and who were misled by the
statements of the trustees, believed that the hierachy's position
was out of line with the country's traditions and ideals and
steadfastly held that the issue was only one between the democracy of the congregation and the autocracy of the clergy. The
impression which the whole struggle left in the average American mind was that Catholicism was a sworn enemy to democratic institutions and thus a dangerous influence in the United

States. The trustees, moreover, had constantly stressed their
desire to escape foreign influences by appointing American pastors, a position which appeared highly laudable to the majority
of Americans. The approval of the hierarchy's stand by the
First Provincial Council in 1829 only served to damn the entire
Catholic church in American eyes. One paper declared it to be
a "singular specimen of papal authority exercised over the
people of a free country" [32] and a group in Pennsylvania protested against "such tyrannical and unchristian acts, so repug-
nant to our republican institutions." [33]

The mounting antipathy to Catholicism caused by the Philadelphia controversy was clearly shown by the Protestant support
afforded the Hogan schismatics. Religious papers printed full
accounts of their stand and praised them editorially, at the same
time refusing the Bishop's party a proper hearing.[34] Thus when
charges were made against Hogan's morality, the Protestant
press was singularly quiet,[35] yet when Bishop Conwell was summoned before the civil courts on charges of "bastardy" trumped
up by the trustees, the event received much undesirable publicity.[36] Similarly a forceful attempt of the Bishopites to prevent
supporters of the trustees from voting in a church election in
1822 called out a mob which included many Protestants, several
being seriously injured in the rioting that followed.[37] Anti-
Catholic sentiment was most openly expressed when the controversy was carried into state politics in 1823 ; a step occasioned
by a petition of the Hoganites to the state legislature asking the
passage of a law which would require lay members of the
churches to select their own pastors and forbid such appointment by any hierarchy. Petitions in support of this measure
argued that the naming of pastors by bishops was equivalent to
their appointment by the Pope and that this was incompatible
with the freedom of American political institutions and deroga-
tory to the character of a republican government. Protestant
support carried the bill through the legislature but it was vetoed

by the governor and an effort to pass it over his veto failed.[38] Despite this, Protestants continued to demand laws which would vest exclusive control of church property in lay trustees,[39] and the ultimate effect of the controversy was to arouse great resentment against the Catholic religious system which seemed intent on perpetuating in America the autocratic systems evolved in despotic Europe.

The Hogan schism, coming as it did concurrently with the Papal Jubilee, the Baltimore Provincial Congress, and the growth of foreign immigration, made it clear that Catholicism, which a short time before seemed headed for early extinction in the United States, was showing new life. Americans began to feel the need of reviving their heritage of antipapal sentiment. Conditions in the 1820's and 1830's were ripe for such a renaissance. The country was then wrapt in the burst of excitement which culminated in the formation of the Anti-Masonic party. Conservative farmers, reading of the rituals and black secrets of Masonry, were more ready to accept such stories about the other great secret organization of which they were beginning to hear, the Catholic church.[40] So Masonry and Catholicism, dread oaths and the Inquisition became linked in the minds of the people.

More important in preparing the American mind for the crusade against Catholicism which was to come were the new tendencies becoming apparent in religion. About 1826 the term "New Measures" began to come into use to designate the means being employed by the churches. The New Measures represented a swing away from the liberalism and Deism which had followed the Revolution toward a rigid fundamentalism which rivaled the stern religion of the Puritans of colonial New England. This new revivalism was introduced by the Reverend Charles G. Finney, whose efforts and success in western New York soon began to attract national attention.[41] As its influence spread, preaching throughout the land became bolder and more

denunciatory, the practice of praying for individuals by name
was begun, converts were pleaded with and led to the anxious
seat, females were encouraged to speak and pray at public meetings, revivals were held everywhere, and religious newspapers
devoted regular space to ecstatic descriptions of the thousands
who were finding their way to the truth. The whole country
was under the influence of a wave of religious excitement;
Protestantism suddenly became a thing to be venerated and
protected, while Catholicism, as an antagonistic system, was
proportionately resented. Those who attacked it became cru-
saders in the popular mind and were assured of a large following.

The new interest in religion which developed through this
revivalism led to the founding of a number of societies and publications which were to aid immeasurably the anti-Catholic
movement. The tract societies, home and foreign missionary
societies, Sunday school societies, and other adjuncts to the formal religious system which were organized at this time all were
to play a part in the crusade against Rome. The first of these to
array itself openly against Catholicism was the American Bible
Society which, since its formation in 1816, had been preparing
for an inevitable conflict with the Catholic church. Its constitution declared that its "sole object shall be to encourage a wider
circulation of the Holy Scriptures without note or comment.
The only copies in the English language to be circulated by the
Society shall be the version now in common use." [42] The Catholic church, believing itself the "divinely appointed custodian
and interpreter of the Holy Writ" [43] insisted that only versions
of the Bible which had been properly approved could be read by
Catholics. A clash developed as soon as the American Bible
Society attempted to spread the Protestant version of the Bible
among Catholics. The indignation of the Catholic hierarchy,
the refusal of poverty-stricken Catholics to accept free Bibles
and papal letters denouncing the society [44] all were interpreted

by Protestants as an attack on the Bible rather than on one version of the Bible.[45] Thus the illusion was created that Papists were hostile to the Scriptures and that their church rested not on divine but on man-made authority. These beliefs bore particular weight with a populace under the fundamentalistic influences of the New Measures.

This supposed Catholic attack on the Bible interested the churches in the No-Popery crusade and led them to take their first exploratory steps against Catholicism. During this early period organized religious efforts against Rome were not attempted, but individual ministers, fired by the dire predictions of the Bible Society which warned that the Jesuits threatened to drive God's word from the land,[46] began preaching an increasingly large number of sermons against Romanism.[47] A convention of the Protestant Episcopal church listened to such a sermon in 1826,[48] and three years later the bishops of that same church issued a pastoral letter on the perils of Popery.[49] These first feeble attempts, while unimportant themselves, indicated the attitude toward Catholicism that the American churches were later to adopt.

Before the churches could take an open stand, their members had to be educated to the dangers of Romanism, and in this process the religious press played a most important part. The founding and continued success of the first religious papers during these years created a powerful force constantly antagonistic toward Catholicism and extremely influential in shaping public opinion along these lines. The first newspaper of this type in the country, the Boston *Recorder,* was founded in 1816 as a Presbyterian organ; in 1819 the *Christian Watchman* was established by the Baptists, and from that time on these weekly newspapers increased rapidly in number and influence. New York's first paper of this type was the New York *Observer,* established in 1823 by two brothers of Samuel F. B. Morse, who was later to gain fame as an anti-Catholic writer as well as

the inventor of the telegraph.[50] This paper, destined to become
the leading American church publication, influencing not only
its readers but also other papers which imitated it, made its
policy toward Rome clear in an early issue: "Many Protestants," the editors wrote, "begin to think that Popery has of
late assumed a more mild form. It is no doubt true that the
Papal church has lost her power, and therefore *cannot* play the
tyrant as heretofore. . . . But Protestants ought to remember
that it is Papal policy to be mild until they have power to be
severe." [51] The *Christian Watchman* was at the same time
preaching the need of constant labor to prevent the world from
returning to the "moral night" of "Popery" which it had
known before the Reformation.[52]

This same intolerant spirit was represented in the thirty religious newspapers which had been founded by 1827;[53] all of
them were distinctly anti-Catholic in tendency, with regular
sections or weekly articles devoted to attacks on Popery. These
ran the gamut of attack; singling out the idolatry,[54] moral
weakness,[55] blasphemy,[56] cruelty,[57] and anti-Christian nature of
Romanism [58] and warning that Protestant vigilance was required to protect America from subjugation by the papal power.
Even secular papers reflected a growing popular trend by editorial attacks on Catholicism.[59] So voluminous had this propaganda become by the end of the 1820's that Bishop England
and other prominent prelates were spending most of their time
defending their faith, and warding off Protestant arguments.[60]
The Baltimore Provincial Council in 1829 deplored the whole
situation when it referred to the Protestant press in a pastoral
letter, saying:

Not only do they assail us and our institutions in a style of vitu-
peration and offense, misrepresent our tenets, vilify our practices,
repeat the hundred-times-refuted calumnies of the days of angry
and bitter contention in other lands, but they have even denounced
you and us as enemies to the liberties of the republic, and have

openly proclaimed the fancied necessity of obstructing our progress, and of using their best efforts to extirpate our religion.

Catholics were warned that the best defense against these attacks was silence and that to return "evil for evil, or railing for railing" would avail little.[61]

A propaganda sufficiently extensive to cause such concern in the Catholic hierarchy must have been effective in winning many converts to the No-Popery cause. Its appeal, however, was limited, for only those religious persons who subscribed to the church papers could learn of Rome's possible threat to America. An equally effective propaganda, which was to have no such limited audience, was at the same time gradually developing in the form of books, pamphlets, and tracts which could be circulated wholesale at a comparatively small cost and eventually reach every literate person in the United States. This direct propaganda was as essential to the success of organized nativism as the religious press.

While a few openly anti-Catholic books and pamphlets had appeared in the United States in the quarter century following the Revolution, this type of propaganda writing was not elevated to an important plane in the No-Popery crusade until the passage of the English Catholic Emancipation bill in 1829. This far-seeing measure, designed to afford certain civil rights to British Catholics, was naturally objected to by the American Protestant press.[62] Its principal importance, however, lay in the controversy which it inspired in England. As soon as the movement to secure the adoption of the bill was fairly begun, protests from English Protestants began to be heard; stories which had been told at the time of the Gunpowder Plot and the Gordon Riots were revived and writers whose numbers were legion attempted to demonstrate to the English people the dangers which lay in any concessions to Catholicism. Dozens of these books and pamphlets found their way to the United States where they were eagerly purchased by Americans newly aroused to the errors of Rome.[63] The success of these English works convinced American writers of the possibility of this form of appeal. The beginnings of the flood of propaganda which was to be loosed in the United States can be traced again to the mother country.

The American authors who sensed this new demand had no specific grievance such as the Emancipation bill which had called into being the British works; hence their attacks on Catholicism were more general and correspondingly more popular. The most common type of work employed learned theological arguments to demonstrate that Romanism was not Christianity; an appeal to which the New Englanders were particularly susceptible.[64] These early American books were probably effective, yet they lacked the wide appeal that was to characterize the later attacks on Rome.

The influence of this American propaganda was sufficiently great to cause concern among leaders of the Catholic church. "How many volumes of religious tracts"; Bishop England wrote, "how many Gospel and Evangelical and Christian periodical publications, teem with misrepresentation and abuse of our creed!"[65] The more outspoken among both the clergy and the laymen could not allow this continued abuse without attempting retaliation through the mediums so successfully employed by nativists: the press and books. Until the 1820's there had been no purely Catholic journals in the United States; the establishment of the first in 1822, the *United States Catholic Miscellany,* indicated the growing influence of the No-Popery crusade and the growing demand for a means of Catholic rebuttal. This paper was founded by Bishop England at Charleston as a medium through which he could answer Protestant attacks, and during the decade in which he remained at the helm it was used principally for this purpose.[66] *The Truth Teller,* established in New York in 1825, attempted to carry on this same work in the northern states aided, after 1829, by *The Jesuit* which was published in Boston. These three small publications assumed the herculean task of answering the calumny of the entire Protestant press.

Catholic defense was attempted through books as well as newspapers. The Reverend John Hughes, destined later to gain prominence as Bishop of New York, in 1827 founded a Catholic Tract Society in Philadelphia for the sole purpose of defending Catholicism and attacking Protestantism.[67] Catholic authors were similarly encouraged to explain the forms of their religion in a manner which could be understood by Protestants, for it was rightly believed that much of the abuse which Catholicism had to endure grew from a lack of understanding of its true principles.[68]

In all probability these Catholic attempts at defense did more harm than good. The labored vindications of Catholicism written by Bishop England, able as they were, were read only by Catholics, for no good Protestant would read a Catholic paper. Instead, objections grew immediately to the establishment of such publications. The three successful journals were a constant indication of the growing power and influence of Catholicism and a perpetual thorn in the side of Protestants. Moreover, the tone adopted by these Catholic publications was often unwise, for the editors were sufficiently carried away by a sincere belief in their own religion to make statements which, although perhaps true, were certainly ill advised and provided much grist for the mills of nativistic writers. The very name of the Boston paper, *The Jesuit,* created a great deal of resentment, until a few of the more thoughtful among the clergy recognized the danger and renamed it the Boston *Pilot*.

Such palliatives were wasted efforts, for by 1830 the stage had been set for the nativistic drama. Many Protestants, stirred by a wave of revivalism, had singled out Popery as their immediate enemy and were beginning to arm themselves against the threatened Romish assault. Immigrants and propaganda were sweeping in from Europe, creating such popular sentiment against Catholicism that the next nativistic step—the enlistment of the great mass of the common people in the anti-Catholic cause—was taken with confidence.

NOTES

[1] Edward Wigglesworth, *The Authority of Tradition Considered at the Lecture founded by the Hon. Judge Dudley in Harvard College, November 5, 1777;* John Tucker, *The Validity of Presbyterian Ordination argued from Jesus Christ's being the Founder, the sole Legislator and Supreme Head and Ruler of the Christian Church . . . a Dudleian Lecture;* John Lathrop, *A Discourse on the Errors of Popery, Delivered in the Chapel of the University in Cambridge, September 4, 1793, at the Lecture founded by the Honorable Paul Dudley, esquire* (Boston, 1793); John Pierce, *The Right of Private Judgment in Religion, Vindicated against the claims of the Romish church, and all kindred Usurpations, in a Dudleian lecture delivered before the University in Cambridge, 24 October, 1821* (Cambridge, 1821).

[2] Bishop Carroll complained to the editor of the *Carlisle Weekly* in 1795 about the general anti-Catholic tone of most religious and secular papers and magazines. *American Catholic Historical Researches,* XI (July, 1894), 133-134. For a typical article of this period reprinted from the *Massachusetts Missionary Magazine* for 1803 see *The Protestant,* April 2, 1831.

[3] The controversy was between the Reverend John Thayer and the Reverend George Lesslie, a Protestant. John Thayer, *Controversy between the the Rev. John Thayer, Catholic Missionary, of Boston, and the Rev. George Lesslie, pastor of a Church in Washington, New Hampshire* (Boston, 1793).

[4] Typical was John McGowan, *The French Convert: being a true Relation of the happy conversion of a noble French lady from the error, and superstitions of Popery to the reformed Religion, by means of a Protestant Gardener.* The work was reprinted from an early English edition and many American editions were published after the first appeared in Boston in 1724. The work was typical of later propaganda in its mild appeal to libidinous instincts. It recounted the adventures of a Catholic lady who was captured by two priests who bore her to a wild spot to ravage her. She threw open her bosom and begged them to plunge a sword to her heart that her honor might be saved. The priests were so intrigued by this sight that they fell to fighting as to who should have her first. She escaped, reached her home and was converted to Protestantism by her Protestant gardener. Others published at the time were: James Crowley, *Reasons for Recantation from the Errors of the Church of Rome* (Baltimore, 1812) and Frederick C. Schaeffer, *The Blessed Reformation* (New York, 1817), which was devoted to an account of the errors of Catholicism which brought on the Reformation.

[5] The best estimates place the number of immigrants reaching the United States between 1790 and 1820 at about 10.000 a year. Max Farrand, "Immigration in the Light of History," *New Republic,* IX (December 23, 1916),

209; Henry P. Fairchild, *Immigration, A World Movement and its American Significance* (New York, 1925), 57–58.

6 Mathew Carey, *Reflections on the Subject of Emigration from Europe with a View to Settlement in the United States* (3rd edition, Philadelphia, 1826), iv–viii. Carey stated that machines in 1826 were doing the work of two hundred million men in England alone and that expenditures for poor relief had increased from £700,000 in 1749, not long before Arkwright's machine went into operation, to £7,329,594 in 1820.

7 F. D. Hutchins, *The Colonial Land and Immigration Commission* (Philadelphia, 1931), 4.

8 The effects of the lumber trade in encouraging Irish emigration are well described in Marcus L. Hansen, "The Second Colonization of New England," *New England Quarterly*, II (October, 1929), 544–546; Thomas W. Page, "The Transportation of Immigrants and Reception Arrangements in the Nineteenth Century," *Journal of Political Economy*, XIX (November, 1911), 734; *House Documents*, 25th Cong., 2nd Sess., No. 1040, 20ff.

9 *Niles' Register*, XXIV (August 30, 1823); XXX (July 29, 1826). This influx was neglected in the official census returns.

10 Typical societies were the Hibernian Society of Baltimore and the Irish Emigrant Association of New York. Thomas F. Meehan, "New York's First Irish Emigrant Society," *United States Catholic Historical Society Records and Studies*, VI (New York, 1913), 202–211.

11 New York *Observer*, October 3, 1835.

12 *Ibid.*, March 28, 1835.

13 *Ibid.*, March 3, 1838.

14 House of Representatives, *Reports of Committees*, 25th Cong., 2nd Sess., No. 1040, 3.

15 *Niles' Register*, XXIV (April 26, 1823), XXIV (August 23, 1823), XXXII (July 21, 1827), XXXVIII (August 14, 1830), XXXVIII (August 21, 1830), XXXVIII (July 3, 1830), LV (January 19, 1839); New York *Observer*, June 2, 1838, January 19, 1839; House *Reports of Committees*, 25th Cong., 2nd Sess., No. 1040, 51.

16 Prescott F. Hall, *Immigration* (New York, 1907), 29.

17 House *Reports of Committees*, 25th Cong., 2nd Sess., No. 1040, 41–48.

18 *Senate Documents*, 24th Cong., 2nd Sess., No. 5, 1–20.

19 House *Reports of Committees*, 25th Cong., 2nd Sess., No. 1040, 51–54.

20 House *Executive Documents*, 24th Cong., 1st Sess., No. 219, 1–3.

21 These laws are conveniently printed in Edith Abbott, *Immigration, Select Documents and Case Records* (Chicago, 1924), 102–108.

22 Friedrich Kapp, *Immigration and the Commissioners of Emigration of the State of New York* (New York, 1870), 45–48.

23 O'Gorman, *History of the Roman Catholic Church*, 291–293.

24 J. Salzbacher, *Meine Reise nach Nord-Amerika im Jahre 1842* (Vienna, 1845). Tables on the growth of the church at the end of the volume.

25 V. F. O'Daniel, *The Right Reverend Edward Dominic Fenwick, O.P., Founder of the Dominicans in the United States* (Washington, 1920), 402.

26 This statement is taken from the address of the Baltimore Provincial Council to the Pope in 1829. O'Gorman, *History of the Roman Catholic Church*, 336–338.

[27] Guilday, *The Life and Times of John England*, II, 68–110.

[28] Peter Guilday, *A History of the Councils of Baltimore (1791-1884)* (New York, 1932), 89–95.

[29] O'Gorman, *History of the Roman Catholic Church*, 299-333.

[30] This account of the controversy is drawn from Joseph L. Kirlin, *Catholicity in Philadelphia* (Philadelphia, 1909), 194–274; and from the standard histories of the Catholic church. Documents particularly helpful in an understanding of the affair are in: John England, *The Works of the Right Reverend John England, First Bishop of Charleston* (Cleveland, 1908), VI, 389–486; "Correspondence between Bishop Conwell of Philadelphia and Bishop Plessis of Quebec, 1821–1825, Relating Principally to the 'Hogan Schism'," *Records of the American Catholic Historical Society of Philadelphia*, XXII (Philadelphia, 1911), 277–279; *Records of the American Catholic Historical Society of Philadelphia* (Philadelphia, 1889–1930), XIII, 21 and ff, XXIII, 20ff, XXIV, 169ff, XXV, 61ff, XXVI, 68ff, XXVII, 146ff; *American Catholic Historical Researches* (Philadelphia, 1883–1911), IX, 120ff, X, 19ff, XVII, 17ff, XXVII, 287ff.

[31] The editor of the Baltimore *Literary and Religious Magazine*, V (February, 1839), 71, stated that he had purchased a bundle of thirty-seven books and pamphlets originating from the Philadelphia schism "at a pretty high price, after strong competition, by a priest who stood nearby." This probably represented only a small part of the literature which the controversy inspired. Many of the anti-Catholic and pro-Catholic publications are reprinted in the *Records of the American Catholic Historical Society of Philadelphia* and in the *American Catholic Historical Researches*, cited above.

[32] *The Philadelphian*, quoted in New York *Observer*, June 28, 1829.

[33] *American Catholic Historical Researches*, XI (July, 1894), 129–132.

[34] See statement by Hogan in the New York *Observer*, August 14, 1824.

[35] *Records of the American Catholic Historical Society of Philadelphia*, XXV, 231.

[36] *Ibid.*, XXV, 340.

[37] *National Gazette*, April 9, 1822.

[38] *Records of the American Catholic Historical Society of Philadelphia*, XXVI, 68–74.

[39] A petition was presented to the Pennsylvania legislature by a group of Protestant citizens praying for such action. *American Catholic Historical Researches*, XI (July, 1894), 129–132.

[40] Charles McCarthy, *The Anti-Masonic Party: a Study of Political Anti-Masonry in the United States, 1827–1840* (Washington, 1903), 539.

[41] W. W. Sweet, *The Story of Religions in America* (New York, 1930), 396–397; Emerson Davis, *The Half Century; or, a History of Changes that have taken Place, and Events that have Transpired, chiefly in the United States, between 1800 and 1850* (Boston, 1851), 355–356. Finney himself frequently preached against Catholicism and encouraged a similar attitude in other revivalistic ministers. *The Protestant*, June 26, 1830.

[42] Henry O. Dwight, *The Centennial History of the American Bible Society* (New York, 1916), I, 25.

[43] *The Catholic Encyclopedia* (New York, 1907–1912), II, 545.

[44] *Ibid.*, II, 545.

⁴⁵ See communication of the Bible Society in the Boston *Recorder,* April 26, 1834.

⁴⁶ New York *Observer,* April 16, 1825, January 23, 1829.

⁴⁷ William Parkinson, *The Romish Anti-Christ. A Sermon Delivered in the Meeting House of the First Baptist Church in the City of New York, Lord's Day, Nov. 28, 1830* (New York, 1831) ; England, *The Works of John England,* III, 452–518. Bishop England felt called upon to answer many of these sermons preached in the south and his replies are printed in his works.

⁴⁸ *Ibid.,* II, 171–209.

⁴⁹ Guilday, *Life and Times of John England,* II, 451.

⁵⁰ New York *Observer,* December 15, 1827; Frank L. Mott, *A History of American Magazines, 1741–1850* (New York, 1930), 373.

⁵¹ New York *Observer,* November 13, 1824.

⁵² *Christian Watchman,* June 12, 1819.

⁵³ New York *Observer,* December 15, 1827. These papers invaded 60,000 homes each week and had an annual circulation of 7,000,000 copies.

⁵⁴ *Ibid.,* January 29, 1825, February 5, 1825, March 19, 1825, November 12, 1825, November 4, 1826, December 16, 1826, March 22, 1828, October 11, 1828, November 21, 1826; *Christian Watchman,* December 25, 1819, January 8, 1820, January 15, 1820, May 6, 1820.

⁵⁵ New York *Observer,* September 23, 1826, April 28, 1827, March 14, 1829.

⁵⁶ *Ibid.,* April 15, 1826, October 27, 1827.

⁵⁷ *Ibid.,* September 23, 1826, December 16, 1826, September 26, 1829, October 3, 1829; *Massachusetts Yeoman,* August 8, 1829; *Christian Watchman,* December 11, 1819, April 15, 1820, March 19, 1830.

⁵⁸ New York *Observer,* June 26, 1824, April 16, 1825, August 16, 1828, April 25, 1829.

⁵⁹ See as example *American Daily Advertiser,* July 26, 1817, and *Massachusetts Yeoman,* November 17, 1827.

⁶⁰ More than half of Bishop England's writings in the latest edition of his published works were devoted to a defense of Catholicism against Protestant attacks. He objected particularly to the bitterness of the *Gospel Advocate, Christian Advocate* and *Mount Zion Missionary.* His replies to these papers are in England, *The Works of John England,* III, 223–423.

⁶¹ O'Gorman, *History of the Roman Catholic Church,* 342–343.

⁶² *The Church Register* (Philadelphia), quoted in J. R. G. Hassard, *Life of the Most Reverend John Hughes* (New York, 1866), 92–93. The Philadelphia *Recorder,* June 27, 1829, on the other hand, favored the passage of the bill and expressed the belief that only by giving Catholics full civil rights and a chance to be educated could they be taught the error of their ways.

⁶³ James Richardson, *The Roman Catholic Convicted upon his Own Evidence of Hostility to the Protestant Churches of Britain* (New York, 1823). Pierce Connelly, *Domestic Emancipation from Roman Rule; a Petition to the Honourable House of Commons* (London, 1829) ; Pierce Connelly, *The Coming Struggle with Rome Not Religious but Political; or, Words of Warning to the English People* (London, 1830) ; J. B. White, *Letters from*

Spain (London, 1822); J. B. White, *Practical and Internal Evidence against Catholicism with Occasional Strictures on Mr. Butler's Book of the Roman Catholic Church; in Six Letters Addressed to the Impartial among the Roman Catholics of Great Britain and Ireland* (London, 1826); *The Conversion and Edifying Death of Andrew Dunn* (Philadelphia, 182-); Anna E. Bray, *The Protestant; a Tale of the Reign of Queen Mary* (New York, 1829); *An Awful Warning; or, the Massacre of St. Bartholomew* (London, 1812); John Coustos, *The Mysteries of Popery Unveiled in the Unparalleled Sufferings of John Coustos at the Inquisition of Lisbon, to which is added, the Origin of the Inquisition and its Establishment in Various Countries; and the Master Key to Popery by Anthony Gavin* (Hartford, 1821); *Father Clement: a Roman Catholic Story* (Boston, 1827).

[64] C. H. Wharton, *Concise View of the Principal Points of Controversy between the Protestant and Romish Churches* (New York, 1817); Jeremiah Odel, *Popery Unveiled; to which is Annexed a Short Recital of the Origin, Doctrines, Precepts and Examples of the Great Church Militant and Triumphant* (Bennington, Vermont, 1821); T. Secker, *Five Discourses Against Popery* (Windsor, Vermont, 1827); Thomas Waddell, *Letters to the Editors of the Catholic Miscellany: Illustrating the Papal Doctrine of Intention: the Opus Operatum, Roman Infallibility, and the Knavery of Popish Writers* (New York, 1830); *An Exposition of the Principles of the Roman Catholic Religion with Remarks on its Influence in the United States* (Hartford, 1830); *The Protestant Catechism, Showing the Principal Errors of the Church of Rome* (Charleston, 1828).

[65] Guilday, *Life and Times of John England*, II, 457.

[66] Mott, *History of American Magazines*, 136. Bishop England devoted much of the space in his paper for two years, 1826-1828, to answering the charges against Catholicism brought by J. Blanco White. England, *Works of John England*, II, 213-562, III, 9-103.

[67] Hassard, *Life of John Hughes*, 77-78. For a full account see "An Early Philadelphia Catholic Truth Society," *Records of the American Catholic Historical Society of Philadelphia*, XXXVIII (March, 1927), 8-14. One of the society's first publications was a book by Hughes attacking the English anti-Catholic novel which had recently been published in Philadelphia, *The Conversion and Edifying Death of Andrew Dunn*. Hughes' book was published under the same title and differed from the other only in that his hero was converted to Catholicism rather than Protestantism.

[68] Roger Baxter, *The Most Important Tenets of the Roman Catholic Church Fairly Explained* (Washington, 1820). The author expressed the hope that his book would be widely read by Protestants in order that they might understand the true nature of the Catholic Church. *Ibid.*, 1.

III

The First Convent Is Burned
1830-1834

BY 1830 the small group of clergymen and others who were beginning to interest themselves seriously in the cause of nativism realized that some unified action was necessary before their efforts could be completely successful. The first step in the achievement of this unification was taken with the establishment of the openly anti-Catholic weekly newspaper, *The Protestant*,[1] the initial number of which appeared in New York on January 2, 1830, under the editorship of the Reverend George Bourne. Bourne personally believed that no reconciliation with Rome was possible and that only through aggressive denunciation could the errors of that church be made known to the American people. This policy dominated *The Protestant* during his editorship.

Subscribers were left in no doubt as to the attitude which the paper would adopt. A prospectus distributed before the publication of the first number declared:

The sole objects of this publication are, to inculcate Gospel doctrines against Romish corruptions—to maintain the purity and sufficiency of the Holy Scriptures against Monkish traditions—to exemplify the watchful care of Immanuel over the "Church of God which he hath purchased with his own blood," and to defend that revealed truth, which Luther and Zuingle; Calvin and Arminius; Cranmer and Knox; Usher and Rutherford; Baxter and Owen; Burnett and Neal; Wall and Gale; Whitefield and Wesley; and all their different followers *ex anima* and *una voce*, have approved, against the creed of Pope Pius IV. and the cannons [sic] of the

Council of Trent and no article will be admitted into the *Protestant,* which does not contribute to these desirable results.[2]

A second and more detailed prospectus described the type of material desired by the editors. The paper's columns, they announced, would be devoted to:

·Narratives displaying the rise and progress of the Papacy; its spirit and character in former periods; its modern pretensions; and its present enterprising efforts to recover and extend its unholy dominion, especially on the western continent. Biographical notices of Martyrs, Reformers and Popish Persecutors. Essays describing the doctrines, discipline, and ceremonies of the Romish Hierarchy; and its desolating influence upon individual advancement, domestic comfort, and national prosperity. Illustrations of Sacred Prophecy relative to the Mystical Babylon. A faithful expose of the moral and religious conditions of Lower Canada, as debased by the prevalence of Roman supremacy.[3]

These promises were rigorously adhered to under Bourne's editorship. A typical issue contained articles on "Code of the Jesuits," "A Canadian Papist Converted," "Roman Excommunication," "Bigotry and Persecution," "Monkish Legends," and "Popery Characterized." [4]

The reception accorded *The Protestant* varied. Some of the religious papers were heartily in sympathy with its program and agreed that only after being educated in the errors of Rome could the American people be made aware of the dangers of Popery.[5] Individual ministers and even ministerial gatherings endorsed the cause which the paper represented and recommended it to their churches.[6] On the other hand the persecuting spirit of *The Protestant* and the violence which characterized its attacks left it open to much abuse. Many moderate Protestants believed that such conduct did not conform to the teachings of Christianity and were especially afraid that the Catholic church would thrive more under persecution than neglect. A large number of clergymen who openly stated their hatred of Catholicism refused to subscribe to the methods chosen by *The Protestant* in its attack upon that religion.[7]

Not only did the lack of sympathy among moderate Protestants for the objectives of this No-Popery paper handicap its growth,[8] but *The Protestant* was further discredited by the mischievous action of a priest, the Reverend John Hughes of Philadelphia, who contributed a series of letters to the publication through the spring and summer of 1830,[9] depicting in absurd terms the designs of the Catholic church on America. These were readily accepted by the editors and printed over the pseudonym of "Cranmer." [10] After publishing a whole series Hughes wrote a confession of his plot to the Catholic *Truth Teller*. *The Protestant* vehemently denied the truth of Hughes' statement, and insisted that he was "guilty of deception, and all the other abominations which it is essential to the craft and character of a Jesuit to perpetuate." [11] Despite this explanation Bourne was seriously discredited by this deceit.

Failure to secure whole-hearted clerical support eventually forced the owners of *The Protestant* to change their policies. Early in 1831 it was announced that a wider class of subjects would be treated in exposing the evils of Popery,[12] but this attracted no greater interest and the subscription list continued to decline. Obviously Protestants were not sufficiently educated in the ways of anti-Catholic reformers to accept the violent denunciation which characterized Bourne's attack on Rome, and his resignation as editor was forced. The helm of *The Protestant* was taken over by the Reverend William Craig Brownlee who was, like Bourne, to become a leader in the anti-Catholic movement.[13] Brownlee showed himself as incapable of moderation as Bourne had been and equally unable to attract the support of the moderate Protestant group on which the paper was dependent.[14] In June, 1832, ownership was transferred to a "group of gentlemen whose opinions of Popery are drawn from the word of God" [15] and the first serious attempt was made to reform the editorial policy.

The new owners were fully aware of the prejudice aroused by Bourne and Brownlee and took pains to allay it immediately. They believed it possible, they said, to uphold the purposes of the Reformation in such a way as to cause offense to no religious person. This would be their object and to this end they were willing to moderate the harsh policies of their paper. "It is not intended," they cautioned, "to soften down the paper, to make it a semi-Protestant, and semi-Papist publication. It is intended that by *solid arguments,* by *documents* and *facts,* the cause of Protestantism shall be sustained." [16] The fear that the connotation of the former name would react against their enterprise caused them to change *The Protestant* into *The Reformation Advocate.*[17] This new weekly journal fared little better than had its predecessor, and in September, 1833, its form was again changed, this time to the monthly *Protestant Magazine.*[18]

The reasons for the shift from a weekly to a monthly publication were explained by the editor in the first issue of *The Protestant Magazine:*

The important cause in which we are engaged, in consequence of the almost total silence of the religious papers formerly, rendered a weekly publication necessary. But happily a great change has of late taken place: articles against popery are now appearing weekly, in almost every part of our country. . . . But to embody for dissemination, and preservation, all the valuable articles which may be written against popery; and especially to elicit from the pens of ready and able writers, well digested, well prepared papers against this great enemy of truth, a Monthly Magazine is thought by many discerning men to be necessary.[19]

He made clear that this change did not mean a lessened attack on Rome:

Deeply convinced of the dangerous tendency of this anti-christian system; of its soul-corrupting, soul-destroying influence; dreading the danger to which our country, if indifferent to its increase in political influence, is exposed; and influenced by a love of country, and by an ardent desire to promote the interests of immortal souls, we have entered upon this work, resolved, as far as in us lies, to defend the great truths of the gospel opposed by popery, and to exhibit those doctrines and practices of Roman Catholics which are contrary to the interests of mankind.[20]

In conformity with this purpose, *The Protestant Magazine* abandoned much of the sensationalism which had characterized *The Protestant* and stressed theological attacks on the papal system.[21]

This policy proved to be a popular one and for a time *The Protestant Magazine* prospered to such an extent that its success threatened to call a rival anti-Catholic publication into the field during 1834. The editors, alarmed at this threat of competition, sought out the backers of the proposed new publication to suggest consolidation, but much to their chagrin found the Reverend George Bourne, whose outspoken tactics had started *The Protestant* on its decline, influential in the project. Instead of merging with Bourne, the editors of *The Protestant Magazine* determined to block his proposed publication and continue to monopolize the field. Hence they continued to issue their monthly magazine and in addition founded a new weekly newspaper, *The Anti-Romanist,* in August, 1834.[22]

Several other newspapers aided these publications in their crusade against Rome by attacking priesthood in all its forms, particularly as exemplified in the Catholic church. Two of the most influential, *Priestcraft Unmasked* [23] and *Priestcraft Exposed* [24] were published during the early 1830's. Typical of their attitude was a declaration of the latter against the Catholic clergy who, it declared, were "covering their hypocrisy with the cloak of *religion,* and with more than the serpent's guile, worming themselves into the confidence and affections of their unsuspecting victims." [25]

This effective newspaper propaganda against Catholicism was instrumental in the creation of the first of the nativistic societies. The group of sincere men who founded and published *The Protestant,* realizing that their cause would be immeasurably aided if it could be given the unity possible only through organization, worked quietly in this direction through 1830 and in January, 1831, were ready to establish the New York Protestant Association. This body, formed "for the express purpose of eliciting knowledge respecting the state of Popery, particularly on the Western Continent" [26] early lapsed into inactivity [27] from which it did not emerge until the elevation of the Reverend W. C. Brownlee to the editorship of *The Protestant.* The new editor, interested in an active organization, arranged a meeting of the New York nativists for this purpose in February, 1832. He recognized the futility of such an attempt unless it had the united support of all who believed as he did and to this end reconciled the differences which had developed between Bourne and the editors of *The Protestant.* With this accomplished the meeting was a complete success. Brownlee presided, and amidst harmony induced by his presence, resolutions were adopted calling the New York Protestant Association again into being and outlining the duties which it was to undertake.[28]

The constitution adopted at this time showed clearly the purpose of the society's backers. The sole object of the association, it declared, was "to promote the principles of the Reformation by public discussions which shall illustrate the history and character of Popery." Meetings for this purpose were to be held monthly, with members of the society admitted free but a nominal admission charge levied against others. All profits from these meetings or from any other sources of revenue were to be expended in publications which would "unfold the true character of Popery." [29] Thus the association was to be di-

rectly a propaganda organization, existing for the sole purpose
of disseminating information against Catholicism, both by
speakers and through publications. The founders believed that
if they could be successful in this, they would drive Romanism
from America. "Popery," they declared, "to be hated needs but
to be seen in its true character, and if the American people can
be induced to look the monster in the face, and observe his
hideous features, they would turn from it with horror and
disgust." [30]

The first public meeting of the society was held in New York
City a few weeks after its formation, with the subject for discussion: "Is Popery that Babylon the Great, which John the
Evangelist has Described in the Apocalypse?" By the beginning
of May the attendance had swelled from three hundred [31] to
fifteen hundred, and the managers, convinced that monthly
gatherings were too infrequent to satisfy those who wished to
hear the debates,[32] not only arranged for regular bi-weekly
meetings but promoted additional gatherings in Brooklyn and
other parts of New York.[33]

Part of this popularity was due to the fact that the meetings
were being attended not only by Protestants seeking to have
their views on Popery confirmed, but by Catholics as well. The
latter came to support their clergy who had early taken an
interest in the association and who welcomed an opportunity to
voice a defense of their religion before a large, although hostile,
audience. The bitter series of debates which followed led to a
minor riot at a meeting held on May 2, 1832, the hall having to
be emptied before the speakers had concluded.[34] To the managers of the association this appeared a popish plot to discredit
its efforts and force an abandonment of the meetings, but they
resolved that they would continue to admit Catholics in the
future as they had in the past.[35] The episode, however, resulted in an order from the bishop of the New York diocese,

forbidding priests to participate in the meetings,[36] and the remainder of the association's gatherings for the year were orderly, although not so well attended.[37]

The popularity of debates between Catholics and Protestants was so well recognized by the leaders of the society that with the opening of the fall season in December, 1832, invitations were extended to a number of priests to come and defend their religion.[38] The continuation of this policy led to several disturbances which attracted attention to the association and aroused Protestant ire. One occurred when Samuel B. Smith, a speaker from the association who was addressing a Baptist gathering in Baltimore in March, 1834, was attacked by a group of Catholics in the audience and fled to escape bodily injury.[39] More serious was a riot in Broadway Hall in New York, a year later. Catholic spokesmen had been specifically invited to this meeting, where the subject for discussion was to be: "Is Popery Compatible with Civil Liberty?" [40] While the debate was going on, the doors were broken down by a mob made up "chiefly, if not exclusively, of Roman Catholics." The speakers managed to escape through a back passage, but the mob leaders stayed for some time, breaking up furniture and destroying the fixtures of the hall.[41] Again the managers of the association immediately announced that despite this attack by Papists they would continue the meetings and not desist until they had "prostrated the beast." [42] From that time on, however, they admitted only those who secured tickets, thus attempting to exclude disorderly elements.[43]

These attacks were principally important in creating popular sympathy for the Protestant Association. Catholics were generally blamed and condemned for the Broadway Hall riot, not only by the nativist and religious press, but by secular papers as well.[44] The New York *Observer* published an account of the attack on Smith under the heading, "Popish Intolerance," [45] and Smith himself popularized the episode by asking: "Must

I be mobbed, as I was in Baltimore, . . . because I use the liberty guaranteed me by my country: the liberty of free discussion?" [46]

The attention focused upon the New York Protestant Association by these attacks and the success which these meetings were enjoying gave a force and unity to the anti-Catholic movement which it had not enjoyed before. Although the society's operations were primarily local, its influence was felt beyond the confines of New York City, for the growing number of speakers giving anti-Catholic sermons in eastern cities constantly spread word of its work among sympathetic Protestants. Some moves were made by the association itself in the direction of national organization, notably in 1832, when it recommended the establishment of Protestant associations in every city as a center for the discussion of "the evils of Popery" and attempted to secure the co-operation of a number of clergymen in carrying out this enterprise.[47] This appeal was evidently unavailing; the time was not yet ripe for the unification of the anti-Catholic forces into one national body.[48]

Although national organization was impossible, the activities of the Protestant Association markedly accelerated the growth of nativistic sentiment and expression. The tone of the religious press was daily becoming more openly hostile to Catholicism, the New York *Observer* in particular publishing a series of articles against Rome from the pen of the Reverend William Nevins, a Baltimore pastor, which was to exert a large influence in the antipapal crusade.[49] There was a marked increase in the number of sermons against Popery; in the larger cities at least one pulpit each Sabbath was occupied by a No-Popery speaker.[50] More and more people were becoming interested and outspoken enemies of Catholicism.

The sporadic debate and rebuttal which went on between anti-Catholic and pro-Catholic writers and speakers led to the development of regular controversies between champions of the two causes. Both parties felt that organized debate would be the most effective device for the presentation of their claims; Protestants, under the impetus of the New York Protestant Association, were eager to convince the people of the horrors of Romanism, while Catholics were equally anxious to show Americans that their religion could be defended and that it was not the hoary iniquity that most Protestants believed it to be. The organized controversies which were to play such an important part in the nativistic movement during the next few years developed naturally to meet this demand.

The first important discussion of this sort was between the Reverend John Breckinridge, a Presbyterian pastor in Philadelphia, and the Reverend John Hughes, then emerging from the obscurity of the priesthood in the same city. In the fall of 1832 Breckinridge addressed a letter to the *Christian Advocate* in which he offered to meet any champion which the opposition could produce on the "broad field of this important and vital discussion. . . . Is the Protestant Religion the Religion of Christ?" [51] Hughes responded to this challenge and for three months the two haggled over the form that their controversy was to take. Finally it was agreed that each contestant should publish articles alternately in *The Presbyterian* and in a Catholic paper which was to be established for the purpose, and that the series should end in six months.[52] Hughes, with money supplied by interested friends, founded the *Catholic Herald* in Philadelphia to serve as the medium for his letters,[53] and on January 21, 1833, published the first article on the Rule of Faith.

At first the controversy was welcomed by the religious newspapers, many of them beginning the ambitious task of reprinting the entire arguments in full;[54] but this they soon abandoned for the debate moved with alarming slowness. After five months of controversy the contestants were still arguing over the first point, the Rule of Faith [55] and journals which had reported their early progress were beginning to wonder if they would go on for decades.[56] The original period was extended to allow at least two points to be argued, but finally on October 3, 1833, Hughes wrote his last letter and Breckinridge replied to it in a spirit of defiance. "I thank God," he wrote, "that the time is not yet come when the *threat* of a Roman priest can make me tremble for my reputation, my liberty, or my hopes of heaven. Even the Bulls of your master become very harmless animals when sent to pasture on our happy soil. Your arrogant and impotent *threats* only show what you *would* do if you *could*." [57] Hughes insisted that the victory was his since Breckinridge had not shown what the Protestant religion was, let alone that it was the religion of Christ. Breckinridge promptly challenged him to an oral debate, but Hughes declined and there the matter rested.

Meanwhile another controversy had arisen in New York City which was attracting almost as much attention. In this the Reverend W. C. Brownlee, president of the New York Protestant Association and pastor of the Dutch Reformed church, was arrayed against three Catholic opponents, the Reverends John Powers, Thomas C. Levine and Felix Verela.[58] The contestants agreed to publish letters in the Catholic *Truth Teller,* and in the Protestant press; no time limit was set and there seems to have been no definite subject of discussion. Like Hughes and Breckinridge, these writers found the Rule of Faith a stumbling block and were concerned with it for some weeks after the contest started in March, 1833, but by the middle of June they had left it behind and were engaged in more general arguments and rebuttal. Brownlee, unrestrained by a definite subject, seized on the occasion to attack Catholicism with such bitter words that the *Truth Teller* objected to having to spread such abuse before its readers. As a result the three priests issued a new challenge, asking Dr. Brownlee to debate the question: "What articles of Faith, found in the Scriptures

in *express* terms must be believed in order to be saved?" [59]
Brownlee refused to be bound; he insisted that this was only
another popish plot to prevent his exposures of Popery and that
he would continue unchecked. His opponents realized that such
abuse could be met only with abuse and from that time on the
controversy lost all dignity. The priests even suggested that
Brownlee should take part in the Catholic Feast of the Asses
which he had ridiculed, writing:

> The Preacher was born and bred with long ears;
> Heigh-ho, my Assy—
> And *still* the Preacher of Asses appears.
> Bray, Preacher Ass, and you shall get grass,
> And straw, and hay too, in plenty. [60]

The proponents of Catholicism finally announced that they
could no longer debate with Brownlee, as he refused to abide by
any subject. "To continue polemic discussion with you," they
wrote, "cannot aid to reputation, for *your* substitute for arguments are [*sic*] falsehood, ribald words, gross invective, disgusting calumny, and the recommendation of an obscene tale.
These have been your weapons from your first to your last
puerile letter." [61] With his opponents withdrawn, Brownlee
went ahead with his letters to the Protestant papers, flaying
Catholicism with the same language to which the priests had
taken exception. [62]

Efforts to force Hughes and Breckinridge again to take up
the gauntlet were repeatedly made, [63] but proved unavailing until
1836. At that time Hughes was persuaded to preside while a
nonsectarian debating society in Philadelphia discussed the effects of Catholicism on civil and religious liberty. When he
arrived he found an agent of Breckinridge waiting to engage
him and was afraid to refuse lest Protestant papers charge that
he had evaded the question. After three evenings of exciting
discussion, Hughes and Breckinridge agreed to meet in a series
of twelve debates before the society on the general question

concerned.[64] Although the large audiences exhibited marked favoritism for Breckinridge[65] and the debates were subsequently published, like all such controversies they settled nothing.

In 1837 another contest attracting even more attention developed in Ohio. The Ohio College of Teachers, meeting at Cincinnati late in 1836, was addressed by a Baptist clergyman, the Reverend Alexander Campbell of Bethany, Virginia, whose remarks were devoted solely to attacking Catholicism. Bishop Purcell of Cincinnati, who was in the audience, objected and for his pains was challenged to a debate by Campbell. They arranged a series of seven meetings and seven subjects were chosen, one to be debated each day.[66] Accounts of this controversy were widely printed[67] and at its conclusion a public meeting of the citizens of Cincinnati expressed satisfaction with the manner in which Campbell had devastated the arguments of the bishop.[68]

The popularity of these controversies inspired a deluge of similar debates which were less well publicized, many of them arranged by debating societies in the larger cities which either drew upon outside speakers or used their own members to discuss various points in Catholic faith. The practice was so general that it was widely believed among the Catholic clergy that all the debates were inspired by the New York Protestant Association as a means of attacking Catholicism.[69] As a result, Catholics in New York were warned to stay away from discussions of their religion[70]—an order which was itself the cause of a controversy carried on through the columns of the New York *Journal of Commerce.*[71]

The last and one of the most important of the early debates involved Bishop John England, long famed as a defender of Catholicism in Charleston, and arose when a local temperance society issued a petition comparing the state's system of licensing liquor-selling to the practice of the Catholic church of selling the privilege to sin before sin was committed. Bishop England refused to allow such a statement to go unchallenged. He demanded the society's authority for its assertion, and when the members were unable to reply, their cause was championed by the Reverend Richard Fuller, a Baptist clergyman, who cited the *Tax Book of the Roman Chancery* published at Rome in 1514 which, he said, authorized and sanctioned the sale of indulgences by the Catholic church. England promptly branded the book a forgery and the two argued at length over this point, eventually drifting into a general discussion of Catholicism and Protestantism.[72] The only sufferer from this controversy was the Charleston *Courier,* in the columns of which letters of both contestants appeared. After the argument was well under way, the editors announced that so much valuable space was being devoted to the question that it would be necessary to charge regular advertising rates for publishing further correspondence.[73] England by this time was ready to close the controversy but Fuller was unwilling and it dragged on until the middle of October, 1839, with both writers discussing everything from the morals of the priesthood to conditions in Ireland.

By the end of the 1830's this form of debate was losing popularity among nativists who slowly realized that the controversies did the anti-Catholic cause little good.[74] Through them, thinking Protestants who had been bred in a hatred of Romanism were learning for the first time that the Catholics did have a sound argument and that many of the charges aimed at Popery were equally repudiated by the Church itself. Propagandists took refuge in the claim that the debates were unfair as priests were pledged to keep no faith with heretics, and so could refuse to tell the truth while Protestant debaters were bound by more rigid ethical standards.[75] Behind this evasion was the grim realization that their champions had not achieved the devastating victories which had been expected.

More to the liking of Protestant writers and speakers was avowed propaganda in which Catholics were given no chance for reply or rebuttal. The stated purpose of these works coincided with the declared objective of the New York Protestant Association and the controversialists: to make known the true character of Romanism in order that Americans might be warned.[76] Yet the type of propaganda which began to appear showed that a subtle change was taking place. The theological arguments which had characterized earlier works were giving way before attacks on the immoral nature of Catholicism. Nativistic propagandists were learning the lesson brought home to the evangelical churches by the New Measures, that sensationalism had far more appeal for the average American than sober arguments.

The effectiveness of this type of propaganda was demonstrated by the favorable reception of several outstanding English No-Popery works; notably Anthony Gavin's *Master Key to Popery,*[77] Scippio de Ricci's *Female Convents. Secrets of Nunneries Disclosed,*[78] and Richard Baxter's *Jesuit Juggling. Forty Popish Frauds Detected and Disclosed,*[79] all of which depicted Catholicism as a highly immoral system in which lecherous priests employed convents to evade the vows of celibacy to which they bound themselves. In these books appeared tales of secret passageways connecting nunneries with the homes of the clergy,[80] of babies' bodies found beneath abandoned convents,[81] and of confessors who abused both their trust and the young ladies whom they confessed. The impression created by these English writers was that convents and monasteries were dens of vice and iniquity in which nuns and monks wallowed in a slough of ignorance and corruption.

This theme found immediate favor and soon American books began to appear disclosing the supposed evils of the convent system. Not only did they reiterate the charges of immorality, but they adapted their arguments to American tastes by asserting that convent schools were to be the medium through which Protestantism was to be subjugated and Popery made supreme in the United States. Many writers were suspicious of the devotion which popish schools showed in educating Protestant children while paying little attention to the educational needs of Catholics. This obviously meant that they were maintained simply to gain converts to Catholicism.[82] "The sole object of all monastic institutions in America," one writer asserted, "is merely to proselyte youth of the influential classes of society, and especially females; as the Roman priests are conscious that by this means they shall silently but effectually attain the control of public affairs." [83] By means of this type of propaganda, Protestant parents were made to believe that in sending their children to a convent school they risked both their daughters' virtue and their country's future.

Much of this calumny was directed against one of the most prominent of the Catholic institutions, the Ursuline Convent school in Charlestown, Massachusetts. The Ursulines had established their religious house in Massachusetts in 1818, and despite a mild persecution, had prospered and constructed a large building on the crest of Mount Benedict. There they conducted a school which attracted the daughters of the wealthier families of Boston and neighboring towns.[84] It was this imposing brick structure which was to arouse Boston Protestants to mob action.

Class antipathies, religious jealousies and economic conditions all combined with the spreading No-Popery sentiment to create a state of mind among the people of Massachusetts whereby such wanton destruction of property was possible. The Charlestown in which the Ursuline convent stood was a rural community whose population was swayed by the superstitions and misbeliefs common to the country people of that day. Those who actually took part in the burning of the convent were from the lower classes; for the most part engaged as truckmen or as brickmakers in Charlestown's brick yards. This group was peculiarly susceptible to the propaganda being circu-

lated against the Catholic church and especially against nunneries, for their natural American curiosity made them read
all disclosures concerning the mysterious building on Mount
Benedict and to believe with unquestioning credulity all that they
read.[85]

The distrust which they felt for the convent was heightened
by the class of pupils which it attracted, drawn largely from
the upper class families of Boston who had rebelled against the
rigid Congregationalism of the public school system.[86] Many
of the families whose daughters attended the Ursuline school
were Unitarians who felt a particular antipathy to the existing
order within the Commonwealth. All of the hatreds bred of
the struggle then going on between liberal and fundamentalist
religion in Massachusetts were centered on the Charlestown
convent. To the lower classes, with whom Congregationalism
was a sacred creed, Catholics and Unitarians seemed to be
combining against their religion. One editor summed up popular sentiment when he wrote: "Atheists and Infidels will be
always ready to sympathize with Catholics, to unite with them
in crushing Protestantism preparatory to the subversion of
Christianity." [87] The issue was clearly drawn when a rival
school was established in Charlestown in 1831, the Charlestown
Female Seminary. Instruction here was in accord with usual
Protestant traditions,[88] and when the liberal Boston families
continued to send their daughters to the convent school, it
seemed obvious that some alliance between Unitarianism and
Catholicism existed.

This success of the Ursulines naturally angered the orthodox
ministers of Boston, for Protestant preference for Catholic
education seemed to typify a crumbling of their entire religious
system. Their alarm was expressed by the General Association
of the Congregational church of Massachusetts which adopted
resolutions urging pastors to labor to save the "country from
the degrading influence of Popery" and recommending that the

district associations "give the subject of Popery, in all its bear-ings, a serious and prayerful consideration." [89]   This inspired a large number of sermons against Catholicism, both in Boston and the neighboring towns.   Most prominent among the minis-ters bent upon exposing papal designs was the Reverend Lyman Beecher, pastor of the Park Street church in Boston, a revival-istic preacher whose fiery sermons had earned his church the popular designation of "Brimstone Corner." [90]   Dr. Beecher, late in 1830, began a series of anti-Catholic sermons in which he attempted to show that Catholicism and despotism were definitely allied and equally opposed to American principles of republicanism.   Popery, he concluded, was dangerous not only to the established religion but also to the established govern-ment.[91]   The wide interest aroused by Dr. Beecher's sermons [92] encouraged other ministers to similar denunciations of Rome [93] and the Boston religious press linked these general attacks with the Ursuline convent by insisting that the pupils who attended were being converted to Popery and warning that the leading citizens of Massachusetts would eventually all be Romanists unless some check could be put on Catholic educational activ-ities.[94]   Bishop Fenwick vainly tried to answer these attacks in a series of sermons, and although his audience was liberally sprinkled with Protestants, the lower classes most affected by anti-Catholic propaganda were not present.[95]   Instead they were being swept along in a current of popular enthusiasm against Popery created by the writers and speakers against Rome and intensified by a religious revival then gripping Boston.[96]

The turbulence fostered in the lower classes by the clergy found expression all through the early 1830's.   In 1829 a group of Americans, aroused by the exhortations of a revivalistic preacher, attacked the homes of Irish Catholics in Boston and stoned them for three days.[97]   Four years later a group of drunken Irishmen beat a native American citizen to death on the streets of Charlestown.   The next night five hundred natives marched on the Irish section, and troops that were called out stood helplessly by while a number of houses were torn down and burned.[98] Posters warning of popish plots began to appear mysteriously about the streets of Charlestown and Boston.[99] Rumors flew in increasing numbers concerning the convent on Mount Benedict: stories of barbarities practiced on the nuns, of a dying man cruelly treated, of the immorality with which it was infested. Parents who considered enrolling their daughters in the Ursuline school were subjected to pressure and plied with dreadful tales of convent life.[100] An anti-Catholic novel, *The Nun,* which was popular just at this time, seemed to confirm many of these fears.[101]

These rumors took on a new meaning with the actual appearance in Boston of an "escaped nun," Rebecca Theresa Reed, who had, according to her own tales, been a sister in the Ursuline convent. The fact that she had been known for years as a commonplace chit of a girl about Charlestown or that the Mother Superior of the Ursulines contended that she had merely been dismissed from a menial position in the sisterhood, did not dull the popular interest in her tales of convent life.[102] Rebecca Reed's account of the dread occurrences within the walls of Mount Benedict and of the plots to carry her off to Canada to check her revelations were generally believed above all denials.[103] Her tales prepared the people to believe the worst when an actual nun, Elizabeth Harrison, a member of the Ursuline order who taught music in the convent school, did "escape" a short time later. Overwork and long hours of teaching had undermined Miss Harrison's health to such an extent that she had become mentally deranged.[104] In this condition, she left the convent on the night of July 28, 1834, ran to the home of a neighboring brick manufacturer, Edward Cutter, and demanded refuge. Cutter took her to her brother in Cambridge, where reason returned, and Miss Harrison, realizing what she had done, immediately asked that Bishop Fenwick be sent for. He visited her the next day and readily granted her request to be allowed to return to the convent.[105]

By that time, however, the mischief had been done. Before Miss Harrison was again at her accustomed post, all Boston had heard her story in an increasingly distorted form. It was generally believed that she had been forced to return and had been cast into a deep dungeon in the cellars of the convent building as punishment.[106] These vague rumors probably would have been soon forgotten but for the publication of an article in one of the Boston papers, the *Mercantile Journal,* on the morning of August 8th, which stated:

MYSTERIOUS

We understand that a great excitement at present exists in Charlestown, in consequence of the mysterious disappearance of a young lady at the Nunnery in that place. The circumstances, as far as we can learn, are as follows: The young lady was sent to the place in question to complete her education, and became so pleased with the place and its inmates, that she was induced to seclude herself from the world and take the black veil. After some time spent in the Nunnery, she became dissatisfied, and made her escape from the institution—but was afterwards persuaded to return, being told that if she would continue but three weeks longer, she would be dismissed with honor. At the end of that time, a few days since, her friends called for her, but she was not to be found, and much alarm is excited in consequence.[107]

These misstatements were copied in the *Morning Post* and the Boston *Commercial Gazette* and immediately caused a flurry of excitement among the sensation-loving populace. Placards were posted which called on the selectmen of Charlestown to investigate, threatening mob violence to the convent unless Miss Harrison was found.[108] Feeling ran high both in Charlestown and Boston.

In the midst of this excitement, the Reverend Lyman Beecher returned to Boston, reaching the city during the week of August

3.[109] On the night of Sunday, August 10, he delivered three violent anti-Catholic sermons in as many churches in Boston, exhorting overflowing audiences to action against Popery;[110] an example which was followed by other Boston clergymen who were always ready to take advantage of the popular antipathy against Rome. Most of the city's pulpits on that Sabbath were given over to denunciations of Catholicism and many of the sermons were directed especially against the Ursuline convent.[111]

In all probability the convent would have been attacked whether or not these sermons were delivered, for there is every reason to believe that the lower classes of Boston and Charlestown had agreed on its destruction even before Miss Harrison's escape and return.[112] It seems clear that a group of truckmen and brickmakers had developed some sort of organization for this specific purpose, that they had held at least two meetings in which ways and means had been discussed, and that they had been prevented from acting before only by a lack of popular support.[113] There is some indication that the leaders of this group were prominent Boston citizens, but this is by no means certain.[114] It is fairly evident, however, that the existence of a plan to destroy the convent was well known among the lower classes at least three days before the actual burning took place and that no move was made against the rioters because public opinion in general gave tacit approval to the project.[115]

Despite this conspiracy, proper action by the Charlestown selectmen would have done much to quell growing resentment and perhaps would have saved the convent. They were, however, unwilling to take any preventive steps because of a personal controversy with Bishop Fenwick in which they were then engaged. Bishop Fenwick had a short time before purchased three acres of land on Bunker Hill to be used as a Catholic cemetery and had applied to the selectmen for permission to bury two children there. The selectmen had replied that the health regulations of the town prevented the burial of any Roman Catholic, although allowing the burial of Protestants. Bishop Fenwick buried the children in the cemetery despite this refusal, and the selectmen brought suit against him. This litigation was pending when excitement over the convent reached its height,[116] and made the selectmen little inclined to exert themselves in behalf of Catholics.

The growing feeling against the Mount Benedict institution finally convinced even the Charlestown selectmen that something must be done. On Saturday, August 9, they visited the convent building and asked to be allowed to make an inspection, but the Mother Superior, taking the attitude that they were responsible for many of the rumors, refused them admittance.[117] However, Edward Cutter, who had sheltered Elizabeth Harrison during her mental derangement, was permitted to talk to Miss Harrison and satisfied himself that she was contended with her lot and not languishing in a hidden dungeon.[118] On the following Monday, August 11, the selectmen were finally allowed to tour the building. They prepared a report for the Boston newspapers, stating that Miss Harrison was "entirely satisfied with her present situation, it being that of her own choice; and that she has no desire or wish to alter it." [119] But when the papers published this report, together with one prepared by Cutter, on Tuesday morning, it was too late. The convent was then a mass of smoldering ruins.

A mob had begun to gather in the school grounds at nine o'clock on the night of August 11, carrying banners and shouting "No Popery" and "Down with the Cross." [120] One Charlestown selectman was present and others were notified, but they insisted that the town's one police officer could handle the situation adequately.[121] While the crowd was milling about, a group of forty or fifty men, evidently well organized and more or less disguised, approached the building and demanded that they be shown the nun who was secreted there. They were told to return the next day when the children would not be awakened and retired, seemingly satisfied.[122] But at eleven o'clock a pile of tar barrels was lighted in a neighboring field, evidently a pre-arranged signal. Fire bells were set ringing and crowds of people began pouring into Charlestown. Fire companies appeared but stood helplessly by as the mob began the attack.[123] The Mother Superior vainly tried to appeal to the throng, first by pleading, then by threatening that "the Bishop has twenty thousand Irishmen at his command in Boston." [124] This only infuriated the crowd. Led by the same forty or fifty organized men who had been active from the first, they burst open the doors and entered the convent building as the dozen sisters present hurried the sixty pupils through a rear door and to a nearby place of refuge.[125] At a little after midnight the torch was applied to both the school and a neighboring farmhouse belonging to the Ursulines. The large crowd stood by until both buildings were consumed by the flames.[126]

Boston was thrown into a furor of excitement by the burning. Rumors spread that bands of Irishmen were marching on the city from neighboring railroad camps and Bishop Fenwick hurriedly dispatched six priests in as many directions to check this onslaught.[127] The bishop also called Boston Catholics together and urged them to remain quiet and depend on the law to see that justice was done.[128] These wise measures did not calm public fears, for everywhere people were apprehensive of some retaliatory step by the Irish and even the Harvard students appointed regular patrols to protect the Yard from attack or vandalism.[129] "I have not," wrote a correspondent, "witnessed such a scene of excitement throughout the whole mass of the phlegmatic and peaceable population of Boston since my residence in the city commenced." [130]

On the night after the attack a mob of men and boys marched to Mount Benedict, burned fences, trees, and all else they could find on the convent grounds, and were only kept from storming a nearby Catholic church by the presence of troops stationed to guard the home of Edward Cutter.[131] The next night a crowd of more than a thousand men wandered the streets of Boston, alarmed by a rumor that Irish laborers were descending on the city. On the following Friday, August 15, rioters burned a Charlestown shanty occupied by thirty-five Irish laborers, but further damage was averted when the drawbridge was raised to prevent the Boston mob which quickly formed from reaching the scene of the blaze.[132]

Excitement such as this in staid Boston clearly indicated the height which popular sentiment against Catholicism had reached. The lower classes, believing that they had struck a decisive blow at Rome, were obviously so anxious to continue their advantage that they would willingly have repeated their destructive tactics at the expense of Irish homes and Catholic churches. The total lack of remorse revealed a deep-seated antipathy toward Catholicism and made it evident that in New England at least, the No-Popery movement had been successfully launched.

NOTES

[1] An attempt to found a No-Popery paper in Boston a year earlier to be called the *Anti-Jesuit and Social and Commercial Advocate* had evidently failed. *Priestcraft Exposed and Primitive Religion Defended*, January 5, 1829.

[2] *Massachusetts Yeoman*, December 19, 1829.

[3] New York *Observer*, November 14, 1829.

[4] *The Protestant*, January 9, 1830.

[5] *Vermont Inquirer*, quoted in *Ibid.*, August 13, 1831; New York *Observer*, November 14, 1829.

[6] Resolutions endorsing *The Protestant* were passed by the Reformed Presbyterian Synod of Philadelphia, the Philadelphia Baptist Association and the Oneida, New York, Presbytery. *The Protestant*, January 16, 1830, February 20, 1830, October 15, 1831, October 22, 1831.

[7] *Ibid.*, June 4, 1831, January 7, 1832. The *Methodist Advocate and Journal* adopted this point of view.

[8] *Ibid.*, January 18, 1830.

[9] *Ibid.*, February 13, 1830 and ff.

[10] The letters so pleased the editors that they wrote a eulogy of the unknown "Cranmer" and urged him to contribute further. *Ibid.*, March 13, 1830.

[11] *Ibid.*, October 30, 1830. The plot was first exposed in July, 1830. *Ibid.*, July 24, 1830, July 31, 1830.

[12] The change was made when David Ayres took over ownership of the paper. Bourne was retained as editor. *Ibid.*, May 7, 1830.

[13] An effort to show the changed policy of the paper was made by securing the endorsement of seventy-three New York clergymen. The development of the New York anti-Catholic press is discussed in some detail in the *Protestant Magazine*, I (August, 1834).

[14] *The Protestant*, June 9, 1832.

[15] *Ibid.*, June 16, 1832.

[16] *Ibid.*, June 30, 1832.

[17] *Protestant Magazine*, I (August, 1834) ; New York *Observer*, November 23, 1833. When Dr. Brownlee gave up his editorship the paper was turned over to its publishers, the firm of Gibson and Irvine, and one of the members of the firm, James Irvine, became editor. It was announced in *The Protestant* itself, June 30, 1832, that the paper was to be published in the interest of the American Reformation Society. There is no extraneous evidence of the continued existence of such a society and this may have been simply a device of the publishers to popularize their enterprise.

[18] *Protestant Magazine*, I (August, 1834). The change from a weekly to monthly publication was effected by a new publisher, C. C. P. Crosby, who purchased the *Reformation Advocate* in September, 1833. The new publisher retained James Irvine as editor.

[19] *Ibid.*, I (September, 1833).

[20] *Ibid.*, I (September, 1833).

[21] The usual issue contained twenty-four pages. It published such articles as : "A Candid Examination of the Doctrines and Usages of Roman Catholics," "Popish Principles Tend to Subvert Civil Liberty," "Letter of Dr. Miller on Popish Education of Children," "Extract from Milton on Popery and the Reformation," and "Catholic Priests Hate the Savior." *Ibid.*, I (September, 1833).

[22] *Ibid.*, I (August, 1834).

[23] A semimonthly paper, published at New York between January 1, 1830, and November 15, 1830.

[24] A semimonthly paper, published at Concord, New Hampshire, during 1834. An earlier paper of the same name, *Priestcraft Exposed and Primitive Religion Defended*, had been published at Lockport, New York, from May 19, 1828, through April 6, 1829. This was a monthly paper.

[25] *Priestcraft Exposed*, April 1, 1834.

[26] *The Protestant*, January 15, 1831. The editor could not help exulting that he had labored to bring into being "something like an organized system of effort to maintain the liberty and prosperity of the Republic, against the machinations of the Pope and the Jesuits."

[27] *Ibid.*, April 30, 1831. A correspondent inquired as to the fate of the association and was informed by the editor that it had done nothing since officers were elected at its initial meeting.

[28] *Ibid.*, February 18, 1832. The organization meeting was held in New York on February 13. Resolutions were offered by Bourne and by Herman Norton, who was likewise to become influential in the whole anti-Catholic movement.

[29] The constitution is printed in *Ibid.*, February 18, 1832. Members were

to pay dues of a dollar a year, although all Protestant ministers were to be admitted free.

30 Circular of the association, printed in *Ibid.,* March 10, 1832.

31 *Ibid.,* March 3, 1832.

32 *Ibid.,* May 5, 1832.

33 *Ibid.,* May 19, 1832.

34 *Ibid.,* May 12, 1832.

35 This conclusion was reached by a committee headed by the president of the association, W. C. Brownlee. *Ibid.,* May 12, 1832.

36 *Ibid.,* June 23, 1832. *The Protestant* branded the order as an example of "that freedom which Papists enjoy in this country."

37 *Ibid.,* May 26, 1832, June 2, 1832, June 16, 1832, June 30, 1832. No meetings were held during the summer months.

38 *Ibid.,* September 29, 1832. A special feature of the first meeting of the fall season was the singing of a new hymn, "The Anthem of the Fall of Babylon," composed for the society.

39 *Protestant Magazine,* I (March, 1834). A speaker in New York in February, 1835, was similarly interrupted but was not forced to abandon the meeting. *American Protestant Vindicator,* February 18, 1835. When the Reverend Robert J. Breckinridge was heckled while giving a series of anti-Catholic speeches in Philadelphia, public interest became so great that his lectures had to be delivered in a larger hall. New York *Observer,* December 27, 1834.

40 *American Protestant Vindicator,* March 4, 1835.

41 This account is taken from an official report issued by the association, printed in the *Christian Watchman,* March 27, 1835; New York *Observer,* March 21, 1835.

42 *American Protestant Vindicator,* March 18, 1835.

43 *Ibid.,* March 25, 1835.

44 The New York *Sun* and the New York *Journal of Commerce* severely indicted the Catholics for their part in the riot. *Ibid.,* March 25, 1835; Boston *Observer,* March 26, 1835; *Downfall of Babylon,* March 28, 1835.

45 March 22, 1834.

46 *Protestant Magazine,* I (April, 1834).

47 *The Protestant,* July 14, 1832.

48 Outside of New York City, the only avowedly anti-Catholic societies at this time were the Irish Protestant societies. Typical were the Orange Association of Philadelphia and the Boston Irish Protestant Association, both of which were devoted to arranging lectures and debates against Catholicism, similar to those organized by the New York Protestant Association. *The Protestant,* August 14, 1830; *American Protestant Vindicator,* June 10, 1835; *Christian Watchman,* October 16, 1835.

49 New York *Observer,* October 26, 1833 and ff. The articles were later published under the title, *Thoughts on Popery* (New York, 1836). Another series in *Ibid.,* December 18, 1830 and ff. entitled "Letters on Popery," pictured affairs in Malta as viewed by a Protestant missionary. During this period several columns of the front page of the New York *Observer* were normally occupied with attacks on Catholics and not infrequently the entire front page

would be devoted to the cause. The *Christian Watchman*, Boston *Recorder*, and other religious newspapers examined showed a similar trend.

50 Bishop Fenwick of Boston complained in 1830 that every pulpit in Boston was given over to attacks on Catholicism. O'Daniel, *The Right Reverend Edward Dominic Fenwick*, 384.

51 John Hughes and John Breckinridge, *Controversy between Rev. Messrs. Hughes and Breckinridge on the Subject, "Is the Protestant Religion the Religion of Christ?"* (Philadelphia, 1833), i–iv.

52 *Ibid.*, vi–xx. It was further agreed that no letter was to fill more than four columns.

53 Hassard, *Life of John Hughes*, 135–142.

54 *Protestant Episcopalian and Church Register*, IV (February, 1833), and ff ; *Protestant Magazine*, I (September, 1833) ; New York *Observer*, March 9, 1833 ; *Episcopal Recorder*, February 16, 1833. The *Christian Watchman* decided that it would not reprint the arguments as few Baptists looked on Popery with anything but horror and it was not necessary to convince them of Catholic error. July 26, 1833.

55 Hughes and Breckinridge, *Controversy*, 1–239.

56 *Protestant Episcopalian and Church Register*, IV (May, 1833).

57 Hughes and Breckinridge, *Controversy*, 470.

58 New York *Observer*, March 9, 1833.

59 *Ibid.*, July 27, 1833.

60 *Ibid.*, August 3, 1833.

61 *Ibid.*, August 17, 1833.

62 *Ibid.*, September 7, 1833 and ff. The letters were printed in the *Christian Intelligencer*, the New York *Observer*, the *Protestant Magazine*, and other religious and nativistic journals. The *Truth Teller* stopped printing the letters as soon as the priests withdrew from the controversy.

63 The *Western Luminary* received a letter from a Catholic offering $2,000 to Breckinridge if he could prove the Protestant religion to be the religion of Christ. *American Protestant Vindicator*, June 17, 1835. Breckinridge continued to give anti-Catholic speeches and sermons in large numbers, however. *Ibid.*, December 17, 1834, December 31, 1834.

64 John Hughes and John Breckinridge, *A Discussion on the Question, Is the Roman Catholic Religion, in any or in all of its Principles or Doctrines, Inimical to Civil or Religious Liberty? and the Question, Is the Presbyterian Religion, in any or in all of its Principles or Doctrines, Inimical to Civil or Religious Liberty?* (Philadelphia, 1836), 3–4. The first subject was debated in six meetings (33–277) and the second in the remaining six meetings (281–546).

65 Hassard, *Life of John Hughes*, 133–160.

66 Alexander Campbell and J. P. Purcell, *A Debate on the Roman Catholic Religion: held in the Sycamore-Street Meeting House, Cincinnati, from the 13th to the 21st of January, 1837* (Cincinnati, 1837), vii–viii.

67 New York *Observer*, November 12, 1837, quoting the *American Baptist* and other religious papers.

68 New York *Journal of Commerce*, February 3, 1837. A similar discussion ranged Bishop John H. Hopkins of the Episcopal church against Bishop

Kenrick of the Philadelphia diocese. Hopkins, however, was not a satisfactory champion for evangelical Protestants; the *American Protestant Vindicator*, March 16, 1838, complained of his "milk and water arguments."

69 Hughes expressed this sentiment in a letter written at the time and printed in Hassard, *Life of John Hughes*, 154.

70 New York *Observer*, January 28, 1837.

71 New York *Journal of Commerce*, January 4, 1837 and ff. The controversy was opened by a Protestant author who signed himself Obsta Principis, charging that this order from the Bishop was typical of efforts of the Church to stop free discussion. He was answered by a Catholic under the signature of Catholicus. The discussion lasted through the early months of 1837.

72 Richard Fuller and John England, *Letters Concerning the Roman Chancery* (Baltimore, 1840), 1–26.

73 *Ibid.*, 155. The Baltimore *Literary and Religious Magazine*, a nativistic publication, offered to undertake the presentation of the arguments, but this was not accepted. V (November, 1839).

74 This was evidenced by the lack of excitement over a controversy taking place in Albany in 1840 between a priest, the Reverend J. Kelly, and an unnamed author of an anti-Catholic pamphlet. The Albany *Argus* and the Albany *Journal* were given over to the letters of the two debaters for several months. *Controversy Between the Author of 'Baptizo Defined' and the Rev. Mr. Kelly* (Albany, 1840).

75 *A History of Popery, Including Its Origin, Progress, Doctrines, Practice, Institutions and Fruits, to the Commencement of the Nineteenth Century* (New York, 1834), 16.

76 *Ibid.*, 3–4; New York *Observer*, March 1, 1834.

77 This book had appeared in England in the eighteenth century, a third edition being published in London in 1773. It was reprinted in America during the Revolution and again in 1812 under the title: *A Master Key to Popery, Giving a Full Account of all the Customs of the Priests and Friars and the Rites and Ceremonies of the Popish Religion* (——, 1812). Subsequent American editions were: *The Master Key to Popery: Customs of Priests and Friars, and Rites and Ceremonies of the Popish Religion, Inquisition, etc.* (Cincinnati, 1834); *A History of Popery: Giving a Full Account of all the Priests and Friars, and the Rites and Ceremonies of the Papal Church* (Hartford, 1845); *The Great Red Dragon, or The Master Key to Popery* (Boston, 1854). It was also printed in part in a number of other anti-Catholic books. The citations are from the 1812 edition.

78 *Female Convents. Secrets of Nunneries Disclosed* (New York, 1834). The author had been a reforming priest in Tuscany in the middle of the eighteenth century. His work was allegedly a compilation of the evidences of immorality in the church which he kept for his own purposes. They had first been published in England during the No-Popery excitement there in 1829.

79 *Jesuit Juggling. Forty Popish Frauds Detected and Disclosed* (New York, 1835). This was an ancient English propaganda work which had frequently been published in that country.

80 Ricci, *Female Convents*, 94.

81 William McGavin, *The Protestant. Essays on the Principal Points of*

Controversy between the Church of Rome and the Reformed (Hartford, 1833), II, 80.

81 New York *Observer*, December 19, 1829, June 18, 1831, August 16, 1834; *Protestant Magazine*, I (September, 1833); Ricci, *Female Convents*, xxi; *A History of Popery*.

83 Ricci, *Female Convents*, xxii.

84 The early history of the Charlestown convent is discussed in E. V. Vogel, "The Ursuline Nuns in America," *Records of the American Catholic Historical Society*, I (1887), 214–243; and in Ephriam Tucker, "The Burning of the Ursuline Convent," Worcester Society of Antiquity *Collections*, IX, 40–41.

85 Frederick Marryat, *A Diary in America* (Philadelphia, 1839), 28. Marryat was told that a majority of the mob which tore down the convent was influenced more by curiosity than any other thing. Marryat sagely remarked that the Americans "cannot bear anything like a secret—that's unconstitutional."

86 Benedict J. Fenwick, "The Destruction of the Ursuline Convent at Charlestown, Mass.," United States Catholic Historical Society, *Records and Studies*, IX (New York, 1916), 187–188. Fenwick was Bishop of the Boston diocese and expressed this view in this letter, written shortly after the burning of the convent.

87 *Massachusetts Yeoman*, January 15, 1831.

88 Charlestown Female Seminary, *Catalogue of the Officers, Teachers and Pupils* (Boston, 1834).

89 *Minutes of the General Association of Massachusetts* (Boston, 1834), 10–11.

90 Thomas Nichols, *Forty Years of American Life* (London, 1864), II, 89.

91 New York *Observer*, January 29, 1831, February 5, 1831.

92 The sermons were printed in the New York *Observer, Christian Watchman, Massachusetts Yeoman, Christian Herald*, Boston *Recorder*, and other papers. They are also in Lyman Beecher, *The Works of the Reverend Lyman Beecher* (Boston, 1852), I.

93 *Christian Watchman*, October 12, 1832.

94 *Ibid.*, January 29, 1830, February 19, 1830, December 17, 1830; *The Protestant*, December 4, 1830, June 4, 1831, June 23, 1832. The amount of instruction in the Catholic religion received by the pupils was a matter of controversy at the time. A circular advertising the Ursuline school stated that the teachers would spare "no pains to adorn their minds with useful knowledge and to form their hearts in virtue. To attain this two-fold object, their first care is to instruct them in the great and sublime truths of Religion." Circular reprinted in Benjamin F. DeCosta, *The Story of Mount Benedict* (Somerville, Massachusetts, 1893), 5. The pupils who attended, however, insisted that they were allowed to practice their Protestant religion unmolested and that no proselyting attempts were made upon them. A series of letters from pupils and their parents testifying to this is printed in Richard S. Fay, *Argument before the Committee of the House of Representatives upon the Petition of Benedict Fenwick and others, with a portion of the Documentary Testimony* (Boston, 1835), 40–50.

95 Boston *Courier*, February 10, 1831. Fenwick's sermons probably did his cause more harm than good, for they were violently criticized by the religious press. The *Christian Herald* called them "boastful and boisterous and assumptive and wholly devoid of Christian meekness." Quoted in New York *Observer*, January 29, 1831. See also *Christian Watchman*, January 21, 1831.

96 This revival was being conducted by the Reverend Charles G. Finney.

97 William Leahy, *The Catholic Church in New England* (Boston, 1899), I, 53.

98 New York *Observer*, December 7, 1833.

99 One poster in 1831 read:

TO THE PUBLIC

Be it known unto you far and near, that all Catholics and all persons in favor of the Catholic Church, are a set of vile impostors, liars, villains and cowardly cut-throats. (Beware of False Doctrines). I bid defiance to that villain,—*THE POPE.*

A True American

100 Louisa Whitney, *The Burning of the Convent; a Narrative of the Destruction, by a Mob, of the Ursuline School on Mount Benedict, Charlestown, as Remembered by one of the Pupils* (Boston, 1877), 17–18. Miss Whitney tells of repeated visits received by her father after he had resolved to send her to the convent school.

101 *Ibid.*, 28–29. The novel was by Miss S. Sherwood.

102 The Mother Superior testified at the trial of the rioters that Miss Reed had insisted on being taken into the convent for six months to prove her worth, hoping then to be admitted into the sisterhood. She had been dismissed at the end of four months. *Trial of John R. Buzzell, the Leader of the Convent Rioters, for Arson and Burglary Committed on the Night of the 11th of August, 1834, By the Destruction of the Convent on Mount Benedict, in Charlestown, Massachusetts* (Boston, 1834), 7.

103 *Report of the Committee Relating to the Destruction of the Ursuline Convent* (Boston, 1834), 7–8.

104 *Ibid.*, 8. *Trial of John R. Buzzell, the Leader of the Convent Rioters*, 7. The Mother Superior testified at the trial that she had been acting queerly for some time.

105 Cutter wrote an account of the affairs of that evening which was published in the New York *Observer*, August 16, 1834.

106 *American Quarterly Review*, XVII (March, 1835), 216; *Report of the Committee Relating to the Destruction of the Ursuline Convent, 9.*

107 *An Account of the Conflagration of the Ursuline Convent . . . by a Friend of Religious Toleration* (Boston, 1834), 5. This is a collection of newspaper extracts made at the time concerning the destruction of the convent.

108 One placard read:

"Go Ahead! To Arms!! To Arms!! Ye brave and free the Avenging Sword unshield!! Leave not one stone upon another of that curst Nunnery that prostitutes female virtue and liberty under the garb of holy Religion. When Bonaparte opened the Nunnerys in Europe he found cords of Infant skulls!!!!!!"

Quoted in *The Charlestown Convent; its Destruction by a Mob on the Night of August 11, 1834; with a History of the Excitement before the Burning, and the Strange and Exaggerated Reports Relating Thereto, the Feeling of Regret and Indignation Afterwards; the Proceedings of Meetings, and Expressions of the Contemporary Press* (Boston, 1870), 70.

[109] Beecher was at this time president of the Lane Theological Seminary at Cincinnati, having accepted that post in 1832. Lyman Beecher, *Autobiography and Correspondence* (New York, 1865), II, 243, 333.

[110] In one church alone the collection amounted to more than $4,000, some indication of the size of his audiences and the popular enthusiasm which he aroused. *Ibid.,* II, 334; *Christian Watchman,* August 15, 1834.

[111] *The Jesuit,* August 16, 1834. The sermon at the Baptist church on Hanover street particularly offended Catholics.

[112] Most Catholic historians have made Beecher responsible for the burning, stating that the mobs rushed directly from his church to Mount Benedict and fired the convent. Shea, *History of the Catholic Church,* III, 473-480; Humphrey Desmond, *The Know Nothing Party* (Washington, 1904), 15-16 and others. Beecher himself denied this. See Beecher, *Autobiography and Correspondence,* II, 335. In this contention Beecher was probably correct, for the respectable persons who listened to his sermons would scarcely take an open part in the rioting that took place, no matter what their personal sentiments might have been.

[113] Testimony of Henry Buck, one of the rioters who turned state's evidence, in the trial of the burners. Buck swore that the conspirators held several meetings in a school house in which detailed plans for the attack were made. Buck's shady reputation, revealed by the defense counsel, makes his testimony unreliable, however. *Trial of John R. Buzzell, the Leader of the Convent Rioters,* 11-12.

[114] The defense counsel in one of the trials stated that the rioters "were ignorant men acting under the instigation of individuals better educated and moving in a higher sphere than themselves." This remark may have been occasioned by a desire to create sympathy for the defendants. *Trial of William Mason, Marvin Marcy Jr., and Sargent Blaisdell, charged with Being Concerned in Burning the Ursuline Convent in Charlestown, (Mass.) on the Night of the 11th of August, 1834* (Boston, 1834), 19.

[115] Evidences of the plot and of rumors concerning it are contained in most of the contemporary literature. See James T. Austin, *Argument of James T. Austin, Attorney General of the Commonwealth, before the Supreme Judicial Court in Middlesex on the Case of John R. Buzzell* (Boston, 1834), 34–35; Whitney, *The Burning of the Convent,* 29, 70; *Report of the Committee Relating to the Destruction of the Ursuline Convent,* 9; Lucy Thaxter, *An Account of Life in the Convent at Mount Benedict, Charlestown.* Manuscript account in the Treasure Room at Widener Library, Harvard University, written by one of the pupils shortly after the burning.

[116] The case was finally tried before the Supreme Judicial Court at the Middlesex Session on October 18, 1834. The town by-laws forbidding burial were declared invalid since the only purpose of such laws should be to regulate public health. The entire controversy is described in *The Jesuit,* November 1, 1834.

117 Whitney, *The Burning of the Convent*, 72–75.

118 His account was printed in the Boston *Morning Post*, August 11, 1834, and reprinted in the New York *Observer*, August 16, 1834.

119 Boston *Morning Post*, August 12, 1834, reprinted in the New York *Observer*, August 16, 1834.

120 *Records of the American Catholic Historical Society of Philadelphia*, XX (June, 1909), 97. The statement was made in a letter published at the time in the *Wahrheitsfreund*, a German newspaper published at Cincinnati.

121 *Report of the Committee Relating to the Destruction of the Ursuline Convent*, 10. The one police officer employed by Charlestown served also as Clerk of the Market and for both offices received a total salary of $50 a year. *Statement of the Expenses of the Town of Charlestown, from March, 1834, to March, 1835* (Charlestown, 1835).

122 Boston *Daily Advertiser*, August 12, 1834, quoted in New York *Observer*, August 16, 1834.

123 The Board of Engineers of the Boston Fire Department published a report on August 13, 1834, exonerating members of the fire companies from any connection with the burning. This report showed that only two companies reached the scene of the fire and both of these withdrew to a point several hundred yards away immediately. *An Account of the Conflagration of the Ursuline Convent*, 22–24.

124 Whitney, *The Burning of the Convent*, 113.

125 *Ibid.*, 125–160.

126 New York *Observer*, August 16, 1834; *Niles' Register*, XLVII (1834); *Report of the Committee Relating to the Destruction of the Ursuline Convent*, 11.

127 New York *Observer*, August 16, 1834; *The Jesuit*, August 16, 1834.

128 *American Quarterly Review*, XVII (March, 1835), 231.

129 Arthur B. Darling, *Political Changes in Massachusetts, 1824–1848* (New Haven, 1925), 105.

130 Boston correspondent of the New York *Journal of Commerce*, quoted in the New York *Observer*, August 23, 1834; *Christian Watchman*, August 22, 1834.

131 Boston *Transcript*, August 13, 1834, quoted in New York *Observer*, August 23, 1834.

132 New York *Observer*, August 23, 1834.

IV
The Flames Spread
1835-1840

THE nation's first reaction to the burning of the Ursuline convent was one of revulsion and horror. Wanton destruction of property and an assault on a group of defenseless women and children offended the conservatism and chivalry blended in most Americans. Particularly did the leading citizens of Boston shrink from responsibility for the outrage. A series of indignation meetings were held in which resolutions were adopted denouncing the mob action,[1] the most important convening at Faneuil Hall with Harrison Gray Otis presiding and most of the leading men of the city represented in the audience. This group agreed that "the destruction of property and danger of life caused thereby, calls loudly on all good citizens to express individually and collectively the abhorrence they feel of this high-handed violation of the laws," [2] and recommended a reward for the capture of the convent burners, state reimbursement to the Ursuline order and more stringent measures to check similar rioting in the future.[3]

This local resentment of mob rule found immediate support throughout the nation. The secular press universally condemned the violence and even the religious newspapers which had been denouncing the convent were heartily repentant, the *Christian Watchman,* the New York *Observer,* the *Western Christian Advocate,* and numerous other journals freely regretting mob rule directed against a religious group in a land which boasted of its liberty and freedom.[4] "The expressions of indignation and

85

abhorrence," said the *Christian Examiner,* "with which the perpetrators of that crime must feel themselves blasted . . . cannot do away with the fact, that they and wretches like them, exist in the bosom of our community." [5] Similarly clergymen placed Christian ethics above their hatred of Catholicism in deploring the burning. "Do you wish to introduce a Protestant inquisition," one asked his congregation, "to establish a religion by law—crush all dissenters from the legal faith, and bring back the age of persecution for opinion?" [6] Even Lyman Beecher, whose antipathy toward Romanism had contributed toward the burning of the convent, condemned the mob's action from his Boston pulpit on the following Sunday.[7] The Catholic press welcomed these repentant statements, but outdid them in its denunciation of the rioters.[8]

Laudable as these sentiments might be, they found little support among the mass of the people, who probably were more pleased than horrified at the destruction of the Ursuline school. Riot might be a poor way to achieve an end, but for the most part the people were so in accord with the end achieved that they quietly welcomed even such a violent attack upon Catholicism as that perpetrated in Charlestown. Thus while editors and ministers were willing to deplore the mob violence, they were quick to add that the Ursuline convent and all convents should be done away with to prevent the conversion of Protestant girls to Catholicism, and the spread of immorality throughout the United States.[9] St. Bartholomew's Day and the Spanish Inquisition were flung back at the Catholic editors who called the convent burning the worst outrage in history. Especially did Protestants resent the repeated insinuations that Lyman Beecher, through his sermons, had been responsible for the outrage. They elevated the issue to one of free speech and demanded that ministers be allowed to make "temperate remarks on the errors of Popery" unmolested by Catholic criticism.[10]

These sentiments were more openly expressed when Bishop

Fenwick tried to re-establish the Ursuline sisters in Boston. They were placed in a house in Roxbury, but inflammatory handbills again appeared and apprehension grew that their new home would be mobbed as was the convent building.[11] The situation was so serious that the citizens of Roxbury, having little faith in the regular law officers, named a Committee of Vigilance which kept a regular watch over the nuns during the remainder of their stay, six of its members being constantly on guard to spread the alarm in case of sudden attack.[12] Not until a year later had feeling died down sufficiently for the Ursulines to be established in Boston, but pupils now refused to attend their school, and in 1838 the Mother Superior and her followers left for Canada.[13]

An even better example of the popular sympathy for the mob which had burned the convent was offered in the trial of the principal rioters. While excitement over the burning was still high, the mayor of Boston offered a reward of $500 for the capture of the leaders and within two weeks thirteen men had been arrested.[14] Eight held for the capital offense of arson were arraigned before the Supreme Judicial Court of Massachusetts on October 10, 1834, and trial was set for December 1. This early date was protested by the attorney general who held that the excitement about Boston and the general approval of the mob's action would make it impossible to get witnesses for the prosecution. All the witnesses that he had approached had received threats, he said, and he himself had received admonitory letters and had been hanged in effigy. The court refused to be moved by these protests and the trial of the first of the rioters, John R. Buzzell, was begun on December 2.[15]

The anti-Catholic nature of the proceedings was demonstrated from the first. The attorney general was denied the right to ask jurors whether they were prejudiced against Catholicism,[16] yet the principal defense attorney was allowed to state in his opening address that the convent did not have charity for its object, that the Mother Superior and nuns had been brought into the court only to make a good impression and that all were pretending to have colds caught on the night of burning. "The prisoner at the bar cannot be convicted without Catholic testimony," he told the jury; "we will endeavor to show what that testimony is worth."[17] This speech set the pattern for the entire trial; a trial which brought Rebecca Reed to the stand to testify concerning the horrors of her life on Mount Benedict, the cross-examination of Bishop Fenwick and the Mother Superior on the immorality of convent life rather than on the matter at issue, and the branding of statements of the two principal prosecution witnesses as "imported foreign testimony" which the jurors should ignore.[18] The presiding judges made no attempt to check this appeal to the jurors' anti-Catholic sentiments in what amounted to an open disregard of justice.

When the jury retired, its decision was a foregone conclusion and the verdict of acquittal, brought in after twenty hours of deliberation, was received with thunderous applause by the crowded courtroom.[19] Immediately upon his release Buzzell was congratulated by thousands of citizens and showered with such a large number of gifts that he had to place a card of thanks in one of the Boston newspapers.[20] After this first acquittal the trial of the remaining rioters was a mere matter of form. They were all released with one exception, a youth who was sentenced to life imprisonment but promptly pardoned after the Catholics of Boston presented a petition asking for his release.[21] The acquittals were accepted with rejoicing by the Protestant press, although the Concord *Freeman* was so aroused by the attorney general's defense of Catholicism that it demanded the abolition of his office.[22]

The obvious satisfaction felt by a majority of the people after the burning of the Charlestown convent continued to be shown over the period of years during which the Ursulines sought compensation for the property which had been destroyed by the mob. The state legislature became immediately involved, when Bishop

Fenwick, shortly after the burning, petitioned for the funds necessary to rebuild the convent. The members of this body, while willing to enact more drastic riot laws,[23] hesitated to vote state funds for the use of Catholics and referred the whole question to a select committee which presented a majority and minority report early in 1835. The majority report denied the right of the Ursulines to reimbursement but, nevertheless, recommended that they be given the sum asked; the minority report refused them any compensation in a bitterly worded general attack on Catholicism.[24] The majority report was immediately attacked by the nativistic press, one editor declaring:

Any man who proposes, or who would vote for the measure, which would rob the treasury of the descendants of the Puritans to build Ursuline Nunneries, after the model of the Ursuline Nunnery at Quebec, and as the headquarters of the Jesuit Fenwick and his 20,000 vilest Irishmen must be a raving lunatic.[25]

This sentiment was so general that the measure was defeated by an overwhelming majority [26] and subsequent attempts to reimburse the Ursulines met a similar fate.[27] It was obvious that the members of the legislature, properly judging public opinion, realized that their constituents harbored such anti-Catholic sentiments that any compromise with Rome would spell their own defeat.

The popular acclaim showered upon the convent rioters, together with their acquittal and the failure of the state to reimburse the Ursulines, not only indicated the popular approval with which their attack had been viewed but encouraged similar epidemics of disorder all over the country. In New England, where the people had had a taste of rioting, mob attacks on Catholic churches became so frequent [28] that many congregations posted regular armed guards to patrol and protect their property, and insurance companies refused to place a policy upon Catholic buildings which were not constructed of noninflammable materials.[29]

Protestants planned to celebrate the first anniversary of the burning of the convent by parading the streets of Charlestown with an effigy of the Mother Superior which was later to be riddled by bullets,[30] but the local selectmen, apprehensive of trouble, refused permission for this display. A Boston military company did destroy an effigy of Bishop Fenwick and a group of riotous men in that city announced their organization as the "Convent Boys" with an avowed intention of destroying all Catholic property.[31] As this mania for rioting spread, attacks became more common through the entire east; [32] the mob spirit extending even into the south where Bishop England hesitated to land a group of nuns coming to establish a school in Charleston lest they arouse the wrath of the people.[33]

The destruction of the Ursuline convent was influential not only in centering attention on the No-Popery crusade and elevating it to a plane of national importance; it was important in that it inspired a new series of propaganda works which were to prove more successful than any preceding them and set a pattern to be followed with great success by nativists for many years. This propaganda was centered about the person of Rebecca Theresa Reed, whose stories had been instrumental in inducing the riot. A group of enterprising Bostonians, led by the editor of the Boston *Advocate*,[34] soon after the burning realized the possibility of capitalizing upon her name and early in 1835 produced her famed *Six Months in a Convent*,[35] a work which was almost universally praised by the press [36] and which was seized upon by a greedy public in a manner little short of phenomenal. The first supply of several thousand copies sent to New York City was exhausted within two hours. Within the first week after publication more than ten thousand copies had been sold and it was conservatively estimated that two hundred thousand copies would be disposed of within a month. By the end of 1835 the book was being republished throughout the United States and England and threatened to break all records for enduring popularity.[37]

Actually *Six Months in a Convent* deserved little of the praise which it inspired. It was a mild account of the author's life, of her tribulations in the Ursuline convent, and of her final escape, none of which could be made particularly exciting. Her revelations of convent life were disappointing to those who had expected intimate details, for they were concerned entirely with the penances which the nuns were forced to perform and were neither immoral nor alarming.[38]

Rebecca Reed's work was important in the anti-Catholic movement not because of its contents, however, but because of the controversy which it aroused. Soon after its appearance it was replied to by the Mother Superior of the Ursuline convent, Sister Mary Edmund Saint George, in *An Answer to Six Months in a Convent Exposing Its Falsehoods and Manifold Absurdities.*[39] After a lengthy introduction attacking Miss Reed's character,[40] the Mother Superior devoted most of her publication to a detailed attack on *Six Months in a Convent,* refuting its statements in a thorough, if dull, manner. This was followed within a short time by *A Review of the Lady Superior's reply to 'Six Months in a Convent,' Being a Vindication of Miss Reed,*[41] in which an anonymous author not only attempted to prove the Mother Superior false but also attacked the whole Catholic system in the United States.[42] The Committee on Publication which had sponsored, and probably prepared, *Six Months in a Convent* was ready with a second volume before the year was out, *A Supplement to 'Six Months in a Convent,' Confirming the Narrative of Rebecca Theresa Reed, by the Testimony of More Than 100 Witnesses,*[43] in which were chronicled the events leading to the burning of the Ursuline convent including the escape of Elizabeth Harrison and the tortures inflicted upon her when she returned.[44]

It was this burst of attack and counterattack which elevated the convent question to a position of importance. "The brands from that burning," one Catholic complained, "have set fires throughout the country, that seem already to have consumed all the Christian virtues and to threaten that religion itself will not escape unscathed." [45] Those fires continued long after Rebecca Reed died in 1838, a victim of consumption which, nativistic editors said, she had contracted while a nun.[46]

An immediate indication of the popular interest in the No-Popery crusade which grew with the burning of the convent and the publication of this propaganda came in the founding of two new anti-Catholic newspapers, both appearing for the first time within a week after the Ursuline school was destroyed. The first of these publications to be offered the public was *The Downfall of Babylon, or the Triumph of Truth Over Popery,* edited from Philadelphia by Samuel B. Smith, who proclaimed himself "late a Popish priest" and whose experiences as a speaker for the New York Protestant Association had brought him some fame. Smith promised to entertain his readers with the inner secrets of the Catholic church gathered from his former associations. "A tale I have to tell," he stated in a prospectus for his paper, "that will shake the mighty Babylon to her centre; at which the darkest night will blush, and nature shrink with horror." [47] True to this prophecy, the *Downfall of Babylon* was from the first a sensational publication, devoted largely to an exposure of the moral corruption of Catholicism. Many of its articles were frankly bawdy accounts of the relationships between priests and nuns,[48] written, Smith explained, to create sympathy for the burners of the Ursuline convent by showing the true nature of the building they had destroyed.[49] This sensationalism won popular favor; additional copies of the early issues had to be printed to meet the demand,[50] and before the end of the year Smith found it advisable to move from Philadelphia to New York in order to supply the many subscribing to his paper.[51]

More influential than the *Downfall of Babylon* was the *American Protestant Vindicator and Defender of Civil and Religious Liberty against the Inroads of Popery,* a bi-weekly newspaper

edited by the Reverend W. C. Brownlee from New York City.[52]
Those who hoped for mild denunciation and a Christian spirit
toward Rome from a paper edited by Brownlee and endorsed by
twelve clergymen were disillusioned by the first issue on August
20, 1834. Brownlee made his stand clear:

> With the deliberate conviction that Popery ought always to be
> loathed and execrated, not only by all Christians, but also by every
> patriot and philanthropist; we shall endeavor to unfold its detestable
> impieties, corruptions and mischiefs. But we engage in this mo-
> mentous controversy with a deep conviction that there is an im-
> portant dissonance between the heinous crime and the bewitched
> transgressors. We shall condemn the monstrous progeny of Baby-
> lon the Great without measure: but we shall not forget that the vast
> majority of the Papists are blind-folded sinners; and we shall ever
> draw a broad line of distinction between Roman Priests, the arch
> servant of the Dragon, and the Beast who from the most hateful
> and inordinately sensual motives are perversely deceitful leaders;
> and the misguided mortals, their wretchedly deluded votaries whom
> they hurry into the bottomless pit of everlasting perdition.[53]

This point of view was subsequently reiterated, the editors maintaining that while they would like to win converts from Catholicism, they believed this impossible until the true nature of the
popish church had been brought home to the American people.
"Our object," they wrote, "is to warn our Protestant friends of
the insidious Jesuitical workings of that abomination, showing
its demoralizing, debasing, character." [54]

Brownlee's views were popularized, not only through the
columns of his publication, but also by lecturing agents whom he
sent traveling about the country, giving speeches against Popery
which were concluded by an appeal for subscriptions to the *American Protestant Vindicator*. The first of these agents began his
tours in New England in the fall of 1834, the editors announcing
that he would not "decline to reason in the spirit of love, and
meekness, and courage with any person . . . on any occasion,
publicly or privately." [55] His efforts were evidently successful, for

during the next years additional lecturing agents were employed, each being given a definite district in which to operate.[56] By 1840 six of these speakers were constantly traveling about the country denouncing Rome with a bitterness typical of the publication which they represented.[57] The *Downfall of Babylon* quickly realized the advantages of these agents, the first being named to represent that paper in October, 1835, with others appointed in the next months.[58] The constant activity of these speakers and the wide range of territory over which they operated gave a decided impetus to the anti-Catholic movement.

Samuel Smith, editor of the *Downfall of Babylon,* in 1836 developed a second means of popularizing his paper and attacking Rome. He announced through the columns of his publication that he would be pleased to receive contributions to publish tracts on Popery which could be distributed free of charge.[59] The first of these pamphlets appeared in the fall of 1836 [60] and was followed by others equally denunciatory of Catholicism.

The success of the *American Protestant Vindicator* and the *Downfall of Babylon* inspired imitation. Both of these nativistic publications were edited from New York and it was felt by many engaged in the crusade against Rome that other local papers would fill an unquestioned need. This demand in the west was supplied by the *Western Protestant,* founded in 1836 by the Reverend Nathan L. Rice and published at Bardstown, Kentucky.[61] In Baltimore, the need for a nativistic journal was filled by the Baltimore *Literary and Religious Magazine,* launched in 1835 and edited by two prominent Presbyterian clergymen, the Reverend Robert J. Breckinridge and the Reverend Andrew B. Cross. Both these editors and the editor of the *Western Protestant* became involved in libel suits growing from charges of immorality or misconduct made against members of the Catholic church,[62] but these enhanced rather than diminished their popularity when obviously prejudiced juries refused to convict them. The growing No-Popery sentiment created by these newspapers and magazines was reflected in the increasingly anti-Catholic tone of the religious and secular press.[63]

The incentive given the nativistic movement by this active No-Popery press led directly to the formation of the first national anti-Catholic societies. The need for such organizations had been felt for some time,[64] particularly by that group of sincere opponents of Rome who were giving vent to their sentiments through the *American Protestant Vindicator* and the New York Protestant Association. Believing, as they did, that the United States could be saved from the curse of Popery only when the American people had been educated to the evils of that religious system, they naturally came to the conclusion that the sporadic efforts of the past would be vastly more effective could their propaganda be shaped along national lines. For this a nation-wide organization was necessary.

The several societies that sprang into being to meet this new-felt demand were modeled directly on well-established counterparts which had been operating successfully in England for many years. There two types of organization had been tried: one designed to convert Catholics to Protestantism and the other seeking to protect England from Popery by convincing the people of the dangers of that religious system. The first type of organization was represented by a number of societies concerned principally with missionary work among the natives of Ireland;[65] the second by the British Society for Promoting the Principles of the Protestant Reformation, formed in 1827 as a means of combating the passage of the Catholic Emancipation act.[66] The work of these British societies was well known in the United States, for their activities were frequently noted in the American nativistic and religious press [67] and their agents had crossed the Atlantic to solicit funds for their struggle with Rome.[68]

The first American societies in imitation of these English models were patterned after those formed to secure the conversion of Catholics to Protestantism. One was the Society for the Diffusion of Christian Knowledge, established in New York in 1835 with the Reverend W. C. Brownlee as its first president. Its avowed purpose was to recommend the Bible to all mankind and in this way to further the principles of the Protestant Reformation. In addition each member was to receive a weekly publication, setting forth some of the distinctive errors of Popery.[69] Evidently the plan was not entirely successful, for the society never exerted much influence in the nativistic cause. Another organization of a slightly different nature, the Canadian Benevolent Association, was also formed in New York in 1835. The guiding spirit in this new enterprise was the Reverend W. K. Hoyt, whose long activity as a missionary in Canada fitted him to direct this society which was designed to stamp out Popery in that province. Brownlee was active in this enterprise as well, being named vice president at its first meeting.[70] A short time later a Society for the Diffusion of Light on the Subject of Romanism was formed at Reading, Massachusetts,[71] and a similar society at Shelburne, Vermont.[72] Yet an attempt on the part of Catholics to form a society dedicated to the promotion of the principles of their religion was branded by nativistic editors as "the embryo of the American Inquisition." [73]

None of these early organizations achieved national prominence. This position was to be secured by another society, obviously modeled on the second type of English organization, The American Society to Promote the Principles of the Protestant Reformation, which came into being early in 1836 as an offshoot of the New York Protestant Association.[74] The Reverend George Bourne and others active in this local society, long dissatisfied with the limited sphere of its operations,[75] felt that the time was ripe for national expansion, and with this in view they issued a call in March, 1836, for representatives of Protestant associations and all other enemies of Catholicism to meet in New York to arrange a means of unified action.[76] Long before this gathering assembled in May, 1836, the directors of the New York Protestant Association had determined the course which it would follow and their plans were carried through without a break. A communication from the New York association was read expressing the conviction that it was the duty of all "Reformed Christians . . . to combine their energies for the illumination of the public mind upon the subjects which are controverted by the Protestant churches and the followers of the Court of Rome"; a resolution was adopted calling for the formation of the American Society to Promote the Principles of the Protestant Reformation; a committee was named to draw up a constitution and promptly reported with a constitution already composed. When this was adopted the Protestant Reformation Society, as it was commonly called, came into being.[77]

The new society was to conduct a double attack on Rome, arousing Protestants to a proper sense of their duties toward Romanism by distributing information on Popery and at the same time laboring to "convert the Papists to Christianity" by means of lectures, tracts, and standard books.[78] Its organization was based on a federal principle, with existing local Protestant societies encouraged to affiliate and combine their energies against Catholicism. This proved an effective system and partially accounts for the rapid expansion of the society. The New York Protestant Association immediately became an auxiliary [79] and within a year branches had been established in Baltimore, Philadelphia, Boston, Trenton, and a number of small communities.[80]

The organization thus developed concentrated and gave direction to anti-Catholic propaganda. As the Protestant Reformation Society accumulated funds, it employed lecturing agents to stir up nativistic feeling in the larger cities and encourage the formation of auxiliary societies which likewise used speakers to attack Catholicism and establish local branches in neighboring regions. Communities immune from the earlier localized propaganda were now subjected to a barrage of No-Popery sentiments. The society attempted to secure the support of the churches by addressing a letter to all evangelical ministers in the eastern states, pointing out its aims and asking that anti-Catholic sermons be made a part of the church service.[81] Similar appeals were made during the next few years,[82] but the society had yet to discover that the most effective way to secure clerical support was by calling on organized church bodies rather than individual ministers.[83]

The continued growth of the Protestant Reformation Society was brought about not only by effective organization, but also through the close alliance which existed between its officers and the *American Protestant Vindicator*. Within a month of the society's formation this anti-Catholic newspaper was adopted as its official organ [84] and from that time on the courses of these two No-Popery agencies were intimately entwined. The society's lecturing agents also solicited funds for the *Vindicator* and meetings were held in eastern cities in which propaganda against Rome was combined with appeals for support for this publication.[85] In return the *Vindicator* gave its whole-hearted editorial approval to every enterprise endorsed by the society.

The activity of these nativistic agencies naturally created a vast amount of interest in their cause. By the middle of the 1830's newspapers, magazines, lecturers, and propaganda agents were co-operating through a national society in spreading calumny against Rome. Ministers were devoting more and more time to denunciations of Catholicism and some were gaining such wide reputations in this field that they were being called about the country to spread their doctrines.[86] It was obvious that these efforts had stirred a new interest in Popery and had created a public anxious to listen to invective against Catholicism or to read books and magazines which showed no mercy in their attack on Rome. Authors soon realized that here was an opportunity both to enrich themselves and to strike a further blow at Catholicism. It was this situation that stimulated the writing of the greatest of the nativistic propaganda works, Maria Monk's *Awful Disclosures of the Hotel Dieu Nunnery of Montreal,*[87] a monumental volume, published in 1836 and frequently reprinted, which was to play a distinguished part in the No-Popery crusade.

Contemporary accounts of Maria Monk's life vary greatly, but the most interesting, if not the most truthful, was that told by the author herself in her several published volumes. In these she told of a Protestant upbringing which ended when she entered the Hôtel Dieu convent in Montreal to be educated, embraced the Catholic faith, and resolved to become a nun. Momentarily wavering in her resolution, she on one occasion left the sisterhood and married, but soon returned and this time received the veil. Her vows being made, she was, according to her story, immediately initiated into the sinful ways of nunneries. She was given instructions by the Mother Superior that she must "obey the priests in all things," and this, she soon found to her "utter astonishment and horror, was to live in the practice of criminal intercourse with them."[88] The children born from these unholy unions were immediately baptized and strangled. "This secured their everlasting happiness," the Mother Superior explained, "for the baptism purified them from all sinfulness, and being sent out of the world before they had time to do anything wrong, they were at once admitted into heaven. How happy, she exclaimed, are those who secure immortal happiness in such little beings! Their little souls would thank those who kill their bodies, if they had it in their power!"[89]

Maria Monk's subsequent life in the convent, as revealed through the *Awful Disclosures,* substantiated these initial revelations. She saw nuns executed for refusing to obey the lustful will of priests [90] and the strangling of two small babies.[91] She discovered a large hole in the basement of the Hôtel Dieu into which the bodies of those murdered were thrown and the secret passage connecting the convent with a neighboring priest's home.[92] Her continued interest in infanticide, Maria Monk finally explained, was due to the fact that she was to have a baby, the father being one Father Phelan. Unable to endure the thought of her own child's murder, she at last determined to escape. This, according to her account, was not difficult. Bursting past a guard as if she were on an important mission, she found herself beyond the walls of the Hôtel Dieu convent.[93]

The first edition of Maria Monk's narrative ended rather abruptly at that point. Any curiosity which her readers may have had as to her subsequent fate was satisfied by a second edition which followed the first almost immediately and contained a lengthy sequel to the original tale.[94] In this she pictured the experiences of the fugitive nun to be as harrowing as those of the cloistered. Attempting to escape from Montreal, she was recognized and forced to return to the city where, in a moment of despair, she tried to drown herself. Her rescue by two passing workmen convinced her that she had been divinely selected to expose the horrors of Popery and she immediately laid plans to go to the United States where her tale might be believed.[95] Her erstwhile husband was induced to provide the necessary funds for the trip, but these were exhausted by the time she reached New York and, alone and friendless, she attempted again to take her own life, this time by starving herself to death in a secluded spot on the edge of the city. Four hunters intervened and carried her to a charity hospital where she, knowing that her baby would be born soon, asked for a Protestant clergyman to whom she might tell her whole story. The minister who responded was so impressed that he asked her to write an autobiography for publication.[96] Thus, according to Maria Monk's own version, the *Awful Disclosures* came into being.

The account of Maria Monk's life given by her mother differed greatly from that contained in the *Awful Disclosures*. The mother, a Protestant living near Montreal, testified that her daughter had never been in the Hôtel Dieu convent and that the whole tale was the product of a brain injured in infancy when the child had run a slate pencil into her head. Maria Monk, the mother insisted, had been a wild girl who was constantly in trouble and had of necessity been confined in a Catholic Magdalen asylum in Montreal. Even there she had erred and had been aided in her escape by a former lover, who was really the father of the child born in New York.[97]

In all probability, the mother's story was substantially correct. It is likely, too, that the man who aided her escape to the United States was the Reverend William K. Hoyt, long active among Canadian Catholics as president of the Canadian Benevolent Association.[98] He undoubtedly took her to New York where he arranged with several other unscrupulous clergymen, among whom were the Reverend J. J. Slocum, the Reverend Arthur Tappan, the Reverend George Bourne, and Theodore Dwight, to employ her as a dupe for their own mercenary schemes. Later Slocum admitted that Maria Monk and Hoyt called upon him to write the story of her life and that he had done so, although he insisted that the account was substantially that dictated by Maria Monk.[99] Subsequent legal proceedings growing from the publication of the *Awful Disclosures* indicated that Slocum actually had been responsible for most of the writing of the book, but that Hoyt, Bourne, and others had given suggestions and taken the largest share of the profits.[100] It is probable that the editors of the *American Protestant Vindicator* were also interested, for just before the *Awful Disclosures* appeared they devoted an unusually large amount of space to articles dealing with the alleged immorality of convent life and even hinted that there was an escaped nun in the city who was soon to write her memoirs.[101]

The manuscript of the book was offered first to Harper

Brothers. This publishing house, although tempted by the prospect of large profits, was unwilling to risk its reputation by printing so scurrilous an attack on Catholicism. An agreement was
eventually arranged through which two employees of the firm,
Howe and Bates, set up a dummy publishing house under their
own names and the book finally appeared in January, 1836.[102]

The publication of the *Awful Disclosures* precipitated a storm
of controversy. The anti-Catholic press did not hesitate to proclaim the work a remarkable exposition of the truth about nunneries,[103] but religious papers, slightly more cautious, simply
gave notice of its publication and agreed that while they could
not vouch for its accuracy, the conditions described were typical
of all convents.[104] Later this caution was abandoned and the
book was given absolute credence by nearly all the religious
press.[105] Others, however, openly questioned the truth of Maria
Monk's story. Posters were distributed about New York attacking her charges as lies and indignant Catholics protested vainly
against the general acceptance of such propaganda.[106] The authorities of the Hôtel Dieu convent properly maintained a dignified silence, but champions rose to their defense with a book
entitled *Awful Exposure of the Atrocious Plot Formed by
Certain Individuals against the Clergy and Nuns of Lower
Canada, through the Intervention of Maria Monk.*[107] Including
denials of statements in the *Awful Disclosures*,[108] and numerous
affidavits demonstrating Maria Monk's falsehoods,[109] this work
was so effective that it was answered by Slocum in a *Reply to the
Priest's Book, Denominated, "Awful Exposure of the Atrocious
Plot Formed by Certain Individuals against the Clergy and Nuns
of Lower Canada, through the Intervention of Maria Monk."* [110]
Here more affidavits upholding Maria Monk were presented [111]
and in addition an attack was made on all convents, with many
citations from the works of Scippio de Ricci and other early No-
Popery writers.[112] These charges and counter-charges led to a
public meeting between Maria Monk and her opponents, which,
rather than settling the question of the truth of her disclosures,

simply intensified public interest in the whole controversy.[113] The New York Protestant Association attempted to capitalize upon this aroused opinion by inciting debates between priests and Protestant clergymen over Maria Monk [114] and, when Catholic representatives failed to respond, blatantly insisted that the author of the *Awful Disclosures* had been vindicated.[115]

As the controversy grew, many partisans on both sides came to the realization that the only solution lay in an examination of the interior of the Hôtel Dieu convent, a step which would forever confirm or repudiate Maria Monk's statements. The first proposed investigation was suggested by the New York Protestant Association, which offered to send a committee including Maria Monk to Montreal for this purpose.[116] Needless to say, this offer was declined by convent authorities, as were similar offers made by Maria Monk herself.[117] Finally two impartial Protestant clergymen were allowed to make the inspection. They returned to New York with the report that all of Maria Monk's accusations were false and that the Hôtel Dieu convent did not even remotely resemble the one which she had described.[118] The backers of the *Awful Disclosures* immediately branded the ministers as Jesuits in disguise and declared that masons and carpenters had completely altered the convent building before the inspection committee had been admitted.[119] A public meeting was held in New York during which resolutions were passed pledging the confidence of those attending to Maria Monk despite this adverse report, and demands were made that a new committee which should include such well-known nativists as Samuel F. B. Morse and Slocum be allowed to make an impartial inspection.[120] A similar meeting was held in Philadelphia and it was suggested that Protestants in other cities show their faith in Maria Monk by united action.[121]

The excitement attendant upon the publication of the *Awful Disclosures* was intensified in the fall of 1836 by the appearance of another fugitive nun in New York City. She was, she explained, Saint Frances Patrick; she had been in the Hôtel Dieu convent while Maria Monk was there, and she was willing to confirm every statement made in the *Awful Disclosures*.[122] The sudden appearance of this new nun probably indicated a rift among New York nativists. Maria Monk had been sponsored by the same group which backed the *American Protestant Vindicator* and undoubtedly had the support of the Protestant Reformation Society, although that organization carefully refrained from connecting itself directly with the scheme. Samuel B. Smith, editor of the *Downfall of Babylon,* envied the new importance gained by this rival publication whose affiliations allowed it to give its readers first-hand information regarding Maria Monk's activities. Smith's position was made clear in a book which he published early in 1836, a *Decisive Confirmation of the Awful Disclosures of Maria Monk, Proving Her Residence in the Hotel Dieu Nunnery, and the Existence of the Subterranean Passages,*[123] in which he was unable to add any new information concerning either Maria Monk or the convent and was forced to confine his narrative largely to an account of his own experiences as a priest.[124] This evidently convinced Smith that he could regain a lion's share of nativistic glory only by sponsoring an escaped nun of his own. Saint Frances Patrick was his candidate for a portion of the popularity being enjoyed by Maria Monk.

Certainly Smith and his paper supplied the publicity attendant on the arrival of Saint Frances in New York. Unable to wait until a full volume of her memoirs could be prepared, Smith published a pamphlet on *The Escape of Sainte Frances Patrick, another Nun from the Hotel Dieu Nunnery of Montreal* [125] which he introduced with a verse:

> Down from the North a torrent comes;
> A moral deluge sweeps our shores;
> Two captives, driven from their homes,
> Come to lament, to weep, deplore
> Their mis-spent days.

Their homes, we say, such homes as those,
The reptiles of the earth would scorn:
Hot-beds of every vice that grows,
And sinks where virtue droops forlorn,
To rise no more.

One tale is told, and horror shrieks;
We stand, aghast, appalled with fear,
And listening now, the echo speaks,
Strikes to the heart, excites the fear;
Alas,—how true! [126]

Smith's pamphlet added few details to the story of the Hôtel Dieu convent already told by Maria Monk. Saint Frances stated that she had been a nun when the investigating committee made its tour and that the entire interior of the building had previously been altered for the occasion. At the time they made their inspection, she said, two strangled babies had been lying in a closet, but the committee had failed to open the door and that deed had remained secret.[127]

Maria Monk and Saint Frances Patrick were brought together at a public meeting and there, tearfully embracing each other, they talked for some time of their mutual convent life.[128] This in itself should have been enough to brand Maria Monk as an impostor, for only the most credulous could believe Saint Frances' story which was almost immediately exposed as a fraud. Yet so great was Maria Monk's hold upon Protestants that greater evidence than her friendship with Saint Frances Patrick was necessary before they began to question the truth of her statements. This doubt came with another investigation of the convent, conducted by Colonel William L. Stone, editor of the New York *Commercial Advertiser*. Stone was a Protestant who had interested himself mildly in the No-Popery crusade. He happened to be in Montreal during the fall of 1836 and sought for and secured permission to make a thorough investigation. He made his examination with Maria Monk's book in his hand, poking into every closet, climbing to a high window to see into an unopened room, and smelling a row of jars in the basement which might have contained lime used in the disposal of infants' bodies.[129] He came away completely convinced and published an account which ended with the pronouncement: "I most solemnly believe that the priests and nuns are innocent in this matter." [130]

This was the most effective setback that Maria Monk had received. Stone was answered by the nativistic newspapers,[131] by the president of the Protestant Reformation Society [132] and by an anonymous pamphlet *Evidence Demonstrating the Falsehoods of William L. Stone*,[133] all insisting that he was either in the pay of the Jesuits or "Stone-blind." Unexpected aid for the backers of the *Awful Disclosures* came from a New York poet who published *The Vision of Rubeta, an Epic Story of the Island of Manhattan*,[134] a volume-length poem satirizing Stone's inspection tour in Hudibrastic verse and with "Illustrations done on Stone." Colonel Stone was pictured as saying:

> A new goldfinder in your sinks of shame
> I come! Prepare. Dead babe hope not to hide,
> Nor friar's sandal, where this wand is guide!
> Aided by which, shall pierce your very stones
> My eagle eyes, and find those little bones! [135]

After a fully described inspection he departed, assuring the nuns:

> Ladies! the charm has work'd; the trial's o'er!
> Virgins ye are, as pure as ever bore.[136]

The *Vision of Rubeta* was promptly answered by a play, *The Critique of the Vision of Rubeta: a Dramatic Sketch in One Act* [137] by one who signed himself "Autodicus." While it may be doubted if this play was ever performed, it probably added immeasurably to the amusement of those interested in the growing volume of literature centering about Maria Monk.

Before this satirizing of Stone's report, his criticism of Maria Monk had obviously done her little good. During the early months of 1837 many of the more conscientious Protestant publications began denouncing her as an impostor.[138] A story was circulated that she had confessed the hoax to Colonel Stone, and while this was vigorously denied by the anti-Catholic press [139] and even by Stone himself,[140] it obviously indicated a growing public distrust. Maria Monk's own conduct did much to accredit these reports. In August, 1837, she suddenly disappeared from New York, only to reappear at a private home in Philadelphia with a tale of having been kidnapped by Catholic priests who were anxious to stop her disclosures of convent life. This may have been arranged by her backers to increase public interest,[141] but more probably was an escapade on the part of Maria Monk who seems to have made the journey to the neighboring city under an assumed name with a male companion.[142] Certainly the final effect of the whole episode was to discredit the author of the *Awful Disclosures.*

There were, however, sufficient people willing to believe her tales of convent life so that a new publication was believed feasible. This appeared in 1837, *Further Disclosures by Maria Monk, Concerning the Hotel Dieu Nunnery of Montreal; also, her visit to Nuns' Island, and Disclosures Concerning That Secret Retreat.*[143] The sensational appeal of the *Awful Disclosures* was not maintained in this new book, which was chiefly interesting for its descriptions of Nuns' Island in the St. Lawrence river where, according to the *Further Disclosures,* nuns from the United States and Canada went to bear illegitimate children.[144] This was the last of Maria Monk's publications. An attempt was made to dress her in nun's clothing and take her on a lecture tour of the eastern cities, but this plan was abandoned because of the opposition of the Reverend W. C. Brownlee, who either had some moral scruples or hesitated to subject his charge to the heckling of an audience.[145]

By this time Maria Monk's popularity was fast fading. She had been cheated out of most of her profits by her backers and a series of lawsuits not only failed to substantiate her claims but exposed the corruption behind her whole venture. Any faith in her that her supporters might have had was dispelled early in 1838 when she again gave birth to a fatherless child and this time made no pretense of naming it after a priest.[146] Only the *American Protestant Vindicator* supported her with the futile charge that her second pregnancy had been arranged by the Jesuits to discredit her exposures.[147] Her downfall from that time on was rapid. She married, but so dissipated her husband's earnings in drink and riotous living that he soon left her.[148] In 1849 she was arrested for picking the pockets of her companion of the moment in a Five Points house of ill fame and died in prison a short time later.[149]

Discredited as she may have been in her later years, Maria Monk's books continued to enjoy unstinted popularity; the three hundred thousand copies of the *Awful Disclosures* sold prior to the Civil War and the editions which have appeared since that time justly earned for it the questionable distinction of being the "Uncle Tom's Cabin of Know-Nothingism."[150] The immediate effect of this volume, however, was to demonstrate both the profits and influence of sensational propaganda. Much of the wave of publication which followed with such telling effect in the creation of anti-Catholic sentiment can be attributed to the widely read and accepted *Awful Disclosures*.

NOTES

[1] The Charlestown meeting nearly precipitated another riot when it blamed the burning on "mobs from the city of Boston," almost arousing retaliation from the inhabitants of that city. New York *Observer*, August 23, 1834; *The Jesuit*, August 16, 1834; *The Charlestown Convent; its Destruction by a Mob*, 22.

[2] *Report of the Committee Relating to the Destruction of the Ursuline Convent*, 2.

[3] *Ibid.*, 2, 13–16.

The Flames Spread, 1835-1840   109

4 *Christian Watchman*, August 15, 1834; *Western Christian Advocate*, August 29, 1834; *American Protestant Vindicator*, August 27, 1834; *An Account of the Conflagration of the Ursuline Convent*, 24-35.

5 *Christian Examiner*, XVII (September, 1834), 131.

6 Caleb Stetson, *A Discourse on the Duty of Sustaining the Laws, Occasioned by the Burning of the Ursuline Convent* (Boston, 1834), 14. This sermon was preached in the First Church, Medford, August 23, 1834. See also: George Curtis, *The Rights of Conscience and of Property; or, The True Issue of the Convent Question* (Boston, 1842), 20-21.

7 New York *Observer*, August 30, 1834; *Protestant Magazine*, I (August, 1834).

8 Foik, "Anti-Catholic Parties in American Politics," *loc. cit.*, 54. The Third Provincial Council of Baltimore, meeting in 1837, was equally frank in denouncing Massachusetts for its failure to protect property or reimburse the Ursulines. Guilday, *A History of the Councils of Baltimore*, 118.

9 *Christian Watchman*, November 26, 1834, January 30, 1835 and ff; *American Protestant Vindicator*, August 27, 1834, September 17, 1834, October 8, 1834, October 22, 1834, February 25, 1835 and ff; Boston *Recorder*, quoted in *Ibid.*, September 12, 1834 and in *An Account of the Conflagration of the Ursuline Convent*, 18; *Vermont Chronicle*, quoted in *American Protestant Vindicator*, September 17, 1834; New York *Observer*, December 27, 1834; R. V. G. Stevens, *An Alarm to American Patriots. A Sermon on the Political Tendencies of Popery, considered in Respect to the Institutions of the United States, in the Church of Church St., Boston, November 27, 1834. Being the Day of Annual Thanksgiving* (Boston, 1834).

10 *Christian Watchman*, August 22, 1834; *Episcopal Recorder*, September 6, 1834. The religious press also discounted the Faneuil Hall meeting by insisting that it was controlled by Jesuits. *Christian Watchman*, October 10, 1834, October 17, 1834; New York *Observer*, October 25, 1834. The *American Protestant Vindicator*, September 3, 1834, went so far as to suggest that the convent had been burned by Catholics as a means of discrediting Beecher and arousing sympathy for their own cause.

11 New York *Observer*, December 27, 1834. The *Christian Watchman*, October 17, 1834, expressed the hope that the nuns would use their new home to educate poor Catholic children rather than Protestants.

12 "The Roxbury Committee of Vigilance," Massachusetts Historical Society *Proceedings*, LIII (1919-1920), 325-331.

13 Shea, *History of the Catholic Church*, III, 489.

14 New York *Observer*, October 23, 1834; *Report of the Committee Relating to the Destruction of the Ursuline Convent*, 3-4.

15 *The Charlestown Convent, its Destruction by a Mob*, 29-30.

16 *Ibid.*, 30-31.

17 *Trial of John R. Buzzell, the Leader of the Convent Rioters*, 15-16. For other accounts of the trial see: *Trial of John R. Buzzell before the Supreme Judicial Court of Massachusetts for Arson and Burglary in the Ursuline Convent at Charlestown* (Boston, 1834); *The Trial of Persons Charged with Burning the Convent in the Town of Charlestown (Mass.) before the Supreme Judicial Court Holden at East Cambridge, on Tuesday, Dec. 2, 1834* (Boston, 1834); *The Trial of the Convent Rioters* (Cambridge, 1834); *Trial of William*

Mason, Marvin Marcy Jr., and Sargent Blaisdell, charged with Being Concerned in Burning the Ursuline Convent in Charlestown (Mass.) on the Night of the 11th of August, 1834 (Boston, 1834); James T. Austin, *Argument of James T. Austin, Attorney General of the Commonwealth, before the Supreme Judicial Court in Middlesex on the Case of John R. Buzzell* (Boston, 1834).

18 *Trial of John R. Buzzell, the Leader of the Convent Rioters,* 1–35; *The Charlestown Convent, its Destruction by a Mob,* 40, 58. Handbills were circulated while the trial was going on, reading:

Liberty or Death!
Suppressed Evidence!

Sons of Freedom! Can you live in a free country,
and bear the Yoke of Priesthood, veiled in the habit
of a profligate Court?

19 *Trial of John R. Buzzell, the Leader of the Convent Rioters,* 35.

20 *The Jesuit,* December 18, 1834.

21 *American Quarterly Review,* XVII (March, 1835), 228–229.

22 Quoted in *Downfall of Babylon,* June 20, 1835. See also: Boston *Observer,* January 15, 1835; New York *Observer,* June 23, 1838; *American Protestant Vindicator,* December 17, 1834, January 7, 1835.

23 "Bill more effectively to suppress Riots," Commonwealth of Massachusetts, *Legislative Documents,* No. 37 (1835), 1–5.

24 "Report on the Convent of Mount Benedict," Commonwealth of Massachusetts, *Legislative Documents,* No. 37 (1835), 1–24. The Catholic arguments are in Fay, *Argument Before the Committee of the House of Representatives upon the Petition of Benedict Fenwick and others, with a portion of the Documentary Testimony.*

25 *American Protestant Vindicator,* January 21, 1835. See also *Christian Watchman,* March 6, 1835.

26 The measure was defeated by a vote of 412 to 67. *Christian Watchman,* March 20, 1835.

27 In 1842 another committee urged reparation upon the legislature which again refused to make the grant. *Documents Relating to the Ursuline Convent in Charlestown* (Boston, 1842), 21–32. In 1846 an inadequate sum was voted and refused by the Ursulines. *American Protestant Magazine,* II (June, 1846). The most serious attempt to secure reparation was made in 1853 and 1854 when a committee of the legislature recommended the appointment of a commission to decide on a proper sum to be paid. Commonwealth of Massachusetts, *House Document No. 75 for 1853,* 1–9. This proposal was defeated by a vote of 120 to 111. *Pilot,* April 16, 1853. Again in 1854 a committee recommended to the legislature the naming of a commission and payment of the amount which it recommended. This measure was decisively defeated, only 26 members of the House voting in favor of it. *Pilot,* May 6, 1854. By this time the *Pilot,* a Catholic paper, was willing to admit that the convent question was dead and that the Ursulines would never be compensated for their loss. It laid the successive defeats entirely at the door of the anti-Catholic sentiment aroused in the legislature by No-Popery speeches and by the nativistic press. *Pilot,* April 23, 1853.

[28] Shea, *History of the Catholic Church,* III, 488; Leahy, *Catholic Church in New England,* I, 63.

[29] Leahy, *Catholic Church in New England,* I, 63.

[30] *Niles' Register,* XLVIII (1835).

[31] "Anti-Catholic Movements in the United States," *Catholic World,* XXII (March, 1876), 814.

[32] Shea, *History of the Catholic Church,* III, 489-499, 635; Leon Whipple, *The Story of Civil Liberty in the United States* (New York, 1927), 61.

[33] England, *The Works of John England,* VII, 44-55.

[34] "The Press and the Convent Question," *New England Magazine,* VIII (June, 1835), 454.

[35] The publication was heralded for a month before the book finally appeared. New York *Observer,* March 21, 1835; *Downfall of Babylon,* March 14, 1835; *American Protestant Vindicator,* March 11, 1835. The book was published in Boston in April, 1835.

[36] For typical reviews see: *Christian Watchman,* March 20, 1835; *American Protestant Vindicator,* April 1, 1835; *Episcopal Recorder,* April 4, 1835; and extracts in *New England Magazine,* VIII (June, 1835), 454. The *Western Monthly Magazine,* XXX (June, 1835), 390-392 was one of the few Protestant journals to condemn the work, although it was universally attacked by the Catholic press.

[37] New York *Observer,* April 18, 1835; *Downfall of Babylon,* April 11, 1835; *American Protestant Vindicator,* May 20, 1835; *Christian Watchman,* November 20, 1835.

[38] Rebecca Theresa Reed, *Six Months in a Convent* (Boston, 1835), 75-93.

[39] Mary Edmond Saint George, *An Answer to Six Months in a Convent Exposing its Falsehoods and Manifold Absurdities* (Boston, 1835).

[40] *Ibid.,* 1-35.

[41] *A Review of the Lady Superior's Reply to 'Six Months in a Convent,' being a Vindication of Miss Reed* (Boston, 1835).

[42] *Ibid.,* 25-51.

[43] *A Supplement to 'Six Months in a Convent,' Confirming the Narrative of Rebecca Theresa Reed, by the Testimony of More than 100 Witnesses* (Boston, 1835).

[44] *Ibid.,* 73-145.

[45] Saint George, *An Answer to Six Months in a Convent,* XXXVII-XXXVIII.

[46] *American Protestant Vindicator,* March 16, 1838.

[47] *Protestant Magazine,* I (July, 1834).

[48] *Downfall of Babylon,* August 14, 1834, and ff.

[49] *Ibid.,* January 3, 1835.

[50] 30,000 copies of the first few numbers had to be printed for distribution. *Ibid.,* May 30, 1835.

[51] *Ibid.,* November 29, 1834. By the end of the first year about 7,000 copies of each issue were being sold. *Ibid.,* December 12, 1835. In January, 1836, the size of the paper was doubled and it was changed from a weekly to a semi-monthly publication. *Ibid.,* January 23, 1836. Some of this growth may have been caused by Smith's energetic promotion schemes. Soon after the paper was launched he addressed a circular letter to many church organizations ask-

ing their support, a device which brought this publication much publicity. *Christian Watchman*, October 3, 1834.

⁵² The individual issues were entitled *Protestant Vindicator* or *American Protestant Vindicator*, the latter form being used through most of the paper's existence. It has been used consistently in this study to avoid confusion. The paper was published by Norwood Bowne and Ira G. Wisner, who were also active in publishing much of the anti-Catholic propaganda of the time under the name, The New York Protestant Press. *American Protestant Vindicator*, December 16, 1835, March 16, 1836.

⁵³ *American Protestant Vindicator*, August 20, 1834.

⁵⁴ *Ibid.*, July 29, 1835.

⁵⁵ *Ibid.*, October 22, 1834. The Reverend Andrew Bruce was the first lecturing agent named by the paper. The policy of naming ministers to these posts was normally followed.

⁵⁶ *Ibid.*, December 25, 1834, January 14, 1835, March 18, 1835, November 18, 1835, February 1, 1837, March 2, 1838.

⁵⁷ *Ibid.*, June 24, 1840. Agents at this time were: the Reverends C. Sparry, C. Shumway, Rufus Pomeroy, Henry Smith, Samuel F. Bunnell, and Epaphras Goodman.

⁵⁸ The first agent appointed was the Reverend C. Sparry. *Downfall of Babylon*, October 24, 1835. A second agent was appointed in the spring of 1836 to work in the New England states while Sparry covered the rest of the country. *Ibid.*, May 28, 1836. The activity of these agents can be judged by the fact that in one week one of them spoke at Providence, Bristol, and Pawtucket, Rhode Island; and Fall River, Taunton, South Reading, West Reading, Reading, Stoneham, and Woburn, Massachusetts. *Ibid.*, November 12, 1836.

⁵⁹ *Ibid.*, June 25, 1836.

⁶⁰ *Ibid.*, November 12, 1836. Seven thousand copies were printed for free distribution. This scheme had probably been suggested to the editor of the *Downfall of Babylon* by a similar activity of *The Protestant* in 1830. The publishers of this first anti-Catholic journal had distributed a series of No-Popery tracts, the first, on *The Worship of the Virgin Mary*, being printed in the fall of 1830. *The Protestant*, September 25, 1830, October 22, 1831.

⁶¹ Benjamin J. Webb, *The Centenary of Catholicity in Kentucky* (Louisville, 1884), 244.

⁶² Rice was sued by a priest after he had published an account in the *Western Protestant* of a nun who claimed to have escaped from a Kentucky convent because this priest had tried to seduce her. The jury reluctantly brought in a verdict forcing Rice to pay damages of one cent and would have certainly acquitted Rice but for the instructions of the court. *American Protestant Vindicator*, July 19, 1837. Breckinridge was sued by the keeper of an almshouse, a Catholic, who took exception when the Baltimore *Literary and Religious Magazine* charged that he was conducting a "papal prison." Baltimore *Literary and Religious Magazine*, V (November, 1839). Breckinridge was released when the jury failed to agree. The entire June, 1840 issue of the Baltimore *Literary and Religious Magazine* was filled with an account of the trial. See also *American Protestant Vindicator*, November 11, 1840.

⁶³ Thus the Presbyterian paper, *Watchman of the South*, founded in 1837, had a regular feature entitled "Selections on Popery." *Watchman of the South*,

August 15, 1839 and ff. Secular papers such as the Pittsburgh *Times* devoted much space to the errors of Romanism. *Downfall of Babylon,* August 27, 1835.

[64] *Christian Watchman,* May 23, 1834, June 27, 1834; *The Protestant,* June 19, 1830; New York *Observer,* February 28, 1835; *American Protestant Vindicator,* June 3, 1835; Samuel F. B. Morse, *Foreign Conspiracy against the Liberties of the United States* (5th ed., New York, 1841), 116–119.

[65] Typical of this type of organization were: the London Hibernian Society, the Irish Evangelical Society, the Irish Society, the Irish Society of London, the Ladies Hibernian Female School Society, the Glasgow Society for Promoting the Religious Principles of the Reformation, the Bristol Reformation Society, the Irish Society of Dublin, and the Baptist Irish Society, all of which were formed between 1806 and 1834. Similar societies also existed on the continent, such as the Protestant Bible Society of Paris, the Evangelical Society of France, and the Evangelical Society of Geneva. Their activities were noticed in *Christian Watchman,* September 25, 1819, September 23, 1830, July 29, 1831, August 10, 1832, June 15, 1838; *The Protestant,* January 16, 1830, November 20, 1830, March 5, 1831; American Home Missionary Society, *Tenth Annual Report* (New York, 1836), 76–77; New York *Observer,* March 12, 1825.

[66] New York *Observer,* July 28, 1827.

[67] *Ibid.,* September 6, 1828, July 18, 1829, July 11, 1829, November 20, 1830, July 16, 1831, June 28, 1834; *Christian Spectator,* June, 1835; *The Protestant,* June 19, 1830, November 6, 1830.

[68] *Christian Watchman,* July 13, 1832.

[69] *Downfall of Babylon,* April 11, 1835. The first publication of the society was *An Apology for the Bible by the Reverend H. Watson* (New York, 1835).

[70] *Ibid.,* July 11, 1835.

[71] *Ibid.,* October 15, 1836. The society was begun with fifty members and had as its objective the spread of anti-Catholic propaganda.

[72] *Ibid.,* May 14, 1836.

[73] *Ibid.,* December 20, 1834.

[74] The New York Protestant Association was active through this whole period in sponsoring yearly lecture series against Catholicism in New York and in sending speakers into neighboring states carrying this same message. *American Protestant Vindicator,* November 12, 1834, November 26, 1834, August 5, 1835, September 23, 1835.

[75] *Ibid.,* September 9, 1835.

[76] *Ibid.,* March 30, 1836, May 4, 1836.

[77] The proceedings of this meeting are printed in full in *Ibid.,* May 18, 1836.

[78] The constitution is printed in *Ibid.,* June 24, 1840, and will be found in Appendix A. It provided for a board of twenty directors in addition to the regular officers. A small yearly fee was charged for membership. Any person contributing twenty dollars was to be made a life member.

[79] The regular lecture series of the association were continued in New York under this arrangement, the national society caring for speakers outside of the city. *Ibid.,* July 13, 1836, February 8, 1837, April 5, 1837, October 18, 1837.

[80] Local societies existed in Washington County and Northumberland

County, New York; and in Union County, Pennsylvania. *Ibid.*, July 20, 1836, December 14, 1836, January 18, 1837, February 1, 1837, March 8, 1837, May 10, 1837, May 31, 1837, July 26, 1837.

81 *Ibid.*, September 21, 1836.

82 *Ibid.*, January 3, 1838, March 23, 1838.

83 An exception to this occurred in 1836 when the society sent a delegation to address the Synod of the Associated Reformed Church, meeting in New York. Brownlee spoke before the assembled ministers for two hours on the evils of Popery and was rewarded by the passage of a resolution in which the society was recommended to the individual churches. *Ibid.*, September 14, 1836.

84 *Ibid.*, June 22, 1836. In March, 1836, the paper had been transferred to Henry K. Stockton, who relinquished his control to the society when it took over the management at this time. Brownlee was retained as editor despite these changes in ownership. *Ibid.*, March 16, 1836.

85 *Ibid.*, June 22, 1836, November 29, 1837. Such a meeting was held on November 16, 1837, in New York, with speeches by Brownlee and others interested both in the society and in the paper.

86 In this group may be placed the Reverends W. C. Brownlee, Robert J. Breckinridge, George Bourne, and numerous others. A series of sermons given by Breckinridge in Richmond, Virginia, had such a profound effect that the ministers of the Protestant churches there combined to express the pious belief that through his efforts alóne the city had been saved from Popery. *Watchman of the South*, September 5, 1839; Baltimore *Literary and Religious Magazine*, V. (September, 1839). See also *American Protestant Vindicator*, October 1, 1834, November 19, 1834, November 26, 1834, December 3, 1834, August 5, 1835, August 12, 1835, January 6, 1836; *Christian Watchman*, October 24, 1834. One oration at the 1835 commencement of the Newton Theological Seminary was on "The Proper Method of Treating the Papists." *Christian Watchman*, August 21, 1835.

87 New York, 1836.

88 Maria Monk, *Awful Disclosures of the Hotel Dieu Nunnery of Montreal*, (New York, 1836), 47.

89 *Ibid.*, 49.

90 *Ibid.*, 97–105.

91 *Ibid.*, 155–157.

92 *Ibid.*, 81–82, 127–128.

93 *Ibid.*, 197–200.

94 The sequel is bound with all regular editions of the *Awful Disclosures*.

95 *Ibid.*, 257–261.

96 *Ibid.*, 262–295.

97 The mother's affidavit is printed in *Ibid.*, 215–220.

98 William L. Stone, *Maria Monk and the Nunnery of the Hotel Dieu; Being an Account of a Visit to the Convents of Montreal, and Refutation of the "Awful Disclosures"* (New York, 1836), 46–48. Stone was impartial and probably more truthful than most of those who entered into the controversy over Maria Monk at the time. Certainly this fact seems borne out by a subsequent visit that Maria Monk made to Montreal with Hoyt, before the *Awful Disclosures* appeared, to bring legal proceedings against the priest who she claimed was the father of her child. While there she lived with Hoyt in a way that allowed a Montreal paper, *L'Ami du Peuple*, to state that "des liaisons

plus intimes" existed between them. Quoted in *American Protestant Vindicator,* November 18, 1835.

99 J. J. Slocum, *Reply to the Priest's Book, Denominated, "Awful Exposure of the Atrocious Plot formed by Certain Individuals against the Clergy and Nuns of Lower Canada, through the Intervention of Maria Monk"* (New York, 1837), 103–112.

100 Maria Monk and Slocum were jointly sued by Hoyt for a share of the profits. New York *Observer,* November 26, 1836. In a second suit brought by Maria Monk through Slocum as next friend against Harper Brothers and others, it was asserted that the copyright on the *Awful Disclosures* had been taken out by Bourne and used by him with the aid of Harper Brothers in such a way that Maria Monk received none of the profits. The court refused to grant her any relief. I *Edward's Chanc. Rep.* 109 (May 16, 1837).

101 *American Protestant Vindicator,* October 14, 1835, October 21, 1835.

102 This was disclosed in the legal proceedings discussed in note 100 above.

103 *Downfall of Babylon,* February 6, 1836. This paper began the ambitious task of reprinting the book in serial form.

104 New York *Observer,* January 23, 1836.

105 *Ibid.,* May 7, 1836, July 9, 1836.

106 *American Protestant Vindicator,* March 9, 1836.

107 New York, 1836.

108 *Awful Exposure of the Atrocious Plot,* 3–71.

109 *Ibid.,* 75–129.

110 New York, 1837.

111 Slocum, *Reply to the Priest's Book,* 15–159.

112 *Ibid.,* 160–176.

113 *Interview of Maria Monk with Her Opponents, the Authors of the Reply to her Awful Disclosures, now in Press, held in this City on Wednesday, August 17* (New York, 1836). Popular interest was also stirred by the publication of *Dreadful Scenes in the Awful Disclosures of Maria Monk* (New York, 1836), a series of illustrations depicting the murder of babies and other events described in the *Awful Disclosures.*

114 *American Protestant Vindicator,* March 9, 1836.

115 *Ibid.,* May 25, 1836.

116 *Ibid.,* July 27, 1836, November 25, 1836. The association continued its offer until Maria Monk was beginning to lose popularity. *Ibid.,* March 22, 1837.

117 *Ibid.,* August 3, 1836; New York *Observer,* August 6, 1836.

118 The clergymen were the Reverend G. W. Perkins and the Reverend W. F. Curry. *American Protestant Vindicator,* July 27, 1836, August 6, 1836, September 14, 1836.

119 *Ibid.,* July 27, 1836, August 3, 1836, November 25, 1836; *Downfall of Babylon,* July 23, 1836.

120 *Downfall of Babylon,* August 20, 1836; New York *Observer,* August 20, 1836; *American Protestant Vindicator,* August 17, 1836. The meeting was held in the rooms of the American Tract Society.

121 *American Protestant Vindicator,* January 18, 1837. The Philadelphia meeting was held on December 29, 1836, and was followed by a second New York meeting on January 16, 1837.

122 New York *Observer,* September 3, 1836; *Downfall of Babylon,* September 17, 1836.

123 New York, 1836.

124 Smith, *Decisive Confirmation, passim.* Smith's work was answered by
G. Vale, *Review of the Awful Disclosures of Maria Monk* (New York, 1836).

125 New York, 1836.

126 Smith, *Escape of Sainte Frances Patrick,* Introduction.

127 *Ibid.,* 7–8.

128 Stone, *Maria Monk and the Nunnery,* 34.

129 *Ibid.,* 22–28.

130 *Ibid.,* 33.

131 *American Protestant Vindicator,* October 12, 1836 and ff.

132 Brownlee issued a long statement which was printed in the New York
Observer, October 16, 1836.

133 New York, 1836. Most of these controversial works were devoted to a
minute examination of arguments and facts. Thus one of the principal points
of Brownlee and of this pamphlet was that Stone could not have made his
thorough inspection in three hours and that his whole account was to be dis-
believed. Pages of print were wasted in attempted proofs of this proposition.

134 Boston, 1838.

135 *The Vision of Rubeta,* 43.

136 *Ibid.,* 162.

137 Philadelphia, 1838. The play was probably written by the author of the
Vision of Rubeta as indicated both by the pseudonym and the fact that it was
not a criticism but a defense of the earlier work, especially against the charge
of immorality. *The Critique,* 1–32.

138 The *Christian Spectator,* III (June, 1835), published a long article on
Maria Monk which began: "If the natural history of 'Gullibility' is ever
written, the impostures of Maria Monk must hold a prominent place in its
pages."

139 *American Protestant Vindicator,* August 9, 1837, August 30, 1837; New
York *Observer,* September 16, 1837. This rumor had it that Maria Monk's
book had been written by the Reverend George Bourne.

140 New York *Observer,* September 30, 1837.

141 This is possible in view of earlier "kidnapping" plots which they had
obviously arranged. One had been rumored even before the *Awful Disclosures*
was published. *American Protestant Vindicator,* November 18, 1835, December 23, 1835. A second attempt was supposedly made in May, 1836, by a group
of priests anxious to secure the reward of $15,000 which Maria Monk said had
been offered by Father Phelan for her return to Montreal. *Ibid.,* June 11,
1836; Slocum, *Reply to the Priest's Book,* 147. All of the attempts were so
crudely managed that they were obviously planned to win publicity.

142 According to Maria Monk's own story she was coaxed to Philadelphia
by six priests, but managed to escape and sought refuge in the home of Dr.
W. W. Sleigh. She stayed there until William Hogan, the ex-priest who had
been excommunicated during the Philadelphia trusteeism controversy and who
was now active in the nativistic crusade, returned with her to New York.
American Protestant Vindicator, September 13, 1837, October 11, 1837. Sleigh
published an account of the whole affair: *An Exposure of Maria Monk's Pretended Abduction and Conveyance to the Catholic Asylum, Philadelphia*
(Philadelphia, 1837). In this he presented affidavits and other evidence to
show that Maria Monk had come to Philadelphia under the name of Jane

Howard and had stayed in a boarding house with a man, even seeking employment as a domestic at a Catholic Asylum. Sleigh, *An Exposure of Maria Monk's Pretended Abduction,* 19-28. Sleigh expressed his opinion as a physician that she was mentally unfit to be at large and should be confined. *Ibid.,* 36. Maria Monk charged in return that Sleigh had been friendly toward her as long as she remained with him, but that he had been disappointed when she left with Hogan. He had then, she said, determined to make some money from the episode by attacking her, as he could not make it by exploiting her. *American Protestant Vindicator,* September 13, 1837.

143 New York, 1837.

144 Monk, *Further Disclosures,* 144-174.

145 Sleigh, *Exposure of Maria Monk's Pretended Abduction,* 32.

146 New York *Observer,* October 6, 1838; *Niles' Register,* LV (1838). Saint Frances Patrick gave birth to an illegitimate child at about the same time. New York *Observer,* October 6, 1838.

147 Statement of Brownlee quoted in New York *Observer,* November 3, 1838. In 1841, when accused of writing Maria Monk's book for her, Dr. Brownlee steadfastly maintained that the story had been dictated by Maria Monk to a Protestant clergyman just as it had appeared. *American Protestant Vindicator,* April 28, 1841. He insisted too that Saint Frances Patrick was a Jesuit in disguise, sent by the convent priests to discredit Maria Monk. *Ibid.,* May 17, 1837, June 9, 1841. Yet when the rumor spread that a third nun had escaped from the Hôtel Dieu convent, Brownlee expressed the hope that she would write her memoirs. *Ibid.,* September 30, 1840.

148 According to the statement, published thirty years later, of a woman who claimed to be Maria Monk's daughter. Mrs. L. St. John Eckel, *Maria Monk's Daughter; an Autobiography* (New York, 1874), 1-15. The daughter tells of her own conversion to Catholicism and most of the book is devoted to a vigorous defense of the Catholic faith.

149 New York *Herald,* quoted in Boston *Pilot,* August 4, 1849, September 8, 1849.

150 A typical post-Civil War edition was: Maria Monk, *The Mysteries of a Convent and the Awful Disclosures of Maria Monk* (——, 1874). The literature on Maria Monk is fairly large, but all of it is either of a popular nature or admittedly prejudiced; hence none of the authors who have dealt with her career have attempted a critical appraisal of contemporary materials. Most of the accounts have been based on Shea, *History of the Catholic Church,* III, 209-212, which is not only prejudiced but inaccurate. Typical is "The Truth about Maria Monk," Catholic Truth Society *Publications,* XIX (London, 1894). Equally prejudiced on the anti-Catholic side is Thomas E. Watson, "The Truth About Maria Monk," *Watson's Magazine* (May, 1916), 3-26. This attempts to prove that Maria Monk's statements were correct and even presents affidavits from two old men who knew Maria Monk's family and who had seen the secret passages beneath the Hôtel Dieu Convent. *Ibid.,* 21-23. The best popular account of her life is in Richardson Wright, *Forgotten Ladies* (Philadelphia, 1928), 121-155. See also R. A. Billington, "Maria Monk and her Influence," *Catholic Historical Review,* XXII (October, 1936), 283-296, and Ralph Thompson, "The Maria Monk Affair," the *Colophon,* Part 17 (1934).

V

Saving the West from the Pope
1835-1840

UNTIL the middle of the 1830's American nativism was directed almost entirely against Catholicism. This had been, and remained, its fundamental appeal, yet so long as the leaders of the movement in the United States confined their energies solely to this one channel, they could not hope to win universal support. Many people were indifferent to the No-Popery agitation or actually hostile toward the type of propaganda being sponsored by the Protestant Reformation Society. Among these were laborers and working men, who, normally hostile toward immigrant competition, might be induced to embrace the nativistic cause if their latent prejudice against foreigners could be aroused. Only when this considerable group had joined with those who felt an equal grievance against Catholicism could nativism hope to secure any of its objectives through political action.

An effective propaganda which developed in the latter part of the 1830's not only aroused Americans against immigrants but also demonstrated to their satisfaction that an alliance existed between these foreigners and the Catholic church to bring about the destruction of the United States. Thus the two phases of nativistic activity were united and were from that time inseparable.

This propaganda told of a plot jointly arranged by the Pope and the despotic monarchs of Europe in order to secure control of the Mississippi valley. This movement had a dual purpose: that region, and eventually the entire United States, would be won to Catholicism and immeasurably increase the strength of the papal church, and at the same time the despots of the old world would be relieved from the constant threat of revolutions inspired by the example of freedom and liberty offered by the American republic. This was to be accomplished by sending Catholic immigrants to the west until their numbers assured them control of that region. They would then rise in armed revolt and establish Popery and despotism in America.

These fantastic arguments were acceptable to many Americans of that day. A generation with sufficient self-esteem to create the concept of manifest destiny was only too ready to believe that the Mississippi valley, the garden spot of the world, was coveted by the Pope temporally as well as spiritually. They could not understand why he should retain his Vatican in outworn Italy when the bountiful lands of the west could be his with proper manipulation. These arguments were, moreover, a challenge to the religious men of America. The Mississippi valley, they believed, was to be the scene of the death struggle between Protestantism and Catholicism. Never in the past had these two antagonistic religious systems had a fair opportunity of testing their strength, for when they had clashed in Europe at the time of the Reformation, the contest had been political, as well as religious, with Catholics and Protestants alike supported by the sword. In America each would have to depend on its own resources in the struggle to achieve control of the vast, sparsely settled area of the west. Supremacy on the American continent and perhaps in the world would be the fruit of victory.

The first predictions of Rome's design on the west came in the 1820's when the religious press began to warn that unless Protestants sent missionaries and Bibles to the Mississippi valley Rome would occupy the region and "build up a system of ignorance, priestcraft, and superstition, such as now casts a blight over some of the fairest portions of Europe." [1] Tangible basis for these

premature fears seemed provided by the French Revolution of
1830. American Protestants believed that the overthrow of despotism and Popery in the old world by this liberal outbreak would
make doubly necessary the Catholic conquest of the west.[2] The
"Romish community" was pictured by one editor as "on the tiptoe
of expectation, indulging the most sanguine hopes . . . of soon
recovering all that it had lost."[3] Other Protestant journals
linked the revival of the Jesuits in 1814 with the entire papal
plot by showing that members of this order were restored to power
so that they could act as spies and advance agents to chart the
American field for eventual conquest.[4] "It is an ascertained
fact," wrote one editor, "that Jesuits are prowling about all parts
of the United States in every possible disguise, expressly to ascertain the advantageous situations and modes to disseminate
Popery. A minister of the Gospel from Ohio has informed us,
that he discovered one carrying on his devices in his congregation; and he says that the western country swarms with them
under the names of puppet show men, dancing masters, music
teachers, peddlers of images and ornaments, barrel organ players,
and similar practitioners."[5] The suppression of the Jesuit order
in Spain in 1835 intensified these fears. "Whither can they fly?"
asked the *Downfall of Babylon.* "Whither but to our own devoted
country?"[6]

This agitation by the religious press found support among a
large group of societies and organizations interested in the advance of Protestantism. As early as 1830 the American Bible
Society urged the uniting of Protestant sects to combat Rome's
influence in the west and expressed the belief that "His Holiness,
the Pope, has, with eager grasp, already fixed upon this fair portion of our Union, and he knows well how to keep his hold."[7]
Similar warnings from the American Education Society,[8] the
British Reformation Society,[9] and the Boston Sunday School
Union[10] attested to the widespread acceptance of this belief. The
Protestant churches were naturally interested and both the Pres-

byterians [11] and Baptists [12] considered the advisability of more concentrated missionary operation in the west to combat the designs of Popery there. Public meetings, at which this problem was presented to the assembled clergymen of several eastern cities, were held in 1834.[13]

At first Protestant suspicion was directed against the entire Catholic church, but in the early 1830's nativistic editors had singled out two Catholic missionary societies which, they asserted, were to carry on the entire papal conquest of the United States: the Association for the Propagation of the Faith, and the Leopold Association. Both of these associations were European missionary societies, formed with the specific purpose of furthering the growth of the Church in Protestant and heathen lands. Of the two, the Association for the Propagation of the Faith was the more influential. It had been formed at Lyons, France, in 1832 as a general missionary society,[14] but many of its efforts were directed toward the United States, where its generous contributions did much to further the growth of Catholicism.[15] It did not, however, attract the scrutiny of the anti-Catholic press as did the Leopold Association, largely because its efforts were world-wide, and the Leopold Association concentrated its attentions on the United States. This latter organization was formed in 1829 in response to the pleas for aid from Bishop Edward Fenwick of the Cincinnati diocese. Its membership was limited to citizens of Austria-Hungary who on joining were pledged to give their prayers and a small weekly sum for its success.[16] At first these funds were sent solely to Cincinnati, but within a short time all the bishoprics in the country were receiving support from this source. The contributions were never large,[17] but the fact that the society was avowedly attempting to strengthen Catholicism in the United States and especially in the west focused American attention on its efforts.

Protestants were especially alarmed because of the apparent success of these societies. Western Catholicism appeared to out-

siders at least to be a vigorous and growing religion, showing
more strength than Protestantism. Foreign travelers repeatedly
commented on the inroads being made by Catholicism in the
Mississippi valley and professed to believe that within a few
years Protestantism would actually be outstripped there. Frederick Marryat believed that "all America west of the Alleghenies
will eventually be a Catholic country . . . as the Catholics are
already in the majority" [18] and similar sentiments were expressed
by many other observers who attributed the rapid Catholic advance to the division among Protestant sects.[19]

It was this situation which centered Protestant attention on
Catholic missionary activities and especially on the Leopold Association. Religious papers first became aware of the operations of
this society in 1834 and immediately began publishing both its
reports and warnings of the danger which threatened because of
its continued existence.[20] These sporadic efforts would probably
have been fruitless had they not interested Samuel F. B. Morse,
inventor of the telegraph, who gained his first fame as an artist
and anti-Catholic propagandist. A descendent of a New England
family and a son of the Reverend Jedidiah Morse of Charlestown,
who had exhibited a flair of nativistic sentiment in preaching
against the Bavarian Illuminati,[21] Morse had been reared in an
atmosphere of antipathy against Rome common in the Massachusetts of his youth, but during his early career as an artist he
had shown none of the characteristics which were to make him
a leading nativistic writer. The change in his attitude came while
he was visiting Rome in 1830, enjoying the pageantry of a Holy
Year. In June of that year, while Morse was watching a papal
procession pass, an event occurred which accounted for much of
his later bigotry:

I was standing [he wrote in his *Journal*] close to the side of the
house when, in an instant, without the slightest notice, my hat was
struck off to the distance of several yards by a soldier, or rather by
a poltroon in a soldier's costume, and this courteous manoeuvre was

performed with his gun and bayonet, accompanied with curses and taunts and the expression of a demon on his countenance. In cases like this there is no redress. The soldier receives his orders and the manner is left to his discretion. . . . The blame lies after all, not so much with the pitiful wretch who perpetrates the outrage, as it does with those who gave him such base and indiscriminate orders.[22]

This episode changed Morse's whole point of view. Heretofore his artistic nature had led him to admire the beauty of Catholic ceremony; now he saw only the harshness of a despotic religious system. His trampled hat was to make him a life-long opponent of Rome.[23]

Upon his return to America, Morse's attention was directed to the Leopold Association by the attacks upon it in the religious press. Feeling that his own European experiences had fitted him to speak with authority on this so-called Catholic plot, he wrote a series of twelve letters under the pen name of Brutus, entitled "A Foreign Conspiracy against the Liberties of the United States" which was published in the New York *Observer* during the autumn of 1834.[24] The importance of the disclosures contained in these letters was immediately recognized. They were widely reprinted in nativistic and religious newspapers [25] and before the end of the year had appeared in book form.

In his *Foreign Conspiracy,* Morse performed the important task of linking immigration and Catholicism and making both equally objectionable in American eyes. He pointed out [26] that Frederick Schlegel, an agent of the Austrian government, had given a series of lectures in Vienna in 1828 in which monarchy and Catholicism were declared interdependent and equally opposed to the republicanism of the United States.[27] Morse believed it no coincidence that the Leopold Association was formed in Vienna a year later, but rather a well-organized attempt against American democracy. If the old monarchies of Europe, and especially Austria, were to survive, they must dam the stream of liberty at its source or be inundated by a flood of rebellion among their own people. It was for this purpose, he said, that the Holy Alliance had been formed.[28] But Austria and the other backward countries of Europe were no match for the vigorous United States and did not dare risk warfare to accomplish their end. Hence they had enlisted the aid of the other great foe of liberty, the Catholic church. Together they were to force their beliefs on the United States, using the Leopold Association to win the west to their cause and sending immigrants in sufficient numbers that the entire country would eventually embrace the doctrines of Popery and despotism.[29] Morse refuted the possibility that the Leopold Association was an altruistic missionary society. "Is it credible," he asked, "that the manufacturers of chains for binding liberty in Europe, have suddenly become benevolently concerned only for the *religious welfare* of this Republican people? If this Society be solely for the propagation of the Catholic faith, one would think that *Rome,* and not *Vienna,* should be its headquarters! that the *Pope,* not the *Emperor of Austria,* should be its grand patron!" [30] Morse urged Protestants to abandon their religious differences and unite against Catholic schools, Catholic officeholders, and especially against lenient immigration laws.[31] "We must first stop this leak in the ship," he wrote, "through which the muddy waters from without threaten to sink us." [32]

The favorable reception accorded this work [33] not only led to its wide circulation [34] but also encouraged Morse to enlarge upon the Catholic plot which he had described in its pages. This he did in a second series of letters entitled "Imminent Dangers to the Free Institutions of the United States through Foreign Immigration," published in the New York *Journal of Commerce* during 1835, and reprinted in book form almost immediately. In these letters Morse enlarged upon the part immigrants were to play in the papal conquest of the United States, charging that nearly all who came were under the direct control of Jesuits who directed their settlement by placing them at strategic points.[35] Austria needed only to place these popish puppets in control of the government, he wrote, and her victory would be won. "They have already sent their chains," Morse warned, "and oh! to our shame be it spoken, are fastening them upon a *sleeping* victim. Americans, you are marked for their prey, not by foreign bayonets, but by *weapons surer of effecting the conquest of liberty* than all the munitions of physical combat in the military or naval storehouses of Europe. Will you not awake to the apprehension of the reality and extent of your danger? Will you be longer deceived by the pensioned Jesuits, who having surrounded your press, are now using it all over the country to stifle the cries of danger, and lull your fears by attributing your alarm to a false cause? Up! Up! I beseech you. Awake! To your posts! Let the tocsin sound from Maine to Louisiana. Fly to protect the vulnerable places of your Constitution and Laws. Place your guards; you will need them; and quickly too.—And first, shut your gates." [36]

The theme of Morse's second work was so similar to that of his first that it did not attain the same popularity.[37] Nevertheless Morse continued his nativistic writings by editing, in 1836, *The Proscribed German Student, being a Sketch of Some Interesting Incidents in the Life and Death of Lewis Clausing; to which is Added, a Treatise on the Jesuits, a posthumous Work of Lewis Clausing*. This account, written by a mentally unbalanced German student who committed suicide in New York in July, 1836,[38] enlarged upon the part to be played by the Jesuits in Europe's conquest of America, picturing them as spies disguised as Protestants, gathering information and seeking out strategic points from which the final attack was to be launched.[39]

Closely rivaling Morse in exposing the Romish designs on the United States was the Reverend Lyman Beecher who had already gained fame among nativists for his sermons preceding the burning of the Ursuline convent. Beecher had a sincere interest in the preservation of the west from papal influence which dated back at least to 1830 when he had considered moving to the Mississippi

valley for the one purpose of personally combating Rome.[40] An
opportunity for this step came in that same year when he was offered the presidency of the Lane Theological Seminary at Cincinnati. Beecher gladly accepted, largely because he felt that the
position offered an opportunity to battle the Pope for possession
of the garden spot of the world.[41] Four years in the west only
strengthened his earlier nativistic convictions and when in 1834
and 1835 he was called upon to tour the east in a money-raising
campaign for his school, he selected a topic quite in keeping with
these beliefs. The result was a powerful sermon which proved so
popular that it was published in book form in 1835 as *A Plea for
the West*.[42]

Naturally interested in education, Beecher amplified the papal
plot as envisaged by Morse, by showing the part which Catholic
schools would play in the Roman conquest of the United States.
Up to this time the proselyting efforts of these schools [43] had not
entirely escaped the attention of the religious press,[44] but it remained for the *Plea for the West* to popularize the issue. Beecher
agreed with Morse that the despotic nations of Europe had determined to stamp out the republicanism of the United States by
winning American converts and by sending popish immigrants
to that country.[45] In this whole process, the schools, he believed,
were to play an important part. Through them, converts to Catholicism would be won, until, eventually, these converts and the
Catholic immigrants would control the nation. Maintaining that
these schools were established purely because of their proselyting
activities, Beecher wrote: "Do they not . . . tax their own people, and supplicate the royal munificence of Catholic Europe to
rear schools and colleges for the cheap and even gratuitous education of Protestant children, high and low,—while thousands
of Catholic children are utterly neglected and uncared for, and
abandoned to vice? Is all this without design?" [46] Beecher concluded that more Protestant schools and colleges must be built to
offset this Catholic influence.[47]

The popular reception accorded the works of Beecher [48] and Morse not only attracted attention to their arguments but inspired a host of imitators and the Catholic plot which they had sketched in outline was filled in by countless writers during the succeeding years. Annual reports of the Leopold Association and the Association for the Propagation of the Faith were widely published in the religious press,[49] with warnings of the fate awaiting America if these activities were continued.[50] Catholic disavowals were brushed aside as worthless. The papal clergy, propagandists maintained, had been taught to keep no faith with heretics and ordinary Catholics were being kept in ignorance until the time to strike,[51] when they would be released from their oath of allegiance to the United States by the Pope,[52] establish the Inquisition in America, and win converts to Catholicism by flame and sword.[53] Already, it was claimed, the Papists were making plans for that day by building inquisitorial chambers beneath their churches and by arming their religious edifices for use in the final attack.[54] Even the foreign military companies which were coming into being in the larger cities seemed to nativists an actual marshaling of papal forces for the conquest of the west.[55] In the south the ever-present fear of a slave insurrection was played upon by writers who conjured up supposed evidence of a Catholic-Negro alliance against Protestant whites.[56]

Propagandists directed much of their attention to foreign immigrants who became, in their eyes, a Rome-directed group of papal serfs, bent on the planned destruction of the United States. Under this impetus the Protestant press began to show greater interest in immigration, printing almost daily statistics of the number of arrivals and stressing constantly the danger in their coming.[57] It was generally agreed that their influence would be harmful rather than good, for so long as they remained Catholics, pledged to support an autocratic system in both church and state, they could never become true advocates of American freedom. As one editor put it:

> Rome's true minions chain them down,
> In ignorance from heel to crown;
> In hopes, perchance, that when the pope,
> Is forced from Europe to elope,
> He here may find a sovereign throne;
> And ready serfs to bend and groan.[58]

Even Protestant immigrants were pictured by propagandists as Jesuits in disguise,[59] and the large number of paupers and criminals among the aliens seemed a deliberate attempt on the part of Rome to undermine and weaken the United States against the anticipated conquest.[60] One book published at the time, *The Flight of Popery from Rome to the West,*[61] described in detail the means through which these immigrants would be used when the Pope actually came to the United States at the head of his armed forces.

The efforts of German colonizing companies, such as the Giessener Auswanderungs Gesellschaft, formed in 1833 to people Missouri, and the Adelsverein with a similar design upon the new lands of Texas[62] were viewed with particular alarm by nativistic writers who decried these settlements as open evidence of popish aggression.[63] Even greater concern was aroused by a London firm, established to aid Irish immigrants in settling a great section of the old northwest and Upper Canada.[64] Although this company never materialized, it did arouse the ire of many nativistic writers.[65] All of these projected colonies seemed attempts on the part of Catholic and foreign capitalists to introduce into the United States groups of aliens who would be so isolated as to resist Americanizing influences. Propagandists pointed out that the American democratic experiment depended on the ability of the new nation to assimilate the migratory streams of the old. Any attempt toward perpetuating European institutions through the establishment of racial colonies in the United States would inevitably lead to disaster.

This persistent propaganda concerning the west [66] eventually interested the society which was most concerned with the spiritual welfare of that region, the American Home Missionary Society. One of the many forces leading to the organization of this society in 1826 had been the fear that Romanism would subdue the Protestant outposts in the Mississippi valley unless support could be given them.[67] As early as 1829 its publication, the *Home Missionary,* and its annual reports, expressed alarm at the increasing number of Catholics in the west,[68] declaring that "the Valley of the Mississippi has been no doubt mapped as well as surveyed, by emissaries from the Vatican." [69] After the appearance of Morse's *Foreign Conspiracy,* the *Home Missionary* became a regular organ for nativistic propaganda, the editor writing in 1839:

> The cause is the cause of the West—for there the great battle is to be fought between truth and error, between law and anarchy—between Christianity, with her Sabbaths, her ministry and her schools, on the one hand, and the combined forces of Infidelity and Popery on the other.[70]

Reports corroborating these editorial fears were received from missionaries in widely separated communities in the west. In 1830 a Missouri agent reported: "It is by no means certain that the Jesuits are not to prevail to a great extent in this western country. Their priests are coming in upon us, and with a zeal that ought to make the Protestant Christian blush,—they are establishing their schools and their nunneries throughout the land." [71] A laborer in Wisconsin a short time later came to the conclusion that cathedrals and convents were being built at strategic points and hinted darkly: "The ignorance of these Romanists is such, that this apparent design must have originated with some one who had more of [a] far reaching plan than they." [72] "The line of Catholic 'posts,'" another missionary reported, "is fast being completed." [73]

The stress placed upon this anti-Catholic appeal by the American Home Missionary Society was clear evidence of the prevalence of eastern nativistic sentiment. Actually the Catholic church

was relatively unimportant in the west and was outnumbered by
the evangelical sects in every state. A vast majority of the reports
from the society's missionaries in the Mississippi valley either
made this clear or failed to mention Catholicism at all.[74] The fact
that the managers of the society carefully selected for publication in the *Home Missionary* and in the annual reports the few
letters which did dwell upon the Catholic danger indicated that
they realized the wide appeal of this fear in the east. They were
willing to play upon this popular apprehension to secure funds for
the project in which they sincerely believed, and their efforts
added much to the ever-increasing stream of propaganda directed
against this phase of Catholic activity. The feeling engendered
in the east by this persistent publication is illustrated in a letter
from a Massachusetts correspondent to the *Western Messenger*:

They tell us here, at least from some pulpits, that the West is
fast becoming the Pope's heritage, and that it will soon be all under
his thumb. Some preachers talk more vehemently against the "Man
of Sin," as they call him, than against sin itself; indeed it seems to
me that many are resolving the whole Christian character into a
cordial hatred of Catholics.[75]

It is small wonder that amidst such distrust of Catholic and foreigner the House of Representatives of the United States should
be called upon by a group of petitioners from Washington
County, New York, to decide whether there was not

a plan in operation, powerful and dangerous, under the management of the Leopold Foundation, for the subversion of our civil and
religious liberties, to be effected by the emigration of Roman Catholics from Europe, and by their admission to the right of suffrage
with us in our political institutions.[76]

The deep-seated and general antipathy toward Rome, attested
by these examples and by the success of the propaganda writers,
found outlet in America's first political nativism in the late 1830's.
The arguments of Morse and Beecher had been essential to the

beginning of such a development. They had shown that immigrants threatened the existence of the United States and that the continuance of the Union depended on a checking or regulation of this alien flow which could be accomplished only by political action. Consequently nativistic papers first began asking for the formation of an anti-Catholic party in 1835 [77] when they realized that a sufficiently large number of people had embraced their cause to make this step possible.

These early attempts at political nativism were sporadic and local. In March, 1835 a few ward meetings were held in New York where nativistic candidates were nominated, but the strength of the movement remained untested when these tickets were promptly absorbed by the Whigs. [78] A more serious effort in June, 1835 resulted in the formation of the Native American Democratic Association, an organization which grew from the efforts of James Watson Webb, editor of the New York *Courier and Inquirer,* and gained such immediate success that a newspaper, the *Spirit of '76,* was founded to popularize its issues. Its platform pledged opposition to foreigners in office, to pauper and criminal immigration, and to the Catholic church. [79] Unfortunately for the success of this first nativistic party, these principles failed to hold together the divergent elements which it attracted. In September, 1835 a schism occurred when one group, wanting to direct the association's activities solely against Catholics, broke away. [80] Despite this difference of opinion an attempt was made to found nativistic parties in other cities and by the fall of 1835 organizations similar to the Native American Democratic Association existed in Brooklyn, Paterson (New Jersey), New Orleans, and Cincinnati. [81]

In New York nativists gained some prominence in the fall elections, and although they did not carry the city, their vote was so menacing that the local Democratic party cast off its foreign supporters. [82] Thus encouraged, New York Native Americans prepared for the spring elections of 1836 with every hope of suc-

cess. They made the mistake of nominating for mayor Samuel
F. B. Morse, who, though a prominent nativist, was also a Democrat and unable to attract Whig support, polling only about two
thousand votes.[83] In the following year, with the panic of 1837
creating dissatisfaction with the older parties and calling attention to the competition provided by alien labor, political nativism
enjoyed its first success in New York. A nativistic ticket was
nominated and carried into office with Whig support, a mayor and
a complete common council being elected.[84]

Similar strength was shown by the movement in other cities.
Citizens of Germantown, Pennsylvania formed a Native American Association and drew up a constitution declaring against foreign officeholders and voters.[85] In Washington seven hundred
persons attended a mass meeting held in July, 1837 and formed
the Native American Association of the United States with similar demands.[86] In New Orleans the Louisiana Native American
Association, which had been formed in 1835,[87] issued an address
deploring the immigration to America of "the outcast and offal
of society, the vagrant and the convict—transported in myriads
to our shores, reeking with the accumulated crimes of the whole
civilized world." [88] Other less important associations were established in smaller cities and towns and enjoyed some local political
success.[89]

By this time nativists were sufficiently united politically to make
stridently vocal their demands. They had two principal griev-
ances against the immigrant : they objected to the political power
which foreigners gained through the franchise, and to the paupers
and criminals among the immigrants who must be supported by
money from American taxpayers. From both of these seeming
injustices they sought relief.

Control of the franchise in national elections was purely a question of federal legislation. Nativists realized that Congress might
be moved by political pressure to change the naturalization laws
and early began petitioning with this end in view, the Native

American Association of Washington being the first to adopt this device. In January, 1838, it presented a petition to Congress, signed by nearly a thousand members, asking for the repeal of the existing naturalization laws [90] and pointing out that the five year probationary period then in use was altogether too short to allow aliens to become versed in the intricacies of the American governmental system. This petition was referred to a select committee by the House of Representatives,[91] one being chosen with a nativist majority so that its report, laid before members of the House in 1838, heartily endorsed the legislation desired by the Native American associations. There was no doubt in the minds of the committee that Morse and other propagandists who had followed him were correct. The despots of Europe, they reported, wanted to stamp out American republicanism and were sending immigrants to the United States for that purpose. These aliens might become valuable citizens after a long period of training, but this could not be accomplished in five years. The committee recommended that the probationary period for naturalization be radically extended, leaving the exact time to the discretion of Congress.[92] This report aroused some opposition [93] but despite this a bill embodying its recommendations was prepared and made some progress in Congress before being pushed aside by more pressing business.[94] Despite renewed demands from petitioners,[95] this was to be the last attempt to change the naturalization laws until the 1840's.

Meanwhile nativists turned their attention to the other grievance which they hoped to remedy—the importation of foreign paupers and criminals. Several states had attempted to check this evil by enacting laws requiring bonds from ship captains importing persons likely to become public charges. Such restrictions, although never operating successfully, provided a means through which a number of states sought protection now.[96] Laws requiring the payment of a head tax for each immigrant brought from Europe were more generally used by states anxious to protect themselves from the burden of pauper support. The money thus collected was to be employed in caring for poor immigrants, erecting hospitals for their care, and generally relieving the state of much of the problem of their support. Although these laws were effective to some extent, they aroused constitutional objections, and in a series of cases in the 1840's the Supreme Court ruled that they interfered with the exclusive right of the federal government to regulate foreign commerce and were hence void.[97]

Unable to solve the problems of pauper immigration by recourse to the states, nativists turned to the national government for relief. The power of Congress to restrict immigration was unquestioned and as early as 1836 petitions from the northeastern states were received requesting legislation which would limit or check the coming of persons likely to become public charges.[98] The immediate result of these petitions was a congressional resolution asking the Treasury department for information on the subject.[99] This served to substantiate the fears of the petitioners, showing that several European governments were using the United States as a dumping ground for their undesirable paupers and criminals and that other aliens, who came voluntarily, had exhausted their resources before landing and immediately became public charges.[100] Despite this evidence and in the face of further petitions from eastern state legislatures,[101] Congress refused to take any action until 1838 when a select committee was appointed to investigate the whole problem, and recommend legislation. This committee's report was so prejudiced as to defeat the ambitions of the nativists. Its members secured information not only from the officials of eastern cities, but also from the Native American Associations of New York and Washington,[102] and the report which they presented was in keeping with this nativistic leaning. "The fact is unquestionable," they concluded, "that large numbers of foreigners are annually brought to our country by the authority, and at the expense of, foreign Governments, and landed upon our shores in a state of absolute destitution and dependence; many of them of the most idle and vicious class; in their personal appearance the most offensive and loathsome; and their numbers increasing with such rapidity by emigration, as to become burdensome to the American people; our own citizens being obliged to contribute largely from their own earnings to support them in idleness." [103] Legislation to stop pauper immigration entirely was recommended.[104]

The report of this committee was allowed to lie neglected while Congress turned to more pressing matters, nor did an attempt to revive it in the next Congress succeed.[105] Obviously politicians believed that the nativistic support that they would gain by furthering these proposals did not balance the alien vote which they would lose by such a step. In this they were correct, but the propaganda of Morse and his followers, linking Catholicism and immigration and making them both equally dangerous to the United States, had nevertheless immeasurably increased nativistic strength. Another group had been added and that slow process through which more and more supporters were won to the anti-Catholic cause was well under way by 1840.

NOTES

[1] New York *Observer*, October 20, 1827. See also *Ibid.*, August 14, 1824, May 2, 1829, December 19, 1829, February 13, 1830; Connecticut *Observer*, quoted in *Ibid.*, January 16, 1830; *Church Register*, June 6, 1829; *Protestant Episcopalian and Church Register*, III (January, 1831); *The Protestant*, January 9, 1830, February 6, 1830, February 20, 1830, November 13, 1830; *Christian Watchman*, February 26, 1830, April 6, 1832, June 27, 1834, December 5, 1834.

[2] New York *Observer*, October 9, 1830, September 20, 1834, January 23, 1836; *Episcopal Recorder*, May 28, 1831; *Christian Watchman*, September 10, 1830, January 24, 1834, January 31, 1834; *The Protestant*, January 1, 1831.

[3] *Protestant Episcopalian and Church Register*, II (January, 1831).

[4] *The Protestant*, January 9, 1830, March 3, 1832; *Spirit of '76*, August 4, 1835; W. C. Brownlee, *Popery an Enemy to Civil and Religious Liberty; and Dangerous to our Republic* (New York, 1836), 204.

[5] *American Protestant Vindicator*, December 25, 1834.

[6] September 26, 1835. *American Protestant Vindicator*, December 25, 1834, September 2, 1835; *The Protestant*, March 3, 1832; New York *Observer*, September 19, 1835; *Christian Watchman*, February 11, 1842.

7 *Massachusetts Yeoman*, April 17, 1830; New York *Observer*, July 21, 1832.

8 *Quarterly Register of the American Education Society*, quoted in New York *Observer*, March 6, 1830.

9 *Ibid.*, August 14, 1830, July 16, 1831.

10 *Ibid.*, December 3, 1831; Beecher, *Autobiography and Correspondence*, II, 219; *Priestcraft Unmasked*, July 15, 1830.

11 *Protestant Magazine*, I (July, 1834); New York *Observer*, July 12, 1834. The Reverend Philo F. Phelps, speaking before the General Assembly of the Presbyterian church in 1834, described this Catholic plot to take over the United States.

12 *Christian Watchman*, June 2, 1832, October 10, 1834. Episcopalian ministers were urged to combat the papal designs on the west by the *Protestant Episcopalian and Church Register*, IV (October, 1833).

13 *American Protestant Vindicator*, October 15, 1834, October 29, 1834.

14 Joseph Freri, *The Society for the Propagation of the Faith and Catholic Missions, 1822-1900* (Baltimore, 1902), 58. The plan and organization of the society are in: *Annales de l'Association de la Propagation de la Foi, Recueil Periodique des Lettres des Évêques et des Missionnaires des Deux Mondes, et de Tous les Documens Relatifs aux Missions et a l'Association de la Propagation de la Foi* (Lyons et Paris, 1823—), I, No. 3 (1824), 31-32.

15 In 1840 the year's contributions amounted to $125,000 and by 1859 the annual aid was as high as $173,000. Freri, *The Society for the Propagation of the Faith*, 27-28; Guilday, *Life of John England*, II, 211-212.

16 Bishop Fenwick sent Father Rese to Europe in 1828 to secure financial aid, and his efforts there led to the establishment of the society, as well as the Ludwig-missionsverein with headquarters at Munich. The Leopold Association was centered at Vienna and its chief patron was Archduke Rudolph. Members were supposed to contribute five kreutzers (about two cents) each week and by authority of Leo XII certain indulgences were allowed them in return for their gifts and prayers. O'Daniel, *The Right Reverend Edward Dominic Fenwick*, 265-361; *American Catholic Historical Researches*, I (1905), 314-316.

17 Between 1829 and 1846 the society sent only $330,000 to America. Raymond Payne, "Annals of the Leopoldine Association," *Catholic Historical Review*, I (1905), 52-57; P. G. Verwyst, *Life and Labors of the Right Reverend Frederick Baroga* (Milwaukee, 1900), 454-456.

18 Marryat, *A Diary in America*, III, 222.

19 *Ibid.*, III, 220; James S. Buckingham, *America: Historical, Statistical and Descriptive* (London, 1841), I, 439; Charles A. Murray, *Travels in North America* (London, 1854), II, 308; Harriet Martineau, *Society in America* (London, 1837), III, 236.

20 *Christian Watchman*, January 17, 1834 and ff; New York *Observer*, January 18, 1834 and ff; *Protestant Magazine*, II (February, March, 1834); the operations of the Association for the Propagation of the Faith had been noticed in New York *Observer*, March 6, 1830, January 26, 1833, May 25, 1833; *Christian Watchman*, February 26-March 19, 1830.

21 Vernon Stauffer, *New England and the Bavarian Illuminati*, in *Columbia University Studies in History, Economics and Public Law* (New York, 1893—), LXXXII (1918), 279.

22 Edward L. Morse, *Samuel F. B. Morse, his Life and Journals* (Boston, 1914), I, 353.

23 This changed attitude was clearly reflected in Morse's journal which he kept at this time. See especially, *Ibid.*, I, 359. Morse's trampled hat became something of a symbol to American nativists. When a man in Cincinnati, Alexander Duncan, claimed to have had his hat knocked from his head during a Catholic procession in that city, the episode was widely commented upon and even offered an excuse for a New York artist to depict the scene in a lithograph. *Western Monthly Magazine*, III (June, 1835); *American Protestant Vindicator*, January 21, 1835; *Christian Watchman*, February 27, 1835.

24 August 30, 1834–November 22, 1834.

25 *Downfall of Babylon*, May 30, 1834 and ff; *Christian Spectator*, VII (June, 1835); *Christian Watchman*, September 19, 1834 and ff; *Protestant Banner*, January 28, 1842. Extracts from the work were also printed in *Zion's Herald*, the Boston *Recorder*, and *The Valley of the Mississippi*. Morse, *Foreign Conspiracy against the Liberties of the United States*, 4th ed., i–ii.

26 Morse, *Foreign Conspiracy*, 15–17.

27 F. Schlegel, *The Philosophy of History* (London, 1835), II, 298.

28 Morse, *Foreign Conspiracy*, 43–46.

29 *Ibid.*, 19–41.

30 *Ibid.*, 41–42.

31 *Ibid.*, 64–68, 71–73, 74, 106, 112–113.

32 *Ibid.*, 143.

33 For favorable reviews see: *Downfall of Babylon*, March 7, 1835; *Christian Spectator*, June, 1835; *Protestant Magazine*, I (July, 1834); *American Protestant Vindicator*, September 3, 1834, September 19, 1834; New York *Observer*, April 11, 1835.

34 A second edition was required almost immediately and annual editions appeared for some time, a fifth edition being published in 1841. Catholic attempts to answer the book, such as an address prepared by Bishop England, were ignored, and the second edition appeared with the boast that the operations of the Leopold Association had not been denied. Guilday, *Life and Times of John England*, II, 209–210.

35 Samuel F. B. Morse, *Imminent Dangers to the Free Institutions of the United States through Foreign Immigration* (New York, 1835), 9–17.

36 *Ibid.*, 25.

37 A second edition was not published until 1854.

38 *American Protestant Vindicator*, July 13, 1836; New York *Observer*, July 23, 1836; *Downfall of Babylon*, July 23, 1836. Clausing suffered from a delusion of persecution at the hands of the Jesuits, dating back to a duel which had resulted fatally for his opponent. He came to Morse's home in New York with the treatise on the Jesuits and Morse harbored him until he took his own life. Even Morse was forced to admit that he was suffering from hallucinations, but insisted that these had grown from the poor treatment he had received at the hands of the Jesuits in his youth. Samuel F. B. Morse, *The Proscribed German Student; being a Sketch of some Interesting Incidents in the Life and Death of Lewis Clausing; to which is added, a Treatise on the Jesuits, a Posthumous Work of Lewis Clausing* (New York, 1836), 7–55.

39 *Ibid.*, 132–217. Morse's last nativistic publication was *The Confessions of a French Priest, to which are added Warnings to the People of the United*

States (New York, 1837). This was so frankly an attempt to appeal to the libidinous tastes of American readers already whetted by the Maria Monk controversy that it suggests that Morse by this time was interested in the commercial possibility of this type of writing. He remained an ardent nativist throughout his life, stating as late as 1854 when he was considered as a Democratic candidate for congress, that his views on Catholicism and immigration were expressed in *Foreign Conspiracy*. Morse, *Samuel F. B. Morse*, II, 332. His anti-Catholic activities are inadequately studied in Francis John Conners, "Samuel Finley Breese Morse and the Anti-Catholic Political Movements in the United States, 1791-1872," *Illinois Catholic Historical Review*, X (October, 1927), 83-122.

40 Beecher to his daughter Caroline, July 8, 1830. Beecher, *Autobiography and Correspondence*, II, 224-225.

41 *Ibid.*, II, 249.

42 Cincinnati, 1835.

43 Bishop Fenwick of the Cincinnati diocese freely admitted the importance of Catholic schools in this connection. O'Daniel, *The Right Reverend Edward Dominic Fenwick*, 393-394.

44 *Downfall of Babylon*, March 28, 1835, August 29, 1835; New York *Observer*, May 2, 1829, December 19, 1829, March 10, 1832, April 29, 1832, July 26, 1834, February 28, 1835, March 14, 1835; *Western Christian Advocate*, February 27, 1835; *Christian Watchman*, February 19, 1830, June 2, 1832, June 27, 1834, August 1, 1834; *American Protestant Vindicator*, September 24, 1834, October 15, 1834; *The Protestant*, January 9, 1830, January 30, 1830, July 17, 1830, December 18, 1830, June 11, 1831; *Episcopal Recorder*, July 16, 1831, July 23, 1831, October 25, 1834.

45 Beecher, *Plea for the West*, 52-55, 117-130.

46 *Ibid.*, 99.

47 *Ibid.*, 182.

48 For favorable reviews of the *Plea for the West* see: *Christian Review*, I (June, 1836); *Christian Spectator*, VII (1835), 481-503; New York *Observer*, June 20, 1835; *American Protestant Vindicator*, July 8, 1835. The editor of the *Western Monthly Magazine* attacked Beecher's arguments in the May, 1835, issue and criticism was so great that he was forced to resign.

49 *Downfall of Babylon*, February 20, 1836; *American Protestant Vindicator*, April 15, 1835, November 4, 1835, May 3, 1837; New York *Observer*, January 23, 1836, November 25, 1837, April 15, 1837; *Christian Watchman*, February 12, 1841, July 16, 1841, March 3, 1843.

50 New York *Observer*, July 26, 1834, March 14, 1835; *Downfall of Babylon*, March 28, 1835; *Christian Watchman*, January 23, 1835, July 24, 1835, January 26, 1838; *Protestant Banner*, May 20, 1842; *Western Christian Advocate*, February 20, 1835; Brownlee, *Popery, an Enemy to Civil and Religious Liberty*, 14-33; Baxter, *Jesuit Juggling*, xviii-xix.

51 S. S. Schmucker, *Discourse in Commemoration of the Glorious Reformation of the Sixteenth Century* (New York, 1838), 125-128.

52 *American Protestant Vindicator*, October 21, 1835.

53 B. F. Ellis, *A History of the Romish Inquisition Compiled from Various Authors* (Hanover, Indiana, 1835), 1-12.

54 *Downfall of Babylon*, August 14, 1834, March 5, 1836; *American Prot-*

estant Vindicator, July 15, 1835, June 8, 1838; *Christian Watchman*, March 13, 1840.

[55] *Spirit of '76*, September 5, 1835, September 8, 1835, September 10, 1835; *Downfall of Babylon*, September 19, 1835; Cyrus Mason, *A History of the Holy Catholic Inquisition* (Philadelphia, 1835), vii–viii.

[56] New York *Observer*, December 27, 1834, February 28, 1835. Tangible basis seemed to be given these fears when Bishop England established a school for slaves in Charleston. Sentiment was so strong that the school was ultimately closed. *Ibid.*, April 11, 1835; Guilday, *Life and Times of John England*, II, 151–156.

[57] New York *Observer*, June 29, 1833, September 20, 1834; *National Intelligencer*, March 21, 1835; *Downfall of Babylon*, January 3, 1835, July 4, 1835, August 8, 1835, July 23, 1836.

[58] *American Protestant Vindicator*, January 20, 1841.

[59] *Spirit of '76*, August 4, 1835.

[60] New York *Observer*, August 3, 1839; *Downfall of Babylon*, June 11, 1836; *American Protestant Vindicator*, December 1, 1841; *Niles' Register*, XLIX (1835), 62; Baltimore *Literary and Religious Magazine*, IV (September, 1838); Morse, *Foreign Conspiracy*, 141–142; Beecher, *Plea for the West*, 54; *Massachusetts Yeoman*, July 9, 1831.

[61] Samuel B. Smith, *The Flight of Popery from Rome to the West* (New York, 1836). Smith was editor of the *Downfall of Babylon*.

[62] Thomas S. Baker, *Lenau and Young Germany in America* (Philadelphia, 1897), 54–55, 61–69.

[63] *Spirit of '76*, September 26, 1835; *Downfall of Babylon*, July 23, 1836.

[64] *Proposed New Plan of a General Emigration Society* (London, 1842).

[65] *Home Missionary*, XIV (February, 1842), XV (July, 1842); *Christian Watchman*, February 3, 1843; *Protestant Banner*, December 1, 1842.

[66] Large public meetings were held in Pittsburgh, Syracuse, and other cities in which speakers stressed the danger of Catholicism in appealing for support for western missionary projects. *American Protestant Vindicator*, June 15, 1836; *Christian Watchman*, November 3, 1843.

[67] American Home Missionary Society, *Eighth Annual Report* (New York, 1834), 10–11. For a full account of the effect of this propaganda on the American home missionary societies see the author's "Anti-Catholic Propaganda and the Home Missionary Movement, 1800–1860," *Mississippi Valley Historical Review*, XXII (December, 1935), 361–384.

[68] *Home Missionary*, II (May, 1829), II (April, 1830), VI (February, 1834); American Home Missionary Society, *Sixth Annual Report* (New York, 1832), 2.

[69] *Home Missionary*, IV (July, 1832), 35.

[70] *Ibid.*, XII (August, 1839), 73.

[71] *Ibid.*, II (April, 1830), 192.

[72] *Ibid.*, XVI (August, 1843), 84.

[73] *Ibid.*, XX (December, 1847), 177.

[74] Professor W. W. Sweet, of the University of Chicago Divinity School, has read thousands of these letters which are now deposited at the Chicago Theological Seminary, Chicago, Illinois. He has informed the author that "rarely is there any reference to the Catholic danger, except, of course, now

and then, on the part of missionaries near such Catholic centers as St. Louis, Detroit and in central Kentucky."

75 I (September, 1835).

76 *House Executive Documents,* 25th Cong., 2nd Sess., No. 154. The petition was dated February 14, 1838. A similar petition from a group of Massachusetts residents had been forwarded on January 5, 1838. *House Executive Documents,* 25th Cong., 2nd Sess., No. 70. Both petitions were referred to the Committee on the Judiciary.

77 *Downfall of Babylon,* July 4, 1835; *Spirit of '76,* July 29, 1835.

78 L. D. Scisco, *Political Nativism in New York State,* in *Columbia University Studies in History, Economics and Public Law* (New York, 1893—), XIII (1901), 23–25.

79 *Ibid.,* 25–27.

80 *Spirit of '76,* September 15, 1835. The schismatic faction refused to return even though the *Spirit of '76* pointed out that if Protestant foreigners were allowed to enter the country Jesuits would disguise themselves as Protestants and attack the government in that way. *Spirit of '76,* September 16, 1835.

81 *Ibid.,* September 4, 1835.

82 Scisco, *Political Nativism in New York,* 27–28.

83 *Ibid.,* 28–30.

84 The Native candidate for mayor was Aaron Clark. *Ibid.,* 30–31.

85 John Hancock Lee, *The Origin and Progress of the American Party in Politics* (Philadelphia, 1855), 16. Lee maintains that the later Native American party grew from this Germantown organization.

86 McMaster, *History of the People of the United States,* VI, 428.

87 *Spirit of '76,* August 24, 1835.

88 *Address of the Louisiana Native American Association* (New Orleans, 1839).

89 McMaster, *History of the People of the United States,* VII, 369–370.

90 *House Executive Documents,* 25th Cong., 2nd Sess., No. 98, 1–7.

91 *Congressional Globe,* 25th Cong., 2nd Sess., 100–101.

92 *House Reports of Committees,* 25th Cong., 2nd Sess., No. 1040, 12–16.

93 William Beatty of Pennsylvania spoke against the report, asserting that its doctrines were those of 1798. *Congressional Globe,* 25th Cong., 2nd Sess., 489.

94 It was read twice and committed after some debate. *Ibid.,* 489.

95 *Ibid.,* 25th Cong., 3rd Sess., 168; *Executive Documents,* 25th Cong., 3rd Sess., No. 162, 1–2; *Senate Documents,* 25th Cong., 3rd Sess., No. 246; *Senate Documents,* 26th Cong., 1st Sess., No. 43.

96 Maryland (1833) and Massachusetts (1837) provided for such bonds. Fairchild, *Immigration,* 81–82.

97 This was the point of view of the court in the so-called Passenger Cases, *Smith v. Turner, Health Commissioner of New York* and *Norris v. City of Boston* (1849), 48 U. S. 282.

98 *Congressional Globe,* 24th Cong., 1st Sess., 373; *House Executive Documents,* 24th Cong., 1st Sess., No. 219; *Senate Documents,* 24th Cong., 1st Sess., No. 342.

99 The principal support for the measures in the Senate came from Massa-

chusetts. *Congressional Globe,* 24th Cong., 1st Sess., II, 414, 614. A similar request that information be supplied by the State department had elicited the reply that no such information was available in that department. *Senate Documents,* 24th Cong., 1st Sess., No. 342.

100 *Senate Documents,* 24th Cong., 2nd Sess., I, No. 5, 1–20.

101 *House Executive Documents,* 25th Cong., 2nd Sess., Nos. 70, 313.

102 *Reports of Committees,* 25th Cong., 2nd Sess., No. 1040, 2–3.

103 *Ibid.,* 9.

104 *Ibid.,* 10.

105 *Congressional Globe,* 25th Cong., 3rd Sess., 159.

VI

Saving the Children for Protestantism
1840-1844

THE principal efforts of nativistic agitators before 1840 had been bent to convert the lower classes to their cause. This desire was reflected in the character of the anti-Catholic newspapers such as the *American Protestant Vindicator* and the *Downfall of Babylon* as well as in the propaganda literature of the 1830's. The violent sensationalism and frank pornography which was the order of the day did little to attract the large group of church-going Americans who made up the bulk of their country's middle class. The failure of the first nativistic political efforts showed that the movement could never be really important until the support of at least a portion of this group had been secured. This realization led to a subtle change in nativistic methods which, beginning in 1840, reached its logical conclusion a decade later; a change through which nativists made an earnest effort to win to their standard the religiously inclined, sober citizens of the United States.

Leaders of the anti-Catholic movement were aware that their best means of appealing to the middle class was through the Bible. If Catholicism could be demonstrated as an enemy of the Gospel, it would become the religious duty of Protestants to destroy American Popery. Propaganda writers tried to show that this was the case, maintaining that the Bible was forbidden to Catholics by their clergy lest they discover in reading the true word of God that their religion was false.[1] The fears were apparently corroborated when priests resisted the efforts of local Bible societies to distribute the King James version of the Scriptures among poor Catholic families in eastern cities. Checked in what they termed their Christian duty, these societies concluded that Catholicism was opposed to the Scriptures in all forms and that the general circulation of the Bible could be achieved only by stamping out Popery.[2]

This conflict between the Bible societies and the Catholic church would probably have remained relatively unimportant had the societies not attempted to enlarge the scope of their activities. However in 1838 members of the Maryland Bible Society adopted resolutions deploring the fact that, while sending God's word to the heathen abroad, they had neglected to see that the Scriptures were read in the schools of their own state, and asking the co-operation of state officials in securing this objective.[3] In the following year this desire assumed national importance when the American Bible Society pledged itself to continuous labor until the Scriptures were read in every classroom in the nation,[4] a resolve which was repeated a year later [5] after both the churches and the religious press had heartily endorsed the society's stand.[6] The seeds of conflict were sown by this action. Catholics, unwilling to allow their children to attend public schools where part of the program of instruction consisted of the reading of an unauthorized version of the Scriptures, were bound to contest the dictates of Protestantism.

The clash between Catholics and Protestants over the use of the Bible in the public schools took its most dramatic form in New York City where the controversy was intensified by the nature of the school system in 1840 when Catholic citizens first began their complaints. New York schools at this time were under the control of the Public School Society, a benevolent association which had been formed in 1805 to care for the instruction of children financially unable to attend religious or private schools. One of the avowed purposes of this society was "to inculcate the sublime truths of religion and morality contained in the Holy Scriptures" so that Bible reading was given a prominent place in the curriculum of the schools under its jurisdiction.[7] After 1813 the society was allotted a portion of the common school fund of the state,[8] this being administered by the Common Council of New York City which decided which educational organizations should share in the public funds.[9] The Public School Society benefited from this arrangement, most of the money available for the city's educational requirements being given it by the council.

The first conflict between this society and the Catholic church came in 1831 when the Common Council deviated from its established course and granted a share of the common school fund to the Protestant Orphan Society. The Roman Catholic Benevolent Society immediately petitioned for a like share, a petition which the Public School Society, visioning a lessening of its funds, resisted vigorously but to no avail.[10] Despite this slight diversion of funds this organization by 1840 had attained a virtual monopoly over the educational facilities of New York City, operating nearly a hundred schools and distributing approximately $130,000 annually, partly from the state common school fund and partly from its own collections.[11]

Catholics had a just cause for complaint against this monopoly. The King James version of the Scriptures was read daily in all of the schools of the society and the regular prayers, singing, and religious instruction were not in accord with Catholic belief. Particular grounds for complaint existed in the textbooks used in the society's schools; all were blatantly Protestant in sympathy and many were openly disrespectful of Catholicism. One spoke of John Huss as a "zealous reformer from popery" who, "trusting himself to the deceitful Catholics," was at last burned at the stake.[12] Another contained a pointedly anti-Catholic dialogue between Hernando Cortez and William Penn in which Penn was made to declare:

Though what thou sayest should be true, it does not come well from thy mouth. A Papist talk of reason! Go to the Inquisition and

tell them of reason and the great laws of nature. They will broil
thee as thy soldiers broiled Guatimozin. Why dost thou turn pale?
Is it the name of the Inquisition or of Guatimozin? Tremble and
shake when thou thinkest that every murder the inquisitors have
committed, every torture they have inflicted on the innocent Indians,
is originally owing to thee.[13]

Equally objectionable was an ecclesiastical history which took
every opportunity to emphasize the corruptions of Catholicism,
depicting Romish missions as mere schemes of ecclesiastical
ambition, and referring to Biblical prophecy as forecasting the
overthrow of the "man of sin, mystery of iniquity, son of perdition." [14] The presence of these books in a public school system
receiving support from the state certainly gave Catholics the right
to demand more just treatment.[15]

This condition, unsatisfactory as it was, might have gone un-
protested, had not Governor William H. Seward interested himself in the matter. Although a Whig, Seward had throughout
his political life shown a marked tendency toward favoring the
alien and the foreign-born, having as a fundamental tenet the
belief that the poorer immigrants must be properly educated before they could be assimilated as good citizens.[16] These views he
expressed in a legislative message delivered in January, 1840,
which precipitated the whole question. Many immigrant children, he said, were being kept from school because of the sectarian
nature of the instruction. To remedy the situation he recommended the "establishment of schools in which they may be instructed by teachers speaking the same language with themselves
and professing the same faith." [17] To Catholics such a declaration seemed a clear invitation, and a group of Catholic churches
in New York which operated free parochial schools immediately
petitioned the Common Council for a share of the state school
fund which that body administered.[18]

The gauntlet thrown down by Catholics was promptly retrieved
by the Public School Society which replied to their claims with

petitions upholding the existing educational system. The society claimed with some justice that favorable action on the Catholic requests would spell its own doom. Should the Common Council grant a share of the school money to one religious group, its petitioners stated, other sects would have an equal claim and the educational funds would be so dissipated that sectarian instruction would displace general education in New York City.[19] Less than a month after the presentation of these petitions, the Common Council voted unanimously against granting a share of the school fund to Catholics. Not only had the latter lost the first tilt but their cause had been subjected to much unfavorable publicity.[20]

The issue, however, was far from settled. Catholics were convinced of the justice of their claims and determined to press them further, a desire indicated by the establishment of the *Freeman's Journal* when the older New York Catholic paper, the *Truth Teller,* refused to agitate the matter.[21] They were given the necessary leadership by the return of Bishop John Hughes to New York in July, 1840. A vigorous, stormy individual, powerful in leadership and indefatigable in contest, Hughes was well qualified to carry the standard of his faith. Two days after he reached New York he attended a meeting of his fellow churchmen and there read a carefully prepared address which indicated the direction his efforts would take. The Public School Society, he said, was filling the minds of Catholic children with errors of fact which would excite them against the religion of their parents. Its books and its teachings were noticeably opposed to Catholicism. Catholics could protect themselves only by securing a share of the school fund and building schools of their own.[22] During the following weeks Hughes held a series of meetings at which he impressed this same belief on most of his followers in New York City.[23]

Having thus prepared the way, Hughes supervised the drafting of a new petition to the Common Council, again insisting that the Public School Society was guilty of sectarian instruction and asking that Catholics be given a share of the school money.[24] This petition was answered by both the Public School Society and the Methodist churches of New York, the trustees of the society insisting once more that their teachings were non-sectarian and the Methodist clergy using the excuse to attack the Catholic version of the Scriptures as upholding the murder of heretics and an unqualified submission to papal authority.[25] With both these petitions widely circulated and public opinion rapidly shaping itself,[26] the Common Council decided to hold a public meeting where Catholics and representatives of the Public School Society could state their views. On October 29, 1840, this debate began.[27]

Bishop Hughes stood alone for the Catholics, while arrayed against him was a whole field of talent gathered from the legal profession and the Protestant clergy. Hughes opened the debate before a crowded hall with a speech which lasted for three hours, explaining the Catholic position in a clear, though heated, manner.[28] His efforts were more than matched by the Protestant rebuttal which lasted two whole days and consisted almost entirely of unreasoned attacks on Catholicism as an anti-Biblical religion. Catholics were represented as irreligious idol worshipers, bent on the murder of all Protestants and the subjugation of all democracies. "I do say," one minister told the sympathetic galleries, "that if the fearful dilemma were forced upon me, of becoming an infidel or a Roman catholic, according to the entire system of popery, with all its idolatry, superstition, and violent opposition to the Holy Bible, *I would rather be an infidel than a papist.*" [29]

The course of this debate presaged the decision which would follow; it was obvious that prejudice was to rule rather than reason. Nevertheless, a committee of the Common Council was named to investigate the schools of the society and to make a final report. When this was given on January 11, 1841, recommending the rejection of Catholic claims, it was adopted by the council with a vote of fifteen to one.[30] Once again Hughes and his followers had met defeat at the hands of a Protestant majority.

More detrimental to the Catholics than this rebuff was the unfavorable publicity which resulted from their efforts. From the outset the religious press was united against them, for no staunch Protestant of that generation could stomach objections to Bible reading. "What better evidence can be given," asked one editor, "than that this church seeks to shut out the light of divine revelation from the minds of its members?"[31] Writers also professed to believe that Catholics were showing their enmity to all education and evidencing the oft-repeated adage that the papal church could ensnare only the ignorant and illiterate.[32] These criticisms became increasingly bitter as Hughes' part in the controversy grew more apparent. The sight of a high churchman openly campaigning to secure funds which Protestants believed to be their own was more than many of them could bear, particularly when they believed that Hughes was seeking this money only to spread his papal beliefs.[33] "They demand of Republicans," one newspaper declared, "to give them funds to train up their children to worship a ghostly monarchy of vicars, bishops, archbishops, cardinals, and Popes! They demand of us to take away our children's funds and bestow them on the subjects of Rome, the creatures of a foreign hierarchy!"[34]

In December, 1840, while the report of the Common Council was being anxiously awaited, rioting and disorder between the rival factions centered further attention on the Catholic ambitions. A meeting of Public School Society sympathizers was unable to proceed when disorderly elements shouted so loudly that the speakers could not make themselves heard.[35] A few months later Brownlee met with a similar reception when he tried to answer Hughes' statements in a public meeting. Catholics in the crowd called the speaker a liar, finally causing the abrupt termination of the lecture.[36] These incidents, magnified by the nativistic press, created new interest in the controversy, and attracted support for the society from James Gordon Bennett's powerful New York *Herald,* the New York *Commercial Advertiser* under the editorship of Colonel William L. Stone,[37] and the New York *Journal of Commerce* which stated that it would refuse to allow Catholics to be singled out for special privileges as a "reward for their bigotry and exclusiveness." [38] In this way a host of persons were made aware of the movement against Catholicism by the activity of the secular press.[39]

When the Common Council refused to grant Hughes' request in January, 1841, the nativistic press prophesied that the Papists would try some new Jesuitical scheme and warned Protestants to be ever on the alert.[40] This prediction proved accurate, for only a month after the Common Council announced its decision Hughes called a meeting of Catholics to name a "Central Executive Committee on Common Schools" which was to prepare a memorial to the state legislature asking for a change in the whole school administration, looking toward completely secular, state-controlled education. Opposed as he was to Godless schools, Hughes nevertheless believed that they alone could do away with sectarian influences in instruction. The petition prepared by this committee was presented to the legislature as a request from the "Citizens of New York" with an attempt being made to keep the religious issue in the background. After some debate it was referred to a select committee of the assembly, and there matters rested as the spring elections of 1841 approached.[41]

With this attempt to involve the state legislature, the school question definitely entered politics. Hughes realized that despite the fairness of his cause, it would be unwise to carry his church into the political arena, for such a course would allow nativists to revive the old cry of the attempted papist union of church and state. Although he took no part in the political agitation preceding the election he was unable to restrain many of his followers. To the religious press, both Catholic and Protestant, the issue was a clear-cut one between two antagonistic religious systems and the principal appeal to voters, through handbills and editorials, was for support on these grounds.[42] The sentiment of the electorate was clearly expressed. The one member of the Common Council who had voted for the Catholic claim was defeated, even though other members of the party were carried into office.[43] This was accepted as a proper rebuff to Catholic political ambitions, and Protestants faced the contest over the school question in the legislature with complete confidence.[44]

More than confidence, however, was needed if they were to be successful there, for Governor Seward was still firmly of the opinion that a share of the school funds should be given the Catholic church.[45] His annual message of January, 1841 was consequently a plea for the Catholic cause. He pointed out the presence of more than twenty thousand children in New York City who were kept from schools by the intolerant instruction offered by the Public School Society and pointed out to the legislature the necessity of change. "I seek the education of those whom I have brought before you," he wrote, "not to perpetuate any prejudices or distinctions which deprive them of instruction, but in disregard of all such distinctions and prejudices. I solicit their education, less from sympathy, than because the welfare of the state demands it, and cannot dispense with it." [46]

Seward's message left two courses open to members of the legislature. They could follow the expressed will of the New York electorate and perpetuate the Public School Society, or they could agree to the demands of the governor as expressed in his annual message. The problem was so delicate that the legislature wisely sought more advice, referring the whole question to the Secretary of State, John C. Spencer, who was also superintendent of the state common schools. Despite influence brought to bear upon him,[47] Spencer prepared an able and impartial report recommending that the general school laws of the state be extended to New York City. The Public School Society was to be done away with and in its place a school commissioner was to be elected in each ward to administer funds and regulate public instruction. In this way sectarian instruction would be impossible, for the Catholic vote would force all commissioners to be strictly impartial, particularly in wards where the foreign element was centered.[48] Spencer's proposal was accepted as a proper solution to the whole school question by the *Freeman's Journal* [49] but naturally aroused the ire of both the Public School Society and the Protestant newspapers which were willing to resort to political pressure to achieve their ends.[50] Members of the legislature, sensing this division between Catholics and Protestants and afraid to settle the matter until after the opinion of the people had been tested once more, postponed consideration of the whole question until January, 1842.[51]

The fall elections of 1841 in New York City were fought largely on this issue, Catholics supporting the Spencer report and Protestants the existing system. Two state senators and thirteen assemblymen were to be chosen from the city, and the fate of the whole question would largely rest with these men. Excitement was great as the election approached. Meetings were held at which the views of either side were aired, the press took a definite stand, and Protestant ministers turned their pulpits into propaganda agencies for the support of the Public School Society.[52] Both Whigs and Democrats realized that the Protestant vote would be united against them, should they endorse Catholic claims. The Whigs, as a result, nominated a ticket pledged against any change in the school system and wrote into their platform a declaration against sectarian schools. The Democrats, more dependent in the past on the alien vote, tried to avoid the issue, although a majority of their candidates for the state Assembly were pledged against any change, as were their two candidates for the Senate.[53]

Hughes realized that the Catholic cause would be disastrously defeated unless drastic action were taken and he determined to play a bold card. Catholic voters were called together at a meeting at Carroll Hall on October 30, four days before the election. There Hughes addressed them, recalling that they had been refused satisfaction by both major parties and that their only hope lay in putting an independent ticket in the field. Before the meeting adjourned, the names of a group of candidates were submitted and Catholics were urged to support them.[54] In all probability Hughes planned this move as a threat to force the Democratic party into line, but in this he was sadly disappointed for the day after the Carroll Hall meeting the Democratic candidates publicly announced that they were now unanimously agreed that any change in the school system was unwise.[55] Hughes was thus forced to carry his ticket into the election, even though he detested a separate Catholic party and believed that all action should be through the regular party channels.[56]

In the main, however, Hughes was not completely dissatisfied with the turn of events. He realized, as did other political leaders of the day, that the immigrant voters held a balance of power and that their diversion from Democratic ranks might well spell defeat for that party. If the Democrats could be defeated, they would not only be rebuffed for deserting their former supporters but would be made to know that such support was necessary in the future. Hughes' views were justified by the election returns. The Whigs swept the polls, going into office with a majority of 290 votes over their opponents, but if the 2,200 voters who supported the Catholic ticket had given their votes to the Democrats, that party would have won an easy victory.[57] Hughes had demonstrated beyond reasonable doubt that the Democrats could not afford to cast off their Catholic supporters if they wanted success.

The legislature which assembled in January, 1842 to settle the whole troublesome question had its task made easier by Governor Seward's opening message. He again called attention to the twenty thousand children in New York City who were deprived of education because of the policy of the Public School Society and recommended the abolition of this society and the substitution of an educational system similar to the one proposed by Spencer before the last legislature, in which a board of commissioners to be selected by the people would apportion the school money among all the schools.[58] Although this suggestion was objected to by supporters of the Public School Society,[59] it was immediately embodied in legislative form in the Maclay bill which was submitted to both houses of the legislature soon after they convened.[60] This measure, for all practical purposes, simply extended the state educational system to include New York City, providing for elective commissioners for each ward who were not only to supervise the schools under them but together constitute a board of education which would control the city's educational system.[61]

Public opinion on the Maclay bill was clearly divided along religious lines, the Protestant press universally denouncing the measure and the Catholic press similarly supporting it. Hughes was popularly supposed to be the author of the bill, [62] a supposition given tangible basis when a petition "half a mile long" and bearing the names of thirteen thousand Catholics was submitted to the legislature, asking that the measure be given favorable treatment.[63] The entire newspaper press of New York City, with the exception of the *Sunday Times* and the Catholic papers, opposed its passage.[64] When a vote was near, friends of the Public School Society called a meeting in front of the City Hall which was attended by more than twenty thousand enthusiastic enemies of Catholicism and which named a committee to present its views to the legislature.[65]

This agitation had little actual effect. The New York legislature which was considering the Maclay bill was Democratic in majority, for the Democrats, although unsuccessful in the fall elections of 1841 in New York City, had swept the rest of the state. This party was anxious to regain Catholic support and recognized in this measure an admirable opportunity for doing so. Consequently the bill was passed by the Assembly immediately,[66] and after some delay, by the Senate in April, 1842.[67] Seward's signature was affixed and the Maclay bill became a law.[68]

News of the passage of this measure precipitated a storm of protest in New York City. The New York *Observer* printed a sorrowful editorial entitled "Triumph of the Roman Catholics." "The dark hour is at hand," it said. "People must only trust in God to be saved from the beast." [69] On the night that the bill was passed, the New York streets were filled with mobs which pursued luckless Irishmen and stoned the windows of Bishop Hughes' home, forcing the calling out of the militia to guard Catholic churches.[70] Whig leaders took advantage of this popular discontent by issuing a statement repudiating the conduct of Seward and declaring their party's opposition to the Maclay bill.[71] Local Democratic spokesmen were afraid to risk the loss of either Protestant or Catholic voters by denouncing or upholding the bill and were reduced to a neutral policy which led eventually to a party split into native-born and Catholic groups.[72]

This discontent and disavowal was to no purpose, for the Maclay bill had become a law and sectarian teaching, in theory at least, was destined to speedy extermination. In practice, however, Catholics were doomed to further disappointment. The new measure placed the New York schools under the supervision of the state superintendent of education who, even before its passage, had recommended a daily reading from the Bible by teachers under his charge.[73] Not content with this, the Whigs immediately bestirred themselves to salvage what they could from the wreckage of the Public School Society by recommending the election of former trustees of this society as educational commissioners in the city's wards. Their propaganda was so effective [74] that opponents of Catholicism throughout the city united into a Union party which gained sufficient ward victories in the June elections to give them complete control of the school board.[75] To make matters worse, the new state superintendent of common schools named in July was William L. Stone, exposer of **Maria**

Monk but long a prominent nativist.[76] The public school Bible was firmly entrenched during his regime and Bishop Hughes, in despair, concentrated his efforts on building parochial schools for the education of Catholic children.[77]

Although Hughes was willing to admit defeat, others of his faith refused to do so. The Maclay bill had forbidden any sectarian teaching in schools sharing the state's funds, and it seemed to many Catholics that this provision might be used to stop the reading of the Protestant Bible to Catholic children. Regardless of the fact that the school board elections in June, 1843, went overwhelmingly in favor of nativistic candidates, commissioners of the fourth ward, where Catholic sentiment was strong, petitioned the Board of Education a month later asking that Bible reading be forbidden.[78] This obviously partisan body replied that the Bible, without note or comment, was not a sectarian book, and that reading from it could not be prohibited under the Maclay bill.[79] Despite this unfavorable interpretation, Catholics were able to obtain some relief. The elective commissioners in charge of education in each ward had the right to select books to be used in the schools under their supervision, and in wards where Catholics were concentrated they did not hesitate to use this power to exclude Bible reading so that by 1844 the practice had been abandoned in thirty-one of the city schools.

The few gains made by Catholics in the New York controversy were more than offset by the unfavorable treatment which they received at the hands of the Protestant press. The controversy seemed to many Protestants to confirm hitherto intangible fears concerning Romanism. Hughes' bold move in forming the Carroll Hall ticket and entering a Catholic party in the field was particularly singled out for abuse. He was pictured as having torn off his mask, revealing himself as the new dictator of New York City [80] and as a "crafty priest" bent on combining crosier and politics.[81] "This is the work," one editor said, "of foreign sectarianism, planting itself in our midst, forming political alliances, and

attaching itself to the fortunes of a party that seek [*sic*] to perpetuate its power even at the expense of everything else."[82]
Hughes' efforts to defend his actions were generally discredited
and the venerable priest was branded a Jesuit who was pledged
to keep no faith with heretics.[83] Even Governor Seward received
his share of this abuse [84] and there is little doubt that his stand
on the school question eventually cost him his office.[85] So universal was this sentiment that when one paper sought to defend
the Maclay bill, its subscription list dropped so rapidly that the
editor was forced to resign.[86] Nor did this No-Popery feeling
die down immediately; for several years each election in New
York City was a signal for renewed agitation against Catholics
for their part in the exclusion of the Bible from the schools.[87]

Although this contest over Bible reading was most spectacular
in New York, similar controversies took place in several other
cities, Philadelphia and Newark being the most prominent.[88]
These were far from universal, but sufficient to give the impression that Catholics were moving all over the country to gain control of the nation's educational facilities, and thus begin their
subjugation of the United States as Morse and Beecher had
warned would be the case.[89] A new group of propaganda writers,
both in the press and through books and pamphlets,[90] agreed that
the sole reason Papists sought to control state educational funds
was to propagate their doctrines of error and win converts from
among Protestants. Even the regular schools were not above suspicion in the eyes of these propagandists who held that many
teachers were disguised Jesuits insinuating themselves into the
schools when Catholic demands for state funds were thwarted.[91]
These arguments were effective and Protestants came to believe
that if they agreed to the papal demands, they would be taxed
to support popish schools whose sole purpose was to win converts against the day when the Pope was ready for his American
conquest.

The effectiveness of this propaganda was dimmed when compared with that directed against the Catholic demand that the Bible be excluded from public schools. To the many religious men and women of that generation a belief in and knowledge of the Word of God was as essential to the preservation of the state as the Constitution. Schools without Bible reading would rear a nation of Godless voters; infidelity and anarchy were synonymous and equally undesirable. National security as well as the Protestant religion required the very training for children against which Catholics were directing their attack.

With this belief generally held, Americans accepted without question the propagandists' assertion that the school controversy clearly demonstrated Rome's enmity to the Scriptures. To Protestants there was only one Bible; because Catholics had objected to the reading of the King James version, they must oppose the reading of any portion of God's word. It was repeatedly asserted by speakers, editors, and writers that Popery was not sanctioned in the Scriptures, and that it was traditional within the Catholic church to forbid the Bible to the people lest they discover the error of their religious system.[92] The Reverend Hiram Ketchum, a prominent nativistic minister, expressed these sentiments before the annual meeting of the American Bible Society in 1844 and so moved the members of this organization that they reiterated their earlier stand, declaring: "that the Bible, from its origin, purity and simplicity of its syle [*sic*] is a book peculiarly appropriate for use in common schools, and cannot be excluded from them without hazard both to our civil and religious liberties."[93] A papal decree in May, 1844, against societies distributing an unauthorized version of the Scriptures in Italy seemed to confirm these beliefs.[94]

Further evidence that Rome was hostile to the Scriptures was provided in October, 1842, when an overzealous missionary priest in Carbeau, New York, justly angered at the distribution of Protestant Bibles among his parishioners by Bible societies, gathered several copies of the Scriptures and publicly burned them.[95] This

"Champlain Bible burning," as it was promptly labeled, immediately was elevated to a national issue by Protestants. Indignation swept the country, fanned particularly by the bold declaration of Hughes' own paper, the *Freeman's Journal:*

> To burn or otherwise destroy a spurious or corrupt copy of the Bible, whose circulation would tend to disseminate erroneous principles of faith or morals, we hold to be an act not only justifiable but praiseworthy. . . .[96]

One editor, with more enthusiasm than accuracy, prophesied that the "27th of October, 1842, will be remembered in the United States as long as the Gunpowder Plot of the 5th of November, 1605, will be remembered in England" [97] and another professed to believe that "the embers of the late Bible conflagration in Carbeau may kindle a flame that shall consume the last vestige of Popery in this land of ours." [98] For a time it appeared that these extravagant claims might be realized. Public meetings of protest were held,[99] books depicting and condemning the affair were hurriedly published,[100] and speakers toured the country arousing Protestants against this latest Catholic outrage.[101] Tales of Catholic attempts to burn Bibles in other states further increased native resentment.[102]

These reported Bible burnings, coming as they did on the heels of the New York school controversy, played an important part in arousing religious, middle-class Americans to the point where they would participate in the No-Popery crusade. Hitherto apathetic and unmoved by the outspoken propaganda of the 1830's, these men and women were at last convinced that Rome was an enemy to be personally combated. Their sincere belief in their religion and their Bible and the newly born conviction that Catholicism was opposed to that Holy Book led more and more of them to take an active interest in organized anti-Catholicism. The great success which the entire movement was to enjoy during the 1840's can be traced in a measure to this new attitude on the part of the middle-class Protestant.

NOTES

[1] *The Protestant,* March 31, 1832; *Downfall of Babylon,* June 27, 1835, November 7, 1835, January 23, 1836, July 23, 1836; New York *Observer,* February 26, 1831, May 28, 1831, June 8, 1833, August 31, 1833 and ff, February 25, 1837, January 26, 1839; *American Protestant Vindicator,* January 12, 1842; *Western Christian Advocate,* November 28, 1834; *Christian Watchman,* March 3, 1837, August 10, 1838, September 2, 1842; *Episcopal Recorder,* May 12, 1834, August 9, 1834, November 22, 1834; McGavin, *The Protestant,* I, 231–293; Ricci, *Female Convents,* xv–xvi; Schmucker, *Discourse in Commemoration of the Glorious Reformation,* 26–27.

[2] American Bible Society, *Twenty First Annual Report* (New York, 1837), 88, *Twenty Fourth Annual Report* (New York, 1840), 60; New York *Observer,* May 23, 1835; *Western Christian Advocate,* July 17, 1835; Shea, *History of the Catholic Church,* III, 623.

[3] Baltimore *Literary and Religious Magazine,* IV (December, 1838). Earlier suggestions of this sort had been made but had not attracted the national attention accorded these resolutions. *The Protestant,* May 21, 1831; *Christian Watchman,* November 4, 1836.

[4] American Bible Society, *Twenty Third Annual Report* (New York, 1839), 87–89; *Watchman of the South,* July 18, 1839; Baltimore *Literary and Religious Magazine,* V (July, 1839). Resolutions to this effect were adopted after a speech by the Reverend Robert J. Breckinridge, in which he warned of the Catholic opposition which such a move would inspire.

[5] American Bible Society, *Twenty Fourth Annual Report,* 79; New York *Observer,* May 23, 1840.

[6] *Ibid.,* September 5, 1840; *Journals of the General Conference of the Methodist Episcopal Church* (New York, 1856), II, 172. A resolution adopted by the General Conference in May, 1840 read: "Resolved, That we highly approve of the use of the Bible as a class book in schools and seminaries of learning, and will use our efforts for its introduction into such schools and seminaries." This view was supported by several books which were being circulated: *Defense of the Use of the Bible in the Schools* (New York, 1830); Thomas S. Grimke, *Address on the Expediency and Duty of Adopting the Bible as a Class Book in Every Scheme of Education, from the Primary School to the University, Delivered at Columbia, South Carolina, in the Presbyterian Church, on Friday evening, 4th of December, 1829, before the Richland School* (Charleston, 1830).

[7] A. Emerson Palmer, *The New York Public School* (New York, 1905), 22; William O. Bourne, *History of the Public School Society of the City of New York* (New York, 1870), 4–26.

[8] *Laws of the State of New York, Passed at the 36th, 37th and 38th Sessions of the Legislature, Commencing November, 1812 and Ending April, 1815* (Albany, 1815), III, 38–39.

[9] The state legislature took this step after the Bethel Baptist Church and other religious organizations had attempted to obtain a share of the fund. *37th Annual Report of the Trustees of the Public School Society of New York, with a Sketch of the Rise and Progress of the Society* (New York, 1842).

10 Palmer, *The New York Public School*, 80–82; Bourne, *The Public School Society*, 124; *The Protestant*, April 28, 1832.

11 Hassard, *Life of John Hughes*, 141–142.

12 Samuel Putnam, *Sequel to the Analytical Reader* (Boston, 1831), 296.

13 *New York Reader, Number Three; Selections in Prose and Poetry from the Best Writers Designed for the Use of Schools* (New York, 1819), 205.

14 C. A. Goodrich, *Outlines of Ecclesiastical History on a New Plan, Designed for Academies and Schools* (Hartford, 1829), 157. Another ecclesiastic history used in schools at the time devoted the first of three volumes to exposing the rise of Popery and its many errors. New York *Observer*, April 12, 1834. Other books used in the New York schools which could be objected to by Catholics were H. H. Wallis, *History of the United States from the First Settlements as Colonies to the Close of the War with Great Britain in 1815* (New York, 1827), 11; Linday Murray, *Sequel to the English Reader* (Bennington, 1821).

15 Catholic objections were made to these passages during the controversy. *American Protestant Vindicator*, February 23, 1842.

16 Seward's belief seems to have dated from a journey which he made through Ireland some years before, and his letters written at that time frequently expressed the opinion that the miserable condition of the people of that country was due to a lack of education. William H. Seward, *Works* (New York, 1853–1861), III, 526–542.

17 *Ibid.*, II, 215.

18 Shea, *History of the Catholic Church*, III, 526.

19 The petitions were printed in full in the New York *Observer*, March 21, 1840. They were dated February 29, 1840.

20 *Ibid.*, May 2, 1840. The council acted on the report on April 27.

21 *Ibid.*, August 1, 1840.

22 *Ibid.*, August 14, 1840.

23 *Ibid.*, August 21, 1840, August 28, 1840.

24 The petition is in Bourne, *The Public School Society*, 189–191.

25 *Ibid.*, 196–197.

26 New York *Observer*, September 26, 1840. The remonstrance by the society stated that the Catholics had been offered a chance to censor the school books used and had refused, fearing that this would handicap them in securing a share of the school fund. This showed clearly, the society believed, that they were after the money alone, and the Jesuitism of the whole movement was thus exposed.

27 Hughes devoted the second part of his address to an attack on Methodism, ending by offering to bet a thousand dollars that the Catholic Bible did not sanction the burning of heretics. This proved a bad move, for the religious press reminded the bishop of the Common Council law against betting. New York *Observer*, November 7, 1840.

28 The society's spokesmen were: Theodore Sedgwick, a lawyer, and the Reverend Hiram Ketchum. Backing them in their arguments were the Reverend Doctors Bond, Rees and Bangs of the Methodist church, Springs of the Presbyterian church, and Knox of the Dutch Reformed Church. Their speeches were printed in a pamphlet: *The Important and Interesting Debate on the Claims of the Catholics to a Portion of the Common School Fund; with the*

Arguments of Council before the Board of Aldermen of the City of New York, on Thursday and Friday, the 29th and 30th of October, 1840 (New York, 1840). Other sources used in compiling this account of the meeting were the New York *Observer,* the New York *Journal of Commerce* and Bourne, *The Public School Society,* 202 ff. The account given by Bourne is especially valuable as it is drawn entirely from the files of the *Freeman's Journal,* a Catholic paper.

[29] *American Protestant Vindicator,* November 11, 1840.

[30] New York *Observer,* January 16, 1841.

[31] *Ibid.,* May 2, 1840.

[32] *American Protestant Vindicator,* October 14, 1840, October 28, 1840, December 23, 1840, December 29, 1841; *Christian Watchman,* June 25, 1841; New York *Observer,* December 19, 1840.

[33] *American Protestant Vindicator,* November 3, 1841 and ff.

[34] *Ibid.,* August 5, 1840.

[35] The meeting was held in Sackett's Drill Room on December 8. New York *Observer,* December 11, 1841.

[36] A meeting held on July 8, 1841. *American Protestant Vindicator,* July 28, 1841.

[37] Hughes wrote a letter to the New York *Courier and Enquirer,* May 17, 1844, reviewing the whole school question and naming these two papers as the most important and troublesome. Hassard, *Life of John Hughes,* 279.

[38] New York *Journal of Commerce,* February 26, 1840.

[39] The New York *Observer,* November 14, 1840, joyfully reported that thousands of converts to the No-Popery cause were being made by the school controversy.

[40] New York *Observer,* January 16, 1841; *American Protestant Vindicator,* January 20, 1841.

[41] Bourne, *The Public School Society,* 350–352.

[42] Typical handbills posted in Catholic sections of the city were reprinted in the New York *Observer,* May 1, 1841; New York *Journal of Commerce,* March 18, 1841 and the *American Protestant Vindicator,* March 31, 1841. Typical of these was the handbill in the New York *Observer:* "Catholics Arouse! To the Rescue! Irishmen to your posts!! The friends of an equal distribution of the School Fund, are called upon to rally! Come early to the polls and deposit your vote for Daniel C. Pentz, the friend of the Catholics; he openly proclaims that he is in favor of an equal distribution of the School Fund. Daniel C. Pentz was the only member of the Common Council, who dared proclaim to the world that he was willing we should have a share of the School Fund. Irishmen, if you would have your children educated, come and vote for Daniel C. Pentz."

[43] New York *Observer,* April 17, 1841.

[44] *Ibid.,* April 24, 1841.

[45] This attitude was expressed in a number of letters written at the time. Seward, *Works,* III, 221, 386–389, 480–489. His idea was clearly shown in one letter when he wrote: "I desire to see the children of Catholics educated as well as those of Protestants; not because I want them Catholics, but because I want them to become good citizens." *Ibid.,* III, 480.

[46] *Ibid.,* II, 280.

47 *American Catholic Historical Researches,* n. s., I, No. 3 (July, 1905), 263.

48 New York *Journal of Commerce,* April 29, 1841.

49 Quoted in *Ibid.,* May 4, 1841.

50 New York *Observer,* June 10, 1841, June 17, 1841. The New York *Journal of Commerce,* May 4, 1841, printed an anti-Catholic article which included an alleged Bill of Excommunication pronounced against William Hogan during the Philadelphia trusteeism controversy. Copies of this issue were placed on the desk of each member of the legislature, carefully opened to this article. The New York *Journal of Commerce* insisted that it was this which brought about the postponement of the bill. *Ibid.,* June 12, 1841. Actually the excommunication oath had been copied bodily from *Tristram Shandy.* Compare with Laurence Sterne, *The Life and Opinions of Tristram Shandy* (New York, 1813), I, 196–204.

51 New York *Journal of Commerce,* June 12, 1841.

52 *Ibid.,* July 1, 1841, July 27, 1841; New York *Observer,* October 9, 1841, October 30, 1841; Baltimore *Literary and Religious Magazine,* VI (November, 1840); Hassard, *Life of John Hughes,* 243–248.

53 New York *Journal of Commerce,* October 25, 1841, October 30, 1841; Scisco, *Political Nativism in New York,* 35.

54 New York *Observer,* November 6, 1841. The statement of the New York *Observer* and other Whig papers that Hughes told his listeners that it would be a sin not to vote as he directed can be readily discounted.

55 New York *Observer,* November 6, 1841.

56 *Ibid.,* December 11, 1841; Hughes to Governor Seward, March 22, 1842, in *Records of the American Catholic Historical Society of Philadelphia,* XXIII (March, 1912), 36.

57 New York *Tribune,* November 12, 1841. The complete vote was as follows:

Whig party	15,980	votes
Democratic party	15,690	"
Catholic party	2,200	"
Nativistic party	470	"

The nativistic party, formed just before the election, polled only a few votes as the Whigs secured the support of most of the sympathizers with this movement because of their stand on the school question.

58 Seward, *Works,* II, 306–308.

59 The New York *Observer,* January 15, 1842, called the governor's plan "a natural offspring of politics and popery." See also New York *Journal of Commerce,* January 7, 1842. The message was heartily praised by the Catholic *Freeman's Journal,* January 8, 1842.

60 New York *Journal of Commerce,* February 27, 1842. The father of the author of this bill was a member of the New York Protestant Association. *Christian Watchman,* April 1, 1842.

61 New York *Observer,* April 16, 1842.

62 New York *Journal of Commerce,* April 4, 1842.

63 New York *Observer,* February 5, 1842.

64 *Ibid.,* February 26, 1842.

65 The meeting was held on March 16. New York *Journal of Commerce*, March 17, 1842.

66 It carried the Assembly with a sixty-five vote majority. *Ibid.*, March 24, 1842.

67 This was occasioned by the submission of the bill to a committee, allowing Whigs to express the hope that the measure was destined to defeat. *Ibid.*, March 24, 1842, April 1, 1842.

68 *Ibid.*, April 16, 1842.

69 April 16, 1842. See also *American Protestant Vindicator*, April 20, 1842, May 4, 1842. These two issues were devoted entirely to mourning the passage of the law. The praise lavished on the measure by the *Freeman's Journal*, May 7, 1842 and ff, did not increase its popularity.

70 New York *Commercial Advertiser*, April 13, 1842.

71 *Ibid.*, April 11, 1842.

72 New York *Herald*, April 14, 1842.

73 New York *Observer*, March 12, 1842. The superintendent at this time was Samuel Young, whose recommendation was dated February 15, 1842.

74 New York *Journal of Commerce*, May 5, 1842, June 1, 1842, June 7, 1842.

75 *Ibid.*, June 8, 1842. The *Freeman's Journal*, June 11, 1842, explained this Protestant victory by claiming the Catholics were unorganized and that they had decided to let the election go by default. The same paper, however, on April 9, 1842, had printed a list of candidates and urged Catholic support for them.

76 New York *Observer*, July 30, 1842. The *Observer* was pleased with the appointment of Stone and commented on the dissatisfaction of Catholics, which was expressed by the *Freeman's Journal*, July 23, 1842.

77 Hassard, *Life of John Hughes*, 251.

78 New York *Observer*, July 23, 1843.

79 *Ibid.*, October 14, 1843.

80 *Ibid.*, November 6, 1841.

81 *Ibid.*, November 20, 1841, contained extracts from most of the New York papers condemning Hughes' policy, the New York *Commercial Advertiser*, New York *Evangelist*, New York *Standard*, New York *Evening Post*, and Hartford *Times* being quoted. See also New York *Journal of Commerce*, November 6, 1841; *Protestant Banner*, December 2, 1842; *Christian Watchman*, December 2, 1842; *American Protestant Vindicator*, November 17, 1841.

82 *National Protestant*, I (December, 1844). The Catholic press defended the step as necessary to combat the organized Protestants. *Freeman's Journal*, November 13, 1841.

83 Hughes issued two statements, one printed in the New York *Observer*, December 11, 1843 and the other in the New York *Courier and Enquirer* in 1844. In both he denied the formation of a Catholic party and insisted that his followers were acting as citizens rather than as adherents to one sect. See *Ibid.*, May 6, 1844. Hughes' speeches and writings on the entire school question are conveniently arranged in John Hughes, *Complete Works of the Most Rev. John Hughes, D.D., Archbishop of New York* (New York, 1866), I, 41–284.

84 *Native American*, April 13, 1844.

85 One of Seward's biographers maintains that the school fund controversy cost him 2,000 Whig votes in the next gubernatorial election, enough to cause his defeat. Seward, *Works,* I, xliii. Again in 1860 Seward's opposition to nativism was one factor preventing his nomination for the presidency on the Republican ticket, for that party was anxious to attract Know-Nothings in the northwest and Pennsylvania. He remained a steadfast friend of the foreigner and immigrant despite this. See Seward, *Works,* III, 258.

86 New York *American Republican,* May 25, 1844.

87 Just before the municipal elections of 1844 the Reverend Hiram Ketchum gave a series of anti-Catholic lectures in New York City which revolved around this question. New York *Observer,* October 26, 1844. Protestants responded by a series of processions on the eve of voting, carrying banners which read: "No Mutilated School Books," and "The Book of Liberty! It Shall not be Excluded from Our Schools." *Ibid.,* April 13, 1844, August 24, 1844; New York *American Republican,* May 28, 1844, June 1, 1844, June 8, 1844; *Native American,* June 11, 1844.

88 New York *Observer,* January 28, 1843, October 7, 1843. Similar attempts were made in Salem, Albany, and elsewhere, and in Detroit Protestant efforts to introduce Bible reading into the schools were successfully blocked. *Christian Watchman,* January 13, 1843; *Freeman's Journal,* January 29, 1842, December 10, 1842, January 21, 1843, January 18, 1845. The *Protestant Banner,* April 22, 1842, had warned that the Catholic success with the Maclay bill would inspire similar attempts in Pennsylvania and other states.

89 A foreign observer commented at the time that Catholics in America were growing increasingly impatient of taxes to support Protestant schools. "This heavy burden," he said, "will be borne only until the Catholics in any State have numbers and political power sufficient to compel a division of the school fund. . . . That day, in several States, cannot be very distant, and is looked forward to with dread by many Protestant Americans." Nichols, *Forty Years of American Life,* II, 84.

90 *American Protestant Vindicator,* October 28, 1835, November 4, 1835, October 28, 1840; New York *Observer,* January 3, 1835, December 2, 1837, February 11, 1843, August 24, 1844; *Western Christian Advocate,* July 24, 1835, October 30, 1835; Herman Norton, *Startling Facts for American Protestants! Progress of Romanism since the Revolutionary War: Its Present Position and Future Prospects* (New York, 1844), 10-11; *Supplement to Six Months in a Convent,* 46-56; Brownlee, *Popery; an Enemy to Civil and Religious Liberty,* 61; *Roman Catholic Female Schools* (New York, 1837); *Education in Romish Seminaries. A Letter in Answer to Certain Inquiries respecting the Propriety of Selecting, as Places of Education, Seminaries Professedly under the Control of Religious Faculties of the Court of Rome* (New York, 1845); Henry James, *Education and the Common Schools* (New York, 1844); *National Protestant Or Anti-Jesuit,* III (April, 1845), 134-135.

91 *Secret Instructions to the Jesuits; Faithfully Translated from the Latin of an old Genuine London Copy* (New York, 1841), Introduction (by W. C. Brownlee), 13-14.

92 A series of lectures on the subject was given in New York during 1843 by the Reverend George B. Cheever and the theme was a popular one among many Protestants ministers. New York *Observer,* June 30, 1843. The New

York *Observer*, July 30, 1842 and ff. printed a series of articles on this same subject. See also *American Protestant Vindicator*, October 20, 1841; New York *American Republican*, May 4, 1844; George B. Cheever, *The Hierarchical Despotism; Lectures on the Mixture of Civil and Ecclesiastical Power in the Governments of the Middle Ages in Illustration of the Nature and Progress of the Romish Church* (New York, 1844), 122–137; *The Crisis, an Appeal to our Countrymen on the Subject of Foreign Influence in the United States* (New York, 1844), 68; *Political Popery; or, Bibles and Schools, with the Condition, Progress and Ulterior Objects of Romanists in the United States* (New York, 1844); John Crowell, *Republics Established and Thrones Overturned by the Bible* (Philadelphia, 1849); Watson, *An Apology for the Bible;* Caesar Milan, *Can I Join the Church of Rome while my Rule of Faith is in the Bible? An Inquiry Presented to the Conscience of the Christian Reader* (New York, 1844); George Borrow, *The Bible in Spain* (New York, 1847); *Rome's Policy Toward the Bible* (Philadelphia, 1844).

[93] New York *Observer*, May 18, 1844.

[94] *Ibid.*, July 27, 1844; *Native American*, July 20, 1844; New York *American Republican*, July 19, 1844, September 18, 1844.

[95] A joint committee of Protestants and Catholics, formed to investigate the burning, reported that forty-two Bibles were destroyed by a missionary from Canada over the protests of the resident Catholic clergyman. All destroyed had been given Catholic families by agents of Protestant Bible societies, usually despite protests that they were not wanted and would not be read. *United States Catholic Magazine,* II (August, 1843); Hughes, *Complete Works,* I, 504. See also: New York *Observer*, December 10, 1842, January 14, 1843; *American Protestant Magazine*, I (September, 1845); *Protestant Banner*, July 20, 1843; *Freeman's Journal*, January 7, 1843.

[96] *Freeman's Journal*, January 21, 1843.

[97] *American Protestant Magazine*, I (September, 1845).

[98] New York *Observer*, January 14, 1834.

[99] *Ibid.*, December 10, 1842; *Christian Watchman*, January 2, 1842, February 24, 1843; *Protestant Banner*, January 19, 1843.

[100] John Dowling, *The Burning of the Bibles* (Philadelphia, 1843); *The Burning of the Bibles; Being a Defense of the Protestant Version of the Scriptures against the Attacks of Popish Apologists for the Champlain Bible Burners* (New York, 1845).

[101] New York *Observer*, February 11, 1843; *Christian Watchman*, March 3, 1843. Cheever also attacked the burning in his *Hierarchical Despotism*, 144, as a revival of the Spanish auto-da-fé in the United States.

[102] Rumors spread that Bibles had been burned near Pittsburgh; in Seymour, Michigan; in Clinton County, New York; and in Mexico, New York. *Protestant Banner*, July 6, 1843, December 15, 1842; *Home Missionary*, XVI (January, 1844); New York *American Republican*, September 7, 1844. The *American Protestant Vindicator*, May 12, 1841, had earlier blamed the burning of an anti-Catholic publishing concern in Baltimore on Catholics and pictured a general popish plot to destroy Protestant property. The reported conversion of one of the "Bible burners" to Protestantism a short time later did not quiet Protestant fears. *Congregationalist*, December 7, 1849; *American and Foreign Christian Union*, I (January, 1850).

VII

The Protestant Organization
Is Strengthened
1840-1844

THE importance of the New York school controversy was quickly realized by that small group of clergymen and editors who headed the country's nativistic organizations. If the thousands of middle-class Protestants who had been jarred from their complacency by Catholic meddling in politics and especially by the attempt to eject the Word of God from the school room could be influenced while their prejudice was still aroused, they might join the existing anti-Catholic societies or support the anti-Catholic press and thus give the movement against Rome strength it had not previously known. Consequently the years during which Catholics were struggling for a share of New York's funds saw a renewed activity on the part of nativistic societies and newspapers and the establishment of new agencies through which all Americans might be won to support the No-Popery crusade.

Especially active in this drive against Catholicism was the Protestant Reformation Society, operating from New York and advantageously situated to take advantage of the controversy raging there. Its officers realized that the new group which the society wished to attract had been antagonistic toward the earlier sensational propaganda and that its policy must be changed to appeal to those who wished to combat Rome through Christian love rather than force. Accordingly a conscious effort was made to increase the number of clerical members of the society.[1] Ministerial lecturing agents were not only multiplied but urged to refrain from violent abuse of Catholics.[2] These tactics attracted large audiences even in such centers of sober Christianity as Harvard and Princeton universities.[3] Some refused to moderate their invective. One, the Reverend Charles Sparry, was mobbed by a hostile audience in Philadelphia [4] and later arrested for selling obscene anti-Catholic literature in Pennsylvania.[5] Others in lectures sponsored by the society included such topics as:

Celibacy of the priests and nuns; History of this modern innovation by ghostly tyranny;—its atrocious consequences. It converts monasteries, nunneries and nations, into one vast brothel. Proof; historical facts.[6]

In 1842 the practice of public lectures in large halls was abandoned and the society instead supplied speakers to individual churches which requested them. The belief that a larger and more diversified religious audience would be reached in this way [7] was evidently justified, for this was the method which was to be continued throughout the remainder of the society's existence.[8]

These speakers were not only effective in spreading anti-Catholic propaganda themselves; the money which they collected was used after 1841 to publish tracts against Rome for free distribution among both Catholics and Protestants. The inauguration of this policy was another indication of the society's desire to cater to the demands of a religious group. Although many of the tracts embodied the well-worn arguments against celibacy and convents, most of them were milder in tone and several were designed entirely to win Catholics to Protestantism.[9] Religious tracts in themselves were attractive to most Evangelical Christians of this generation, and their moderate tone commended the work of the Protestant Reformation Society to public favor.

The popularity of both the cause and methods of this society was shown by an increased membership and a growing number of auxiliaries. At Reading (Massachusetts), Washington, Pittsburgh, Louisville, and other cities active branches were formed, as well as other Protestant societies not affiliated with the national organization.[10] At Princeton interest was so great among the students of the Theological School that they named a "Committee on the Romish Church, Public Morals and Infidelity," to which was committed the task of diffusing knowledge of Popery not only among the students but also among the townspeople.[11] New Yorkers likewise, believing that the danger of Catholicism was great enough to warrant the existence of another society, founded the American Protestant Union in May, 1841. Headed by Samuel F. B. Morse, this union announced itself as opposed to the "subjugation of our country to the control of the Pope of Rome, and his adherents and for the preservation of our civil and religious institutions" and proposed to operate as a "national defense society" in the interests of Protestantism.[12] At the same time a movement was under way to bring all anti-Catholic societies into a national organization.[13]

An even more impressive indication of the desire of Protestants to organize against Rome was offered by the small local societies which sprang into being spontaneously in many cities and towns. Most of these had no connection with larger societies and simply represented the wish-fulfillment of thousands of Protestants who sought a means of anti-Catholic expression. In Philadelphia the number of these local groups was so large that they were able to co-operate in forming a Union of Protestant Associations which sponsored speeches against Catholicism [14] and eventually set up a Protestant Institute for the dissemination of information on Popery.[15] Membership in these organizations was sufficiently large that plans to construct a Protestant hall as a headquarters were seriously considered,[16] and a Philadelphia Protestant Beneficial Association was formed in 1842, open to all members of Protestant associations and no others.[17]

The unprecedented activity and change in methods among

anti-Catholic societies were both matched by the rapidly growing nativistic press. Older papers, finding that their calumny had to be modified if they were to endure, introduced a score of new publications advocating a labor of love to secure the conversion of Catholics to Protestantism. The Christian charity which characterized this new period was alien to the nature of Samuel B. Smith, editor of the *Downfall of Babylon,* and his publication quietly passed from existence. Brownlee, as publisher of the *American Protestant Vindicator,* was more tolerant, and although he continued to denounce Popery, his paper more and more expressed the belief that Catholics should be saved rather than exterminated. "I do persecute them [Catholics]," he wrote, "in the same manner as I would persecute my neighbor, who is fast asleep in his bed, and his house on fire. I persecute him by rushing in through the flames, and dragging him, his wife and little ones out of doors, to a place of safety." [18] Another earlier journal, the Baltimore *Literary and Religious Magazine,* had always devoted itself to theological arguments designed to appeal to clerical enemies of Rome rather than laymen, and the transformation which it effected was occasioned by the retirement of one of its editors, Andrew B. Cross, in December, 1841, rather than by any change in policy. The name of the monthly publication was changed to the *Spirit of the XIX Century,* and it continued under the editorship of Robert J. Breckinridge. The new magazine, like the old, was a financial failure [19] and finally expired at the end of 1843, the editor explaining that the many new anti-Catholic journals then being published made his unnecessary.[20]

Breckinridge's assertion was certainly true, for the early 1840's saw new publications being founded all over the country. Baltimore supported the *Pilot and Transcript* which attempted to portray the dangers of Catholics in politics, and the *Saturday Visitor,* a general No-Popery paper established in 1841. A Presbyterian minister, the Reverend A. A. Campbell, founded the

Jackson Protestant in Jackson, Tennessee, and circulated it through the southwest until his death in 1848. In the lower south the New Orleans *Protestant* began a successful career in 1844. In Albany a monthly publication, *The Reformation Defended Against the Errors of the Times,* was founded in the same year, and farther to the west, at Cincinnati, *The American Protestant,* edited by two local clergymen, was influential after its establishment in 1845.[21]

One new anti-Catholic paper which typified the spirit of the nativists was the *Protestant Banner,* published in Philadelphia and first appearing early in 1842 under the editorship of the Reverend Joseph F. Berg, who was already well known as a No-Popery writer. "Our motto," Berg wrote in an early issue, "is Light and Love; whilst in the conscientious discharge of our duty, we bear testimony against the delusions of Popery, it will be with the earnest wish and prayer that God may seal his own truth, snatch our mistaken brethren from the toils of priestcraft, and save their souls from death." [22] This policy proved successful, for the *Banner* continued publication for a number of years,[23] employing lecturing agents and the usual devices through which the nativistic press extended its influence.[24]

One of the most successful of the new publications of this period was a monthly magazine, the *National Protestant,* edited by the Reverend Charles Sparry and first appearing in November, 1844. Sparry had become famous as a lecturing agent for his bitter denunciations of Rome, and the popularity of his magazine, which reflected these same views, showed that there were many who still scorned toleration and wanted to hear only the worst of Popery. Sparry announced from the first that he had no interest in converting Catholics "to Christianity"; most of them, he said, could not read, and the rest were not worth saving.[25] Instead he wanted to "develop the pestilential attributes and fearful consequences of Romanism, wherever it either sways, or is tolerated—and to sound the alarm to Protestants, so that they may be on their guard against the wiles of Jesuitism, and the snares of the Devil, under the name of Popery." [26]

The three thousand who had subscribed by the time the second number of the *National Protestant* appeared [27] convinced Sparry that his enterprise would be successful and he promptly entered upon an extensive promotion program, securing no less than thirty-three clergymen as lecturing agents before the year was out and constantly enlarging and improving his publication.[28] This overexpansion was to prove his downfall, for in May, 1845, he was forced to sell half his interest in the magazine to the Reverend H. Righter who found the financial affairs badly muddled and, the better to settle them, bought out Sparry entirely, Sparry as part of the bargain promising that he would refrain from publishing a similar magazine.[29] Righter was unable to straighten out the affairs of the *National Protestant* and on his first opportunity sold its publication rights to the Reverend D. Mead, who changed its name to *The National Protestant Magazine or the Anti-Jesuit* but otherwise continued the same policy.[30] Under this name the magazine continued to be published for some time, attaining a large circulation and employing a number of lecturing agents.[31]

Sparry meanwhile had been regretting the bargain which kept him from re-entering the publishing field. When Righter transferred ownership of the *National Protestant* to Mead, Sparry considered that his own obligation no longer held and entered the field once more as editor of the *North American Protestant Magazine or the Anti-Jesuit,* the first issue of which, appearing in April, 1846, showed that Sparry still believed in violent denunciation of Popery.[32] Both this magazine and the *National Protestant* continued as rival publications until 1847 when they were absorbed by another nativistic publication.[33]

The increased popular interest in the No-Popery crusade shown by the success of these papers and magazines, was reflected also in the religious journals. Anti-Catholic articles began to appear in increasing numbers on their pages; the New York *Observer, Christian Intelligencer, Christian Watchman* and others of equal prominence published weekly attacks on Romanism, usually couched in the language of tolerance which recently had met with such popularity. The *Freeman's Journal* summed up the situation well when it declared:

> One fact, in connection with these papers, continually occurs with force to us and that is, how large a proportion of the raw material, out of which these papers are prepared, consists of topics connected with "Popery," either violent attacks, bitter denunciations, malicious representations, mendacious sketches and stories, false perversions of fact, or uncharitable inferences and constructions. . . . No matter what their creed or profession; confession or platform; all, both orthodox and heterodox, Calvinist and Lutheran, high and low church, unite in an indiscriminate onslaught upon the Catholic.[34]

Even secular journals such as the *New England Magazine* showed as much devotion to the cause as the more openly Protestant papers.[35] Wherever the church-going, evangelical Christian of that day looked, he found arguments and invective against Rome.

There remained for nativists, however, the task of securing the support of the churches themselves. If these powerful evangelical organizations could be persuaded to encourage organized anti-Catholicism from the pulpit, new converts to the No-Popery cause could be readily secured. The New York school controversy had prepared the way by showing Catholic enmity to the Bible, and nativistic writers quickly seized upon this in asking for church support. Clergymen were warned that unless they awoke "from their dreamy confidence and false charity," and roused their energies to a "universal and persevering opposition to that artful, insinuating, and dangerous traitor, the Popish Priesthood; ere long we may realize the terrors, cruelties, tortures, and massacres which our ancestors endured." [36] They were reminded that Luther had not hesitated to take sides and were told that if he had not, all the world might yet be in the "spiritual gloom of the miserable, servile, superstition-crushed beggars of Naples and of Rome." [37] They were assured that they must definitely align themselves, that they could no longer remain neutral in the great controversy between the true and false religion.[38] "It may be, in a degree," wrote one editor, "the battle of the Reformation over again. For the prince of the power of the air has long chafed under his defeat and the loss of his dominion in that contest, nor will he rest until he has made one mighty effort to recover his lost possessions." [39]

Nearly all of the Protestant denominations in the United States responded to this appeal but none with more enthusiasm than the Presbyterians whose heritage of antagonism toward Rome fitted them to take full advantage of the excitement over the New York controversy. The General Assembly of the church, as early as 1830, had passed resolutions against Romish persecutions in Switzerland [40] and two years later overwhelmingly rejected the report of a committee which recommended acceptance of the validity of Catholic baptism.[41] In 1834 again, the assembled Presbyterian clergymen had heard a bitter No-Popery sermon which warned them of a papal plot to subdue the United States and stamp out Protestantism.[42]

The early attempts on the part of the General Assembly to deal with the Catholic question culminated in 1835 when a report of its Board of Education was devoted entirely to an exposition of the papal plot to convert America to Romanism and recommended that ministers and educators be specially trained "to meet and discomfit in the field of argument . . . this ever-growing and ever-to-be-dreaded system." [43] The principal objection to this report, disclosed in the debate which followed, was that it was not sufficiently denunciatory of Rome. To offset this, a new committee was named on the "Prevalence of Popery in the West," headed by the Reverend Robert J. Breckinridge, a prominent nativist. Critics dissatisfied with the mildness of the previous report had no cause for complaint concerning the resolutions submitted by this committee. The Pope was denounced as the Anti-Christ, the "Man of Sin and the Son of Perdition"; the Catholic church was declared to be not a church of Christ but an apostate from God, corrupted by "various profane exorcisms, idolatrous incantations and unauthorized additions, mutilations and ceremonies"; and seminaries under Presbyterian control were urged to train all candidates for the ministry specifically in the Catholic controversy that they might meet and defeat the Romish priesthood in America.[44]

Such outspoken calumny as this was unacceptable to a majority of the clergymen attending the General Assembly, and although the resolutions were defended by Breckinridge and others, they were finally laid upon the table. It was not until several days later that new resolutions were submitted which, although only slightly less outspoken than those of the Breckinridge committee, met the approval of the Assembly:

Resolved, That it is the deliberate and decided judgment of this General Assembly, that the Roman Catholic church has essentially apostatized from the religion of our Lord and Savior Jesus Christ; and therefore cannot be recognized as a Christian Church.

Resolved, That it be recommended to all in our communion to endeavor by the diffusion of light by the pulpit, the press and all other christian means, to resist the extension of Romanism, and lead its subjects to the knowledge of the truth, as it is taught in the word of God.

Resolved, That it is utterly inconsistent with the strongest obligations of Christian parents to place their children for education in Roman Catholic Seminaries.[45]

Fairly launched on the road to nativism by the acceptance of this report, the Presbyterian church was unable to continue its aggressive attitude in the following years. When members gathered for the General Assembly of 1836, the seeds of controversy which were to flower in the schism of the following year had already been sown. In 1837 the conflict between liberal and fundamental groups led to the expulsion of nearly 100,000 church members who were forced to organize themselves as the New School Presbyterians. Not until this internal strife abated could No-Popery again become important, despite the efforts of Breckinridge and others who sought a reconciliation of the divergent branches in order to allow the church to present a united front against Catholicism.[46] For several years the only action against Romanism by Presbyterians came through individual synods.[47]

Although the schism was not to be completely healed for many years, the first heat of controversy soon cooled, and by 1841 the Presbyterians were again ready to turn their attention to the problem of Catholicism. The General Assembly of the Old School had by this time felt the influence of the New York controversy, and after listening to two sermons denouncing Rome, it adopted resolutions which were to shape its policy for several years:

Resolved, That a preacher be appointed to deliver a discourse before the next Assembly on some general topic connected with the controversy between Romanists and Protestants.

Resolved, That this Assembly most earnestly recommends to the bishops of the several congregations under our care, both from the pulpit and through the press, boldly though temperately, to explain and defend the doctrines and principles of the Reformation, and to point out and expose the errors and superstitions of popery.

Resolved, That this Assembly solemnly and affectionately warn all our people of the danger and impropriety of supporting, or in any manner, directly or indirectly, patronizing or encouraging popish schools and seminaries.

Resolved, That this Assembly recommend to the special attention of all our people the works on the Reformation and Popery, which have been already, and may be still further issued by our Board of Publication.

Resolved, That the delegates of the several presbyteries be called on at the next meeting of the Assembly, to report what has been done in compliance with these resolutions.[48]

The adoption of these resolutions meant that a new and "mighty machine" [49] had been set in motion against Catholicism, with eleven hundred ministers pledged to make their pulpits organs for nativistic propaganda.[50]

Although the Old School Assembly had agreed to listen to a sermon on Popery only in the following year, the plea delivered by the Reverend Robert J. Breckinridge proved so popular that these sermons were made an annual feature.[51] Members under this influence had another opportunity to express their dislike of Catholicism in 1845 when they were asked to deal again with the question of the validity of Romish baptism. A spirited debate ensued, based principally on the problem of whether the Catholic church was Christian or non-Christian, and even those bold enough to defend Catholic claims prefaced their remarks with denunciations of the papal church. The vote was decisive, the Assembly refusing to accept the validity of Catholic baptism with only eight favoring such a step and one hundred and sixty-nine opposed.[52] Clearly the Presbyterians could be listed among the sects openly antagonistic to the Catholic church.

The Methodist church was less violent in its reaction to Catholicism than the Presbyterian. Although there had been indications of growing antipathy on the part of the church members for some time,[53] it was not until 1844 that the Methodists were ready to take any united action. In that year the address of the bishops to the General Conference was devoted largely to a denunciation of Popery and an exposition of papal ambitions. "These last few years," the bishops wrote, "have been marked with a renewed, and simultaneous, and mighty movement of Papal Rome to recover that domination and influence which she so reluctantly yielded to the champions of Scriptural truth. . . . The establishment of schools and colleges, literary and theological, with a design to wield the mighty engine of education to mould the minds of the rising generation in conformity to the doctrines of their creed, and the forms of their worship, is no unimportant or inefficient part of that extensive system of policy which is now in operation. . . . Romanism is now labouring, not only to recover what it lost of its former supremacy in the Reformation, but also to assert and establish its monstrous pretensions in countries never subject either to its civil or ecclesiastical authority. With these weapons the Papal power has invaded Protestant communities with such success as should awaken and unite the energies of the evangelical Churches of Christ in every part of the world." [54]

This report brought members of the General Conference face to face with the problem of Catholicism and obviously called for proposals similar to those adopted by the Presbyterians three years earlier,[55] but before these could be made, the attention of the conference was diverted to graver matters. Members found themselves embroiled in the slavery controversy, and before the convention adjourned, the division into northern and southern branches had taken place. After 1844 Methodist attention was absorbed in this schism and in efforts at reconciliation; the menace of Catholicism in America was forgotten.

The Congregational church was faced with no such schism, and the attention which it could pay to the problem of Popery was proportionately greater. Its lack of a central organization made any united action impossible, but individual associations, particularly in the New England states, early expressed alarm at the advance of American Catholicism.[56] These first efforts were given a certain centralization in 1834 when a deputation from the Congregational Union of England visited the United States and left with the warning that Popery must be exterminated or it would triumph.[57] The Massachusetts General Association was sufficiently alarmed to urge its ministers to labor "in the spirit of prayer and Christian love, and in all suitable ways to save our country from the degrading influence of popery," [58] and all the associations from that time on devoted increasing attention to Catholicism.

It was not, however, until news of the action of the Presbyterian General Assembly in 1841 was officially conveyed to the

Congregational associations that they expressed their true feelings.[59] A committee, named by the General Association of Massachusetts in 1843 to recommend the course which Congregationalists should follow toward Rome,[60] reported a year later that the danger was greater than at any time since the Reformation and that the "persecuting arm of the apostate church,—which has been weakened ever since the reformation by Luther,—will be invigorated, and will again send the sword and the faggot, where they have long been unknown." [61]   The Leopold Association, Catholic idolatry, and Romish enmity to the Bible were all included in the report, which concluded by urging all ministers to instruct their congregations "concerning the character of the Catholic church, and to warn them against the sophistry, and the arts, and the efforts of Antichrist." [62]   The acceptance of these recommendations, not only by the Massachusetts Association, but by others as well, added several hundred additional clergymen to those already denouncing Catholicism from their pulpits.[63]

Equal support for the nativist cause was given by the Episcopal church, not because of any inherent sympathy between the conservative members of this sect and the No-Popery agitators, but because of the English Oxford movement, the full effect of which was felt in America from the early 1840's until long after the original Oxfordians had found haven within the Catholic church.   Its impact on the Episcopalian church in the United States was particularly great because of the condition of that church at the time.   Members of this sect had, in common with those of other denominations, felt the effect of the conflict then going on between liberalism and fundamentalism and had separated into two groups, the high churchmen on the one hand, the low churchmen, or evangelicals, on the other.   The high church party as early as 1835 had adopted the name "Anglo-Catholic" and under the leadership of Bishop John Henry Hobart made rapid advances, much to the alarm of many who could not distinguish it from Catholicism.[64]   The effect of the teachings of the Oxford group on such a divided church was bound to be great. American Protestants as early as 1839 had begun to brand the Oxfordians as Papists in disguise [65] and it was now believed that they were winning over many high church Episcopalians to Rome. Weight was given these suspicions and the whole question crystalized when the Catholic Bishop Francis Patrick Kenrick of Philadelphia addressed an open letter to the bishops of the American Episcopal church, asking them to follow their English brethren and return to the fold from which they had strayed.[66] Earnest as this appeal may have been, its results were unfortunate, for from that time on the issue was between Catholicism and high churchism on the one hand and Protestantism and low churchism on the other.

Low church bishops, opponents of the Anglo-Catholic movement, quickly realized the situation and did not hesitate to utilize the No-Popery cry in their own behalf, urging their clergy to resist the growing impulse toward Rome found both in English Tractarianism and American ritualism.[67] Thus in Virginia Bishop Richard Channing Moore besought the ministers of his diocese "to hold fast the great principles of the Protestant Reformation . . . and to give no place nor countenance, no not for an hour, *to these abominations of Popery* issuing from Oxford." [68] In Connecticut, Vermont, Ohio, and other states similar warnings were voiced by churchmen who were willing to combat Oxfordism by denouncing the Romanism with which that movement was associated in the popular mind.[69] Bishop John Henry Hopkins of Vermont wrote a number of learned books to prove the errors of Catholicism,[70] Bishop Alexander Griswold, of the Eastern diocese, venerated as one of the leaders in the church's early development, and Bishop Charles P. McIlvaine of Ohio showed a similar prejudice,[71] and the Reverend H. A. Boardman was willing to enter into a controversy to uphold his Protestant principles.[72] Even high churchmen objected to being linked with Catholicism. "Must we," one asked, "be

claimed as advocates for monkery with all its abominations, or
for Jesuitism with its unspeakable iniquities, because we laud the
'Catholic feelings' of self renunciation, mortification, subjection
of the individual will, and devotion to the life and work of
Christ, that furnished the spark of life with which these monsters
stalked abroad to conquest?" [73]

The sharp division of opinion within the Episcopal church,
crystalized by these expressions from its leaders, probably had a
great effect in winning converts to the No-Popery cause. Partici-
pants in this controversy had either to be enemies of the Oxford
movement and nativistic or high church and pro-Catholic, for no
compromise was possible. The latter ground was inacceptible to
most Americans, and Episcopalians found themselves, as a result, arrayed with the more evangelical sects in denouncing Romanism. Advantageous as this may have been from the point of
view of the organized nativists, it was dangerous in the extreme
for the church, a schism being narrowly averted in 1843.[74] The
feeling engendered by this threatened disunion was so great that
for many years thereafter the pamphlet warfare continued, serving as a constant reminder to many Episcopalians of the threat
of Catholicism.

The other American churches were only slightly less active
than the Presbyterians, the Methodists, and the Episcopalians.
Although the Baptists had no central body to take united action
against Catholicism, individual conferences of the clergy repeatedly went on record as being willing to combat Romish designs
in any way possible.[75] The Free Will Baptists were sufficiently
aroused to agree "that it is the duty of every Christian and every
philanthropist to do what he can by writing, printing, speaking,
prayer, and holy living, and by any and every other proper
method, to promote the principles of Christianity, and thus to
counteract the principles and operations of Popery." [76] Similarly
the General Synod of the Dutch Reformed church, after listening
to a sermon against Popery by the Reverend W. C. Brownlee in

1837, recorded its sentiments as in accord with those of this prominent nativist.[77] The Lutheran church acted only through its synods, but these showed every tendency to follow the other evangelical sects in denouncing Rome. One synod, that of western Pennsylvania, in 1836 instructed its clerical members to labor against Rome in every possible way [78] and two years later agreed on an annual sermon on Romanism,[79] the first of which, delivered in 1838 by the Reverend S. S. Schmucker, was a bitter attack on Catholicism.[80] By 1840 the Lutheran church had decided to publish a Protestant Almanac devoted to an exposition of the errors of Popery,[81] and four years later the official *Lutheran Observer* announced its determination to join the anti-Catholic ranks.[82]

By the middle of the 1840's the American churches were able to present a virtually united front against Catholicism. Swept away by the pleas of organized nativists, they had accepted the challenge to make America the scene of a new Reformation in which Popery would be driven from the land and the work of Luther and Calvin brought to a successful end.

In this task the churches were ably supported by several of the religious and humanitarian societies which were so influential among Protestants of that day. So effectively did nativists woo these organizations that many of them exerted an influence as great as that of the Protestant Reformation Society itself. This was particularly the case of the American Tract Society, which was not only whole-heartedly opposed to Catholicism but in a position to make its opposition felt.[83] This was accomplished largely through its publications, many of the tracts and books issued either for gratuitous circulation or for sale being exposures of papal pretensions in America or attacks on the theology of Romanism.[84] In 1842, following an anti-Catholic sermon before the annual meeting, the society agreed to adopt a second device which was to prove effective, a system of colportage in which missionary agents would work among Catholics, distributing tracts and endeavoring to secure conversions to Protestantism.[85]

This system was immediately successful; after it had been operating a year the managers of the society joyfully reported that their colporteurs had begun a new Reformation in America and looked forward to the time when all Papists would have been returned to Christianity by their efforts.[86]

The same anti-Catholic spirit which inspired these efforts was shown by the American Education Society, which, like the American Bible Society, was drawn into the No-Popery crusade by the New York controversy when it seemed that American schools were being attacked by Catholics. Its members in 1841 listened to the Reverend Lyman Beecher plead for better educational facilities to offset the influence of "Popish schools" and from that time on they enthusiastically supported the nativistic cause.[87]

This marshaling of the nation's religious forces lacked only one thing to make it completely effective. Virtually all the denominations had indicated a willingness to combat Rome, yet they were still divided and unable to offer a solid front against papal aggressions. If the Protestant sects could be persuaded to abandon their differences and unite in one powerful evangelical body, Catholicism might be driven from America and the new Reformation become a reality. Nativistic editors repeatedly stressed the necessity of such unity,[88] and soon after the school controversy had aroused the interest of religious bodies, an effort was made toward its realization. In 1842 a convention was held in New York composed of delegates from various denominations with the avowed purpose of uniting all churches in order to secure the evangelization of the world. Although those attending felt sufficiently encouraged to arrange a similar convention a year later [89] they actually accomplished nothing and the attempt was soon abandoned. Religious jealousies were too acute to be forgotten, and the gulf between the sects was so great that a more immediate danger was necessary before it could be bridged.

As soon as this sectarianism became apparent, nativists turned their attention to a new method of attack on the problem. If the denominations, as national organizations, could not be made to unite, unity might be accomplished within specific areas. There the initiative would rest on individual clergymen, who might be willing to co-operate sufficiently to make it appear that a Protestant alliance had actually been formed. The first effort in this direction was made in Philadelphia in 1842 when a group of clergymen addressed a letter to all ministers in the city, pointing out the need of "united counsel and effort among true Protestants" and urging them to meet to arrange such a course.[90] Sixty-one of the Protestant clergy in the city responded to this call, representing most of the evangelical sects. They agreed unanimously on the "importance of united action for the protection and defence of the rights and principles which distinguish the Protestant Churches of this country, from the threatening assaults of Romanism" and decided that for this purpose they would form themselves into an American Protestant Association.[91] This organization was soon perfected, nearly a hundred ministers of Philadelphia becoming charter members.[92]

The constitution adopted by this group of clergymen asserted that Popery was in its "principles and tendencies, subversive to civil and religious liberty, and destructive to the spiritual welfare of men" and that it could be combated only through united church action. The members were pledged "to give to their several congregations instruction on the differences between Protestantism and Popery," to further the circulation of the Bible and anti-Catholic books, and to "awaken the attention of the community to the dangers which . . . threaten these United States from the assaults of Romanism." The way was left open for expansion by a provision that similar Protestant organizations could be formed in other cities and even within Philadelphia, thus building up a national organization of Protestant clergymen opposed to Catholicism.[93]

The officers of the association, aware that this expansion must be undertaken immediately, lost no time in issuing a widely circulated *Address* [94] calling on their clerical brethren everywhere to unite against the common foe.[95] This call met with a quick response; in the same month that it was issued a Cincinnati Protestant Association was formed, and before the parent society was a year old similar associations had been formed at Albany, Baltimore, and Pittsburgh, and others were being projected in cities all over the country.[96] Meanwhile subordinate branches of the association were formed within Philadelphia, co-operating in common projects but carrying on individual programs within their own districts.[97]

The principal effect of the American Protestant Association was to interest ministers in the No-Popery cause and encourage them to deliver sermons against Catholicism; many of the pulpit denunciations of the 1840's can be traced to its influence. It also instituted monthly lectures on Popery which proved so popular that they soon became a weekly feature.[98] The association decided that it would be inexpedient either to publish anti-Catholic works or send out lecturing agents, as those two fields were already sufficiently supplied,[99] but it continued for some years as an active propaganda society within the limits which it set for itself.

In its second year the association broadened its activities by sponsoring a new magazine, *The Quarterly Review of the American Protestant Association,* the first issue of which appeared in January, 1844.[100] This newest addition to the anti-Catholic journals typified the aims of the society which published it; it was obviously designed to furnish its clerical subscribers with material for No-Popery sermons and arguments. The first number contained a plea to the clergy to join in the crusade against Rome,[101] and it continued to voice this demand throughout its brief career.[102]

The example set by the American Protestant Association in Philadelphia was imitated by the clergymen of Baltimore who, in March, 1843, formed the Society of the Friends of the Reformation. The moving spirit in this enterprise was the Reverend

Robert J. Breckinridge, whose activities as a nativist had well fitted him to be its leader. The clergymen who supported this society agreed that their purpose was "to maintain, defend and promote among the several denominations of Christians to which the members belong the principles of the Reformation and of civil and religious liberty, against all encroachments and errors whatever." [103] The plan of operation of the Friends of the Reformation was similar to that used by the Philadelphia association; public meetings in the Baltimore churches were relied on to a large extent in spreading the gospel against Popery, the funds collected at these meetings being used to publish tracts and books against Romanism.[104]

By 1844 nativism had assumed an enviable position in America. The churches had been enlisted in the cause and were not only spreading calumny against Rome but were making individual efforts to unite against the common foe. Many Protestants firmly believed that a new Reformation was in progress, and that the Breckinridges, Hogans and Brownlees of that day were playing a part comparable to that played by Calvin and Luther centuries earlier. In vain did the Fifth Provincial Council of Catholic Bishops implore members of their faith to refute "all those atrocious calumnies which deluded men . . . constantly circulate by every possible means against our holy religion." [105] Catholic rebuttal went unheeded; America had embarked on a crusade and was intent on carrying it to a conclusion. "Truly a great revolution in public sentiment is already accomplished," wrote the editor of an anti-Catholic journal in 1843, "when in the same city, the same cause which in 1832 endangered a man's life, in 1835 jeoparded his character, and as late as 1840 exposed him to indictment, fine and imprisonment—in 1843 looms gloriously up on the top of a general movement of the piety of the community, and becomes the very center of Christian unity." [106] No-Popery had at last reached a place where it could bid for national power.

NOTES

[1] *American Protestant Vindicator*, February 17, 1841. The society sought to secure such memberships by asking church congregations to make their pastors life members of the society. This was evidently successful, for the files of the *American Protestant Vindicator* during these years are filled with letters of thanks from ministers for such memberships.

[2] *Ibid.*, January 20, 1841.

[3] *Ibid.*, January 20, 1841; *National Protestant*, II (November, 1845).

[4] New York *Observer*, February 20, 1841; *American Protestant Vindicator*, February 17, 1841, March 3, 1841.

[5] *United States Catholic Magazine*, II (December, 1843), 757. The work being sold consisted of extracts from a Catholic book, Den's *Moral Theology*, only the obscene passages being published.

[6] *American Protestant Vindicator*, December 1, 1841.

[7] *Ibid.*, February 9, 1842.

[8] New York *Observer*, January 20, 1844.

[9] These tracts were published in the *American Protestant Vindicator* during 1840 and 1841, as well as being printed in pamphlet form.

[10] *American Protestant Vindicator*, December 23, 1840, June 9, 1841, May 18, 1842; *Protestant Banner*, April 6, 1842. The society at Reading was the Female Protestant Association, formed to sponsor sermons on Romanism and circulate free tracts exhibiting its errors.

[11] *American Protestant Vindicator*, May 18, 1842.

[12] New York *Observer*, June 12, 1841.

[13] *American Protestant Vindicator*, August 11, 1841, September 22, 1841; *Christian Watchman*, May 11, 1838. Although these Orange societies played their part they were not primarily responsible for the nativistic movement as most Catholic historians have said. See Guilday, *Life and Times of John England*, II, 379.

[14] *Protestant Banner*, December 31, 1841, January 14, 1842, March 25, 1842.

[15] *Ibid.*, October 14, 1842.

[16] *Ibid.*, February 11, 1842, February 25, 1842. Subscriptions were collected for this building but no information has been found as to the fate of this money.

[17] *Ibid.*, July 15, 1842.

[18] *American Protestant Vindicator*, July 28, 1841.

[19] *Spirit of the XIX Century*, I (January, 1842). Perhaps another reason for the change was the $2,000 owed the Baltimore *Literary and Religious Magazine* from unpaid subscriptions. These had been placed in the hands of a commercial agency for collection, which might have been made easier through the suspension of the older publication and the creation of a new one in its place.

[20] *Ibid.*, II (December, 1843).

[21] The author has been unable to locate the files of any of these papers or magazines. References to them have been found in other nativistic papers. See especially *American Protestant Vindicator*, December 23, 1840, May 12, 1841, May 18, 1842; *American Protestant Magazine*, II (August, 1846); New York *Observer*, August 30, 1845; *Freeman's Journal*, August 31, 1844, November 16, 1844.

[22] *Protestant Banner*, February 25, 1842.

23 In December, 1843, the Reverend Channing Webster was named associate editor with Berg. *Ibid.,* December 7, 1843. Two years later, in 1845, one of the publishers, C. L. Hughes, retired, and his interests were assumed by J. B. Lippincott Co. *Ibid.,* March 27, 1845.

24 The Reverend Edward D. Smith was named lecturing agent in May, 1842, and others were subsequently added. *Ibid.,* May 20, 1842.

25 *National Protestant,* I (April, 1845).

26 *Ibid.,* I (April, 1845).

27 *Ibid.,* I (December, 1844).

28 In addition Sparry employed sixty-one traveling agents to solicit subscriptions. *Ibid.,* I (April, 1845), II (May, 1845).

29 Although Sparry agreed that he would not publish another nativistic magazine, he did succeed in securing the plates of the May issue of the *National Protestant* which was about to go to press at the time the transfer was made. He violated his agreement and published the issue, so that two numbers of the May number were printed, one bearing the name of Sparry, the other of Righter. The American Antiquarian Society has the two copies, identical in every respect except the editors' names.

30 The change was made with the January, 1846 issue.

31 *Ibid.,* III (October, 1846). At this time about 5,000 copies of the *National Protestant* were sold monthly, and it was advertising for twenty more lecturing agents to work on a salary basis. In October, 1846 the magazine again changed hands, being sold by Mead to C. Billings Smith, who modified its tone and continued as its editor until it was absorbed into the *American Protestant Magazine* in 1847.

32 *North American Protestant Magazine or the Anti-Jesuit,* I (April, 1846).

33 They were united with the *American Protestant Magazine. American Protestant Magazine,* II (March, 1847). It was announced that the *National Protestant* had been acquired some months before, the *North American Protestant Magazine or the Anti-Jesuit* just completing the arrangements for amalgamation. For origins of the *American Protestant Magazine,* see below, p. 248.

34 *Freeman's Journal,* November 2, 1844. The *Freeman's Journal* believed that this was done to excite Protestants and in this way loosen their purse strings.

35 A typical volume of the *New Englander,* that for the year 1844, included the following anti-Catholic articles: "Western Colleges and Theological Seminaries," 58–65; "The Protestant Principle," 66–80; "Review of the Errors of the Times," 143-174; "Miracles," 208-221; "What are the Ministers to do in the Great Controversy of the Age," 222-232; "Romanists and the Roman Catholic Controversy," 233-255; "Apostolic Succession," 273-296; "The Roman Catholic Faith," 414-419; "The Philadelphia Riots," 470-483; "Review of Dr. Stone's Mysteries Opened," 510-527; "The Roman Catholic Faith," 568-588. The *Freeman's Journal* complained in 1845 that the New York *Journal of Commerce* and the New York *Commercial Advertiser* were as anti-Catholic in tone as the religious papers. *Freeman's Journal,* May 31, 1845.

36 *The American Text Book of Popery: being an Authentic Compend of the Bulls, Canons and Decretals of the Roman Hierarchy* (New York, 1844), 371.

[37] John S. C. Abbott, *Sermon on the Duties and Dangers of the Clergy and the Church* (Boston, 1842), 13.

[38] *New Englander*, II (April, 1844); *American Protestant Vindicator*, March 3, 1841; *Christian Watchman*, September 2, 1836, April 30, 1841; *Addresses of Rev. Leonard Bacon and Rev. E. N. Kirk at the Christian Alliance held in New York, May 8, 1845, with the Address of the Society and the Bull of the Pope against It* (New York, 1845), 12–13; *National Protestant*, I (February, 1845), I (April, 1845); Charlotte Elizabeth, *Falsehood and Truth* (New York, 1842), viii–ix; Baxter, *Jesuit Juggling*, viii–xi.

[39] *National Protestant*, I (January, 1845).

[40] New York *Observer*, June 5, 1830. The New York *Observer*, a Presbyterian paper, reported the proceedings of the General Assembly in full.

[41] *Ibid.*, June 1, 1833.

[42] The sermon was delivered by the Reverend Philo F. Phelps. *Protestant Magazine*, I (January, 1834), reprinted it in full.

[43] The committee report was presented on May 22. New York *Observer*, May 30, 1835.

[44] *Ibid.*, June 20, 1835.

[45] *Ibid.*, June 20, 1835; *Downfall of Babylon*, July 4, 1835; *American Protestant Vindicator*, June 17, 1835.

[46] Bishop Hughes, in a letter to Bishop Purcell, January 2, 1837, reported that Breckinridge was trying to effect a reconciliation for this purpose. Hughes commented on the fact that while the Presbyterians were thus engaged, the attacks on Catholicism had materially lessened. Hassard, *Life of John Hughes*, 172–173.

[47] Thus the Synod of Philadelphia, in its 1837 meeting, listened to a sermon on "The Dangers of Education in Roman Catholic Seminaries" in which it was stated that the Papists sought to gain control of the United States through control of schools. Baltimore *Literary and Religious Magazine*, IV (May, 1838). Earlier action by synods had inspired the General Assembly to adopt its aggressive policy toward Catholicism, particularly the Indiana Synod which in 1832 had named a committee to investigate Popery and the Philadelphia Synod which in 1833 had adopted a series of resolutions against Romanism. *Protestant Magazine*, I (January, 1834), I (June, 1834); *Christian Watchman*, May 25, 1832; *American Protestant Vindicator*, August 27, 1834, December 28, 1836; *The Protestant*, June 4, 1831, October 29, 1831, April 21, 1832, June 9, 1832; *Protestant Banner*, April 6, 1843.

[48] New York *Observer*, June 12, 1841.

[49] *American Protestant Vindicator*, June 9, 1841.

[50] The reports of the various presbyteries at the next session of the Assembly indicated that this practice was general. New York *Observer*, May 28, 1842.

[51] Breckinridge's sermon was on the Rule of Faith. New York *Observer*, May 28, 1842. It was printed in full in the *Spirit of the XIX Century*, I (July, 1842). In 1843 the sermon was delivered by another leading nativist, the Reverend N. L. Rice of Cincinnati. New York *Observer*, June 3, 1843.

[52] *Ibid.*, May 31, 1845, June 7, 1845; *Protestant Banner*, April 22, 1842; *United States Catholic Magazine*, V (February, 1846), 114.

[53] In 1830 an attempt had been made in the General Conference to delete

the term "Catholic Church," from the creed. This had failed, but had led to a definition of the term as meaning "the church of God in general." *Journals of the General Conference of the Methodist Episcopal Church*, I, 434, 450–479. Four years later, in 1834, a similar anti-Catholic sentiment had been expressed when the conference agreed to establish religious magazines in the west, largely to offset Catholic influences there. *Ibid.*, II, 53–54.

[54] *Ibid.*, II, 167-169.

[55] The addresses of the Conference to the Wesley Methodist Conference in England and to the Evangelical Association, both adopted early in the session, spoke joyfully of the coming conflict with Rome. *Ibid.*, II, 175, 181–184.

[56] Action was taken by the Maine and Massachusetts associations. *The Protestant*, July 31, 1830, August 14, 1830.

[57] Andrew Reed and James Matherson, *A Narrative of the Visit to the American Churches by the Deputation from the Congregational Union of England and Wales* (London, 1835), II, 77–80. In the speeches which the delegates gave on leaving the United States they again urged the necessity of being constantly on guard against Catholic aggression. *Christian Watchman*, September 26, 1834.

[58] New York *Observer*, July 5, 1834.

[59] *Minutes of the General Association of Massachusetts* (Boston, 1842), 19.

[60] *Ibid.*, 10; *Minutes of the General Association of Massachusetts* (Boston, 1843), 13. A committee was named in 1842 but evidently did little, for another was appointed a year later. This consisted of the Reverend William Allen, the Reverend George Allen, and the Reverend B. B. Edwards.

[61] William Allen, *Report on Popery Accepted by the General Association of Massachusetts, June, 1844* (Boston, 1844), 10.

[62] *Ibid.*, 28.

[63] *Minutes of the General Association of Massachusetts* (Boston, 1844), 7; New York *Observer*, July 6, 1844.

[64] Sweet, *Story of Religions in America*, 383-385.

[65] *Watchman of the South*, July 11, 1839; New York *Observer*, December 28, 1839 and ff; *American Protestant Vindicator*, April 28, 1841; Baltimore *Literary and Religious Magazine*, VII (May, 1841); *New Englander*, II (January, 1844), 143–147; *Christian Watchman*, September 16, 1842, January 20, 1843; *Protestant Banner*, January 28, 1842; *Western Christian Advocate*, April 10, 1835. Several books were published to show that Oxfordism and Romanism were the same, among which may be mentioned: Thomas Smyth, *The Prelatical Doctrine of Apostolic Succession Examined, and the Protestant Ministry Defended Against the Assumptions of Popery and High Churchism* (Boston, 1841); Thomas Smyth, *Ecclesiastical Republicanism; or, the Republicanism, Liberality and Catholicity of Presbytery in Contrast with Prelacy and Popery* (New York, 1842); Henry Anthon, *The True Churchman Warned Against the Errors of the Time* (New York, 1843).

[66] New York *Observer*, July 24, 1841. The letter was printed in the *Spirit of the XIX Century*, I (November, 1842).

[67] Typical charges to the clergy of different dioceses on this subject were: Thomas C. Brownell, *Errors of the Times; A Charge Delivered to the Clergy of the Diocese of Connecticut at the Annual Convention Holden in Christ Church in the City of Hartford, June 13, 1843* (Hartford, 1843); Charles P.

McIlvaine, *The Chief Dangers of the Church in these Times: A Charge Delivered to the Clergy of the Diocese of Ohio at the Twenty Sixth Annual Convention of the Same, Gambier, September 8, 1843* (New York, 1843).

⁶⁸ *American Protestant Vindicator*, June 23, 1841. The convention went on record as denouncing the Oxford tracts as "Popery in disguise." New York *Observer*, June 12, 1841.

⁶⁹ The Bishops of the church in 1844 addressed a letter to all seminaries, asking what was being taught "concerning the heretical character of the Roman Church." *Freeman's Journal*, November 23, 1844.

⁷⁰ J. H. Hopkins, *The Novelties Which Disturb Our Peace: Four Letters Addressed to the Bishops, Clergy and Laity of the Protestant Episcopal Church in the United States* (Philadelphia, 1844); *Lecture on the British Reformation* (Boston, 1844); *An Humble Address to the Bishops, Clergy and Laity of the Protestant Episcopal Church in the United States, on Tolerating Among Our Ministry of the Doctrines of the Church of Rome* (n.d., n.p.). Hopkins also challenged Bishop Hughes to a public discussion of the issues involved. *Freeman's Journal*, February 4, 1843.

⁷¹ Alexander Griswold, *The Reformation; A Brief Exposition of Some of the Errors and Corruptions of the Church of Rome* (Boston, 1843). This work was chiefly concerned with showing the vast gulf which separated Christianity from Romanism.

⁷² Boardman's denunciation of Oxfordism was answered by Bishop George W. Doane of New Jersey, one of the few prominent defenders of Newman. New York *Observer*, March 27, 1841. Doane's views were best expressed in a larger work, *Puseyism, No Popery* (Boston, 1843).

⁷³ William L. Whittingham, *A Letter to the Right Reverend Francis Patrick Kenrick* (New York, 1841), 11. Whittingham was Bishop of Maryland.

⁷⁴ Division was averted largely through the efforts of William A. Muhlenberg, who called himself an Evangelical Catholic, and strove constantly for a reconciliation of the opposing factions. The conflict is well described in Sweet, *Story of Religions in America*, 385.

⁷⁵ *The Protestant*, June 4, 1831; *Christian Watchman*, June 9, 1837, July 28, 1837, June 7, 1839, September 15, 1843.

⁷⁶ *American Protestant Almanac for the Year of Our Lord 1841* (New York, 1841), 7.

⁷⁷ *The Acts and Proceedings of the General Synod of the Reformed Protestant Dutch Church in North America convened at Kingston, New York, June, 1848* (New York, 1848), 60. Earlier anti-Catholic sentiments had been expressed by the official organ of the church, the *Magazine of the Reformed Dutch Church*, II (August, 1827), II (September, 1827), II (October, 1827), II (December, 1827).

⁷⁸ *American Protestant Vindicator*, January 25, 1837. In 1837 the Lutheran Synod of South Carolina heard an anti-Catholic sermon delivered by the Reverend John Bachman. England, *The Works of John England*, I, 58–79. Bachman's sermon was answered by England through the columns of the *United States Catholic Miscellany*. His answer is in *Ibid.*, I, 79–228.

⁷⁹ Schmucker, *Discourse in Commemoration of the Glorious Reformation*, iii. The resolution recommended that "a discourse on the Reformation be annually delivered by each member of the Synod before the people of his

charge, and . . . that one should annually be delivered before the Synod, on the same topic."

80 Schmucker's sermon was printed in book form under the title, *Discourse in Commemoration of the Glorious Reformation of the Sixteenth Century* and was entirely anti-Catholic.

81 *American Protestant Vindicator,* June 24, 1840.

82 *Lutheran Observer,* quoted in the *National Protestant,* I (February, 1845). The editor stated that if any subscribers objected, he would lay down his pen, for he felt it his duty to battle the Old Man of Sin.

83 Thus in Pennsylvania, Nicholas Murray, then a student at the Princeton Theological Seminary, helped organize the local branch of the society and insisted that one of its first publications should be *The History of Andrew Dunn,* an anti-Catholic work which had been circulated in England and Ireland. Nicholas Murray, *Memoirs* (New York, 1862), 99.

84 Among the anti-Catholic books and pamphlets published by the society were: *The History of Andrew Dunn* (1835) ; W. Nevins, *Thoughts on Popery* (1836) ; *Tracts on Romanism* (1836); *Roman Catholic Female Schools* (1837) ; *On Purgatory and Infallibility* (1839) ; *False Claims of the Pope* (1842) ; Austin Dickinson, *Thoughts for Catholics and Their Friends* (1844) ; *Destruction of the Inquisition at Madrid* (1844) ; Merle D'Aubigne, *History of the Great Reformation,* 3 vols. (1844) ; Mrs. Austin Dickinson, *The Mother of Saint Augustine* (1845) ; Isaac Orchard, *Friendly Suggestions to an Emigrant by an Emigrant* (1845) ; *The Conversion of Luther* (in German, 1845) ; *The Reformation in Europe* (1845) ; *The Spirit of Popery* (1844). All of the works were published in New York. American Tract Society, *Annual Reports,* 1835–1846. The Society also recommended a model Christian library which should be in every school, including such anti-Catholic works as Nevins, *Thoughts on Popery.* New York *Observer,* May 23, 1840.

85 The sermon was delivered by the Reverend E. N. Kirk. American Tract Society, *Twenty-eighth Annual Report* (Boston, 1842), 10–12 ; *Ibid., Twenty-ninth Annual Report* (Boston, 1843), 4. The nature of the system was indicated when the society named a converted Romanist as its first colporteur. *Ibid.,* 47.

86 *Ibid.,* 47. The society included in its report for 1843 a long list of conversions from Popery. *Ibid.,* 48–51. The annual meeting for 1844 adopted a resolution praising the colportage system as "An important means of evangelization . . . for the large and increasing immigrant German and Roman Catholic population." *Ibid., Thirtieth Annual Report* (Boston, 1844), 4.

87 Resolutions were offered and speeches delivered by the Reverend V. D. Johns of Baltimore, the Reverend George B. Cheever and the Reverend L. N. Green. New York *Observer,* May 20, 1843. A similar meeting was held three years later. *Ibid.,* May 23, 1846.

88 *American Protestant Magazine,* I (September, 1845) ; William Hogan, *Auricular Confession and Popish Nunneries* (Boston, 1845), 199–200; Rufus W. Clark, *Popery and the United States, Embracing an Account of Papal Operations in Our Country, with a View of the Dangers Which Threaten Our Institutions* (Boston, 1847), 19.

89 *Christian Watchman,* March 24, 1843.

90 *Address of the Board of Managers of the American Protestant Associa-*

tion, with the Constitution and Organization of the Association (Philadelphia, 1843), 5. The letter was dated November 2, and was signed by twenty-six clergymen, headed by the Reverend C. C. Cuyler and the Reverend H. A. Boardman.

91 *Ibid.,* 6. The meeting was held on November 8.

92 A meeting in which a constitution was adopted and the organization perfected was held on November 22. Ninety-four ministers, representing twelve denominations, signed the constitution. Officers elected at this meeting were headed by the Reverend E. E. Backus as president. *Ibid.,* 6–11. The high church Episcopalians alone refused to have any connection with the association and denounced it through their official organ, *The Churchman. Freeman's Journal,* February 4, 1843.

93 *Address of the Board of Managers of the American Protestant Association,* 7–8. Sections of the constitution were also printed in the New York *Observer,* January 21, 1843; *Christian Watchman,* February 3, 1843. The entire constitution will be found in Appendix A.

94 One hundred thousand copies of this address were circulated. *Protestant Banner,* February 16, 1843.

95 *Address of the Board of Managers of the American Protestant Association,* 19–42.

96 *Protestant Banner,* March 2, 1843; New York *Observer,* March 11, 1843; American Protestant Association, *First Annual Report* (Philadelphia, 1843), 9–10. A similar organization, the Protestant Association of New York, had been launched a short time before but evidently had no connection with the Philadelphia group. *American Protestant Vindicator,* June 11, 1842.

97 The *Protestant Banner* carried weekly notices of the meetings and activities of these associations.

98 American Protestant Association, *First Annual Report,* 5–6.

99 *Ibid.,* 7–8.

100 *Quarterly Review of the American Protestant Association,* I (January, 1844). The decision to start publication was reached by the Board of Managers only a month after the first annual meeting.

101 *Ibid.,* I (January, 1844).

102 The first editor was the Reverend Rufus W. Griswold and the magazine was published by a company headed by Herman Hooker. New York *Observer,* May 11, 1844. In October, 1845, Hooker transferred his interests to William S. Young, who continued the publication. *Quarterly Review of the American Protestant Association,* II (October, 1845). Young almost immediately sold control of the magazine to the *American Protestant Magazine* and after October, 1845 it was merged in this newer publication.

103 *Spirit of the XIX Century,* II (May, 1843).

104 Eight public lectures were held during the first season of the society's existence, with an estimated attendance of ten thousand persons. *Ibid.,* II (May, 1843).

105 The council met at Baltimore in 1843. Quoted in O'Gorman, *History of the Roman Catholic Church,* 344.

106 *Spirit of the XIX Century,* II (May, 1843).

VIII

No-Popery Enters National Politics

1840-1844

AMERICA'S first important outburst of political nativism came in the 1840's. Nurtured by the anti-Catholic propaganda which had been so carefully shaped during the preceding decades, thousands of voters who had been convinced of the papal designs on the country and its Bible were ready to resort to the ballot box for protection. Their demands led to the formation of the first important No-Popery party. Local at first, it gradually grew until it secured control of some states and even threatened to become national in scope.

Two factors were responsible for this outburst of political nativism: one, a hatred of Catholicism bred by the forces of organized No-Popery; the other, a fear of the immigrant, not only as a Catholic, but as a menace to the economic, political, and social structure which Americans had reared with such care in the new world. The anticipated crumbling of tested institutions before the alien onslaught and the challenge of the foreigner to the individual security of natives were as essential to the success of this nativistic party as the propaganda of the Protestant Reformation Society.

Foreign immigration did appear to be mounting in an alarming way. Goaded by increasingly unsatisfactory economic conditions in Germany and Ireland and aided by improved methods of ocean transportation, foreigners entering the United States passed the hundred thousand mark in 1842 and continue to increase with such rapidity that five years later they had more than doubled in number. Between 1830 and 1840 the immigrants amounted to only about 3 per cent of the total population; in the following decade they were nearly 7 per cent.[1] Such a large alien influx would necessarily have caused discontent in a nationalistic country long accustomed to virtual independence from European influences, but in this case dissatisfaction was made even greater by an effective propaganda demonstrating the evils of immigration and pleading for measures to check the spread of those evils. A whole school of writers of the 1830's and 1840's was determined to convince Americans that immigration should be stopped or rigidly regulated.

These propagandists found one of their strongest arguments in the public burden of supporting foreign-born paupers. Many of the aliens were extremely poor. With their meager resources exhausted by the passage across the Atlantic and their bodies ravaged by the miserable conditions on the immigrant vessels, they were unable to support themselves and immediately became objects of public charity.[2] The disproportionately large number of foreign-born in almshouses was repeatedly emphasized by writers who made a conscious effort to depict them as lazy and indolent, content either to accept public charity or beg upon the streets but unwilling to do the necessary hard work which the country required.[3] "The evil," one writer warned, "fungus like, is rapidly growing by what it feeds upon; and it has now so fastened itself upon the whole body of the American people that it hangs a loathsome mass upon every community and corporation throughout our once pure and healthful country. Three-fourths of this pauperism is the result of intemperance, moral depravity and sheer idleness." [4]

There was little doubt in the minds of most propagandists that these paupers were dumped on America's shores by European countries anxious both to be rid of their responsibility, and to undermine the United States.[5] The old world despots, it was said, deliberately planned to dissipate the Republic's resources and disrupt its social structure so that the eventual papal conquest of America could be accomplished more easily. "Republicanism," said one author, "is destined to swallow the whole serpent brood of monarchies, unless it receives its death sting here. War has been tried, and as it failed when the giant was an infant, it would be worse than a forlorn hope now." [6] Nativists explained the large number of criminals among the aliens and the increase in crime since their coming in the same way. America was being made a Botany Bay for the European countries, they believed, both because their countries wanted to drain off their undesirable population and because the lawless elements would further weaken the United States and make easier its conquest.[7]

Social arguments against the immigrants were equally effective, particularly the charge that the alien invasion was lowering the whole moral tone of the community. The lack of respect on the part of foreigners for such an American institution as the Puritan Sabbath was a source of never-ending regret to New Englanders both in New England and in the west.[8] Equally annoying to many was the Irish devotion to whiskey and the German to beer, which aroused the antagonism of temperance advocates everywhere. In many of the larger cities, they complained, most of the grog shops were kept by Irish with the open connivance of their priests.[9] Temperance societies agreed their work was handicapped by the excessive drinking common among Europeans, one officially reporting that this "refuse of European population, has been one of the most formidable obstructions to this cause." [10]

It was natural, in the eyes of nativists, that such a morally dissolute group as the foreigners should breed lawlessness and disorder. In this complaint Americans had some justification, for immigrants did tend to continue the feuds of the old country on the soil of the new. Native citizens began to hear of Orangemen and Ribbonmen and Corkonians; they began to witness street brawls and warfare between the rougher elements of the foreign-born. "Who are the political, street, canal and railroad rioters?" asked one editor. "Foreigners! Men always ready and prepared to enter into any fray, whose object may be to resist the authorities." [11] A wit of the day remarked that while Saint Patrick was the name of an order, Saint Patrick's day "is more associated with the idea of disorder" since the coming of the Irish.[12]

Agitators had some basis for their claims, for rioting covered the country in the wake of the immigrant stream. From the eastern cities it spread west and south and north as alien workmen followed the advancing lines of railroads and canals across the country. In New York and Philadelphia each election after 1834 was the occasion for violent street fighting between rival Irish factions or between natives and foreigners. Bloodshed was common and deaths were not infrequent. In 1834 in New York Irishmen armed with stones and cudgels put the mayor, sheriff, and a posse to flight and terrorized the city.[13] A year later police who tried to quell Irish fighting in the Five Points area were driven back and the turmoil was not ended until a man had been killed.[14] The spring elections of 1842 brought a pitched street battle in New York between Irish and Orangemen aided by native Americans.[15] Minor incidents also precipitated much fighting; in 1835 the beating of a boy by an Irishman called out a mob which required special action by the Common Council before peace could be restored [16] while a few months later a similar period of mob rule followed the attempt of an Irishman to take a horse away from two small boys.[17] An official effort to capture pigs running loose on the streets of New York in 1844 was so successfully resisted by their Irish owners that a period of rioting followed.[18] Boston's Broad Street riot in 1837, growing from a clash between an Irish funeral procession and a native fire company, inaugurated a reign of disorder there, and other eastern cities were little better off.[19]

This same turbulent spirit marked the westward march of the aliens. Foreign-born laborers on the Baltimore and Ohio railroad turned Maryland into a battlefield which called troops from Washington and brought resolutions from the native citizens accusing the rioters of being Catholic "ruffians, and murderers, combined together, under the most solemn ties, to carry into effect such hellish designs as their passions or *prejudices* may prompt them to commit." [20] In 1839 the same state witnessed another pitched battle between Irish and German workers on the Chesapeake and Ohio canal, which ended only when troops shot down ten of the rioters.[21] From Florida, Indiana, Connecticut, and other states came news of disorder and bloodshed among foreign workmen.[22] Irish exuberance was visited not only on their fellow countrymen but frequently was turned upon natives. In Detroit, Irishmen, having imbibed too deeply of both patriotism and whiskey on July 4, 1835, attacked citizens on the principal street of the city until they were disbanded by mobs of natives.[23] A similar incident occurred in upper New York state two years later when a group of Irish began stopping citizens, asking them if they were Catholics or Protestants and beating the Protestants. In Pennsylvania, drunken foreigners attacked and damaged a Lutheran church.[24] More serious troubles, such as the Bread Riots in New York in 1837 and the Slavery Riots in Philadelphia in 1842 were also blamed upon foreigners or foreign influence.[25]

The Germans in the west proved as capable of creating disturbances as the Irish in the east. Bloodshed followed a parade of German military companies in Cincinnati in 1842 when one of the officers of the company killed a small boy who had been annoying him.[26] Louisville had its taste of turmoil when a German paper warned its readers to go to the polls armed during an election in 1844. The warning, translated and printed in the Louisville *Journal*, caused such resentment that the editor was forced to flee from enraged natives, and a period of disorder followed.[27] Rioting in St. Louis during 1840 was responsible for the death of at least one man,[28] and that city as well as others in the middle west witnessed mob rule when anti-Catholic lecturers were attacked by foreign mobs.[29]

This rioting and disorder naturally alarmed many Americans. Their country, long quiet and peaceful, now seemed teeming with violence. Mob rule was displacing the ordinary forces of law wherever the foreigners were centered. Popery and slavery, northern nativists agreed, were responsible for this transition, and most of the people agreed with them. "How is it possible." one writer asked, "that foreign turbulence imported by ship loads, that riot and ignorance in hundreds of thousands of human priest-controlled machines, should suddenly be thrown into our society and not produce here turbulence and excess? Can one throw mud into pure water and not disturb its clearness?" [30] Particularly alarming to many was the fact that in several riots where civil authorities had failed to quell the battling foreigners, priests had accomplished the task easily. This was taken as evidence of the marshaling of immigrants under priestly control so that they would be ready to strike when the time came to overthrow the government.[31]

Nativists were willing to believe that the alien tide had brought not only disorder but political corruption on a scale never before seen in the United States. The immigrants usually voted in a body and normally supported Democratic candidates, a thing which aroused the wrath of Whigs. This clannish method of voting gave rise to the charge that foreigners cast their ballots as they were told to, and the belief was general that Catholic priests were bartering votes for political favors.[32] Both the Whig and Democratic parties were denounced for truckling to aliens by appointing the foreign-born to profitable offices in state and local governments.[33] "The Republican principle is reversed," wrote the editor of one anti-foreign paper. "Instead of officeholders being the servants of the people, they actually lord it over their masters and dictate to them as imperiously as would the Autocrat of all the Russias to his serfborn subjects." [34]

Faulty naturalization laws were responsible for most of the immigrant's political activity, nativists believed. They argued that the five-year probationary period preliminary to naturalization was too short, that it had been fixed by the framers of the government only as a means of pleasing the French and Irish who had aided the United States during the Revolution, and that it was not intended to be permanent. [35] This, they said, was especially the case as so many of the aliens were both so steeped in ignorance that they were unable to comprehend the complicated political system of the United States and unwilling to learn because of their despotic upbringing. [36] "It would be necessary to un-educate them," one writer said, "and then to re-educate them before they could be fitted intellectually and morally to perform the solemn and responsible duties which devolve upon an American Citizen." [37] If the probationary period could be lengthened, foreigners would be properly educated before assuming the duties of citizenship and the frauds attendant on voting would be lessened. [38] This plea of propagandists for a longer period before naturalization was to be taken up by the nativistic parties and made the basis of their platforms.

Probably the most effective argument against the immigrant was the charge that foreign-born workers were depriving Americans of jobs, or, through competition, lowering the wage scale in American industries. Until 1837 these claims had no basis, for the United States was a land of limitless opportunity with work enough for all, but with the panic of that year the situation changed, and as industry struggled toward recovery during the following years, nativists more and more took the opportunity to excite native workmen against immigrant competitors. [39] One newspaper summed up the prevailing view of a large portion of the working class when it said:

Our laboring men, native and naturalized, are met at every turn and every avenue of employment, with recently imported workmen from the low wages countries of the old world. Our public improvements, railroads, and canals are thronged with foreigners. They fill our large cities, reduce the wages of labor, and increase the hardships of the old settler.[40]

The popularization of this belief probably drove many laborers into the nativistic parties which promised them relief from this competition.

The discontent aroused by these propagandists found its political expression in the organization of Native American parties based upon nativistic principles. To Americans who were actually alarmed by the invasion of their country by Catholics and foreigners, this seemed necessary. The Democrats had apparently bartered their birthright for foreign votes; the Whigs, although flirting occasionally with nativistic ideas, had refused to translate these ideas into political action; a third party seemed the only recourse for enemies of Papist and immigrant. The movement toward such a party was spontaneous; communities in the west and south as early as 1839 formed local Native American associations which gradually multiplied in numbers and influence,[41] spurred on by the leadership of the New Orleans Native American Association.[42]

The new party, however, could not hope to get fairly under way until it had invaded the eastern seaboard cities where nativistic propaganda had been most effective. Its growth there was independent of the movement in the west and was due to the prolonged Democratic control of New York and Philadelphia and the favors accorded the foreign-born by that party.[43] To protest this practice a group of disgruntled New York natives organized an American party in June, 1843, which within a few months had attained a city-wide organization and adopted the name, American Republican party.[44] In October, 1843, a newly established nativistic paper, the *American Citizen,* became its official organ,[45] and in the fall elections of that year it astounded all observers by polling more than eight thousand votes.[46] In only five months this lusty new party was making a bid for power.

From that time on, its spread was so rapid that in the spring elections of 1844 American Republican candidates were swept into office in New York and it was clear that the Whigs were to be temporarily eclipsed by this nativistic infant.[47] Jubilant members of the party immediately laid plans for expansion over the rest of the country.[48] This proceeded rapidly under the impetus of the New York success: branches were established in every county of New York state and New Jersey; [49] in May a southern wing was launched at Charleston, South Carolina; and two months later Boston welcomed the organization after a series of No-Popery sermons from nearly all of the city's pulpits had aroused the people.[50] During the fall of 1844 the movement was strengthened in the south and east,[51] and traveling agents began covering the country establishing new units.[52]

The first attempt at combining these local units into a wider organization was made in New York, where an American Republican state convention was called for September, 1844.[53] Divergent views on methods to be employed in the state forced the disruption of this meeting,[54] and the American Republicans faced the fall elections of 1844 with no central organization, even in the state where their strength was greatest. The disaster which many expected in view of this divergence was averted by the national situation which was ideal for the purposes of the nativists. The Whigs, representing the aristocratic elements of society and naturally leaning toward nativism, had nominated Henry Clay for the presidency and Theodore Frelinghuysen for the vice presidency. Frelinghuysen especially, through his long connection with evangelical and Bible associations, was particularly acceptable to the nativists,[55] and Whig politicians in New York, sensing this, set out to secure American Republican backing, promising Whig support for American Republicans in local elections in return for American Republican support for Clay in the national canvass.[56] This presaged success for the nativists and made certain the importance of nativism as an issue along the eastern seaboard.

The campaign was marked by the enthusiasm of American Republican supporters who, visioning victory, were anxious to make their success impressive. Giant mass meetings at which speakers denounced Catholics and foreigners with equal vigor were held in New York and Philadelphia.[57] Every attempt was made to arouse the religious prejudice of voters; in Philadelphia placards were posted throughout the city calling on the Protestant churches to array themselves against Popery by supporting Clay and the local nativistic candidates.[58] Even the official songs of the American Republicans urged:

Then strike up "Hail Columbia!" boys, our free and happy land,
We'll startle knavish partisans and break the Jesuit's band.
We'll snap the reins, spurn party chains and priestly politics
We swear it by our father's graves—our sires of Seventy Six![59]

The success of this form of appeal was shown in the election returns. Although the Whigs failed to carry the country, their political allies, the American Republicans, emerged triumphant in the two local contests where their strength was concentrated. In New York City the nativistic ticket was completely victorious, and in Philadelphia three of the four congressmen chosen were advocates of American ideals.[60] "At the only two points where our principles are understood," boasted an official organ of the party, "we have triumphed by overwhelming majorities. Let us regenerate perfectly the city and county, and then each become a missionary for the next four years to redeem his country from foreign influence."[61]

Encouraged by this success, leaders of the American Republicans decided that they no longer needed to lean on the staff of Whig support and discarded it immediately after the election.[62] They were by this step committed to a more vigorous policy of expansion, for if the party was to attain the success visioned by many of its members, it must have an effective national organization. Pennsylvania members of the party suggested a national convention as the first step in this process,[63] and on July 4, 1845, that convention met at Philadelphia with every state and territory in the union represented. Little actually was accomplished by this assembly; the name of the party was changed from American Republican to Native American, resolutions were adopted denouncing foreigners and Catholics, and an *Address* was issued asking for support.[64] This first national convention of overzealous Americans could do no more, for already the star of nativism was on the wane.[65] New forces which were to bring the eventual eclipse of this nativistic party were at work.

The principles which the American Republican party advocated with such enthusiasm during its brief career showed how thoroughly its members had become imbued with nativistic propaganda. In its public documents the party adhered to three major objectives: (1) to change the naturalization laws in such a way that foreigners would have to dwell in the United States twenty-one years before being naturalized, (2) to restrict authority over naturalization to the federal courts, and (3) to reform the gross abuses arising from party corruption. In addition to these principal aims a number of minor reforms were agitated: a restriction of public officeholding to natives, a continuation of the Bible as a schoolbook, the prevention of all union between church and state, a lessening of the number of street riots and election disorders, a guarantee of the right to "worship the God of our fathers according to the dictates of our own consciences, without the restraints of a Romish priest, or the threats of a Hellish Inquisition."[66]

It was upon the first of the major reforms that members of the party showed most complete agreement. They pointed out that Americans were forced to live in the country twenty-one years before voting and insisted that an equal time should be required of the foreigner, steeped in ignorance and the traditions of despotism.[67] "At this moment," wrote the party managers in New York, "there exists on the continent of Europe, in the heart of its most despotic government, a society protected by the crown of Austria, patronized by the most unflinching supporters of civil and religious despotism . . . for the express purpose of exporting to this country, (free America) the abject slaves of their country, who, bound in fetters of civil and religious serfdom, would be incapable in twice twenty-one years, of understanding the principles of civil and religious freedom which alone fit a man to become an American citizen." [68] Almost equal unanimity of feeling existed for the need of placing only Americans in office, reforming political corruption, and restricting naturalization to the federal courts.[69]

The American Republican party was far less outspoken when dealing with Catholics; its leaders realized they must move cautiously to escape the charge of proscription. Party pronouncements were couched in general phrases planned to give no offense but its leaders could not hide their intolerant attitude toward Rome. They admittedly believed that the Catholic church was grasping for power in America and that if the United States was to be ruled by Americans rather than the Pope, political organization was necessary to oppose this great religious machine.[70] Even the first national convention of the party gave over much of its report to a denunciation of Catholicism without mentioning that church by name,[71] and individual ward meetings, feeling no restraining influence, clearly demonstrated by their outspoken attacks on Rome the important part that No-Popery played in the formation and success of the party.[72]

The legislative program of the American Republican party was based upon this platform. Of necessity, the reforms that it advocated could be secured only through the action of the national government, for most of them concerned naturalization and hence came within the province of the federal government

alone. The party thus found itself in an unfortunate position, being unable to utilize locally its strength in the eastern states and with insufficient power nationally to achieve its ends. Even in New York and Pennsylvania where its supporters were most numerous, attempts to introduce nativistic provisions into new state constitutions being framed at the time failed,[73] but a change in the New York immigration laws, made in 1847 and restricting the importation of pauper immigrants, was due in part to nativistic activity.[74]

Nationally, American Republican representatives had pledged themselves to secure a twenty-one-year probationary period before naturalization, and it was to this end that their principal efforts were directed. The first demand for such a step came from the western states where the people, feeling the influence of the growing American Republican party in 1844, began petitioning Congress to enact such a measure. The House of Representatives was faced with the problem of dealing with these petitions first in May, 1844, and with little hesitation decided to follow the "gag rule" policy which was operating so successfully with antislavery petitions, laying the whole matter on the table rather than referring it to the proper committee.[75] Nativistic indignation at this move was loudly expressed; a mass meeting in Philadelphia attended by fifteen thousand American Republicans agreed to work for the defeat of those who had voted against their claims, and extolled their congressional champions as "possessed of some slight recollections of those principles for which our fathers bled—the good old principles of Saxon liberty—the principles which cost to John, his power—to James, his throne—to Charles, his head—to George, his provinces;—principles which are destined to supply for *both* the vitiated factions which disturb 'the last hope of the free,' their grave and epitaph."[76]

This reaction, and particularly the threat of retaliation, may have had some effect, for many congressmen must have been

uncertain of the political influence which this new and as yet
untested political party could exert. At least they made no further attempt to relegate the flood of similar petitions which followed to the table, but referred them all to the Judiciary committee where they accumulated through 1844.[77] As the months
passed and the volume of demand from petitioners did not di-
minish, Congress reluctantly came to the conclusion that it could
no longer evade the issue. By December, 1844, it was ready to
act, seizing on a resolution submitted by Senator Henry Johnson of Louisiana which called on the Judiciary committee of the
Senate to "inquire into the expediency of modifying the naturalization of [*sic*] laws of the United States, so as to extend the
time allowed to enable foreigners to become citizens; to require
greater guard against fraud in the steps to be taken in procur-
ing naturalization papers; and to prevent, as far as is practicable,
fraud and violence at elections." [78] This sweeping motion, embodying the principal points in the platform of the American
Republicans, was introduced on December 11; five days later
debate in the Senate was begun, after Johnson had amended his
own bill to add the words, "and to prohibit the introduction of
foreign convicts into the United States." [79]

All of the pent-up nativistic feelings, long curbed in the legislature, were loosed in the debate on Johnson's motion. Nevertheless, outspoken as some advocates of the measure might be,
others recognized in the whole controversy an opportunity to
better their political fortunes at little risk. Most of the congressmen who favored the American Republican stand spoke enthusiastically for a reform of abuses in the naturalization system but
avoided, in an obviously deliberate way, any mention of the
twenty-one-year probationary period which was at the very root
of the party's demands. Clearly many senators were willing to
court the favor of this new party if they could do so without
alienating the foreign vote.

Senator Johnson himself set the pattern for the debate on his resolution. He insisted that fraud and corruption had crept into the government through the operation of the existing law, which moreover had by its too liberal features attracted to the United States thousands of ignorant immigrants to compete with American workmen. "This question soars far above party considerations," he said. "It is a question upon which depends, not only the purity of our political institutions, but the preservation of the government itself. All parties . . . are equally interested in guarding against a repetition of the abuses complained of, which, if not prevented in the future, may ultimately destroy our government." [80] Other speakers who followed Johnson imitated his method, most of them painting dismal pictures of election fraud, voting by unnaturalized aliens, and unmitigated corruption at the polls. This support and the general nature of the measure meant that it would have little opposition; when the vote was taken, it was found to have carried easily.[81] The Judiciary committee was thus launched on a probe of the entire naturalization system.

The committee shaped its investigation to conform to the obvious intent of the supporters of the Johnson resolution as disclosed in the debate.[82] From the first it concerned itself not at all with the nativistic demand for a longer period preceding naturalization but confined its probing to an inquiry into voting frauds. This it accomplished well; agents were sent into the leading cities and ports, witnesses were summoned, and the whole election machinery thoroughly raked over.[83] The report which was finally submitted on March 3, 1845, was a damning criticism of the then-existing naturalization process. It showed that fraudulent citizenship papers were being obtained through party manipulation, that judges and court officials were tools of political machines and violated their oaths constantly, and that in many places foreign paupers were marched from the almshouses to the polls by party henchmen. In Louisiana, the committee found, conditions were particularly bad, with foreigners controlling the voting places and refusing to allow native citizens to cast their ballots.[84]

To remedy this corruption, the Judiciary committee recommended the passage of a measure which, although embodying many of the changes insisted upon by the American Republicans, passed over in silence their demand for a twenty-one-year probationary period preceding naturalization. The elaborate machinery that it provided was well suited to end fraud, but despite this the bill was allowed to die in the Senate without further action.[85]

While nativistic champions were seeing their hopes frustrated in the Senate, the House of Representatives was becoming the scene of an even more violent contest in which the American Republican party was actively involved. There an innocent resolution from Massachusetts asking for a change in the naturalization laws, presented in December, 1845, became the center of an extended debate, largely through the efforts of Lewis C. Levin, of Pennsylvania.[86] Actually the sole question at issue was whether the Massachusetts resolution should be referred to a select committee or allowed to die in the Judiciary committee.[87] Yet Levin insisted on pressing the matter to determine the exact strength of the American Republicans in this branch of the legislature and to demonstrate to the nation that this new party was a force to be reckoned with in politics.

That this was the purpose of Levin and other nativistic champions was clearly demonstrated in the debate which lasted from December 17 to December 30, 1845. Levin frankly stated that he represented the American Republican party which would soon have a million voters in its ranks, and that his party wanted the whole question of naturalization brought into the open where honest opinions could be expressed, rather than buried in committee.[88] He believed, he said, that a papal plot was under way to subdue the United States and that this was to be accomplished by the millions of immigrants sent from the despotic countries of the old world to control elections in the new. Congress alone had power to protect the country, through its exclusive control over the alien, and that control should be exercised immediately if the nation was to be saved from Romish domination.[89] This bold statement, while supported by others who held similar views,[90] was in general condemned by later speakers,[91] and in the wave of revulsion which followed it the House agreed without serious division to refer the Massachusetts memorial to the Judiciary committee rather than the select committee which Levin preferred.[92] The native Americans had insisted upon a show of strength and had found their own so slight that not even a roll call was necessary.

After this clear expression of sentiment on the part of the House, the Judiciary committee naturally acted unfavorably upon the Massachusetts resolution. Its report, rendered in February, 1846, reviewed the whole question of naturalization and decided that "no alteration of the naturalization laws is necessary for the preservation of the rights, interests and morals of the people, or from the guarding of the ballot-box against every improper influence." [93] Native American newspapers promptly branded the report as breathing the spirit of Benedict Arnold and a "servile, truckling, pope's-toe-kissing resolution," [94] but the die had been cast. Until the Know-Nothing agitation brought a revival a few years later, nativism as a legislative issue was dead.[95]

The American Republican party, while unable to foster a successful program in Congress or in the states, nevertheless was an important factor in creating antagonism against aliens and Catholics. The speeches of its congressional champions were widely reprinted, and the newspapers and lecturing agents which it sponsored did much to mold public sentiment into channels desired by its leaders. Most of the publications of the party were centered in New York, where leadership was supplied by the New York *American Republican,* a daily paper founded early in 1844. Its success was so immediate that by the fall of that year it boasted a circulation second only to the New York *Sun,* and a weekly edition was being published to satisfy out-of-city readers.[96] The columns of this paper were filled constantly with articles against foreigners and Catholics.

The first party organ of this type in Philadelphia was the *Native American,* upholding, after its first appearance on April 11, 1844, an editorial platform corresponding closely to the platform of the American Republicans whom it represented:

The principles of this Paper are—That Native-born Americans are competent to make and administer their own laws.

That, in framing their institutions, they are not bound to consult the judgment or feelings of the inhabitants of any other portion of the globe.

The EVILS we complain of are—

That the cheap rate at which American privileges are granted has invited to this country the less worthy part of the population of the Old World—and that this population has been used by political demagogues to their own benefit and the detriment of the country.

The REMEDIES we propose are—

To extend the Period of Naturalization—

To elect none but Natives to office—

To reject foreign interference from all our institutions, social, religious and political.[97]

The strenuous defense of this policy by the editors and their frequent attacks on Catholicism attracted sufficient readers by September, 1844, to encourage them to launch a second nativistic publication, the *National American,* for national circulation.[98]

A third type of party organ appeared in 1845 with the founding of the *Native Eagle and American Advocate.* This daily newspaper was designed to attract the working class into the American Republican party; its platform called for the "protection to American labor, by protecting the American laborer," [99] and its editors demanded restrictions on the immigrant as a voter, maintaining that the ease with which aliens were naturalized lured thousands to the United States to compete with American workers.[100] This same view was expressed by many of the other papers which sprang into existence in a number of cities to

capitalize upon the success of the American Republican party.[101]
The constant propaganda which they voiced against immigrants
and Catholics proved effective, particularly among the lower
classes.

National magazines also were founded as party organs for the
American Republicans and furthered the propaganda which the
party was sponsoring. Most prominent among these publications
were the *Metropolitan Magazine and Republican Review* and the
American Republican Magazine, both founded in New York in
1844.[102] Each contained news of the party and articles attacking
Catholicism and foreign immigration.

These propaganda forces created by American Republican
success were a new and powerful influence in the advance of nativism. The party's publication and lecturing agents,[103] added to
those already sponsored by the anti-Catholic societies, appealed
particularly to eastern workers who were always ready to believe
that immigrant laborers would prove dangerous competitors.
Stemming from this new source and nurtured in the carefully
fostered intolerance which had been instilled into Americans for
two decades, organized nativism by the middle 1840's seemed
destined to flourish unchecked upon American soil.

NOTES

[1] The total number of arrivals officially recorded in 1842 was 104,565 and in
1847, 234,968. It was realized at the time that these official estimates were
approximately fifty per cent below the actual number of arrivals. J. C. G.
Kennedy, *Preliminary Report on the Eighth Census* (Washington, 1862), 13–
14; J. D. B. DeBow, *Statistical View of the United States, Embracing its Territory, Population—White, Colored and Slave—Moral and Social Condition,
Industry, Property and Revenue; the Detailed Statistics of Cities, Towns, and
Counties; being a Compendium of the Seventh Census* (Washington, 1854),
122.

[2] The conditions on immigrant ships at this time were unbelievably bad.
Owners sold their excess ship space to agents whose only interest was to fill
it with as many passengers as possible. The immigrants were crowded together into unsanitary quarters for voyages of six weeks or more and were
peculiarly susceptible to the ravages of disease. The conditions are well described in Kapp, *Immigration and the Commissioners of Emigration,* 19–43.

[3] *Downfall of Babylon*, January 7, 1835, June 27, 1835, June 11, 1836; *Christian Watchman*, May 15, 1840; *Massachusetts Yeoman*, July 9, 1831; *Niles' Register*, XLIX (September 26, 1835), 62; *Spirit of '76*, October 1, 1835; New York *Observer*, April 18, 1835, December 7, 1839, November 27, 1841, October 28, 1842; New York *American Republican*, July 23, 1844, July 26, 1844; *Native American*, April 26, 1844; Baltimore *Literary and Religious Magazine*, IV (September, 1838); Morse, *Foreign Conspiracy*, 141–142; Beecher, *Plea for the West*, 54; *The Crisis*, 25–30.

[4] *The Crisis*, 31.

[5] New York *Observer*, December 7, 1839, January 4, 1845; New York *American Republican*, June 25, 1844; New Orleans *Native American*, quoted in *Ibid.*, October 3, 1844; *Native Eagle*, December 3, 1845; *Native American*, April 24, 1844, August 3, 1844, August 9, 1844, August 13, 1844, October 29, 1844; *The Crisis*, 3–4, 6, 24, 32, 34, 44.

[6] New York *American Republican*, May 31, 1844.

[7] *National Protestant*, I (February, 1845); *The Crisis*, 43.

[8] New York *Observer*, August 30, 1828; *The Protestant*, December 18, 1830; *Downfall of Babylon*, December 27, 1834, January 3, 1835, January 17, 1835, February 14, 1835, July 11, 1835, March 6, 1836; New York *Evangelist*, quoted in *Freeman's Journal*, November 27, 1844; Baxter, *Jesuit Juggling*, XV–XVI. The *Christian Watchman* also complained that public "pugilistic combats" were engaged in and attended largely by foreigners. *Christian Watchman*, September 23, 1842.

[9] *Protestant Magazine*, I (May, 1834); *Downfall of Babylon*, June 25, 1836. Nativistic editors were placed in a quandary with the arrival in the United States in the early 1840's of Father Mathew, an Irish priest who devoted himself to temperance reform among his own people with considerable success. As religious men, they were universally supporting temperance, yet it was against their principles to admit that a priest could do anything that was praiseworthy. Some editors welcomed Father Mathew and even went so far as to say that he had more chance of getting into Heaven than the Pope and all his cardinals. New York *American Republican*, May 27, 1844. Others saw in his efforts only another popish plot to collect money for the advancement of Catholicism or to unite all Catholics in temperance societies which would really be military organizations making ready for the conquest of America. Baltimore *Literary and Religious Magazine*, VI (December, 1840), VII (May, 1841); *Spirit of the XIX Century*, I (May, 1842); *Christian Watchman*, June 19, 1840; *Congregationalist*, July 20, 1849.

[10] The New York Temperance Society so resolved. New York *Observer*, May 8, 1841. See also *Ibid.*, May 19, 1838, June 11, 1842. Actually the immigrant press constantly advocated temperance and many a Saint Patrick's day toast was drunk in cold water under this influence. *Freeman's Journal*, July 2, 1842 and ff.

[11] *Native American*, September 17, 1844.

[12] George A. O'Beckett, *The Comic Blackstone* (Philadelphia, 1844).

[13] New York *Observer*, April 19, 1834; *Protestant Magazine*, I (May, 1834).

[14] New York *Observer*, June 27, 1835; *Downfall of Babylon*, July 4, 1835, July 11, 1835.

[15] McMaster, *History of the People of the United States*, VII, 373.

[16] New York *Observer*, June 27, 1835.

[17] *Spirit of '76*, September 25, 1835.

[18] New York *American Republican*, September 4, 1844.

[19] *Niles' Register*, XLVI (June 24, 1834); *Massachusetts Spy*, June 14–July 12, 1837; *Freeman's Journal*, August 3, 1844, August 10, 1844, July 27, 1844.

[20] *Downfall of Babylon*, December 27, 1834; New York *Observer*, December 6, 1834.

[21] New York *Observer*, August 31, 1839, September 7, 1839, November 2, 1839.

[22] *Ibid.*, September 5, 1835, January 23, 1836; *Native American*, September 30, 1844.

[23] New York *Observer*, July 25, 1835; *Downfall of Babylon*, August 1, 1835.

[24] *American Protestant Vindicator*, September 6, 1837; *Native American*, August 27, 1844; *Freeman's Journal*, August 31, 1844.

[25] *Protestant Banner*, August 19, 1842.

[26] New York *Observer*, August 20, 1842; *Freeman's Journal*, August 20, 1842.

[27] Arthur C. Cole, "Nativism in the Lower Mississippi Valley," Mississippi Valley Historical Association *Proceedings*, VI (1912–1913), 265.

[28] New York *Observer*, October 3, 1840.

[29] *Native Eagle*, April 14, 1846; *Native American*, April 11, 1844.

[30] Morse, *Imminent Dangers*, Introduction.

[31] New York *Observer*, December 27, 1834; *Downfall of Babylon*, October 20, 1834; Beecher, *Plea for the West*, 93.

[32] *Protestant Magazine*, I (December, 1833); *Spirit of '76*, July 29, 1835, October 6, 1835; *American Protestant Vindicator*, April 20, 1836, December 23, 1840; *Christian Watchman*, April 24, 1835; New York *Observer*, November 12, 1836, December 13, 1834, January 16, 1841, October 16, 1841, February 11, 1843, April 27, 1844; New York *American Republican*, April 25, 1844, May 2, 1844; *Native American*, May 22, 1844, October 21, 1844; *The Crisis*, 13; *The Trial of the Pope of Rome, the Anti-Christ or Man of Sin Described in the Bible, for High Treason against the Son of God. Tried at the Sessions House of Truth before the Right Hon. Divine Revelation, the Hon. Justice Reason and the Hon. Justice History. Taken in Short Hand by a Friend to Saint Peter* (Boston, 1844), 164.

[33] *Native Eagle*, December 19, 1846; *Native American*, May 18, 1844, May 24, 1844, October 3, 1844; *The Crisis*, 9, 12, 24.

[34] *Native American*, August 19, 1844.

[35] *Native American*, July 9, 1844.

[36] *Ibid.*, July 17, 1844, July 29, 1844; *The Crisis*, 7–8, 35–37.

[37] New York *American Republican*, April 26, 1844. Even Daniel Webster endorsed these sentiments in a speech in Boston following the Whig defeat in 1844, a defeat which he laid at the door of foreign-born voters. *Native American*, November 12, 1844. He was answered by the Catholic champion, Brownson. O. A. Brownson, *Works* (Detroit, 1882–1887), X, 17 ff.

[38] There was much actual fraud in the naturalization process at this time and reaction against this accounts for much of the support given nativists. See

Senate Documents, 25th Cong., 2nd Sess., No. 173. In New York Governor Seward devoted a special message to the legislature to the subject. Seward, *Works,* II, 395–404. Conditions, bad as they were, were exaggerated in the nativistic press. *Native American,* April 11, 1844, April 17, 1844; New York *American Republican,* May 3, 1844; *The Crisis,* 41–44.

³⁹ *Native American,* June 4, 1844, June 21, 1844, June 24, 1844, November 13, 1844; *The Crisis,* 18–22, 54–56.

⁴⁰ *Native American,* November 29, 1844.

⁴¹ John Bach McMaster, *With the Fathers* (New York, 1896), 94–95.

⁴² *Address of the Louisiana Native American Association, passim.*

⁴³ New York *Journal of Commerce,* October 23, 1843. Democratic favor was expressed by granting market licenses and petty offices to foreigners.

⁴⁴ Anna E. Carroll, *The Great American Battle; or, The Contest between Christianity and Political Romanism* (New York, 1856), 264. According to the story told by Miss Carroll, a group of sympathizers with nativism happened to meet in a blacksmith's shop and there decided to form a new party.

⁴⁵ New York *Journal of Commerce,* November 3, 1843.

⁴⁶ *Ibid.,* November 22, 1843. The total vote in this election was as follows:

Democratic party	14,410 votes
Whig party	14,000 "
American Republican party	8,690 "
Walsh Democrats	320 "
Antislavery party	70 "

⁴⁷ The American Republican candidate, James Harper, of the firm of publishers bearing his name, was elected mayor by the following vote:

American Republican party	24,509 votes
Democratic party	20,538 "
Whig party	5,297 "

A comparison of this vote with that in the fall elections of 1843 in footnote 46, *ante,* shows that nearly all of the nativists' strength came from the Whigs, the Democratic vote remaining about the same in both elections. New York *American Republican,* April 26, 1844.

⁴⁸ *Address to the People of the State of New York by the General Executive Committee of the American Republican Party of the City of New York* (New York, 1844), 8.

⁴⁹ New York *American Republican,* June 26, 1844. The party had been established in Philadelphia in December, 1843, aided by the political situation in that city at the time. Irish voters had attempted to rebuke the Democratic party by deserting it in 1842 and returning in 1843. This demonstration of the strength of the Irish vote, causing defeat for the Democrats when they were out of the party, led to considerable nativistic excitement. *Native American,* April 25, 1844; Lee, *The Origin and Progress of the American Party in Politics,* 17.

⁵⁰ New York *Observer,* February 8, 1845. A native American association had existed there since the fall of 1844. *Freeman's Journal,* August 3, 1844.

⁵¹ By this time the party had been established in Virginia, Maryland, Georgia and Mississippi, as well as in such eastern cities as Washington, Pitts-

burgh, Buffalo, Rochester, Utica and Albany. New York *American Republican*, October 9, 1844; *Native American*, August 24, 1844; *National Protestant*, I (December, 1844).

52 New York *American Republican*, October 9, 1844.

53 *Address to the People of the State of New York by the General Executive Committee of the American Republican Party of the City of New York*, 8. The convention was called to meet at Utica on September 10.

54 New York *American Republican*, September 24, 1844.

55 *Ibid.*, September 2, 1844, October 14, 1844.

56 Scisco, *Political Nativism in New York State*, 49.

57 New York *American Republican*, September 26, 1844, October 2, 1844, October 5, 1844, October 14, 1844; *Native American*, October 1, 1844.

58 *Native American*, October 8, 1814. The papal plot to subdue America was a popular theme for party speakers at this time. George P. Gifford, *An Address . . . before the Bunker Hill Native ·American Association in the Town Hall, Charlestown*, September 17, 1844 (Charlestown, 1844), 1–12. The efforts of Catholics to drive the Bible from the public schools was also a prominent theme for writers of campaign literature. *An Honest Appeal to Every Voter; the Bible in the Schools* (New York, 1844), 1–16.

59 P. de LeRee, *The American Republican Songster* (New York, 1843), 3–5.

60 *Native American*, October 9, 1844; Scisco, *Political Nativism in New York State*, 50–51.

61 *Native American*, November 4, 1844.

62 Scisco, *Political Nativism in New York State*, 52.

63 *Proceedings of the Native American State Convention held at Harrisburg*, February 22, 1845 (Philadelphia, 1845), 3.

64 *Address of the Delegates of the Native American National Convention, Assembled at Philadelphia, July 4, 1845, to the Citizens of the United States* (Philadelphia, 1845).

65 A second national convention was held in 1847 which adopted resolutions similar to those adopted two years before and endorsed Zachary Taylor, the Whig candidate, as the presidential choice of the party. Carl F. Brand, "History of the Know Nothing Party in Indiana," *Indiana Magazine of History*, XVIII (1922), 49–50.

66 *An Honest Appeal to Every Voter; the Bible in the Schools*, 16.

67 *Address to the People of the State of New York*, 3–7; *Address of the American Republicans of Charleston, South Carolina*, printed in the New York *American Republican*, September 24, 1844; *Address of the Executive Committee of the American Republicans of Boston to the People of Massachusetts* (Boston, 1845), 13; New York *American Republican*, April 25, 1844, September 6, 1844.

68 *Address of the Executive Committee of New York City*, printed in New York *American Republican*, April 26, 1844.

69 *Address to the People of the State of New York*, 6–7; *Address of the Executive Committee of the American Republican Party of Boston*, 14; *Address of the Louisiana State Native American Convention*, printed in the *National Protestant*, I (January, 1845); New York *American Republican*, August 6, 1844.

[70] *Proceedings of the Native American State Convention held at Harrisburg,* 11–13; *Address to the People of the State of New York,* 5–6; *Address of the Executive Committee of the American Republican Party of Boston,* 10–11.

[71] *Address of the Delegates of the Native American National Convention, passim.*

[72] New York *Observer,* April 13, 1844, August 24, 1844; New York *American Republican,* April 24, 1844, June 1, 1844, September 6, 1844; *Native American,* May 1, 1844, August 7, 1844; *Native Eagle,* December 9, 1845, July 15, 1846. This feeling among members of the party was so strong that one of the leading Catholics of the day, Orestes Brownson, believed that the whole movement was aimed at Catholicism and that its other phases were merely attempts to disguise this fundamental issue. H. F. Brownson, *Life of O. A. Brownson* (Detroit, 1898-1900), II, 107. This view must be discounted, but it is probable that anti-Catholicism was the most powerful single factor in driving members into the party.

[73] McMaster, *History of the People of the United States,* VII, 370; *Native Eagle,* July 22, 1846. Attempts were made to insert a clause restricting office-holding to the native-born into the Pennsylvania constitution in 1841, and confining the governorship to a native in the New York constitution of 1846.

[74] The New York law was changed as the result of an investigation begun in 1842 which disclosed frequent abuse and fraud in the system then in operation. The new law forced ship captains to pay one dollar head tax on each alien brought into the country in addition to posting a bond of $300 to be forfeited if the alien became a public charge, and created an Immigration Commission to supervise the whole matter. This was one of the acts held unconstitutional in the Passenger Cases in 1849. Kapp, *Immigration and the Commissioners of Emigration,* 59-60; Fairchild, *Immigration,* 80-81.

[75] *Congressional Globe,* 28th Cong., 1st Sess., 674. The motion to lay the memorial on the table rather than refer it to the Judiciary committee was made by William H. Hammett, and was carried by a vote of 128 to 26.

[76] *Native American,* June 6, 1844, June 8, 1844, June 13, 1844. The meeting was held in front of the State House in Philadelphia on June 7.

[77] Many of the petitions were introduced by Senator W. S. Archer who constantly favored immediate action. On June 7, 1844 he presented a memorial from the citizens of Philadelphia in this way. *Congressional Globe,* 28th Cong., 1st Sess., 694. On June 11 he introduced eleven more petitions and his speech in favor of them was answered by Senator James Buchanan of Pennsylvania and Senator William Allen of Ohio. *Ibid.,* 28th Cong., 1st Sess., 704-705. Others who introduced the memorials commonly stated that they had little sympathy with the objects of the petitioners. Thus on June 1, 1844, Senator James Buchanan introduced a petition from the citizens of Philadelphia, *Ibid.,* 28th Cong., 1st Sess., 675–676; on June 3 he presented a similar petition, *Ibid.,* 28th Cong., 1st Sess., 677; on June 5 E. J. Morris of Pennsylvania presented eight petitions in the House, *Ibid.,* 28th Cong., 1st Sess., 690; on June 6 Senator D. W. Sturgeon of Pennsylvania presented a memorial from citizens of that state, *Ibid.,* 28th Cong., 1st Sess., 690; and on June 7 offered another similar petition, *Ibid.,* 28th Cong., 1st Sess., 694; on June 8 Senator Buchanan presented five more, all from Philadelphia. *Ibid.,* 28th Cong., 1st Sess.,

607; on June 13 Senator Rufus Choate of Massachusetts presented three memorials from Pennsylvania citizens, *Ibid.,* 28th Cong., 1st Sess., 718; on June 14 similar memorials were introduced by Senator Thomas Benton of Missouri and Senator Buchanan, *Ibid.,* 28th Cong. 1st Sess., 727; on June 15 Senator E. H. Foster of Tennessee presented one memorial and Senator Archer of Virginia three more, all from Pennsylvania, *Ibid.,* 28th Cong., 1st Sess., 736; on the same day a similar memorial was offered in the House, *Ibid.,* 28th Cong., 1st Sess., 742; on December 10, J. R. Ingersoll of Pennsylvania presented a petition from his native state and asked that it be referred to a select committee of nine, a request that was refused by the House, the memorial going instead to the Judiciary committee, *Ibid.,* 28th Cong., 2nd Sess., 18.

78 *Ibid.,* 28th Cong., 2nd Sess., 19.

79 *Ibid.,* 28th Cong., 2nd Sess., 32.

80 *Ibid.,* 28th Cong., 2nd Sess., 32.

81 *Ibid.,* 28th Cong., 2nd Sess., 33.

82 A resolution submitted by Senator Alexander Barrow of Louisiana and passed on December 17, 1844, further stressed the necessity of investigating this phase of the question. *Ibid.,* 28th Cong., 2nd Sess., 38.

83 A resolution adopted by the Senate on December 26, 1844, authorized the Judiciary committee to take testimony through commissioners. *Ibid.,* 28th Cong., 2nd Sess., 67. Agents were sent to New York, Philadelphia, Baltimore and New Orleans. *Ibid.,* 28th Cong., 2nd Sess., 303. Petitions were presented all through the period in which the committee was deliberating, approving its work, and recommending a thorough investigation. See *Ibid.,* 28th Cong., 2nd Sess., 37, 38, 67, 303.

84 *Senate Documents,* 28th Cong., 2nd Sess., No. 173.

85 *Ibid.,* 28th Cong., 2nd Sess., No. 173, 198–202. The proposed law received the universal commendation of the nativistic press. *Native Eagle,* December 12, 1845.

86 These resolutions were generally worded and made no specific suggestions for change, other than that laws be passed which would end the existing corruption. *Ibid.,* 29th Cong., 1st Sess., 52, 67.

87 The House Judiciary committee had shown its attitude in January, 1845 when it reported unfavorably on several petitions to introduce the twenty-one-year naturalization period. *Reports of Committees,* 28th Cong., 2nd Sess., No. 87, 1–6. The committee had reported favorably on a bill similar to the Senate measure to end fraud in naturalization. *Congressional Globe,* 28th Cong., 2nd Sess., 224. For full reports of the speeches on this measure and the measure itself see *Ibid.,* 28th Cong., 2nd Sess., Appendix, 192–231.

88 *Ibid.,* 29th Cong., 1st Sess., 68. Levin was to remain a legislative champion of nativism through the whole period preceding the Civil War. Despite his convictions, his wife was converted to Catholicism ten years before her death in 1881, and his son also became a Catholic. *American Catholic Historical Researches,* VII (April, 1911), 189.

89 Levin's speech was printed in full in the *Congressional Globe,* 29th Cong., 1st Sess., Appendix, 6–50.

90 These included Robert C. Winthrop of Massachusetts, William Campbell of New York, Thomas M. Woodruff of New York, William Yancey of Alabama, Robert Dale Owen of Indiana, Robert J. Ingersoll of Pennsylvania,

and Washington Hunt of New York. *Congressional Globe,* 29th Cong., 1st Sess., 69–74, 105–107.

⁹¹ Those who spoke against the Levin proposal included Richard Bradhead and Cornelius Dorough of Pennsylvania, William B. Maclay of New York, William W. Payne of Alabama, Leonard H. Simms of Missouri, Alexander B. Sims of South Carolina, Henry Bedinger of Virginia, James Dixon of Connecticut, and Stephen A. Douglas of Illinois. *Ibid.,* 29th Cong., 1st Sess., 69–74, 113–118.

⁹² *Ibid.,* 29th Cong., 1st Sess., 118.

⁹³ *Ibid.,* 29th Cong., 1st Sess., 353.

⁹⁴ *Native Eagle,* February 16, 1846, March 2, 1846. The Catholic press heartily opposed any changes in the existing law, thus demonstrating to nativists the connection between Popery and immigration. *Freeman's Journal,* October 5, 1844, December 21, 1844, January 4, 1845.

⁹⁵ Levin, who remained in Congress for some years, made several attempts to revive the nativistic issue on minor questions but without success. Thus in 1846 he tried to secure passage of a measure restricting enlistments in a company being raised for the Mexican War to native-born Americans, but his suggestion was promptly rejected by Congress. *Congressional Globe,* 29th Cong., 1st Sess., 605–609, 655, 832.

⁹⁶ New York *American Republican,* August 19, 1844. An earlier paper of the same type, the *American Citizen,* had been established in 1843. New York *Journal of Commerce,* November 4, 1843.

⁹⁷ *Native American,* April 11, 1844.

⁹⁸ *Ibid.,* September 19, 1844. The editor of the new publication was Hector Orr, a well-known nativistic editor and writer.

⁹⁹ *Native Eagle,* December 1, 1845.

¹⁰⁰ *Ibid.,* December 1, 1845.

¹⁰¹ Among the definitely native American papers established at this time were the following: *The American Ensign* (Philadelphia); *The Weekly American Ensign* (Philadelphia); *The American Republican* (Boston); *The Daily American* (Jeffersonville, Indiana); the Lancaster *American Republican* (Lancaster, Pennsylvania); *The Native* (Harrisburg, Pennsylvania); and *The Pennant and Native American* (St. Louis), all founded in 1844. In the next year the following papers were added: *The Weekly Eagle and Advocate* (Philadelphia); *The American* (New York); the New York *American Sentinel* (New York); the Pittsburgh *American Eagle* (Pittsburgh); *The American Citizen* (Cincinnati); *The American* (Poughkeepsie); and the Harrisburg *Statesman and Native American Advocate* (Harrisburg, Pennsylvania). In 1846 new papers founded were: *The American Press and Republican* (Lancaster, Pennsylvania); the Ann Arbor *American* (Ann Arbor, Michigan); *The American Vineyard* (Detroit, Michigan); the Worcester *Native American* (Worcester, Massachusetts); *The Native American* (New Orleans); *The Republican and Constitutionalist* (New Orleans); and the Baltimore *American Republican* (Baltimore). The above list has been secured from notices in the following papers and publications: *Native American,* July 10, 1844, August 14, 1844, August 27, 1844, November 2, 1844, November 14, 1844; *Native Eagle,* December 1, 1845, December 20, 1845, December 8, 1846; *Proceedings of the Native American Convention at Harrisburg,* 5. Established papers embracing

the American Republican cause included: the New Haven *Courier* (New Haven, Connecticut); the Baltimore *Clipper* (Baltimore); Windsor *Journal* (Windsor, Vermont); *Daily Mercury* (Bangor, Maine); Charlotte *Journal* (Charlotte, North Carolina); Newark *American Citizen* (Newark, New Jersey); Lexington *Inquirer* (Lexington, Kentucky); China *Republican* (China, New York); Shelby *News* (Shelby, Kentucky); Lancaster *Union and Sentinel* (Lancaster, Pennsylvania); Norfolk *American* (Norfolk, Virginia); New Orleans *Topic* (New Orleans); *The American Flag* (Trenton, New Jersey); *Bunker Hill Aurora* (Boston); *Morning Courier* (Louisville, Kentucky); *Public Index* (Portsmouth, Virginia). The above list has been taken from references in the following periodicals: *Native American*, November 7, 1844, November 13, 1844, November 20, 1844; *National Protestant*, I (December, 1844); Benjamin Tusca, *Know Nothingism in Baltimore* (New York, 1925), 4.

[102] The first issue of the *American Republican Magazine* contained patriotic stories and verse, articles on "The Insolence of Foreigners" and "The Constitution," and news of party activities. *American Republican Magazine*, I (October, 1844).

[103] Lecturing agents were employed by the central state organization of the party to popularize their cause. *Proceedings of the Native American State Convention at Harrisburg*, 9.

IX

The Philadelphia Riots of 1844

FOR more than a decade before the middle 1840's forces had been at work to create antipathy toward Rome; societies, lecturers, newspapers, magazines, churches, ministers, and a political party had all been enlisted in the cause. An intolerance unusual in a democratic land had been bred in thousands of people. This prejudice against Popery led inevitably to violence and bloodshed, for such depth of feeling as that created by the anti-Catholic agitators demanded physical expression in this forceful generation. This outburst occurred in Philadelphia during the summer of 1844, when natives and foreigners clashed in a series of riots which turned the City of Brotherly Love into a chaos of hatred and persecution.

Philadelphia was well equipped for its part in the struggle. The population of the city itself was largely American—an old society with a heritage of intolerance toward new forces—but the many suburbs were filled with alien workers who manned the city's industrial establishments. This geographic cleavage between the two antagonistic groups had caused trouble before; the city had known several pitched battles between fire companies and between American and foreign workers on the railroads and in the textile mills.[1] Election rioting was also common, and had reached its peak in the spring of 1844 when Irish and Americans had fought openly on the streets of one of the suburbs.[2] Much of this violence was attributable to the Protestant-Catholic antagonism which the American Protestant Association had aroused by making most of the city's pulpits organs for antipapal attacks. Local debating societies and tract societies had similarly been interested in the No-Popery crusade during the early 1840's and had combined with ministerial and political speakers to create in the people a general antipathy toward Rome.[3] In such an atmosphere of suspicion and distrust, any suspected Catholic aggression would certainly spell trouble.

The spark which set off the smouldering hatred was an educational controversy similar to that of New York. Inspired by the efforts of Bishop Hughes to secure a share of the school fund, Bishop Francis Patrick Kenrick of the Philadelphia diocese had, on November 14, 1842, addressed a letter to the Board of Controllers of the public schools complaining that the Protestant Bible was being read to Catholic children and that religious exercises were being made a daily part of the instruction. He respectfully asked that the Catholic children be allowed to use their own version of the Bible and that they be excused from other religious instruction.[4] In January, 1843, the school board complied with this request, allowing children to read from any version of the Bible which their parents selected.[5]

Dissatisfaction with this action developed slowly during the following year, stirred by the American Protestant Association which promptly seized upon the issue as one worthy of its undivided efforts.[6] Pamphleteers and the local religious press were unrestrained in their condemnation of the Controllers' action and demanded that Protestants throw every obstacle in the path of Catholics who sought to introduce un-Christian education. "The interference of foreign prelates," wrote one author, "and of a foreign ecclesiastical power, should perish at our threshold. Let a grave be sunk, then, over which even the great Papal hierarch himself cannot step." [7] This challenge was accepted without question by a large part of the population. When a school board member of the suburb of Kensington tried to stop Bible reading in a local school, a mass meeting was held to demand his resignation.[8] A similar public gathering was staged in Independence

Square, Philadelphia, on March 11, 1844, where a large audience heard speeches against Catholicism and resolved:

> That the present crisis demands that without distinction of party, sect, or profession, every man who loves his country, his Bible, and his God, is bound by all lawful and honorable means to resist every attempt to banish the Bible from our public institutions.[9]

In vain did Bishop Kenrick publish a second letter to the Controllers on the following day, stating that he "did not object to the use of the Bible, providing Catholic children be allowed to use their own version." [10] The time had come when such a palliative could no longer quiet Protestant fears. Resentment throughout Philadelphia and its suburbs continued to grow.

During the early weeks of April a mounting tension was apparent among both Protestants and Catholics, particularly in the suburb of Kensington, an industrial section where Irish laborers were concentrated in large numbers. The first actual clash came late in the month, when a group of American Republicans announced that they would hold a meeting in the third ward of that city. Irish resentment at such an invasion of their territory was great, and threats were openly made that if the natives persisted in their intention, their meeting place would be burned to the ground.[11] Undeterred by this warning, the natives assembled on the night of May 3, only to be routed by an Irish mob.[12] Driven from their meeting, the remnants of the nativists gathered in a safe place and passed a series of resolutions:

> That we, the citizens of Kensington in mass meeting assembled, do solemnly protest against this flagrant violation of the rights of American citizens, and call upon our fellow citizens at large, to visit with their indignation and reproach, this outbreak of a vindictive, anti-republican spirit, manifested by a portion of the alien population of Third Ward Kensington.
>
> *Resolved,* That in view of the above transaction, we invite our fellow-citizens at large to attend the next meeting to sustain us in the expression of our opinions.

Resolved, That when we adjourn we adjourn to meet in a mass meeting on Monday afternoon at 4 o'clock, at the corner of Second and Maseer [*sic*] streets.[13]

This second meeting was little more than a gauntlet thrown at the feet of Irishmen ever eager to retrieve it. Bloodshed was being openly welcomed, nor was the situation eased by the attitude of the anti-Catholic press. On the morning of Monday, May 6, the day on which the postponed meeting was to be held, the *Native American* proclaimed:

NATIVE AMERICANS

The American Republicans of the city and county of Philadelphia, who are determined to support the NATIVE AMERICANS in their Constitutional Rights of peaceably assembling to express their opinions on any question of Public Policy and to *Sustain them against the assaults of Aliens and Foreigners* are requested to assemble on *THIS AFTERNOON,* May 6th, 1844, at 4 o'clock, at the corner of Master and Second streets, Kensington, to express their indignation at the outrage on Friday evening last, and to take the necessary steps to prevent a repetition of it. *Natives be punctual and resolved to sustain your rights as Americans, firmly but moderately.*[14]

Such an appeal would naturally attract rowdies from the lower classes, who would be ready to riot if given the slightest excuse.

Those who anticipated trouble were not disappointed. Several thousand strong, the American Republicans had scarcely gathered at the appointed meeting place when a heavy rain drove them in a bedraggled procession through the streets of the Irish section of Kensington to the Market House. Just as they were entering this building, several shots rang out, fired either from the windows of the Hibernia Hose Company house, an Irish fire company, or from the mob itself. The meeting was thrown into a turmoil immediately. One of the marchers, a young man named George Shiffler, who had been struck and mortally wounded, was carried from the meeting by four men amid general confusion, where spectators were able to hear only one gray-haired man who shouted "On, On Americans. Liberty or Death." Before order could be restored, a band of Irish laborers stormed the building; the natives lost courage and made a hasty retreat for the second time.[15]

Before nightfall another meeting of native Americans had been hurriedly assembled to lay plans for the burial of George Shiffler and the others who had been killed in the fighting. At its conclusion, those present again invaded the Irish quarter in Kensington and attacked several Irish homes before the militia arrived. "When the natives had got their blood up," one nativistic newspaper remarked with some bitterness, "and were fast gaining the ascendancy, the peace officers thought it high time to interpose the authority of the law." [16]

The dawn of a new day found the whole city in the grip of intense excitement. Crowds gathered at every corner, listening to volunteer speakers exhort against Catholicism. A procession was hastily formed and marched through the streets bearing a torn American flag on which was painted: "This is the flag that was trampled under foot by the Irish papists." A proclamation by Bishop Kenrick deploring Catholic participation in the disorder did little good, for when copies were hurriedly posted throughout the city they were torn down and made into cockade hats by the natives. Two Irishmen, recognized as among the preceding night's rioters, were captured by a group of Americans and taken to an alderman's home while a mob followed at their heels shouting, "Kill them. Kill them. Blood for blood." [17] The editor of the *Native American* completely lost his sense of balance; his paper, appearing with its columns shrouded in black, boldly demanded reprisal and more bloodshed:

Heretofore we have been among those who have entered our solemn protest against any observations that would bear the slightest semblance of making the Native cause a religious one, or charging upon our adopted fellow-citizens any other feeling than that of a mistaken opinion as to our views and their own rights. We hold back no longer. We are now free to declare that *no terms whatever* are to be held with these people.

Another St. Bartholomew's day is begun on the streets of Philadelphia. The bloody hand of the Pope has stretched itself forth to our destruction. We now call on our fellow-citizens, who regard free institutions, whether they be native or adopted, to arm. Our liberties are now to be fought for;—let us not be slack in our preparations.[18]

Spurred on by this ill-advised warning, native Americans assembled that afternoon in the State House yard. Orators tried to warn them against bloodshed and cautioned them to keep the peace, but their words were answered by cries of "No, No," from the crowd. After adopting a number of resolutions asserting the right of peaceful assembly and charging the Papists with an attempt to drive the Bible from the schools, the natives banded together and again marched into Kensington. Traversing the Irish section shouting insults and damaging Irish homes, the mob was soon locked in armed conflict with equally riotous foreigners. The Hibernia Hose Company house was stormed and demolished; before midnight more than thirty houses belonging to Irishmen had been burned to the ground, and only the tardy arrival of the militia put an end to the holocaust.[19]

The third day of rioting climaxed this period of disorder. Crowds began gathering on the streets of Kensington early in the afternoon, shouting against the Pope and demanding vengeance for the natives who had been killed. To observers many of the attackers seemed to be well organized and bent solely on the systematic destruction of Irish homes, for within a few hours whole blocks of houses were in flames. The militia appeared but proved powerless before the pillaging mob. Protestant Irish and Americans all over Kensington hastened to protect themselves by fastening large signs bearing the legend "Native American" upon the doors of their houses, or lacking these, hastily displaying a copy of the newspaper of that name. The crowd always stopped before such a sign to cheer.[20]

Roaming the streets, the rioters finally came to Saint Michael's Catholic church. A rumor that arms were concealed within the building proved sufficient grounds for attack, and while the presiding priest fled in disguise,[21] the torch was applied. As flames consumed the church and an adjoining seminary,[22] the rioters marched on St. Augustine's church. A hurry call was dispatched for the mayor, who had been neglecting his duties to celebrate his daughter's birthday,[23] but his speech to the crowd from the steps of the structure, in which he stated that the building was unarmed and that he himself had the key, had an opposite effect from that intended. The mob, now assured that the building was not defended, brushed past the few militia available, burst open the doors, and set fire to the church.[24] Throughout the city priests and nuns trembled for their lives,[25] and Kensington was fast assuming the aspect of a war-torn town as Irish refugees fled with their belongings.[26]

The burning of Saint Augustine's church marked the peak of mob rule. Philadelphia awakened on the morning of May 9, sobered by a chorus of criticism resounding throughout the nation. "Who would not give worlds," wrote the editor of the *Spirit of the Times,* "to wipe off the foul blot from the disgraced name of our city? . . ."[27] Even the *Native American* appeared in chastened form, declaring: "No terms that we can use are able to express the deep reprobation that we feel for this iniquitous proceeding; this wanton and uncalled for desecration of the Christian altar."[28] A mass meeting, called at the insistence of the mayor, met that afternoon and agreed to the appointment of special policemen in each ward to keep order. These officers were immediately sworn in and patrolled the streets of Kensington all that night.[29] There was no further evidence of trouble and quiet seemed to have settled on a mollified and sobered Philadelphia.

This calm was deceptive, for beneath the surface tension was still high. Isolated groups continued to destroy Catholic property despite the efforts of officials,[30] and on the following Sunday all Catholic churches were closed by the bishop who feared further violence.[31] Signs posted about the city a few days later proclaiming "Fortunio and his Seven Gifted Servants" created a flurry of excitement when the rumor spread that the mysterious words contained a papal order to Catholics to arm themselves, a rumor which was dissipated when they were found to be an advertisement of a local theater.[32] An Irishman who was seen purchasing a dray load of muskets nearly caused another riot until he explained that this purchase was part of a commercial transaction.[33] The nativistic press and the American Republican party did little to aid the return of peace to the city. Both began a concentrated effort to gloss over the stigma of church burning and remind the people that the trouble had started when Irish laborers had fired on defenseless Americans peaceably going about their business. "The murderous assault on American citizens," stated an official proclamation of the native Americans, "the trampling under foot and tearing into shreds the American flag, . . . is the cause, the origin of the whole trouble. . . . Disgraceful as is the burning of the Churches . . . is it an outrage of a greater character than that which sends the souls of men without a moment's time for preparation, to the bar of God's judgment?"[34] Through the deliberate efforts of nativists, those who had been killed in Kensington became martyrs; concerts were given in behalf of their families, a ship was built by American labor and dedicated to them, and on July 4 a procession of seventy thousand people escorted carriages containing their widows and orphans through the streets of the city.[35] Amid scenes such as these the horrors of the May rioting were soon forgotten.

The excitement of the Independence Day celebration led to a renewal of mob rule a day later. A clash between Irish laborers and a group of American Republicans, together with widespread rumors that arms were being smuggled into the Church of Saint Philip de Neri in Southwark, another suburb, attracted a turbulent group of natives to that Catholic edifice by nightfall on July 5. Fortunately no attack was made until the sheriff could arrive; the crowd then demanded.that he search the church for arms. Twelve muskets were found and exhibited to the rioters, who, unappeased, demanded a second investigation, this time by a group of twenty men from their own ranks. This search disclosed seventy-five more guns together with a quantity of ammunition, supplies probably stored there by an ill-advised pastor as a precautionary measure during the earlier period of church burning. Wise counsel prevailed among members of the searching party, and they kept all knowledge of their find to themselves, fearing violence should the mob learn of the firearms. Disgruntled, the crowd around the church finally dispersed about midnight when the military forces arrived.[36]

By the following morning news of the committee's find had leaked out, and at nine o'clock a crowd gathered around the church. All that day they milled about, checked from violent action only by large forces of the militia who were ranged before the church doors. By night the mob was pressing so close upon the militiamen that orders were given to fire. Before this command could be carried out, a prominent citizen, Charles Naylor, protested and for his pains was promptly arrested and clapped into the church, where he was held under guard by an Irish military company, the Hibernia Greens, which had been assembled. Angry as was the mob at this action, the order to fire had its effect, and the crowd broke up without further delay.[37]

Before leaving the scene, however, leaders of the rioters issued an ultimatum that unless Naylor was released by noon of the following day, he would be taken by force. When crowds began assembling on the next morning, Sunday, July 7, they had prepared themselves to carry out this threat. Two cannons were procured from ships at the wharves and at twelve o'clock these were hauled before the church doors, but wet powder prevented their being fired. Frustrated in this method of attack, the mob secured a log, and using this as a battering ram, broke down the doors of the church and emerged in triumph with Naylor. But the presence of the Hibernia Greens had been discovered, and the rioters now issued a new demand; unless that military company was removed, the church would be burned. Realizing the seriousness of this threat, the Hibernians marched to the street where they were attacked and at least one member of the company was killed.[38]

Returning to the church after this foray, the rioters brushed aside spokesmen who pleaded for peace, entered the building and would probably have set fire to it, had they not been checked by natives who assumed the task of guardians. A continued increase in the size of the mob through the afternoon warned law officers that an attack might come at any time and that strong measures were necessary to protect the Catholic property. They dispatched a hurried call for military aid, and by nightfall a company of troops had turned the square on which the church was located into an armed fortress, with barricades erected and cannon commanding the principal avenues of approach. A second military company on the way to the scene became engaged with a group of native rioters, and in the confusion an order was given to fire; one volley from the soldiers left seven citizens dead and a score wounded. When word of this spread through the city, new crowds poured into the vicinity of Saint Philip de Neri's church, intent on revenge. A cannon was procured and fired point blank into the soldiers about the door. The military answered, and cannon and musket fire persisted on both sides for several hours. Not until another company had been called out to capture the rioters' cannon was peace restored to the war-torn city.[39]

Sensing the hostility which had been aroused against the military companies by the night's activity, the mayor ordered them withdrawn early the following morning. This proved a wise move, for although gangs roamed the streets all the next day and thousands of Catholic families left the city, no further damage was done. The arrival of the governor of the state to plead for peace brought some order, but for days the streets of Philadelphia were crowded with excited men and women. When the city took stock of its brief interlude of mob rule, it found that thirteen citizens had been killed and more than fifty wounded in the three days of fighting.[40]

Although Philadelphia publicly mourned its dead and openly deplored its period of carnage, many even among the more substantial citizens were secretly exultant. Quaker merchants, who spoke indignantly of the outrage in public, returned to their shops to express the sincere belief that "the Papists deserve all this and much more," and, "It were well if every Popish church in the world were leveled with the ground." [41] Official inquiries reflected this same spirit of intolerance. A city investigating committee laid the blame for the riots entirely on the Irish who had broken up a peaceful procession of American citizens.[42] The Grand Jury's presentment, brought in after the close of the first period of rioting, ascribed the trouble to

the efforts of a portion of the community to exclude the Bible from our Public Schools.—The Jury are of opinion that these efforts in some measure gave rise to the formation of a new party, which called and held public meetings in the District of Kensington, in the peaceful exercise of the sacred rights and privileges guaranteed to every citizen by the Constitution and laws of our State and Country.—These meetings were rudely disturbed and fired upon by a band of lawless, irresponsible men, some of whom had resided in our country only for a short period.—This outrage, causing the death of a number of our unoffending citizens, led to immediate retaliation, and was followed up by subsequent acts of aggression in violation and open defiance of all law.[43]

A second Grand Jury called to report on the causes of the Southwark riots in July blamed them solely on the Catholics who had armed the church of Saint Philip de Neri.[44] Equal resentment was aroused by the efforts of the city to pay for the property destroyed; all the chicanery of the law was resorted to by stubborn nativists, and it was not until many years later that the Church of St. Augustine was restored with public funds. Saint Michael's church, lying beyond the official jurisdiction of the city, was never paid for.[45] In every way Philadelphians showed little remorse for their violence.

Meanwhile the excitement engendered by events in Philadelphia had spread to New York. There the influential New York *American Republican* told the story of the Kensington riots under a headline "The Voice of Blood," saying:

They have commenced the war of blood. Thank God, they are not yet strong enough to overcome us with brute force. There is yet time to stay the bloody hand of tyranny. A revolution has begun. "Blood will have Blood." It cannot sink into the earth and be forgotten. The gory vision will rise like the ghost of the murdered Banquo, and call for revenge.[46]

These inflammatory statements fell on the ears of a group of native Americans eager for trouble, for one of their processions in Brooklyn had engaged in a battle with a group of Irish only a few days before fighting broke forth in Philadelphia.[47] Conditions were ripe for violence even more serious than that in the latter city.

That New York remained outwardly calm during this period of strife was due to the vigorous efforts of Bishop John Hughes, who took a firm stand from the very start. He publicly declared that "if a single Catholic Church were burned in New York, the city would become a second Moscow." The Catholics of Philadelphia, he believed, were responsible for the trouble there. "They should have defended their churches," he wrote, "since the authorities could not or would not do it for them. We might forbear from harming the intruder into *our house* until the last, but his *first* violence to our church should be promptly and decisively repelled." [48] Such an attitude, belligerent as it was, was necessary, for only through open threats could bloodshed have been averted in New York in those troubled days.

As soon as news of the first Kensington riot reached New York, native Americans there moved into action. A large mass meeting was held on the night of May 7 where, after denouncing the Catholic aggression and appropriating rewards for the capture of the Irish rioters, a call was issued for a second mass meeting of all the citizens of New York, to meet in Central Park on May 9. [49] Hughes fully realized the danger of such an assembly, for a delegation from Philadelphia was to be present to exhibit the national flag which had allegedly been torn and trampled at Kensington. Excitement stirred by this exhibition might lead to rioting and church burning in New York. His first step was to ascertain from legal authorities that the state law did not require the city to compensate Catholics for any churches destroyed by mobs. Clearly Catholics must protect their own property. Hughes promptly stationed between one and two thousand men, fully armed, about each church and hurried from the presses a special edition of the *Freeman's Journal,* warning his watchers to keep peace as long as possible but to defend their property at all costs. [50]

These warlike preparations were viewed by American Republicans with resentment and alarm. A hasty conference with the mayor made clear that the civic authorities believed bloodshed could be averted only by abandoning plans for the Central Park mass meeting, and the party leaders were at last won to this view. On the afternoon of May 9, just before the meeting was to assemble, placards were posted about the city announcing that it had been postponed because of the existing tension and the danger of rioting. [51] Had the meeting been held, bloodshed would probably have ensued; Bishop Hughes deserves credit for saving New York from a period of mob rule such as that which had racked Philadelphia. The New York American Republicans made no further attempt to appeal to the prejudices of the people, and the city enjoyed a calm which was in marked contrast to the turbulence of Philadelphia.[52]

Although the Philadelphia outburst had stirred interest in nativism, it had done little good and much harm to the anti-Catholic cause. Bloodshed and rioting had followed in the wake of the American Republicans; respectable citizens throughout the country shrank from a party which sanctioned mob rule. That the almost universal condemnation of the church burning and property destruction was deeply felt by the nativists was shown by the vigorous efforts which they made to defend themselves. They insisted that the rioting had been precipitated by foreigners who attacked an innocent group of Americans [53] and that this was but the first blow of a popish plot to take over the United States by armed conquest.[54] Members of Congress were forced to listen to such accusations when the spokesman of the American Republicans, Lewis C. Levin, said in the House of Representatives:

Drilled bands of armed foreigners rushed with impetuous fury upon native-born Americans who carried no weapons but what equal rights had given them. In the majesty of freemen, they stood armed only with moral power. The element opposing them was physical force. It was an imported element,—an European weapon—one peculiar only to the feudal institutions of the Old World.[55]

"We love not riots," wrote another editor, "we abhor bloodshed; but it is idle to suppose that Americans can be shot down on their own soil, under their own flag, while in the quiet exercise of their constitutional privileges, without a fearful retribution being exacted." [56]

Members of the party continued to stress this view during the next few years, constantly minimizing the church burning, insisting that American Republicans had had no part in that outrage, and stressing the killing of natives by foreign mobs. George Shiffler, the first American to fall, became a martyr in their eyes.

and lithographs depicting his death were displayed in most of
their homes.[57] In 1845 and 1846 while thousands looked on with
approbation the anniversary of the Kensington riot was celebrated with elaborate ceremonies in the market house where the
first shots were fired.[58] "While the Republic retains a place
among the Nations of the earth," declared a nativistic paper on
May 6, 1846, "this day will remain enshrined in the hearts of
Native Americans." [59]

These vain hopes were devoid of realization. The Philadelphia riots, with their bloodshed, property destruction, and church
burning deeply shocked the majority of Americans whose natural conservatism led them to view any attack on private property
with suspicion. Particularly alarmed were the sober, church-going citizens who had been attracted to the anti-Catholic cause by
the New York school controversy and who now shrank from a
continued alliance with such a lawless group as the nativists had
demonstrated themselves to be. The American Republican party
which had been advancing with such rapid strides, found its path
strewn with obstacles and its supporters deserting in large numbers. Upon all the forces of No-Popery lay the curse of popular
disapproval, and nativism entered into that period of quiescence
from which it was only to emerge with the growth of the Know-
Nothing party.

NOTES

[1] The history of these disturbances is traced in the *Native American*, July
16, 1844.

[2] The rioting had centered in Spring Garden, *Ibid.*, May 29, 1844. Similar
racial riots had occurred in another suburb, Kensington, a year earlier. *Protestant Banner*, January 19, 1843.

[3] New York *Observer*, January 21, 1843.

[4] The letter is printed in the New York *Observer*, January 28, 1843, and in
the American Protestant Association, *First Annual Report*, 24–25; *Protestant
Banner*, January 19, 1843; *Freeman's Journal*, January 21, 1843. A Philadelphia
priest had publicly suggested such a step a year before. *Ibid.*, January 29, 1842.

[5] New York *Observer*, January 28, 1843. The Controllers stated that no
action was necessary concerning hymn singing and religious instruction as
those things had been specifically forbidden by an order issued in 1834 in
response to Catholic protests.

6 American Protestant Association, *First Annual Report*, 7. The association was particularly active at this time, holding a series of monthly, and after November, 1843, weekly, lectures against the Catholic claims. *Protestant Banner*, October 26, 1843, November 9, 1843.

7 Walter Colton, *A Reply to the Allegations and Complaints Contained in Bishop Kenrick's Letter to the Board of Controllers of the Public Schools* (Philadelphia, 1844). The entire pamphlet was published in the *Quarterly Review of the American Protestant Association*, I (January, 1844). This extract is from this source, 21–22. See also *Protestant Banner*, April 4, 1844.

8 Philadelphia *Public Ledger*, quoted in McMaster, *History of the People of the United States*, VII, 376–377. The meeting had been called in response to an inflammatory demand published by the *Protestant Banner*, March 7, 1844. "The decisive blow has been struck," this editor wrote, "the Pope reigns in Philadelphia! Infidel politicians have bowed the neck to the 'Priest-Kings' of Europe, and sold their country and their God for the votes of foreign paupers."

9 New York *Observer*, March 16, 1844.

10 *New Englander*, II (July, 1844), 472–473.

11 *Native American*, April 26, 1844.

12 *Ibid.*, May 4, 1844; New York *Observer*, May 11, 1844.

13 *Native American*, May 4, 1844.

14 *Ibid.*, May 6, 1844.

15 There was, and is, much dispute as to whether the natives or Irish precipitated this riot by firing the first shot. Extracts from eighteen secular and religious newspapers, published in the *Protestant Banner*, June 20, 1844, indicate that the initiative was taken by the Irish. They were undoubtedly provoked into this action by abusive comment from the natives and perhaps even by minor attacks on their homes, although there is no trustworthy contemporary evidence of this. Other details of the rioting have been drawn from the New York *Observer*, May 11, 1844; *Native American*, May 7, 1844; New York *American Republican*, May 10, 1844; *New Englander*, II (July, 1844), 475–479; *United States Catholic Magazine*, III (June, 1844), 379–384. Most accounts of the episode have been based on Shea, *History of the Catholic Church in the United States*, IV, 46–55, who states, probably incorrectly, that the native Americans marched directly from their meeting to attack Irish homes without any provocation. The *Freeman's Journal* stated at the time that amidst the confusion of the natives' meeting a shot was fired at an Irishman who was trying to escape into the Hibernia Hose Company headquarters and that this Irishman, Patrick Fisher, was the first rioter to die. *Freeman's Journal*, May 9, 1844. Later evidence advanced in the trial of twelve of the rioters seemed to indicate that an Irishman was responsible for the first shot. *Ibid.*, September 21, 1844, September 24, 1844, September 28, 1844, October 5, 1844, October 26, 1844. November 2, 1844.

16 New York *Observer*, May 11, 1844.

17 New York *American Republican*, May 7, 1844, May 8, 1844, May 9, 1844, May 10, 1844; *Native American*, May 7, 1844.

18 *Native American*, May 7, 1844.

19 New York *Observer*, May 11, 1844; *Native American*, May 8, 1844. Evidence produced at trials of the rioters indicated that the natives were

already well organized and that they marched and fired in regular military array. *Freeman's Journal,* September 24, 1844.

20 *Native American,* May 9, 1844.

21 "The Very Reverend T. J. Donaghoe," *Records of the American Catholic Historical Society of Philadelphia,* XXIII, No. 2 (June, 1912), 75-77. Donaghoe was pastor of the church and only managed to escape after the mob had gathered around the building.

22 *Native American,* May 9, 1844; New York *Observer,* May 11, 1844.

23 "The Anti-Catholic Riots of 1844 in Philadelphia," *American Catholic Historical Researches,* XIII, No. 2 (April, 1896), 53. An account of the riots by a Catholic eyewitness.

24 *Native American,* May 9, 1844.

25 A letter written by Sister M. Gonzoga, a nun in a Catholic orphan asylum in Philadelphia, at midnight on May 9, describes the tense situation well. It is printed in the *American Catholic Historical Researches,* VIII, No. 2 (April, 1891), 89-90.

26 "The Anti-Catholic Riots of 1844 in Philadelphia," *loc. cit.,* 52.

27 Quoted in "The Philadelphia Anti-Catholic Riots of 1844," *American Catholic Historical Researches,* n.s., VII (July, 1911), 233.

28 *Native American,* May 9, 1844.

29 *Ibid.,* May 10, 1844.

30 *Ibid.,* May 11, 1844. A group of natives were caught destroying tombstones in a Catholic cemetery.

31 "The Philadelphia Anti-Catholic Riots of 1844," *loc. cit.,* 231.

32 New York *American Republican,* May 13, 1844.

33 *Ibid.,* June 15, 1844.

34 *Native American,* May 15, 1844.

35 *Ibid.,* May 28, 1844, July 3, 1844, July 6, 1844, August 8, 1844.

36 This account of the riot is drawn from the New York *Observer,* July 13, 1844; New York *American Republican,* July 8, 1844; *Native American,* July 8, 1844; *New Englander,* II (October, 1844), 624-631; *Protestant Banner,* July 18, 1844. The Grand Jury justified the pastor for keeping arms, as ordinary law enforcement officials had proven incapable of protecting Catholic property. *Freeman's Journal,* August 17, 1844.

37 New York *Observer,* July 13, 1844; *Native American,* July 8, 1844. The *Freeman's Journal,* July 13, 1844, held that this heroic action by Naylor was occasioned by his desire to win popular support for his own political ends. He had been a member of Congress and was planning to run for office again.

38 New York *Observer,* July 13, 1844; *Native American,* July 8, 1844. A description of the rioting by the captain of the Hibernia Greens is in the *Freeman's Journal,* August 3, 1844.

39 *Native American,* July 8, 1844; New York *Observer,* July 13, 1844; *Freeman's Journal,* July 13, 1844.

40 *Native American,* July 9, 1844.

41 A Catholic worker in Philadelphia at the time is responsible for this statement, having observed his employers, all substantial merchants, speak against the rioting in public and utter the quoted sentiments in private. "The Anti-Catholic Riots of 1844 in Philadelphia," *loc. cit.,* 51.

42 New York *American Republican,* May 13, 1844.

[43] The presentment was printed in the *Native American*, June 17, 1844, and the New York *American Republican*, June 17, 1844. Catholics were so aroused by the prejudiced tone of this presentment that they named a committee of five to draw up an answer. *Protestant Banner*, July 4, 1844.

[44] *Native American*, August 5, 1844.

[45] "The Anti-Catholic Riots of 1844 in Philadelphia," *loc. cit.*, 64.

[46] May 9, 1844.

[47] A native American meeting in Brooklyn had been disturbed when Irish stoned some of the speakers. On the homeward march, the natives passed a Catholic church, from which emerged a group of Irishmen who attacked the rear of the procession. The fight which followed lasted for several hours although there was no serious bloodshed. The Irish had probably been gathered to defend the church from attack and were unable to resist the temptation to stir up a battle. *Native American*, April 11, 1844.

[48] Hassard, *Life of John Hughes*, 276.

[49] New York *American Republican*, May 8, 1844.

[50] Hassard, *Life of John Hughes*, 276-278.

[51] New York *American Republican*, May 10, 1844.

[52] In St. Louis news of the Philadelphia mob rule nearly led to an attack on a Jesuit college and medical school. Students of the school, due to gross negligence, had left sections of human bodies and other anatomical specimens lying about the college grounds where they were seen by passers-by. Rumors spread that the Inquisition had been established in St. Louis and that these remains were the ghostly relics of Protestant martyrs. A mob formed, and only an armed force of Irish who surrounded the building for several hours, prevented the destruction of the school. John O'Hanlon, *Life and Scenery in Missouri* (Dublin, 1890), 92-93. O'Hanlon was a priest in St. Louis at the time and an eyewitness to the episode.

[53] New York *American Republican*, May 13, 1844, July 4, 1844, July 16, 1844; New York *American Republican*, July 13, 1844, July 20, 1844; New York *Journal of Commerce*, quoted in *Ibid.*, July 13, 1844; *Native American*, May 14, 1844; Pittsburgh *Chronicle*, May 10, 1844, quoted in *Ibid.*, May 14, 1844; *Protestant Banner*, May 16, 1844; *Proceedings of the Native American State Convention at Harrisburg*, 16-24. According to the New York *American Republican*, all the New York papers with the exception of the *Plebeian*, the *Tribune*, the *Sun*, and the *Freeman's Journal* laid the rioting on foreigners rather than natives.

[54] New York *Observer*, May 25, 1844; New York *American Republican*, May 8, 1844. It was also charged that the riots had been stirred up by priests in order to discredit the American Republicans. *Protestant Banner*, July 18, 1844; *Native American*, May 15, 1844; New York *American Republican*, May 9, 1844; *The Crisis*, 76.

[55] *Congressional Globe*, 29th Cong., 1st Sess., Appendix, 49.

[56] New York *American Republican*, May 8, 1844.

[57] *Native Eagle*, November 3, 1846.

[58] *Ibid.*, April 6, 1846.

[59] *Ibid.*, May 6, 1846.

X

The Period of Decline
1845-1850

BEFORE the wave of revulsion against nativists for their part in the Philadelphia riots had spent itself, new issues had risen to absorb the interest of the American people. For the next six years the political caldron boiled merrily while statesmen wrangled over the Oregon boundary, the Mexican War, the Wilmot Proviso, and the whole question of slavery in the territories. Native sons marched forth to fulfill the promises of manifest destiny or grew absorbed in the compelling oratory of Webster, Calhoun, Benton, and Clay. With the nation in immediate danger, either from a foreign foe or internal disruption, the more intangible fears of papal conquest were forgotten. Such a sternly Puritanical body as the New England Society of New York could drink a toast to the Pope in Rome and call forth only feeble protests from the press.[1]

But even as nativism was being eclipsed, forces were at work which were to lead to its more vigorous revival. The mere fact that the Mexican War was fought against a Catholic power was sufficient to provide grist for the mills of prejudice. The east heard repeated rumors of Catholic desertion to the enemy and of popish plots to poison native American soldiers,[2] while in the army luckless Catholics were driven to Protestant religious services where they were forced to listen to violent denunciations of their faith. President Polk's effort to alleviate their lot by appointing Catholic chaplains to accompany the invading armies aroused protests from nativistic and religious newspapers,[3] personal abuse,[4] and the demand that this "flagrant outrage upon the constitution . . . be frowned upon and denounced by every friend of the liberties of the country and its free institutions." [5] Similarly, Polk's attempted use of Bishop John Hughes of New York as a peace mediator stirred such a hornet's nest of criticism that Hughes reluctantly refused to act.[6] Even the successful conclusion of the war failed to quiet nativists' fears, for they professed to see in the acquisition of a Catholic-populated domain only a new plot to surround the United States toward eventual papal subjugation.[7]

More important than the Mexican War in keeping alive the ancient fear of Catholicism was the new tide of immigration which was surging upon American shores. Earlier alien invasions, which had caused such alarm in the 1830's, shrank to insignificance when compared with the flood which engulfed the land in the late 1840's and early 1850's. In 1845, for the first time, the 100,000 mark was passed, by 1847 more than 200,000 were arriving each year; by 1850, 300,000; and finally, in 1854 the movement reached its peak when official records showed that 427,833 foreign-born had landed in the United States. Taking 1844 as a standard of comparison, immigration figures had multiplied by three in 1847, by four in 1850, and by five and one half in 1854. This was startling enough, but alarmists pointed out that the official statistics failed to take into account thousands of aliens who entered irregularly, and maintained that the actual number of immigrants was fifty per cent greater than it appeared.[8] Many Americans believed that nearly half a million foreigners swarmed over the land in 1850 and that by 1854 three quarters of a million were arriving each year.

This unusual influx was due not only to the magnetic influence of opportunity in the new world and to the growing importance of "America letters" but also to abnormal conditions in Ireland and Germany, from whence came more than three quarters of the immigrants. In Ireland the potato blight of 1846, wiping out

the means of subsistence for thousands of tenant farmers, was
followed by mortgage foreclosures and evictions on a wholesale
scale. Peasants long close to the soil were forced to utilize the
New Brunswick lumber ships to reach America and a chance to
begin life anew. In Germany a similar blight and the institutional
changes which followed the Revolutions of 1848 completely demoralized the peasant population and sent more than a million
farmers to the United States to recuperate their vanished fortunes.[9]

The normal difficulties attendant on the assimilation of these
two large racial groups were intensified by the inclination of the
immigrants to concentrate in the northeast and middle west. The
Irish showed a marked preference for the eastern cities and mill
towns and so filled New England and the middle states that they
threatened to absorb the native Americans rather than be absorbed themselves. Boston by 1850 contained a foreign-born
population almost equaling its native-born; five years later the
natives were outnumbered by some 10,000. In Rhode Island
more than one fifth of the population in the 1850's proudly admitted an old world birth.[10] "The Irish and Germans in America," wrote an English traveler, "increase with much greater
rapidity than the Americans of an older stock. So remarkably
is this the case, that there must, in a few years, be an Irish
majority even in such old states as Massachusetts and Rhode
Island." [11]

While the Irish were threatening to inundate New England,
the Germans were causing similar alarm in the middle west.
They naturally drifted to that region, attracted by the cheap
transportation on the cotton vessels plying between New Orleans
and continental ports.[12] From New Orleans they made their way
up the Mississippi and its tributaries, to be joined in the fertile
northwest by a similar stream of Germans who had come across
country after landing in New York. These sturdy peasants
showed no tendency, as did the Irish, to drift into the cities; they

became such valued farmers that one state, Wisconsin, established a regular immigration service to lure them to its borders, and other western states openly welcomed their coming.[13]

This combination of favorable trade routes and friendly reception brought more than 270,000 Germans to the northwest by 1850; a decade later this number had increased to over a million.[14] In Wisconsin the foreign-born were almost as numerous as natives, in other western states the proportion was only slightly more favorable to Americans, and in many of the cities, such as St. Louis, the native-born were definitely outnumbered. A traveler observed: "Nearly half of Cincinnati is German; and crossing a canal that divides the northern part of the city from the southern is popularly termed 'going over the Rhine.' It is much the same at Chicago and St. Louis. At Milwaukee, the Germans appeared to me to occupy nearly or quite a third of the city." [15]

Only the south escaped the full impact of the immigrant invasion. Both Germans and Irish avoided the states below the Mason-Dixon line—the Irish because sparse settlement and lack of industrial opportunity deterred them, the Germans because they hesitated to compete with slave labor. As a result there were only 260,000 foreign-born in all the south in 1850, and the number did not increase appreciably during the next few years.[16] Although the south did not have to face the social and economic adjustments which immigration forced on the north, it resented the additional population strength which the alien gave that section. As its own minority position became increasingly clear, the south's bitterness against the foreign-born mounted proportionately.[17]

Each section of the nation, then, felt deeply concerned at the immigrant invasion. In the northeast the tradition of American supremacy was being challenged by the foreign-born; in the west natives were awakening to the fact that aliens were usurping political and economic leadership; and in the south the foreigner was resented for the additional strength that he gave the north.

Immigration had conjured up a host of problems which, although largely ignored through the 1840's when the nation was absorbed in other matters, were soon to give the nativist cause new impetus.

Almost as important as the alien influx in keeping alive nativistic prejudice were the liberal revolutions which shook western Europe in 1848. The proprietory interest taken by Americans in all such uprisings made them peculiarly susceptible to the lessons drawn by anti-Catholic propagandists from the old world's troubles.[18] If the revolutions should succeed, writers promptly pointed out, monarchists and Catholics would be driven from their homes and forced to seek refuge elsewhere. What would be more natural than that they should turn to the United States? There they would be protected by the toleration extended all creeds and sects. There, too, in an undeveloped country, they would have their best chance to recuperate ancient powers, win converts, and perhaps eventually recover in the new world all that they had lost in the old.[19] One editor expressed the general alarm when he wrote:

> Have we not reason to believe that now, while popery is losing ground in Europe, that this land presents to the Pope a fine field of operations, and that here he is endeavoring by every means in his power, to establish his falling throne, and that he is now sending out his minions to accomplish his fiend-like purpose, to prepare the way before him, that he may make a grand a triumphant entree [*sic*] into this country when he shall be hurled from his tyrannous and polluted throne in Europe? [20]

These warnings took on new meaning with the fall of Rome and the flight of Pope Pius IX; prophecy seemed to be fulfilling itself and American liberty endangered as never before.[21]

Nor did the failure of the uprisings quiet American apprehension. Mixed with regret that the cause of liberty had suffered a setback was the fear that a new and more vigorous Catholic church, strengthened by victory and secure in its despotic allies, would again turn to the task of subduing the United States.

Popery, writers warned, was now bolstered with the bayonets of European rulers; Protestants must be ever-vigilant lest they lose all that they had gained since the Reformation.[22]

The failure of these varied forces—the Mexican War, mounting immigration, and the European uprisings—to arouse more general resentment against Catholicism convinced nativists that something was wrong. Events which but a few years before would have stirred a universal clamor now went unnoticed save for half-hearted notices in the religious press. The realization was gradually brought home to those directing the destinies of organized anti-Catholicism that time-tried methods no longer sufficed and that only a complete overhauling of their propaganda machinery would bring the success they had formerly enjoyed.

Particularly susceptible to this belief were the leaders of the Protestant Reformation Society. Although the need of attracting the more moderate group won to their cause by the New York school controversy had forced them to temper their methods, they still lived in a day when the lurid tales of a Maria Monk, the invective of a Breckinridge or a Brownlee or a Samuel Smith, and the imagined plots of a Morse were the best instruments with which to shape popular opinion. Criticism of this type of propaganda had frequently been voiced. Typical of many attacks was a book by David M. Reese, *Humbugs of New York,* in which he classed anti-Popery with antislavery and prohibition "among the humbugs of the times, for the obvious reason that both Popery and Anti-Popery are impostures upon the public." [23] Reese made it clear that he objected not to attacks on Catholicism but to their un-Christian form and demoralizing influence. "Tales of lust, and blood, and murder," he wrote, "such as these with which the ultra-Protestant press is teeming, in all the loathsome and disgusting details in which they are recited; and especially when they are represented as transpiring under the cloak of religion, and the criminals occupying and disgracing the holy office of the ministry, are adapted in the very nature of things to strengthen the hands of infidelity and irreligion." [24] Another writer expressed a similar sentiment when he said: "The taste for these publications and the excitement produced by them, are the natural product of the false alarm which the Jesuitism of our own country had attempted to raise against the Jesuitism of Rome. Here is rogue chasing rogue—Jesuit in pursuit of Jesuit—but the older rogue is the wiser, because he has been longer in practice." [25]

Criticisms such as these might have been ignored by the Protestant Reformation Society, had not tangible evidence of their weight in the form of declining membership, the indifference of the religious press, the rapid growth of the American Protestant Association, and the storm of resentment following the Philadelphia riots convinced many of the society's leaders that drastic reforms were necessary. The reorganization which ensued was begun early in 1844 and by the time the revulsion which followed the Philadelphia riots had died down, a new society was fairly launched, ready to accept a policy dictated by the needs of the times.

Opportunity for this change came late in 1843, when the Reverend W. C. Brownlee, who had served as president of the Protestant Reformation Society since its inception, retired from active labors. His successors were wise enough to realize the stigma which had been attached even to the name of their society; hence in January, 1844, they allowed it to pass quietly from existence and reared in its place a new nativistic organization, the American Protestant Society.

Although this new society was pledged to battle the "superstition" and "spiritual darkness" of Popery, its constitution reflected what its founders believed to be a spirit of tolerance and Christianity:

Believing coercion in religious opinions, and the spirit of denunciation, to be inconsistent with the spirit of Christianity, the means to be employed to secure the objects of the Society are Light and

Love; in the use of these means, the Society will aim to enlighten Protestants concerning the nature, operation, and influence of Romanism, as well as to guard against its encroachments upon our civil and religious institutions, as to awaken Christian feeling and Christian action for the salvation of Romanists, by the employment of the Press, Lecturing Agents, Missionaries, and Colporteurs to circulate Bibles, Tracts, and Books upon the subject—looking unto God for success in this work.[26]

Thus the society was to have a dual objective: warning Protestants of the dangers inherent in the Catholic system and bringing about the "salvation of Romanists" by converting them to Protestantism.

It was this second aim that distinguished the new organization from the Protestant Reformation Society and accounted for much of its success. Monthly concerts of prayer for the conversion of Papists were inaugurated in the New York churches,[27] and armed with this spiritual endorsement, missionaries sallied forth to spread among Catholics their new message of "light and love." Within a short time special groups were singled out for conversion: the Portuguese fishermen of the New England coast,[28] the French inhabitants of the northeast, the German settlers in the west.[29] Although the society's managers warned that results would probably be few,[30] the annual reports were filled with glowing accounts of conversions which had been made and the amount expended on these agents increased from $3,000 in 1844 to $20,000 in 1848.[31]

Although these domestic missionary operations were generally approved by the Protestant churches, the society's efforts abroad brought it more popular support. These interests were centered in the island of Madeira, where the Reverend Robert R. Kalley and the Reverend M. J. Gonsalves, the latter an agent of the society, were seeking converts. The political and religious activities of these two agents aroused such resentment among Catholics that both the missionaries and those they converted were

subjected to a mild persecution.[32] Kalley finally made his way to
the United States with tales of men and women who had been
imprisoned for publicly denying the doctrine of transubstantiation, and the American Protestant Society, sensing the popular
appeal of a group persecuted by modern Rome, immediately made
his cause its own. Money necessary to bring the Madeira Protestants to the United States was raised, and in 1848 the first
group of about sixty arrived, with others following during the
year.[33]

Having encouraged some 400 of these converts to come to
New York, the American Protestant Society was faced with the
embarrassing task of providing for them and settling them in
new homes. Funds were necessary, and these were solicited
through a number of public meetings, the first held at the Broadway Tabernacle in New York. An overflow audience listened
to violent anti-Catholic speeches, heard the Madeira exiles sing
hymns and give testimony of Catholic persecution, and contributed handsomely to the collection that was taken up.[34] This success encouraged similar meetings in other cities; for a time the
refugees were shuttled about the country for group appearances,
then they were divided up to accompany Gonsalves, Kalley, and
the regular agents of the society on speaking tours which allowed
additional thousands to hear of the persecution that they had
endured.[35] Protestants of Jacksonville, Illinois, were so moved
by the sufferers' pleas that they contributed farms on which the
exiles might settle, and by October, 1849, most of them had established themselves comfortably in their new homes.[36] If Protestants, said the Catholic *Freeman's Journal,* "intend carrying out
the farm system they may do a large business in the conversion
line." [37] Despite such cynical comments, the Madeira group convinced many religious men and women of the American Protestant Society's sincere desire to win converts for Protestantism.

These missionary activities gradually broke down the barriers
which the churches, long accustomed to denunciation and sensa-

tionalism from anti-Catholic speakers, had erected against the society's lecturing agents. The managers of the society, aware of this prejudice, had taken pains to combat it; four lecturing agents who had been inherited from the Protestant Reformation Society were dismissed when they failed to temper their invective, and new agents were selected who would appeal to the milder antipathies of respectable audiences.[38] As churches realized the change which had taken place, they began opening their doors to the society's speakers.[39] The religious press, too, soon showed a willingness to accept and praise their messages. Typical was the comment occasioned by an address of Herman Norton, an agent of the society:

We have had so many fiery spirits among us and so much mischief has been done by fierce denunciation, that it was no easy task for Mr. Norton to overcome the prejudice which was arrayed against him. But the thing has been done in the most surprising manner. Baptist and Methodist and Presbyterian and Dutch and German Reformed churches are open to a hearing of the claims which he urges.[40]

Commendation such as this meant that the lecturing system could expand; the initial twelve agents were soon augmented by others who carried on an effective campaign through the latter 1840's.[41]

The publications of the American Protestant Society were both more tolerant and more numerous than those of any previous organization. By 1849 more than 2,200,000 pages of tracts were being circulated yearly, some bearing such titles as *Awful Effects of the Confessional,* but a greater number printed in French, German, and Portuguese as well as English, designed to appeal to Catholics who might possibly be converted.[42] Anti-Catholic books were printed and the production of such works was encouraged by yearly prizes.[43] A library established in New York City made these publications, as well as other books on Popery, available to interested ministers and laymen.[44]

It was in the journalistic field, however, that the American Protestant Society enjoyed most success. The most influential of the earlier anti-Catholic journals, the *American Protestant Vindicator,* ceased publication with the retirement of Brownlee as its editor in 1843 and its place was immediately taken by a bi-weekly newspaper, *The American Protestant,* sponsored by the society.[45] A year later this enterprise was abandoned as unsuccess-ful, and the monthly *American Protestant Magazine* founded.[46] This journal reflected the spirit of the society that it represented, its editors announcing in their first issue:

It is our purpose in this work to make prominent our relations and duties to the Roman Catholic population of the United States. This will be done not in a controversial manner. During the heat and hurry of controversy, we fear that many have lost sight of their true position with respect to the Romanists among us. This we wish to present by statements of facts and the true grounds of obligation, rather than by the denunciation of ignorant men, who may be walking in the light with which they are favored. The Protestant community must be made to feel that they are called to labor for the best welfare of the papal population, not merely by the American Protestant Society, nor by any other Society, but the Providence of God summons them, and the authority of His word calls them into this vineyard.[47]

The success of this policy was indicated by the popularity of the *American Protestant Magazine.* Within a few months it absorbed the *Quarterly Review of the American Protestant Association* and in 1847 the *National Protestant* and the *North American Protestant Magazine or Anti-Jesuit.*[48] By this time its circulation "exceeded the expectations of its most sanguine friends" [49] and its editors felt justified in founding a similar magazine for Germans in America, *Der Freie Deutsche Katholik.*[50]

By 1847 the American Protestant Society had established itself as the most successful among nativistic organizations. Its membership was constantly increasing and the auxiliary societies which it had established in eastern cities were showing a lusty growth.[51] Equally encouraging were the financial returns. In 1844 the society's income was about $6,000; a year later this had increased to more than $7,000 and members were boasting that the proceeds of the American Board of Commissioners for Foreign Missions had been even less when that organization was two years old.[52] By 1847 the receipts were $19,000, considerably more than the American Bible Society could vaunt at its fourth meeting,[53] and by 1849 they had mounted to nearly $30,000.[54] Optimistic members were justified in believing that the American Protestant Society had taken its permanent place among the religious societies of its day.

More important than the material accomplishments of this organization, however, were the lessons that nativists could learn from its success. They could see that organized anti-Catholicism had to depend on the churchgoing middle classes for its greatest support. From this realization, it was but a step to the belief that the direct aid of the churches was as essential as the support of those who attended them. Organized religion was necessary in any reform and the society's deliberate efforts to enlist the churches of America in their crusade brought to No-Popery its first major successes.

Lecturing agents again were used for this purpose. They were sent to the church conventions, both national and local, which assembled annually, there to outline to the gathered clerics the purposes of the society which they represented.[55] The response was universally encouraging, both in financial contributions and in pledges of support exemplified in such resolutions as that adopted by the Presbytery of Georgia:

Resolved: that in view of the increase of the adherents of Romanism, and of the influence of that system of error throughout our land by means of efforts, zealous advocates, and also of emigration from foreign lands, we cordially commend to the Churches under our care, the American Protestant Society.[56]

Several thousand ministers of the gospel each year heard agents of the society speak against Catholicism and were sufficiently swept away to pass commendatory resolutions of this type.

One result of this activity was a marked increase in the number of anti-Catholic sermons preached in individual churches.[57] Many ministers gave whole services over to the No-Popery cause or regularly included prayers against the anti-Christ, the most popular invocation of this sort reading:

O Lord God, thou hast commanded us to wait upon thee and to call upon thee in the day of trouble, and thou hast promised to hear and answer us. . . . Be thou our sun and shield, that if Popery is destined to gain the ascendency in our land, we may be armed to meet and triumph over its attendant evils; may we remember that not only from seeming but from real evils thou canst and will enduce good; that in leading thy church triumphantly over all her enemies thou art glorifying thyself, whilst thou art preparing her for thy presence above.[58]

Other clerics, duly impressed, hurriedly studied the history and principles of Catholicism that they might be better prepared for the struggle which the American Protestant Society prophesied as inevitable.[59]

The society and others interested in its work were not content with these individual efforts. Lack of unity among the Protestant sects had long been recognized as their greatest weakness in the battle with Rome, both by Protestants who urged the necessity of a united front [60] and by Catholics who took every occasion to ridicule Protestant division.[61] "How degrading is the spectacle that Protestantism is made to present," remarked the *Freeman's Journal*, "when its ministers are found disputing among themselves, on all subjects of hope, faith and charity; unable to arrive at unity, except when marshaled into the ranks of Protestant Bigotry, to deliver anti-Popery lectures, and to assail the only denomination that never goes out of its way to meddle with them." [62] Even impartial foreign observers pointed out that the "chaotic condition of the Protestant community, divided into warring sects, increases the power of a church whose characteristic is unity." [63] Criticisms such as these, particularly from the hated Catholic journals, aroused such resentment that many Protestants sought a means of uniting the hitherto divergent sects.

The first attempt in this direction was international in scope but participated in by most of the American denominations which sent delegates to a World Convention and Evangelical Alliance in London in August, 1846. Those attending united in deploring the "existing divisions" in the Christian church and made some progress in drafting articles of faith which would be acceptable to all the denominations represented. However, they soon became so involved in debating the admission of slaveholding delegates that the meetings ended in confusion, and nothing was accomplished. [64]

More important was an American convention, called by a group of clergymen and laymen representing the Baptist, Methodist Episcopal, Methodist Protestant, Congregational, and Presbyterian churches, to meet at Binghamton, New York, on July 22, 1847. Although the American Protestant Society disclaimed responsibility for the meeting, its guiding hand was clearly apparent, for the speakers included Herman Norton, Lyman Beecher, M. J. Gonsalves, and others active in its behalf, and the resolutions that were finally adopted specifically singled out the society for praise:

Resolved: that the efforts of the abettors of Romanism to supplant our free institutions are now so apparent, and so openly avowed, especially by the princes and crowned heads of Europe, that every intelligent observer must see the danger to which we are exposed; and must appreciate the necessity for active exertions on our part to avert it.

Resolved: that the time has come when all Protestants, of whatever name, should unite their energies, their counsels and their prayers, in the work of enlightening the Romanists, and converting them to the religion of the Bible—thus forming in reality a "Holy Alliance," beloved and honored by every friend of humanity, and hated only by tyrants and the workers of iniquity.

Resolved: that we regard the plans and operations of the American Protestant Society as admirably adapted to promote both the temporal and eternal welfare of the Roman Catholics of our country, and at the same time to secure the perpetuity of our free institutions, by defeating the machinations of those despots in the old world, who, for the sake of their tottering thrones, are attempting to subvert our liberties.[65]

These resolutions were the only accomplishments of the Binghamton convention. The several hundred delegates willingly listened to rabid speeches against Rome and talked in impassioned tones of the need of Protestant consolidation, but insurmountable obstacles blocked the path to unity. The American Protestant Society evidently hoped to arrange other Protestant conventions to create interest in both Catholicism and the society itself, but none was held.[66]

Despite this single failure, the managers of the American Protestant Society by 1849 had every right to review their work with a glow of pride. Their efforts had turned the war against Rome into a religious crusade and everywhere American churchgoers were showing a quickening interest. Speeches and books against Catholicism were increasing, No-Popery orators were invading even college commencements,[67] and Protestants were displaying an interest in Romanism which would have been considered unusual even in 1844. The many curious Protestants attending Catholic churches aroused just resentment; "during the interesting part of the performance," wrote one correspondent of the *Freeman's Journal,* "they stand on tip-toe on the kneeling-board to obtain a good view; when the music pleases them they listen in silent admiration; when the interest of either Mass or music lags, conversation, not always confined to an under tone, beguiles the time." [68] Such general interest in Catholicism gave nativistic leaders renewed hope for the success of their cause.

Perhaps the best indication of Protestant confidence was the revival of written and oral controversies with Catholics. The outspoken discussions which had enlivened the 1830's had been abandoned, partly because of the effectiveness of Catholic arguments, partly because many Americans, hitherto entirely ignorant of Catholicism, had been convinced that there was much to be said in behalf of that church. The revival of these same controversies in the late 1840's indicated a sturdy Protestant assurance; there was no longer any fear that champions of nativism might be bested by those of Rome.

The part that Brownlee and the Breckinridges had played in the earlier controversies was taken over now by the Reverend Nicholas Murray, a prominent Presbyterian clergyman who held a pastorate at Elizabethtown, New Jersey. Murray was Irish-born, of Catholic parentage. He had emigrated to the United States as a young man and after his conversion to Presbyterianism had risen rapidly in the councils of that church, finally assuming its leadership in 1849 as moderator of the General Assembly.[69] Murray felt that his Catholic upbringing peculiarly fitted him to expose the evils of Popery; hence in February, 1847, he began addressing weekly letters to Bishop John Hughes through the columns of the New York *Observer,* signing them "Kirwan" in honor of Dean Walter Blake Kirwan, a famed eighteenth century Irish convert from Catholicism.[70] His arguments were written with moderation but were nevertheless firm; Catholicism, he maintained, was an enemy of the Bible, of morality and of liberty and would remain an enemy so long as its autocratic hierarchy held to anti-Scriptural beliefs. His inevitable conclusion was that Catholics should leave their church and seek the truth in Protestantism:

You are hoodwinked and manacled by a system of the grossest fraud and delusion; you are denied the common birthright of a citizen of the world—seeing with your own eyes and hearing with your own ears. You are robbed of the only volume that can guide you—and are forbidden to enter the way of life, save through the gate which is guarded by your priests. O! Suffer the entreaties of one who suffered as you now do under the galling chains of papal tyranny. Break the fetters which priests have forged, and in which they have bound you.[71]

The popularity of Murray's letters amazed even the author. They were published in whole or in part in nearly all religious periodicals and when reprinted in book form in June, 1847, 10,000 copies were disposed of within two weeks with sales at the end of a year reaching more than 100,000.[72] By the summer of 1847 Murray had been revealed as the author and was immediately besieged with letters urging him to continue his attacks on Rome. "Allow me to say," wrote one admirer, "yours is the hand to sweep through this whole domain of error. It would be an occasion of deep regret if you should not carry forward to its completion a work which you have so happily begun. The Christian public expect, may I not say, demand it of you. . . . Your country, whose political as well as religious interests are threatened with deadly invasion, demands it." [73] Goaded on by these requests, Murray began a second series in the New York *Observer* in October which, like the first, was addressed to Hughes.[74] The letters showed less polish and delicacy than the first (Murray explained that they were addressed to Catholics rather than Protestants and had to be cruder in form to have any appeal) and were devoted to bitter attacks on extreme unction, penance, miracles, relics, indulgences, the Mass, and other beliefs of the church. The last two letters pleaded with Catholics to come out from their sinful ways.[75]

Through the two series, Murray had obviously been seeking to embroil Hughes in a controversy. Other nativists took up the cry,[76] and finally Hughes announced that he was ready to answer Murray through any medium mutually agreeable.[77] In a calmer moment he recognized the futility of rebuttal, but it was too late now to back down. An attempt to do so brought from the New

York *Observer* the sly remark: "When the bishop announced his intention of meeting these letters he stated that he had not read them. . . . Their perusal may have led to his change of purpose." [78] Hughes began his reply early in 1848, publishing his letters in the *Freeman's Journal* and confining them to specific answers of Murray's arguments.[79] The New York *Observer* tried vainly to enmesh the two authors in a controversy comparable to the Hughes-Breckinridge affair of a decade before, offering to publish Hughes' letters if the *Freeman's Journal* would print those of Murray,[80] and engaging Murray to reply to each letter of Hughes through its own columns.[81] When Hughes finally withdrew from the lists, Protestants accepted Murray as their new champion and joyfully hailed the triumphant third series of letters which he promptly published.[82]

The Murray-Hughes controversy was only one of many. Everywhere Protestants, confident in their new position, sought to best Catholics through arguments and rebuttal. In Iowa a Catholic bishop and a Baptist minister engaged in a long dispute; [83] in Philadelphia the Reverend Joseph F. Berg published an analysis of an encyclical letter of Pope Pius IX and challenged Bishop F. P. Kenrick to a public debate on the issues involved; in Boston the Reverend Edward Beecher singled out Bishop Kenrick as the recipient of public letters attacking in general the theological beliefs of Catholics; in Cleveland a controversy raged between a Protestant clergyman styling himself "Veritas" and a Catholic who signed his articles "Catholicus;" [84] in Washington a Protestant minister and the Catholic president of Georgetown University engaged in an oral debate,[85] and the *Nation* was the medium of controversy on Catholicism and Protestantism.[86] Two antagonists in Jersey City came to grips over the Catholic school system; [87] thirty Protestant clergymen in St. Louis grew so incensed over the publications of the Catholic editor, Orestes Brownson, that they challenged him to public debate,[88] and two rival editors in Louisville filled their papers with arguments up-

holding and attacking Catholicism.[89]   The editor of the New
York *Daily Times* again lured Bishop Hughes into the field by
publishing letters to which the prelate took exception.[90]   A Protestant minister and a Catholic bishop in Savannah, Georgia, not
only agreed on a written controversy but set up a committee of
three Protestants, three Catholics, and a Jew to judge who had
won.[91]   Throughout the country appeared the challenge of the
Reverends Robert J. Breckinridge of Baltimore, N. L. Rice of
Cincinnati, and William S. Plumer of Virginia to debate any
three Catholic clergymen anywhere and at any time on the subject "Is the Romish Church the Church of Christ?" [92]

These controversies were indicative of the spirit which by the
end of the 1840's permeated the ranks of organized nativism.
Bolstered by a latent public opinion which had been aroused by
the Mexican War, the European uprisings of 1848, and an alarming immigration, nativists had equipped themselves with an active society and a close alliance with the Protestant churches.
Thus armed, they waited with confidence the renewal of general
popular support for their cause.

NOTES

[1] New York *Observer*, January 1, 1848; *Freeman's Journal,* January 29,
1848.   Other religious papers did not notice the matter.   This same society
had listened to an anti-Catholic address by the Reverend George Cheever in
1842. *Freeman's Journal,* December 31, 1842.

[2] *Order of United Americans,* October 21, 1848; *Native Eagle,* May 12,
1846; *The Know Nothing Almanac; or, True American's Manual for 1855*
(New York, 1855), 58; *An Alarm to Heretics; or, An Exposition of Some
of the Evils, Villainies and Dangers of Papacy, also a Vindication of and an
Outline of the True American Platform* (Philadelphia, 1854), 10.

[3] *American Protestant Magazine,* II (December, 1846); New York *Observer,* July 18, 1846; William Hogan, *High and Low Mass in the Catholic
Church; with Comments* (Boston, 1846), 45–46.

[4] A Presbyterian clergyman threatened to launch such a newspaper attack
on Polk that he would be driven from office unless the Catholic chaplains were
withdrawn.   Polk ignored both the threat and the eventual attack. *The Diary
of James K. Polk during his Presidency, 1845–1849* (Chicago, 1910), II, 187–
188, III, 103–105.   See also *Freeman's Journal,* August 7, 1847, December
18, 1847.

[5] New York *Observer*, July 18, 1846. The American army's attitude toward Catholics is described in the *Freeman's Journal*, September 16, 1848, August 9, 1851, August 23, 1851.

[6] Polk planned to use Hughes to "disabuse the minds of the Catholic Priests and people of Mexico in regard to what they most erroneously supposed to be the hostile design of the government and people of the United States upon the religion and church property of Mexico." *Diary of James K. Polk*, I, 408. Typical attacks on the plan are in *Native Eagle*, May 27, 1846, May 30, 1846; New York *Observer*, December 18, 1847. See also Thomas F. Meehan, "Archbishop Hughes and Mexico," United States Catholic Historical Society *Records and Studies*, XIX (September, 1929), 32–37.

[7] *Order of United Americans*, August 12, 1848.

[8] These estimates were based on computations of the normal rate of population increase in the United States and on the few figures furnished by Canadian authorities on immigration from that dominion. *DeBow's Review*, III (March, 1848); Louis Schade, *Immigration into the United States from a Statistical and National Point of View* (Washington, 1856), II; Jesse Chickering, *Immigration into the United States* (Boston, 1848); DeBow, *Compendium of the Seventh Census*, 124–125; Condon, "Irish Immigration into the United States since 1790," *loc. cit.*, IV, 88.

[9] The causes of emigration from Ireland and Germany at this time are best treated in two articles by Marcus L. Hansen: "The Second Colonization of New England," *loc. cit.*, II, 539–560, and "The Revolutions of 1848 and German Emigration," *Journal of Economic and Business History*, II (August, 1930), 630–655.

[10] G. H. Haynes, "The Causes of Know Nothing Success in Massachusetts," *American Historical Review*, III (October, 1897), 73; C. Stickney, "Know Nothingism in Rhode Island," *Brown University History Seminary Papers* (Providence, 1894), 8. In 1850 12.65 per cent of the population of the northeastern states was foreign-born, 19.84 per cent of the middle states and 12.75 per cent of the middle western states. DeBow, *Compendium of the Seventh Census*, 121.

[11] Nichols, *Forty Years of American Life*, II, 78.

[12] *Ibid.*, II, 68–69; *American Union*, October 20, 1849. By 1850 New Orleans was second only to New York as a port of entry, mute testimony to the large number of Germans who were taking this route to the middle west. Cole, "Nativism in the Lower Mississippi Valley," *loc. cit.*, VI, 259.

[13] Theodore C. Blegen, "The Competition of the Northwestern States for Immigrants," *Wisconsin Magazine of History*, III (September, 1919), 4–10, 23–26. Wisconsin created a Commissioner of Emigration in 1852, authorized to employ agents and use advertising to attract Germans to that state. The office was abolished in 1855, probably because of opposition from nativist factions.

[14] DeBow, *Compendium of the Seventh Census*, 61; Kennedy, *Preliminary Report on the Eighth Census*, 18–19.

[15] Nichols, *Forty Years of American Life*, II, 69.

[16] Caroline E. MacGill, "Economic History, 1607–1865," in *The South in the Building of the Nation* (Richmond, 1909–1910), V, 595–606.

[17] Southern population at this time was increasing at between 25 and 30

per cent for each decade, northern population at a rate of 40 per cent. Southerners believed the difference was due to immigration. DeBow, *Compendium of the Seventh Census,* 96.

[18] A few nativists insisted that the revolutions, like all past European uprisings, had been stirred up by the Pope for his personal aggrandizement and could accomplish nothing. *North American Protestant Magazine or Anti-Jesuit,* I (April, 1846); *American Protestant Magazine,* II (March, 1847).

[19] *American Protestant Magazine,* IV (September, 1848), IV (March. 1849); *Order of United Americans,* September 9, 1848; *The Protestant Annual; Exhibiting the Demoralizing Influence of Popery, and the Character of its Priesthood* (New York, 1847), 117; American Protestant Society, *Fifth Annual Report* (New York, 1848), 25; *Sixth Annual Report* (New York, 1849), 4–5.

[20] *Protestant Annual,* 117.

[21] *Congregationalist,* June 1, 1849, October 19, 1849; New York *Observer,* December 30, 1848.

[22] New York *Observer,* December 22, 1849, September 25, 1851; *Congregationalist,* December 26, 1851, January 2, 1852; Robert Gault, *Popery, the Man of Sin and the Son of Perdition* (New York, 1855), vi–vii.

[23] David M. Reese, *Humbugs of New York; being a Remonstrance Against Popular Delusion, whether in Science, Philosophy, or Religion* (New York, 1838), 210.

[24] *Ibid.,* 217.

[25] *Protestant Jesuitism* (New York, 1836), 30–31.

[26] The constitution is printed in American Protestant Society, *Second Annual Report* (New York, 1845), 27–28. It may be consulted in Appendix A.

[27] *American Protestant Magazine,* II (February, 1847).

[28] American Protestant Society, *Second Annual Report,* 14–16. Missionaries able to speak the language of the group with whom they were to work were chosen.

[29] *Ibid.,* 17.

[30] *Ibid.,* 3–4.

[31] *Ibid.,* 28; American Protestant Society, *Fifth Annual Report,* 27.

[32] Kalley and Gonsalves both maintained this persecution was solely on religious grounds. Robert R. Kalley, *Persecutions in Madeira in the Nineteenth Century* (New York, 1845), 15–49; M. J. Gonsalves, *The Testimony of a Convert from the Church of Rome: Narrative of the Religious Experience and Travels of the Reverend M. J. Gonsalves. Also a Narrative of Signorina Florencia D'Romani* (Boston, 1859), 1–32. The Catholic press, on the other hand, insisted that the Madeira exiles were outlaws, who had been punished only for civil offenses. *Freeman's Journal,* May 19, 1849, December 22, 1849; *Pilot,* November 10, 1849.

[33] *American Protestant Magazine,* IV (November, 1848), IV (December, 1848), V (June, 1849); *Protestant Banner,* July 4, 1844.

[34] *American Protestant Magazine,* V (November, 1849); *Freeman's Journal,* May 19, 1849. Appeals were also made for food and clothing for the exiles. *American Protestant Magazine,* V (October, 1849).

[35] Gonsalves, *Testimony,* 33–68; *Congregationalist,* October 26, 1849, November 2, 1849; *American Protestant Magazine,* V (June, 1849), V (November, 1849).

[36] The president of Illinois college played a leading part in securing the land. *American Protestant Magazine*, V (July, 1849), V (September, 1849), V (December, 1849).

[37] May 19, 1849.

[38] *Circular Issued by the American Protestant Society, December 1847* (New York, 1847), 8–9; American Protestant Society, *Second Annual Report*, 10. The society normally secured converted Catholics as its lecturing agents.

[39] American Protestant Society, *First Annual Report* (New York, 1844), 7–8.

[40] New York *Evangelist*, quoted in *American Protestant Magazine*, I (December, 1845). For similar comments see *Ibid.*, I (April, 1846).

[41] American Protestant Society, *First Annual Report*, 11.

[42] American Protestant Society, *Sixth Annual Report*, 24–25. Thirty-three different tracts were published in 1849.

[43] American Protestant Society, *Second Annual Report*, 10. The usual practice was to give two premiums, one of $100, the other of $25.

[44] American Protestant Society, *First Annual Report*, 10.

[45] *Ibid.*, 9.

[46] New York *Observer*, June 14, 1845. The new magazine had 24 pages in each number and sold for one dollar a year.

[47] *American Protestant Magazine*, I (June, 1845).

[48] *Ibid.*, II (January, 1847), II (March, 1847). See above, pp. 170–171 for earlier history of these magazines.

[49] *Ibid.*, III (May, 1848); New York *Observer*, May 27, 1848. One popular feature of the magazine was a children's department, added in II (November, 1846). Parents were urged to recommend this to their offspring that they might be "secured from the errors and dangers of Popery." *Ibid.*, II (January, 1847).

[50] *Ibid.*, II (November, 1847). After six months of publication this new magazine had a circulation of about 500 copies monthly. American Protestant Society, *Fifth Annual Report*, 23–24.

[51] No evidence exists as to the number of these auxiliaries, but such representative societies as the Female Protestant Society of Savannah, Georgia, the Emory College Protestant Society, and the Baptist Protestant Society of Brooklyn indicate that they were widely scattered. They were supposed to hold monthly meetings to discuss Popery and to maintain libraries through which anti-Catholic books could be circulated. *American Protestant Magazine*, III (November, 1847), III (February, 1848), IV (June, 1848).

[52] American Protestant Society, *Second Annual Report*, 28; New York *Observer*, May 4, 1844, May 24, 1845. The boast was made at the annual meeting of the society.

[53] American Protestant Society, *Fourth Annual Report* (New York, 1847), 27–28, 40.

[54] New York *Observer*, May 19, 1849.

[55] Agents were heard by such representative bodies as the Annual Conference of the Methodist Protestant churches, the General Synod of the Dutch Reformed church, the General Conference of the Methodist Episcopal church, the Baptist State Convention of Pennsylvania, the General Association of Massachusetts Congregational churches, the combined Synods of New York

and New Jersey, and countless individual presbyteries, synods and associations. The agents were indefatigable workers; one described a typical day's activity in which he spoke before the Synod of Utica, New York, at Oswego on Saturday night, the Methodists of Oswego on Sunday morning, the Presbyterians on Sunday afternoon and the Baptists on Sunday night. Each issue of the *American Protestant Magazine*, I–V (1845–1849) is crowded with accounts of these meetings. See also *Minutes of the General Association of Massachusetts* (Boston, 1848), 12; New York *Observer*, October 28, 1848.

[56] *American Protestant Magazine*, III (June, 1847).

[57] New York *Observer*, July 24, 1847.

[58] *American Protestant Magazine*, II (February, 1846).

[59] Typical was the action of the Association of Protestant Ministers of Cincinnati which, in 1848, named a committee to report on "Romanism in the Nineteenth Century" for the education of its members. *Ibid.*, III (May, 1848).

[60] Andrew A. Lipscomb, *Our Country; its Danger and Duty* (New York, 1844), 107–109; George W. Bethune, *The Strength of Christian Charity; a Sermon Preached Before the Foreign Evangelical Society, New York, May 5, 1844* (Philadelphia, 1844), 33; Gardiner Spring, *A Dissertation on the Rule of Faith; delivered at Cincinnati, Ohio, at the Annual Meeting of the American Bible Society* (New York, 1844), 100–101.

[61] *Freeman's Journal*, February 15, 1845, March 15, 1845, May 17, 1845, May 31, 1845.

[62] *Ibid.*, February 19, 1842.

[63] Nichols, *Forty Years of American Life*, II, 87.

[64] *United States Catholic Magazine*, V (November, 1846).

[65] *American Protestant Magazine*, III (September, 1847). See also *Ibid.*, III (August, 1847).

[66] *Ibid.*, III (September, 1847).

[67] *Freeman's Journal*, August 27, 1842. The Reverend George Cheever, a prominent anti-Catholic speaker, delivered a commencement address at Dartmouth in which he ascribed all progress to the Reformation and all decline to Romanism.

[68] *Ibid.*, March 3, 1849.

[69] Murray, *Memoirs*, 1–187, 256–259.

[70] New York *Observer*, February 6, 1847–May 8, 1847.

[71] Nicholas Murray, *Letters to the Right Reverend John Hughes, First Series* (New York, 1847), 99.

[72] New York *Observer*, June 19, 1847; Murray, *Memoirs*, 281. The volume was translated into German and widely circulated among Germans in the western part of the United States. Murray, *Memoirs*, 282.

[73] New York *Observer*, September 25, 1847.

[74] *Ibid.*, October 2, 1847–December 4, 1847.

[75] Nicholas Murray, *Letters to the Right Reverend John Hughes, Second Series* (New York, 1847), *passim;* Murray, *Memoirs*, 302.

[76] *American Protestant Magazine*, II (May, 1847).

[77] *Freeman's Journal*, December 4, 1847.

[78] January 15, 1848.

[79] *Freeman's Journal*, July 1, 1848–August 5, 1848. Hughes' letters were

subsequently issued in book form under the title *Kirwan Unmasked* (New York, 1848).

[80] The *Freeman's Journal* refused to accept this challenge. New York *Observer*, July 8, 1848, July 15, 1848.

[81] New York *Observer*, July 15, 1848–September 16, 1848.

[82] Hughes finally withdrew when business compelled him to leave the country. The third series was published under the title *Bishop Hughes Confuted. Reply to the Right Reverend John Hughes* (New York, 1848). Murray's influence continued large; his books were republished in the United States and translated into many foreign languages, editions appearing in Ireland, Ceylon and India, as well as other corners of the world. He continued his written attacks on Catholicism, publishing *Romanism at Home. Letters to the Hon. Roger B. Taney, Chief Justice of the United States* (New York, 1852) and a series of letters on Popery in Europe in the New York *Observer*, January 6, 1853 and ff. So great was his influence that converted Catholics in the United States were for some time referred to as Kirwanites.

[83] *Home Missionary*, XV (March, 1843).

[84] *American Protestant Magazine*, III (June, 1847).

[85] *Congregationalist*, April 19, 1850.

[86] *Pilot*, February 24, 1849.

[87] J. Kelly and A. W. McClure, *The School Question; a Correspondence between Rev. J. Kelly . . . and Rev. A. W. McClure, Jersey City* (New York, 1853). The controversy was carried on through the Jersey City *Daily Telegram*.

[88] *Pilot*, February 4, 1854.

[89] T. J. Jenkins, "Know Nothingism in Kentucky and its Destroyer," *Catholic World*, LVII (July, 1893), 517–518. The controversy was between George D. Prentice, editor of the Louisville *Journal*, and Benedict J. Webb, editor of the *Catholic Advocate*.

[90] *American and Foreign Christian Union*, V (October, 1854).

[91] *Ibid.*, II (September, 1851). The controversy was begun when Bishop F. Xavier Gartland took exception to a review in a Savannah paper of Achilli's *Dealings with the Inquisition* and wrote a reply attacking Protestant belief in general. He was answered by a Baptist minister who issued the challenge which was promptly accepted.

[92] *Protestant Banner*, August 15, 1844.

XI

Organizing for Victory
1850-1854

SO LONG as the nation was haunted by the spectre of sectional strife, nativism's popular appeal was limited, but with the Compromise of 1850 the situation abruptly changed. For four years north and south were to live in peace, the slavery issue settled, the fear of disunion forgotten. Americans once more were ready to listen eagerly to tales of papal conquest and to vote for candidates who promised to end the invasion of foreign hordes. Not until the latter part of 1854, when the full effects of the Kansas-Nebraska act were realized, did the United States again sublimate its hatred of Catholics and immigrants into the hatred from which grew a civil war.

Nativists made good use of these years of quiescence. Before they could convince the nation that vague fears of Romanism should be translated into political action, they found it necessary to strengthen their organization, capitalize fully upon blunders of the Catholic hierarchy, and emphasize their propaganda against both the Papist and foreigner as never before. In all of these things, but particularly in rebuilding their societies to meet the needs of the times, they were immeasurably aided by the situation in Europe.

To the religious American of 1849 or 1850 two things appeared certain: that Catholicism was declining rapidly on the continent and that it was making a last vigorous stand in England and the United States. In Italy the establishment of the Roman Republic of 1849 seemed to indicate that even that stronghold of Catholicism would welcome Protestantism.[1] In France antagonistic elements within the Church created the illusion that a lusty Protestant minority was struggling to be heard.[2] In Germany, reaction against the exhibition of a seamless coat of Christ centered in a Silesian priest, Johannes Ronge, whose efforts to establish a German Catholic church independent of Rome appeared to Americans to be a new Reformation sweeping the Man of Sin from the Rhine country.[3] All over Europe Catholics were showing evidences of apparent dissatisfaction with their church; Protestantism might yet triumph in those traditionally papal lands.

Religious Americans were equally certain that Catholicism was seeking to entrench itself in their own country and in England. In the United States the steady flow of Catholic immigrants and the unprecedented growth of their church convinced even the most skeptical. In England the so-called "Papal Aggression" of 1850 was equally alarming. There a Papal Bull setting up a hierarchy of English bishops deriving title from English sees offered positive proof to many Protestants, already alarmed by the Romeward drift of the Oxford group, that Pius IX was extending the spiritual arm of the church over the realm. An outraged populace forced Parliament to pass the Ecclesiastical Titles Bill, forbidding Roman Catholics the use of titles taken from any territory or place within the United Kingdom, but even this failed to allay Protestant fear.[4]

Still the situation in England was less alarming than that on the continent. American Protestants had no doubt that their English cousins could protect themselves, for the "Papal Agression" had led to a strengthening of anti-Catholic forces; a Protestant Alliance had been formed in 1851 to co-ordinate the efforts of those opposed to Rome,[5] and a short time later the eight British No-Popery societies merged into one powerful body.[6] But if Europe were to be saved, outside aid would be necessary, and American propagandists began preaching the need of antipapal missionary efforts abroad, the success of which, they pointed out, would not only fulfill Biblical prophecy by ending Romanism but would purify the stream of immigration at its source and assure the continuance of the United States as a Protestant power.[7] The conversion of Europe thus became a cardinal point in the American nativistic program.

This type of activity had not been completely neglected in the past. For some time two small societies had been engaged in the herculean task of driving Popery from Europe. The older of these was the Foreign Evangelical Society, formed in 1839 with its principal objective the winning of converts to Protestantism in France.[8] By 1849 its income of about $25,000 yearly was spent in maintaining missionaries both in France and in other Catholic countries.[9] The second society, the Christian Alliance, dated from 1842 and was concerned with the diffusion of "useful and religious knowledge among the natives of Italy, and other papal countries." [10] Its principal boast was the special denunciation it had received in an encyclical letter of Gregory XVI; the publicity naturally resulting had made the Christian Alliance the better known of the agencies working for the conversion of papal Europe.[11]

By the late 1840's, then, the United States was equipped with three anti-Catholic societies; the American Protestant Society operating at home, the Foreign Evangelical Society in France, and the Christian Alliance in Italy. The inefficiency of their overlapping efforts was apparent and a union inevitable. This merger was first suggested at a meeting of the Foreign Evangelical Society in 1843.[12] Four years later, when the *American Protestant Magazine* began advocating such a step,[13] the first move was taken. Meetings of representatives of the three societies were held through the spring of 1848, and by May of that year a satisfactory agreement was reached. A new society was to be formed, known as the American and Foreign Christian Union. Within this organization the older societies would remain intact;

the American Protestant Society would continue its efforts to Protestantize the United States while the Foreign Evangelical Society and the Christian Alliance would dispatch missionaries to France and Italy. But to the world at large, and particularly to the churches from which they hoped to solicit funds, a united front would be presented.[14]

This plan of union was accepted with alacrity by the Christian Alliance at its spring meeting in 1848. The members of the American Protestant Society showed some hesitancy; their organization was the most prominent of the three involved, and the consolidation would entail some sacrifice, but they finally accepted the arrangement at the society's annual meeting in May, 1848.[15] The Foreign Evangelical Society soon entered the fold,[16] and by the spring of 1849 it was possible for agents of the three societies to meet in New York and arrange final details of the union.[17]

The object of the American and Foreign Christian Union, according to its constitution, was to "diffuse and promote the principles of Religious Liberty, and a pure and Evangelical Christianity, both at home and abroad, wherever a corrupted Christianity exists." This was to be accomplished through the usual means: lecturing agents and missionaries were to be employed, while the press, the churches, and co-operating societies were to be pressed into service.[18] The society's methods were to be those of "light and love"; Catholics were to be "converted to Christianity" and the Protestant population both enlightened on the errors of Rome and induced to aid in the mighty work of evangelizing the world. The constitution of the society breathed a spirit of what its authors thought was toleration; "Popery" and "Romanism" were not even mentioned, and Catholicism was referred to only as corrupted Christianity. This was a far cry from the days of the Protestant Reformation Society, whose members refused to concede that Catholicism could be Christianity, no matter how corrupt.

The new society enjoyed remarkable success in its every enterprise. Funds poured into its coffers in unbelievable amounts, reaching nearly $80,000 in 1854.[19] Much of this was allotted to missionaries and lecturing agents; by 1854 more than 120 of these earnest men were roaming the country, speaking whenever there was an opportunity and working zealously to save Catholic souls wherever they might be found.[20] The society attempted to place these agents at strategic points, particularly at ports of entry such as New York and New Orleans, where Catholic immigrants could immediately be converted to Protestantism.[21] Many of these agents labored assiduously in the cause; one estimated that in two months he traveled 13,500 miles, visited eight states, preached 127 times, delivered seventy-nine addresses, wrote 330 letters, and visited 2,261 families.[22] Although a majority were employed in the home field, fifteen or twenty each year journeyed to Europe to beard Catholicism in its native haunts.

The society's other activities were on a corresponding scale. The anti-Catholic library which it established in New York City was boasted to be the most complete in the world.[23] The free lectures on Catholicism inaugurated in large eastern cities were sufficiently inflammatory to attract huge throngs. At least one riot was precipitated when disorderly elements in Newark attempted to stop the speaker's rantings.[24] The following extract from a typical speech explains both their popularity and the attacks upon them:

Catholicism is, and it ever has been, a bigoted, a persecuting, and a superstitious religion. There is no crime in the calendar of infamy of which it has not been guilty. There is no sin against humanity which it has not committed. There is no blasphemy against God which it has not sanctioned. It is a power which has never scrupled to break its faith solemnly plighted, wherever its interests seem to require it; which has no conscience; which spurns the control of public opinion; and which obtrudes its head among the nations of Christendom, dripping with the cruelties of millions of murders, and haggard with the debaucheries of a thousand years, always ambitious, always sanguinary, and always false.[25]

The dissemination of such calumny proved so lucrative that in 1854 the society purchased a New York building to serve as head-quarters and confidently prepared to take its permanent place among American religious organizations.[26]

The American and Foreign Christian Union championed two causes which added immeasurably to its prestige. The first was that of two Tuscan peasants, Francisco and Rosa Madiai, who had, according to word reaching America, been sentenced to long terms of imprisonment for reading a Protestant Bible. Catholics protested in vain that the Madiai family was being punished for the civil offense of plotting against the Tuscan state;[27] Americans preferred to believe the New York *Observer* when it said: "The two Madai [*sic.*], and multitudes besides them, are in the prisons of Tuscany for no other crime than *Protestantism,* and under this edict, some of these prisoners will in all probability suffer martyrdom, unless the Christian world lifts up its voice of remonstrance, and makes its indignant tones to be heard along the shores of the Mediterranean."[28]

The American and Foreign Christian Union took upon itself the task of fomenting and directing American protest. Its first step was to arrange a giant mass meeting, held at the Metropolitan Hall in New York City on January 7, 1853. An enthusiastic audience heard the mayor and innumerable speakers denounce Catholicism and find in the Madiai affair justification for all that had been said concerning Catholic enmity to the Bible. Resolutions expressing sympathy with the sufferers and calling on the President of the United States to bring about their release were adopted, and a fund was collected to ease the suffering they were enduring in their Tuscan dungeon, some $12,000 being raised for this purpose.[29] Similar meetings in Boston, Baltimore, and other cities [30] evinced such popular sympathy for the Madiai that religious organizations and individuals joined in urging the federal government to intervene in their behalf.[31] Even the New York legislature, swept away by the enthusiasm of the moment, passed resolutions:

Resolved, that the Legislature of the State of New York have regarded with deep solicitude and regret the recent persecutions to which Francisco Madiai and his wife, Rosa Madiai, have been subjected in the kingdom of Tuscany, for the alleged crime of reading the Holy Scriptures.

Resolved, that the congratulations with which the State of New York formally and by public act hailed in 1847 the efforts of Pius IX to ameliorate the condition of the Italian people and bestow upon them the incalculable blessings of national independence and constitutional freedom, make eminently proper at this time a formal and public remonstrance against cruel and flagrant oppressions in that same land.

Resolved, that the President of the United States be respectfully requested to exert his best influences with the Government of Tuscany to obtain, as a favor, asked by a people which welcomes all strangers and protects all religions, permission for the Madiai and their fellow-prisoners for the same offence to emigrate to this country.[32]

Although the national government took no formal action in response to these petitions, Lewis Cass, in the Senate, branded the action of the Duke of Tuscany as "one of the most flagrant violations of the rights of conscience recorded in the long chapter of religious intolerance," [33] and President Fillmore at one time considered a note requesting the release of the Madiai.[34] The two peasants continued to languish in their cells, unaware that they had done much to strengthen the society which had defended them.

Even more popular interest was aroused by the second cause embraced by the American and Foreign Christian Union: an effort to secure, through diplomatic action, complete liberty of conscience and action for all Protestant missionaries in Italy. The reaction against the liberal revolutions in that country was interpreted by most Americans as an attack on Protestantism, for many of the revolutionists were of that religious faith, and the Italian government was inclined to view all Protestants as potential enemies of the state. News began to filter into the press of

Americans who had been punished for preaching or reading from the Bible and of Italian Protestants who were being made to suffer for their faith. The imprisonment of an agent of an English evangelical society aroused particular resentment.[35] Protestants felt that the American government should formally protest these apparent violations of religious liberty and secure for Americans the right to worship according to the dictates of their own consciences in any country of the world.

The American and Foreign Christian Union, sensing the popular sentiment behind this demand and realizing the threat to its own foreign operations should Protestant missionary activities abroad be stamped out, was quick to sponsor the cause of Italian religious liberty. The success of the Madiai meeting suggested a similar procedure now. Plans for such a gathering were laid during the closing months of 1853, and on January 26, 1854, thousands jammed the Broadway Tabernacle to listen to denunciations of Catholicism and to adopt resolutions pleading for congressional action.[36] Similar resolutions from the Methodist General Conference and the Old School Presbyterian General Assembly, together with many from individuals [37] forced the Senate to act. Lewis Cass, who introduced the question there in April, 1854, urged the adoption of a resolution requiring the state department to negotiate treaties guaranteeing Americans religious freedom in foreign lands and in the debate that followed found many who agreed with him.[38] No action was taken at the time, but Cass persisted and finally secured a vote on March 1, 1855. At that time the resolutions were adopted without a roll call.[39]

The society's success was due, however, not only to its own efforts but also to two powerful allies: the religious press and the churches. Its own publication set a pattern which was followed by other journals. The *American and Foreign Christian Union,* a monthly magazine that replaced the *American Protestant Magazine,* was devoted to spreading a pure Christianity "among people at home and abroad who know only a corrupting one" and to enlightening "its readers respecting the nature and position of Romanism and other forms of error which have usurped the place of 'truth as it is in Jesus'." [40] Like the society that sponsored it, this new journal was mild and conciliatory, pleading for the salvation of Catholics and dwelling benevolently on conversions reported by missionaries. In similar vein were the *Missionary Intelligencer* and the *Missions-Blatt des Amerikanischen und Auswaertigen,* two other monthly magazines which the society published for the benefit of its agents and those whom they hoped to save. [41]

The spirit reflected in the pages of these publications helped revive the flagging interest of the religious press. During the early 1850's paper after paper shook off its lethargy and gave whole-hearted support to the anti-Catholic crusade. Such influential journals as the New York *Observer* and the *Congregationalist,* which had been almost void of No-Popery articles since 1844, now devoted an increasing amount of space to the cause, an example followed by most of the 125 religious magazines and newspapers then published in the United States. [42] New anti-Catholic publications sprang into being on the crest of this mounting popular interest. The *Protestant Union* was started in Pittsburgh, the *True Catholic* expressed the views of Protestant clergymen in Louisville, Kentucky, and the *Northern Protestant and American Advocate* sought to carry the crusade to the region about Newberry, Vermont. In Boston the *Christian Alliance* aroused the ire of Catholics. The Milwaukee *Banner* won for itself the questionable distinction of being the leading anti-Catholic paper of the northwest and that position in the south was claimed by the *Interpreter and New Orleans Creole.* New Yorkers could choose among the *Protestant Advocate,* the *True Freeman's Journal and Protestant Standard* and the New York *Crusader* when seeking nativistic fare. [43] Readers of these papers could run the gamut from softly spoken pleas for the conversion of Catholics to bitterly worded attacks on the immorality of the confessional or the plotting of the Jesuits.

Even more influential than the press was the second ally of the American and Foreign Christian Union, the church organizations. Managers of the society recognized the value of the pioneering work done by the American Protestant Society in soliciting the aid of religious groups and they adopted similar methods immediately, sending several speakers to address each annual gathering of the clergy of various denominations. The substitution of a group of speakers for the one normally employed by the American Protestant Society had its obvious advantages; they could command more time, attract more attention, and exert a greater personal influence over the assembled ministers.[44] Many of the churches co-operated sufficiently to devote a whole session to agents of the society, the New School Presbyterian General Assembly taking this step in 1851 and the Methodist General Conference a year later.[45] The reception was universally favorable; all of the churches adopted resolutions commending the society's work and some instructed their clergy to deliver regular sermons against Catholicism.

Probably these efforts of the American and Foreign Christian Union would have been sufficient to bring most of the American churches under the No-Popery banner. Actually other forces were playing into the hands of the society's managers and helping solidify religious opinion against Catholicism. The belief that Rome was opposed to the Bible was brought home anew to Protestants of the 1850's both by a persistent propaganda [46] and by those European events which had led the Senate to debate the question of Italian religious liberty. Equally alarming to evangelical Americans was Catholic competition in the mission field. As one writer put it:

One of the most fearful manifestations of hostility to God and his Church, on the part of the Romanists at the present day, consists of their determined opposition to Protestant missions. Wherever the

missionary of the cross plants himself . . . he is almost sure to be
encountered by the priests of Rome. Wherever he goes they are
close upon his track, to counteract his efforts, to defeat his designs,
to belie his religion, and turn aside the poor heathen, if possible,
from the faith of the gospel. It is in efforts such as these that the
emissaries of Rome discover most clearly their character and religion.[47]

Missionaries, to whom the idolatry of Rome was as distasteful
as the idolatry of paganism, resented particularly the aid given
papal missionaries by Catholic powers in Europe and mournfully
reported to the American Board of Commissioners for Foreign
Missions that so long as Rome's agents were backed by the guns
of warships, competition with them was impossible.[48]

These things naturally inclined the churches to the nativistic
cause, but more important in luring them into the fold was the
attitude of the American and Foreign Christian Union. The anti-
Catholic campaign of this society was no longer one of sensationalism and abuse; instead its object was the salvation of papal
souls. In this churches could readily co-operate. Hence during
the 1850's sects which had been guilty of un-Christian intolerance toward Rome hastily changed their tactics, while others,
formerly indifferent, girded themselves joyfully for the fray.

The hasty about-face of the Old School Presbyterians was
typical. Since 1842 ministers and laymen who gathered for this
church's annual General Assembly had listened to a sermon on
Popery, usually of the most bitter sort, and similar sermons were
customarily delivered before individual synods at their yearly
conventions.[49] In 1852 the advisability of discontinuing these
sermons was brought before the General Assembly. Many of the
delegates believed that such a step would be taken as a sign of
defeat in the contest with Popery; a majority, however, held that
the Presbyterian church would always be known as the "uncompromising opponent of Romanism" and that the continued re-
iteration of this fact was not necessary. These sermons, they

pointed out, had antagonized many Catholics and made their conversion more difficult. This argument proved effective and the General Assembly voted to substitute for these open attacks on Catholics more subtle efforts to save their souls.[50]

Other American churches showed this same attitude, although many individuals and some sects held to the older policy of denunciation. Methodists, although particularly proud of the number of Catholics converted, still boasted that seven tenths of their members were violent enemies of Catholicism.[51] The New School Presbyterians, solemnly pledged to win Papists to the Gospel by methods of "light and love," nevertheless debated the validity of "Romish baptism" with as much vehemence and hatred as ever.[52] The Episcopalians, rankled by the depletion of their ranks because of the Oxford Movement, were for the most part uncompromisingly opposed to Rome.[53] The General Synod of the Reformed Protestant Dutch church expressed its attitude in a resolution adopted in 1853:[54]

Resolved, That this Synod feel themselves called upon, as representing one of the branches of the great Protestant family, to maintain unflinchingly and firmly the entire faith once delivered to the saints, and to avoid the doing of anything which may actually or by implication give the sanction of their name to any of the erroneous doctrines of the Church of Rome, or any sentiments which may in any way favor the corrupt tenets of the Mother of Abominations.

The Seventh Day Adventists held unfalteringly to the belief that Popery, the child of Satan, was responsible for the hated First Day Sabbath, and even the Swedenborgians were told that their prophet believed the church of Rome to be the Babylon of Biblical prophecy.[55]

Although the churches might voice such epithets, they were, like the organized nativists, more concerned with saving Catholics than denouncing them. Energies previously expended by religious groups in railing against Rome found new outlet in missionary activities abroad. These were both nonsectarian and sectarian in nature. Groups of individuals from many denominations might unite to missionize a particular European nation, or a whole church might swing its influence against Catholicism in Italy, France, or Ireland. One nonsectarian group was formed to bring Canada within the Protestant fold; [56] another undertook the ambitious task of winning Ireland from Popery and was ready to boast by 1853 that 30,000 Irishmen had abandoned "the idolatry of Romanism and made open and bold profession of conversion to the truth of the Gospel." [57] A similar project for Italy was launched in Boston in 1850, leaders of all the Boston Protestant churches uniting into a Christian union to evangelize that center of Popery.[58]

More important were efforts in this same direction by existing church organizations. The Presbyterian church had been conscious for some time of the need of missionaries in Europe; its Board of Foreign Missions had explored the field as early as 1844 and had decided to participate in proselytism. "The Papal crusade," the Board reported to the church, "is against the truth, wherever it is found—the warfare is against the liberties of the world. We cannot, therefore, avoid this contest, unless we deem the truth, and everything dear to the Christian and to man not worth contending for. In such a contest there can be no neutrals; it is between Christ and anti-Christ, and there is no middle ground." [59] Thus it was clearly the duty of the church "to aid in filling this land with Bibles, that the fountain may be purified from which such bitter waters flow." [60] At first this was accomplished by contributing funds to existing missionary societies, particularly the Evangelical Society of Geneva and the Evangelical Society of France,[61] but many believed that more direct participation was desirable. An effort to establish a Presbyterian mission in Rome failed,[62] but in 1851 the General Assembly agreed to send special missionaries to papal lands, and from that time on the Board of Foreign Missions divided its efforts between the heathen and Catholics.[63] Similarly, papal missionaries were appointed by the Methodist General Conference in 1852,[64] while the Dutch Reformed church agreed to aid such projects,[65] and the Congregationalists and the Baptists were only prevented from acting by their decentralized organization.[66] The editor of the *Western Christian Advocate,* a Methodist journal, expressed the point of view of thousands when he joyfully reported that his brethren had agreed to "go and beard the lion in his den; and if they escape with life the first time, let them go again . . . and renew the assault, till it shall become clear to all men, that the Pope is the greatest tyrant in Europe, and that American popery is the most perfect specimen of Hypocrisy and Turpitude, the earth has ever seen." [67]

In this attempt to reform Catholics and to warn the United States of the evils of the papal system, the American and Foreign Christian Union and the churches were ably supported by the religious societies then thriving in such large numbers. Both the American Bible Society and the American Tract Society, long active in the cause, were virtually converted into nativistic organizations during this period. Each was concerned with winning converts from among the ranks of American Catholics; the Bible Society by distributing the Holy Book,[68] the Tract Society by the use of colporteurs who could plead with deluded Papists and save them from the faith in which they had been born.[69] To this end, members of the latter society not only adopted resolutions at each annual meeting endorsing this method of redeeming Roman souls,[70] but tempered the tone of their tracts, that Catholics might read and be converted. Although such works as *The Spirit of Popery* still appeared, the trend was toward milder titles, such as *The Christian Catholic, The Catholic Question* and *What Do Protestants Believe.*[71] These were published in German, French, Spanish, Italian, and other languages which would make them available to the large American immigrant population.

A third society with a marked No-Popery bias and a long record of opposition to Rome was the American Home Mission-

ary Society. Every development of the late 1840's tended to drive
this organization closer into the arms of the nativists; the rising
immigrant tide threatened to offset the work of its missionaries
in the west, the European revolutions and the conservative reaction that followed raised again the spectre of foreign despots
seeking the conquest of the United States through a union with
Popery, and the addition of the Mexican territory with its Catholic population substantiated the belief that America was being surrounded by papal foes bent on its destruction. The goal set by
the American Home Missionary Society—establishing a "pure
religion, undefiled" throughout the United States—was becoming more and more identical with that of the American and Foreign Christian Union, for as Catholicism increased, Popery
rather than infidelity became the great obstacle to evangelical
Christianity.

Spurred on by these forces and by a swelling propaganda
which detailed the means Rome would employ to establish itself
in the west,[72] the American Home Missionary Society resolved
as early as 1845

that the influence which the Protestant Missionary exerts for the
proper organization, regulation, and general welfare of society at
the West, entitles him to the confidence and support, not only of the
Christian, but also of the Patriot.[73]

This resolution, aimed by obvious implication against the efforts
of Catholicism in the Mississippi valley, opened the way for an
oratorical attack on Popery which was not silenced for more than
a decade. At each subsequent annual meeting the members listened to at least one speaker flay Romanism and plead for Protestant support in thwarting the Man of Sin. These same fears
were echoed by clerical members of the society who were delegated to deliver sermons on home missions before eastern congregations. First to touch on the dangers of Catholicism was the
Reverend Horace Bushnell in his sermon of 1847 on *Barbarism,
the First Danger*.[74] With few exceptions each sermon from that

date until 1856 dealt at some length with the means to be used
to defeat Papists in the struggle for the west.[75] All agreed with
the Reverend Albert Barnes, who in 1849 pictured the Mississippi
valley as "the great battle field of the world—the place where
probably more than anywhere else the destinies of the world are
to be decided," [76] and were ready to voice an enthusiastic nega-
tive when the Reverend Henry Smith asked in 1854: "Shall we
accept the splendid trappings of the Papacy, its stupendous Cathedrals, its pealing organs, its scarlet robes, its genuflexions and
images, and incense, and host and unction—and with them, let us
not forget, its chained Bible, its night of mind, its ecclesiastical
despotism, its Papal interdicts, its annals, its indulgences, its
inquisitorial dungeons and its auto-da-fé?" [77]

The American Home Missionary Society was aided in its task
of saving the west for Protestantism by a number of lesser domestic missionary societies, such as the Massachusetts Home Missionary Society, the Maine Missionary Society, the Missouri
Home Missionary Society, and the Boston Ladies' Association
for Evangelizing the West.[78] Members of the last-named society
felt so strongly on the Catholic problem that in 1845 they publicly condemned the spread of Popery through "the aid of foreign
gold and patronage and the zealous co-operation of their own
deluded victims," [79] while the others were scarcely less outspoken
in their denunciation of Romish designs.

Equally helpful both to the American and Foreign Christian
Union and to the American Home Missionary Society were the
several Protestant societies primarily interested in educational
work in the Mississippi valley. Beecher and other early propagandists had insisted that the parochial school was to be a principal weapon in Rome's conquest of the west. These warnings
seemed to be corroborated by missionaries who reported a rapidly growing Catholic educational system to which Protestants
were forced to subject their children because of the lack of
Protestant schools.[80] The issue seemed a clear one to many

churchgoers: Catholic education would lead to a Catholic west, Protestant education to a Protestant west. One eastern clergyman summed up popular thought when he told his congregation:

There, Brethren—there our great battle with the Jesuit, on western soil, is to be waged. We must build College against College. If the musty atmosphere of a Jesuit School suits the freeborn western youth; if the repetition of scholastic modes of discipline can captivate the child of the prairies, then we may fail in the contest. But all experience has confirmed our anticipation, that America is a field on which the open, manly, Christian discipline of a Protestant College must annihilate the rival system of Jesuitical instruction.[81]

These warnings made it the obvious duty of Protestants interested in the promulgation of their faith to provide means for establishing schools in the Mississippi valley. Several societies were organized to this end. The most prominent was the Society for the Promotion of Collegiate and Theological Education at the West, formed at Boston in 1843. From its inception this society emphasized the need of Protestant schools to offset the work of Jesuits in the west.[82] The public meetings that it held to secure financial support were entirely given over to denunciation of Catholicism, one resolving:

That the association of Catholics and Catholic potentates of Europe, united to secure the uncontrolled direction of education in the Western States, demands the prayerful attention, the sympathetic action, of our entire nation.[83]

Its speakers, too, dwelt on this popular theme in soliciting funds. "The Jesuits," one declared, "are willing, nay, longing, nay, plotting and toiling, to become the educators of America. Let them have the privilege of possessing the seats of education in the west, and of moulding the leading minds of the millions that are to inhabit there, and we may give up all our efforts to produce in the west what Puritanism has produced here." [84]

The Catholic danger was similarly pointed out by another education society, the Ladies' Society for the Promotion of Education at the West. The meeting at which this society was formed was addressed by two avowed nativists, the Reverend E. N. Kirk and the Reverend Edward Beecher, who devoted their speeches to an attack on Catholicism and the need for Protestant education to offset its influence.[85] The society continued to stress nativistic arguments for the benefit of its members and those to whom it appealed for support,[86] even setting up a separate fund for the education of Catholic children who could be induced to attend Protestant schools.[87]

So effective was the propaganda of societies interested in perpetuating Protestantism in the west that many of the churches felt called upon to embark on domestic missionary projects aimed primarily against Catholicism. The Congregational, Presbyterian, Lutheran, and German Reformed churches operated through the American Home Missionary Society and felt no need for special action other than resolutions spurring that organization to greater efforts against Rome.[88] However, the Dutch Reformed church, with no such affiliation, sent missionaries into the west in 1848, and the Baptist Home Mission Society and the Western Baptist Educational Association constantly solicited support to subdue Popery in the Mississippi valley.[89]

Despite the earnestness of these appeals, an overtone of confidence marked the attitude of religious and humanitarian leaders when they viewed Catholicism in the early 1850's. As staunch defenders of their faiths, they could not believe that the Divine Plan included the eventual defeat of Protestantism at the hands of Rome. Instead, they saw the whole growth of American Catholicism simply as God's wondrous means of winning His peoples to the evangelical truth. Why else, they asked, had God delayed the colonizing of North America until the Reformation gave the true Bible to man? Why had He allowed the lowly savage to hold the first settlers on the seaboard until they had developed and strengthened their religion and religious institutions? Why had He held back the influx of Catholic foreigners until these preparations for their arrival had been completed? The design was obvious. God had planned the entire settlement of the United States only as a means of enticing Europe's priest-ridden peasants to a land where their conversion was possible. If proof of such a plan was needed, Protestants had only to look to California. For God had hidden the gold of that region beneath the soil so long as Popery dominated there, only to reveal its presence after annexation by the Protestant United States had opened the way to the conversion of seekers after wealth.[90]

There was little doubt among religious men as to their success in this crusade against Catholicism. "If Protestantism cannot cope with Popery on this free soil," one speaker before the American Home Missionary Society declared, "in the midst of Bibles and Sabbaths and schools and seminaries; then I say let us give up the contest, and hasten back to Rome and get absolution as speedily as possible." [91] Armed with this confidence, the ministerial adherents to the antipapal cause were beginning to believe that immigration should not be discouraged, but that Catholic aliens should be welcomed to America and converted with all possible dispatch. They pictured themselves as actors in a new Reformation in which the United States was to play the leading rôle; their cues were from Heaven and were to be obeyed without question.

This optimism was indicative of the new spirit which permeated nativistic ranks by the middle 1850's. Entrenched in their smoothly functioning organizations, backed by a united religious press and by nearly all of the non-Catholic sects, in agreement with most of the religious societies of the day, and confident in their belief that Divine backing was theirs, nativists were in a stronger position than ever before. They had won back the support that the Riots of 1844 had lost them. They had secured the adherence of the middle-class, churchgoing Americans without which no reform could be successful. Organized nativism had accomplished much in one brief decade.

NOTES

[1] Theodore Dwight, *The Roman Republic of 1849; with Accounts of the Inquisition and the Siege of Rome* (New York, 1851), 32–34.

[2] New York *Observer,* April 10, 1847; *Congregationalist,* April 29, 1853.

[3] *Protestant Banner,* March 13, 1845; New York *Observer,* May 24, 1845 ff., December 16, 1847; *American Protestant Magazine,* I (November, 1845); *National Protestant Magazine or Anti-Jesuit,* I (April, 1845), II (October. 1845); *John Ronge, the Holy Coat of Treves, and the New German Church* (New York, 1845). American interest was aroused when 200 German Catholics in Cincinnati announced they were forsaking Catholicism because of the teachings of Ronge. *National Protestant,* III (November, 1845).

[4] New York *Observer,* November 30, 1850, January 23, 1851; *Congregationalist,* November 22, 1850, December 13, 1850, January 3, 1851, January 10, 1851, January 17, 1851, February 28, 1851, January 30, 1852. American writers also frequently complained against the Catholic request for funds for Maynooth college which Parliament finally refused. New York *Observer,* July 8, 1852; *American and Foreign Christian Union,* V (May, 1854); *Congregationalist,* January 20, 1854.

[5] New York *Observer,* July 24, 1851, January 1, 1852.

[6] A conference was held for this purpose in London in May, 1854, attended by representatives of the Protestant Reformation Society, the Protestant Association, the Protestant Alliance, the Church Protestant Defense, the Evangelical Alliance, the Islington Protestant Institute, the Scottish Reformation Society and the National Club. *American and Foreign Christian Union,* V (September, 1854).

[7] *Congregationalist,* August 29, 1851; New York *Observer,* August 21, 1851, October 16, 1851; *Home Missionary,* XXVI (April, 1853); Robert Baird, *Sketches of Protestantism in Italy Past and Present, Including a Notice of the Origin, History and Present State of the Waldenses* (Boston, 1847), introduction; Samuel M. Hopkins, *Protestantism in the Middle of the Nineteenth Century* (Auburn, New York, 1849), 1–36; Nicholas Murray, *The Decline of Popery and its Causes. An Address Delivered at the Broadway Tabernacle January 15, 1851* (New York, 1851), 20–21; Gault, *Popery, the Man of Sin,* 6–7.

[8] The society had originated when French Protestants appealed to the United States for missionary funds following the Revolution of 1830. Americans interested in this work conceived the idea of perpetuating it through a regular organization. *American Union,* June 2, 1849; American Protestant Society, *Sixth Annual Report,* 44–45.

[9] The society's operations and fund-raising methods were similar to those of the American Protestant Society. It held public meetings, appealed to churches for support and endorsement, and encouraged sermons describing its activities. For typical accounts of these activities see *Protestant Banner,* June 1, 1843; New York *Observer,* May 12, 1849; *The Acts and Proceedings of the General Synod of the Reformed Protestant Dutch Church in North America Convened at Kingston, New York,* 237; *Minutes of the General Association of Massachusetts* (Boston, 1839), 10; *Ibid.* (Boston, 1844), 6; *Ibid.* (Boston. 1845), 10–11.

10 The society was formed on December 12, 1842, as the Philo-Italian Society and was reorganized and renamed during the summer of 1843. New York *Observer*, January 21, 1843, April 13, 1844, May 17, 1845, May 16, 1846; *Addresses of the Rev. Leonard Bacon and Rev. E. N. Kirk at the Christian Alliance, 7–9*. The quotation is from the constitution of the society which is printed in this pamphlet.

11 The "Papal Bull," according to the society, stated: "Against the plots and designs of the members of the Christian Alliance, we require a peculiar and most lively vigilance from those of your order." *Addresses of the Rev. Leonard Bacon and Rev. E. N. Kirk at the Christian Alliance, 38–39*. Protestants interpreted this as an attack on the Bible, for the society claimed that it had been circulating the Scriptures in Italy. See *Native American*, July 20, 1844; New York *Observer*, July 27, 1844; New York *American Republican*, July 19, 1844, September 18, 1844; *Protestant Banner*, August 1, 1844, January 2, 1845; *Minutes of the General Association of Massachusetts* (Boston, 1845), 10–11; *Freeman's Journal*, August 3, 1844.

12 *Protestant Banner*, June 1, 1843.

13 *American Protestant Magazine*, III (May, 1847).

14 American Protestant Society, *Fourth Annual Report, 29, Fifth Annual Report, 29–32, Sixth Annual Report, 25–28*.

15 *American Protestant Magazine*, V (April, 1849), V (June, 1849); New York *Observer*, May 27, 1848.

16 The society could not enter the union until several legacies had been received. American Protestant Society, *Fifth Annual Report, 32*.

17 American Protestant Society, *Sixth Annual Report, 41*.

18 "Address of the American and Foreign Christian Union to the Public," printed in American Protestant Society, *Sixth Annual Report, 44-45*. The Address is also printed in the New York *Observer*, June 30, 1849; *Congregationalist*, June 8, 1849, and a number of other papers.

19 The society's income was as follows:

       1850............$58,885.84
       1851............ 56,265.82
       1852............ 56,649.91
       1853............ 69,602.84
       1854............ 79,611.91
       1855............ 63,867.28
       1856............ 69,572.00
       1857............ 76,296.93

Expenditures balanced income excepting in 1855, when an unexpected drop in revenue caused a deficit of $2,524.41. These figures have been compiled from the *Annual Reports* of the society.

20 American and Foreign Christian Union, *Second Annual Report* (New York, 1851), 36; *Third Annual Report* (New York, 1852), 30–41; New York *Observer*, January 30, 1851, May 12, 1853.

21 New York *Observer*, May 11, 1850.

22 American and Foreign Christian Union, *Fifth Annual Report* (New York, 1854), 47; *Congregationalist*, March 22, 1850.

23 American and Foreign Christian Union, *Fourth Annual Report* (New York, 1853), 44.

²⁴ A special agent, the Reverend Patrick J. Lea, devoted his entire time to these free lectures, a second agent, the Reverend David Magill, later being added. Lea lectured through the east, Magill largely in the middle west. American and Foreign Christian Union, *Fifth Annual Report*, 49–50; New York *Observer*, May 11, 1850, December 14, 1850, June 3, 1852, May 12, 1853; *American Union*, June 2, 1849; *Congregationalist*, June 1, 1849; *American and Foreign Christian Union*, V (January, 1854).

²⁵ Richard Pike, *Romanism, A Sermon* (Boston, 1854), 10–11.

²⁶ American and Foreign Christian Union, *Fifth Annual Report*, 51–52.

²⁷ *Pilot*, January 22, 1853, January 29, 1853, February 26, 1853, March 19, 1853; *Freeman's Journal*, January 15, 1853, February 19, 1853; Hassard, *Life of John Hughes*, 363–364.

²⁸ December 23, 1852. See also *American and Foreign Christian Union*, III (December, 1852), IV (March, 1853), IV (April, 1853); *Congregationalist*, March 4, 1853; Rufus W. Clark, *Romanism in America* (Boston, 1855), 178–180.

²⁹ Full reports of the meeting were published in the New York *Observer*, January 13, 1853; *Freeman's Journal*, January 15, 1853; *American and Foreign Christian Union*, IV (February, 1853).

³⁰ *American and Foreign Christian Union*, IV (March, 1853), IV (April, 1853); *Pilot*, June 4, 1853; American and Foreign Christian Union, *Fifth Annual Report* (New York, 1854), 19–20.

³¹ The New School Presbyterians at their General Assembly in 1853 adopted such resolutions. New York *Observer*, June 2, 1853. The *American and Foreign Christian Union*, IV (March, 1853), urged all members of the society to send petitions to the president asking his intervention.

³² *Congregationalist*, February 4, 1853.

³³ *Congressional Globe*, 33rd Cong., 1st Sess., Appendix, 682.

³⁴ *Pilot*, January 22, 1853; *Freeman's Journal*, January 22, 1853.

³⁵ The agent was Margaret Cunninghame and, according to American accounts, she was imprisoned in the same cell in Tuscany that had formerly held Rosa Madiai. New York *Observer*, November 17, 1853 ff.; *American and Foreign Christian Union*, V (December, 1853). The *Freeman's Journal* approved the closing of a Protestant chapel in Rome by the Pope on the grounds that Protestantism in Italy was as much political as religious and could do much harm. *Freeman's Journal*, January 11, 1851. For other Protestant objections to these practices see New York *Observer*, April 22, 1852, May 26, 1853; *Congregationalist*, January 10, 1851, January 31, 1851, January 9, 1852, June 17, 1853, August 26, 1853, November 25, 1853; *American and Foreign Christian Union*, I (March, 1850); *National Protestant Magazine or the Anti-Jesuit*, I (April, 1846); Dwight, *The Roman Republic of 1849*, 11–16; Murray, *Romanism at Home*, 32; Robert Lowell, *Five Letters Against Certain Pretensions of the Papal Church* (Newark, 1853), 7–20; *An Alarm to Heretics*, 5; *Startling Facts for Native Americans* (New York, 1855), 69; Lewis D. Campbell, *Americanism; a Speech Delivered at the American Mass Meeting held in Washington City, February 29, 1856* (Washington, 1856), 3; Carroll, *Great American Battle*, 105, 303; Joel T. Headley, *History of the Persecutions and Battles of the Waldenses* (New York, 1852), *passim*.

³⁶ Full reports of the meeting were published in the New York *Observer*,

February 2, 1854, and in a 64-page supplement to the *American and Foreign Christian Union*, V (February, 1854).

37 *Journals of the General Conference of the Methodist Episcopal Church*, III, 37, 201; New York *Observer*, May 20, 1852, June 9, 1853; *Freeman's Journal*, February 12, 1853.

38 The Senate Committee on Foreign Affairs recommended the adoption of such resolutions as early as February, 1853. *Congressional Globe*, 32nd Cong., 2nd Sess., 658. No action was taken until Cass reopened the debate in April, 1854. Nearly all speakers favored the resolutions, only one Catholic champion being found in Stephen R. Mallory. *Ibid.*, 33rd Cong., 1st Sess., 835, 1187, 1194-1195. Cass' speech is printed in full in *Ibid.*, 33rd Cong., 1st Sess., Appendix, 682-691 and typical petitions such as inspired the action in *Ibid.*, 789-790, 929.

39 The resolutions were before Congress again on December 19, 1854 for further debate. *Ibid.*, 33rd Cong., 2nd Sess., 80-81, 1032; *American and Foreign Christian Union*, V (June, 1854).

40 *American and Foreign Christian Union*, I (January, 1850).

41 American and Foreign Christian Union, *Fifth Annual Report*, 26; *Sixth Annual Report*, 12-16. These two journals were not financially successful, but the *American and Foreign Christian Union* reached a circulation of nearly 15,000 copies monthly and by 1853 was paying the society a profit of more than $5,000 yearly. *American and Foreign Christian Union*, IV (February, 1853).

42 Thus the *Congregationalist*, December 21, 1849, inaugurated a regular weekly department entitled "Movements of the Papacy."

43 The author has been unable to locate files of any of these papers. They are referred to and fully described in *Protestant Banner*, March 13, 1845; *Pilot*, February 3, 1849; *Freeman's Journal*, January 14, 1854; *American and Foreign Christian Union*, V (January, 1854), V (April, 1854); John M. Henni, "Letters of the Right Reverend John Martin Henni and the Reverend Anthony Urbonek," *Wisconsin Magazine of History*, X (August, 1926), 93.

44 Reports of these activities are in the New York *Observer*, June 2, 1849, May 27, 1852, June 10, 1852, July 1, 1852, June 9, 1853; *Congregationalist*, July 5, 1850; *Minutes of the General Association of Massachusetts* (Boston, 1849), 10; and in nearly every number of the *American and Foreign Christian Union* between 1850 and 1856.

45 New York *Observer*, May 29, 1851; *Journals of the General Conference of the Methodist Episcopal Church*, III, 3.

46 Nearly every anti-Catholic book of this period attempted to show that Catholicism was opposed to the Bible. Supposed instances of Catholic Bible burning were widely circulated. New York *Observer*, May 25, 1850; *American and Foreign Christian Union*, II (April, 1851), V (July, 1854); Carroll, *Great American Battle*, 311–312. Public meetings were also held where the people could be told of Rome's hostility toward the Scriptures, one such meeting in New Jersey being presided over by the governor of the state and attended by several thousand people. New York *Observer*, March 10, 1849.

47 Enoch Pond, *No Fellowship with Romanism* (Boston, 1843), 229–230.

48 *Presbyterian Quarterly Review*, I (December, 1852), I (March, 1852); *National Protestant*, III (December, 1845); *National Protestant Magazine or the Anti-Jesuit*, I (February, 1846); New York *Observer*, February 15,

1840, April 3, 1841, July 6, 1844, September 14, 1844. It was rumored that Marcus Whitman and other Protestant missionaries in western America had been murdered by Jesuits who were anxious to pre-empt that field for themselves. *American Protestant Magazine,* IV (January, 1849).

49 Edward P. Humphrey, *A Discourse on the Spiritual Power of the Roman Catholic Clergy. Delivered at Louisville before the Synod of Kentucky, October 13, 1849* (Louisville, 1850), 3.

50 The debate is printed in full in the New York *Observer,* June 3, 1852.

51 *Journals of the General Conference of the Methodist Episcopal Church,* III, 179; Augustus A. Longstreet, *Know Nothingism Unveiled* (Washington, 1855), 3. An interesting picture of a Methodist minister's reaction to Catholicism is in J. B. Finley, *Autobiography* (Cincinnati, 1854), 255–257.

52 New York *Observer,* June 1, 1854, June 8, 1854.

53 Daniel Washburn, *The Man of God Who Was Disobedient unto the Word of the Lord. A Sermon Preached on the Occasion of Reading the Sentence of Deposition of L. Silliman Ives, to the Congregation of Trinity Church, Pottsville, Pa.* (Philadelphia, 1854), 3–40. Ives had deserted the church and embraced the Catholic faith.

54 New York *Observer,* June 16, 1853. The resolution was adopted by opponents of the so-called Mercersburg theology which, a majority of the members of the Synod believed, tended to "undermine the principles of the Reformation in favor of the Papacy."

55 *Pilot,* October 6, 1849, quoting an Adventist paper, *The Herald; Second Advent Review and Sabbath Herald* (1850), 17; Ellen Gould White, *The Great Controversy between Christ and Satan* (New York, 1858), 83; *Popery Adjudged; or, The Roman Catholic Church Weighed in the Balance of God's Word and Found Wanting, Extracted from the Works of Emanuel Swedenborg* (Boston, 1854), 3–42.

56 This was the French Canadian Missionary Society which in 1850 was employing eight missionaries in French Canada and in addition had established several schools there. *Congregationalist,* August 2, 1850.

57 *Ibid.,* February 4, 1853. See also New York *Observer,* June 17, 1848, June 2, 1849; *Home Missionary,* XXV (October, 1852).

58 *Freeman's Journal,* December 21, 1850; *Congregationalist,* November 8, 1850.

59 Board of Foreign Missions of the Presbyterian Church of the United States of America, *Eighth Annual Report* (1845), 25.

60 *Ibid.,* 26.

61 Nearly $32,000 was sent these societies between 1844 and 1851, allowing 28 ministers and 42 colporteurs to be maintained in the Catholic countries of Europe. *Ibid., Eighth Annual Report* (1845) to *Fifteenth Annual Report* (1852).

62 This proposal was well received by the General Assembly in 1849, but no action was taken. New York *Observer,* June 2, 1849.

63 *Ibid.,* June 5, 1851. The General Assembly was told two years later that the missionary's efforts had been highly successful. *Ibid.,* June 2, 1853.

64 *Journals of the General Conference of the Methodist Episcopal Church,* III, 77. Proposals for a Methodist mission in papal Europe had been advanced as early as 1850. *Congregationalist,* March 8, 1850.

65 *The Acts and Proceedings of the General Synod of the Reformed Protestant Dutch Church in North America convened at Kingston, New York*, 286.

66 *Congregationalist*, February 28, 1851; *American and Foreign Christian Union*, II (November, 1851).

67 Quoted in *Congregationalist*, August 13, 1852.

68 The American Bible Society was particularly concerned because, it reported, priests either refused to allow Catholics to accept Bibles distributed by the society's agents, or destroyed Bibles that had been distributed. *Congregationalist*, August 31, 1849. On the other hand the Catholic Boston *Pilot*, May 7, 1853, warned against agents of the Bible society, charging that they obtained Catholic Bibles by false promises and destroyed them. See also *Congregationalist*, November 29, 1850; April 7, 1854; New York *Observer*, May 20, 1848, May 19, 1849, May 12, 1853; *American and Foreign Christian Union*, V (April, 1854). Anti-Catholic speeches were regularly given at the society's annual meetings. American Bible Society, *Thirty First Annual Report* (1847) to *Thirty Eighth Annual Report* (1854).

69 The colporteur system had been inaugurated by the society in 1841, but not until after 1846, when the Reverend J. M. Stevenson of Dayton, Ohio, vigorously pointed out its advantages as a means of converting Catholics, was it fully developed. American Tract Society, *Thirty Second Annual Report* (1846), 9–10, 29–30.

70 These resolutions were usually introduced by violent anti-Catholic speeches. Typical are those printed in *Ibid., Thirty Fourth Annual Report* (1848), 2–8; *Thirty Seventh Annual Report* (1851), 9 and ff.; *Thirty Eighth Annual Report* (1852), 12–14; New York *Observer*, November 29, 1845, May 15, 1847.

71 The lists of tracts published yearly by the society were printed in the *Annual Reports*.

72 A discussion of this propaganda will be found in the author's "Anti-Catholic Propaganda and the Home Missionary Movement, 1800–1860," *loc. cit.,* 361–384.

73 American Home Missionary Society, *Nineteenth Annual Report* (1845), 3.

74 Horace Bushnell, *Barbarism, the First Danger* (New York, 1847), *passim*.

75 E. N. Kirk, *The Church Essential to the Republic* (New York, 1848), 12, 21–22; Albert Barnes, *Home Missions* (New York, 1849), 29–34; David N. Riddle, *Our Country for the Sake of the World* (New York, 1851), 24–25; Leonard Bacon, *The American Church* (New York, 1852); L. P. Hickok, *A Nation Saved from its Prosperity only by the Gospel* (New York, 1853), 9–13; Henry Smith, *The True Christian Pulpit Our Strongest National Defense* (New York, 1854), 26; *Home Missionary*, XXI (February, 1849), XXII (November, 1849), XXVI (September, 1854), XXVI (October, 1854).

76 Barnes, *op. cit.,* 34.

77 Smith, *op. cit.,* 26.

78 *Home Missionary*, XVII (May, 1844), XVII (December, 1844), XVIII (December, 1845), XIX (October, 1846), XX (October, 1847), XXIII (September, 1850); American Home Missionary Society, *Sixteenth Annual Report* (1842), 71, *Seventeenth Annual Report* (1843), 82.

⁷⁹ Boston Ladies' Society for Evangelizing the West, *Second Annual Report* (Boston, 1844), 4. Before passing the resolution members listened to an anti-Catholic address delivered by the Reverend E. N. Kirk.

⁸⁰ American Home Missionary Society, *Sixteenth Annual Report* (1842). 98–99, *Twenty Seventh Annual Report* (1853), 113–115, *Nineteenth Annual Report* (1845), 92; *Home Missionary*, V (February, 1833), VI (April, 1834), XIV (April, 1842), XXIV (October, 1851).

⁸¹ E. N. Kirk, *The Church and the College* (Boston, 1856), 29. Many sermons stressed the need of Protestant educational activities in the west to offset Catholic facilities: N. Porter, *A Plea for Libraries* (New York, 1848), 15, 22–26; John Todd, *Colleges Essential to the Church of God* (New York, 1848), 11–12; Absalom Peters, *Collegiate Religious Institutions* (New York, 1851), 25; Edwin Hall, *Colleges Essential to Home Missions* (New York, 1853), 6, 15, 31; E. N. Kirk, *The Church and the College* (Boston, 1856), 28–30; H. B. Smith, *An Argument for Christian Colleges* (New York, 1857), 26.

⁸² Society for the Promotion of Collegiate and Theological Education at the West, *Second Annual Report* (New York, 1845), 23.

⁸³ *Proceedings of the Public Meeting in behalf of the Society for the Promotion of Collegiate and Theological Education at the West, held in Park Street Church, Boston, May 28, 1845; including the Addresses of Rev. Drs. Hopkins, E. Beecher, Bacon, and L. Beecher* (New York, 1845), 11; New York *Observer*, June 7, 1847; *National Protestant*, VI (December, 1845).

⁸⁴ *Proceedings of the Public Meeting*, 10.

⁸⁵ *History of the Formation of the Ladies' Society for the Promotion of Education at the West; with Two Addresses Delivered at its Organization by the Rev. Edward Beecher, D.D., and the Rev. E. N. Kirk* (Boston, 1846), 16.

⁸⁶ Ladies' Society for the Promotion of Education at the West, *Second Annual Report* (Boston, 1848), 13–15; *Third Annual Report* (Boston, 1849), 28–29; *First Annual Report* (Boston, 1847), 29–38.

⁸⁷ *Ibid., Fourth Annual Report* (Boston, 1850), 44.

⁸⁸ *Home Missionary*, XV (January, 1843); New York *Observer*, July 5, 1834; Allen, *Report on Popery*, 26–27; Board of Missions of the General Assembly of the Presbyterian Church in the United States of America, *Annual Report for 1848* (Philadelphia, 1848), 45–46; *Annual Report for 1854*, 21–24.

⁸⁹ *The Acts and Proceedings of the General Synod of the Reformed Protestant Dutch Church in North America*, 280, 308–310; Board of Domestic Missions of the Reformed Protestant Dutch Church, *Nineteenth Annual Report* (New York, 1851), 14–15; American Baptist Home Mission Society, *Twelfth Annual Report* (New York, 1844), 13–14; *Thirteenth Annual Report* (New York, 1845), 15–16; *Fourteenth Annual Report* (New York, 1846), 17; *Fifteenth Annual Report* (New York, 1847), 18–19; *Sixteenth Annual Report* (New York, 1848), 5; *Twentieth Annual Report* (New York, 1852), 34; *Christian Watchman*, March 30, 1832, September 27, 1833, May 30, 1835, February 10, 1843.

⁹⁰ American Home Missionary Society, *Sixteenth Annual Report* (1842), 83–85; *Seventeenth Annual Report* (1843), 99; *Twenty Fifth Annual Report* (1851), 109; *Twenty Seventh Annual Report* (1853), 90–91; *Western Christian Advocate*, February 20, 1835; *Congregationalist*, November 30, 1849, August 9, 1850, January 11, 1850; *Home Missionary*, XX (August, 1847), XXI

(January, 1849), XXIII (October, 1850), XXIV (September, 1851); Edward Beecher, *The Papal Conspiracy Exposed and Protestantism Defended in the Light of Reason, History and Scripture* (Boston, 1855), 373.

[91] American Home Missionary Society, *Seventeenth Annual Report* (1843), 99.

XII

The Catholic Church Blunders
1850-1854

BEFORE nativistic sentiment could take political form, lower-class support had to be added to that already gained from the middle class. During the early 1850's two things operated to drive the masses into the arms of anti-Catholic agitators: the uncompromising and sometimes arrogant attitude of the Catholic hierarchy, and the fear of the immigrant, politically, socially, and economically. In these two things, nativists found their most forceful arguments when appealing to the working class.

The arrogance of the Catholic hierarchy which provided Protestant writers with such effective ammunition could be attributed to the new and strange position of Catholicism in the United States. The Church's traditional policy had been shaped in European countries where it operated in close co-operation with the government; there it could afford to be domineering, even at the expense of antagonizing its few enemies. In America, however, governmental support was lacking and the enemies of Catholicism far outnumbered the Catholics themselves. This situation called for compromise and caution but the whole tradition of the Church, and the whole philosophy of its hierarchy, opposed such a policy. Powerful and overbearing in Europe, Catholicism naturally sought to be domineering in America, even though the two situations had little in common.

This spirit had been quiescent during the early years of the Republic but with the flood of immigration from papal countries during the 1840's and 1850's the attitude of many Catholics changed abruptly. The Church was growing so rapidly that it would, its members believed, soon dominate the American religious scene. Restraint seemed no longer necessary, and priests and laymen sloughed off their earlier timidity and began to pattern their actions on those of their fellows in Catholic Europe. Bold expressions by Catholic priests which would be certain to arouse Protestant antagonism were bandied about freely.[1] New churches were no longer quietly put into service; now they were dedicated with pomp and ceremony, traditionally frowned upon by simplicity-loving Americans.[2] Catholic editors, such as Orestes Brownson, whose *Quarterly Review* was widely circulated, pleaded with their fellow churchmen to proclaim their religion openly.[3] Others heaped abuse on the Protestant sects, one stating: "Our object is to show, once more, that Protestantism is effete, powerless, dying out though disturbed only by its proper gangrenes, and conscious that its last moment is come when it is fairly set, face to face, with Catholic truth."[4] Protestants could find in these words little of the apologetic humility they had come to associate with Catholicism.

Most outspoken among the churchmen who fostered this new attitude was the spiritual leader of the Catholic church in America, Archbishop John Hughes of New York. Ill-suited by temperament and training to any compromising policy, he was blindly loyal to the Catholic church and strove constantly to make that church stronger and better. There can be no doubt of his success, but there can be no doubt too that his actions and utterances aroused considerable resentment among Protestants.

One legitimate means of furthering Catholicism, Hughes believed, was to attack Protestantism. His most effective public thrust was delivered in November, 1850, when he spoke before the congregation of St. Patrick's Cathedral, New York, on "The Decline of Protestantism and Its Causes." Pagan and Protestant nations were both crumbling before the force of Rome, Hughes said, and would continue to do so until all the world was under the spiritual rule of the Holy Mother church.

There is [he said] no secret about this. The object we hope to accomplish in time, is to convert all Pagan nations, and all Protestant nations, even England with her proud Parliament and imperial sovereign. There is no secrecy in all this. It is the commission of God to his church, and not a human project. . . . Protestantism pretends to have discovered a great secret. Protestantism startles our eastern borders occasionally on the intention of the Pope with regard to the Valley of the Mississippi, and dreams that it has made a wonderful discovery. Not at all. Everybody should know it. Everybody should know that we have for our mission to convert the world—including the inhabitants of the United States,—the people of the cities, and the people of the country, the officers of the navy and the marines, commanders of the army, the Legislatures, the Senate, the Cabinet, the President, and all! [5]

Such declarations as these, no matter how sincere, were ill-timed. Protestants who had for years disregarded the warnings of Morse and his followers as the ravings of fanatical alarmists now heard an acknowledged church leader freely admitting that a Romish plot did exist. The Pope did intend to move to the Mississippi valley; he did seek to subjugate free America!

Protestant protest was immediate. Nativists were wise enough to realize that they would gain more by popularizing Hughes' statements than by refuting them, and extracts from his speech were widely printed in both the religious and secular press. [6] Rebuttal was not neglected, however. The American and Foreign Christian Union hurriedly summoned a public meeting where three speakers reiterated the usual arguments against Popery and urged Protestant unity in this new crisis. [7] The Reverend Nicholas Murray was called from retirement by the petition of a group of New York clergymen to deliver a two-hour address before a large audience on "The Decline of Popery and Its Causes." [8] In Philadelphia a similar petition circulated by ministers and laymen brought the Reverend Joseph F. Berg to the lecture platform, there to attempt a labored refutation, point by point, of all that Hughes had said. "If the principles which belong to the great charter of human rights are losing favor with the masses of mankind," Berg told his audience, "if the people of any nation under heaven are weary of the enjoyment of that liberty which secures to every man the largest amount of personal comfort, wealth and happiness compatible with the equal rights of his neighbor to the same; if the inhabitants of any civilized country are longing for the chains of despotic authority or reaching forth their hands that they may be manacled, or bowing their necks in voluntary servitude to the yoke of tyranny —then I will admit Protestantism is declining." [9]

The alarm stirred by Hughes' ill-chosen remarks, important as it was, was still slight when compared to that aroused by other Catholic moves for which the New York Archbishop was largely responsible. For the efforts of Archbishop Hughes, more than any other person, lay behind the revival of controversies centering around those two ancient sources of friction, Bible reading in the schools and trusteeism. From these controversies in the 1850's grew a popular hatred of Catholicism more openly expressed than at any other time in the history of the nation.

The education controversy was actually a delayed continuation of the struggle that had racked New York City a decade before. Many Catholic leaders who had at that time hesitated to follow Hughes' vigorous example now felt that the time was ripe to strike for a share of the school funds. They were encouraged in this attitude by articles appearing in the *Freeman's Journal* and other Catholic papers during the autumn of 1852 urging Catholics everywhere to unite in demanding public money for the support of their own schools or, if this could not be obtained, the passage of laws forbidding the reading of Protestant Bibles in state-operated educational institutions.[10] Although there is no proof that Hughes inspired these proposals, the fact that the *Freeman's Journal* was his official paper makes it probable that

the campaign was shaped in his fertile brain. If such was the
case, he had every reason to be gratified at the results. His fellow
churchmen swung into action in a dozen states; legislatures were
swamped with Catholic petitions praying for a division of school
funds, and Catholic voters were threatening political eclipse for
politicians bold enough to deny their wishes.[11] Within a few
months the issue had become one of major importance in every
state which boasted even a sizable Catholic population.

Protestant reaction was immediate and violent—as well it
might be, for the Catholic attack was so sudden and far reaching
that its ramifications touched every corner of the land. In Cincinnati indignant Protestants carried the issue to the voters and
after a tumultuous election won a resounding victory.[12] In Baltimore 10,000 persons gathered outside the hall in which the state
legislature was meeting and raised their voices against truckling
to Rome's demands.[13] In Oswego, New York, whole-hearted
approval was given a teacher who severely whipped a Catholic
child for refusing to read the Protestant Bible.[14] In Albany the
New York legislature, goaded by Protestant demands, very
nearly reversed its liberal stand of the past decade by passing a
law forbidding sectarian institutions to share in the school funds
and requiring Bible reading in all state schools.[15] In every state
the American and Foreign Christian Union hurried its agents to
the legislatures as lobbyists against Catholic demands,[16] while in
numerous cities its members marched the streets chanting a
parody which began:

> Roman, spare that Book,
> Keep off thy bloody hand.[17]

It was in Ellsworth, Maine, that this struggle over Bible reading took its most violent form. After Catholics there had sought
and been refused a share of the school funds, they found a champion in one Lawrence Donahoe, who, rather than allow his daughter to read a Protestant Bible, withdrew her from school and

instructed her himself, finally sending a bill to the state for the expenses of her education. This seemingly innocent action brought out hostile mobs that battled openly in the streets. For a time the situation was serious; the Ellsworth *Herald,* a pro-Protestant paper, advertised:

> 1000 MEN WANTED. To Protestant laborers everywhere, we say, Come to Ellsworth and come quickly! for your services may yet be needed in more ways than one! [18]

Fortunately both factions were content to appeal to the law courts which eventually handed down a decision upholding the Protestant contention and making Bible reading definitely legal within the state. "If," the Maine supreme court held, "Locke and Bacon and Milton and Swift are to be stricken from the list of authors which may be read in the schools because the authorities of one sect may have placed them among the list of heretical writers whose work it neither permits to be printed nor sold nor read, then the right of sectarian interference in the selection of books is at once yielded. . . . Thus the power of selection of books is withdrawn from those to whom the law entrusts it, and by the right of negation, is transferred to the scholars. The right, as claimed, undermines the power of the state. It is the will of the majority that shall bow to the conscience of the minority, or of one." [19] This decision, unfair as it was, governed nearly all state courts for a generation.

Despite this Protestant victory, Catholic attempts to drive the Bible from the schoolroom or secure a share of educational funds seemed to nativists a major aggression. In their eyes the whole attack was another Rome-controlled plot against those fundamental American institutions, the Bible and the school. This they did not doubt; how else, they asked, could the simultaneous demand arising in every corner of the nation be accounted for? That these demands could have been made with such unanimity without orders from the Pope seemed to nativists inconceivable.[20] Churches, ministers, and the press all joined in urging Protestant resistance, and the *American and Foreign Christian Union* expressed a general sentiment when it declared that the Bible would not be expelled from American classrooms "so long as a piece of Plymouth Rock remains big enough to make a gun flint out of." [21]

From the point of view of American Catholics, this attitude was most unfortunate. They could not send their children to public schools; there they would be subjected to a religious instruction contrary to the faith of their fathers. There too a mild persecution awaited most Irish lads; they were hooted at as "Paddies" and taunted with all the ingenious epithets that young nativists could devise. Yet parochial schools were expensive to maintain, particularly for the poorer immigrant families who were forced to contribute to the public schools through taxation. Parochial schools, moreover, were frowned upon by many sincere patriots who believed that they encouraged racial differences and slowed the process of assimilation. A dilemma thus faced the immigrants for which, at that time, there was no answer.

Unfortunate as was the school controversy from the Catholic point of view, the trusteeism conflict of the same period was even more disastrous. Although there is some question as to the part Hughes played in his church's efforts to secure educational funds, there is no doubt as to his rôle in this struggle over the control of church property. His vigorous handling of the whole matter during the 1840's and 1850's created schisms and antipathies which offered a golden opportunity to nativists.

The formula of a trusteeism controversy was the same now as it had been in the 1830's. Rebellious laymen, operating through a board of trustees, refused to vest control of church property in the clergy. Inevitably schism and scandal followed as the trustees were led to meddle in spiritual affairs and appoint their own pastors. Inevitably, too, the resulting confusion provided admirable material for nativistic writers.

Although the 1840's and 1850's witnessed many conflicts of this nature—notably one in Louisiana which aroused bitter feeling throughout the south—the New York controversies centering about Hughes were most spectacular and important. These had their origin in a law passed by the legislature in 1784 requiring that lay trustees chosen by the congregation should control all church property within the state. Under this law ownership of all Catholic churches built in New York in the early nineteenth century had been vested in trustees; a process which was undisputed as the state was without a bishop until 1815. With the arrival of a bishop an attempt was made to secure hierarchical control but a number of the churches resisted and the struggle was on. Here again the conflict was intensified by racial animosities; the older French Catholic groups contending with the growing Irish Catholic faction.[22]

It was into this contest that Hughes had been thrown as coadjutor Bishop of the New York diocese in 1838. He immediately issued a pastoral address to the congregation of St. Patrick's Cathedral, admitting the civil right of the trustees to control the church property but warning that any interference on their part with the clergy or sacraments would lead to an interdict.[23] Although this warning proved sufficient to check a threatened rebellion against ecclesiastical authority, Hughes knew that future trouble could only be averted if property control was vested in the hierarchy.[24] He dared not make the demand, for the law of 1784 was still upon the statute books, but a carefully worded appeal in 1842 caused most congregations in the diocese to volunteer to deliver up their property.[25] The sole exception was the trustees of the St. Louis church in Buffalo, who resisted briefly [26] before being forced to acknowledge their error and promise obedience in the future.

Hughes' firm stand had thus ended this phase of the New York trusteeism controversy, but the solution was far from permanent. The apparently acquiescent wardens of the Buffalo church had found defeat bitter and were awaiting an opportunity for retaliation. This came in 1846, when the New York diocese was divided and a new bishop, the Reverend John Timon, was placed in control of the district around Buffalo. For a time the St. Louis trustees tried the patience of the new appointee by slightly overstepping their authority, but they did not rebel openly until 1849, when Bishop Timon, acting under orders from the Baltimore Council of that year, made an attempt to secure control of the property. Relying on the state law, the trustees refused to surrender, and on June 14, 1851, the church was placed under an interdict.[27]

Hughes, now an archbishop and directly concerned, reasoned that the trustees would remain adamant so long as they were supported by the state's civil authorities. Not until the law of 1784 was removed from the statute books would the incorrigible trustees back down. Hence in 1852 Hughes secured the introduction of a measure into the New York legislature which would allow ecclesiastical authorities to hold title to church property. He hoped that its passage would strike at the roots of trusteeism by depriving the rebellious wardens of legal authority for their acts.

The Taber bill, as it was called, aroused the usual Protestant opposition. The New York *Observer* warned that any legislature passing such an act would be "selling out to the Pope," and the *Congregationalist* wondered who could "be so blind as not to see the cloven hoof, or so deaf as not to hear the clank of Inquisitorial chains in such a movement!" [28] Petitions calling for the defeat of Hughes' measure were showered on the legislators, each of whom received a long poem, allegedly signed by Archbishop Hughes, which began:

> Sweet Protestants, attend to me,
> Dear goose and gull and pigeon.
> We want to have equality
> In matters of religion.

But what that means let me expound,
And don't suppose we hate you:
I'll tell you how—should we get ground—
We mean to tolerate you:
Yes, when we once have gained our end; and that
    is Domination,
We'll tolerate you with a tol—derolderolderation.[29]

Impressed, the legislature defeated the bill, an act probably in accord with public opinion.[30]

Disastrous as was this decision to Catholics, the repercussion resulting from the Taber bill threatened to be even more serious. This was occasioned by the plight of the St. Louis church trustees. They had defied the interdict and had in 1854 been excommunicated. When this final step was taken against them, they prepared a careful statement to the legislature, pointing out that they had been subjected to the pain of excommunication simply because they had obeyed a state law, and asking the rigid enforcement of the statute of 1784.[31]

Protestant sympathizers in the legislature, still rankled by Hughes' attempt to push through the Taber bill, promptly drafted a measure which would force lay ownership of all church property within the state and make clerical ownership definitely illegal.[32] Debate on this Putnam bill, as it was called, was bitter and soon spread beyond the legislative chambers. Ablest defender of the Protestant cause was Senator Erastus Brooks, whose bold statement that Hughes owned five million dollars' worth of property in New York City, all of which was to be turned over to the Pope on demand, embroiled its author and Hughes in a new controversy.[33] The Archbishop replied in a semihumorous letter to the New York *Courier and Enquirer,* challenging Brooks to prove his claim. This letter was the first of a long series between the two men which, although settling nothing, attracted a great deal of attention.[34]

The fate of the Putnam bill was never in doubt and the debate which inspired the Brooks-Hughes controversy had little to do with its passage. The success of the measure was predetermined both by the strong nativistic feeling in the legislature and by the existing political situation in the state. The same body which debated the Putnam bill had just elected William H. Seward to the United States Senate, an action which naturally infuriated nativists, who resented his tolerance toward the foreign-born. Members of the legislature who had voted for Seward were anxious to make peace with the nativist faction and gladly supported the Putnam bill to show their constituents that a vote for Seward was not necessarily a vote for the Pope or Hughes.

The bill, enacted in 1855, if enforced, would have upset the entire Catholic church system in New York. Fortunately the state officials were wiser than the legislature; they made no attempt to apply the measure, and it was finally repealed in 1863.

While Hughes was waging a losing battle in New York, his fellow churchmen in other states were finding similar opposition when they tried to assume control of church property. In Massachusetts, in New Jersey, and in Connecticut bishops attempting to follow the example of the New York archbishop found their efforts blocked by stubborn trustees ably supported by nativists.[35] In Arkansas a legislative measure which would have allowed bishops to hold church property was defeated after one of the lawmakers had given a violent anti-Catholic address, bolstering his remarks by reading from Dowling's *History of Romanism*. The legislature then adjourned to listen to a sermon on "The Man of Sin." [36] "Such," remarked the Boston *Pilot*, "is the civilization of Arkansas." [37] In Pennsylvania and in Connecticut the legislatures, responding to petitions from rebellious trustees who had been threatened with excommunication, adopted bills similar to the Putnam act of New York, refusing incorporation to any religious body unless control of its property was vested in lay members.[38] In other states as well, attempts were made to pre-

vent clergymen from holding church property.[39] A general legislative attack on this vulnerable spot in the Catholic structure
seemed fairly launched.

Actually the church suffered less from these laws—which were
never enforced—than from the controversies that inspired them.
With trusteeism again before the public, nativists had an excellent chance to preach the undemocratic nature of a religion which
refused to allow the people control of their own churches and to
decry the manner in which Popery sought to evade American
laws.[40] The trusteeism controversy was particularly unfortunate
from the Catholic standpoint in that it led to the American visit
of Monsignor Gaetano Bedini, whose coming precipitated a
period of mob violence which played a large part in arousing
lower class interest in the No-Popery crusade. Bedini arrived in
the United States in 1853, accredited as a papal nuncio and empowered to settle trusteeism conflicts in Buffalo and Philadelphia.
Quickly terminating these in favor of the clergy, he began a tour
of the United States to visit prominent Catholics and bestow
upon them the papal blessing.

Few moves could have been more impolitic. Even before
Bedini began his swing across the country, the nativistic press
had prepared Protestants for his coming by misrepresenting his
innocent mission as a carefully planned journey which would end
in the subjugation of American freedom. "He is here," the New
York *Observer* stated positively, "to find the best way of riveting
Italian chains upon us which will bind us as slaves to the throne
of the most fierce tyranny the earth knows." [41] Lecturers mounted
their rostrums to warn their countrymen that Bedini was an
advance agent of the Inquisition and that he was authorized to
establish secret societies whose members would systematically
poison Protestant Americans.[42] The redoubtable Kirwan, controversialist of the late 1840's, began another series of letters in
the religious press to warn the people of this new crisis.[43] All
these propagandists stressed particularly Bedini's part in the

Italian uprisings of 1848 and 1849; he had, they said, been a staunch defender of monarchy and had personally been responsible for the death of Ugo Bassi and some hundred other Italian patriots.[44]

The efforts of these speakers and writers in depicting Bedini as a cloven-hoofed enemy of freedom and evangelical religion paled in comparison with those of a new defender of nativism who made the attack on the papal nuncio his own personal crusade. This fiery champion was an Italian ex-priest, Father Alessandro Gavazzi, whose experiences in behalf of the liberal cause in the Italian revolutions had convinced him that Popery and liberty were incompatible.[45] Determined to devote his life to "stripping the Romish harlot of her garb," he had renounced the priesthood and fled to England, where his lectures attracted so much attention that the American and Foreign Christian Union invited him to come to the United States.[46]

Gavazzi's first American appearance was in New York, where, on March 23, 1853, he addressed a large meeting which had been arranged by the American and Foreign Christian Union.[47] Those who heard him recognized in this ex-priest a new nativistic leader. He was a commanding personality—six feet tall, beardless, but with long black hair and compelling eyes—clothed in the somber garb of a monk with a blazing cross interwoven over his breast. He spoke rapidly, in an excited manner and with an "almost savage physical energy." [48] His lecture—"a ferocious discourse," according to the *Freeman's Journal*—struck a new note in nativistic spell-binding. He was not, he told his audience, a Protestant, for it was useless to protest against Popery. "No! No!" he said, "Popery cannot be reformed. . . . Therefore I go by myself and not protest at all. *Destruction to Popery!* No Protestantism; no protestations. Nothing but annihilation! Therefore I do not call myself a Protestant. I am a Destroyer." [49]

This message of hate won Gavazzi an immediate following. In a series of lectures in New York and other cities he told

audiences of Popish plots and designs on America so fantastic
that only his compelling presence made them believed.[50] His most
vitriolic words he saved for Bedini, that "Bloody Butcher of
Bologna," as he termed him. That despotic priest, Americans
were told, had been long a foe of liberty and freedom in Italy; it
was he who had ordered the assassination of Ugo Bassi and it
was he, personally, who had tortured that patriot before the end
came.[51] Gavazzi convinced the thousands who heard him that
Bedini was a formidable foe bent on undermining the foundations of American liberty.

Forewarned, the nation waited Bedini's tour, ready to harry
this papal minion from the land. At Boston great crowds on
the Common burned his effigy and threatened the home of the
bishop where he was staying. At Wheeling, West Virginia, the
mob spirit ran so high that civil authorities were powerless and
Bedini was only saved from assassination by the prompt action
of several hundred Irishmen who armed themselves and guarded
both his person and the Catholic churches of the city. At Pittsburgh a group of rowdies manhandled him as he entered the
bishop's carriage. At Baltimore he was again burned in effigy
and several bullets were fired into his room. When rumor reached
New Orleans that he would visit there, placards appeared about
the city announcing:

> BEDINI, THE TIGER, who is Guilty of the Murder
> of Hundreds of Patriots, their Wives and Chil-
> dren in Italia, who Ordered that Ugo Bassi, the
> Patriotic Catholic Priest be Scalped before he
> was Executed; Will this Abominable Servant of
> Despoty Receive the same Honors as the Heroes
> of Freedom, or will we Follow the Action of the
> Brewers of London against Haynau![52]

Bedini's worst reception awaited him at Cincinnati, where
large numbers of Germans, who took particular exception to his
rôle in the Revolutions of 1848, had been goaded on by an out-

spoken local press. On the night that Bedini arrived some 2,000 citizens marched through the streets carrying an effigy of the priest, a gallows, and banners which proclaimed: "DOWN WITH BEDINI," "NO PRIESTS, NO KINGS, NO POPERY," "THE GALLOWS BIRD BEDINI," and "DOWN WITH THE RAVEN BUTCHER." The marchers planned to pass the house where Bedini was staying, then burn his effigy in the neighboring yard of a Catholic church, but special police were on hand and clashed with the rioters, some twenty persons being injured before the procession was broken up.[53] Two weeks later another mob did succeed in burning Bedini's effigy, but neither this nor the arrest of the police officers responsible for the earlier firing satisfied nativists, who felt that the attack upon them had been engineered by Bedini and his Catholic friends.[54] The affair turned sentiment against Bedini throughout the nation; when he finally sailed from New York, the mob waiting at the dock to attack him was so large that the police were helpless, and he had to be smuggled aboard his ship after it was well down the harbor.[55]

Bedini's disastrous visit was principally important for the physical violence which it inspired. Rioting, in complete disfavor among nativists since Philadelphia's outburst in 1844, had been suddenly revived. The lower classes, with their tastes whetted by this interlude, welcomed the opportunity of wreaking their own brand of vengeance on Popery. The years which followed 1853 were years of almost constant turbulence and disorder; mob rule replaced the soft-spoken words and "Christian spirit" so stressed by nativists. This rioting did much to make the restless elements of the lower fringe of society feel their importance in the anti-Catholic crusade.

In this respect it is significant that the visit of Alessandro Gavazzi, whose haranguing tongue led to the revival of mob activity, had been arranged by the American and Foreign Christian Union. This august and "tolerant" organization obviously was bidding for popular support, for its managers must have known from Gavazzi's European record that his appeal was to the mob and that trouble would follow in his wake. If this was their expectation, they were not to be disappointed. Gavazzi not only helped make Bedini's tour one of constant turbulence; his own lectures stirred such a riotous spirit as the United States had not known for a decade. The first outbreak of disorder in which he directly figured took place in Quebec, where he had gone after lashing American audiences with his invective. There his bawdy descriptions of convents proved too much for his auditors; they rose against him, and Gavazzi, although defending himself for some time with a chair, was finally pitched into the battling mob and only miraculously escaped serious injury.[56] Two days later at Montreal the building in which he was speaking was attacked, and troops who had been on hand in anticipation of trouble only added to the confusion by firing into the crowd that poured from the lecture hall.[57] Some fifty persons were injured, and several killed before the fighting ended. Gavazzi returned to the United States with his popularity so enhanced that an enthusiastic committee awaited him in New York.[58]

His success was principally important because it convinced hundreds of rabble-rousers that nativism offered a fertile field for their invective. These fanatics blossomed suddenly over the entire country, holding forth from lecture platforms and churches or, as was more common, from any street corner to which they could attract a crowd. Some were regular ministers; the evangelical sects of New York in 1851 sanctioned street preaching as a means of bringing religion to the people, and other cities quickly followed this example.[59] Others were simply zealous Protestants impelled by vindictive natures to voice their hatred of Popery. A few recognized in the collections that were taken up a fruitful, if hazardous, source of income. All dwelt upon the popular theme: Popery was a grasping, tyrannical and immoral religious system which should be driven from America as speedily as possible.

These messages of hate were certain ᴛᴏ cause trouble, for turbulence and disorder stalked the land in that restless decade of the 1850's. The lawlessness of the Mississippi valley frontier was permeating the seaboard, where tempers were already ragged and nerves on edge as a result of the slavery controversy. Reformers, drawn from the lunatic fringe of society and impatient of the rational attainment of their ends, encouraged physical violence to stamp out opposition. Bands of women were raiding bar rooms, breaking glasses, staving in whiskey kegs, and pouring liquor into the street. Mobs were hunting down antislavery agitators or turning with equal enthusiasm to fight for the freedom of a runaway slave. Amid such unrest, each anti-Catholic street preacher became a potential mob leader, inspiring his listeners to attacks upon Catholic churches and property or Catholics themselves. Wherever they went, these agitators left a wake of rioting and disorder. "The logic of the Stillingfleets and Chillingworths has lost its force," remarked ᴏne Catholic paper. "Its place is now supplied by trumpets, brickbats and knives. The ancient propagators of Christianity fled on the eve of tumult; our nineteenth-century preachers take pride in creating one." [60]

Most of these preachers were obscure men who gained fame only through the chaos they inspired; others earned a justifiable notoriety. Most prominent among these was an itinerant wanderer, John S. Orr, more generally called the Angel Gabriel, a name given him because he always spoke clothed in a long white gown and summoned his hearers by blasts on a brass horn. Orr leaped into prominence in Boston in May, 1854, when he made several speeches, going from place to place with an eager mob at his heels. As was inevitable under these conditions, a clash with a group of Irish laborers occurred, and Orr's followers, with their appetites thus whetted, attempted to burn a Catholic church at Mount Bellingham. Police arrived in time to protect the building, but the crowd refused to disperse until given the cross from the top of the edifice. The police finally agreed to this, a boy was sent up the steeple to throw the cross down, and it was publicly burned. An attempt was then made to attack another church in East Boston, but by this time troops had been assembled, and the rioters were forced to disband.[61]

The fame growing from these events followed the Angel Gabriel to New York.[62] On Sunday, June 11, he spoke to a large audience from the steps of the city hall, then headed for Brooklyn with a crowd of more than a thousand persons following him. A whole army of special police had been drafted for the occasion and only these precautions allowed the day to pass quietly, for about 10,000 people had gathered to hear Orr. As the mob was returning to Manhattan ferries, it clashed with a group of Irish, but no serious damage resulted.[63]

This comparative peace was not duplicated when the Angel Gabriel returned to New England; his path there was one of continuous disorder. At Nashua, New Hampshire, a mob rushed directly from his lecture to attack the Irish settlement. He spoke at Bath, Maine, with such telling effect that his hearers stormed a Catholic church, displayed an American flag from the balcony, and then burned the building to the ground. A short time later he incited another church burning in Palmyra, New York.[64] Inspired by these successes, the Angel Gabriel returned to Boston, the scene of his first triumphs. This proved his undoing. When he attempted to speak in Charlestown late in August, 1854, he was arrested and charged with creating a disturbance and selling handbills on the Sabbath. Although a mob tried to release him from the Boston jail, he was tried and convicted.[65] Other cities followed the example of Boston; everywhere officials, afraid of property damage, refused him permission to speak. When he disregarded such a ruling in Washington, he was clapped into jail for two weeks.[66] Finally convinced that his American audiences were denied him, the Angel Gabriel left for British Guiana, where his preaching stirred the natives to such an extent that they arose against the Portuguese Catholics of that country.[67]

The rabble-rousing tactics Orr used so successfully in New England were duplicated in New York by a street preacher named Daniel Parsons, who boasted a long career as a speaker from docks and market places before his anti-Catholic addresses brought him fame. Parsons gained his first notoriety late in November, 1853, when he was interrupted in a vehement attack on Catholicism by several hecklers. On successive Sabbaths his audiences were greatly increased until by December 11 he had a gathering of some 10,000 waiting to hear him. Police who were on hand to prevent trouble arrested Parsons in the middle of his sermon, and the crowd, greatly enraged, laid siege to the mayor's home and threatened such violence that that worthy ordered Parsons' release.[68] Feeling was still high, and on the following Wednesday a mass meeting was held in Central Park where resolutions were adopted upholding Parsons and demanding the mayor's resignation. Trouble obviously was brewing, Archbishop Hughes sensed the situation and issued a proclamation that was intended to ease the tension but which actually had an opposite effect:

If there be, as it has been insinuated, a conspiracy against the civil and religious rights which are secured to you by our Constitution and laws, defeat the purpose of that conspiracy by a peaceful and entirely legal deportment in all the relations of life. But on the other hand, if such a conspiracy should arise, unrebuked by the public authorities, to a point really menacing with destruction any portion of your property, whether your private dwellings, your churches, your hospitals, orphan asylums, or other Catholic institutions, then, in case of an attack, let every man be prepared in God's name to stand by the laws of the country and the authorities of the city in defense of such rights and property.[69]

Protestants interpreted this as a declaration of war, but a manifesto from the mayor calling for peace calmed their ruffled feelings and the following Sunday passed quietly. A crowd of more than 20,000 which gathered to hear Parsons and two other street preachers dispersed without disorder when the speeches were over.[70] Parsons and his cohorts continued to hold forth in New York, unmolested by authorities, for several years.[71]

Although the Angel Gabriel and Parsons were most notorious, other fanatics were just as influential in stirring up hatred of Catholicism. One who called himself Father Leahy had a colorful career of rioting and arrest before being sentenced to life imprisonment in Wisconsin after killing a man in a quarrel.[72] Another, the Reverend G. G. Achilli, reached America from Italy in 1853 and gained a wide reputation for his descriptions of the Inquisition and priestly immorality.[73] Perhaps the most ingenious of the group was the Reverend L. Giustiniani, who traveled about with a troup of Germans, "converting" them to Protestantism in each city. His tactics aroused so much resentment among Catholics that the Cincinnati church in which he was speaking in 1853 was destroyed by a mob.[74]

Police and civil authorities were helpless in trying to restrain either these speakers or the crowds that they attracted; popular sentiment, particularly among the lower classes, was too much in their favor. Thus in Pittsburgh a street preacher entered a Catholic church, made his way to the pulpit during services, and harangued the congregation on Popery, knowing that the authorities were unable to take proper steps against him.[75] When police tried to stop a blind preacher who had been holding forth in the markets of Baltimore, the crowd which formed was so menacing that he was released.[76] The arrest of a fanatic named Kirkland in Cincinnati in 1853 caused such dissension that a committee of 100 citizens demanded the mayor's resignation.[77] Police who carted a Boston street preacher to jail on three successive Sundays in 1854 had a howling mob at their heels, constantly threatening trouble.[78] Only in Oswego, New York, was a satisfactory means found of checking these rabble-rousers. There Catholics attended the sermons of a wandering preacher and shouted so loudly that he was unable to make himself heard.

After three days of attempting to outroar his hecklers, the speaker left town.[79]

Nowhere, however, was the popular support of these itinerant preachers better shown than in Pittsburgh. There one Joseph Barker, goading authorities beyond endurance by his anti-Catholic oratory, was arrested and sentenced to a year in jail. Popular indignation knew no bounds. In the next mayoralty campaign Barker's friends announced that he would be a candidate and this fanatical individual, who was still languishing in the local lockup, was elected to the office by a substantial majority. His term as mayor was a sad one for Pittsburgh Catholics, yet he was kept from re-election only by a narrow vote.[80]

Little wonder that, with anti-Catholic sentiment so great, these street preachers could incite such disorder. Frequently crowds of excited Protestants, whipped to angry resentment by the exhortations of some wandering orator, rushed directly to a Catholic church, bent on its destruction. A dozen churches were burned during the middle 1850's; countless more were attacked, their crosses stolen, their altars violated, and their windows broken.[81] At Sidney, Ohio, and at Dorchester, Massachusetts, Catholic houses of worship were blown to pieces with gunpowder, probably placed by plotting nativists.[82] In New York City a mob laid siege to the prominent cathedral of St. Peter and St. Paul, and only the arrival of the police saved the building.[83] In Maine Catholics who had had one church destroyed were prevented from laying the cornerstone of a new one by hostile Protestants, and statues of priests were torn down or desecrated.[84] So general were these attacks that a Catholic historian, writing many years later, believed that there existed "a general conspiracy to destroy the church property of Catholics." [85]

Priests suffered from this Protestant hostility almost as much as their churches. Mobs were constantly threatening them or subjecting them to public abuse. At least two were severely beaten on their way to administer the last rites to the dying.[86] The citizens of Ellsworth, Maine, aroused by a contest over Bible reading in the schools, carried matters to the extreme when the local priest was tarred and feathered and ridden from town on a rail.[87] Although a mass meeting was called to condemn this disgraceful deed, the rioters found tacit approval even in the secular press, and a grand jury refused to hold any of them for trial.[88] One priest, writing from Portland, Maine, described the popular attitude toward himself and his fellow churchmen:

> Since the 4th of July I have not considered myself safe to walk the streets after sunset. Twice within the last month I have been stoned by young men. If I chance to be abroad when the public schools are dismissed, I am hissed and insulted with vile language; and those repeated from children have been encouraged by the smiles and silence of the passers by. The windows of the Church have frequently been broken—the panels of the Church door stove in, and last week a large rock entered my chamber rather unceremoniously about 11 o'clock at night.[89]

Attacks such as these were not confined solely to churches and priests; Americans found in this interlude of rioting a long-sought opportunity to renew their ancient enmity toward convents. Attention was directed to these structures by the inevitable crop of escaped nuns who appeared miraculously now just as they had in the 1830's. One, who called herself Sister Agnes and who claimed to be a second Maria Monk, toured the country, recounting immoral tales of convent life to all who would pay to hear.[90] Two others, Milly McPherson and Olivia Neal, were the subject of considerable speculation when they vanished just after making good their "escape" from Catholic institutions; nativists firmly believed that both had been murdered by priests.[91] Still others penned voluminous documents of convent life, such as that by an anonymous author: *The Escaped Nun; or, Disclosures of Convent Life and the Confessions of a Sister of Charity.*[92] Most notorious among the fence-climbing sisterhood of this generation, however, was Josephine M. Bunkley, the story of whose life as a novice in the Sisterhood of St. Joseph at Emmetsburg, Maryland, was one of the best sellers of the day.[93] Miss Bunkley differed from other propagandists of her sort in that she actually had been in the convent; the Mother Superior freely acknowledged that the girl had been a novice for ten months, that she had appeared happy and contented during that period, and that her elaborate "escape" was both unconventional and unnecessary, as she was free to go at any time.[94] Protestants ignored this straightforward statement to gloat over Miss Bunkley's revelations of priestly immorality.

The antagonism aroused by these tales and by the frequent press notices of girls lured into nunneries and forced to take the veil,[95] led both to demands that states legislate convents out of existence [96] and to physical attacks on these "Popish brothels" designed to force the release of nuns who, many Protestants honestly believed, were confined in dungeons against their will. In New Orleans, Galveston, and Charleston, mobs stormed convents, shouted insults at the nuns, and were only prevented from doing serious damage by police intervention. Sisters of Mercy in Chicago were subjected to repeated annoyances, not the least of which was being dragged into court by overzealous Protestants who sought to secure their release by legal means. Sober-minded citizens had to aid Catholics in protecting an Ohio convent of the Sisters of Notre Dame when it was attacked by a mob.[97] Even Providence, traditional center of tolerance, was so stirred by tales of immorality which were published in the Providence *Journal* that a group of Sisters of Mercy stationed in the city were subjected to repeated insults. Finally, in March, 1854, the paper boldly stated that an American girl was confined in this nunnery against her will. Despite a denial of the charge by the girl herself, a mass meeting was called, and only hurried action by authorities, aided by armed Irishmen, prevented the destruction of the building.[98]

These disgraceful attacks on houses of worship, priests, and

nuns clearly indicate the enthusiasm with which the lower classes
had, by the middle 1850's, embraced the cause of anti-Catholicism. What amounted to a popular hysteria was gripping many
sections of the country. A rumor that Irish serving girls had
been instructed to poison the food of their Protestant employers
swept over New England early in 1855; instead of being laughed
away, this absurd tale was so seriously believed that many honest
servants lost their jobs.[99] A priest reported that he could not
travel to a neighboring city without causing suspicions to fly
through the countryside that he was returning laden with poison
to be used by his parishioners in killing all Protestants.[100] The
entire city of Bangor, Maine, was thrown into a panic one morning in 1854 when mysterious symbols were discovered on many
houses; these, rumor had it, were families marked for destruction by the Inquisition. Excitement was only allayed when it was
found that an itinerant German hair dresser had been distributing advertisements and had marked the houses he had can-
vassed.[101] In most towns placards and posters constantly warned
Protestants to be on their guard against popish attack; even the
paper used by storekeepers to wrap parcels admonished Americans against the evils of Rome.[102] The United States, having experienced one burst of national hysteria in 1798, was experienc-
ing another now, just as great in some sections as that of a half
century before.

Probably the state of the popular mind is best illustrated by two
trivial incidents. One concerned an Irish serving girl in Charlestown, Massachusetts, who had been converted to the Freewill
Baptist faith by the family which employed her. This young lady,
after spreading rumors of Catholic attempts to restore her to the
fold, mysteriously disappeared on the night of February 12,
1853. Two days later Boston and Charlestown newspapers were
beginning to give credence to the rumor that she had been abducted by priests. Excitement grew. On February 23 handbills
were spread through Charlestown, reading:

SHE MUST BE FOUND!

All people opposed to religious oppression and the IMPRISONMENT of a Human Being for Opinion's Sake are requested to meet at Richmond street, Charlestown, on Wednesday Evening, March 2.

City officials believed that the selection of a meeting place adjacent to a Catholic church was not mere coincidence, and promptly called out the militia. This precaution was timely, for the mob tore down an Irish dwelling and was only restrained from destroying the church by the presence of troops. Feeling remained high, with almost constant rioting on the streets of Charlestown, until Hannah Corcoran returned on March 5, as quietly as she had disappeared. Protestant ministers were notified and the next morning, a Sunday, joyfully announced from the city pulpits that the girl was back, "still strong in the faith of our Lord and Savior, Jesus Christ." Where Hannah stayed during her absence will probably always remain a mystery. Her mother, a Catholic, insisted that the girl had gone to Philadelphia to seek employment and had only returned to quiet fears growing from her disappearance. Hannah herself told a romantic story of being drugged by priests who sought to reconvert her to Catholicism and only allowed her to return when they feared mob violence to their churches. Be that as it may, Protestant friends showered so many gifts upon her that she was able to retire from the servant girl class and depart for school, having profited greatly by her notoriety.[103]

The absurdity of the Hannah Corcoran incident was equalled only by another that took place in Washington, D. C. In 1852 a block of marble arrived in that city, a gift of the Pope to the American people, and intended for the Washington monument, then under construction. Objections immediately arose; one pamphlet, *The Pope's Stratagem: "Rome to America!" An Ad-*

dress to the Protestants of the United States, against placing the Pope's block of Marble in the Washington Monument, urged Protestants to hold indignation meetings and contribute another block to be placed next to the Pope's "bearing an inscription by which all men may see that we are awake to the hypocrisy and schemes of that designing, crafty, subtle, far seeing and far reaching Power, which is ever grasping after the whole World, to sway its iron sceptre, with bloodstained hands, over the millions of its inhabitants." [104] A number of these meetings were held, resentment steadily mounted, and finally, in the spring of 1854, a mob forced its way into the shed where the Pope's gift was being stored, secured the block, and threw it into the Potomac.[105]

In these attacks on Catholicism there was none of the tolerance and love for which organized nativists had been pleading for a decade. There was only hysterical fear and fanatical hate. The blunders of the Catholic church—the ill-advised comments of some of its leaders, the struggle over school funds, and the trusteeism controversy—had again brought the lower classes firmly within the nativistic fold, to join the churchgoing group previously attracted by the American and Foreign Christian Union. As a result, the anti-Catholic forces were numerically stronger than at any time before in the country's history.

NOTES

[1] *Congregationalist,* September 15, 1854.

[2] *Freeman's Journal,* December 11, 1852. In the three years, 1845–1847. 191 new Catholic churches were erected in the United States and the number continued to increase in proportion. *Ibid.,* June 10, 1848.

[3] Brownson, *Life of O. A. Brownson,* II, 98–102. Brownson also believed in practicing what he preached. While dining at an inn in Andover one Friday he called the landlord and asked in a voice so loud that all in the room could hear, "Why don't you have something in your house that a good Christian can eat?" The landlord explained that he had exceptionally good steaks and roasts. Brownson answered: "Why don't you have fish? No Christian eats meat on Friday."

[4] *Freeman's Journal,* March 4, 1848. *The Shepherd of the Valley,* a Catholic paper published in St. Louis, took this same tone through the period.

[5] John Hughes, *The Decline of Protestantism and its Causes* (New York, 1850), 26; *Freeman's Journal*, November 23, 1850.

[6] Thus New York *Observer*, November 23, 1850; *American and Foreign Christian Union*, I (December, 1850). The *Freeman's Journal*, November 30, 1850, and December 7, 1850, reprinted hostile comment from nearly all of the New York papers, secular as well as religious.

[7] *American and Foreign Christian Union*, II (January, 1851); *Freeman's Journal*, December 14, 1850. The speakers were the Reverends Dowling, Cheever, and Cox, and the meeting was held in the Broadway Tabernacle.

[8] Murray, *Memoirs*, 308–309; Nicholas Murray, *The Decline of Popery and its Causes; an Address Delivered at the Broadway Tabernacle January 15, 1851* (New York, 1851).

[9] Joseph F. Berg, *Lecture Delivered in the Music Fund Hall on Tuesday, November 26, 1850, in Answer to Archbishop Hughes on the Decline of Protestantism* (Philadelphia, 1850), 5–6. A few months later Berg again attacked Hughes through the medium of a pamphlet *Trapezium; or, Law and Liberty vs. Despotism and Anarchy* (Philadelphia, 1851) in which he reiterated his former arguments and proved that Protestantism was the parent of liberty and Catholicism the father of despotism. His arguments were supported by Abel C. Thomas, whose pamphlet *Triangle. The Catholic Question Considered. Both Disputants Answered* (Philadelphia, 1851) attempted to prove that Berg was correct in claiming Catholicism to be the enemy of liberty.

[10] *Freeman's Journal*, September 18, 1852, October 23, 1852, October 30, 1852, December 25, 1852; New York *Observer*, September 30, 1852. The *Shepherd of the Valley* and other prominent papers adopted a similar point of view, following the lead of the *Freeman's Journal*.

[11] *Pilot*, February 12, 1853, February 26, 1853, April 23, 1853; *Freeman's Journal*, April 9, 1853; *Congregationalist*, January 28, 1853.

[12] New York *Observer*, March 31, 1853; *Congregationalist*, April 29, 1853.

[13] *Pilot*, April 23, 1853; New York *Observer*, April 14, 1853.

[14] Shea, *History of the Catholic Church*, IV, 479. The student was punished and expelled with the express sanction of the trustees. Excitement over the affair caused the burning of a convent at Palmyra by a mob.

[15] New York *Observer*, December 29, 1853, April 6, 1854; *Pilot*, March 5, 1853.

[16] American and Foreign Christian Union, *Fifth Annual Report* (1854), 20.

[17] *Freeman's Journal*, October 15, 1853.

[18] *Pilot*, May 6, 1854. See also *Freeman's Journal*, November 18, 1854; New York *Observer*, November 24, 1853. Conditions were not improved when two Catholics broke into the public school building and destroyed all Bibles they could find there.

[19] *Donahoe v. Richards*. 38 Maine, 379. The arguments before the court were intensely anti-Catholic in tone. They are printed in New York *Observer* August 31, 1854. This decision, making it possible for school authorities to force the reading of the King James version of the Scriptures, remained the leading case on the subject for many years, despite Catholic objections. Students were expelled from Boston and New York schools as late as 1858 and 1859 for refusing to read the Protestant Bible. It was not until 1890 that the *Egerton Bible Case*, tried in the Wisconsin courts, reversed the decision in

Donahoe v. Richards and made it possible for Catholic children to attend public school without having their religious beliefs interfered with.

²⁰ New York *Observer*, March 17, 1853; *Congregationalist*, April 22, 1853; American and Foreign Christian Union, *Fourth Annual Report* (1853), 20–25.

²¹ *American and Foreign Christian Union,* IV (September, 1853). Several church assemblies, notably the New School Presbyterians and the Reformed Protestant Dutch church, passed resolutions attacking the Catholic stand, while the Old School Presbyterians were already on record as favoring Protestant Bible reading in the schools. New York *Observer*, May 30, 1846, June 2, 1853, June 16, 1853. Individual ministers also gave the matter their attention; thus in Cincinnati the Reverend N. L. Rice gave a series of sermons on the subject and in Boston the Reverend Rufus W. Clark gave over two lectures of a series against Popery to the question of Bible reading in the schools. Other clergymen frequently touched on the matter. *Ibid.*, October 14, 1852; Clark, *Romanism in America* (last two sermons); Pike, *Romanism, a Sermon*, 25–26. Nearly every anti-Catholic book or publication of this period has much space devoted to the question. The Protestant attitude toward the entire Catholic educational system was shown by the failure of the Massachusetts legislature to issue a charter for the College of the Holy Cross in Worcester when it applied for incorporation in 1849 after seven years of successful operation. Speeches in the legislature were strongly anti-Catholic; see *Pilot*, April 14, 1849; *Congregationalist*, October 19, 1849; *Freeman's Journal*, May 12, 1849; *Speeches of Mr. Hopkins of Northampton on the Bill to Incorporate the College of the Holy Cross, in the City of Worcester, Delivered in the House of Representatives, April 24th and 25th, 1849, with an Introductory letter to the members of the House* (Northampton, 1849). When the adverse vote was announced the Boston *Pilot* remarked: "Thank God that the free constitution of the United States does not leave us in the power of these Puritans." *Pilot*, April 28, 1849.

²² J. Talbot Smith, *The History of the Catholic Church in New York* (New York, 1905), 40–68.

²³ Hassard, *Life of John Hughes*, 193–194.

²⁴ This had been announced as the accepted policy of the Church by decrees of the Baltimore Councils in 1829, 1837, and 1840. Guilday, *History of the Councils of Baltimore*, 81–134.

²⁵ This was embodied in a pastoral letter, which was printed in the New York *Journal of Commerce*, October 22, 1842. It aroused the usual Protestant rejoinder; the *Journal of Commerce* maintaining that this was the "arbitrary interference of a foreign potentate" with American institutions. *Ibid.*, September 17, 1842–November 19, 1842.

²⁶ Hassard, *Life of John Hughes*, 261–264.

²⁷ John M. Farley, *The Life of John Cardinal McCloskey* (New York, 1918), 185–186; *Freeman's Journal*, July 19, 1851.

²⁸ New York *Observer*, June 30, 1853; *Congregationalist*, April 2, 1852.

²⁹ *American and Foreign Christian Union,* IV (September, 1853).

³⁰ *Congregationalist*, July 22, 1853.

³¹ The petition was printed in the New York *Tribune*, January 9, 1855.

³² The measure, drawn up by Senators James O. Putnam, Thomas R. Whitney, and Erastus Brooks, provided that on the death of any clerical officer,

church property held by him should escheat to the state. The escheat was only to be granted to the congregation after it had incorporated itself as provided under the Act of 1784. The Catholic church alone would suffer, for Protestant churches normally employed a method of lay control. *Laws of the State of New York Passed at the 18th Session of the Legislature* (Albany, 1855), 338.

33 W. S. Tisdale (ed.), *The Controversy between Senator Brooks, and John, Archbishop of New York, over the Church Property Bill* (New York, 1855), 11-23.

34 Hughes offered to build a $2,000,000 library for the education of legislators if Brooks could prove he owned $5,000,000 worth of property. The debate hinged largely on whether a 999-year lease constituted ownership. Letters of the controversialists were edited by Tisdale with a nativistic slant, and also by Hughes under the title of *Brooksiana* (New York, 1855). They were also widely reprinted in the religious and nativistic press. See *Congregationalist*, April 27, 1855; *Pilot*, May 12, 1855; W. S. Tisdale, *The Know Nothing Almanac and True Americans' Manual for 1856* (New York, 1856), 23-25; *Pope or President? Startling Disclosures of Romanism as Revealed by its Own Writers* (New York, 1859), 280.

35 New York *Observer*, November 24, 1853; *Congregationalist*, March 2, 1855; Shea, *History of the Catholic Church*, III, 490-491.

36 New York *Observer*, February 17, 1849.

37 March 24, 1849.

38 *Pilot*, March 3, 1855; *Connecticut Courant*, May 26, 1855; *Congregationalist*, February 24, 1854; New York *Observer*, February 16, 1854; *American Catholic Historical Researches*, XI (July, 1894), 129-132.

39 *Pilot*, March 3, 1855. The American and Foreign Christian Union attempted to set up a lobby in every state legislature to campaign for laws of this type. American and Foreign Christian Union, *Fifth Annual Report* (1854), 20-21.

40 New York *Observer*, July 24, 1851, July 6, 1854; *American and Foreign Christian Union*, V (January, 1854); *Pilot*, April 21, 1855; Thomas, *Triangle*, 23; Carroll, *Great American Battle*, 313-314; *Pope or President*, 275-277; *The Origin, Principles and Purposes of the American Party* (————, 1855), 31; E. H. Derby, *The Catholic: Letters Addressed by a Jurist to a Young Kinsman Proposing to Join the Church of Rome* (Boston, 1856), 171.

41 New York *Observer*, August 25, 1853. See also *Ibid.*, November 10, 1853; *Congregationalist*, January 13, 1854; Tisdale, *Controversy*, vii; *Pope or President*, 290-291; *The Sons of the Sires; a History of the Rise, Progress and Destiny of the American Party* (Philadelphia, 1855), 32.

42 Such a series was delivered in America by Signor Gajani in 1853. *Pope or President*, 240-243, 290.

43 New York *Observer*, February 16, 1854 and ff.

44 *Congregationalist*, November 11, 1853; *Pope or President*, 295-297. Actually Bassi was an apostate priest who had joined Garibaldi's troops. He was tried by a regular Austrian court martial and executed. Bedini's connection with the trial grew simply from the fact that he was in Bologna when it took place.

45 *The Life of Father Gavazzi* (London, 1851), 1-64.

46 *American and Foreign Christian Union,* III (May, 1853).

47 The address was given at the Broadway Tabernacle on March 23, 1853. The American and Foreign Christian Union kept secret its own part in sponsoring Gavazzi; the meeting was supposedly arranged by a committee of twenty men and no mention was made of the nativistic society in newspaper accounts. New York *Observer,* March 17, 1853.

48 His address was so described by a Catholic who, despite his hostility, was obviously much impressed. *Pilot,* June 16, 1853. See also *Freeman's Journal,* April 3, 1853.

49 New York *Observer,* March 31, 1853.

50 Gavazzi's lectures in New York were printed in two separate volumes. One, *The Lectures Complete of Father Gavazzi as Delivered in New York; Reported by an Eminent Stenographer and Revised and Corrected by Gavazzi Himself; to which is Prefixed the Life of Gavazzi by G. B. Nicolini* (New York, 1853) was the official edition, so recognized by Gavazzi, and has been used in this study. The other, *Lectures in New York, reported in full by T. C. Leland, Photographer; also the Life of Father Gavazzi, Corrected and Authorized by himself, together with reports of his Addresses in Italian to his Countrymen in New York, Translated and Revised by Madame Julie de Marguerittes* (New York, 1853) was not authorized by Gavazzi and people were warned by him not to purchase it. New York *Observer,* July 21, 1853.

51 Gavazzi, *Lectures,* iv–v; *Pilot,* May 7, 1853.

52 *Pilot,* January 14, 1854, February 4, 1854, February 11, 1854; *Congressional Globe,* 33rd Cong., 1st Sess., 223; *Freeman's Journal,* December 17, 1853, January 14, 1854.

53 New York *Observer,* January 12, 1854; *Pilot,* January 7, 1854, January 14, 1854; *Freeman's Journal,* December 31, 1853, January 14, 1854. The *Freeman's Journal* complained that any attempt to interfere with Gavazzi led to a charge of interference with freedom of speech and that the Germans who had taken part in the Bedini rioting were looked upon as martyrs by the rest of the people.

54 *Pilot,* January 28, 1854.

55 *Ibid.,* January 28, 1854. The hostile demonstrations against Bedini were so violent that governmental officials feared diplomatic consequences. This view was expressed to the Senate by Lewis Cass of Michigan who publicly deplored this treatment of an agent of another power. Senators William Dawson of Georgia, Edward Everett of Massachusetts and Stephen A. Douglas of Illinois joined with Cass in denouncing the mob violence. Nativists found their champion in Senator John B. Weller of California, who defended the American actions. The state of public opinion was indicated by the fact that although Cass and others who defended Bedini spoke in silence, Weller aroused such cheers that the Senate galleries had to be cleared. *Congressional Globe,* 33rd Cong., 1st Sess., 223–228. The only result of the debate was the passage of a resolution asking the president to submit information on Bedini's visit. This he did on January 27, 1854, and the matter was then dropped. *Senate Documents,* 33rd Cong., 1st Sess., No. 23.

56 Montreal *True Witness,* quoted in *Pilot,* June 18, 1853; *New York Observer,* June 16, 1853.

57 *American Union,* July 2, 1853; New York *Observer,* June 16, 1853; *Pilot,* June 18, 1853. Although both Catholics and Protestants held indigna-

tion meetings, a jury that investigated the rioting could find no direct blame on either side. *Pilot,* June 25, 1853, July 2, 1853, July 30, 1853.

58 New York *Observer,* December 14, 1854.

59 All the Protestant sects excepting the Episcopalians joined in supporting and encouraging street preaching. *Ibid.,* November 13, 1851, November 20, 1851, April 29, 1852; McMaster, *History of the People of the United States,* VIII, 81.

60 *Pilot,* June 17, 1854.

61 *Ibid.,* May 13, 1854; *Freeman's Journal,* May 20, 1854.

62 One of Orr's co-workers, Samuel G. Moses, had remained in New York while Orr was in New England, denouncing Popery so successfully that he stirred up several minor riots on successive Sundays. The most serious took place on June 4 when a group that had been listening to Moses clashed with an Irish faction. Pistols were fired, heads were broken, and it was necessary to call out the militia before fighting was stopped. New York *Observer,* June 8, 1854.

63 *Ibid.,* June 15, 1854.

64 *Pilot,* July 8, 1854, July 15, 1854, August 19, 1854; New York *Observer,* July 13, 1854.

65 *Pilot,* August 26, 1854.

66 *Ibid.,* October 7, 1854, October 21, 1854.

67 New York *Tribune,* March 24, 1856. A man who claimed to be a close friend of Orr stated that he was not a Scotchman, as his name implied, but a native of Demerara, the son of a Scotch father and West Indian mother. *Pilot,* July 29, 1854. It was incorrectly stated by several papers at the time that Orr's name was Sandy MacSwish. *Ibid.,* July 22, 1854.

68 New York *Observer,* December 22, 1853; *Freeman's Journal,* December 17, 1853.

69 Quoted in Shea, *History of the Catholic Church,* IV, 463-464.

70 New York *Observer,* December 22, 1853; *Freeman's Journal,* December 24, 1853.

71 Minor riots occurred in New York on nearly every Sunday during 1854, caused by street preachers and those who tried to heckle them. This was despite the fact that Catholics were repeatedly urged by their clergy and their press not to attend such gatherings. *Pilot,* May 13, 1854, August 12, 1854; *Freeman's Journal,* February 11, 1854, April 8, 1854; New York *Observer,* June 22, 1854.

72 The colorful career of this scoundrel may be traced in the following newspapers: New York *Observer,* September 30, 1848; *Pilot,* January 27, 1849, February 10, 1849, October 20, 1849; *Freeman's Journal,* May 13, 1848, May 27, 1848, June 3, 1848, February 17, 1849, March 10, 1849, February 16, 1850, April 19, 1851, March 27, 1852, May 1, 1852, September 11, 1852; *Congregationalist,* March 23, 1850, April 12, 1850, May 2, 1851; *American Union,* April 19, 1851, May 14, 1853; *American and Foreign Christian Union,* III (May, 1852). Reasons for the rioting that Leahy caused can be seen from the title of one of his lectures, delivered in Charleston: "The Unchristian Treatment of Females in the Confessional, by Popish Priests, according to the standard of Popish Theology." The poster, reproduced in the *Freeman's Journal,* March 27, 1852, states that: "Ladies and Youths are positively prohibited from coming to this Lecture, as some awful disclosures will be made." An

earlier attempt on Leahy's part to speak in Charleston had resulted in a controversial book of some importance. Permission had been refused him by the city council, largely due to the efforts of John Bellinger, a Catholic. Bellinger published his reasons for this stand, using the occasion to attack Protestantism and particularly the theology of Luther. He was replied to by the Reverend John Bachman and a prolonged controversy followed, the letters eventually being published by Bachman under the title: *A Defense of Luther and the Reformation Against the Charges of John Bellinger and Others* (Cincinnati, 1853).

[73] *American and Foreign Christian Union,* I (January, 1850); *Congregationalist,* February 1, 1850, March 1, 1850, April 12, 1850, August 23, 1850, February 6, 1852; *Pilot,* September 15, 1849, May 21, 1853, March 17, 1855; *Freeman's Journal,* June 18, 1851, July 24, 1852.

[74] *Freeman's Journal,* October 9, 1847, December 2, 1848, August 4, 1849; *United States Catholic Magazine,* V (March, 1846), V (July, 1846); New York *Observer,* April 7, 1853.

[75] Shea, *History of the Catholic Church,* IV, 76–77.

[76] New York *Herald,* July 27, 1853.

[77] *Pilot,* May 21, 1853, May 28, 1853.

[78] *National Intelligencer,* June 22, 1854.

[79] *Pilot,* October 28, 1854.

[80] *Freeman's Journal,* December 1, 1849, November 2, 1850, January 25, 1851, September 25, 1852.

[81] *Pilot,* January 1, 1853, June 16, 1853, July 22, 1854, September 2, 1854, September 16, 1854, December 9, 1854; *American Union,* May 17, 1851; *Freeman's Journal,* January 1, 1853.

[82] New York *Observer,* July 13, 1854; *Pilot,* July 15, 1854, July 29, 1854; Pike, *Romanism, a Sermon,* 18–22; Shea, *History of the Catholic Church,* IV, 543.

[83] New York *Observer,* November 16, 1854.

[84] *Pilot,* November 10, 1849, November 24, 1855.

[85] Shea, *History of the Catholic Church,* IV, 510.

[86] *Pilot,* July 28, 1849, June 2, 1855.

[87] *Ibid.,* July 8, 1854, October 28, 1854; New York *Observer,* October 26, 1854.

[88] *Pilot,* October 28, 1854, November 4, 1854, November 11, 1854; *American and Foreign Christian Union,* V (December, 1854).

[89] *Pilot,* October 28, 1854.

[90] *American Union,* August 13, 1853.

[91] Milly McPherson was reported to have fled from a convent in Bardstown, Kentucky, in 1836 to escape the attentions of a priest. The incident had aroused a great deal of interest at the time as the editors of the *Western Protestant* had gone so far as to name the priest who had attempted to seduce her. This justly indignant cleric promptly entered a libel suit against the publication, and was awarded one cent in damages by a reluctant jury. Milly McPherson conveniently vanished, and it was frequently charged thereafter that she had been abducted and murdered by the priests to prevent her from revealing the truth. New York *Observer,* June 11, 1836, July 15, 1837; *Downfall of Babylon,* July 9, 1836; N. L. Rice, *Romanism the Enemy of Education, of Free Institutions and of Christianity* (Cincinnati, 1853), 360–361. Olivia Neal

was alleged to have been a Carmelite nun in Baltimore who escaped in 1838. The Reverend Robert J. Breckinridge attempted to capitalize on the episode, but his designs were frustrated when civil authorities took charge of Miss Neal and competent doctors pronounced her insane. Despite this, crowds of irate Protestants menaced the convent for three days after the escape, and nativists for many years insisted that Miss Neal had been murdered by priests. *American Protestant Vindicator*, May 27, 1835, November 11, 1835, July 22, 1840; Baltimore *Literary and Religious Magazine*, V (September, 1839), V (October, 1839), VI (January, 1840), VI (July, 1840), VI (August, 1840); Robert J. Breckinridge, *Papism in the United States in the Nineteenth Century* (Baltimore, 184-), 240 ff.; Schmucker, *Discourse in Commemoration of the Glorious Reformation*, 119-121.

92 This book contains the revelations of three escaped nuns, for it includes, in addition to the narrative that provides the title, "The Orphan Nun of Capri" and "The Confessions of a Sister of Charity."

93 Josephine M. Bunkley, *The Testimony of an Escaped Novice from the Sisterhood of St. Joseph, Emmetsburg, Md.* (New York, 1855). Miss Bunkley "escaped" on November 10, 1854.

94 New York *Observer*, November 30, 1854; *Congregationalist*, December 8, 1854; *Pilot*, November 9, 1854, December 16, 1854, December 30, 1854.

95 *Congregationalist*, February 1, 1850, April 26, 1850, August 27, 1852; Cross, *Priest's Prisons for Women*, 34-38.

96 *The Know Nothing Almanac*, 45; Bunkley, *Testimony of an Escaped Novice*, 333-334; *The Escaped Nun*, 233; *Freeman's Journal*, April 5, 1851; Edward J. Morris, *Remarks of Honorable E. Joy Morris, of Philadelphia, in the House of Representatives of Pennsylvania, February 12, 1856, Against the Introduction of the Monastic System and the Secret Religious Orders of the Church of Rome into that Commonwealth, Delivered on the Final Passage of the Bill to Incorporate the Third Order of Franciscans, in Cambria County, into a Body Politic* (Philadelphia, 1856), 1-16.

97 Shea, *History of the Catholic Church*, IV, 273, 617-618; McMaster, *History of the People of the United States*, VIII, 76-77; Vogel, "Ursuline Nuns in America," *loc. cit.*, I, 223-224; *Freeman's Journal*, September 14, 1850.

98 *Pilot*, March 31, 1855.

99 *Ibid.*, May 12, 1855.

100 *Ibid.*, July 1, 1854.

101 New York *Observer*, July 20, 1854.

102 *Pilot*, July 1, 1854.

103 *Hannah Corcoran, the Missing Girl of Charlestown. The Mysterious Disappearance Unraveled. The Convent and the Confessor. Attempt at Abduction Foiled! A Full and Complete Report of the Riot at Charlestown* (Boston, 1853), 1-13; Thomas F. Caldicott, *Hannah Corcoran: an Authentic Narrative of her Conversion from Romanism; her Abduction from Charlestown. and the Treatment she Received during her Absence* (Boston, 1853), 1-90; *Pilot*, March 12, 1853, July 30, 1853; *American Union*, July 23, 1853, May 6, 1854.

104 The pamphlet was written by John F. Weishampel and was published at Philadelphia in 1852.

105 *Pilot*, March 25, 1854, July 1, 1854, May 12, 1855.

XIII

The War Against the Immigrant
1850-1854

ALMOST as important as the fear of Catholicism in driving the lower classes into the nativists' fold were the material forces centering around foreign immigration. Many Americans believed that the influx of aliens threatened their established social structure, endangered the nation's economic welfare, and spelled doom for the existing governmental system. They sought in political nativism protection from the social, political, and economic evils which seemed inevitably linked with the immigrant invasion.

Propagandists played an important part in magnifying the effects of the alien impact, but their work was not essential. The average American had only to look about him to find tangible evidence of the propagandist's worst fears. He could see quiet city streets transformed into unsightly slums by the foreigner's touch. He could see corrupt political machines thriving upon foreign votes and deadlocked political parties struggling for the support of untrained aliens. He could see the traditional policy of American isolation threatened by immigrant blocs seeking to embroil the United States in the affairs of their homelands. He could see intemperance, illiteracy, pauperism, and crime, all increase with the coming of the foreigner. He could see alien labor, content with a lower standard of living, taking over more and more of the work which American hands had formerly performed. Here were arguments which required no propagandist embroidery.

Nor did Americans need to be reminded of the social effects of this immigration. Advocates of prohibition laws, with success seemingly within grasp as state after state followed the example of Maine in enacting temperance legislation, found their progress threatened by "a noisy, drinking and brawling rabble" [1] of Irish and Germans. "They bring the grog shops like the frogs of Egypt upon us," one writer complained,[2] and the temperance societies warned that the success of their cause depended upon a check of immigration.[3] Similarly, the friends of the Puritan Sabbath viewed with increasing alarm the open defiance with which foreigners treated that venerable American institution; particularly were the German beer gardens a thorn in the flesh of those who strove to keep the Sabbath day holy.[4] Other reformers who were striving to awaken the United States to the need of universal education saw their plans frustrated when they learned that in 1850 only 6.58 per cent of the foreign-born were attending school as compared to 20 per cent of the native population.[5] The moral and intellectual purity of the United States seemed threatened; indeed many believed that the aliens were leading the nation into a decadence which would rival that of ancient Rome.

These alarmists found particular cause for apprehension in the pauperism and crime that followed in the wake of the alien. This situation had been bad in the 1830's; it was far worse now, for most of the foreigners came from famine-stricken Ireland or Germany and were destitute before they left their native shores. Unable to pay for proper transportation, they crossed the Atlantic herded into the dank and unsanitary holds of slow sailing vessels where illness and death were fellow-passengers.[6] Those who survived were in no condition to cope with life in a new land. "Many of them," wrote the commissioner of a New York almshouse, "had far better been cast into the deep sea, than linger in the pangs of hunger, sickness and pain, to draw their last agonized breath in the streets of New York. They came, however, in rags and tatters, pale and ghostly shadows shrouding their pinched and haggard features, scarcely able to utter the sound of complaint, and staggering with the feebleness of dire prostration to the doors of our institution." [7] Nor were these conditions confined to the eastern seaboard. At St. Louis hundreds had to be carried from the river vessels that brought them from New Orleans. Regular cabs were dispatched to meet each ship for this purpose, and as soon as possible a special hospital was erected near the shore for ill or dying immigrants. [8]

These conditions meant increasing tax rates as cities and states struggled with the problem of pauperism. By 1850 one pauper for every 317 natives and one for every thirty-two foreigners was receiving public support. [9] In Massachusetts nearly $400,000 each year went to the care of the poor, and many towns were being driven toward bankruptcy by the steadily increasing burden. [10] New York was spending $800,000 each year on charity, and Louisiana was supporting twice as many foreign as native paupers, despite the relatively smaller number of aliens in the population. [11] "A vast influx of foreign pauperism," complained the Boston Society for the Prevention of Pauperism, "ready made and hatched abroad, combined of the worst and most intractable elements constituting such a social pest . . . has been thrown upon us; and difficulties and embarrassments unknown to the men of an earlier day . . . have multiplied apace." [12]

The criminal record of the immigrant caused equal concern. In 1850, of the 27,000 persons convicted for criminal offenses, more than half were foreign-born, although foreigners then constituted only about eleven per cent of the population. Virginia, with almost no aliens, boasted only one arrest for every 23,000 persons in the ten-year period preceding 1850; Massachusetts with its larger immigrant population had one convict for every 7,586 inhabitants. [13] Clearly the foreign-born, removed from the restraints of the old world and intoxicated by the freedom of the new, had not yet adjusted themselves to the standard of a society which they appreciated more than they understood. [14]

This social disruption made admirable material for propagandists. Nativistic, religious, and secular newspapers printed almost daily statistics illustrating the increase in pauperism and crime and warned that immigration was responsible.[15] The ancient argument that Europe's despotic nations were intentionally weakening the United States by sending their paupers and criminals to this land was used by scores of writers and editors.[16] "America," declared one, "has become the sewer into which the pollutions of European jails are emptied," [17] and another asked: "Have we not a right to protect ourselves against the ravenous dregs of anarchy and crime, the tainted swarms of pauperism and vice Europe shakes on our shores from her diseased robes?" [18] No American could read the daily press and escape the conviction that immigration must be checked if his country and its institutions were to survive.

The political ramifications of the alien invasion were as important as the social. With the foreigner came corruption and graft to change the traditional routine of American politics. In this process the immigrants at first were only tools of the natives. Befuddled aliens were met at the docks by politicians, they were placed under the care of minor bosses, they were fraudulently naturalized by machine-controlled judges, and they were marched to the polls to vote as they were told. Little wonder that these foreign-born gained a faulty picture of a democracy or that they soon entered into the political game themselves. Thus corrupt foreign politicians were created; Irish and German names began to appear on the ballots, and natives, long accustomed to rule, found their position challenged by officeholders and voters who appreciated the opportunities of democracy more than its responsibilities.

This situation was particularly alarming because the rapid increase of foreign voters made it appear inevitable that they would eventually rule the land. Thus in Boston between 1850 and 1855 the native-born voters increased 14.72 per cent; those

of foreign birth 194.64 per cent.[19] Although the foreign-born
in Boston were accumulating at a more rapid rate than elsewhere,
the same story could be told to a lesser degree of every city and
state in the north, and many Americans agreed with a nativistic
speaker when he prophesied that "in fifteen years the foreign
population will exceed the native." [20]   Much apprehension was
occasioned by the fact that in many communities the even balance between the parties placed the foreign-born in control although they were outnumbered by natives. Each party recognized the importance of the immigrant vote and bid for it openly
by offering minor offices and other political plums to alien leaders
who held the balance of power.[21] Tangible proof of this situation
seemingly was provided in the election of 1852 when the foreign-
born helped elect a Democrat, Franklin Pierce, to the presidency.
When Pierce named a Catholic postmaster general and appointed
several foreign-born Democrats to diplomatic posts, nativists
and Whigs were convinced that he was paying an election debt
and that immigrant voters controlled the United States.[22]

Actually, the foreign-born voted the Democratic ticket consistently, and carping against the immigrant's political power
came largely from disgruntled Whigs or indelible nativists. Millard Fillmore was speaking as both when he declared that the
foreign vote was "fast demoralizing the whole country; corrupting the ballot box—that great palladium of our liberty—into an
unmeaning mockery where the rights of native born citizens are
voted away by those who blindly follow their mercenary and self-
ish leaders." [23] Yet some truth probably lay behind these charges,
for impartial observers agreed that "political parties seek . . .
[the immigrants'] support; they are taken into account in the
framing of political platforms, in the acts of legislatures, in the
policy of governors." [24] Certainly nativists could see more truth
than humor in the current joke concerning the schoolboy who
was called upon to parse "America." "America," he stated, "is a

very common noun, singular number, masculine gender, critical case, and governed by the Irish." [25]

The solidarity of the foreign-born vote, whether cast for Whigs or Democrats, created the impression that the immigrants were all acting in accord with a general command and that that command came from the Catholic church. Nativists who thought that priests bartered the political power of their parishioners for favors and protection for Catholicism were afraid that this unholy alliance would spell the doom of both Protestantism and democracy; Protestantism would not be able to stand against a Catholic church receiving state support, and democracy would soon crumble in the hands of such corrupt leaders. [26]

Propagandists who pointed out these supposed evils had three proposed remedies. They suggested, first, that laws of the various states be changed to limit voting to naturalized immigrants, rather than allowing any alien who had lived in the state for six months or a year to enjoy the privileges of the ballot box. This, they said, would remove much of the corruption then rampant in local elections. Their second proposal was the oft-repeated demand for a twenty-one-year probationary period preceding naturalization. [27] Thirdly, they insisted that only natives be placed in either elective or appointive offices. [28] Countless writers and editors stressed these three solutions to the problem of the immigrant in politics; countless other Americans were convinced that their nation would be saved only if voting were limited to naturalized citizens who had lived for twenty-one years in the United States and if all foreign-born were denied political office. It is significant that these propagandists' demands were incorporated bodily into the platforms of the nativistic parties of the 1850's.

The immigrants were objected to not only on social and political grounds but also because their coming threatened the traditional American policy of isolation. The foreign-born carried to the United States an active interest in the affairs of their native lands. Many of them, their primary allegiance still east of the Atlantic, sought to force their adopted country to participate in old world quarrels with which it had no direct concern. On more than one occasion their overenthusiastic activity seriously embarrassed the United States diplomatically. Americans who were blindly loyal to the dictum of Washington's Farewell Address felt a natural resentment.

The Irish were particularly troublesome in this respect. With their untiring devotion to the "auld sod" they were constantly aroused in behalf of their countrymen who were striving to secure the repeal of the union with England. Societies of "Repealers" were formed throughout the east in the 1840's, money was collected to aid Daniel O'Connell and other leaders, and the view was regularly expressed that America should intervene in behalf of Ireland.[29] These demands assumed new proportions with the Oregon Boundary dispute in 1846, Irish Americans insisting that war with England would bring freedom to Ireland and territory to the United States.[30] Again during the Young Irish uprising of 1848 they tried to force American entry, holding out the well-worn bait of Canada as a reward for a combined Irish-American victory.[31] This continued Irish insistence on war with a friendly neighboring power naturally antagonized Americans.[32]

More alarming than the Irish, however, were the Germans who were driven to the United States by the failure of the liberal revolutions of 1848. A few of this group were revolutionary radicals who carried from the old world the advanced ideas that had forced them to seek refuge in the new. Their grandiose schemes included the creation in America of a Germanized nation which could spread its doctrines of liberty and revolution over the world. This was to be accomplished by the radical revision of the governmental, social, and economic institutions of the United States, and to bring this about a number of revolutionary societies were formed, the German Social Democratic Association at Richmond, the American Revolutionary League at Philadelphia, the Free Germans at Louisville, the Republikanischer Freiheitsverein at Pittsburgh, and countless others. Although differing in name, these German societies were united in ideals: they sought a complete change in the government of the United States by which the president and senate would be abolished; slavery, Bible reading, formal Christianity, and the Puritan Sabbath done away with; and the common people vested with the complete right to rule.[33] In 1854 representatives of all of the organizations holding to these beliefs met in Cleveland and formed a national Central Union of Free Germans, drawing up a platform opposed to slavery, despotism, and the Bible.[34]

The intellectual conquest of the United States was only the first step in the elaborate schemes of these German radicals. They proposed to make America the center of a world revolutionary movement leading eventually to a universal anti-Christian state, ruled by the masses and with kings, rulers, and priests conspicuously absent. This became the objective of the Volksbund für die alte und neue Welt, formed in 1852, with branches in every important city where Germans had settled. A national convention of this society in the fall of 1852 issued an address to the American people, announcing its determination to create a Universalrepublik, and pamphlets, speakers, and the German press kept its radical views before the country.[35]

These activities had a profound effect on Americans. Immigrants who had been welcomed in good faith were abusing their trust; they seemed determined to build in the United States "a crystal palace of *Nothing to Do* in an eldorado of *Much to Get.*" [36] Their societies threatened to make America the center of a world revolutionary movement and plunge the nation into the boiling caldron of European politics; their members intended to sacrifice the land where they found sanctuary on the altar of their own radical theories. So violent was the revulsion of American feel-

ing against the Germans that one legislature, at least, refused to
incorporate an innocent German Turnverein because of the fear
that it might be a disguised anarchistic society.[37]

The American attitude toward European revolutionaries and
their threatened foreign entanglements was best illustrated in
the Kossuth affair. Louis Kossuth was a Hungarian patriot who
had taken a leading part in his country's ill-fated attempt to win
independence from Austria in 1848 and 1849. Americans, comparing that struggle with their own war for independence,
watched with ill-concealed rejoicing; they were openly sorrowful when the revolutionists were defeated and Kossuth fled to
Turkey.[38] The Senate simply reflected popular sentiment when,
in February, 1851, it invited Kossuth to visit America and asked
the president to place a warship at his disposal for the journey.[39]
This was done, and after some delay occasioned by Kossuth's
desire to visit England, he arrived in the United States on December 5, 1851.

New York outdid itself in its reception for the Hungarian
patriot. As he was conveyed across the bay from Staten Island
salutes thundered, sailors and spectators cheered, bands played,
and the whole harbor took on a festive air. When his ship passed
Governors Island, a salute of 31 guns was fired; from the New
Jersey shore 120 more guns echoed across the bay. More than
200,000 people who jammed the Battery cheered so wildly that
they drowned out Kossuth's attempts to address them. After a
pageant that rivaled even the one staged for Lafayette, Kossuth
was escorted through the milling streets of Manhattan at the head
of a giant parade. One editor wrote:

People are going crazy; some don't know whether they are standing on their head or their heels—others know but don't care. Aldermen are all on the qui-vive; printer's devils and newspaper reporters
are knocking one another down; military gents are polishing their
swords and boots; cabs are getting a new coat of paint; carpenters
are erecting skeleton arches on Broadway; the Bowery is alive with

people decorating stores and houses; thunder and lightning are in demand, and so are imitation Russian bears for targets.[40]

Kossuth's reception was due in part to the fact that he was a symbol of Protestantism as well as of liberty. From the first he and the revolution with which he was associated were frowned upon by the Catholic hierarchy and press; Hughes called him a "humbug" before he reached America,[41] Brownson labeled him "one of the most dangerous characters now living" [42] and the *Freeman's Journal* believed that he was a "demagogue, a tyrant, and an enemy of Christianity," and that his fellow revolutionists were "vipers too pestiferous and disgusting to be longer endured in society." [43] These comments impressed on Protestants the need of publicly worshipping Kossuth as a means of reproving Hughes and his coreligionists.[44] On the first Sunday that the Hungarian was in New York, a Baptist minister preached a sermon on "The Coming of Kossuth, Illustrative of the Second Coming of Christ," and a short time later a delegation representing all the Protestant clergy of the city sought him out to pledge their support.[45] Kossuth recognized the advantage of this aid, and many of his speeches were strongly anti-Catholic.[46]

As long as Kossuth was willing to accept the acclaim of American Protestants, all was well. He had come to the United States, however, not as an exile but as a revolutionary leader seeking funds and support to renew the cause of his "poor down-trodden Hungary." His first reception convinced him that these things would be cheerfully given him, hence he soon began asking for money, for American recognition of the Hungarian Republic, and for intervention against both Austria and Austria's ally, Russia.[47] The changed attitude toward Kossuth following these requests showed the suspicion with which the people viewed any tampering with the policy of isolation.

This coolness was not noticeable at first; he was received in Philadelphia with as much enthusiasm as in New York.[48] But when he reached Washington, a division of sentiment became apparent. First to desert the bandwagon were southerners, who were alarmed at the support given Kossuth by abolitionists, and who were afraid that any American intervention in Europe might pave the way to a similar intervention in the domestic affairs of the south. Slaveholders, determined to protect their property from northern interference, feared this above all else.[49] During the congressional debate on the type of reception to be given Kossuth, this slavery question split the members along sectional lines, with southerners urging that the congressional greeting to the Hungarian be as dignified and chilling as possible. Some northerners agreed with the southern representatives, for they wanted it impressed on Kossuth that America's attitude was and ever would be one of "friendship with all nations, entangling alliances with none." [50]

News of this debate spread beyond the walls of the capitol building. When Kossuth finally arrived in Washington, there were no booming cannon and no parades to greet him; only a crowd of curious people waited to see his reception by the Senate committee which had been appointed to escort him to the White House.[51] Although the Hungarian was received on the floor of both the House and Senate, every effort was made to keep the ceremonies strikingly simple.[52] The speeches at the congressional banquet tendered him were so mild and noncommittal that, as one southern paper put it, Seward felt called upon to interrupt constantly to assure Kossuth that he was welcome.[53]

This reversal of public opinion was even more obvious as Kossuth continued his tour of the country. In the middle west he was received in something of the same spirit as in New York, but wise observers pointed out that material contributions to his cause were singularly lacking and that western enthusiasm had probably been arranged by politicians anxious to attract the German vote of that region.[54] The southern attitude toward the Hungarian leader was one of open hostility. He went first to Louisville, where the aldermen had been given a banquet for their refusal, four times repeated, to invite Kossuth to visit the city.[55] His arrival occasioned no public excitement, no crowds gathered about his hotel, and the one address which he delivered to a small group of Germans turned popular sympathy still more against him.[56] St. Louis with its large German population was more enthusiastic, but at New Orleans, Montgomery, Mobile, Augusta, and Charleston there was no public welcome or demonstration of any sort. The legislatures of Louisiana, Alabama, and Georgia publicly condemned both Kossuth and his cause.[57] Southerners were clearly opposed to intervention, either in Europe or within their own borders.

If Kossuth expected a repetition of his first reception when he returned north, he was doomed to disappointment. The northern press had turned against him while he was in the south. The New York *Times,* which had earlier hailed the Hungarian as a "Peter the Hermit of a New Crusade," was now pointedly opposed to any American intervention in European affairs.[58] The *National Intelligencer* believed that "Paine's 'Age of Reason' and Kossuth's 'New Crusade' are kindred emanations of dangerous minds, and both are heresies fatal to the established truth." [59] Little wonder that on his return to New York few of the 200,000 who had wildly cheered his first arrival knew that he was back. His second journey to Washington attracted no attention whatsoever.[60] Only in New England was Kossuth still popular; invited by the legislatures of most of the New England states to visit that region, he was escorted in triumph to Boston and there found some of the acclaim denied him by the rest of the nation.[61] New Englanders obviously put their hatred of slavery and Catholicism, now closely associated with Kossuth's name, above their fear of foreign entanglements. But in this New England stood alone. Kossuth finally left the country in July, 1852, going aboard his ship without a single person to bid him Godspeed on his journey.[62] How marked must have been the contrast in his eyes between that solitary departure and the reception he had received only a short time before.

One salient fact had been impressed on Americans by Kossuth's visit. They had been made to realize, as never before, that foreigners, whether they were famous patriots like Kossuth or humble immigrant farmers, were willing to sacrifice the United States in the interest of their home lands. Clearly if the number of immigrants increased, and if they secured political power, they might embroil the United States in many disastrous European affairs. The one way to forestall such a catastrophe was to restrict immigration or limit the immigrant's use of the franchise. Many Americans were convinced of the plausibility of these nativistic arguments by Kossuth's visit.

The fear of foreign entanglements, political corruption, and social degradation all were important in arousing antagonism against immigrants, but more influential than all of these was the general belief that aliens were taking jobs away from American workers. Discontent grew in proportion to the increase of alien laborers; natives began to complain of lessened opportunities, of a lowered standard of living, and of declining pay as factory owners adjusted their wage levels to the point where they could secure foreign-born workers. Propagandists saw to it that these rankling beliefs were nurtured. They compared the high standards of American labor with those of Europe and pointed out that foreign workers "feed upon the coarsest, cheapest and the roughest fare—stalk about in rags and filth—and are neither fit associates for American laborers and mechanics, nor reputable members of any society." [63] They insisted that as long as immigration was allowed to flow unchecked, the living standard of American workers would decline.

Actually there was little truth in these arguments. The alien laborers were simply taking over menial tasks and elevating American workers to a higher level. In a country approaching an occupational limit, excessive immigration might have caused hardship, but the United States was expanding rapidly economically, and the whole process benefited rather than harmed the natives. Nor did immigrant labor lower the wage scale markedly. Wages showed no downward trend in the seven-year period preceding 1855, and industries employing immigrant labor maintained as high or higher levels than those using only native workers.[64]

But although wages might remain constant and employment opportunities grow no less, the whole economic situation of the early 1850's caused the American worker grave concern. The United States in those years was going through an inflationary period, caused partly by the development of new industries centering about the railroad, the reaper, the sewing machine, the clipper ship, and other inventions—partly by the gold discoveries in California which dumped some $50,000,000 in specie on the nation's money markets in one year. As usual in a period of expansion, prices rose more rapidly than wages. Workers did not understand these complex economic forces; they knew only that since the coming of foreigners their living standard had been lowered. They were ready to protest by demanding the restriction or end of foreign immigration. They did protest: some, like those in New Jersey and Massachusetts, rioted against the hiring of aliens by city and state governments;[65] others joined the nativistic parties.

Native laborers were further aroused by the lawlessness of the aliens with whom they were forced to compete. The Irish, particularly, were a turbulent lot, and conflicts between them and native factions were inevitable. Frequently the Irish were to blame for the trouble. Thus one group of canal workers posted a warning forbidding any "damned Yankees" to work there, and threatening all who did so with "powder and ball" which would "send them to hell." [66] In nearly every state armed conflicts between native and Irish or German workmen were common.[67]

American laborers, reading exaggerated reports of these affairs, feared for their lives as well as their jobs.

These workers, thus aroused, made excellent tinder for the nativistic parties which were to flare in the 1850's. Their drift into those parties was aided by several patriotic and benevolent associations formed among them during the 1840's and 1850's. These societies not only filled native workers with nativistic sentiments; they also served as models for the political organizations that were to come into being a little later.

Most important among these workingmen's organizations was the Order of United Americans, formed in New York in 1844 as a benevolent and patriotic society which promised to protect its members both against a poverty-stricken old age and immigrant competition.[68] Membership was restricted to American-born laborers. The order was to be, according to the plans of its managers, in no sense political; the constitution that they drew up stated specifically:

> We disdain all association with party politics; we hold no connection with party men: but we avow distinctly our purpose of doing whatever may seem best to us, for sustaining our National institutions, for upholding our National liberties, and for freeing them wholly from all foreign and deleterious influences whatever. Whenever it shall appear to us that foreign interests, political or religious, are operating in any manner injurious to our country, we shall hold it to be our duty to resort to all lawful means to counteract them. But we declare our steadfast adherence to that feature of our institutions, which secures to every man protection of his civil and religious rights.[69]

This declaration, vague as it was, was rigidly adhered to, and the Order of United Americans remained a nonpolitical organization, even though its members commonly supported nativistic parties.[70]

The principles of the Order of United Americans proved sufficiently popular to allow a rapid expansion; by 1855 chapters were thriving in 16 states and its membership lists included some 50,000 names.[71] This success was partly due to the effective system of organization that its managers had hit upon. The society was a secret one with its members being initiated and forced to learn elaborate handclasps, passwords and other awe-inspiring mysteries. The basis of the organization was the local chapter, which sent three delegates to a State Chancery where state policies were decided upon. These State Chanceries, in turn, named delegates to an Arch Chancery which was the national legislative head of the order.[72] Many features of this organization were taken over bodily by the Know-Nothing party when it came into being.

The success of the Order of United Americans brought a number of imitators into the field. One of these was the United Daughters of America, formed in March, 1845, as a women's auxiliary of the older society. In the same year the Order of United American Mechanics and the United Sons of America were founded in Philadelphia. Although these societies were similar to the Order of United Americans in that all encouraged mutual aid and benevolence and advocated a reformation of the naturalization laws and the checking of immigration of foreign laborers, efforts to unite them into one body consistently failed.[73]

The propaganda carried on by these patriotic benevolent societies was important. The usual methods were employed: speakers were sent out, addresses were arranged on immigration and Catholicism, and publications, designed to circulate primarily among workingmen, were sponsored.[74] In all these activities the Order of United Americans was most prominent. The weekly newspaper which was established as its official organ in July, 1848, the *Order of United Americans,* and the monthly magazine that it founded in January, 1851, *The Republic, a Monthly Magazine of American Literature, Politics and Art,* both remained influential organs for some years.[75] The Order of United American Mechanics also published a weekly paper, *The Ameri-*

can Mechanic.[76] The theme most stressed by these propaganda publications was the need of protecting American workers against the competition of immigrant labor. As the *Republic* expressed it:

> The interests of our mechanics and working men and women, who have been sorely pressed by the unfair competition and combinations of pauper Europeans, will receive attention at our hands and we . . . shall strive ever to keep alive the glowing, and warm into full life the latent fires of patriotism that dwell in their hearts, and to inspire them, and all, with a true sense of their dignity as free men, free women—virtuous and patriotic *Americans.*[77]

This they did so successfully that newspapers and magazines of this type became effective instruments in the education of American nativists.[78]

These societies and their publications, focusing attention as they did on foreign immigration and its dangers, played a prominent part in creating the anti-Catholic, anti-foreign sentiment upon which the Know-Nothing party was nurtured. They convinced many workingmen that their prosperity depended on restricted immigration. In this sense they, and the alien influx which inspired them, contributed to the many forces which had by the early 1850's aroused a sentiment in the United States conducive to the development of political nativism.

NOTES

[1] Brownson, *Works*, XVIII, 259.

[2] *American Protestant Magazine*, IV (February, 1849).

[3] New York *Observer*, May 18, 1850. See also: Nichols, *Forty Years of American Life*, II, 74; George M. Towle, *American Society* (London, 1870), II, 277; *Congregationalist*, June 7, 1850; John C. Pitrot, *Americans Warned of Jesuitism; or, the Jesuits Unveiled* (New York, 1851), 117–118; John P. Sanderson, *Republican Landmarks. The Views and Opinions of American Statesmen on Foreign Immigration* (Philadelphia, 1856), 39–40, 230; Francois Pepin, *A Narrative of the Life and Experiences of Francois Pepin who was for more than Forty Years a Member of the Papal Church, Embracing an Account of his Conversion, Trials, and Persecutions in Turning to the True Religion of the Bible* (Detroit, 1854), 36–39; O'Hanlon, *Life and Scenery in Missouri*, 144–145.

⁴ *Congregationalist,* November 22, 1850; Clark, *Romanism in America,* 98.

⁵ DeBow, *Compendium of the Seventh Census,* 150, 153; *Pilot,* March 17, 184.

⁶ *Native Eagle,* December 31, 1846; *Pilot,* March 17, 1849; Page, "The Transportation of Immigrants," *loc. cit.,* 735. In one group of immigrants about whom records were kept when they sailed for America in 1854, 20,000 of the 98,000 making the journey died before reaching the United States. Kapp, *Immigration and the Commissioners of Emigration,* 23.

⁷ *Executive Documents,* 29th Cong., 2nd Sess., No. 54, 9.

⁸ O'Hanlon, *Life and Scenery in Missouri,* 140–141. Several countries were still sending their paupers to be dumped in the United States. Irish Poor Law Commissioners were empowered in 1849 to borrow money to assist emigration and although their poor were sent to Canada, many made their way eventually to the United States. Many Swiss and German states likewise shipped their public charges directly to this country. *Executive Documents,* 29th Cong., 2nd Sess., No. 54, 1–8; No. 161.

⁹ DeBow, *Compendium of the Seventh Census,* 163.

¹⁰ *Ibid.,* 168; Haynes, "Causes of Know Nothing Success in Massachusetts," *loc. cit.,* 77–78. Brook Farm had been transformed into a haven for paupers by Roxbury in 1849. *American Union,* May 26, 1849.

¹¹ DeBow, *Compendium of the Seventh Census,* 163–164.

¹² Boston Society for the Prevention of Pauperism, *Twenty Third Annual Report* (Boston, 1855), 7.

¹³ DeBow, *Compendium of the Seventh Census,* 165–167.

¹⁴ The Irish press insisted that aliens were discriminated against in arrest and that a drunken American was never molested but a drunken Irishman was always clapped into jail by the police. *Pilot,* May 12, 1849. This may have accounted in some degree for the heavier criminal record of the foreign-born, as may the fact that a few criminals were still being sent to the United States by other countries. *American Union,* December 15, 1849.

¹⁵ *American Union,* November 11, 1848, June 7, 1851, January 24, 1852, January 31, 1852; New York *Observer,* October 14, 1852, June 15, 1854; *Native Eagle,* September 22, 1846; *Order of United Americans,* July 29, 1848; *Republic,* II (October, 1851); *Home Missionary,* XIX (September, 1846), XXI (September, 1848), XXIII (April, 1851); Samuel C. Busey, *Immigration, its Evils and Consequences* (New York, 1856), 107–116; Thomas R. Whitney, *A Defense of American Policy* (New York, 1856), 180–187; D. G. Parker, *A Compilation of Startling Facts; or, Romanism against Republicanism* (Chicago, 1856), 95–105; Sanderson, *Republican Landmarks,* 29–31; Carroll, *Great American Battle,* 344.

¹⁶ *Native Eagle,* April 14, 1846, March 7, 1846; *American Union,* January 4, 1851, May 17, 1851; *Order of United Americans,* September 2, 1848; Busey, *Immigration,* 66–76; *Know Nothing Almanac,* 33; Sanderson, *Republican Landmarks,* 48–80; *Sons of the Sires,* 68; W. H. Ryder, *Our Country; or, the American Parlor Keepsake* (Boston, 1854), 56–57; Campbell, *Americanism,* 3; *Republic,* I (March, 1851); *Home Missionary,* XVII (March, 1845); *American Protestant Magazine,* IV (November, 1848).

¹⁷ *Protestant Banner,* February 1, 1844.

18 W. R. Alger, *An Oration Delivered before the Citizens of Boston, July 4, 1857* (Boston, 1857), 28.

19 Haynes, "Causes of Know Nothing Success in Massachusetts," *loc. cit.,* 74 note. See also DeBow, *Compendium of the Seventh Census,* 123; Joseph Schafer, "Know-Nothingism in Wisconsin," *Wisconsin Magazine of History,* VIII (September, 1924), 9–10.

20 John Bell, *Speech Delivered at a Mass Meeting of the American Party held at Knoxville, Tenn., September 22, 1855* (Nashville, 1855), 7–8. For similar expressions of sentiment see *Native Eagle,* November 3, 1846; *American Protestant Magazine,* IV (August, 1848); Carroll, *Great American Battle,* 206–207; George Robertson, *The American Party* (Lexington, Kentucky, 1855), 2.

21 *Native Eagle,* March 31, 1846; *Republic,* II (September, 1851); Carroll, *Great American Battle,* 108; Robertson, *The American Party,* 2–3; *Know Nothing Almanac,* 30; *Origin, Principles and Purposes of the American Party,* 13; Busey, *Immigration,* 138–145.

22 Nativists pointed out that Pierce had a popular vote 214,694 larger than Scott, the Whig candidate. They claimed that 367,320 foreign-born voters all cast their ballots for the Democrat. Busey, *Immigration,* 145–147; *Origin, Principles and Purposes of the American Party,* 108–109, 150.

23 Millard Fillmore, *The Millard Fillmore Papers. Publications of the Buffalo Historical Society* (Buffalo, 1907), XI, 347–348.

24 Towle, *American Society,* II, 278–279.

25 *Native Eagle,* November 18, 1846.

26 *Congregationalist,* September 10, 1852, April 8, 1853; *Pilot,* January 1, 1853; *American Union,* January 1, 1853; *Order of United Americans,* July 22, 1848; *DeBow's Review,* III (March, 1848); *American Protestant Magazine,* III (June, 1847); *National Protestant,* I (February, 1845); *Origin, Principles and Purpose of the American Party,* 36; Robertson, *The American Party,* 15; *Sons of the Sires,* 30–31, 46; Carroll, *Great American Battle,* 315–316; Whitney, *Defense of American Policy,* 64–77; Thomas R. Whitney, *An Address on the Occasion of the Seventh Anniversary of the Alpha Chapter, Order of United Americans* (New York, 1852), 16–17; Franklin (pseud.), *Know Nothingism; or, the American Party* (Boston, 1855), 7.

27 *Origin, Principles and Purposes of the American Party,* 21–25; Robertson, *The American Party,* 19–20; Campbell, *Americanism,* 3–4; Franklin, *Know Nothingism,* 9; Sanderson, *Republican Landmarks,* 151–174; *Sons of the Sires,* 64–65; Ryder, *Our Country,* vii; *The Wide Awake Gift and Know Nothing Token for 1855* (New York, 1855), 40–41, 107–108; Bell, *Speech Delivered at a Mass Meeting of the American Party,* 12–14; *Native Eagle,* July 2, 1846, January 16, 1848; *Republic,* I (April, 1851); *Romanists Disqualified for Civil Power: Proved from the Decrees of the Council of Trent, and other Authentic Documents of the Romish Church* (New York, 1855), 4; and other Know-Nothing literature of the period.

28 Carroll, *Great American Battle,* 328–329; *Sons of the Sires,* 41–48; *Origin, Principles and Purposes of the American Party,* 26.

29 Accounts of such meetings are in Seward, *Works,* III, 153–163, 254–256; and in the *Freeman's Journal,* November 13, 1841, February 26, 1842, Sep-

tember 17, 1842, June 17, 1843, July 22, 1848. A national convention of the local organizations was held in 1842. *Report of the Proceedings of the National Repeal Convention of the Friends of Ireland in the United States of America, held in the City of Philadelphia, February 22nd and 23rd, 1842* (Philadelphia, 1842). Typical nativistic comments on these activities are in New York *Observer*, June 12, 1841; *American Protestant Vindicator*, September 8, 1841, October 6, 1841, November 3, 1841, April 6, 1842; *The Crisis*, 51–52; Hogan, *Auricular Confesson and Popish Nunneries*, 159–161; L. Giustiniani, *Intrigues of Jesuitism in the United States of America* (New York, 1846), 153.

30 *Native Eagle*, April 15, 1846.

31 *Pilot*, February 17, 1849; New York *Observer*, May 1, 1847; *Order of United Americans*, August 12, 1848.

32 Thus the *Freeman's Journal*, September 18, 1852, urged its readers to vote for any candidate who was hostile toward England. See also *Congressional Globe*, 32nd Cong., 1st Sess., 407–408, 527–531, 1469; New York *Observer*, September 22, 1851; *Familiar Letters to J. B. Fitzpatrick, Catholic Bishop of Boston, by an Independent Irishman* (Boston, 1854), 38–45.

33 Platforms of these societies, with copious comments, are printed in New York *Observer*, July 3, 1851, March 18, 1852; Busey, *Immigration*, 14–20; Sanderson, *Republican Landmarks*, 219–222; *Republic*, II (December, 1851); Carroll, *Great American Battle*, 170–171; Whitney, *Defense of American Policy*, 170–178; J. W. Laurens, *The Crisis; or, The Enemies of America Unmasked* (Philadelphia, 1855), 59–71; J. L. Chapman, *Americanism versus Romanism: or, the Cis-Atlantic Battle between Sam and the Pope* (Nashville, 1856), 301–311.

34 The meeting was held on February 23, 1854. New York *Observer*, April 6, 1854. Louisville later became the national headquarters for this Union.

35 *Freeman's Journal*, March 6, 1852; Baker, *Lenau and Young Germany*, 71–77.

36 Whitney, *Address on the Seventh Anniversary of Alpha Chapter, Order of United Americans*, 10–11.

37 The New York legislature refused the incorporation. *Pilot*, April 8, 1854.

38 This was shown especially by the large mass meetings held in many cities to pass resolutions encouraging the Hungarian cause. At New York 20,000 people attended such a gathering, at Philadelphia a meeting almost as large not only passed the usual resolutions but raised a large sum of money to aid the Hungarians, at Cincinnati 15,000 people gathered to urge the United States to recognize Hungarian independence and at Louisville similar action was taken. In New York an Association of Nations was organized to encourage this European struggle for freedom, and at Little Rock, Arkansas, The Central Southern Association to Promote the Cause of Liberty in Europe was created for the same purpose. Money was subscribed in large amounts all over the country and at least one company of volunteers left New York in 1849 to aid the Hungarian cause. *National Intelligencer*, August 29, 1849; New York *Tribune*, August–September, 1851; Ellis P. Oberholtzer, *The Literary History of Philadelphia* (Philadelphia, 1906), 307–308; New York *Observer*, September 1, 1849; *American Union*, December 22, 1849. Many newspapers looked upon the failure of the uprising as the end of liberty in Europe. *National In-*

telligencer, October 6, 1849; New York *Tribune,* September 6, 1849; *Dollar Newspaper,* September 12, 1849; New Orleans *Daily Picayune,* September 8, 1849; Cincinnati *Commercial,* September 8, 1849.

[39] *Congressional Globe,* 31st Cong., 2nd Sess., 710. This had been suggested by a resolution of the Ohio Assembly received on February 9, 1850. *House Miscellaneous Documents,* 31st Cong., 1st Sess., No. 38.

[40] Philadelphia *Ledger,* December 6, 1851. Kossuth's reception was best described in the New York *Herald,* December 6, 1851.

[41] Hassard, *Life of Hughes,* 341–343. See also *Freeman's Journal,* February 9, 1850, February 7, 1852, for similar comments.

[42] Brownson, *Life of Brownson,* II, 418.

[43] June 16, 1849, January 31, 1852. The *Pilot,* August 18, 1849, September 15, 1849, was an exception, and welcomed Kossuth to America, although it soon changed its tune.

[44] N. M. Gaylord, *Kossuth and the American Jesuits* (Lowell, 1852), 1–23; New York *Observer,* December 11, 1851.

[45] *National Intelligencer,* December 17, 1851; *Report of the Reception of Kossuth* (New York, 1852), 99 ff.; New York *Observer,* December 25, 1851. Kossuth was made a life member of the American and Foreign Christian Union by an enthusiastic clergyman who contributed the necessary $30. *American and Foreign Christian Union,* III (April, 1852).

[46] New York *Observer,* December 18, 1851, January 15, 1852.

[47] These views were expressed by Kossuth in speeches made during his New York stay and published in *Report of the Reception of Kossuth,* 32 ff. In one speech before the New York Bar he frankly admitted that his purpose was to plunge the United States into a war with Russia and Austria in behalf of Hungary. *Ibid.,* 325.

[48] Philadelphia *Public Ledger,* December 25, 1851; P. H. Skinner, *The Welcome of Louis Kossuth, Governor of Hungary, to Philadelphia, by the Youth* (Philadelphia, 1852).

[49] *Alexandrian Gazette,* December 24, 1851. This southern attitude was shown in a threat of southern Democrats to bolt the party should it adopt the principle of "intervention" and by the fact that southern Whigs offered a platform in the Whig National Convention of 1852 definitely repudiating any such step. *National Intelligencer,* June 17, 1852.

[50] The debate is in the *Congressional Globe,* 32nd Cong., 1st Sess., 32–85.

[51] *National Intelligencer,* December 31, 1851.

[52] *Congressional Globe,* 32nd Cong., 1st Sess., 199; *National Intelligencer,* January 6, 1852.

[53] New Orleans *Picayune,* January 23, 1852. The New York *Tribune,* favorable to Kossuth, termed the banquet, "dignified, pertinent and characteristic, but no great sensation." January 10, 1852.

[54] New York *Herald,* February 7, 1852. See also John W. Oliver, "Louis Kossuth's Appeal to the Middle West—1852," *Mississippi Valley Historical Review,* XIV (March, 1928), 481–495.

[55] *National Intelligencer,* March 4, 1852.

[56] *Ibid.,* March 12, 1852, March 13, 1852.

[57] *Ibid.,* January 16, 1852, April 13, 1852; New York *Herald,* February 10, 1852, April 11, 1852, April 20, 1852; New Orleans *Picayune,* January 11,

1852, March 17, 1852; *Senate Miscellaneous Documents,* 32nd Cong., 1st Sess., No. 48.

⁵⁸ *National Intelligencer,* February 5, 1852.

⁵⁹ *Ibid.,* February 28, 1852.

⁶⁰ *Ibid.,* April 14, 1852.

⁶¹ Vermont, Rhode Island, Massachusetts and Maine issued invitations. *Senate Miscellaneous Documents,* 32nd Cong., 1st Sess., No. 25 and No. 26; *National Intelligencer;* January 13, 1852; Boston *Courier,* April 13, 1852; *Kossuth in New England* (Boston, 1852), 10-65; George S. Boutwell, "Kossuth in New England," *New England Magazine,* X (July, 1894), 525-543.

⁶² New York *Herald,* July 17, 1852.

⁶³ *Native Eagle,* April 1, 1846. See also: *Ibid.,* December 29, 1845, March 3, 1846; *Congregationalist,* April 12, 1850; *Order of United Americans,* October 28, 1848, November 25, 1848, February 10, 1849; Busey, *Immigration,* 80-81; Sanderson, *Republican Landmarks,* 234; Whitney, *Address on the Seventh Anniversary of Alpha Chapter, Order of United Americans,* 5; Tisdale, *Know Nothing Almanac,* 19-20; Whitney, *Defense of American Policy,* 306-316; *Red Cross of Catholicism in America; Startling Exposure of an Infernal Catholic Plot. Know Nothings Set at Defiance. Use of Fire Arms in Cathedrals. Confessions and Secret Correspondence* (Boston, 1854), 5.

⁶⁴ DeBow, *Compendium of the Seventh Census,* 164; James P. Hambleton, *History of the Political Campaign in Virginia in 1855* (Richmond, 1856), 324.

⁶⁵ *Republic,* I (May, 1851), II (December, 1851). In California similar sentiment led to organized efforts to keep the foreign-born from operating mines. *American Union,* October 27, 1849; *Pilot,* April 7, 1849; *Freeman's Journal,* September 14, 1850.

⁶⁶ New York *American Republican,* May 20, 1844.

⁶⁷ *Congregationalist,* August 11, 1854; New York *Observer,* March 9, 1850, February 19, 1852; *American Union,* February 23, 1850, August 10, 1850, April 5, 1851; *Native Eagle,* February 13, 1846, March 28, 1846. The *Freeman's Journal* pleaded with Irish workmen to stop rioting and keep order, September 6, 1851.

⁶⁸ Carroll, *Great American Battle,* 251-260. Included in the list of founders were such prominent nativists as James Harper, William Atkinson, and Thomas R. Whitney. An informal meeting to discuss the organization was held at the home of R. C. Root early in December, 1844, and the actual founding took place on December 21, 1844.

⁶⁹ From the preamble of the constitution, printed in *Order of United Americans,* April 21, 1849.

⁷⁰ The sole exception to this was in 1856, when the Arch Chancery of the order nominated Millard Fillmore, Know-Nothing candidate, as its presidential choice. *Fillmore Papers,* II, 361. In 1860 it reverted to its usual practice, although urging members to support one of the compromise candidates and thus aid in preserving the Union. *Address of the Arch Chancery of the Order of United Americans to the Order throughout the United States* (New York, 1860), 2-8.

⁷¹ *Defense of American Policy,* 271-272.

⁷² *Ibid.,* 265-271.

⁷³ *Ibid.,* 312-315; *Republic,* I (June, 1851), II (October, 1851).

[74] *Order of United Americans,* February 24, 1849; *Republic,* II (December, 1851). Typical of the addresses sponsored by the order was Jacob Broom, *An address delivered at Castle Garden, February 22, 1854, before the Order of United Americans, on the Occasion of their Celebration of the 122 Anniversary of the Birthday of George Washington* (New York, 1854).

[75] In 1849 the name of the *Order of United Americans* was changed to *The Continental.* The first issue of the *Republic* appeared in January, 1851.

[76] This was published at Poughkeepsie, New York. *Order of United Americans,* March 31, 1849.

[77] *Republic,* I (January, 1851).

[78] These publications were not only extremely nativistic, they were also extremely patriotic. Thus the first issue of the *Republic* contained stories and articles entitled: "The Flood, a Tale of the Pioneers," "The Young Martyr; a Life Scene of the Revolution," "The Old Corporal's Story," "The Surprise of Ticonderoga," "The Tory and his Sister; a Life Scene of the Revolution," and numerous patriotic verses and sentiments.

XIV

The Literature of Anti-Catholicism

NO clear understanding of the depth or scope of the nativistic movement is possible without a consideration of the vast flood of propaganda loosed against the Catholic church in the first half of the nineteenth century. Conflicts over trustee-ism, Irish rioting, lawlessness and disorder, foreign pauperism, school controversies, and political Popery—all these were im-portant in fomenting a spirit of intolerance among the people. But had not a legion of writers made this growing sentiment the basis of an effective literary campaign, the No-Popery crusade would have been far less fruitful.

The average Protestant American of the 1850's had been trained from birth to hate Catholicism; his juvenile literature and school books had breathed a spirit of intolerance; his illicit dips as a youth into the parentally condemned but widely read Ned Buntline tales had kept his prejudice alive; his religious and even his secular newspapers had warned him of the dangers of Popery; and he had read novels, poems, gift books, histories, travel accounts, and theological arguments which confirmed these beliefs. Only the unusually critical reader could distinguish be-tween truth and fiction in this mass of calumny; more were swept away to a hatred of Catholicism which endured through their lives.

Bishop England, writing in the early 1830's, ascribed the mounting nativistic sentiment first to the Protestant clergy who measured their zeal by the number and intensity of their attacks on Popery, second to the "poisoning of the wells of history," third to the misuse of the sciences and fourth to the abusive spirit of American writers.[1] Had he revised his estimate a decade later, he would most certainly have elevated the literature of anti-Catholic protest to a position of influence equal to or greater than that of the Protestant pulpit. This form of writing first began to be used extensively about the middle of the 1830's, growing partly because of the popularity of the books of Maria Monk and Samuel F. B. Morse, partly because of the increased interest of the religious press,[2] and partly because by this time the wide sales awaiting this type of work had been demonstrated. By 1838 an observer complained that books on the subject had become so numerous that it was impossible to read them all, and bookstores were established in the larger cities to deal solely in anti-Catholic works.[3]

The motives that led individuals to contribute to this flood of anti-Catholic literature were varied. Probably most of the writers sincerely believed that Popery was a menace either to their country or their religion and simply sought to win others to that view. Others may have been inspired by a desire to achieve some political end, either the creation of nativistic parties or the vilification of the Democratic party to which a majority of the Catholic foreigners gave their allegiance. More, undoubtedly, penned attacks on Rome to share in the profits from the wide sale of books of this type. "The abuse of the Catholics," one writer complained in 1835, ". . . is a regular trade, and the compilation of anti-Catholic books . . . has become a part of the regular industry of the country, as much as the making of nutmegs, or the construction of clocks."[4] Many of the most outspoken anti-Catholic works came from writers inspired largely by the hope of financial gain; men like Samuel B. Smith, William Hogan, the Reverend Charles Sparry, and numerous others appear to have made at least a haphazard living from the No-Popery crusade. This commercial motive was particularly prominent among the publishers and distributors of anti-Catholic writings. Venders of books against Rome penetrated into every corner of the nation, visiting farm and city homes alike, to appear with benevolent mien, an anti-Catholic message, and a series of volumes against Popery. Every agent of the numerous publishing houses that dealt in this type of literature was an ally of the Protestant cause and a spokesman against Rome.[5]

All types of reading matter were utilized by those who employed the printed word to shower calumny on Catholicism. Children whose primary instruction was from one of the primers in common use were accustomed to crude engravings of Protestant martyrs and to sentiments placing Popery in alignment with heathenism and infidelity.[6] Infant minds were shaped to believe that "to be a Catholic, was to be a false, cruel and bloody wretch," and that Popery included everything that was vicious and vile.[7] The school training was often supplemented by parental instruction, for the women of America embraced the No-Popery cause with more enthusiasm than the men.[8] Sincerely believing that their prejudice should be shared by their offspring, they instilled into their children an enduring hatred of Catholicism.

Through childhood these early beliefs were strengthened by a persistent literature which was readily available. Nativistic writers had early recognized the need of stories which would "infuse into the youthful mind the proper sentiments that ought to be entertained respecting Jesuitical craftiness and deception." [9] The first of these tales appeared in 1835, *Edwin and Alicia; or, the Infant Martyrs,*[10] but this was soon supplanted in popular favor by the works of Charlotte Elizabeth Tonna, whose pen name "Charlotte Elizabeth" graced at least nine children's books published in America between 1841 and 1845.[11] Mrs. Tonna was an English writer whose early life had been spent in the shadow of the prisons where Protestant martyrs had suffered under Bloody Mary. She had been given Foxe's *Book of Martyrs* to read when only five, and had then and there decided to devote her life to Protestantism, a resolution which was strengthened by several years' residence in papal Ireland.[12] Her great contribution, she believed, was to influence young minds with sentiments that would offset the work of popish educators.[13] Her stories were dull, pious, and argumentative, apparently little adapted to readers of any age, but their popularity showed that she gauged her audience well. The pattern was the same in all her books: a pious family, a daughter or son lured to Popery by the insidious machinations of a neighboring priest, long Biblical arguments between the father and the erring child, and eventually righteousness triumphant with the child, and usually the priest as well, saved for Protestantism. Unappetizing as this fare might be, the large number of Charlotte Elizabeth's books printed in the United States was mute evidence of their wide consumption.

On reaching adulthood, the children trained on these No-Popery tales could continue to read attacks on Catholicism in nearly every form; novels, plays, and verse were bent to the use of propagandists and made to depict the evils of Rome. The success of the first anti-Catholic novel, *Father Clement,* accounted for the appearance of many similar literary efforts.[14] One fruitful theme was the Ursuline convent in Charlestown, for the attention focused on that structure by its destruction assured the popularity of any work concerning it. The most prolific of the convent theme writers was Charles W. Frothingham of Boston; three of his works, *The Convent's Doom; a Tale of Charlestown in 1834, Six Hours in a Convent; or, the Stolen Nuns,* and *The Haunted Convent,* were immensely successful, one selling forty thousand copies in the first week of publication and going through five editions within a year.[15] All of his stories concerned Protestant girls who had been spirited away by priests to the Charlestown convent, there to remain in gloomy cells until rescued by their lovers. Other fiction writers, while not localizing their scenes, described convent life to be as immoral and soul-destroying as that depicted by Maria Monk.[16]

The novelists who utilized anti-Catholic topics emphasized the harmful effects of nearly every practice of the Church. Several books of fiction described the suffering of Protestant martyrs who faced popish Inquisitors,[17] others unfolded the mental and spiritual anguish of misguided persons who had been seduced by Rome's agents and who suffered the tortures of the damned before again finding the haven of Protestantism,[18] still others reversed the process and recounted the punishment inflicted on converts from Catholicism by priests who sought their forceful return.[19] More in keeping with popular taste were books detailing the part to be played by Jesuits in the papal conquest of the United States, appearing under such titles as *Stanhope Burleigh; the Jesuits in our Homes* and *The Female Jesuit; or, the Spy in the Family.*[20] All of these novels had one thing in common: they were sprinkled with long arguments, usually between the Protestant hero and the Catholic villain, on the evils and dangers of Rome, arguments in which the papal defenders were always decisively bested. These were monuments either to the sincerity of the authors or to the theological bent of the readers, but their ultimate result was effective propaganda. Certainly they were widely read, for when a mild anti-Catholic novel by Catherine Sinclair, *Beatrice; or, the Unknown Relatives,* appeared in 1853, it was confidently expected that sales would exceed those of *Uncle Tom's Cabin.*[21]

The success of these works of fiction inspired other literary efforts against Rome. A play based upon Jesuit intrigue and hypocrisy, *The Jesuit; a National Melodrama in Three Acts,* appeared in New York in 1850.[22] Verse, running the gamut from doggerel acrostics to ponderous volumes in Elizabethan meter, was available both in book form and in nativistic publications.[23] Travel accounts which pictured Italy and other Catholic countries as backward because of papal influence and openly poked fun at the miracles and ceremonies of the Church were popular during the 1840's and 1850's.[24] Although many of these reflected only a normal American intolerance toward Catholicism, others, notably the Reverend Nicholas Murray's *Men and Things*

As I Saw Them in Europe, made the revelation of popish error their primary concern.[25]

History, too, shared in the literary crusade against Rome. A broad province was open to the historian who cared to show that Romanism always had been a corrupt and harmful influence and many took advantage of the opportunity.[26] Most of the historical works were concerned with the Middle Ages or the period of the Reformation; etched in a language which was openly hostile to Catholicism, they depicted the Popes as a succession of dissolute scoundrels and the Church as the mother of abominations. Deservedly the most popular among these studies was a *History of the Great Reformation in the Sixteenth Century,* a well written four-volume work from the pen of J. H. Merle D'Aubigne.[27] Widely circulated and often reprinted,[28] its seemingly scholarly approach veiled a devastating attack on Catholicism which must have influenced even the more learned men of the day. American history was also retold by No-Popery writers, with Jesuits pictured as constantly driving Indians against the frontiers and the papal plot to subdue the United States traced from the first settlement.[29] One point at issue between Catholic and anti-Catholic scholars was the relative part played by Catholicism and Protestantism in introducing toleration into America, the controversy between those who sought this honor for Rhode Island and Maryland stirring newspaper comment and the publication of several books in the 1850's.[30]

A greater popularity than that enjoyed by these historical works was reserved for the gift books and almanacs with which the enemies of Rome flooded the United States. Gift books with their ornate bindings and colored "embellishments," and almanacs with their weather forecasts and miscellaneous editorial comments, were as essential to the pre-Civil War generation as the Bible. Nativists realized this and stressed both forms of publication. Starting in the 1840's, American Protestant Almanacs began to appear yearly,[31] and gift books were not long in following their example. Published under such titles as *The Native American, a Gift for the People* and *Our Country; or, the American Parlor Keepsake*,[32] they were filled with story, verse, and arguments against Catholicism and were read in many American homes.

Although these novels, plays, histories, travel books, almanacs, and gift books played a part in formulating and giving direction to anti-Catholic prejudice, they were less influential than the numerous unvarnished propaganda works published at the same time. Hundreds of writers flooded the country with books and pamphlets, some attacking special features of the papal church, others spinning a web of testimony and invective against all phases of Romish policy and practice. A survey of this mass of material indicates that these propagandists had three principal objectives: first, to show that Catholicism was not Christianity, but an idolatrous religion, the ascendency of which would plunge the world into infidelity; secondly, that Popery was by nature irreconcilable with the democratic institutions of the United States and was determined to insure its own existence by driving them out; and thirdly, that the acceptance of the moral standards of the Catholic church would be suicidal to the best interests both of Protestantism and the nation. It was about these three principal contentions that most of the arguments were built.

The task of demonstrating the idolatrous nature of Catholicism was undertaken by innumerable writers. The pages of history, the writings of the church fathers, and the annals of the Church both in Europe and America—all were diligently searched by propagandists. Probably the most influential of these writers was an obscure New York pastor named William Nevins, who published a series of letters in the New York *Observer* in 1833 and 1834 which were later collected and printed by the American Tract Society as *Thoughts on Popery*.[33] This simple, straightforward exposition of the Protestant point of view was so easily understandable to the layman that Nevins' book enjoyed greater

popularity than any other comparable study. "Nothing has yet
been issued," declared the American Tract Society, "which so
lays open the deformities of Popery to common minds or is so
admirably adapted to save our country from its wiles, and to
guard the souls of men from its fatal snares." [34]   Another Protestant champion was the Reverend Joseph Frederick Berg, a
Philadelphia minister, whose many books lacked the popular appeal of Nevins', but whose theological attacks on Catholicism
were widely read and frequently quoted. [35]   Dozens of lesser
authors who attracted little attention as individuals created a
volume of propaganda which could not be ignored.

These writers were principally concerned with proving that the
Bible and history sanctioned Protestantism alone and that Romanism was anti-Scriptural. They maintained that the Protestant religion began with Christ's birth and not, as Catholics asserted, with the Reformation. Protestantism, they agreed, had
been obscured for several centuries by the blackness of Popery;
it was, as one put it, a flower held in the dead grasp of Rome until
God's gardener, Luther, transplanted it to the soil of Ridley and
Latimer for a new vigorous growth. [36]   In proof they analyzed
the principles of Catholicism to show that its tenets were not
sanctioned by the Bible and that the early church fathers were
not familiar with them. The peculiar features of Popery, they
concluded, originated between the second and sixteenth centuries
while the world was held in the corrupt grasp of papal Rome. In
support of this view, propagandists pointed out that the distinctive features of Catholicism had been borrowed directly from
heathen practices and had no connection with pure Christianity
and that they tended to lead worshippers toward infidelity. [37]

Thus the papal claim to spiritual infallibility was given no
credence; the Pope, writers asserted, had not the "shadow of a
shade" of right to a preponderant place in the religious affairs of
the world. Such an assumption was opposed, they said, both to
the clear statement of the Bible and to historical truth. They

denied that Peter had ever been at Rome, let alone that he had
founded his church there; they condemned Peter to a place among
the Apostles similar to that held by Judas, and they charged that
forgeries and fraud had been resorted to by Popes seeking un-
warranted power. Moreover, the whole course of history demonstrated that papal infallibility was a mere legend; how, it was
asked, could that tenet be reconciled with doctrinal differences
within the Church and with the numerous schisms that racked
Catholicism during the course of centuries? The conclusion was
inevitable: Popery had less unity and infallibility than Protestantism with its universal faith in the Scriptures.[38]

Similarly Protestant propagandists tried to show that the
Catholic doctrine of transubstantiation had no place in Christian
practice, that it was an adaptation from heathen idolatry, and
that its practice subverted the ideals of Christ. The principal attack on this doctrine was directed against its origin, the words
uttered by Christ, "This is my body; this is my blood." Catholics
were ridiculed for accepting this metaphorical statement in its
literal sense:

> 'Tis true that Christ by figure said,
> "This is my body,"—pointing to the bread,
> Just as he said in parable before,
> "I am the Vine—the Rock—the Way—the Door";
> But these mean not, nor any proof afford,
> That Christ bore grapes, was stone, or made of board;
> Just as absurd, this figure could design,
> That Christ had made himself of bread and wine.[39]

Writers maintained that the church fathers made no mention of
transubstantiation, and this was accepted as proof that the doctrine had been added by medieval Popes to increase their own
power. The fact that priests still continued to practice this idolatrous mummery aroused intense indignation among propagandists. "What are your Eastern fire-eaters, sword-swallowers, and
dervishes, to a Popish priest?" one asked. "Why, it would be

easier to swallow a rapier, ten feet long, or a ball of fire as large as the mountain Orizaba, than to metamorphose flour and water into the *great and holy God,* who created the heavens and the earth, and all that is therein." [40] Another writer headed an article on transubstantiation, "Popish Cannibals, God-Makers and God Eaters." [41] Frequently told was the story of a priest who refused to partake of the host after being informed that the original bread had contained arsenic. Protestants agreed that Catholics, in worshipping bread, were worshipping matter and thus were well on the road to paganism. [42]

Charges of the idolatrous nature of Romanism seemed substantiated by Catholic adoration of the Virgin Mary. This, in the eyes of many, was unadulterated heathenism; they believed that Catholics had erected graven images of the Virgin and of saints and worshipped at the feet of these rather than at the feet of God or His Son. It was solemnly asserted that the Ten Commandments had been corrupted by the papal hierarchy to omit the second of God's divine laws and thus open the path to idolatry. Superstition had secured such a hold on Catholics, propagandists stated, that bits of wood supposedly from the cross were venerated more than Christ and offerings before the bones of saints overbalanced those dedicated to the Lord. "If in the next village to ours," declared one enemy of Rome, "in enlightened New England, the inhabitants were all pagans, and bowed down daily in a temple of Jupiter or Venus, we are persuaded the holy majesty of Heaven would be less insulted and less offended, than He is by the actual worship of Mary and the saints by a multitude among us who bear the name of Christians." [43] Catholics persisted in this practice, authors insisted, despite the Biblical warnings against praying to more than one Lord and bowing down to graven images. [44]

Even the most bitter No-Popery writers admitted that Catholics had not consciously strayed from the clear road to salvation, but were led from this path by a false and designing priesthood.

Such practices as those of transubstantiation and the worship of saints and images clearly had been improvised by the early Popes for their own aggrandizement and to strengthen the Church. For most of the other objectionable doctrines of Catholicism, propagandists could find a mercenary explanation; priests, they said, had devised beliefs and practices simply to wring treasure from the dupes who embraced Romanism. The doctrines of purgatory and extreme unction and the use of penances and confession were cited as proof.

The "lucrative fiction of purgatory" [45] was branded as "one of the most unscriptural dogmas and pick-pocket doctrines in the Romish church." [46] Priests were criticized for refusing to release the souls of the poor from torment while guaranteeing an immediate heavenly journey to the rich who bought salvation.[47] Similarly, extreme unction was pictured as a man-made doctrine that enabled priests to force dying men to will their fortunes to the Church.[48] Penances were scoffed at by most writers as unsanctioned by the Bible, unhealthy in their effects, and valuable only for the wealth they brought to Rome.[49] For the doctrine of confession propagandists had an equal scorn, showing that it had no basis in Scripture and that Judas was the only person in the Bible who had confessed his sins to another.[50] One author summed up the Protestant view in verse:

> 'Twere worse than madness to believe,
> Man can his brother worm forgive,
> Or yield unto the contrite one
> That peace which comes from heaven alone.[51]

The anti-Scriptural doctrine of confession had been devised, it was said, to exact money for the priesthood and give them control over worshippers.[52]

No less destructive of spiritual well-being, Protestants were told, were the ceremonies and ritualism of Catholic worship. Americans, with their tastes adjusted to the rigorous simplicity of the frontier, naturally viewed the papal processions, the elaborate clerical garb, the impressive ceremony of the mass, the feasts, the incense, and the holy water with misgiving and distrust. "Will the Roman Catholic ask his priest," wrote one author, "whom he now sees crossing himself, what is the use or meaning of all this crossing, capering and twirling of his limbs and body? Assuredly, while he is *devoutly* offering to the Father of heaven and earth the Holy Mass, there can be no devils or demons playing or dancing around his sacred person, which he might drive away by these *divine* antics." [53] Protestants believed that these features of Catholicism, like many others, had been contrived by the clergy to elicit liberal contributions from awed worshippers. [54]

An even better example of clerical deception, according to the propagandists, could be found in Catholic miracles. Writers explained each miracle as the work of some scoundrelly priest who willingly used fraud to make dupes of his flock. Repeatedly told were stories of the clotted blood of Saint Januarius at Naples which flowed when Napoleon so ordered, of the Weeping Virgin of the same city who likewise performed at Napoleon's command, and similar tales designed to show that miracles were the work of men rather than of God. [55] In 1844 attention was centered on this type of propaganda when the Holy Coat of Treves, supposedly worn by Christ, was exhibited in Europe, attracting more than a million pilgrims and performing countless miracles. Nativists disapproved of this "disgusting blasphemy and trickery" [56] and expressed indignation at the presence of such superstition in the nineteenth century. [57] "We have often said," one declared, ". . . that the man who can bolt such a monstrous lump of superstition as Popery itself, could swallow anything—nay, if he has been able to take *it* down, with all its legends, fables, and absurdities, it is only wonderful that he can find room for anything more." [58]

Another proof of the anti-Scriptural nature of Popery was found by propagandists in the prophetic books of the Bible. There they unearthed references to a Babylon on seven mountains, a Beast with seven heads and ten horns, a "Man of Sin, the Son of Perdition, who opposeth and exalteth himself above all that is called God," a "Wicked One," "whose coming is after the working of Satan, with all power and signs and lying wonders." To Protestants it seemed that God had pictured the rise of Popery in these mystic words; the seven mountains and the seven heads referred obviously to the seven hills of Rome, the ten horns could mean only the ten kingdoms of the Roman Empire, the Man of Sin was certainly the Pope who tried to exalt himself above God, and the "lying wonders" were clearly the miracles of Catholicism. The number of the "Beast" had been foretold in the Scriptures as "666" and nativistic writers, after elaborate computations, showed that this symbol applied to Popery.[59] Moreover the Bible had declared that the "Man of Sin" "causeth all, both small and great, rich and poor, free and bond, to receive a mark on the right hand, and on their forehead." This must refer, writers claimed, to the mark placed on the foreheads of Catholics on Ash Wednesday and to the marking of the hands and heads of priests during the ordination ceremony. Such evidence as this was sufficient to convince many that Catholicism was truly the "Man of Sin," the "Son of Perdition," the "Scarlet-Colored Woman," the "Whore of Babylon," the "Beast which Sitteth on Seven Mountains," the "Wicked One." Its coming had been foretold and its downfall predicted; it was a sinful and false religious system, an anti-Christ, opposed by God and bent on the destruction of true Christianity.[60]

These Scriptural arguments, available everywhere in religious journals and propaganda books, undoubtedly affected many of the men and women who read them. The reason now seemed clear for the popish aversion to the Bible. No religious system so completely condemned by the Scriptures could endure if the word of God were widely circulated. Protestants agreed with one writer when he declared:

Popery is a compound of all that is senseless in Pagan idolatry and polluting in Heathen sensual festivity—a direct contradiction to Christianity. It is emphatically the Antichrist—the Apocalyptic Babylonish mystery condemned to utter destruction.[61]

A second type of anti-Catholic propaganda stressed the enmity between Popery and democracy. The United States, writers declared, could thrive only so long as its tradition of liberty and freedom was perpetuated. Catholicism was a religious system so intimately connected with monarchy and despotism as to be fundamentally incompatible with American institutions. Patriotic as well as religious citizens, then, should oppose this mighty Romish machine, for the future of democracy and Christianity alike rested upon its extinction.

Propagandists attempted to prove this premise by showing that the papal system was itself completely despotic. At its head, they said, was the Pope, maintained by a system of idolatry which elevated him above God in the eyes of Catholics. The entire hierarchy was so organized in the lower ranks that the Pope could exercise immediate authority over the most humble of worshippers. Within that religious system liberty had vanished and an autocracy reminiscent of the Dark Ages had been created.[62]

This absolute power, according to anti-Catholic writers, had always been used to stamp out freedom of thought and action. They warned that the supremacy of Catholicism in America would mean the end of a free press and free speech; that the Index would stamp out the literature upon which cultural advance rested; that the Inquisition would still the agents of science; that reform and progress would be permanently arrested. This, it was agreed, had been the fate of all papal countries through the course of history. Particularly stressed was the effect that papal domination would have on religious liberty; Catholics were represented as pledged to kill all heretics and the oath allegedly taken by bishops binding them to "persecute and oppose" all "heretics, schismatics and rebels to our Said Lord," was frequently cited.[63] Should Catholicism ever fasten its grip on America, one propagandist wrote:

All knees would bend, or be broken, before "His Holiness" of Rome; all tongues would sing paeans to the tenant of the Vatican, or be plucked out by the roots; the crosier and the sword would beat the bones of heresy to dust; daring Galileos would sup in dungeons on horrors; emperors and kings, and, maybe, presidents, would go a-toe-kissing, and perchance be glad to expiate some rebellious deed by a two days' shiver, *en deshabille,* in wintry weather, in a Pope's ante-chamber. . . . Then there would be a rare time for shaven monks—an imperial field of plunder and rapine.[64]

The Inquisition provided authors with their most effective argument when they sought to show the intolerant and tyrannous nature of Catholicism. "It is vain to deny," one wrote, "that Popery has been the cause of the most bloody wars and the most cruel persecutions, so that millions have been the victims of this perversion of the gospel and anti-Christian system of religion." [65] Tales of massacres, such as that of St. Bartholomew's Day, were retold by many writers; Protestant martyrs were made to live again on countless pages, and the tortures of the Inquisition were realistically depicted.[66] An author portrayed the usual Protestant point of view when he wrote: "The Inquisition, beyond all other institutions that ever appeared in the world, evidences the deepest malignity of human nature. Nothing, in all the annals of time, ever exhibited so appalling and hateful a view of fallen and degenerate men, demoralized to the lowest ebb of perversity by Romanism and Popedom." [67]

The obvious Catholic rebuttal—that the Inquisition and persecution both belonged to an earlier day and had long since been abandoned by the Church—Protestants met by hurling back the clergy's own assertion that Catholicism never changed. Moreover, they pretended to find modern instances of the Inquisition: an Inquisition building in Madrid which was used as late as 1820, British soldiers in Malta, Protestant missionaries in Ireland,

converts from Catholicism in Madeira and Italy who were persecuted for their beliefs, and Inquisitorial chambers in Rome,
rivaling those of the Dark Ages, brought to light by the Revolution of 1849.[68] Even in the United States, propagandists stated,
the Inquisition was beginning to function, for converts to Protestantism were beaten by priests, rebellious churchmen mysteriously made to disappear, and clergymen noted for their attacks
on Rome themselves attacked and their lives endangered.[69]
These persecutions were insignificant only because Catholicism
had not established itself; once its power was secured no Protestant would be safe from the sword or faggot.

Particularly would this be true when the Pope assumed in
America the temporal power that he had claimed through the
ages and still asserted whenever possible. The question of
whether that power could be exercised in the nineteenth century
provided one of the sorest points of controversy between Catholics and Protestants. Catholic writers asserted that although a
temporal power had been exercised by the Papacy in past centuries,
changed conditions had forced its abandonment years before.[70]
The Protestant rebuttal again flaunted the Catholic assertion
that the Church never changed; temporal power had been advanced once, they said, and would be advanced again in any
country where Popery gained the ascendancy. Not only did this
temporal authority threaten the future security of the United
States, but it was an immediate menace to the country because so
long as Papists were bound to obey all commands of the Pope, he
might at any time order them to take up arms against their government.[71] "A religion," one propagandist wrote, "which com-
pels its chiefs to swear, in the hour of sacred investiture, to yield
nothing to 'principalities or powers'; that can conflict with the
will and interests of their one and only sovereign, the temporality-
grasping 'Successor of St. Peter,' is a political element and authority to be watched, and met, and baffled wherever the people
would rule the State, or govern their own temporal affairs." [72]

These controversies over temporal power bulked large in the mass of propaganda directed against Catholicism, but they were dwarfed by the still larger volume of books and pamphlets attacking the immorality of the papal system. Writers here had a two-fold opportunity: they could demonstrate the degrading effects of Popery, and they could appeal to an audience wider and more varied than that attracted by theological or patriotic arguments. Probably many of the writers who described Catholic immorality looked upon the No-Popery crusade as a business enterprise. The works of William Hogan, Samuel B. Smith, and the Reverend Charles Sparry were sufficiently licentious and popular to sell well. One of them, at least, went too far, for Sparry was arrested for vending obscene writings when peddling one of his own books.[73]

No other explanation can account for the flood of indecent expositions of Catholic immorality which marked the propaganda of this period. Both the effectiveness and the profits of this type of work were demonstrated by Maria Monk's *Awful Disclosures,* and although most of the writers could not parade as escaped nuns, they could depict the confessional, convent life, and priestly celibacy in terms as lurid as those used in this pioneering volume. Titles such as *Open Convents; or, Nunneries and Popish Seminaries Dangerous to the Morals and Degrading to the Character of a Republican Community,*[74] and *Priest's Prisons for Women; or, a Consideration of the Question, whether Unmarried foreign priests ought to be permitted to erect prisons, into which, under pretense of religion, to seduce or entrap, or by force compel young women to enter, and after they have secured their property, keep them in confinement, and compel them, as their slaves, to submit themselves to their will, under the penalty of flogging or the dungeon,*[75] indicate a desire to captivate popular interest, particularly among the lower classes. Probably the most widely read book of this type was *Rosamond; or, a Narrative of the Captivity and Sufferings of an American Female*

*under the Popish Priests in the Island of Cuba, with a full dis-
closure of their manners and customs, written by herself.*[76] In
this vulgar little volume the author, Rosamond Culbertson, recounted her adventures as mistress of a Cuban priest, climaxing
her revelations of their love life by describing a clerical plot to
capture negro boys, kill them, and grind them up into sausage
meat. One reason for her popularity can be found in the remark
with which she concluded her description of this insidious design: "Those who bought and eat these sausages," she wrote,
"said they were the best sausages they ever eat." [77] Such works
extended anti-Catholic propaganda to readers who would have
scorned theological arguments. Even the nativistic societies recognized their value, for the Protestant Reformation Society offered a fifty-dollar premium for the best work on "The
Happiness and Horrors of a Roman Catholic Priest in
never being allowed to marry a beautiful, young and virtuous
wife." [78]

These books neglected no phase of Catholicism which could
possibly be attacked on moral grounds. Propagandists maintained that all Papists were taught to lie and perjure in the interests of their religion. How, they asked, can such persons be
moral? Trained in minor sin by their priests, they descend naturally to the lower ranks of iniquity until "impiety, immorality,
falsehood, frauds in business, perjury, theft, murder, infanticide
and regicide" are as natural to them as their religion itself.[79] The
immorality inherent in the papal system was increased, Protestants believed, by the system of indulgences which still thrived in
Catholic countries. This encouraged crime by assuring criminals
pardon for their dark deeds. Moreover, priests goaded their flocks
into evil acts to increase the revenues of the church.[80] Writers
were not surprised to find crime more common in papal countries
than in those where Protestantism was dominant.[81]

The confessional, too, anti-Catholic writers insisted, led Romanists into sin. They pointed out that the confessional gave a

priest absolute control over his subjects. He could command them to sin in any way, particularly to spy on Protestants or murder them in the interests of the Church. Above all, confession allowed criminals to have their sins forgiven.[82] One propagandist asked: "Would the people be afraid of the ague, if it could be cured by merely swallowing a glass of water? Or, would any one be afraid to rob or murder, if he could get off by washing his hands? Confession is almost as easy, where you have only to whisper a word in the ear of the priest, without fearing a postponement of absolution." [83]

Far more attention, however, was paid the confessional as a means for priestly iniquity. A host of writers painted the clerical members of the Catholic church as lecherous rogues who used this instrument of their holy office simply as a device for the seduction and ruin of their fair penitents. To Protestants this conclusion seemed inevitable from the nature of the confessional. By it the priest could forgive all sins, including those which he himself might commit. "Persuade a woman that if she sins, you can forgive her as thoroughly and effectually as Almighty God could forgive her," wrote one, "and you take away every check from vice." [84] Propagandists naturally concluded that the confessor's box served as a prelude to the most revolting of sexual practices.[85]

This would have been bad enough, they said, had the priests confined their evil deeds to married women and others already accustomed to the practices they were forced to endure. Instead, the confessors, by insinuating questions and improper suggestions, corrupted and seduced innocent girls. Thus initiated into a life of sin, their young victims drifted down the crimson path to end their lives in convents as priests' mistresses. Although most authors hesitated to reveal the lewd conversations through which this seduction was accomplished, several examples found their way into print; examples which explain the popularity of this type of exposure.[86] A description of the confessional, as

outspoken as the author "with due regard to *decency*" could give,
follows:

First let the reader figure to himself, or herself, a young lady,
between the ages of from twelve to twenty, on her knees, with her
lips nearly close pressed to the cheeks of the priest, who, in all
probability, is not over twenty-five or thirty years old. . . . When
priest and penitent are placed in the above attitude, let us suppose
the following conversation taking place between them, and unless
my readers are more dull of apprehension than I am willing to believe, they will have some idea of the *beauties of Popery*.

CONFESSOR. What sins have you committed?
PENITENT. I don't know any, sir.
CON. Are you sure you did nothing wrong? Examine yourself
well.
PEN. Yes; I do recollect that I did wrong. I made faces at school
at Lucy A.
CON. Nothing else?
PEN. Yes; I told mother that I hated Lucy A., and that she was
an ugly thing.
CON. (Scarcely able to suppress a smile in finding the girl per-
fectly innocent) Have you had any immodest thoughts?
PEN. What is that, sir?
CON. Have you not been thinking about men?
PEN. Why, yes, sir.
CON. Are you fond of any of them?
PEN. Why, yes; I like Cousin A. or R. greatly.
CON. Did you ever like to sleep with him?
PEN. Oh, no.
CON. How long did these thoughts about men continue?
PEN. Not very long.
CON. Had you these thoughts by day, or by night?
PEN. By ————.

In this strain does this reptile confessor proceed until his now
half-gained prey is filled with ideas and thoughts, to which she has
been hitherto a stranger. He tells her that she must come tomorrow
again. She accordingly comes, and he gives another twist to the
screw, which he has now firmly fixed upon the soul and body of his
penitent. Day after day, week after week, and month after month

does this hapless girl come to confession until this wretch has worked up her passions to a tension almost snapping, and then becomes his easy prey.[87]

Protestant readers understood the significance of conversations of this nature because they believed that the practice of celibacy made every priest a wanton individual whose unnatural desires removed the last vestiges of moral sense which Catholic teachings had allowed him to retain. This un-Scriptural doctrine, propagandists asserted, was at the basis of the universal corruption marking the whole history of the Papacy.[88] "Licentiousness takes the lead of the vices among these ungodly Priests," one writer declared. "They obtain constant access to the Nunneries. Their appetites and passions are without restraint. Their unbridled lust stalks forth in broad daylight; and deeds of iniquity are daily committed by them, which are enough to make the savage of the wilderness blush. . . ." [89] Nor were these conditions confined to antiquity or to the Catholic countries of the old world; propagandists who boasted of being former "Popish priests" recounted experiences from their own past to show that the lusts of a celibate clergy were as common in the United States as in Europe.[90]

This sinful path into which priests were led by celibacy accounted in large degree, Protestants believed, for their avaricious characteristics. Writers insisted that vows of poverty were as little regarded as vows of chastity, that priests in every country were accumulating wealth, and that the purses of the poor were wrung dry to satisfy their greedy desires. Propagandists demonstrated that only barren fields were left in the wake of Catholicism, by comparing Protestant countries such as the United States with Catholic countries such as Italy, Ireland, or Spain.[91] The lesson in their reasoning was clear; if Catholicism should gain the upper hand in America, not only the moral but the economic welfare of the people would be sacrificed to satisfy the desires of a sin-steeped clergy.

Moreover, any success for Catholicism would mean an extension of the convent system, and this propagandists considered the worst of all iniquities invented or practiced by Rome. They viewed these religious retreats as "slave factories," "Popish brothels," "priests' harems" and "baptized brothels"; with their pleasure-mad inhabitants principally occupied in satisfying the lust of priests. What other results could be expected, Protestants asked, when clergymen trained in immorality and barred from normal practices by their vows of celibacy, were placed in daily contact with attractive young women whose sins they could both foster and forgive? Writers admitted that in America there were no foundling hospitals such as those erected by European convents to care for the illegitimate children of nuns. Abortion and infanticide had been effectively substituted, they said, and were "common in nunneries throughout this country." [92] "No tongue can express so much iniquity as can be found and has been and now is practiced in these Romish brothels," wrote one nativist. "Noble and virtuous girls who piously seclude themselves from the world are seduced and made the miserable victims of the lust of priests. Children are born and slaughtered by these devotees of wickedness. Not one, not ten, not twenty, nor fifty— not an hundred, nor yet a thousand, but more than ten times that number are born to die with a few moments of life." [93] Only through the abolition of convents by law, Protestants agreed, could the purity of American women and the sanctity of the American home be maintained.

These accounts of Catholic immorality were accepted without question by perhaps a majority of the evangelical Protestants in America. They came to consider even the priests in their own communities as dissolute rakes, deserving neither courteous treatment nor toleration. On several occasions members of the Catholic clergy were arrested, charged with rape or seduction through the confessional, and in trials which aroused the indignation of impartial observers, sentenced to pay fines or to imprisonment.[94] Protestants refused even to grant a priest justice when he was accused of moral laxity.

By the 1850's, then, propagandists had taught American Protestants that Popery was unsanctioned by the Bible or history, that it was determined to usurp universal power, and that it would inflict upon them tortures and corruption reminiscent of the Dark Ages. Before this onslaught of prejudiced literature, American tolerance gave way to a blind, misunderstanding hate. Probably one writer only slightly distorted the common sentiment when he said:

> We regard the Pope as an impostor; and the Mother Church as the mother of abominations. We don't believe in the close-shaven, white-cravated, black-coated priesthood, who profess to "mortify the flesh" by eschewing matrimony and violating nature. We don't believe in the mummeries of prayers in unknown tongues; nor in the impious assumption of the power to forgive sins—to send the soul of a murderer to heaven, or to curse the soul of a good man down to the other place. We don't believe in Nunneries, where beauty that was made to bloom and beam on the world is immured and immolated, not to say prostituted.[95]

Anti-Catholic propaganda had produced a state of mind where, as one Catholic expressed it, "whenever the question relates to the church, the Protestant waives the ordinary rules of law, logic and good sense, and proceeds on the presumption that every man is to be counted guilty till he succeeds in proving his innocence." [96]

NOTES

[1] Quoted in Guilday, *Life of John England,* II, 456.

[2] Religious newspapers began to show their marked interest in anti-Catholicism in 1830. By 1835 it could be stated that for several years the entire religious press, with but few exceptions, had been given over to the attack. *The Protestant,* January 1, 1831; *Western Monthly Magazine,* III (June, 1830).

[3] *American Protestant Vindicator,* December 16, 1835, May 12, 1841; Reese, *Humbugs of New York,* 226–227.

[4] *Western Monthly Magazine,* III (June, 1835), 379. This issue contained an article on "The Catholic Question" which, although unsympathetic toward

the crusade against Rome, gave an interesting analysis of the methods employed and their effectiveness. The *Freeman's Journal* expressed a similar sentiment when its editors wrote, on September 18, 1852: "Verily, the hatred of
Rome covers a multitude of sins. Whoever wishes to gain honor, reputation
and renown in the United States need only write a book against the 'Harlot
of Babylon.' The blacker he paints her, the more profitable will it be for him."

5 *Ibid.*, 381.

6 *Ibid.*, 380; Martineau, *Society in America*, II, 234.

7 William Cobbett, *A History of the Protestant Reformation in England
and Ireland; showing how that Event has Impoverished and Degraded the
Main Body of the People in those Countries* (New York, 1832), 5–6.

8 Bishop England believed that "there are no minds over which this prejudice has a more extensive and better established dominion than those of generous and amiable females." Quoted in Guilday, *Life of John England*, II, 455.

9 New York *Observer*, April 25, 1835.

10 S. Sherwood, *Edwin and Alicia; or, the Infant Martyrs* (New York,
1835). *The Downfall of Babylon*, April 25, 1835, praised this work for its
"moral and anti-Popish tone."

11 Her books included *Alice Benden; or, the Bowed Shilling: and Other
Tales* (New York, 1841); *Glimpses of the Past; or, the Museum* (New York,
1841); *The Church Visible in All Ages* (New York, 1845); *Falsehood and
Truth* (New York, 1842); *Dangers and Duties* (New York, 1841); *The
Happy Mute* (Boston, 1842); *The Siege of Derry; or, Sufferings of the Protestants: a Tale of the Revolution* (New York, 1844); *Second Causes; or,
Up and Be Doing* (New York, 1843); *Personal Recollections* (New York,
1843). In addition she published books of travel and books designed for adult
readers describing the persecuting nature of Popery. She contributed short
stories to American nativistic publications as well. See New York *Observer*,
April 24, 1841; *American Protestant Vindicator*, May 26, 1841.

12 Elizabeth, *Personal Recollections*, 13–165.

13 Elizabeth, *Falsehood and Truth*, viii–ix.

14 This work had been reprinted from an English edition. A new edition
was required in 1843, published at Baltimore at that time. Both the Reverend
Robert J. Breckinridge and L. Giustiniani testified that they had been won to
the support of the anti-Catholic cause by reading this book. *Spirit of the Nineteenth Century*, II (July, 1843).

15 All of Frothingham's books were published in Boston in 1854. *The Convent's Doom* went through five editions in one year, *Six Hours in a Convent*
through eight editions in two years. An earlier novel of the same type had
been: Harry Hazel, *The Nun of St. Ursula; or, the Burning of the Convent;
A Romance of Mt. Benedict* (Boston, 1845). Like Frothingham, the author of
this work insisted that he was concealing through fiction the actual chain of
events leading to the destruction of the convent. *The Chronicles of Mount
Benedict: a Tale of the Ursuline Convent, the Quasi Production of Mary
Magdalen* (Boston, 1837) was a Catholic novel which answered these arguments and reduced most of the statements made by nativists concerning the
convent to absurdities.

16 Typical of this type of work were: Rachel MacCrindell, *The School
Girl in France; or, The Snares of Popery: a Warning to Protestants against*

Education in Catholic Seminaries (4th edition, Boston, 1846) ; Rachel Mac-Crindell, *The Convent; a Narrative Founded on Fact* (New York, 1853) ; Rachel MacCrindell, *The English Governess* (New York, 1844) ; James M. Campbell, *The Protestant Girl in a French Nunnery; or, the School Girl in France* (New York, 1845).

17 J. C. Meeks, *Pierre and his Family; or, a Story of the Waldenses* (New York, 1841) ; W. C. Brownlee, *The Whigs of Scotland* (New York, 1839) ; Lawrence Bungener, *The Priest and the Huguenot; or, Persecution in the Age of Louis XV* (Boston, 1854).

18 *The Conversion and Edifying Death of Andrew Dunn* (New York, 1835).

19 *Recantation; or, the Confessions of a Convert to Romanism* (New York, 1846) ; *Helen Mulgrave; or, Jesuit Executorship: being Passages in the Life of a Seceder from Romanism* (New York, 1852).

20 Helen Dhu, *Stanhope Burleigh: the Jesuits in Our Homes* (New York, 1855) ; Edmund Farrenc, *Carlotina and the Sandfedesti; or, a Night with the Jesuits at Rome* (New York, 1853) ; L. Giustiniani, *Intrigues of Jesuitism in the United States of America* (New York, 1846) ; John C. Pitrot, *Paul and Julia; or, the Political Mysteries, Hypocrisy, and Cruelty of the Church of Rome* (Boston, 1855) ; *Carlington Castle; a Tale of the Jesuits* (New York, 1854) ; *The Red Cross of Catholicism in America; Startling Exposé of an Infernal Catholic Plot* (Boston, 1854) ; *The Female Jesuit; or, the Spy in the Family* (New York, 1851) ; *Despotism; or, the Last Days of the American Republic* (New York, 1856) ; *Sequel to the Female Jesuit* (New York, 1853). A Catholic answer to these works was in *Proselytizing; a Sketch of Know Nothing Times* (Cincinnati, 1854).

21 *Pilot*, June 4, 1853. The book was published at New York in 1853. Other novels by Catherine Sinclair were *Modern Flirtations* (New York, 1853) ; *Modern Society* (New York, 1850) and *Shetland and the Shetlanders; or, the Northern Circuit* (New York, 1840).

22 New York, 1850. The play, written by T. W. Whitley, took advantage of the Mexican War for its setting and portrayed the struggle of an American naval officer and a Jesuit for the hand of a Mexican girl. It pictured the Jesuit as a cunning rascal, well deserving of his ultimate death. There is no evidence that the play was ever performed.

23 Typical of the acrostics which were popular was one from the *Know Nothing Almanac*, 12 :

> Parent of errors, masterpiece of sin ;
> Owned by Satan, all corrupt within ;
> Pride, superstition, bigotry, and blood,
> Endear her to the foe of earthly good,
> Relentless on the human soul she preys,
> Yes, claims the right to save it, and betrays.

The classical verse was typified by Joseph Turnley, *Priestcraft; or, the Monarch of the Middle Ages* (London, 1850), a dramatic poem more than one hundred pages in length.

24 Joel T. Headley, *Letters from Italy* (New York, 1845) ; Sinclair, *Shetland and the Shetlanders;* Charlotte Elizabeth, *Letters from Ireland* (New

York, 1843) ; James Jackson Jarves, *Italian Sights and Papal Principles, seen through American Spectacles* (New York, 1856).

25 Murray, *Memoirs*, 311–319. Another book of this same type was L. DeSanctis, *Rome, Christian and Papal: Sketches of its Religious Monuments and Ecclesiastical Hierarchy, with Notices of the Jesuits and the Inquisition* (New York, 1856). This was written in the form of conversation between a priest, a Puseyite and a Protestant who visit parts of Rome and argue over the miracles and ceremonies which they witness.

26 For a list of these histories see Bibliography.

27 New York, 1846.

28 New York *Observer*, January 7, 1837, February 24, 1838; *American Protestant Vindicator*, June 24, 1840.

29 Typical of these works was C. W. Webber, *Sam; or, the History of Mystery* (Cincinnati, 1857). Several Catholic histories of the United States were also available, showing little more tolerance than those of the anti-papal writers. Thus Thomas D. McGee, *The Catholic History of North America* (Boston, 1855), 5–9, announced that it would prove that Catholics were alone responsible for the discovery and settlement of America, for all missionary work among the Indians, and largely for the independence of the country and its subsequent development.

30 *Congregationalist*, May 7, 1852, May 28, 1852, June 18, 1852; Carroll, *Great American Battle*, 187–190. The Catholic view was best presented in G. L. Davis, *The Day Star of American Freedom* (New York, 1855), an attempt to show that all toleration was due to Catholic influence in Maryland.

31 For a list of these almanacs and gift books see Bibliography.

32 Hector Orr, *The Native American, a Gift for the People* (Philadelphia, 1845) ; William H. Ryder, *Our Country; or, the American Parlor Keepsake*.

33 William Nevins, *Thoughts on Popery* (New York, 1836).

34 American Tract Society, *Twenty Second Annual Report* (New York, 1836), 105. This sentiment was agreed to by the New York *Observer*, April 2, 1836, and one bookseller advertised that he had been converted from Catholicism by the book. *Ibid.*, June 30, 1838.

35 Berg was pastor of the Second Reformed Protestant church of Philadelphia. His numerous books included: *Lectures on Romanism* (Philadelphia, 1844) ; *The Confessional; or, an Exposition of the Doctrine of Auricular Confession as Taught in the Standards of the Roman Church* (3rd edition, New York, 1841) ; *The Great Apostasy Identified with Papal Rome; or, an Exposition of the Mystery of Iniquity and the Marks and Doom of Anti-Christ* (Philadelphia, 1842) ; *Mysteries of the Inquisition* (————, 1846) ; *Oral Controversy with a Catholic Priest* (————, 1843) ; *A Synopsis of the Moral Philosophy of Peter Dens as Prepared for the Use of Romish Seminaries and Students of Theology* (New York, 1841).

36 *National Protestant*, I (April, 1845), II (October, 1845); *Southern Presbyterian Review*, IX (July, 1855); *American and Foreign Christian Union*, I (November, 1850), IV (January, 1853) ; *American Text Book of Popery*, 61–126; Thomas H. Horne, *A Protestant Memorial* (New York, 1844), 49–78; Griswold, *The Reformation; A Brief Exposition of some of the Errors and Corruptions of the Church of Rome*; J. H. Hopkins, *The Church of Rome in her Primitive Purity Compared with the Church of Rome at the*

Present Day (New York, 1835); William H. Odenheimer, *The True Catholic No Romanist* (New York, 1842); William B. Sprague, *Contrast Between True and False Religions* (New York, 1837); W. C. Brownlee, *Sketch of the History of the Western Apostolic Churches from which the Roman Church Apostatized* (New York, 184-); Beecher, *Papal Conspiracy Exposed*, 229–237; *The Lives of the Popes from A.D. 100 to A.D. 1853* (New York, 1853), 565; Joseph Turnley, *Popery in Power; or, the Spirit of the Vatican* (London, 1850); Clark, *Romanism in America*, 11–21; John Cumming, *Lectures on Romanism, being Illustrations and Refutations of the Errors of Romanism and Tractarianism* (Boston, 1854), 137–139; Berg, *Answer to Archbishop Hughes*, 8–9; Derby, *The Catholic*, 3–5; Samuel Edgar, *Variations of Popery* (New York, 1848), 46–60. These writers even tried to show that many Catholic saints had really been Protestants, existing before increasing corruption created the Catholic church. See W. C. Brownlee, *The Religion of the Ancient Irish and Britons not Roman Catholic, and the Immortal Saint Patrick Vindicated from the False Charge of being a Papist* (2nd Edition, New York, 1841).

37 *The Protestant*, March 31, 1832; New York *Observer*, May 25, 1833; *American Protestant Vindicator*, March 3, 1841, May 2, 1842; *North American Protestant Magazine or Anti-Jesuit*, I (April, 1846); *Congregationalist*, February 14, 1851, December 17, 1852, October 20, 1854; Cheever, *Hierarchical Despotism*, 34–41; *American Text Book of Popery*, 27–35; Derby, *The Catholic*, 128–136; Clark, *Romanism in America*, 131–154; Gavazzi, *Lectures*, 279–292; Lipscomb, *Our Country*, 84; John Poynder, *Popery in Alliance with Heathenism; Letters Proving the Conformity which Subsists between the Romish Religion and the Religion of the Ancient Heathens* (London, 1835); L. Giustiniani, *Papal Rome as it is, by a Roman* (Baltimore, 1843), 59–90.

38 McGavin, *The Protestant*, I, 687, II, 28; Cheever, *Hierarchical Despotism*, 10–14; Pond, *No Fellowship with Romanism*, 125–126; Nevins, *Thoughts on Popery*, 40–43; Horne, *Protestant Memorial*, 85–93; Beecher, *Plea for the West*, 168–169; Allen, *Report on Popery*, 20–21; Edgar, *Variations of Popery, passim;* Beecher, *Papal Conspiracy Exposed*, 212–273; *Romanism Incompatible with Republican Institutions* (New York, 1844), 5–20; Lipscomb, *Our Country*, 50–54; Cumming, *Lectures on Romanism*, 159–201; Berg, *Answer to Archbishop Hughes*, 9; Gavazzi, *Lectures*, 54–65, 134–149; *Pope or President*, 1–35; Gault, *Popery, The Man of Sin*, 337–350; Derby, *The Catholic*, 157–176; D'Aubigne, *History of the Great Reformation*, I, 11–13; White, *Practical and Internal Evidence*, 81–105; *Southern Presbyterian Review*, I (June, 1847); *Congregationalist*, January 7, 1853; *Western Christian Advocate*, November 20, 1935; Philadelphia *Recorder*, January 29, 1831; *Christian Watchman*, February 19, 1830; *American Protestant Magazine*, I (March, 1846), IV (February, 1849); *An Inquiry into the Fundamental Principles of the Roman Catholics, in Five Letters Addressed to a Roman Catholic* (Washington, 1822), 4–7.

39 *American Protestant Almanac for 1841*, 11.

40 William Hogan, *Synopsis of Popery as it Was and as it Is* (Hartford, 1854), 160–161.

41 *North American Protestant Magazine or Anti-Jesuit*, I (April, 1846).

42 *Quarterly Review of the American Protestant Association*, I (April,

1844) ; New York *Observer*, August 24, 1833 ; Baltimore *Literary and Religious Magazine*, IV (October, 1838) ; *Protestant Episcopalian and Church Register*, IV (August, 1833), IV (October, 1833) ; *American Protestant Vindicator*, December 15, 1844 ; *Western Christian Advocate*, January 30, 1835 ; *Episcopal Recorder*, February 22, 1834 ; *National Protestant Magazine and Anti-Jesuit*, III (February, 1846) ; *Christian Watchman*, March 18, 1820 ; Allen, *Report on Popery*, 15–16 ; McGavin, *The Protestant*, I, 406–488 ; Nevins, *Thoughts on Popery*, 103–105 ; Edgar, *Variations of Popery*, 382–436 ; Gavazzi, *Lectures*, 98–129 ; Cumming, *Lectures on Romanism*, 332–420 ; Clark, *Romanism in America*, 26–75 ; *Inquiry into the Fundamental Principles*, 10–17 ; Hogan, *High and Low Mass*, 147–169.

43 Allen, *Report on Popery*, 20.

44 New York *Observer*, January 30, 1830, October 2, 1830, April 20, 1833 ; *Downfall of Babylon*, October 3, 1835 ; *American Protestant Vindicator*, June 23, 1841 ; *Episcopal Recorder*, January 7, 1832, November 2, 1833, August 9, 1834, August 16, 1834 ; *Christian Watchman*, January 22, 1830, September 8, 1831, August 1, 1834 ; *The Protestant*, October 23, 1830, January 7, 1832 ; *Congregationalist*, August 24, 1849, November 23–December 7, 1849, December 14, 1849, February 14, 1851, June 11, 1852, June 30, 1852, October 8, 1852, March 9, 1855, October 27, 1854 ; Philadelphia *Recorder*, March 26, 1831 ; Nevins, *Thoughts on Popery*, 65–69, 95–100 ; *History of Popery*, 236–276 ; McGavin, *The Protestant*, I, 293–380 ; Pond, *No Fellowship with Romanism*, 138–139 ; Hogan, *High and Low Mass*, 18–35 ; *What is Romanism* (London, 1850), Nos. 3–26 ; Edgar, *Variations of Popery*, 457–468 ; Cumming, *Lectures on Romanism*, 259–331 ; Murray, *Romanism at Home*, 124–125 ; Gault, *Popery, the Man of Sin*, 315–332 ; Gavazzi, *Lectures*, 341–351 ; *Protestant Episcopalian and Church Register*, IV (October, 1833) ; *Southern Presbyterian Review*, VIII (January, 1855) ; *Home Missionary*, XVIII (July, 1845) ; *North American Protestant Magazine or Anti-Jesuit*, I (April, 1846) ; *American Protestant Magazine*, III (March, 1848) ; *American and Foreign Christian Union*, IV (August, 1853).

45 Brownlee, *Popery, an Enemy to Civil and Religious Liberty*, 67.

46 Hogan, *High and Low Mass*, 108–109.

47 *Quarterly Review of the American Protestant Association*, III (July 1845) ; New York *Observer*, December 18, 1830, January 1, 1831, August 21, 1833, August 29, 1840 ; *American Protestant Vindicator*, July 22, 1840 ; Philadelphia *Recorder*, February 19, 1831 ; Nevins, *Thoughts on Popery*, 152–158 ; *History of Popery*, 221–236 ; McGavin, *The Protestant*, I, 532–570 ; Hogan, *High and Low Mass*, 116–134 ; Edgar, *Variations of Popery*, 491–509 ; *On Purgatory and Infallibility* (New York, 1839).

48 *American Protestant Vindicator*, July 22, 1840, September 2, 1840 ; *Quarterly Review of the American Protestant Association*, IV (October, 1845) ; McGavin, *The Protestant*, II, 204–217 ; Nevins, *Thoughts on Popery*, 109–112 ; *Startling Facts for Native Americans*, 55 ; Edgar, *Variations of Popery*, 444–450 ; Gavazzi, *Lectures*, 239–240 ; *A Book of Tracts, Containing the Origin and Progress, Cruelties, Frauds, Superstitions, Miracles, Ceremonies, Idolatrous Customs of the Church of Rome; with a Succinct Account of the Rise and Progress of the Jesuits* (New York, 1856), 165–171.

49 New York *Observer*, January 8, 1831 ; *Downfall of Babylon*, Septem-

ber 19, 1835, April 2, 1836; *American Protestant Vindicator,* October 28, 1840; Philadelphia *Recorder,* February 12, 1831, March 26, 1831, February 5, 1831; *Congregationalist,* March 19, 1852; *National Protestant,* II (September, 1845); Nevins, *Thoughts on Popery,* 112–116; Hogan, *High and Low Mass,* 53–91; Edgar, *Variations of Popery,* 36–43; D'Aubigne, *History of the Great Reformation,* III, 18–21; Beecher, *Papal Conspiracy Exposed,* 135–136.

50 Nevins, *Thoughts on Popery,* 149.

51 *Protestant Magazine,* I (November, 1833).

52 New York *Observer,* May 1, 1824; Philadelphia *Recorder,* March 8, 1831; *Episcopal Recorder,* April 12, 1834; *Congregationalist,* April 18, 1851; *National Protestant,* I (February, 1845); Schmucker, *Discourse in Commemoration of the Glorious Reformation,* 10; Gavazzi, *Lectures,* 216–222.

53 Hogan, *High and Low Mass,* 54.

54 *Downfall of Babylon,* December 27, 1834; *Christian Watchman,* July 28, 1843; *American Protestant Vindicator,* May 24, 1837; *Congregationalist,* March 19, 1852; *Home Missionary,* XII (May, 1839); *American Protestant Magazine,* IV (October, 1848); Edgar, *Variations of Popery,* 44; Hogan, *High and Low Mass,* 61; Murray, *Romanism at Home,* 42–57; *The Ceremonies of the Holy Week in the Papal Chapel of the Vatican* (————, 1839); G. D. Emerlina, *Frauds of Papal Ecclesiastics; to which are added Illustrative Notes from Letters of Gilbert Burnett and Gavin's Master Key to Popery* (New York, 1835), 120–135.

55 *Protestant Episcopalian and Church Register,* I (September, 1830), IV (August, 1833); *National Protestant,* II (October, 1845), I (April, 1845); *Home Missionary,* VI (April, 1834); *American Protestant Magazine,* IV (June, 1848); Baltimore *Literary and Religious Magazine,* V (August, 1839); New York *Observer,* January 25, 1834, September 5, 1840; *Congregationalist,* October 11, 1850, March 14, 1851, March 21, 1851; *Episcopal Recorder,* April 30, 1836; *Downfall of Babylon,* March 19, 1836; Hogan, *Synopsis of Popery,* 161–166; Emerlina, *Frauds of Papal Ecclesiastics,* 5–7, 59–63; Giustiniani, *Papal Rome as It Is,* 250–262; *Book of Tracts,* 172–194; *Know Nothing Almanac,* 42; *Startling Facts for Native Americans,* 52–53; Murray, *Romanism at Home,* 93–115; Baird, *Sketches of Protestantism in Italy,* 253–254; Baxter, *Jesuit Juggling,* 184–187.

56 New York *American Republican,* August 30, 1844.

57 *Quarterly Review of the American Protestant Association,* II (April, 1845); *John Ronge, the Holy Coat of Treves and the New German Church* (New York, 1845); J. Marx, *History of the Robe of Jesus Christ, Preserved in the Cathedral at Treves* (New York, 1845).

58 *American Protestant Vindicator,* June 24, 1840.

59 Two examples of this type of computation will illustrate the general method. One writer found that the Latin name assumed by the Pope, Vicar General of God Upon Earth, when given its numerical equivalents, produced the number 666:

V I C A R I V S G E N E R A L I S D E I I N T E R R I S
5 I 100 I 5   50 I 500 I I   I

These figures added made the required sum. Another attempted to show that Pius, the then Pope, bore that number, by citing 2 Thess., ii, 8: "I say turn that wicked one upside down; and it is so." P I O 9, turned upside down, gave the number 666; the P and the 9 by some stretch of the imagination becoming two sixes, and the I and the O, by an even greater stretch of the imagination, being united to make the other six. Baltimore *Literary and Religious Magazine*, V (October, 1839) ; *American Protestant Magazine*, IV (October, 1848). An entire book, devoted to such computations, and reprinted from an English edition of 1701, was Robert Fleming, *An Extraordinary Discourse on the Rise and Fall of Papacy; or, the Pouring out of the Vials in the Revelation of St. John, Chapter xvi, containing Predictions Respecting the Revolutions of France, the Fate of its Monarch; the Decline of Papal Power* (New York, 1848).

⁶⁰ New York *Observer*, December 18, 1830, January 10, 1835, October 10, 1840, July 5, 1845 and ff.; *American Protestant Vindicator*, March 31, 1841; *Downfall of Babylon*, August 8, 1835; *Quarterly Review of the American Protestant Association*, I (April, 1844) ; *North American Protestant Magazine or Anti-Jesuit*, I (April, 1846) ; *American Protestant Almanac for 1841*, 21–27; *American and Foreign Christian Union*, II (December, 1851), IV (September, 1853) ; *Protestant Banner*, September 2, 1842; *American Text Book of Popery*, 36–41 ; *History of Popery*, 404–410; Allen, *Report on Popery*, 6–9; Beecher, *Papal Conspiracy Exposed*, 214–215; Spring, *Dissertation on the Rule of Faith*, 99; Gault, *Popery, the Man of Sin*, 17–33. In addition a number of books dealt specifically with this problem. Among these may be listed J. N. Campbell, *Papal Rome Identified with the Great Apostasy Predicted in the Scriptures. The Substance of three Discourses Addressed to the First Presbyterian Church in Albany* (Albany, 1838) ; W. C. Brownlee, *The Roman Catholic Religion Viewed in the Light of Prophecy and History; its Final Downfall and the Triumph of the Church of Christ* (New York, 1844) ; F. J. Berg, *The Great Apostasy Identified with Papal Rome; or, an Exposition of the Mystery of Iniquity and the Marks and Doom of Anti-Christ* (Philadelphia, 1847) ; *The Two Apocalyptic Beasts in St. John's Revelation Fully Explained with an Accurate Engraving* (New York, 1842).

⁶¹ *The Protestant*, January 30, 1830.

⁶² *Downfall of Babylon*, August 29, 1835, September 26, 1835, July 23, 1836; New York *Observer*, December 19, 1840; *Republic*, I (March, 1851) ; *American Protestant Almanac*, 2 ; Allen, *Report on Popery*, 13 ; Cheever, *Hierarchical Despotism*, 69–89; McGavin, *The Protestant*, I, 83 ; Frederic Shobere, *Persecutions of Popery; Historical Narratives of the Most Remarkable Persecutions Occasioned by the Intolerance of the Church of Rome* (New York, 1844), 179; Schmucker, *Discourse in Commemoration of the Glorious Reformation*, 97–98 ; White, *Practical and Internal Evidence*, 117–125 ; Hogan, *High and Low Mass*, 77 ; Pike, *Romanism*, 23–25 ; Murray, *Romanism at Home*, 38–39 ; Edgar, *Variations of Popery*, 152–177; Beecher, *Papal Conspiracy Exposed*, 28–50; Arthur B. Fuller, *Liberty versus Romanism. Two Discourses Delivered in the New North Church* (Boston, 1859), 11.

⁶³ *American and Foreign Christian Union*, II (September, 1851), II (November, 1851), IV (December, 1853) ; *Home Missionary*, XXIV (June, 1851), XXIV (December, 1851) ; New York *Observer*, October 25, 1835, January 16, 1841, June 3, 1848; *Downfall of Babylon*, November 14, 1835; *American Protestant Vindicator*. September 16, 1840; *Congregationalist*, May 24, 1849, June 1, 1849, January 31, 1851, March 12, 1852, June 18, 1852, Febru-

ary 11, 1853, June 10, 1853, November 18, 1853; American and Foreign Christian Union, *Fourth Annual Report*, 4–5; *The Crisis*, 75; Schmucker, *Discourse in Commemoration of the Glorious Reformation*, 78–79; *Know Nothing Almanac*, 27–29; Tisdale, *Controversy over Church Property*, 15, 45; *Startling Facts for Native Americans*, 57–58; Murray, *Decline of Popery*, 24–26; Murray, *Romanism at Home*, 29–30, 151–152; Carroll, *Great American Battle*, 172; Gonsalves, *Testimony of a Convert from the Church of Rome*, 41; Robertson, *American Party*, 16; *Protestant Annual*, 30; Clark, *Romanism in America*, 76–104; *Familiar Letters to Fitzpatrick*, 7–20; *Sons of the Sires*, 52–53; D. G. Parker, *A Compilation of Startling Facts; or, Romanism against Republicanism* (Chicago, 1856); Fuller, *Liberty versus Romanism*, 4–8; Brownlee, *Popery an Enemy to Civil and Religious Liberty*, 35–36, 83–98; *Our Country; or, the American Parlor Keepsake*, 92–103; White, *Practical and Internal Evidence*, 153–224; John N. McLeod, *Protestantism; the Parent and Guardian of Civil and Religious Liberty* (New York, 1843); Humphrey, *A Discourse on the Spiritual Power of the Roman Catholic Clergy*, 4–20; *The Wide Awake Gift and Know Nothing Token*, 68–70; Dwight, *The Roman Republic of 1849*, 225–226; Beecher, *Papal Conspiracy Exposed*, 13–15; William L. Hubbell, *The Birth, Growth, Position and Perils of the American Republic; and the Duties of its Citizens* (Waterbury, Connecticut, 1856), 10–22; Robert C. Grundy, *The Temporal Powers of the Pope Dangerous to the Religious and Civil Liberties of the American Republic* (Maysville, Kentucky, 1855), 11; Gavazzi, *Lectures*, 206–207; *Sam; or, the History of a Mystery*, 533.

64 *Wide Awake Gift and Know Nothing Token*, 70.

65 Allen, *Report on Popery*, 24–25.

66 Nearly every book, pamphlet, or newspaper directed against Catholicism devoted some attention to the Inquisition and to papal cruelty. The references are too numerous to be cited.

67 Edgar, *Variations of Popery*, 262.

68 *Episcopal Recorder*, September 21, 1833; *Christian Watchman*, August 4, 1843; New York *Observer*, August 9, 1834, November 7, 1835, November 12, 1842, May 6, 1843, July 15, 1852; *Congregationalist*, August 5, 1853; *American Protestant Vindicator*, November 25, 1840; *Home Missionary*, XXV (November, 1852); *North American Protestant Magazine or Anti-Jesuit*, I (April, 1846); *American Protestant Magazine*, I (January, 1846), IV (August, 1848); *American and Foreign Christian Union*, II (October, 1851); *Quarterly Review of the American Protestant Association*, II (April, 1845); Kalley, *Persecution in Madeira in the Nineteenth Century; The Protestant Exiles of Zillerthal; their Persecution and Expatriation on Separating from the Church of Rome and Embracing the Reformed Faith* (New York, 1844); Tisdale, *Know Nothing Almanac*, 35–36; *Sons of the Sires*, 121–125; *Pope or President*, 124–125, 140–158; Gavazzi, *Lectures*, 370; Pierce Connelly, *Reasons for Abjuring Allegiance to the See of Rome* (London, 1852), 30; *Footprints of Popery; or, Places where Martyrs Have Suffered* (Boston, 1846), 190–191; Frederick Saunders and Thomas B. Thorpe, *A Voice to America; or, the Model Republic, its Glory and its Fall* (New York, 1855), 179–189. An enterprising New York showman capitalized on the interest in the Inquisition by exhibiting a model Inquisitorial building depicting the tortures commonly employed. New York *Observer*, December 10, 1842.

69 *The Protestant*, March 6, 1830, February 11, 1832; *Downfall of Babylon*,

March 14, 1835, June 13, 1835; New York *Observer*, August 27, 1836, March 12, 1842; *Congregationalist*, March 29, 1850; *American Protestant Magazine*, II (June, 1846), II (September, 1846); *Home Missionary*, VI (April, 1834); Baltimore *Literary and Religious Magazine*, VI (February, 1840), VII (August, 1841); American Protestant Society, *Fourth Annual Report*, 10; American Home Missionary Society, *Twenty Seventh Annual Report*, 124–125; *Protestant Annual*, 200–204.

70 This assertion was made by the Baltimore Provincial Council, as well as by individual Catholic writers and speakers. *Congregationalist*, June 28, 1850; *Pilot*, February 10, 1855; *Freeman's Journal*, August 3, 1844; Brownson. *Works*, XVIII, 345; *Letter of an Adopted Catholic Addressed to the President of the Kentucky Democratic Association of Washington City, on Temporal Allegiance to the Pope, and the Relations of the Catholic Church and Catholics, both Native and Adopted, to the System of Domestic Slavery and its Agitation in the United States* (Washington, 1856), 2–5. These claims were substantiated by official papal decrees of these years in which Pius IX specifically denied any temporal power for himself or his successors. These are conveniently collected in *The Encyclical Letter of Pope Pius IX and the Syllabus of Modern Errors*, dated December 8, 1864 (——————), 10–12.

71 *The Protestant*, September 18, 1830; *Western Christian Advocate*, December 19, 1834; *American Protestant Vindicator*, November 12, 1834; *Congregationalist*, July 13, 1849, November 1, 1850; *National Protestant* I (December, 1844); *The Crisis*, 73–74; *American Text Book of Popery*, 166–178; Pond, *No Fellowship with Romanism*, 154–164; Cheever, *Hierarchical Despotism*, 179–180; Saunders, *Voice to America*, 215–228; *Protestant Annual*, 50–51; Edgar, *Variations of Popery*, 210-238; Robertson, *American Party*, 16; *Origin, Principles and Purposes of the American Party*, 31–35; Beecher, *Papal Conspiracy Exposed*, 92–109; Gavazzi, *Lectures*, 131; Lipscomb, *Our Country*, 66–74; Chapman, *Americanism versus Romanism*, 68–121; Brownlee, *Popery, an Enemy to Civil and Religious Liberty*, 138–157; Murray, *Decline of Popery*, 10–16; *Startling Facts for Native Americans*, 49; Connelly, *Reasons for Abjuring Allegiance to the See of Rome*, 28–30; Carroll, *Great American Battle*, 196–305, 319–323; *Papal Diplomacy and the Bull "In Coena Domini"* (London, 1848), 1–63; *False Claims of the Pope* (New York, 1842); Pierre C. P. Daunou, *Outline of the History of the Court of Rome and of the Temporal Power of the Popes* (Philadelphia, 1837); John C. Pitrot, *Review of the Speech of Hon. J. R. Chandler of Pennsylvania on the Political Power of the Pope* (Boston, 1855), 1–72.

72 *Wide Awake Gift and Know Nothing Token*, 67.

73 Sparry was arrested in Spottsville in 1843. *Protestant Banner*, November 23, 1843. The book that he was selling was his *Extracts from the Theological Works of Peter Dens on the Nature of Confession and the Obligation of the Seal* (New York, 1843). Nativists asserted that Peter Dens' books were used in Catholic schools, yet were so immoral that a Protestant minister could be arrested for selling one openly.

74 Written by Theodore Dwight and published in New York in 1836.

75 Written by Andrew B. Cross and published at Baltimore in 1854. The work first appeared as a series of letters in the Baltimore *Clipper*.

76 New York, 1836. This work was evidently sponsored by Samuel B.

Smith, for most of it was published serially in his *Downfall of Babylon*, April 2, 1835 ff. Its sales as a book were reputedly so large that a second edition was required only a few weeks after the first. *Downfall of Babylon*, June 11, 1836.

[77] Culbertson, *Rosamond*, 188–189.

[78] *American Protestant Vindicator*, October 26, 1836.

[79] *American Protestant Vindicator*, October 29, 1834, July 8, 1840, September 30, 1840; *Congregationalist*, December 8, 1854, May 25, 1855, *National Protestant*, II (May, 1845), II (July, 1845), II (August, 1845); Hogan, *Auricular Confession and Popish Nunneries*, 191; Cheever, *Hierarchical Despotism*, 116–119; Emerlina, *Frauds of Papal Ecclesiastics*, 39; Schmucker, *Discourse in Commemoration of the Glorious Reformation*, 48–49; Samuel B. Smith, *Synopsis of the Moral Theology of the Church of Rome from the Works of Saint Ligori* (New York, 1836), 160; Elizabeth, *Second Causes; or, Up and Be Doing*, 191–193; Webber, *Sam; or, the History of a Mystery*, 527; Pitrot, *Americans Warned of Jesuitism*, 114–116; Beecher, *Papal Conspiracy Exposed*, 110–124; Gavazzi, *Lectures*, 296; Baird, *Sketches of Protestantism in Italy*, 253–254; Edgar, *Variations of Popery*, 277; Connelly, *Reasons for Abjuring Allegiance to the See of Rome*, 31; *Know Nothing Almanac*, 38–42; *Protestant Annual*, 13–18.

[80] *Episcopal Recorder*, July 6, 1833; New York *Observer*, December 25, 1830, February 16, 1854; *National Protestant*, II (July, 1845); *Quarterly Review of the American Protestant Association*, III (January, 1845), III (July, 1845); Pond, *No Fellowship with Romanism*, 135–136; Schmucker, *Discourse in Commemoration of the Glorious Reformation*, 41–42; Sinclair, *Shetland and the Shetlanders*, 35; Hogan, *Synopsis of Popery*, 173–176.

[81] New York *Observer*, December 5, 1840, March 18, 1852; *American Protestant Vindicator*, January 6, 1841, July 28, 1841; *Downfall of Babylon*, April 18, 1835; Hogan, *Auricular Confession and Popish Nunneries*, 55–57; Pond, *No Fellowship with Romanism*, 147–149; Ricci, *Female Convents*, 67; Beecher, *Papal Conspiracy Exposed*, 419.

[82] *American and Foreign Christian Union*, III (April, 1852), IV (May, 1853); Hogan, *Auricular Confession and Popish Nunneries*, 168; Cheever, *Hierarchical Despotism*, 189; Gavazzi, *Lectures*, 240–241; Baird, *Sketches of Protestantism in Italy*, 255; *Pope or President*, 61–69; *Startling Facts for Native Americans*, 60–61; *Protestant Almanac*, 170; *American Protestant Vindicator*, April 14, 1841, December 15, 1841; *Downfall of Babylon*, April 2, 1836.

[83] *Pope or President*, 68–69.

[84] Hogan, *Auricular Confession and Popish Nunneries*, 67.

[85] *Downfall of Babylon*, April 4, 1835, April 11, 1835; *American Protestant Vindicator*, September 16, 1840; New York *Observer*, July 15, 1852; Hogan, *Auricular Confession and Popish Nunneries*, 64–67; Giustiniani, *Intrigues of Jesuitism*, 66; Gavazzi, *Lectures*, 225–237; *Pope or President*, 37, 69; Beecher, *Papal Conspiracy Exposed*, 172–185; Bunkley, *Testimony of an Escaped Novice*, 26; Berg, *The Confessional;* M. Michelet, *Spiritual Direction and Auricular Confession* (Philadelphia, 1845); *Popery Exposed; or, the Secrets and Privacy of the Confessional Unmasked* (New York, 1845).

[86] Emerlina, *Frauds of Papal Ecclesiastics*, 139; Pond, *No Fellowship with Romanism*, 132–133; *American Text Book of Popery*, 330–336; Schmucker,

Discourse in Commemoration of the Glorious Reformation, 60–62; *Supplement to Six Months in a Convent,* 236–237; Hogan, *Synopsis of Popery,* 170–171; *Pope or President,* 48; Pepin, *A Narrative of the Life and Experiences of Francois Pepin,* 27; *American and Foreign Christian Union,* I (January, 1850); *Congregationalist,* September 14, 1849.

[87] Hogan, *Auricular Confession and Popish Nunneries,* 33–34.

[88] *Downfall of Babylon,* March 21, 1834, December 20, 1834; *American Protestant Vindicator,* October 14, 1835; *Episcopal Recorder,* September 14, 1833, February 15, 1834; New York *Observer,* February 3, 1844, May 25, 1844; Baltimore *Literary and Religious Magazine,* IV (April, 1838), IV (June, 1838); *National Protestant,* II (May, 1845), II (July, 1845); *Congregationalist,* September 21, 1849, November 29, 1850, January 12, 1855; Schmucker, *Discourse in Commemoration of the Glorious Reformation,* 37; *American Text Book of Popery,* 300–307; *Pope Alexander VI and his Son, Caesar Borgia* (Philadelphia, 1844); Hogan, *Auricular Confession and Popish Nunneries,* 48–60; Emerlina, *Frauds of Papal Ecclesiastics,* 138–146; White, *Practical and Internal Evidence,* 125–162; Baxter, *Jesuit Juggling,* 210–226; *Startling Facts for Native Americans,* 75–78; Cross, *Priest's Prisons for Women,* 25–30; Chapman, *Americanism versus Romanism,* 266–267; Connelly, *Reasons for Abjuring Allegiance to the See of Rome,* 22; *Know Nothing Almanac,* 26; Edgar, *Variations of Popery,* 108–118, 537–572; Hogan, *Synopsis of Popery,* 126–127; *Protestant Annual,* 211–214; *Book of Tracts,* 8–50; Beecher, *Papal Conspiracy Exposed,* 149–153; D'Aubigne, *History of the Great Reformation,* I, 25–27; Murray, *Romanism at Home,* 164–165; Bunkley, *Testimony of an Escaped Novice,* 139; *Pope or President,* 41–48; Pitrot, *Americans Warned of Jesuitism,* 142–144; Giustiniani, *Papal Rome as It Is,* 185–194.

[89] *Downfall of Babylon,* March 5, 1836.

[90] *Ibid.,* October 24, 1835; *National Protestant,* II (May, 1845); Beecher, *Papal Conspiracy Exposed,* 155–165; Hogan, *Auricular Confession and Popish Nunneries,* 46–47; *Pope or President,* 45.

[91] *American Protestant Vindicator,* October 28, 1840; *Priestcraft Exposed,* October 1, 1834; *Downfall of Babylon,* May 16, 1835; New York *Observer,* January 27, 1849; *Congregationalist,* January 4, 1850, January 9, 1852, July 6, 1855; *American and Foreign Christian Union,* I (September, 1850); *National Protestant,* III (December, 1845); *American Protestant Magazine,* IV (July, 1848); *Southern Presbyterian Review,* II (December, 1848); *Home Missionary,* XIX (January, 1847), XXI (March, 1853); Emerlina, *Frauds of Papal Ecclesiastics,* 150–154; Hogan, *Synopsis of Popery,* 62–63; Ricci, *Female Convents,* xvii; Brownlee, *Popery an Enemy to Civil and Religious Liberty,* 49–51; *Romanism Incompatible with Republican Institutions,* 76–78; Beecher, *Papal Conspiracy Exposed,* 145–146; Carroll, *Great American Battle,* 172–173; Murray, *Romanism at Home,* 148; Gavazzi. *Lectures,* 85–86; Derby, *The Catholics,* 9–10; Gault, *Popery, the Man of Sin,* 417–419; Farrenc, *Carlotina,* vi; *Sons of the Sires,* 51; Clark, *Romanism in America,* 99–103; Saunders, *Voice to America,* 345–362; Murray, *Letters to Hughes, First Series,* 45–52; William Sparrow, *Romanism and Protestantism Compared as to their Temporal Influence* (Alexandria, Virginia, 1852), 6–8; Napoleon Roussell, *Catholic and Protestant Nations Compared in their*

Threefold Relations to Wealth, Knowledge and Morality (Boston, 1855). Catholic rebuttal was contained not only in the Catholic press but also in such books as James Balmes, *Protestantism and Catholicity Compared in their Effects on the Civilization of Europe* (Baltimore, 1851).

⁹² *Spirit of '76*, August 4, 1835; New York *Observer,* November 26, 1836; Hogan, *Auricular Confession and Popish Nunneries,* 59–63; Emerlina, *Frauds of Papal Ecclesiastics,* 149; Smith, *Synopsis of the Moral Theology of Saint Ligori,* 231–232; Schmucker, *Discourse in Commemoration of the Glorious Reformation,* 53; *Protestant Annual,* 63; Baird, *Sketches of Protestantism in Italy,* 244; Murray, *Romanism at Home,* 78–79; Samuel P. Day, *Monastic Institutions; their Origin, Progress, Nature and Tendency* (Dublin, 1844), x–xi; Dwight, *Open Convents,* 144–156; *Lorette. The History of Louise, Daughter of a Canadian Nun: Exhibiting the Interior of Female Convents* (New York, 1833), 2–214; *Christian Watchman,* August 15, 1836; Baltimore *Literary and Religious Magazine,* V (October, 1839); Hogan, *Synopsis of Popery,* 132; Giustiniani, *Intrigues of Jesuitism,* 54; Dwight, *Roman Republic of 1849,* 210-211; Connelly, *Reasons for Abjuring Allegiance to the See of Rome,* 7; Gavazzi, *Lectures,* 91; *The Escaped Nun,* 263; Carroll, *Great American Battle,* 316; *Pope or President,* 108–110.

⁹³ A. McMurray, *Awful Disclosures! Murders Exposed! Downfall of Popery! Death Bed Confession! Death Bed Confession and Renunciation of the Right Rev. Bishop McMurray, Bishop of the St. Mary's Roman Catholic Church, Montreal, Canada* (Buffalo, 1845), 27.

⁹⁴ *American Protestant Vindicator,* July 28, 1841, September 28, 1841; New York *Observer,* May 28, 1842, June 1, 1842, June 29, 1854, July 6, 1854; *Congregationalist,* November 22, 1850; *Freeman's Journal,* July 23, 1842, July 15, 1854; Shea, *History of the Catholic Church,* III, 654.

⁹⁵ *Wide Awake Gift and Know Nothing Token,* 98.

⁹⁶ Brownson, *Life of O. A. Brownson,* II, 21.

XV

The Rise of Know-Nothingism
1850-1854

THE forces which had, for half a century, been breeding antagonism toward the foreigner and Catholic took political form in the early 1850's with the rise of the American, or Know-Nothing, party. Virtually unheard of until 1854, this singular organization enjoyed phenomenal success and for a time seemed destined to endure as a permanent addition to the parties of the United States. But by 1856 its meteoric career was ended, its unity sacrificed on the altar of sectionalism, and its popular appeal dissipated in the clashing interests from which grew a civil war.

The origins of the party which enjoyed this spectacular rise and fall are shrouded in mystery.[1] If its enthusiastic members are to be believed, George Washington was the first Know-Nothing and the party's ancestors included the Federalists and the nativistic organizations of the 1840's.[2] Less romantic, but more probable, is the explanation that the party was hatched in the mind of Charles B. Allen of New York, who, in 1849, gave it a nucleus by forming a secret patriotic society known as the Order of the Star-Spangled Banner.[3] From this feeble beginning the whole giant structure of the Know-Nothing party was to grow.

Just what led Charles Allen to form this lodge will probably never be known. Doubtless he was familiar with both the popular appeal of nativism and the charm of a secret society. Perhaps he realized that political nativism, dormant since the collapse of the Native American party several years before, was due for a vigorous revival. Certainly he knew that all over New York men were forming nativistic clubs and societies and that popular interest in Catholicism and immigration was greater than at any time since 1844.[4] Any patriotic organization with sufficiently popular objectives could count on a reasonable success.

The Order of the Star-Spangled Banner, as originally conceived by Allen, was not to enter the political arena directly, but was to support the more nativistically inclined among the nominees of existing parties, hoping in this way to insure the election of men hostile to foreign and Catholic influence.[5] There was nothing either startling or new in this plan, and for two years the order remained unimportant, never boasting a membership of more than thirty and having no influence whatsoever even in local politics. Its rise began in April, 1852, when Allen relinquished his control to James W. Barker, a prominent dry goods merchant with a gift for organization. Under Barker's leadership expansion went on rapidly and within four months more than a thousand members were enrolled and its influence was felt in the municipal elections of 1852. At this time the order was still completely unknown, so efficiently had its secrets been guarded, and although the press was conscious of the working of some hidden political force, this was blamed on the Order of United Americans.[6]

This first success came at a singularly opportune time. The presidential election of that year placed Franklin Pierce, a Democrat, in office, and both Whigs and nativists agreed that the foreign-born vote was largely responsible for his success.[7] Smarting under this defeat, many Whigs were ready to cast their lot with any nativistic party which would allow them revenge. Here was an opportunity for the Order of the Star-Spangled Banner—but an opportunity of which it was ill-equipped to take advantage. Its organization was still primarily local, for while

a State Wigwam had been established to encourage the founding
of branches in New York state, this body had neither the authority nor the ability to extend the order throughout the union. The
few chapters which existed outside the state had been established
by former members of the New York locals who, moving elsewhere, simply duplicated in their new situation the organization
with which they were familiar. By the close of 1853 branches
had been formed in New Jersey, Maryland, Connecticut, Massachusetts, and Ohio, but no real bond held them together other
than the common interest of their members in political nativism.[8]
Any central governing body which would have given them cohe-
sion was lacking.

The greatest obstacle in the path of an effective national organization was a schism within the New York society. There a
faction became discontented with the inefficient operation of the
State Wigwam and in December, 1853, set up a rival Grand
Council which, like the Wigwam, made a pretense of controlling
the local chapters throughout the state. Both of these bodies
issued charters and dissipated more energy in factional disputes
than in founding new branches.[9] Harmony was essential for
expansion, and the state leaders, realizing this, finally managed
to heal their differences in May, 1854. They did this by combining the Grand Council and the State Wigwam into a single
governing body to be known as the Grand Council for the State
of New York.

New York members of the Order of the Star-Spangled Banner, with their own house in order, were now ready to give attention to a national organization. Even before their local differences
were entirely settled they sent out a call for a national convention
to meet on May 14, 1854, in New York City. The small attendance did not justify any constructive steps, and this first convention adjourned after issuing an invitation for a second meeting
to be held in New York in June, 1854. This time delegates from
thirteen states were present, and it was possible to devise and

adopt a governmental system to which the order adhered throughout its existence.[10]

A federal system of organization was employed. At the basis of the structure were the Local, or District, Councils, each of which existed by authority of a charter granted by the central governing body of the state in which it was located. These local councils had a large degree of self-government, choosing their own officers, enacting their own by-laws, and initiating their own members. Above them were the City or County Councils, made up of one delegate from each of the District Councils. Their function was to supervise the political activity of the District Councils and select the county or city candidates which the order was to support.

These local units were under the control of a state Grand Council, made up of three delegates from each District Council, and governed by a Grand-President and other elective officials. The Grand-President not only supervised the political activities of the order in the state; he was also responsible for the expansion of the society. To this end he appointed deputies in each district to recruit new local councils and keep up enthusiasm in the old. The political candidates whom the order backed in state elections were chosen by the Grand Council.

At the top of this elaborate pyramid was the National Council, composed of seven delegates from each Grand Council and two from each territory in which the order was established. This National Council exercised a delegated authority vested in it through the constitution of the order and was limited in its actions by that constitution. It was authorized to decide all matters pertaining to national politics, including the nomination of the order's candidates for the presidency and vice presidency of the United States, fix the ritual which the state and local councils were to follow, punish any dereliction of duty on the part of members, and provide for the general welfare of the organization. The National Council chose its own officers by ballot and these officers, particularly the president, were given a large amount of power over state and district councils.

This complex governmental system played an important part in the rapid expansion of the Order of the Star-Spangled Banner. Friction was done away with by the council system, for the local chapters were virtually independent in selecting their candidates for office, the state councils were equally unmolested in regulating state politics and the National Council enjoyed a comparable position for the nation as a whole. Managers of the order had actually erected an efficient, nation-wide political machine with an unusual solidarity and a minimum of friction.

No less important than this organization in accounting for the success of the Order of the Star-Spangled Banner was the ritual which it adopted and the garb of secrecy with which it was clothed. These devices were employed partly to allow the members to escape the stigma which the Philadelphia riots had fastened on nativistic political organizations and partly because fraternal societies and the Order of United Americans had demonstrated their wide appeal. Grips, passwords, signs, phrases of recognition, signals of distress, and other well-tested formulæ were successfully used by the order during its formative years and probably lured many curious Americans into its ranks.[11]

The ritual provided for initiation into two degrees of membership.[12] To be eligible for the first degree, a candidate had to assure the order that he was of proper age, that he had been born in the United States, that his parents were Protestants, and that he was not married to a Roman Catholic. This first obstacle passed, the objects of the order were then explained to the candidate: "Are you," he was asked, "willing to use your influence and vote only for native-born American citizens for all offices of honor, trust or profit in the gift of the people, the exclusion of all foreigners and Roman Catholics in particular, and without regard to party predilections?" If the candidate could subscribe to these objectives, he was required to swear renunciation of all other party allegiance, to abide by the will of the party in supporting nominees for office, and to work persistently for a change in the naturalization laws.

Having sworn allegiance to the order, the candidate was entrusted with the secrets which lent it so much charm. The elaborate ceremony by which each member gained admission to a lodge meeting was explained, the passwords were given him, together with the sign of recognition, the grip, the challenges, and the warnings which might be issued. He was told that meetings were to be announced by the distribution of heart-shaped bits of white paper, and that if danger threatened, these were to be red. He was made acquainted with the cry of distress, cautioned that it must be used only rarely, and instructed as to his procedure when that cry was heard. He was taught to make the sign of caution by drawing his thumb and forefinger across his eyes when any member was speaking too boldly. Such delightful secrets as these made many a candidate glad that he had decided to cast his lot with the order.

Holders of the second degree were eligible both for office within the Order of the Star-Spangled Banner and to represent it as nominees in regular political contests; the ritual by which they were initiated and their instructions varied accordingly. They were told "that, if it may be done legally, you will, when elected or appointed to any official station conferring on you the power to do so, remove all foreigners, aliens, or Roman Catholics from office or place, and that you will in no case appoint such to any office or place in your gift." The president of the local lodge, in addressing those newly admitted to the second degree, urged them to train the youth of the land in truly American principles and "above all else, keep alive in their bosoms the memory, the maxims and the deathless example of our illustrious Washington."

The members who gloried in this elaborate ritual were united by two major principles: opposition to the foreigner and opposition to the Catholic. This was clearly shown by the section of the constitution of the National Council which dealt with the order's objectives:

The object of this organization shall be to protect every American citizen in the legal and proper exercise of all his civil and religious rights and privileges; to resist the insidious policy of the Church of Rome, and all other foreign influence against our republican institutions in all lawful ways; to place in all offices of honor, trust, or profit, in the gift of the people, or by appointment, none but native-born Protestant citizens, and to protect, preserve, and uphold the Union of these states and the Constitution of the same.[13]

Thus, in the Order of the Star-Spangled Banner, the principles advocated by nativists for half a century came into full fruition.

Although both the order and the party into which it grew professed vehement enmity for immigrants, the motive behind the whole Know-Nothing movement was hatred of Catholicism. Official party pronouncements and opinions of members obviously reflected far more fear of the Papist than of the foreigner. It was reported at the time that several Protestant aliens who were zealous against Popery were members of the order and certainly official spokesmen for the party openly welcomed foreign-born Protestants.[14] But with Catholics there was no such equivocation. Every Know-Nothing firmly believed that Papists should be barred from every office in the national, state and local governments and, if possible, driven back to the priest-ridden lands from whence they had come. The Know-Nothing party was really a No-Popery party, despite all the gloss and fine phrases in its pronouncements.

This fact alone accounts for its unity, for on more material matters the Know-Nothings were as divided as other political organizations in that era of sectional strife. American campaign pamphlets issued in the north and south read like those of entirely different parties.[15] Southern Know-Nothings wanted territorial expansion into regions where cotton culture could spread; northern Know-Nothings were opposed. Southerners favored a low tariff; northerners believed that American labor should be protected from foreign competition by high tariff barriers. The northerners in the party worked consistently for a homestead bill; southerners replied that the public domain should not be given away to every idler. Northern nativists wanted governmental aid for internal improvements; southern nativists were heartily opposed. If members of the party had been able to express themselves on slavery, they would have shown the same division which existed among Democrats or Whigs. Only one force held members of the Know-Nothing party together, and that was their hatred for the Catholic church.

With this one bond of unity—something that the major parties lacked—the Know-Nothings swept to a series of political triumphs which startled the nation. The appearance of the party was spectacular. The first rumor that some new secret force was operating in politics began to spread in the autumn of 1853 when candidates who had been defeated for local offices let it be known that a dread nativistic society had conspired against them,[16] but as late as March, 1854, the Order of United Americans was believed to be responsible.[17] The spring elections of 1854 saw the order make its first dramatic bid for power. Its members decided on their own candidates and made their way to the polls to vote accordingly, often writing in the names of men who had not been nominated. The result was phenomenal. Whole tickets not even on the ballots were carried into office. Men who were unopposed for election and who had been conceded victory found themselves defeated by some unknown Know-Nothing. Even though the opposition parties were caught by surprise and failed to make their best showing, intelligent observers realized that here was a new political force that must be reckoned with.[18]

Through the summer of 1854 the Know-Nothings, elated by these victories, continued to increase with amazing rapidity.

Their enemies were helpless; they could not strike back, for they did not even know the name of the party which had suddenly become such a political force.[19] Everyone seemed anxious to support and popularize this growing nativistic organization. "Know-Nothing Candy" was sold, together with "Know-Nothing Tea" and "Know-Nothing Toothpicks." A clipper ship launched in New York in 1854 was christened *The Know Nothing*. Omnibuses and stage coaches were given this popular name by operators anxious to attract customers.[20] A poem was widely sold under the same title and nativistic books began to appear with the large letters "K. N." printed on their jackets.[21] The Know-Nothings had become the rage of the day, and members of the organization looked forward with confidence to the fall elections of 1854.

The anticipation with which the party faced its first major political contest was justified by the results. It carried Massachusetts and Delaware and, through a combination with the Whigs, Pennsylvania. Throughout the northern and border states it showed surprising strength, for many of the Republican and anti-Nebraska Democrats placed in office were Know-Nothings. About seventy-five congressmen were sent to Washington pledged to carry the nation into a war against the Pope and his minions. Massachusetts was the scene of the party's greatest victories; there the governor and all state officers were Know-Nothings, the state Senate was made up entirely of representatives of this party, and the state House of Representatives was composed of one Whig, one Free Soiler and 376 Know-Nothings.[22]

These victories were repeated a year later. Rhode Island, New Hampshire, and Connecticut were added to Massachusetts as Know-Nothing states in New England. Among the border states Maryland and Kentucky went solidly Know-Nothing, while Tennessee only held to the Democratic standard by a small majority. In New York, Pennsylvania, and California, state officers elected were for the most part adherents of this new party. In the south the invasion of Know-Nothing lodges had been delayed until the spring and summer of 1854, yet so rapidly was the region organized that the party very nearly carried Virginia, Georgia, Alabama, Mississippi, and Louisiana and did elect minor officials in Texas. In Louisiana and the southern states east of the Mississippi the total Know-Nothing vote was only 16,000 less than that given its opponents. In the northwest the American party showed less strength, due to the large number of foreign-born there, but in Wisconsin it held a balance of power between Republicans and Democrats and helped place the Republican candidate in office.[23]

In view of these decisive victories, it is not surprising that the Know-Nothings confidently expected to place their candidate in the White House in 1856. This view was reluctantly shared by many impartial observers and even by the party's avowed enemies. The New York *Herald* was convinced that the Americans would carry Massachusetts, Rhode Island, Maine, Connecticut, New York, New Jersey, Pennsylvania, Delaware, Louisiana, and Ohio in the presidential election. This would give them 140 of the 149 electoral votes necessary for success. The *Herald* gloomily predicted that the remaining nine votes would probably be forthcoming.[24] Henry Wilson estimated that the Know-Nothings could command 1,250,000 popular votes, enough to make them a dangerous enemy in the election and probably enough to give them victory.[25] Even such Catholic papers as the Boston *Pilot* accepted the inevitability of a Know-Nothing president after 1856.[26]

The rise of the Know-Nothing party effected a change of major importance in the American political scene. The forces responsible deserve detailed examination. Why did hundreds of thousands of Americans desert the well-established parties and support this intolerant organization which promised war on Catholics and foreigners? Three forces were operating that together accounted for the rise of Know-Nothingism: the confusion of party alignments, the slavery controversy, and the growth of a sincere nativistic sentiment. Alone no one of these forces was sufficient to bring Know-Nothing success; all three were necessary before political nativism could become important.

The confusion that swept over the American political parties between 1852 and 1860 is well known. Voters who marched to the polls in 1854 and 1855 were befuddled by a welter of names and issues with literally dozens of parties in the field: Democratic, Know-Nothing, Anti-Nebraska, People's, Free Soil, Fusion, Hard Democratic, Soft Democratic, Temperance, Rum-Democrats, Anti-Maine-Law Democrats, Union Maine Law, Whig, Adopted Citizen, Republican, and even Know-Something. In one election in Connecticut twenty-three different parties were represented among the candidates, and this situation was not unusual.[27] The Know-Nothings naturally profited from this jumble. Their unity, which might have meant little under ordinary conditions, meant much when the opposition was so completely scattered. In many instances the party was successful, not because it controlled a majority of votes cast, but because those voting against Know-Nothings scattered their strength among a dozen candidates and parties.

More important than this confusion of party alignment in explaining the success of the Know-Nothings was the growing importance of the slavery question. The passage of the Kansas-Nebraska act in 1854 plunged the nation into a controversy that was only to be settled by a civil war. The older parties were unable to withstand this tempest; the Whigs, inherently the weaker, died a speedy death, and Democratic support of popular sovereignty lost that party many of its northern members. Northern Whigs and Democrats and southern Whigs were left stranded with no party allegiance, for many of them refused to support either the proslavery Democratic party or the antislavery Republican party that had been born of the struggle. They drifted naturally into the Know-Nothing party, which was not only neutral on the vital issue of slavery but loudly promised to preserve the union.[28]

Equally influential in swinging support to the Know-Nothing party was the nativistic sentiment which had been moulded so carefully by a generation of propagandists. This sentiment was at its height in the early 1850's. The upper classes had been won to the cause by the American Protestant Society, the American and Foreign Christian Union, and the churches; they were convinced that war against Rome was a new crusade necessary to protect their Bible and their faith. The lower classes had been recruited by inflammatory lecturers and street preachers, and by a persistent and effective propaganda. They had been taught that their economic, social, and political welfare would be endangered through continued foreign immigration. These beliefs had been effectively insinuated into every level of society.

The Compromise of 1850, settling the slavery problem apparently for all time, allowed these sentiments to find political expression. People no longer worried about expansion or the Wilmot Proviso or the status of slaves in the territories. They were a little "tired of talk about rum and talk about niggers." [29] What was more natural than that they should turn to the Know-Nothing party with a sense of relief? It offered them an opportunity to show their enmity to the Pope, and rebuff the Papists and aliens who threatened their country. Thousands of people joined the Know-Nothing party in all sincerity, not because they did not know where to turn concerning slavery, but because they believed that their land needed protection from foreign foes.

These three forces, all operating at the time, together accounted for the success of Know-Nothingism. But the party's victories in 1854 and 1855 were not nation-wide. It enjoyed its greatest triumphs in the northeast and the border states, was nearly successful in the south, and showed little strength in the middle west. Obviously sectional influences were at work and the true reasons for Know-Nothing success can only be found by a survey of the economic, social, and political conditions in the regions where it met victory and defeat.

In the south the few Catholics and immigrants who might have aroused apprehension were concentrated in either Louisiana or Maryland. (See maps, pp. 400–401.) Even in those states Catholics had been established so long that no one could seriously suspect them of ultramontanism or of designs on their country, and the weight of the alien burden was scarcely felt outside of New Orleans and a few other coastal cities. Nevertheless the rural conditions and isolated settlements made southerners naturally suspicious of new forces and they were ready to believe the dire tales of No-Popery writers and the awful warnings of ministers. Many whose knowledge of Catholicism was gained solely from propagandists feared that religion as an individual fears the dark—Romanism to them was something unknown yet horrible. Immigrants were objected to on more tangible grounds. Those who remained in the south lacked either the ambition or the resources to reach northern farms and greatly increased the region's pauper burden. More resentment was aroused by the belief that all aliens were abolitionists—for southerners failed to distinguish between the Irish and Germans in this respect— and that the northern states were being peopled by hordes hostile to southern institutions. There they would increase the balance of power against the south, give the north eventual legislative control of the nation, and in some not too distant future lead the attack on southern domestic institutions. Particularly alarming was the fact that so many immigrants settled in the upper Mississippi valley which still hung in the balance between north and south. The freedom-loving foreigners might drive that neutral section into the arms of the north. Many southerners joined the Know-Nothing party to voice these objections to Catholics and aliens.

The American party, as the Know-Nothings were officially

called, also gained southern support by its compromising attitude toward slavery. The large landholders of the Black Belt and Mississippi Flood Plains, who were interested more in protecting existing property rights than in extending slavery into new areas, had been left without a haven when the Whig party expired and the Democratic party embraced the doctrine of popular sovereignty. Southern Know-Nothing leaders realized this and constantly sought to attract this group, drafting party platforms and pronouncements which embodied the same conservative principles formerly employed by the Whigs.[30] They were only partially successful in this aim. An analysis of the elections from 1848 to 1860 (see maps, pp. 402–406) shows little correlation in the lower south between the Whig areas of 1848 and 1852, the Constitutional Union areas of 1860, and the Know-Nothing areas in the state elections of 1855 and the presidential election of 1856. Despite this, Know-Nothing strength was concentrated in the rich soil regions and probably represented conservative sentiment. In North Carolina the traditional Whig regions swung almost solidly into the ranks of the American party.

It can safely be assumed, then, that southern Know-Nothings were motivated both by nativistic sentiments and by a desire to compromise the troublesome slavery question. If they had been interested in compromise alone, there would have been more correlation between the areas supporting Bell in 1860 and those carried by Know-Nothing candidates in 1855 or 1856. If they had been swept away purely by the No-Popery crusade, the American party vote would not have been concentrated in the rich soil regions but would have extended into the back country where the illiterate population was particularly susceptible to the arguments of nativists. Obviously neither factor alone explains Know-Nothing success in the south. Both contributed to give that party its near victories.

The triumphant course of Know-Nothingism in the border states, on the other hand, was probably due more to the ramifications of the slavery issue than to the work of anti-Catholic propagandists. Here, as in the lower south, immigration and Catholicism caused no serious concern. Maryland and Kentucky were sprinkled with Catholics and aliens, but both groups were numerically unimportant except in a few scattered areas. Natives in the border states, particularly in the regions where the revivalistic churches were centered, doubtless hated both Papists and immigrants, but they feared far more the effects of any serious sectional conflict. They knew that their states would be the battleground in a civil war between north and south and that only continuous compromise would delay that war. After the rise of the sectional parties in 1854 they had no choice but to vote the Know-Nothing ticket.

This explanation alone accounts for the nearly complete and strangely enduring success of the American party in that section. In 1854 and 1855 it carried Delaware, Maryland, California, and Kentucky and very nearly added Tennessee and Virginia to this list. Maryland was the only state to cast its electoral vote for the Know-Nothing candidate in 1856 and continued to support the party down to 1860. Within these states the same regions that voted Whig in 1848 and 1852 and supported either Bell or Douglas in 1860 were solidly Know-Nothing in 1855 and 1856. (See maps, pp. 402–406.) Clearly the American party was successful there because it was a compromise party, not because it promised to protect America from the Pope.

In the northwest the No-Popery agitators aroused little enthusiasm. Natives of that region were in daily contact with aliens and realized that foreigners were not the designing creatures pictured by propagandists, but sober, hard-working farmers. Moreover, westerners were too absorbed in the task of wringing wealth from nature's stubborn soil to be frightened by vague threats of popish invasion. Their concern was with material progress and they were willing to welcome any aid, even from Catholics and immigrants. "Our German settlers," one Illinois editor wrote in 1855, "are valuable acquisitions to the State and are doing good service in opening up its waste places to the hand of cultivation. . . . It is seldom, indeed, that we hear of one being in the poor house or under the care of a pauper committee." [31]

This attitude kept the Know-Nothing party from any major successes in the northwest. Ironically enough it was forced to content itself with the same secondary role there that was played by the foreign-born. During the middle 1850's each of the northwestern states supported, in addition to the regular Democratic and Republican parties, two large independent groups, made up of Know-Nothings on the one hand and immigrants on the other. The conduct of neither group was absolutely predictable, so both major parties consistently bid for their support. The foreign-born normally voted with the Democrats while the Know-Nothings cast their lot with the Republicans rather than nominate candidates of their own. Under their influence the Republican party in many northwestern states took on a decided nativistic tint, but was never willing to favor the entire American platform. [32]

The anti-Catholic sentiment which did exist in the northwest was almost certainly sincere. The people of this section wanted no compromise on slavery; they steadfastly opposed any extension of the southern institution that would throw them into competition with bond labor. Moreover the Republican party was launched in this section and from the first provided an outlet for those who put slavery above nativism. The fact that the Know-Nothings enjoyed even minor success in this region is testimony to the effectiveness of the No-Popery crusade.

Only in the northeast did the American party parallel its victories in the border states. If the desire to compromise on the slavery issue had been the sole force driving people into the Know-Nothing ranks, this section would have reacted as did the northwest. New Englanders particularly, and the inhabitants of New York and Pennsylvania to a lesser degree, abhorred that southern institution as thoroughly as the farmers of Wisconsin or Michigan. They had no wish to evade the issue and within a short time were to give freely of money, energy and life that northern institutions and ideas might triumph in the south. They were equipped with the means of expressing their dislike of slavery, for the Republican party invaded the northeast shortly after it was founded in the middle west. They were, like the inhabitants of the northwest, discouraged from embracing political nativism by the presence of large numbers of foreigners who promised to demolish any party openly favoring immigration restriction. In other words, the situation in the northeast was in every way similar to the situation in the northwest. Logically, the two sections should have reacted the same way to the stimulus of nativistic agitators. Actually the northeastern states supported the American party more solidly than those of any other section. Massachusetts, Rhode Island, New Hampshire, Connecticut, Pennsylvania, and New York returned Know-Nothing majorities in 1854 or 1855.

The only explanation for this variation between northeast and northwest is the greater effectiveness of anti-Catholic propaganda in the eastern states. It was in these states that the No-Popery crusade had centered for three decades. There ministers and propagandists had instilled hatred of Rome into the minds of a people whose Puritan tradition made them ready to believe the most devastating criticism of Catholicism. They voted for Know-Nothing candidates because they were convinced that the Catholic church and foreign immigration threatened the perpetuation of the institutions and ideals of their forefathers. To these New Englanders in 1854 and 1855, slavery seemed a less immediate menace than Popery and foreign invasion.

The success of the Know-Nothing party, then, cannot be attributed to any one thing. Contributing to it were the charm and efficiency of the party itself, the confused political alignments of the 1850's, and the desire of many to delay the inevitable conflict, as well as the welter of propaganda which organized nativists had fostered so carefully. In the south the hope of compromise and fear of Popery were probably equally important, in the border states Know-Nothings were actuated more by the hope of preserving the union than by alarm over Catholicism, and in the north hatred of Rome seemingly was responsible for most of the success that the American party enjoyed.

NOTES

1 The party left virtually no records. The papers of its central governing unit passed from one secretary to another until they finally disappeared. Most of the founders and early leaders of the party were comparatively unimportant men and their papers have consequently not been preserved. Accounts of the origin and growth of the Know-Nothing movement hence must be drawn from printed sources which are extremely unreliable, for they were written either by the friends or foes of nativism who were undoubtedly guilty of misrepresentation and deliberate falsehood.

2 *Know Nothing Almanac*, 17–20; Carroll, *Great American Battle*, 83–97.

3 The statements on the origin of the party are drawn from Carroll, *Great American Battle*, 263–271 and Whitney, *Defense of American Policy*, 281ff. Both of these writers were official propagandists of the party, but the factual account of its growth that they present may probably be believed.

4 In 1852 there were more than 60 small nativistic organizations in New York City and it is reasonable to presume that some had been founded by 1849. Scisco, *Political Nativism in New York State*, 84.

5 Carroll, *Great American Battle*, 268.

6 Whitney, *Defense of American Policy*, 283; Scisco, *Political Nativism in New York State*, 86–87.

7 In this election both Pierce and the Whig candidate, Winfield Scott, had been accused of nativistic leanings; Pierce because his native state of New Hampshire had just refused to remove from its constitution a religious test which discriminated against Catholic officeholders, and Scott because he had expressed sympathy with the nativists' stand in the early 1840's. Although Scott vehemently insisted that his views had changed, Pierce probably did gain much of the foreign-born vote, as was natural for the Democratic candidate. Many Catholics, however, voted against Pierce as a means of rebuking the intolerance of New Hampshire, and an attempt was made to get Hughes to endorse this stand. *American Catholic Historical Researches*, IX, No. 4 (October, 1892), 149.

8 Carroll, *Great American Battle*, 269–270; Whitney, *Defense of American Policy*, 284; Tusca, *Know Nothingism in Baltimore*, 9.

9 Carroll, *Great American Battle*, 269.

10 The first constitution was adopted on June 17, 1854. A second, varying only in detail from the first, was accepted on November 24, 1854. This second

constitution is printed in N. W. Cluskey, *Political Text Book and Encyclopaedia* (Washington, 1857), 47ff. The earlier constitution, probably in inaccurate form, is printed in Hambleton, *Political Campaign in Virginia*, 47ff.
The second constitution has been used for this discussion, together with a
constitution of a subordinate council printed in Cluskey, *Political Text Book*,
50-53. The organization of the order is well described in Scisco, *Political
Nativism in New York State*, 100-107, and in Brand, "History of the Know
Nothing Party in Indiana," *loc. cit.*, 177-179. There is a less satisfactory account in Desmond, *Know Nothing Party*, 56ff.

[11] Probably many members were attracted by this secrecy. Many years
later Ulysses S. Grant testified that he joined a Know-Nothing Lodge because
he wanted to see what went on in the meetings. Ulysses S. Grant, *Personal
Memoirs* (New York, 1885-1886), I, 169. The term "Know-Nothing" is indicative of the mystery surrounding the order. This was popularly applied by
outsiders because members answered every question with "I know nothing
about it."

[12] Information about the ceremonies and ritual of the Know-Nothing lodges
is scattered and probably untrustworthy. Most accounts of the ritual printed
at the time appeared in hostile newspapers as exposures of Know-Nothingism and can hardly be relied on. What appears to be a more accurate
summary appeared in Cluskey, *Political Text Book*, 55-58. This agrees in
substance with a manuscript copy used by George H. Haynes in preparing
"A Chapter from the Local History of Know-Nothingism," *New England
Magazine*, XV (September, 1896), and with a "Form for Initiation and
Installation in the American Party," a manuscript in the possession of the
Connecticut State Library at Hartford, Connecticut. All copies of the ritual
examined show variation in wording, but this does not mean that any one is
inaccurate, for there was undoubtedly a wide divergence between forms used
in different states and even in different cities. In essence, if not in wording,
nearly all accounts, including those published in hostile newspapers, agree.

[13] Cluskey, *Political Text Book*, 57.

[14] *Remarks on the Majority and Minority Reports of the Select Committee
on Secret Societies of the House of Delegates of Maryland* (New York, 1856),
6-7; Carroll, *Great American Battle*, 125, 162-170.

[15] See Carroll, *Great American Battle*, 146-150, for the northern view and
Origin, Principles and Purposes of the American Party, 44-47, for that of the
south. This last work was probably written by Henry Winter Davis, a prominent member of the party from Maryland.

[16] John P. Senning, "The Know Nothing Movement in Illinois, 1854-
1856," *Illinois Historical Society Journal*, VII (April, 1914), 16-17.

[17] Both the *American Union*, March 4, 1854, and the New York *Journal
of Commerce*, quoted in the *Pilot*, February 18, 1854, estimated the national
strength of the Know-Nothings at 5,000.

[18] The Boston *Pilot*, June 3, 1854, insisted that all opposition voters had
stayed away from the polls in order to test the strength of this mysterious
nativistic party. If they had voted, the editor insisted, the Know-Nothings
would never have won such victories.

[19] This confusion is illustrated in a Democratic campaign pamphlet issued
in Pennsylvania in 1854, *A Few Words to the Thinking and Judicious Voters*

of Pennsylvania (——, 1854), 38–39. George W. Julian in his *Political Recollections, 1840–1872* (Chicago, 1884), 142, reports that when meetings were called to protest the proscriptive action of this secret party they were met by superior Know-Nothing forces which "silenced them by savage yells."

20 *American Union,* May 13, 1854.

21 *Know Nothing: a Poem for Natives and Aliens* (Boston, 1854). A typical book with the letters "K.N." inscribed is Charles W. Frothingham, *The Convent's Doom; a Tale of Charlestown in 1834* (5th edition, Boston, 1854).

22 *Whig Almanac and United States Political Register for 1855* (New York, 1855), 40–54.

23 *Tribune Almanac and Political Register for 1856* (New York, 1856), 53–64. The following monographs give excellent descriptions of the election: Laurence F. Schmeckebier, *History of the Know Nothing Party in Maryland,* Johns Hopkins University, *Studies in History and Political Science,* XVII (Baltimore, 1899), 20; Ulrich B. Phillips, "Georgia and State Rights," *American Historical Association Report,* II (1901), 177–178; Cole, "Nativism in the Lower Mississippi Valley," *loc. cit.,* 271; Schafer, "Know Nothingism in Wisconsin," *loc. cit.,* 14–20; Desmond, *Know Nothing Party,* 67.

24 Quoted in the *Pilot,* July 8, 1854.

25 Henry Wilson, *History of the Rise and Fall of the Slave Power in America* (Boston, 1872–1877), II, 422.

26 *Pilot,* September 30, 1854.

27 A Hartford election in 1854. Connecticut *Courant,* December 2, 1854.

28 This is the traditional explanation for the rise of the Know-Nothing party. It was set forth first in classic form by Hermann Von Holst in his *Political and Constitutional History of the United States* (Chicago, 1885), V, 379. He has been followed by most of the general historians. See Channing, *History of the United States,* VI, 129–137; Theodore C. Smith, *Parties and Slavery* (The American Nation, A History, XVIII) (New York, 1906), 115–116; James Ford Rhodes, *History of the United States from the Compromise of 1850* (New York, 1920), II, 7–15.

29 This was the way in which Edward Everett Hale accounted for the rise of the party. Quoted in Haynes, "A Chapter from the Local History of Know Nothingism," *loc. cit.,* 88.

30 Thus in Mississippi the Know-Nothings followed in Whig footsteps by insisting that repudiated state bonds be paid off in full. Cole, "Nativism in the Lower Mississippi Valley," *loc. cit.,* 273.

31 Illinois *Journal,* July 25, 1855, quoted in Senning, "The Know Nothing Movement in Illinois," *loc. cit.,* 12. An excellent discussion of the whole Know-Nothing movement in the middle west is in M. Evangeline Thomas, *Nativism in the Old Northwest, 1850–1860* (Washington, 1936).

32 In all probability the Republicans promised to push nativistic measures in return for Know-Nothing support. Thus the abolition of the Wisconsin immigration agencies by the Republicans in 1855, just after the party had won a major election with Know-Nothing aid, looked suspiciously like the carrying out of a campaign promise.

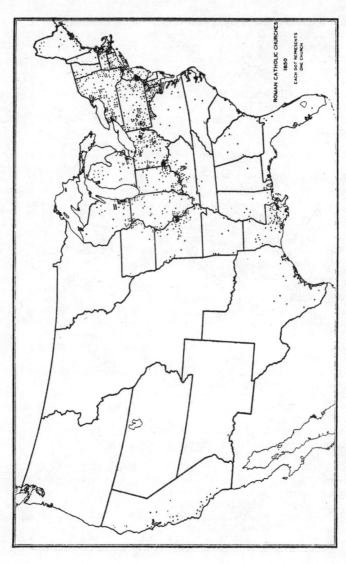

ROMAN CATHOLIC CHURCHES
1850
EACH DOT REPRESENTS
ONE CHURCH

ROMAN CATHOLIC CHURCHES IN THE UNITED STATES, 1850

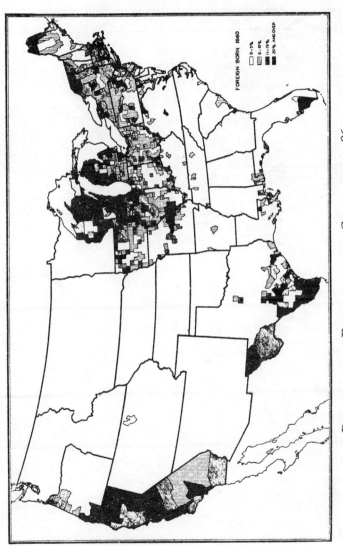

FOREIGN BORN 1860
☐ 0-3%
▨ 4-6%
▦ 11-19%
■ 20% AND OVER

PERCENTAGE OF FOREIGN-BORN BY COUNTIES IN 1860

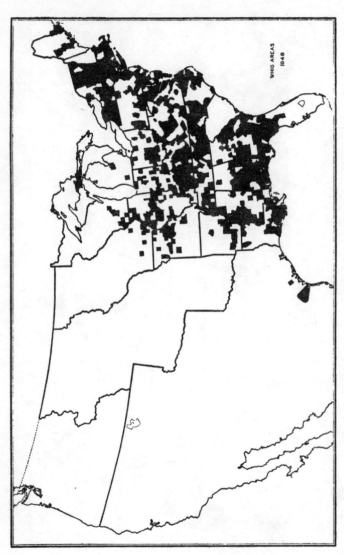

WHIG AREAS
1848

WHIG AREAS IN THE PRESIDENTIAL ELECTION OF 1848

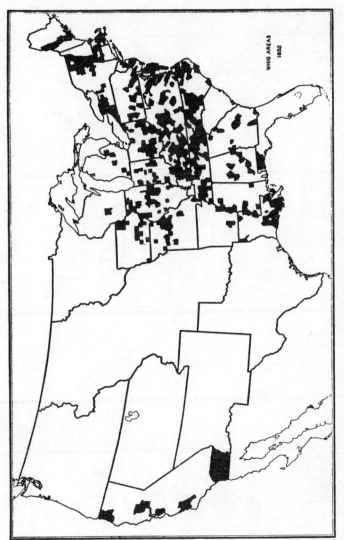

WHIG AREAS
1852

WHIG AREAS IN THE PRESIDENTIAL ELECTION OF 1852

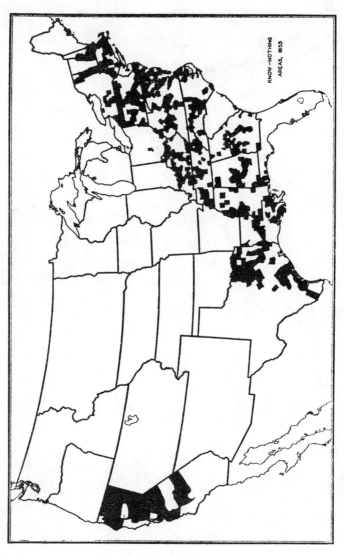

KNOW-NOTHING AREAS, 1855

KNOW-NOTHING AREAS IN THE CONGRESSIONAL AND STATE ELECTIONS OF 1855

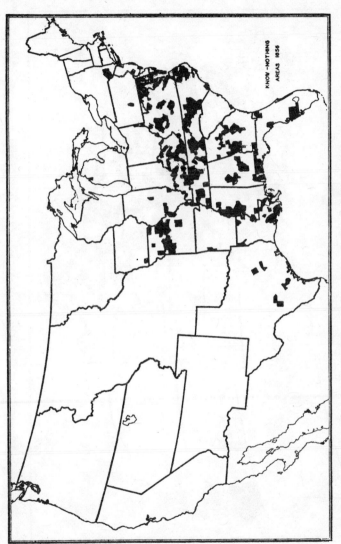

KNOW-NOTHING
AREAS 1856

KNOW-NOTHING AREAS IN THE PRESIDENTIAL ELECTION OF 1856

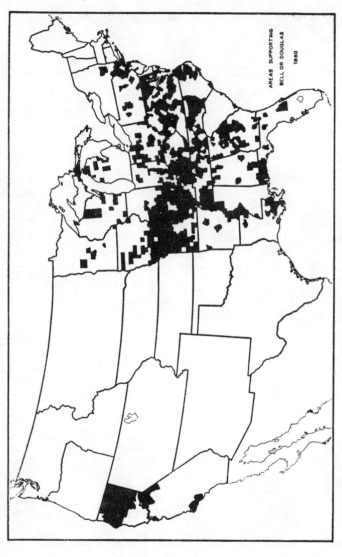

AREAS SUPPORTING
BELL OR DOUGLAS
1860

AREAS SUPPORTING BELL OR DOUGLAS IN THE PRESIDENTIAL ELECTION OF 1860

XVI

Know-Nothingism in Action
and Decline
1854-1860

THE rise of the Know-Nothing party in the elections of 1854 and 1855 placed nativists in a position where they could, for the first time, translate their theories into practice. For a generation they had been advocating legislation to protect the United States from the Papist and foreigner. Now they controlled a number of state legislatures and had a considerable representation in the national Congress. These legislative bodies became political laboratories where they could attempt to practice what they had preached. The almost complete failure of the Know-Nothings to carry into effect the doctrines of anti-Catholic and antiforeign propagandists contributed to the rapid decline of this nativistic party.

It is easy to understand why the party's adherents failed to sweep the national Congress into a crusade against Rome. At no time did the Know-Nothings control either the House of Representatives or the Senate, although in the 34th Congress they held the balance of power between Democrats and Republicans. As a minority group they could only secure their ends by co-operating with either major faction. This co-operation was not forthcoming in behalf of schemes to attack Catholicism, for both Democrats and Republicans recognized the foolhardiness of such a stand. Not only would it alienate thousands of foreigners and fair-minded persons, but it would have no chance of success, for constitutional amendments alone would allow interference with religious freedom or religious tests for office-holders. Hence Republicans and Democrats persistently turned a cold shoulder to all Know-Nothing overtures in this direction.

This stand on the part of the major parties left the nativists with so little strength that the final political result of a half century of tumult and shouting against Popery resolved itself into a few speeches in Congress. The first debate in which defenders of Protestantism expressed themselves took place in the closing months of 1854 and was occasioned by a severe attack on Know-Nothingism by William S. Barry, a representative from Missis-sippi. Barry, in the midst of an extended denunciation of the party, remarked that the Pope had no temporal power and that Catholicism, as a result, could do no harm to the United States.[1] Nathaniel P. Banks of Massachusetts immediately took the floor, both to defend the Know-Nothings and to insist that the Pope did exercise temporal power.[2] This was emphatically denied by L. M. Keitt of South Carolina and J. R. Chandler of Pennsyl-vania. The latter argued that the temporal power had no spirit-ual basis and had not been exercised for centuries. He was, he told his fellow congressmen, a Catholic. But, he said, "if, by any providence, the Bishop of Rome should become possessed armies and a fleet, and, in a spirit of conquest, or any other spirit, should invade the territory of the United States, or assail the rights of our country, he would find no more earnest antagonists than the Roman Catholics. And for myself, if not here in this hall to vote supplies for a defending army, or if too old to take part in the active service, I should, if alive, be at least in my chamber, or at the foot of the altar, imploring God for the safety of my country and the defeat of its invaders."[3]

These remarks brought into the lists W. R. Smith of Alabama, who was to become the leading congressional spokesman of nativism. He launched now into a bitter attack on the whole

Catholic system, ridiculing Chandler's contention regarding temporal power, and dwelling especially on the part that the Jesuits were to play in the papal conquest of the United States. He pictured the Jesuit as "prowling about the country with his tablet and his pencil, culling all information, looking into everybody's business, peeping over every man's shoulder, winding himself into every man's confidence; lifting the curtain of every man's window; and with his meek mysterious eyes shining like a saint, does he not hurry away to reveal this information wherever it is of sufficient importance." [4] Every man, Smith insisted, must labor to save the United States from these hidden foes; every Protestant must be "a sentinel on the watch-towers of liberty." [5] Smith, despite his enthusiasm, had nothing constructive to offer, and after his remarks Congress turned to more important matters.

The assembling of the 34th Congress in December, 1855, began a new debate on Catholicism which lasted through much of the session. The forty-three Know-Nothings in this body held such a clear balance of power that neither Democrats nor Republicans could enact legislation without their aid.[6] In this situation nativistic spokesmen felt free to voice demands they would not have dared utter on previous occasions. These were frequently expressed during the two months of balloting necessary to elect a speaker for the House of Representatives.[7] Again William R. Smith of Alabama was the leading Know-Nothing spokesman, ably seconded by Thomas R. Whitney of Pennsylvania whose long activity in nativistic circles had at last elevated him to Congress. These two, together with L. M. Cox of Kentucky and Jacob Broom of Pennsylvania, spent much of this two-month period making violent speeches against Catholicism, to no apparent purpose other than to satisfy the constituents who had placed them in office.[8]

Although these few speeches represented the sole political outcome of the prolonged anti-Catholic campaign, the Know-

Nothings had more support when they attempted to deal with the problem of immigration. This was a less dangerous subject, for it was generally agreed that pauper and criminal immigration should be checked and the enforcement of the naturalization laws improved. The Know-Nothings, pledged to prohibit the introduction into the United States of the physically and morally unfit, and to seek a twenty-one-year probationary period before the naturalization of aliens, offered a platform attractive to eastern laborers, southern planters, and western farmers as well as to avowed nativists. All of these groups believed that their political or economic welfare would suffer from a continued alien influx.[9]

Nevertheless the Know-Nothing demand for a twenty-one-year period before naturalization had little chance of adoption.[10] The matter was forced on Congress by petitions from New England states,[11] and in December, 1854, Senator Stephen Adams of Mississippi introduced a bill embodying the nativists' proposal. His speech in support of the measure made it clear that he favored this action not only to protect the ballot box but also to discourage all immigration. "I sympathize with the poor and unfortunate in every country," he said, "but am Native American enough to prefer that the tyrannical Governments which produce these paupers should take care of them, and believing as I do, that the facility with which they become citizens serves as a great stimulant to immigration, I desire to see it changed." [12] Adams' bill was referred to the Committee on the Judiciary and never reported out.[13] A similar fate that met an identical bill in the House made it clear that Know-Nothing strength was not yet sufficient to secure even this fundamental objective of the party.[14]

With the opening of the 34th Congress a year later, the party's adherents took new heart, hopefully believing that they could barter their influence in return for Democratic or Republican support. Adams promptly reintroduced his bill and it was as promptly referred again to the Committee on the Judiciary.[15]

This time, however, the measure was reported back to the Senate, on April 21, 1856, with the committee's recommendation that it should not pass.[16] An impassioned plea from Adams did no good, and the measure on which the Know-Nothings had staked their prestige was allowed to die without a vote.[17] A similar bill that Thomas R. Whitney had introduced in the House was reported out of committee there in July, 1856, but this too was never voted on.[18] A majority of the people of the nation might admit that the naturalization system was fraudulent, but they obviously preferred a better administration of existing laws to the enactment of new ones. Certainly the failure of the Know-Nothings to force a test vote on one of their favorite measures lost the party public confidence and hastened its decline.

In seeking to deal with pauper and criminal immigration, the Know-Nothing party found greater support but supposedly insurmountable constitutional barriers stood in the way of any reform. The measure that received party sanction was introduced into the House early in January, 1855, by a representative from Massachusetts. It made illegal the introduction into the United States of all foreign paupers, criminals, idiots, lunatics, insane, and blind persons.[19] This, advocates of the measure maintained, was necessary to protect the states from the burden of pauper support and the nation from the weakening influence of impoverished foreigners, many of whom, it was hinted, had been sent for this specific purpose by European nations anxious to sap the strength of the American republic.[20] The bill's opponents based their arguments solely on constitutional grounds. They insisted that the Constitution nowhere gave Congress the power to pass such a measure and that its enactment would seriously infringe upon the reserved rights of the states. Congress had only the authority to establish uniform rules of naturalization; it did not have the right to prohibit the importation of certain classes of immigrants, no matter how desirable that might be.[21]

In the end these views of the opposition prevailed. After a

long debate the whole question was referred to the House Committee on Foreign Affairs, which reported out its conclusions in August, 1856. The committee was strongly nativistic in sympathy, so much so that it relied for information on such propaganda works as Whitney's *A Defense of American Policy* and Sanderson's *Republican Landmarks,* to show that aliens brought poverty, intemperance, crime, and atheism to American soil. "Thousands [of foreigners] have come hither," the report read, ". . . to fill our streets as beggars, or to become the inmates of our alms-houses, and other charitable institutions. . . . Our country has been converted into a sort of penal colony to which foreign governments ship their criminals. It is not only the thriftless poor who come hither, spending their last cent in crossing the Atlantic, to add to the burden of our poor laws . . . but inmates of the prisons of Europe are sent hither by their governments to prey upon society and to contaminate our people with their vices." Despite this evil, the committee reluctantly concluded that constitutional limitations prevented any congressional action and urged the states to pass laws against foreign paupers and criminals under their police powers.[22] When a committee as nativistically inclined as this one came to such a conclusion, it was clear that Know-Nothing attempts to attain even their mildest objective would be frustrated.

Within the states, however, obstacles such as those blocking national legislation against foreigner and Catholic were lacking. In several states the Know-Nothings had clear majorities in the legislatures, constitutional limitations were less important, and popular support was strong. If the nativistic formula were to be applied anywhere, this was certainly the place. Yet here again the party failed, and the collapse of these Know-Nothing legislatures did much to end the whole nativistic movement.

Massachusetts offered the best opportunity for Know-Nothing legislation. The legislature chosen in the fall of 1854 and meeting in January, 1855, was made up almost entirely of members of the party, who also dominated the rest of the state administration. Enthusiastic as were these governing officials against Catholicism and immigrants—the legislature was labeled "Our Praise-God-Bare-Bones-Parliament" by the Boston *Pilot* [23]—they were able to do nothing, for they lacked the necessary legislative experience. Only thirty-four had served in the assembly before, and a great majority were mechanics, laborers, clerks, school teachers, and ministers who understood nothing of the governmental process and were ill equipped to learn. One wag suggested that the election sermon for this legislature should be based on Job 8:9: "For we are but of yesterday, and know nothing." [24]

This poorly trained and inexperienced group proved utterly unable to solve the problems that faced it. The Know-Nothing governor, in his inaugural address, suggested several reforms, stressing particularly the need of modifying the state laws concerning pauper aliens. Yet this important matter was not taken up until near the end of the session and then only referred to a committee. Similarly, several amendments to the state constitution were proposed: one restricting the franchise to those who could read and write English, another excluding from the voting lists all who had not resided in the country for twenty-one years and been legally naturalized, and a third confining office holding to the native born. Of these the first was voted down, and no action was taken on the other two until the last day of the session when they were hurriedly passed. These amendments, representing almost the entire constructive side of Know-Nothing rule in Massachusetts, met a speedy death at the hands of a later legislature.[25]

Even more disastrous were the assembly's bungling attempts to deal a blow at Catholicism. Various bills designed to give the state control of education were introduced and lost in the legislative shuffle, only one, requiring the daily reading of the Bible "in the common English version" in the public schools, being passed.[26] More important was the work of a "Nunnery Committee" appointed by the legislature to report on Catholic convents within the Commonwealth. Such an investigation had long been demanded by propagandists,[27] and a similar committee had been appointed by the English parliament only a short time before.[28] Hence it was not unnatural that citizens of one of the towns should petition the legislature asking that Massachusetts have such a commission or that the assembly should respond by naming one in February, 1855.[29]

Although the legislature had been asked to appoint only a "Nunnery Committee," some of the more intelligent members pointed out that no convents existed in the state and that if the commission were to serve any purpose, its powers must be enlarged. As appointed, it was authorized to visit "such theological seminaries, boarding schools, academies, nunneries, convents, and other institutions of like character as they may deem necessary" and report its findings to the legislature.[30] Armed with this broad grant, the committee began its tour of inspection in March, 1855. Its conduct from the first aroused hostile sentiment over the entire state. At Worcester, where Holy Cross college was visited, the committee reported favorably not only on that Jesuit institution, but also on the local wines that were consumed freely at state expense.[31] At Roxbury, where a harmless Catholic school was singled out for an inquisitorial survey, some twenty investigators appeared although only seven were on the committee. The whole party tramped over the school building, frightening the children, treating the nuns with little respect, and poking into closets and corners to find the dread evidences of Popery which propaganda writers had convinced them should be there. After thoroughly disrupting the school, the whole party adjourned to an elaborate dinner where champagne flowed freely— although sale of this beverage was forbidden in the state.[32] At Lowell members of the committee and their friends not only imbibed freely of local liquors but also charged the state expenses incurring from their relationships with a woman "answering to the name of Mrs. Patterson" who was notorious for her easy virtue.[33]

This was too much. The Boston *Daily Advertiser* printed a detailed account of the committee's disgraceful conduct at Lowell, and the press immediately took up the hue and cry.[34] Amidst the clamor the legislature ended the commission's tours and ordered its chairman, Joseph Hiss of Boston, before the House for punishment. He was exonerated of charges of ill-treating the nuns and pupils of Roxbury, but the legislature agreed that his conduct at Lowell deserved reproach, and on May 10, by a vote of 137 to 15, he was expelled from the assembly.[35] A satirist summed up prevailing opinion when he wrote:

> One after one the honored Bay-leaves fade,
> And ancient glories wither in the shade;
> The solon's [*sic*] of the state, at duty's call,
> Have hissed a loving member from the hall.
> Take courage, Joseph, in thy great ado;
> The world has hissed the Legislature, too.[36]

Nevertheless it is noteworthy that 150 members of the legislature absented themselves from the House rather than vote against Hiss.

Despite the stigma cast upon the Massachusetts legislature by the Nunnery Committee, the session dragged on while members collected the increased pay they had voted themselves. The session was the most expensive the state had known to that time and accomplished the least.[37] Yet the voters were sufficiently loyal to the principles of Know-Nothingism to return another nativistic assembly in 1855, although only about one sixth of the members of the first Know-Nothing legislature were re-elected. The preachers, doctors, and shophands were left at home, and merchants and lawyers were called to govern the state, but this second legislature, like the first, was unable to pass any measure favored by the party.[38]

Maryland's record under Know-Nothing rule was no better than that of Massachusetts. There nativists were particularly concerned with convents and with the nuns believed to be forcefully detained in these popish prisons. When the legislature assembled in 1855, it was showered with requests for the release of these unfortunate females. These petitions were referred to a select committee on which Know-Nothings were in a majority. Despite this, the committee reported unanimously against legislative action, stating its belief that no persons were confined in convents by force and that the writ of habeas corpus offered ample protection. A proposal to reject the committee's report and push through some type of anticonvent legislation was lost in the rush of a closing session. Other pet doctrines of the party met a similar fate. Petitions to change the naturalization laws were buried in committees and even a resolution requesting Congress to modify its naturalization procedure was never acted on.[39]

The incompetence and failure of the Massachusetts and Maryland legislatures were duplicated in other states where Know-Nothings either gained control or held the balance of power. In California no nativistic legislation was passed even though the party had a clear majority in the legislature.[40] In Connecticut a literacy test for the franchise and a bill forcing the corporate rather than individual holding of all church property were sole monuments to a year of Know-Nothing rule.[41] Resolutions of the Connecticut legislature on naturalization were referred to a joint committee from which they never emerged.[42] In Indiana, where the legislature was generally supposed to be controlled by Know-Nothings, an amendment to the state constitution limiting the suffrage to citizens of the United States never advanced beyond a second reading.[43] Massachusetts adopted a literacy test in 1857 similar to the one Connecticut had accepted two years earlier, and these two laws were the only legislative results of a period of Know-Nothing rule.

The complete failure of the Know-Nothing party both in Congress and in the state legislatures made its inherent weaknesses clear. Horace Greeley had been correct when he wrote in 1854 that the party "would seem as devoid of the elements of permanence as an anti-Cholera or anti-Potato-rot party would be." [44] Know-Nothingism had nothing permanent to offer. Its principles were inimical to those on which the American nation had been founded; its demands were of a sort that could never be realized in a country constituted as was the United States. Thus the party's success contributed to its failure, for its leaders, once in power, were helpless, and the people, realizing this, began to desert the organization as rapidly as they had joined.

This inevitable decline was hastened by elements of weakness within the party. One was the secrecy with which the members had surrounded themselves. Admirable as this had been in luring curious Americans into the order, it became a boomerang as soon as the party gained recognition and power. Rumors began to fly of dread plots hatched against democracy within the Know-Nothing conclaves. Criticism followed close on the heels of the rumors. The Richmond *Examiner* compared the mysterious meetings of the order of those of the Thirty Tyrants of Athens and the Council of Ten of Venice. [45] Henry Ward Beecher wrote in the *Independent* that "one might as well study optics in the pyramids of Egypt, or the subterranean tombs of Rome, as liberty in secret conclaves controlled by hoary knaves versed in political intrigue." [46] A prominent southern judge complained that he objected to the Know-Nothings because of their "night working, their needless swearing," while an equally well-known northern politician branded the order "a horrid conspiracy against decency, the rights of man, and the principle of human brotherhood." [47]

As this sentiment grew, legislative attacks on the Know-Nothing tactics became fairly common. Maryland was the scene of an investigation which ended in a widely publicized report condemning the party's secrecy as essentially anti-American,[48] while other state legislatures passed resolutions of a similar nature.[49] The national Congress was called on to debate the question when a member of the House introduced a resolution in February, 1855:

Resolved, that, in the opinion of this House, the existence of secret oath-bound political associations, having in view an interference with the sanctity of the ballot box and the direction of the course of national and municipal legislation, is inconsistent with, and dangerous to, the institutions of republicanism and directly hostile to the genius of this Government.[50]

Although this resolution was defeated, it led to a debate in which the Know-Nothing secrecy was the target for thrusts from Democratic and Republican speakers.[51] In Congress and out, by the middle of 1855, the order was being heartily condemned for its "dark-lantern" methods.

More effective than these serious arguments was the ridicule which opponents of the party heaped upon its aims and ritual. Burlesque accounts of the initiation pictured candidates for membership being seized by a Revolutionary war veteran, whirled around three times, and asked such questions as "Should Uncle Sam's farm, or Brother Jonathan's nation, ever be threatened by the cannibals of the uninhabited regions around the South Pole, or by the Goths and Vandals who drove the Romans into the Mediterranean Sea, will you take up arms, pitchforks, stove pipes, wooden nutmegs, saw logs, and swear by the great horn spoon to lick all creation?"[52] Similarly the name "Know-Nothing" was played upon relentlessly; "Owe-Nothing," "Say-Nothing," and "Do-Nothing" societies were proposed and even formed.[53] Particularly trying to the order was the fun poked at its objectives. These were absurd enough in themselves: the Know-Nothings were trying to make people believe that imagined popish armies and Jesuit spies threatened the security of a strong nation. Leaders of the party who had conjured up such phantoms felt keenly the thrust of a critic who said: "The pretended Know-Nothing apprehension lest a successor to Julius II should acquire supremacy over the American Union, is as absurd an anachronism, as would be the anticipation of a Carthaginian invasion, or the subjection of the country by mail-clad warriors of a descendant of William of Normandy." [54] Ridicule such as this was more than the party could stand. [55]

Equally trying to the Know-Nothings were the efforts of journalists to penetrate the order's barrier of secrecy. Local chapters were so harassed by the curious that they frequently had to hold their meetings in out-of-the-way places. [56] Diligent newspaper reporters caused trouble by trying to worm their way into meetings or bribe members into revealing what went on there. A series of "exposures" of Know-Nothing secrets began early in January, 1854, when the *Freeman's Journal* published the constitution of the Guard of Liberty, a nativistic military company, and boasted that the ritual of Know-Nothingism had been revealed. [57] Other journalists were soon so hot on the trail that in May, 1854, the president of the order forcibly removed a trunk full of records from the office of a minor official who was reported to be negotiating their sale to a newspaper. [58] Despite these precautions, inklings of the true nature of the party found their way into the papers [59] and in the fall of 1854 the Richmond *Examiner* printed an authentic copy of the ritual and constitution. [60] Other exposures followed, until by the middle of 1855 the secrets of Know-Nothingism were well known to every person in the country who could read. [61] By this time the nativistic press was urging the party to forsake its "dark-lantern" methods, stressing particularly the fear of appearing ludicrous in the eyes of the world. [62] Delegates to a national convention in June, 1855, responded by declaring that the principles of the order would henceforth be openly avowed and recommended that the local councils no longer conceal their existence or their places of meeting. [63] But by this time the mischief had been done.

While in use, this Know-Nothing secrecy had been harmful both because of its absurdity and because it allowed enemies to lay at the order's door blame for much of the rioting that characterized the 1850's. This was a serious charge during that turbulent decade. Bloodshed and lawlessness were common, with men and boys going about armed and pitched battles of unbelievable intensity every-day occurrences during political campaigns. The Know-Nothings did not originate these practices, but the precipitation of this intensely emotional order into an already riotous political scene made elections in which it participated models of violence and disorder. This opened the party to the charge that its secret conclaves plotted forceful methods to keep foreigners from the polls.[64] The Know-Nothings could not deny this so long as their meetings were closed to the outside world.

There is little doubt that the party encouraged violent methods. Fringed about it were several clubs and political societies whose members were pledged to enforce their nativistic principles by any lawless means. First of these adjuncts to be formed was the Order of the American Star, whose members were distinguished by wide white felt hats and the rallying cry of "Wide Awake." The "Wide Awakes," as they came to be called, attracted the rougher elements of the population, anxious to share in the self-assigned duty of protecting anti-Catholic street preachers and harrying the foreign-born from the polls on election day. In the van of the Wide Awakes there sprang up a host of clubs that at least professed American principles: the Black Snakes, Tigers, Rough Skins, Red Necks, Thunderbolts, Gladiators, Ranter, Eubolts, Little Fellows, Rip Raps, Screw Boats, Stay Lates, Hard Times, Dips, Plug Uglies, and Blood Tubs.[65] The Democrats were not immune to this organizing spirit and countered with such clubs as the Bloody Eights, Double Pumps, Calithumpians, Ferry Road Hunters, Gumballs, Peelers, Pluckers, Shad Hoes, Bloats, Butt Enders and Sag Nichts.[66]

Conflicts between these lawless groups were certain on every election day, for the Know-Nothing clubs were pledged to keep the foreign-born from voting, and the Democratic organizations were equally determined to protect the rights of immigrants at the polls. Police were helpless when these affrays began, and sober citizens were forced to stay at home rather than risk their lives amidst the pitched battles that developed around every polling place. In Baltimore, where conditions were particularly bad, a cannon was mounted outside one voting booth during one election; in another the Rip Raps and the New Market Fire Company faced each other in platoon formation and fired volley after volley until the less experienced fire company broke ranks and retreated. Eight were killed and fifty wounded on that election day. Even when there was no open fighting, good citizens were afraid to vote, for Know-Nothing workers filled the polling places with shoemaker's awls attached to their knees ready to "persuade" voters to support the American ticket. By 1856 Baltimore had reached the stage where only Know-Nothings could vote in some wards and only Democrats in others.[67]

In every American city the story was the same. In New Orleans four men were killed when native and foreign factions clashed. In Lawrence, Massachusetts, 1,500 Americans stormed the Irish section and destroyed homes and churches. In St. Louis the 1854 elections led to a riot in which ten men were killed and several wounded.[68] More serious was a battle which developed in Louisville on August 5, 1855. There the native factions had been aroused by a No-Popery campaign being carried on by the Louisville *Journal*. When a group of them marched through the German sector, fighting began which only ended after more than twenty men had been killed and several hundred wounded. Louisville long remembered that "Bloody Monday" with regret.[69]

Probably the Know-Nothings were no more to blame for these disgraceful incidents than the Democrats. Actually the full stigma of this period of mob rule fell upon the party; the press agreed that it alone was responsible for the election disorders that were sweeping the nation. This charge the Know-Nothings could not refute, for their pledge of secrecy prevented them from making more than general replies. Some members went so far as to condone the rioting, even the peaceful and conservative John Bell of Tennessee declaring:

> It is better that a little blood shall sprinkle the pavements and side-walks of our cities now, than that their streets should be drenched in blood hereafter; or that the highways and open fields of our country should drink up the blood of citizens, slain in deadly conflict, between armed bands—it may be between disciplined legions—Native Americans on one side, and foreigners supported by native factions, on the other.[70]

Although expressions like this were not general, they increased the apprehension with which sober citizens viewed a party capable of such lawless deeds.

Less important than this disorder in causing the decline of Know-Nothingism, but of some influence nevertheless, was disintegration within the party's ranks. Members found they could not agree even on fundamental principles. In the southwest, and particularly in Louisiana, Catholics from the older families joined Know-Nothing lodges as a means of protesting the newer immigration of Irish and Germans. After failing in an effort to force the party to abandon its religious proscription, they deserted the national organization, carrying on a separate existence within their state and nominating Catholics to office.[71] Other southern states were more or less sympathetic with this stand, partly because of sectional loyalty and partly because a complete absence of Catholics made them apathetic to the whole problem; Virginia, South Carolina, Missouri, and California abolished the religious test for their local councils before the end of 1855.[72] On the other hand the northwestern states were willing to approve the party's No-Popery stand, but objected to its proscription of foreigners. The Indiana State Council in July, 1855, agreed to accept as members all naturalized citizens save Catholics, and in Illinois the party split into the "Sams" and the "Jonathans" over this question.[73] Clearly disunion that no party could stand was setting in.

These factors—legislative failure, criticism and ridicule of the party's secrecy, rioting and bloodshed, internal dissension—would probably have brought an eventual end to the Know-Nothing party. Its immediate Waterloo, however, was the reopened slavery question. Amidst the heat of discussion that followed the repeal of the Missouri Compromise—amidst tales of "Bleeding Kansas" and border warfare and the frantic pleading of emigrant aid companies—the nebulous fears of foreign influence and papal invasion were forgotten. By the middle of 1855 the nation had divided into two warring camps. The Know-Nothing party, built on a basis of union and nationalism, could no more survive these sectional forces than the union itself.

The division of the American party over the slavery issue occurred only after its leaders had taken every possible step to preserve unity. By the fall of 1854 many of them recognized the growing seriousness of the problem and one, Kenneth Raynor of North Carolina, sought to solve it. At the Cincinnati meeting of the National Council, held in November, 1854, he proposed the establishment of a third degree of membership, to be known as the Union degree. Those who took this degree were to pledge absolute fidelity to the union, to "discourage and denounce any attempt coming from any quarter . . . to destroy or subvert it or to weaken its bonds," to seek an amicable adjustment of all political differences that threatened its continuance, and to vote only for men who opposed disunion.[74] The new degree was adopted and immediately proved popular; within six months 1,500,000 members had solemnly agreed to stand together against sectional forces from either north or south.[75]

These efforts were utterly futile. As the sectional gulf widened with the passing months, northern and southern Know-Nothings drifted farther apart, unable to agree on a program that would keep the party, let alone the nation, united. Northern political leaders, swept along on the antislavery tide, began to look upon the whole Know-Nothing movement as a new southern conspiracy. The south, they pointed out, was satisfied with the Kansas-Nebraska act, and could afford to distract northern attention by conjuring up visions of papal aggression and foreign influx. This northern view was clearly expressed by one leader when he wrote that the Know-Nothing movement was a

well-timed scheme to divide the people of the free States upon trifles and side issues, while the south remained a unit in defense of its great interest. It was the cunning attempt to balk and divert the indignation aroused by the repeal of the Missouri restriction, which else would spend its force upon the aggressions of slavery; for by thus kindling the Protestant jealousy of our people against the Pope, and enlisting them in a crusade against the foreigner, the South could all the more successfully push forward its schemes.[76]

Thus it became the patriotic duty of every northerner who opposed the extension of slavery to desert the Know-Nothing party and join the Republican; many Know-Nothing lodges actually followed this path.

Southerners, meanwhile, were beginning to feel that Know-Nothingism was only abolitionism in disguise. Its lodges, they believed, were centers of antislavery sentiment, cleverly concealed beneath the veneer of nativism.[77] This "fiery consistency of abolitionism" alone, their leaders told them, held the party together in the north.[78] Southerners were susceptible to these arguments because they recognized in the very foundations of the Know-Nothing party a principle dangerous to southern institutions. The nativists were insisting on a strong union and nationalism; the south was veering consistently away from any such governmental centralization and toward state's rights. "Sir," one congressional speaker declared in attacking this phase of Know-Nothingism, "those who would consolidate the Government in order to preserve it, are harpies defending the feast which the harpies would fain devour." [79]

These southern fears were not without foundation. As passions bred by the slavery controversy increased, northern Know-Nothing leaders openly sought to align their party with the abolitionists. A large part of the inaugural address of the Know-Nothing governor of Connecticut consisted of an attack on the Kansas-Nebraska act, and the legislature elected with him passed resolutions condemning both this measure and the Fugitive Slave act.[80] The Know-Nothing assembly in Massachusetts adopted a personal liberty law and demanded the removal of the state judge who had enforced the Fugitive Slave act in the case of Anthony Burns.[81] Northern Know-Nothing lodges, equally unable to contain themselves, were frequently outspoken on this vital issue. One convention, at Norfolk, Massachusetts, resolved that

Whereas, Roman Catholicism and slavery being alike founded and supported on the basis of ignorance and tyranny; and being, therefore, natural allies in every warfare against liberty and enlightenment; therefore, be it

Resolved, That there can exist no real hostility to Roman Catholicism which does not embrace slavery, its natural co-worker in opposition to freedom and republican institutions.[82]

Reports of these activities, together with sentiments of a similar nature from individuals in the north,[83] were widely circulated through the south. Little wonder that southern Know-Nothings grew distrustful of the northern wing of their party.

This swing of northern Know-Nothings toward abolitionism was due partly to the spirit of the times and partly to a deliberate plot on the part of several of their leaders. A number of minor northern politicians had entered the party determined to use it to further the antislavery cause. Most notable among this group was Henry Wilson of Massachusetts. He had joined a lodge in March, 1854, and even though he was completely out of sympathy with the proscriptive aims of his fellow members, had rapidly worked his way upward in the party's councils.[84] Chosen United States senator by the Know-Nothing legislature, Wilson was ready to capitalize upon the opportunity. He wrote to a friend: "I saw that one of three things must happen—that the anti-slavery men must ignore their principles to make a national party; or they must fight for the supremacy of their principles, and impose them upon the organization, which would drive off the Southern men: or they must break up the party." [85] The first of these alternatives Wilson would not accept. Hence he determined either to win the Know-Nothing party to an antislavery stand or wreck it and thus make room for a party that would express northern sentiment.

Wilson's chance came during a meeting of the National Council in June, 1855. Southern delegates were in the majority, and the party's platform committee finally brought in a majority and minority report, the former upholding slavery and the latter opposed. Debate on these planks was vigorous and heated; at one time a southerner threatened Henry Wilson, leader of the northern delegates, with a loaded revolver. Finally, after three days of futile wrangling, the proslavery report was adopted, stating that:

> It is the sense of this National Council that Congress ought not to legislate on the subject of Slavery within the Territories of the United States, and that any interference by Congress with Slavery as it exists in the District of Columbia would be . . . a breach of the National Faith.[86]

On the morning after this plank was accepted Wilson brought the northern delegates together. They issued an "Appeal to the People" which declared the signers' principles to be those of nativism and antislavery, and publicly bolted the party.

During the following months the northern State Councils, one by one, endorsed this action of their representatives.[87] An attempt to form a Know-Something party which would advocate

nativism, temperance and antislavery soon failed, and there began a wholesale exodus of former Know-Nothings into the Republican party.[88] The Boston *Pilot* jubilantly remarked: "Sam
has lived too fast. He has lived a hundred years in one. He is
already old, crazy and tottering. He has to lean on a black, woolly
headed staff. He is a little, worn-out, weazened, stunted, dried-
up, helpless, toothless, brainless, heartless, soulless, miserable,
malignant dwarf." [89]

Attempts that were made to continue the Know-Nothing party
as a national organization after June, 1855, were largely of
southern origin. Southerners stoutly maintained that adherence
to the Know-Nothing standard was doubly necessary since the
Republicans and Democrats had become sectional and no longer
represented the entire nation.[90] Northerners refused to be won
by such persuasion; the American party was actually a southern
party after June, 1855. This was particularly unfortunate, for
in its first southern political contest in Virginia in May, 1855, its
candidates were decisively beaten by Democrats.[91] With its
prestige thus shaken, the party lost a succession of elections in the
south during the next few months, failing to carry a single state.
The Know-Nothings were able to win elections only in the
north, yet northern support had been lost through the action of
southerners who were unable to contribute victories in their own
section.

Thus divided, the party approached the presidential election
in 1856 with no chance of victory. Its leaders, however, were
still hopeful. If they could patch up internal differences and
carry the border states, they might succeed in throwing the election into the House of Representatives. No sectional candidate
could be chosen president there, and a Know-Nothing might be
placed in office. The first step was to heal the breach between the
party's northern and southern wings. This was attempted at a
meeting of the National Council in Philadelphia in February,
1856. The objectionable proslavery plank that had been written

into the platform the preceding June was removed, and in its place was inserted a hybrid clause demanding congressional non-interference with all "domestic and social affairs" in the territories and condemning the Pierce administration for the repeal of the Missouri Compromise.[92] Here, indeed, was fence straddling carried to an absurd degree.

More than this, however, was needed to restore harmony to this section-torn party. When the national convention assembled, northern delegates refused to be bound by the platform suggested by the Council and demanded that no candidates be nominated who did not favor congressional action to bar slavery from the territory north of 36° 30'. A resolution to this effect was tabled by southern votes, and the northern members again withdrew, leaving southerners in complete control. Millard Fillmore, whose signing of the Fugitive Slave act of 1850 had made him unpopular in the north and who was also the Whig candidate, was nominated for the presidency.

Fillmore was an unfortunate choice. His record as president had been unimpressive and most northerners looked upon him as an avowed advocate of the slavocracy. Nor could he win the votes of sincere nativists. He had joined a Know-Nothing lodge in 1855, hoping to reap political reward by membership in the party, but his past utterances indicated no enmity either for Catholics or foreigners. By a strange freak of fate he was in Europe and had just sought and obtained an audience with the Pope when news of his nomination reached him, a fact that turned many Know-Nothings against him.[93] Actually nativism was almost forgotten by Fillmore during his campaign. He mentioned the danger of unrestricted foreign immigration in a few speeches,[94] but most of his campaign was devoted solely to means for preserving the union.[95]

Nor did other members of the party stress nativism in the election of 1856. It is true that the American platform demanded that native-born citizens should alone hold public office, that political station be closed to all who recognized "any allegiance or obligation of any description to any foreign prince, potentate, or power," and that legislation should be enacted requiring the twenty-one-year probationary period before naturalization.[96] It is true, too, that an attempt was made to discredit the Republican candidate, John C. Fremont, by proving him a Catholic; pamphlets under such titles as *Fremont's Romanism Established, Colonel Fremont's Religious History. The Authentic Account. Papist or Protestant. Which?* and *The Romish Intrigue. Fremont a Catholic* [97] tried to show that the Republican leader was a member of the church of Rome and a Jesuit. But for the most part, the Know-Nothings confined their campaign literature to pleas for the preservation of the union, warning that the election of either sectional candidate would lead to disaster.[98] In the heat of the slavery controversy, the American party had forgotten the issues that gave it birth.

Nor were the other parties ready to assume the mantle of nativism which the Know-Nothings had discarded. The Democrats, loyal to their foreign-born supporters and conscious of the poor showing the Know-Nothing party had made in the south, declared in their platform against the "attempt to enforce civil and religious disabilities against the rights of acquiring and enjoying citizenship in our own land." [99] The Republican managers were tempted to appeal to New England votes by favoring an anti-Catholic program but abandoned such ideas when they found sentiment at the national convention almost unanimously opposed.[100] The Republican platform did not even mention the subject.

The American party was thus left as a compromise party, the binding thread of nativism that had held its members together obscured and forgotten. The result was disastrous. Fillmore received a popular vote of some 800,000 but the electoral vote of only one state, Maryland. His strength was centered in the border states and in the south; one seventh was from the north, three sevenths from the south, and the remainder from the border states.[101] His northern vote came partly from sincere Know-Nothings and partly from former Whigs who still clung to the hope of compromise; it was concentrated largely in New York, New Jersey, and Pennsylvania, and to a lesser extent in Ohio, Indiana, and Illinois. The New England states had deserted the Know-Nothing standard almost completely. The great strength that the party showed in Maryland, Delaware, Kentucky, Tennessee, Missouri, and California probably did not represent nativistic feeling so much as it did a desire to compromise on the question of slavery. Similarly the Know-Nothing vote in the south came from the traditionally conservative Whig planters whose property interests might be threatened by the aggressive proslavery stand of the Democrats. (See map, p. 405.)

Although the American party actually polled about 25 per cent of the popular vote cast in 1856, its electoral vote was so small that it seemingly suffered a crushing defeat. The blow was so decisive that the party could never hope to recover. It lingered on in Maryland and other border states until the outbreak of the Civil War, but now it was only a compromise party with its nativistic principles completely abandoned.

Thus did the slavery issue sound the death knell of Know-Nothingism. This greater sectional problem and a civil war alone proved strong enough to break the hold that the Monks, the Breckinridges, the Beechers, the Morses, the Brownlees, and the Gavazzis had on overzealous American Protestants.

NOTES

[1] *Congressional Globe,* 33rd Cong., 2nd Sess., Appendix, 53–60.

[2] *Ibid.,* 33rd Cong., 2nd Sess., Appendix, 48–53.

[3] *Ibid.,* 33rd Cong., 2nd Sess., Appendix, 68, 111–116. Chandler's speech was widely circulated in pamphlet form under the title *The Temporal Power of the Pope—a Full and Authentic Report of the Brilliant Speech of the Hon. Joseph R. Chandler of Pennsylvania in the House of Representatives of the United States, Jan. 11, 1855* (Philadelphia, 1855). Chandler was answered not only in Congress and by the nativistic journals but in a pamphlet, Robert C.

Grundy, *The Temporal Powers of the Pope Dangerous to the Religious and Civil Liberties of the American Republic; a Review of the Speech of the Hon. Joseph R. Chandler delivered in the House of Representatives of the United States, January 10* [sic] *1855* (Maysville, Kentucky, 1855). The author believed that the age of miracles was not past when a Catholic could stand on the floor of Congress and defend the Pope of Rome.

4 *Congressional Globe,* 33rd Cong., 2nd Sess., 97.

5 *Ibid.,* 33rd Cong., 2nd Sess., 103.

6 The House was made up of 83 Democrats, 108 Republicans (of whom 70 had been or were members of Know-Nothing lodges) and 43 Know-Nothings. The Democrats had a clear majority in the Senate, with 42 Democrats, 15 Republicans and five Know-Nothings.

7 Both major parties selected candidates for the position who were also Know-Nothings, the Democrats Humphrey Marshall of Kentucky and the Republicans Nathaniel P. Banks of Massachusetts. The Know-Nothing candidate was H. M. Fuller of Pennsylvania. Banks was finally selected.

8 *Congressional Globe,* 34th Cong., 1st Sess., 166–173; *Ibid.,* 34th Cong., 1st Sess., Appendix, 967–969, 1082–1085, 1136–1143. Smith's speech was widely reprinted in religious and nativistic newspapers and was issued in pamphlet form. It was replied to by "An Adopted Catholic" in *Letter of an Adopted Catholic Addressed to the President of the Kentucky Democratic Association of Washington City, on Temporal Allegiance to the Pope, and the Relations of the Catholic Church and Catholics, both Native and Adopted, to the System of Domestic Slavery and its Agitation in the United States* (Washington, 1856).

9 Even the Boston *Pilot,* a Catholic and Irish paper, agreed that there was something to be said for the Know-Nothing stand on immigration. This view was adopted, it explained, because Irish immigration had virtually ceased and German immigration was increasing. This was bringing to America large numbers of infidels who should not be allowed to share in the government. *Pilot,* March 18, 1854.

10 The decisive defeat of this proposal during the Native American agitation of the 1840's prejudiced opinion against it. An attempt of Lewis C. Levin of Pennsylvania to introduce such a measure into the House of Representatives in 1850 had aroused scarcely any interest. *Congressional Globe,* 31st Cong., 1st Sess., Part I, 219.

11 Massachusetts and Rhode Island sent such petitions. *Senate Miscellaneous Documents,* 33rd Cong., 2nd Sess., No. 19; *House Miscellaneous Documents,* 34th Cong., 1st Sess., No. 40.

12 *Congressional Globe,* 33rd Cong., 2nd Sess., 26.

13 *Ibid.,* 33rd Cong., 2nd Sess., 26.

14 *Ibid.,* 33rd Cong., 2nd Sess., 447. The House bill was introduced by Nathaniel G. Taylor of Tennessee and was allowed to expire in the hands of the Committee on the Judiciary.

15 *Ibid.,* 34th Cong., 1st Sess., 350, 616.

16 *Ibid.,* 34th Cong., 1st Sess., 980.

17 *Ibid.,* 34th Cong., 1st Sess., 1409–144.

18 *Ibid.,* 34th Cong., 1st Sess., 641, 1692. The bill, when reported out unfavorably by the Committee on the Judiciary on July 21, 1856, was immediately referred to the Committee of the Whole on the State of the Union and never

taken up again. The one speech in its favor was delivered by H. W. Hoffman of Maryland on July 29.

[19] The measure originated in the Committee on Commerce in response to numerous requests from state legislatures and bore the stamp of approval from that body. At about the same time resolutions were introduced in the Senate calling for similar action there. *Ibid.*, 33rd Cong., 2nd Sess., 166–167, 357.

[20] *Ibid.*, 33rd Cong., 2nd Sess., 389–391; *Ibid.*, 33rd Cong., 2nd Sess., Appendix, 83–84. A. R. Sollers of Maryland in the House and James Cooper in the Senate were the principal supporters of the bill.

[21] Leading exponents of this point of view were Robert Breckinridge of Kentucky in the House, and Richard Bradhead of Pennsylvania and James C. Jones of Tennessee in the Senate. *Ibid.*, 33rd Cong., 2nd Sess.; 393, 783, 1181.

[22] *Reports of Committees,* 34th Cong., 1st Sess., No. 359, 1–152.

[23] February 3, 1855.

[24] George H. Haynes, "A Know Nothing Legislature," *American Historical Association Report for 1896,* 178–179.

[25] *Ibid.*, 181–182.

[26] *Ibid.*, 182.

[27] Just before the legislature met the Reverend Rufus W. Clark had delivered a series of No-Popery sermons in Boston in which he urged the appointment of such a committee. *Congregationalist,* November 24, 1854.

[28] The appointment of this committee was fully discussed in Boston by the *Pilot,* March 25, 1854, April 1, 1854, April 29, 1854 and ff.

[29] The petition was presented by residents of Foxborough. Charles Hale, *A Review of the Proceedings of the Nunnery Committee of the Massachusetts Legislature; and Especially Their Conduct . . . on occasion of the Visit to the Catholic School in Roxbury, March 26, 1855* (Boston, 1855), 9–15.

[30] Haynes, "Know Nothing Legislature," *loc. cit.*, 183.

[31] *Pilot,* March 10, 1855.

[32] Hale, *Review of the Proceedings of the Nunnery Committee,* 17–40; *Pilot,* April 7, 1855.

[33] Hale, *Review of the Proceedings of the Nunnery Committee,* 60–61. Mrs. Patterson's charge was $1.25. The *Pilot* noted that one member of the committee had visited "nuns of the type who got him intoxicated and stole $71 from him." April 14, 1855.

[34] Hale, *Review of the Proceedings of the Nunnery Committee,* 16.

[35] *Ibid.*, 53–59.

[36] Quoted in Desmond, *Know Nothing Party,* 132.

[37] Haynes, "Know Nothing Legislature," *loc. cit.*, 185.

[38] *Ibid.*, 186–187.

[39] Schmeckebier, *History of the Know Nothing Party in Maryland,* 33–34.

[40] Peyton Hurt, "The Rise and Fall of the 'Know Nothings' in California," California Historical Society *Quarterly,* IX (March–June, 1930), 48.

[41] *National Intelligencer,* October 9, 1855; *Connecticut Courant,* May 26, 1855, July 21, 1855, October 20, 1855.

[42] *Senate Journal,* May Session, 1855, 41.

[43] Brand, "Know Nothing Party in Indiana," *loc. cit.*, 181–182.

[44] *Tribune Almanac and Political Register for 1855,* 23.

[45] Quoted in Hambleton, *Political Campaign in Virginia,* 160–162.

46 Quoted in Desmond, *Know Nothing Party*, 86–87.

47 Longstreet, *Know Nothingism Unveiled*, 8; Julian, *Political Recollections*, 141. The Springfield *Republican* shared in these sentiments when its editor wrote on March 31, 1854: "Secret political organizations, in a Republican government, are in the last degree reprehensible." Quoted in George S. Merriam, *The Life and Times of Samuel Bowles* (New York, 1885), II, 124–125.

48 Schmeckebier, *History of the Know Nothing Party in Maryland*, 30–33; *Remarks on the Majority and Minority Reports of the Select Committee on Secret Societies.* The committee, named by a Know-Nothing legislature at the insistence of a Democratic governor, was Know-Nothing in majority. The majority report favored secret societies, the minority report condemned them bitterly. The *Remarks* cited above were violently anti-Know-Nothing and condemned the majority report.

49 A typical resolution sent by the Maine legislature to Congress declared that "secret oath bound political associations are hostile to a Republican form of government; destroy the rights of the minorities and the independence of the citizens; corrupt the purity of the ballot box and become patent engines by which cunning, ambitious and unprincipled men are enabled to subvert the power of the people, and usurp for themselves the reins of government." *Senate Miscellaneous Documents*, 34th Cong., 1st Sess., No. 58.

50 *Congressional Globe*, 33rd Cong., 2nd Sess., 571–572. The resolution was introduced by William H. Witte of Pennsylvania.

51 A motion to suspend the rules that this resolution might be debated was lost, although if all Democrats had voted for it it would have carried. Every Democrat and Republican who had voted against the motion felt called upon to explain that this did not mean that he favored the Know-Nothings. These speakers usually ended by attacking the secrecy of the order. *Ibid.*, 33rd Cong., 2nd Sess., 349ff., 648–649.

52 *The Know Nothings. An Expose of the Secret Order of Know Nothings; the most Ludicrous and Startling Yankee "Notion" ever Conceived* (New York, 1854). A similar satirical account was: William Swinson, *An Expose of the Know Nothings* (Philadelphia, 1854), 1–10. Another pamphlet *A Few Words to the Thinking and Judicious Voters of Pennsylvania* (——, 1854), attempted to ridicule the Know-Nothing candidate for governor of the state by representing his initiation into the order in absurd terms.

53 *American Union*, May 6, 1854; *Pilot*, April 29, 1854.

54 *Remarks on the Majority and Minority Reports of the Select Committee on Secret Societies*, 22–23.

55 The seriousness of these charges was shown by attempted Know-Nothing rebuttals. They maintained that secrecy had been used by the Revolutionary fathers, by the framers of the Constitution, by the Senate, and by older political parties. They insisted, too, that secrecy was necessary to fight Romanism, "the most secret and formidable association that human ingenuity has ever devised." *Sons of the Sires*, 21; Robertson, *American Party*, 7–10; Carroll, *Great American Battle*, 225–226; Bell, *Speech Delivered at a Mass Meeting of the American Party*, 8–9; *Wide Awake Gift and Know Nothing Token*, 55–62; Saunders, *Voice to America*, 363–372; Franklin, *Know Nothingism*, 12. These same views were expressed by the party's representatives in Congress. *Congressional Globe*, 33rd Cong., 2nd Sess., 71, 84, 97.

434   *The Protestant Crusade, 1800-1860*

[56] Brand, "Know Nothing Party in Indiana," *loc. cit.*, 74, cited the example of a lodge that had to meet in the middle of a cornfield to escape the curious.

[57] *Freeman's Journal*, January 29, 1854. The Guard of Liberty was a minor nativistic military company having about 300 members.

[58] Sisco, *Political Nativism in New York State*, 96–97.

[59] New Orleans *Delta*, quoted in *American Union*, April 15, 1854.

[60] *Pilot*, September 2, 1854. The Richmond *Examiner* published its expose on August 8, having obtained the information from the Democratic politician, Henry A. Wise, who had secured it from the governor of Illinois. The *Examiner* article is printed in Hambleton, *Political Campaign in Virginia*, 46–54.

[61] Hartford *Daily Times*, February 20, 1855; *Congregationalist*, May 4, 1855; Philadelphia *Register*, April 5, 1855; New York *Tribune*, May 5, 1855.

[62] *Connecticut Courant*, March 31, 1855 ff. The *Know-Nothing Crusader*, the New York *Express*, and the Philadelphia *Sun* also campaigned for such a reform and the Pennsylvania and Delaware Councils passed resolutions declaring for an open constitution. Brand, "Know Nothing Party in Indiana," *loc. cit.*, 197.

[63] Cluskey, *Political Text Book*, 46.

[64] *Remarks on the Majority and Minority Reports of the Select Committee on Secret Societies*, 7–8.

[65] McMaster, *History of the People of the United States*, VIII, 86.

[66] Schmeckebier, *History of the Know Nothing Party in Maryland*, 43–44.

[67] *Ibid.*, 37–38, 86–88; Tusca, *Know Nothingism in Baltimore*, 7, 15–17, 23; Bernard C. Steiner, *The Life of Henry W. Davis* (Baltimore, 1916), 82–83.

[68] *Pilot*, July 15, 1854, August 19, 1854, March 26, 1855; *Freeman's Journal*, April 1, 1854, July 15, 1854, November 18, 1854.

[69] *Pilot*, April 21, 1855, May 19, 1855, August 18, 1855; New York *Tribune*, August 8, 1855; Hartford *Times*, August 15, 1855; Tisdale, *Know Nothing Almanac*, 22.

[70] Bell, *Speech Delivered at Knoxville*, 14.

[71] The controversy between the Louisiana State Council and the National Council is well described in two works by Charles Gayarre, leader of the state Know-Nothings. *Address on the Religious Test to the Convention of the American Party Assembled in Philadelphia on the 5th of June, 1855* (New Orleans, 1855), 1–26; and *Address to the People of Louisiana on the State of the Parties* (New Orleans, 1855), 1–32.

[72] Brand, "Know Nothing Party in Indiana," *loc. cit.*, 197; Desmond, *Know Nothing Party*, 102–103.

[73] Brand, "Know Nothing Party in Indiana," *loc. cit.*, 198–199; Senning, "Know Nothing Party in Illinois," *loc. cit.*, 28.

[74] Wilson, *History of the Rise and Fall of the Slave Power*, II, 21.

[75] Julian, *Political Recollections*, 144–145.

[76] *Ibid.*, 141–142.

[77] *Remarks on the Majority and Minority Reports of the Select Committee on Secret Societies*, 8, 31; *Letter of an Adopted Catholic*, 1, 6; Hambleton, *Political Campaign in Virginia*, 127; *Congressional Globe*, 33rd Cong., 2nd Sess., Appendix, 69–70, 267, 270–271, 351–353.

[78] *Congressional Globe*, 33rd Cong., 2nd Sess., Appendix, 66.

[79] *Ibid.,* 70.

[80] *Connecticut Courant,* May 5, 1855, June 2, 1855.

[81] William G. Bean, "An Aspect of Know-Nothingism—The Immigrant and Slavery," *South Atlantic Quarterly,* XXIII (October, 1924), 322. On one occasion handbills were circulated in Boston calling on the Know-Nothings to rise against a foreign military company that had aided in the return of a runaway slave. *Pilot,* June 3, 1854.

[82] Quoted in *Congressional Globe,* 33rd Cong., 2nd Sess., Appendix, 59.

[83] *Pilot,* July 22, 1854.

[84] Elias Nason, *The Life and Public Services of Henry Wilson, Late Vice President of the United States* (Boston, 1876), 135–137.

[85] *Ibid.,* 131–132.

[86] New York *Tribune,* June 15, 1855. This account of the meeting is drawn from *Ibid.,* June 6 ff., from Wilson, *History of the Rise and Fall of the Slave Power,* II, 423–433, and from Nason, *Life of Henry Wilson,* 138–140.

[87] Typical was the "Springfield Platform" drawn up by the Massachusetts Know-Nothings. Nason, *Life of Henry Wilson,* 142–145.

[88] Brand, "Know Nothing Party in Indiana," *loc. cit.,* 196.

[89] August 18, 1855.

[90] Bell, *Speech Delivered at Knoxville,* 15–17; *Origin, Principles and Purposes of the American Party,* 6; Robertson, *The American Party,* 25–39; Carroll, *Great American Battle,* 145–146; Anna E. Carroll, *The Union of the States* (Boston, 1856), 20–30; Campbell, *Americanism,* 8.

[91] This Virginia campaign is described in detail in Constance M. Gay, "The Campaign of 1855 in Virginia and the Fall of the Know-Nothing Party," *Richmond College Historical Papers,* I (Richmond, 1916), 309–325; in John S. Wise, *The End of an Era* (Boston, 1899), 54–55; and in Hambleton, *Political Campaign in Virginia, passim.* The latter book is a collection of newspaper extracts, speeches and other material having to do with the election.

[92] Wilson, *History of the Rise and Fall of the Slave Power,* II, 508.

[93] Fillmore, *Millard Fillmore Papers,* XI, 355–357.

[94] *Ibid.,* XI, 16–17.

[95] See especially *Ibid.,* XI, 17–29. Many of his campaign speeches are printed in full in this collection.

[96] Edward Stanwood, *A History of Presidential Elections* (Boston and New York, 1884), 195–196.

[97] All three pamphlets were published in 1856. None bears a place of printing. The charges were answered by a Republican campaign pamphlet, *Colonel Fremont Not a Roman Catholic* (——, 1856). Actually Fremont was an Episcopalian. The rumor that he was a Catholic originated in his marriage by a Roman Catholic priest.

[98] Carroll, *Union of the States,* 43–54; *Indictment: The People of the United States versus James Buchanan of Pennsylvania; a True Bill! National Grand Jury, Sam, Foreman* (New Orleans, 1856), 1–4. The Massachusetts Historical Society owns a large collection of Know-Nothing campaign pamphlets donated by R. C. Winthrop, and most of them are of this character. The party spokesmen in Congress were similarly confining most of their speeches in 1856 to pleas for union. See Henry Winter Davis, *Speeches and Addresses Delivered in the Congress of the United States, and on Several*

436   *The Protestant Crusade, 1800-1860*

Public Occasions (New York, 1867), 61–62. The Democrats concentrated their campaign literature directed against the Know-Nothings to a rebuttal of this claim. See *Proceedings of the Democratic and Anti-Know-Nothing State Convention Held in the City of Montgomery, January 8th and 9th, 1856* (Montgomery, 1856), 10.

99 Stanwood, *History of Presidential Elections,* 202.

100 This was done by proposing a series of anti-Know-Nothing resolutions from the floor of the convention. The hearty applause convinced Republican managers that this was the correct procedure. George Schneider, "Lincoln and the Anti-Know Nothing Resolutions," *McLean County Historical Society Transactions,* III (Bloomington, Illinois, 1900), 89–90. For expressions of Republican leaders on the question see Julian, *Political Recollections,* 147–149; Nichols, *Forty Years of American Life,* II, 90; George W. Julian, *Speeches on Political Questions* (New York, 1872), 109ff., and 126ff.

101 *Tribune Almanac and Political Register for 1857* (New York, 1857), 44–64.

Appendix

CONSTITUTION OF THE AMERICAN SOCIETY, TO PROMOTE THE PRINCIPLES OF THE PROTESTANT REFORMATION [1]

Whereas, the principles of the court of Rome are totally irreconcilable with the gospel of Christ; liberty of conscience; the rights of man; and with the constitution and laws of the United States of America.—And whereas, the influence of Romanism is rapidly extending throughout this Republic, endangering the peace and freedom of our country—Therefore, being anxious to preserve the ascendancy of "pure religion and undefiled," and to maintain and perpetuate the genuine truths of Protestantism unadulterated; with devout confidence in the sanction of the Great Head of the Church to aid our efforts in withstanding the "power and great authority of the Beast, and the strong delusion of the False Prophet," we do hereby agree to be governed by the following Constitution:

I. This Society shall be called "The American Society, to promote the principles of the Protestant Reformation."

II. To act as a Home Missionary society—to diffuse correct information concerning the distinctions between Protestantism and Popery—to arouse Protestants to a proper sense of their duty in reference to the Romanists—and to use all evangelical methods to convert the Papists to Christianity by Lectures, and the dissemination of suitable Tracts and standard books upon the Romish controversy.

III. Any person who subscribes to the principles of this Constitution, and who contributes in any way to the funds of this Society, may be a member, and shall be entitled to a vote at all public meetings.

IV. The officers of this Society shall be a President, Vice-Presidents, a Treasurer, a Foreign Secretary, a Corresponding, and a Recording Secretary,—all to be elected by members of this Society.

[1] From the *American Protestant Vindicator,* June 24, 1840.

437

V. This Society shall annually elect an Executive Committee of twenty gentlemen residing in New York city, and its vicinity, five of whom shall be a quorum, to do business, provided the President, or some one of the officers be one of them present. They shall enact their own bye [*sic*] laws, fill vacancies in their body, employ agents, and fix their compensation, appropriate the funds, call special meetings of the Society, and zealously endeavor to accomplish the object of the institution.

VI. Any Society or Association founded on the same principles, may become auxiliary to this Society; and the officers of each auxiliary Association shall, ex-officio, be entitled to deliberate at all meetings of the Society, for the transaction of its affairs.

VII. This constitution may be amended by a vote of two-thirds of all the members present at any annual meeting of the Society, which shall be held on the second Tuesday of May, and should it be prevented from taking place at that time, all the officers elected at the former annual meeting shall hold over until such meeting shall be duly called and held.

VIII. Any person contributing the sum of twenty dollars, or more, to the funds of the Society, shall be constituted a life member; and those who have made donations, or otherwise rendered eminent service in the cause, shall be entitled to honorary membership.

Constitution of the American Protestant Association [2]

Whereas, we believe the system of Popery to be, in its principles and tendency, subversive of civil and religious liberty, and destructive to the spiritual welfare of men, we unite for the purpose of defending our Protestant interests against the great exertions now making to propagate that system in the United States; and adopt the following constitution:—

Article I. This Society shall be called the American Protestant Association.

Article II. The objects of its formation, and for the attainment of which its efforts shall be directed, are—

1. The union and encouragement of Protestant ministers of the gospel, to give to their several congregations instruction on the differences between Protestantism and Popery.

[2] *Address of the Board of Managers of the American Protestant Association with the Constitution and Organization of the Association, 7-8.*

2. To call attention to the necessity of a more extensive distribution, and thorough study of the Holy Scriptures.

3. The circulation of books and tracts adapted to give information on the various errors of Popery in their history, tendency, and design.

4. To awaken the attention of the community to the dangers which threaten the liberties, and the public and domestic institutions, of these United States from the assaults of Romanism.

Article III. This Association shall be composed of all such persons as agree in adopting the purposes and principles of this constitution and contribute to the funds by which it is supported.

Article IV. The officers of the Association shall be a President, three Vice-Presidents, a treasurer, a corresponding secretary, a recording secretary, and two lay directors from each denomination represented in the Association, to be elected annually; together with all the ministers belonging to it; who shall form a Board for the transaction of business of whom any seven, at a meeting duly convened, shall be a quorum. The stated meetings of the Board to be quarterly.

Article V. The Board of managers shall, at the first meeting after their election, appoint an executive committee, consisting of a minister and layman from each of the denominations represented in the association, of which the secretaries and treasurer shall be ex-officio members. This committee to meet as often as they may find necessary for the transaction of the business committed to them, and to report quarterly to the Board of managers.

Article VI. The duties of the Board shall be, to carry out, in every way most expedient in their view, the ends and purposes for which this Association is organized; and to aid and encourage the formation of similar associations in the various parts of the United States; and to render an annual report of their proceedings to the Association, at their annual meeting on the second Tuesday in November.

Article VII. The Board of managers shall have power to enact such by-laws as may not be inconsistent with this constitution, and to fill all vacancies that may occur between the annual meetings.

Article VIII. This constitution shall be subject to amendments only at the annual meetings of the Association, by a vote of two thirds of the members present at such meeting.

CONSTITUTION OF THE AMERICAN PROTESTANT SOCIETY [3]

Whereas the influence of Romanism is rapidly extending over this Republic, endangering the freedom and the institutions of our country, by withholding the "Word of God" from large masses of minds, leaving them in ignorance, and under the influence of superstition: And whereas we desire to secure the permanency of our free institutions, and through them the liberty of conscience, to maintain and perpetuate "pure religion and undefiled," and also to rescue from error and from sin those who are in spiritual darkness, we adopt the following

CONSTITUTION

Article I

As this Society is of a national character, it shall be called "The American Protestant Society."

Article II

The object of this Society is to diffuse throughout the United States the principles of the Protestant religion, for the purpose of enlightening the minds both of Protestants and of Romanists respecting the doctrines and the duties revealed in the Word of God, and to diffuse correct information concerning the distinctions between Protestantism and Romanism.

Article III

Believing coercion in religious opinions, and the spirit of denunciation, to be inconsistent with the spirit of Christianity, the means to be employed to secure the objects of the Society, are Light and Love; in the use of these means, the Society will aim to enlighten Protestants concerning the nature, operation, and influence of Romanism, as well to guard against its encroachments upon our civil and religious institutions, as to awaken Christian feeling and Christian action for the salvation of Romanists, by the employment of the Press, Lecturing Agents, Missionaries, and Colporteurs, to circulate Bibles, Tracts, and Books upon the subject—looking unto God for success in this work.

[3] American Protestant Society, *Second Annual Report*, 27–28.

Article IV

As it is a prominent object of this Society to diffuse correct information on the subject of Protestantism and Romanism, the Society will moreover appoint a Committee of literary gentlemen, who will receive donations of books, and money for the purchase of books, in order that a Library may be collected, that shall embrace the standard works on these subjects that have been published by Protestant and by Roman Catholic writers; which Library shall be kept in connexion with the Depository of the Society, and be under the control of its Executive Committee, for the use of Protestant Ministers of all denominations, and of literary gentlemen, who may desire to resort to it for the purposes of reference.

Article V

The Officers of the Society will be a President, Vice Presidents, Recording Secretary, a Corresponding and Foreign Secretaries, and a Treasurer.

Article VI

The Society will annually elect an Executive Committee, to consist of at least twelve gentlemen, residing in New-York, five of whom shall be a quorum for the transaction of business. The Officers of the Society are *ex-officio* members of the Executive Committee. The Committee shall have power to fill their own vacancies, and enact their own by-laws.

Article VII

The Executive Committee shall appoint the editor of *The American Protestant;* also Committees on Agencies, on the Printing Department, and on the various business of the Society.

Article VIII

Any Society or Association formed on the same principles, in any part of the United States, may become auxiliary to this Society.

Article IX

Any person who subscribes to this Constitution and contributes three dollars annually, may be a member of this Society, and be entitled to vote at all public meetings; a contribution of the sum of twenty-five dollars constitutes a life member; and fifty dollars, a life director.

Article X

The annual meeting of the Society shall be the fourth Wednesday in April of each year, when this Constitution may be altered by a vote of two-thirds of the members present.

CONSTITUTION OF THE AMERICAN AND FOREIGN CHRISTIAN UNION [4]

Preamble

Whereas there have been formed in this country, at different times, three Societies: The American Protestant, The Foreign Evangelical, and the Christian Alliance; all having in view substantially the same great work, viz. *The Diffusion of Evangelical Truth wherever a corrupted form of Christianity exists, at home and abroad.* And, whereas it is deemed practicable to merge these Societies into one, which shall prosecute their several objects, thus diminishing the number of appeals to the Churches, as well as expense and labor, it is deemed expedient that a new organization be formed, which shall undertake the work and assume the responsibilities of the above-named Societies, and conduct its affairs according to the following

CONSTITUTION

Article I. This Society shall be known by the name of THE AMERICAN AND FOREIGN CHRISTIAN UNION.

Article II. The objects of this Society shall be, by Missions, Colportage, the Press, and other appropriate agencies, to diffuse and promote the principles of Religious Liberty, and a pure and Evangelical Christianity, both at home and abroad, wherever a corrupted Christianity exists.

Article III. Any person contributing three dollars a year shall be a Member of the Society; a contribution of thirty dollars at one time shall constitute a Member for Life; and the donation of one hundred dollars shall constitute a Director for Life. All Life Mem-

[4] American Protestant Society, *Sixth Annual Report*, 41-42.

Appendix

bers and Life Directors of the American Protestant Society, the Foreign Evangelical Society, and the Christian Alliance, shall be Life Members and Life Directors of this Society. Life Directors shall have the privilege of meeting with the Board of Directors and participating in their deliberations and discussions.

Article IV. The control and disposal of the funds, property, and estate of the Society, shall be vested in a Board of 32 directors, (one-half at least of whom shall be laymen, and 18 at least of whom shall reside in the city of New-York and its vicinity), who shall be chosen by the Society at its annual meeting; and, in default of an election, the Directors last chosen shall hold their office until others are elected; eight of whom shall constitute a quorum for the transaction of business at any meeting regularly convened. The Board shall be divided into four classes of eight members each, one of which shall go out at the end of each year, but shall be re-eligible. The Board shall be chosen from the several evangelical denominations; but no more than one-fourth part from any one denomination. The Board shall fill all vacancies that may occur in its own body, appoint a President, Vice-Presidents, a Treasurer, and Secretaries for the Home and Foreign Departments, and such other officers, and such committees as the interests of the Society may require. The President, Vice-Presidents, Treasurer, and Secretaries shall be, ex-officio, members of the Board.

Article V. The Board shall annually elect an Executive Committee of nine members. The President, 1st Vice-President, and Treasurer shall be, ex-officio, members of this committee, and five shall constitute a quorum for the transaction of business. The Executive Committee shall be charged with the business of the Society at home and abroad, shall form their own by-laws, and keep regular minutes of their transactions, and prepare an annual report of their proceedings, to be submitted to the Society, under the direction of the Board, and also report to the Board at their regular meetings as often as required.

Article VI. The Board shall meet at least once in three months, form their own rules for the transaction of business, and, when necessary, convene the Society. They shall take such security of the Treasurer as shall be deemed proper, employ such means for the accomplishment of the objects of the Society as occasions and exigencies may require, and keep regular minutes of their proceedings.

Article VII. The annual meeting of the Society shall be held on the Tuesday preceding the second Thursday of May in each year, when the Directors shall be chosen, the Treasurer's accounts presented, and the proceedings of the foregoing year reported.

Article VIII. The Board of Directors shall meet within fifteen days after the annual meeting of the Society, for the election of their officers and the appointment of the committees.

Article IX. The Board of Directors may admit, as an Auxiliary, any Society organized to labor in the same fields, according to the same principles, and upon the same plans proposed by this Society.

Article X. No alteration shall be made in this Constitution, except by the Society at an annual meeting, on the recommendation of the Board of Directors, and by a vote of two-thirds of the members present.

Bibliography

The following bibliography [1] is divided into three parts. The first attempts to list all newspapers, magazines, reports of societies, publications of nativistic parties, books and pamphlets directed againt Catholicism or immigration which appeared in the United States between 1800 and 1860. Foreign books are included only where external evidence indicates their influence in America, and works printed before 1800 only when they are referred to in the text. This section of the bibliography makes no pretense of being exhaustive. The author has searched some two dozen libraries in New England and the middle states for anti-Catholic references, yet each new collection examined yields new titles.

The second part includes other primary materials used in the compilation of this work: public documents, newspapers and periodicals, reports of societies, and miscellaneous books and pamphlets. The third lists the secondary materials consulted. This section is confined to those books and articles that deal primarily with nativism during the period studied, or that have been referred to repeatedly. Secondary works employed only once or that are well known have been omitted.

I. Anti-Catholic Publications

1. Newspapers and Periodicals

The American Banner (Chicopee, Massachusetts), January 13, 1848– ?. A weekly newspaper published by the Order of United Americans.

[1] A portion of this bibliography has been published by the author under the title: "Tentative Bibliography of Anti-Catholic Propaganda in the United States (1800–1860)," *Catholic Historical Review*, XVIII (January, 1933), 492–513.

The American and Foreign Christian Union (New York, New York), January, 1850–December, 1861. A monthly magazine, the organ of the American and Foreign Christian Union.

The American Protestant (New York, New York), 1845–1849. A monthly magazine.

The American Protestant (New York, New York), January, 1844–May, 1845. A semi-monthly magazine issued by the American Protestant Society. Replaced by the *American Protestant Magazine*.

The American Protestant Magazine (New York, New York), June, 1845–December, 1849. Official monthly journal of the American Protestant Society. Suspended publication when its place was taken by the *American and Foreign Christian Union*.

The American Protestant Vindicator and Defender of Civil and Religious Liberty Against the Inroads of Popery (New York, New York), 1834–1842. Semi-monthly newspaper. Official organ of the American Protestant Reformation Society.

The American Republican Magazine (New York, New York), October, 1844– ? . A monthly magazine published by the American Republican party.

The Anti-Romanist (New York, New York), July, 1834– ? . A weekly journal maintained for a short time by publishers of the *Protestant Magazine*.

The Baltimore Literary and Religious Magazine (Baltimore, Maryland), 1835–1841. Anti-Catholic monthly magazine. Its editors suspended publication at the end of 1841 and launched in its place the *Spirit of the XIX Century*.

The Colonial Protestant and Journal of Literature and Science (Montreal, Quebec, Canada), March, 1848– ? . A monthly anti-Catholic magazine for Canadian readers.

The Continental (New York, New York), May 19, 1849– ? . A weekly newspaper representing the Order of United Americans and continuing the newspaper, *Order of United Americans*.

Daily American Organ (Washington, D. C.), November 13, 1854–November 14, 1856. Published daily by an association of Native Americans.

The Downfall of Babylon; or, the Triumph of Truth over Popery (Philadelphia and New York), August 14, 1834–July, 1837. Weekly and semi-monthly.

The Jackson Protestant (Jackson, Tennessee), ? –1846. A weekly that suspended publication in 1846.

The Know Nothing and American Crusader (Boston, Massachusetts), 1854–1855. Published weekly.

Metropolitan Magazine and Republican Review (New York, New York), 1844– ?. The first monthly magazine founded by the American Republican party.

The National Protestant (New York, New York), November, 1844–September, 1846. A monthly magazine. In 1846 the name was changed to the *National Protestant Magazine or the Anti-Jesuit,* and in 1847 it was absorbed by the *American Protestant Magazine.*

The Native American (Philadelphia, Pennsylvania), April 11, 1844–?. Daily organ of the American Republican party of Philadelphia.

The Native American (Washington, D. C.), 1837–1840. Weekly.

The Native Eagle and American Advocate (Philadelphia, Pennsylvania), December 1, 1845– ?. Daily newspaper devoted to the interests of the American Republican party.

The New Orleans Protestant (New Orleans, Louisiana), 1844– ? Weekly.

The New York American Republican (New York, New York), 1843– ?. A daily newspaper.

The New York Crusader (New York, New York), 1854– ?. Official organ of the Know-Nothing party in New York City.

The North American Protestant Magazine or the Anti-Jesuit (New York, New York), April, 1846– ?. A monthly magazine.

The Northern Protestant and American Advocate (Newbury, Vermont), 1848– ?.

The Order of United Americans (New York, New York), July 15, 1848–May 12, 1849. Official organ of the Order of United Americans. Published under the title: *O.U.A.* Continued as *The Continental.*

The Pennant and Native American (St. Louis, Missouri), 1844– ?. Daily newspaper of the American Republican party.

Priestcraft Exposed and Primitive Religion Defended (Lockport, New York), May 19, 1828–April 6, 1829. A monthly paper attacking priestcraft in all its forms.

Priestcraft Exposed (Concord, New Hampshire), 1834– ?. Semimonthly.

448   *The Protestant Crusade, 1800-1860*

Priestcraft Unmasked (New York, New York), January 1, 1830–November 15, 1830. Semi-monthly.

The Protestant (New York, New York), January 2, 1830–December, 1832. Weekly. The first anti-Catholic newspaper.

The Protestant (Williamsburg, New York), April, 1852– ?. A monthly magazine.

The Protestant Banner Set for the Defense of Truth (Philadelphia, Pennsylvania), December 3, 1843–April 24, 1845. Semi-monthly organ of the Union Protestant Association of Philadelphia.

The Protestant Magazine (New York, New York), September, 1833–August, 1834. Monthly.

The Quarterly Review of the American Protestant Association (Philadelphia, Pennsylvania), January, 1844–October, 1845. Absorbed into the *American Protestant Magazine.*

The Reformation Advocate (New York, New York), 1832–September, 1833. Weekly. Suspended publication when its place was taken by the *Protestant Magazine.*

The Reformation Defended against the Errors of the Times (Albany, New York), 1844.

The Republic: a Monthly Magazine of American Literature, Politics and Art (New York, New York), January, 1851–December, 1852. Published by the Order of United Americans.

The Spirit of the XIX Century (Baltimore, Maryland), 1842–1843. A monthly anti-Catholic magazine.

The Spirit of '76 (New York, New York), 1835– ?. A daily nativistic newspaper.

The True Catholic (Louisville, Kentucky), 1845– ?. An anti-Catholic weekly newspaper operated by the Protestant clergymen of Louisville.

The True Catholic, Reformed Protestant and Free (Baltimore, Maryland), 1843– ?. A monthly magazine.

The True Freeman's Journal and Protestant Standard (New York, New York), January, 1854– ?. A New York anti-Catholic weekly.

The Weekly American Republican (New York, New York), 1844– ?. A weekly organ of the American Republican party.

The Western Protestant (Bardstown, Kentucky), 1836– ?. A weekly anti-Catholic journal.

2. Reports of anti-Catholic Societies

American and Foreign Christian Union, *Annual Reports.* New York, 1850–1861.

American Protestant Association, *Address of the Board of Managers of the American Protestant Association, with the Constitution and Organization of the Association.* Philadelphia, 1843.

American Protestant Association, *First Annual Report of the American Protestant Association, together with a Sketch of the Addresses at the First Anniversary, November 18, 1843.* Philadelphia, 1843.

American Protestant Society, *Annual Reports.* New York, 1844–1849.

American Protestant Society, *Circular Issued by the American Protestant Society, December, 1847.* New York, 1847.

Christian Alliance, *Addresses of Rev. Leonard Bacon and Rev. E. N. Kirk at the Christian Alliance held in New York, May 8, 1845 with the Address of the Society and the Bull of the Pope Against It.* New York, 1845.

3. Publications of Nativistic Parties

Address of the American Republicans of the City of Philadelphia to the Native and Naturalized Citizens of the United States. Philadelphia, 1844.

Address of the Arch Chancery of the Order of United Americans to the Order throughout the United States. New York, 1860.

Address of the Delegates of the Native American National Convention, Assembled at Philadelphia, July 4, 1845 to the Citizens of the United States. Philadelphia, 1845.

Address of the Executive Committee of the American Republicans of Boston to the People of Massachusetts. Boston, 1845.

Address of the Louisiana Native American Association to the Citizens of Louisiana and the Inhabitants of the United States. New Orleans, 1839.

Address to the People of the State of New York by the General Executive Committee of the American Republican Party of the City of New York. New York, 1844.

Address of the Third Ward American Republican Association, to their Fellow Citizens. The Position of the Party in Relation to

the Public School Question, and the False Issue Attempted to
be Created by Bishop Hughes. New York, 1844.

*The American's Text Book: being a Series of Letters, Addressed by
"an American," to the Citizens of Tennessee, in Exposition
and Vindication of the Principles of the American Party.* Nashville, 1855.

Bell, John, *Speech Delivered at a Mass Meeting of the American
Party held in Knoxville, Tenn., September 22, 1855.* Nashville, 1855.

*A Brief Review of the Origin and Object of the Native American
Party. By a Native American.* Philadelphia, 1844.

*Colonel Fremont's Religious History. The Authentic Account.
Papist or Protestant, Which?* ——, 1856. American party
campaign pamphlet.

Cox, Leander M., *Speech of Hon. L. M. Cox, of Kentucky, delivered in the House of Representatives, July 26, 1856, in Defense
of the Principles of the American Party, and the Approaching
Presidential Election.* Washington, 1856.

*Defense of the American Party; a Speech of Dr. Harmon before
the Baton Rouge Convention.* New Orleans, 1856.

Franklin (pseud.) *Know Nothingism; or, The American Party.*
Boston, 1855.

The Fillmore and Donelson Songster. ——, 1856.

Fillmore on the Great Questions of the Day. The Arrival, Reception, Progress, and Speeches of Millard Fillmore. New York,
1856.

Fremont's Romanism Established. ——, 1856. American party
campaign pamphlet.

Gayarre, Charles, *Address to the People of Louisiana on the State
of the Parties.* New Orleans, 1855.

Gayarre, Charles, *Address on the Religious Test to the Convention
of the American Party Assembled in Philadelphia on the 5th
of June, 1855.* New Orleans, 1855.

Gifford, George P., *An Address . . . Before the Bunker Hill
Native American Association in the Town Hall, Charlestown,
September 17, 1844.* Charlestown, 1844.

*A History of Election Riots in New Orleans and the Exposure of
the Systematic Violence and Corruption of the Modern Democracy.* New Orleans, 1856. American party campaign pamphlet.

An Honest Appeal to Every Voter; the Bible in the Schools. New York [1844?]. American Republican campaign pamphlet.

Immigration and the Present Mode of Naturalization Dangerous to the South and to the Union of the States. New Orleans, 1856. American party campaign pamphlet.

Indictment: The People of the United States versus James Buchanan of Pennsylvania; a True Bill! National Grand Jury, Sam, Foreman. New Orleans, 1856. American party campaign pamphlet.

The Know Nothings. Cause and Effect. ——, (1854?). American party campaign pamphlet.

Know Nothing Songster. Compiled and Composed by "a Native." Boston, 1854.

Lee, John Hancock, *The Origin and Progress of the American Party in Politics.* Philadelphia, 1855.

LeRee, P. de, *The American Republican Songster.* New York, 1843.

Letters to the People from Washington Hunt, Daniel D. Barnard, and Sam Houston. Buffalo, 1856. American party campaign pamphlet.

Levin, Lewis C., *The Union Safe! The Contest between Fillmore and Buchanan! Fremont Crushed!* New York, 1856. American party campaign pamphlet.

Mass Meeting of the Citizens of Washington, September 27, 1854. ——, 1854. Minutes of a meeting of the American party.

The Origin, Principles and Purposes of the American Party. ——, 1855.

Ourselves and Our Candidates. New York, 1844. American Republican campaign pamphlet.

Phillips, Philip, *Letter of Hon. P. Phillips, of Mobile, Ala., on the Religious Proscription of Catholics.* ——, 1855. American party pamphlet.

The Popish Intrigue: Fremont a Catholic!!! ——, 1856. An American party campaign pamphlet.

Principles and Objects of the American Party. New York, 1855.

Proceedings of the Native American State Convention held at Harrisburg, February 22, 1845. Philadelphia, 1845.

Rayner, Kenneth, *Reply of Hon. Kenneth Rayner, to the Manifesto of Hon. Henry A. Wise.* Washington, 1854. American party pamphlet.

Read! Digest! Act! A Few Facts or Reasons why or for Whom I May Vote!!! by a New York Merchant. Millard Fillmore, the Candidate of the American Party. New York, 1856.

Robertson, George, *The American Party.* Lexington, Kentucky, 1855.

Smith, William R., *The American Party and its Mission. Speech of Mr. Smith, of Alabama, delivered in the U. S. House of Representatives, January 15, 1855.* ——, 1855.

Stockton, Robert F., *Speech of Commodore Robert F. Stockton, on the Past, Present and Future of the American Party. Delivered in the City of Camden, N. J., August 4th, 1859.* Camden, 1859.

4. Books and pamphlets

Achilli, D., *Dealings with the Inquisition; or, Papal Rome, her Priests and her Jesuits.* New York, 1851.

An Alarm to Heretics; or, an Exposition of some of the Evils, Villainies and Dangers of Papacy, also a Vindication of and an Outline of the True American Platform. Philadelphia, 1854.

Allen, William, *Report on Popery Accepted by the General Association of Massachusetts, June, 1844.* Boston, 1844.

Alvard, Henry, *Romanism in Rome.* Boston, ——.

The American Keepsake; or, Book for Every American. Boston, 1845.

American Protestant Almanac for the Year of Our Lord 1841. New York, 1841.

The American Protestant Almanac for the Year of Our Lord 1846. New York, 1846.

The American's Text Book: being a Series of Letters Addressed by an American to the Citizens of Tennessee in Exposition and Vindication of the Principles and Policy of the American Party. Nashville, 1855.

The American Text Book of Popery: being an Authentic Compend of the Bulls, Canons and Decretals of the Roman Hierarchy. New York, 1844.

Anthon, Henry, *The True Churchman Warned against the Errors of the Time.* New York, 1843. A warning against Puseyism and Romanism.

An Awful Warning; or, the Massacre of St. Bartholomew. London, 1812.

Bachman, Luther, *A Defense of Luther and the Reformation*

against the Charges of John Bellinger and Others. Cincinnati, 1853.

Bacon, T. S., *Both Sides of the Controversy between the Roman and the Reformed Church.* New York, ——.

Baird, Robert, *History of the Waldenses, Albigenses and the Vandals; with an Essay on their Present Condition.* New York, 1847.

Baird, Robert, *The Life of Ramon Monsalvatge, a Converted Spanish Monk of the Order of the Capuchins.* New York, 1845.

Baird, Robert, *Sketches of Protestantism in Italy Past and Present, Including a Notice of the Origin, History, and Present State of the Waldenses.* Boston, 1847.

Barca, Calderon de la, *Life in Mexico During a Residence of Two Years in that Country.* London, 1843.

Barclay, Robert, *The Anarchy of the Ranters and . . . the Hierarchy of the Romanists . . . Refuted in . . . [an] Apology for the Quakers.* Philadelphia, 1770.

Barnett, D., *Truth and Error Contrasted, Wherein the Great Apostasy as Prefigured in Cain, Baloom and Korah is Pointed Out.* Dublin, 1838.

Barrow, Isaac, *A Treatise on the Pope's Supremacy.* London, 1851.

Baxter, Richard, *Jesuit Juggling. Forty Popish Frauds Detected and Disclosed.* New York, 1835.

Bayne, Thomas, *Popery Subversive of American Institutions.* Pittsburgh, 1856.

Bayssiere, Pierre, *A Letter to My Children on the Subject of my Conversion from the Romish Church, in which I was Born, to the Protestant, in which I hope to Die.* London, 1829.

Bayssiere, Pierre, *Conversion of Pierre Bayssiere from the Romish Church to the Protestant Faith, in a Letter to his Children.* New York, 1833.

Beecher, Edward, *The Papal Conspiracy Exposed and Protestantism Defended in the Light of Reason, History and Scripture.* Boston, 1855.

Beecher, Lyman, *A Plea for the West.* Cincinnati, 1835.

Belisle, Orvilla S., *The Arch-Bishop: or Romanism in the United States.* 4th edition, Philadelphia, 1855.

Bennett, T. A., *Confutation of Popery.* Cambridge, 1801.

Berg, Joseph Frederick, *Church and State; or, Rome's Influence*

upon the Civil and Religious Institutions of our Country. ——,
1851.

Berg, J. F., *The Confessional; or, an Exposition of the Doctrine of
Auricular Confession as Taught in the Standards of the Roman
Church.* 3rd edition, New York, 1841.

Berg, J. F., *The Great Apostasy Identified with Papal Rome; or, an
Exposition of the Mystery of Iniquity and the Marks and
Doom of Anti-Christ.* Philadelphia, 1842.

Berg, J. F., *The Jesuits: a Lecture Delivered in the Music Fund
Hall.* Philadelphia, 1852.

Berg, J. F., *A Lecture Delivered on Monday Evening, December 23,
1850, on the Jesuits.* Boston, 1851.

Berg, J. F., *Lecture; Delivered in the Music Fund Hall on Tuesday,
November 26, 1850, in Answer to Archbishop Hughes on the
Decline of Protestantism.* Philadelphia, 1850.

Berg, J. F., *Lectures on Romanism.* Philadelphia, 1840.

Berg, J. F., *Mysteries of the Inquisition.* ——, 1846.

Berg, J. F., *The Old Paths: or, a Sketch of the Order and Discipline
of the Reformed Church before the Reformation, as Maintained by the Waldenses Prior to that Epoch, and by the Church
of the Palatinate in the Sixteenth Century.* Philadelphia, 1847.

Berg, J. F., *Oral Controversy with a Catholic Priest.* ——, 1843.

Berg, J. F., *A Synopsis of the Moral Philosophy of Peter Dens as
Prepared for the use of Romish Seminaries and Students of
Theology.* New York, 1841.

Berg, J. F., *Trapezium; or, Law and Liberty vs. Despotism and
Anarchy.* Philadelphia, 1851.

Binder, William E., *Madelon Hawley; or, The Jesuit and his Victim; a Revelation of Romanism.* New York, 1860.

Boardman, H. A., *The Intolerance of the Church of Rome.* Philadelphia, 1845.

*A Book of Tracts, Containing the Origin and Progress, Cruelties,
Frauds, Superstitions, Miracles, Ceremonies, Idolatrous Cus-
toms of the Church of Rome: with a Succinct Account of the
Rise and Progress of the Jesuits.* New York, 1856.

Borrow, George, *The Bible in Spain.* New York, 1847.

*The Boston Pilot's Attempt to Sell Adopted Citizens to the Whig
Party Exposed by a Catholic Citizen of Boston.* Boston, 1853.

Bower, Archibald, *The History of the Popes: From the Foundation
of the See of Rome to A.D. 1758.* Philadelphia, 1846.

Brainerd, Thomas, *Our Country Safe from Romanism.* Philadelphia, 1843.

Bray, Anna E., *The Protestant; a Tale of the Reign of Queen Mary.* New York, 1829.

Breckinridge, R. J., *An Address to the American People.* Baltimore, 1836.

Breckinridge, R. J., *Papism in the United States in the Nineteenth Century.* Baltimore, ——.

Broom, Jacob, *Defense of Americanism. Speech of Hon. Jacob Broom, of Pennsylvania; delivered in the House of Representatives, August 4, 1856.* Washington, 1856.

Brown, T., *Popery Perverts the Gospel.* Glasgow, 1836.

Browning, W. S., *A History of the Huguenots.* Philadelphia, 1845.

Brownlee, William Craig, *The Apocalyptic Beasts, seen in Vision by St. John in his Holy Revelation, by Catholicus.* New York, 1843.

Brownlee, W. C., *The Doctrinal Decrees and Canons of the Council of Trent, translated from an edition printed at Rome in 1564.* New York, 1842. With introduction and notes by Brownlee.

Brownlee, W. C., *Letters in the Roman Catholic Controversy.* New York, 1834.

Brownlee, W. C., *Popery an Enemy to Civil and Religious Liberty, and Dangerous to Our Republic.* New York, 1836.

Brownlee, W. C., *The Religion of the Ancient Irish and Britons not Roman Catholic and the Immortal St. Patrick Vindicated from the False Charge of Being a Papist.* 2nd edition, New York, 1841.

Brownlee, W. C., *The Roman Catholic Religion Viewed in the Light of Prophecy and History; its Final Downfall and the Triumph of the Church of Christ.* New York, 1844.

Brownlee, W. C., *Romanism in the Light of Prophecy and History: its final Downfall: and the Triumph of the Church of Christ.* New York, 1857.

Brownlee, W. C., *Secret Instructions to the Jesuits; Faithfully Translated from the Latin of an Old Genuine London Copy.* New York, 1841. Another edition, New York, 1857.

Brownlee, W. C., *Sketch of the History of the Western Apostolic Churches from which the Roman Church Apostatized.* New York, ——.

Brownlee, W. C., *The Whigs of Scotland*. New York, 1839. On Catholic persecution.

Brownlow, W. G., *Americanism Contrasted with Foreignism, Romanism and Bogus Democracy in the Light of Reason, History, and Scripture in which Certain Demagogues in Tennessee and Elswhere are shown in their true Colors*. Nashville, 1856.

Bullfinch, S. G., *Romanism*. Boston, 1849.

Bungener, Lawrence, *The Priest and the Huguenot; or, Persecution in the Age of Louis XV*. 2 v. Boston, 1854.

Bunkley, Josephine M., *The Testimony of an Escaped Novice from the Sisterhood of St. Joseph, Emmetsburg, Md.* New York, 1855.

The Burning of the Bible; being a Defense of the Protestant Version of the Scriptures against the Attacks of Popish Apologists for the Champlain Bible Burners. New York, 1845.

Busey, Samuel C., *Immigration: Its Evils and Consequences*. New York, 1856.

Caldicott, Thomas F., *Hannah Corcoran: an Authentic Narrative of her Conversion from Romanism; her Abduction from Charlestown, and the Treatment she Received during her Absence*. Boston, 1853.

Campbell, Alexander and J. P. Purcell, *A Debate on the Roman Catholic Religion: held in the Sycamore-Street Meeting House, Cincinnati, from the 13th to the 21st of January, 1837*. Cincinnati, 1837.

Campbell, George, *Alarms in Regard to Popery: an Address to the People of Scotland*. London, 1840.

Campbell, James M., *The Protestant Girl in a French Nunnery; or, the School Girl in France*. New York, 1845.

Campbell, John D., *Papal Rome Identified with the Great Apostasy Predicted in the Scriptures. The Substance of three Discourses addressed to the First Presbyterian Church in Albany*. Albany, 1838.

Campbell, Lewis D., *Americanism; a Speech Delivered at the American Mass Meeting held in Washington City, February 29, 1856*. Washington, 1856.

Carlington Castle; a Tale of the Jesuits. New York, 1854.

Carroll, Anna E., *The Great American Battle; or, the Contest between Christianity and Political Romanism*. New York, 1856.

Carroll, Anna E., *The Star of the West, National Men and National Measures.* New York, 1856.

Carroll, Anna E., *The Union of the States.* Boston, 1856.

Cassels, S. J., *Christ and Anti-Christ; Jesus Proved to be the Messiah and the Papacy Proved to be the Anti-Christ.* Philadelphia, 1847.

Caveat against Popery. Baltimore, 1791.

The Ceremonies of the Holy Week in the Papal Chapel of the Vatican. ——, 1839.

Chapman, J. L., *Americanism versus Romanism; or, the cis-Atlantic battle Between Sam and the Pope.* Nashville, 1856.

The Character of the Rev. W. Palmer, M.A., of Worcester College, as a Controversialist; particularly with Reference to his Charge against Dr. Wiseman, of Quoting, as Genuine Works of the Fathers, Spurious and Heretical Productions, considered in a letter to a Friend at Oxford. Baltimore, 1844.

Chase, S., *The Doctrine, History and Moral Tendency of Roman Catholic Indulgences.* Watertown, New York, 1841.

Cheever, George B., *The Hierarchical Despotism; Lectures on the Mixture of Civil and Ecclesiastical Power in the Governments of the Middle Ages in Illustration of the Nature and Progress of the Romish Church.* New York, 1844.

Cheever, George B., *The Right of the Bible in our Public Schools.* New York, 1854.

Chillingworth, W., *The Works of W. Chillingworth, A.M. Containing his Book Entitled: The Religion of Protestants a Safe Way to Salvation, Together with his Sermons, Discourses and Controversies.* Philadelphia, 1840.

The Christian Catholic. New York, 1854.

A Chronological Table of the Papacy and the Persecution of Christians from the Christian Era to the Present Century. New York, 1845.

Clark, Rufus W., *Popery and the United States, embracing an Account of Papal Operations in Our Country, with a View of the Dangers which Threaten our Institutions.* Boston, 1847.

Clark, Rufus W., *Romanism in America.* Boston, 1855.

Clemen, R., *Geschichte der Inquisition in Spanien.* Columbus, Ohio, 1850.

Cobbin, I., *The Book of Popery; a Description of the Origin, Progress, Doctrines, etc., of the Papal Church.* Philadelphia, ——.

The Colporteur and Roman Catholic: a Dialogue. New York, 1847.

Colton, Walter, *A Reply to the Allegations and Complaints Contained in Bishop Kenrick's Letter to the Board of Controllers of the Public Schools.* Philadelphia, 1844.

Connelly, Pierce, *Domestic Emancipation from Roman Rule; a Petition to the Honourable House of Commons.* London, 1829.

Connelly, Pierce, *Reasons for Abjuring Allegiance to the See of Rome.* 15th edition, London, 1852.

Controversy between the Author of "Baptizo Defined" and the Rev. Mr. Kelly. Albany, 1840.

The Conversion of Luther. New York, 1845.

The Conversion and Edifying Death of Andrew Dunn. Philadelphia,
———.

Cooper, Samuel, *A Discourse on the Man of Sin; Delivered in the Chapel of Harvard College, in Cambridge, New England. September 1, 1773, at the lecture founded by the Hon. Paul Dudley.* Boston, 1774.

Cotter, J. R., *The Mass and Rubrics of the Roman Catholic Church Translated into English.* New York, 1845.

Cousin, Victor, *Jaqueline Pascal; or, a Glimpse of Convent Life at Port Royal.* New York, 1853.

Coustos, John, *The Mysteries of Popery Unveiled in the Unparalleled Sufferings of John Coustos, at the Inquisition of Lisbon, to which is added, the Origin of the Inquisition and its Establishment in Various Countries; and the Master Key to Popery by Anthony Gavin.* Hartford, 1821.

Cramp, J. M., *A Text Book of Popery; comprising a Brief History of the Council of Trent, a Translation of the Doctrinal Decrees, etc.* New York, 1831.

The Crisis; an Appeal to our Countrymen on the Subject of Foreign Influence in the United States. New York, 1844.

Cross, Andrew B., *Letters on the Papal System.* Baltimore, 1854.

Cross, Andrew B., *Priests' Prisons for Women.* Baltimore, 1854.

Crowell, John, *Republics Established and Thrones Overturned by the Bible.* Philadelphia, 1849.

Crowley, James, *Reasons for Recantation from the Errors of the Church of Rome.* Baltimore, 1812.

Culbertson, Rosamond, *Rosamond; or, A Narrative of the Captivity and Sufferings of an American Female under the Popish Priests in the Island of Cuba, with a full disclosure of their manners and customs, written by herself.* New York, 1846.

Cumming, John, *Lectures on Romanism, being Illustrations and Refutations of the Errors of Romanism and Tractarianism.* Boston, 1854.

D'Aubigne, J. H. Merle, *The Authority of God: or, the True Barrier against Romish and Infidel Aggressions.* New York, 1851.

D'Aubigne, J. H. Merle, *History of the Great Reformation in the Sixteenth Century.* New York, 1846.

Daunou, Pierre C. F., *Outline of the History of the Court of Rome and of the Temporal Power of the Popes.* Philadelphia, 1837.

Davis, E. S., *Seven Thunders; or, the Mighty Crash of Europe's Royal and Papal Thrones.* New York, 1855.

DeCarmenin, Louis M., *A Complete History of the Popes of Rome, from Saint Peter, the First Bishop, to Pius the Ninth, the Present Pope.* New York, 1847.

Defense of the Use of the Bible in the Schools. New York, 1830.

DeHass, F. S., *Romanism Unmasked.* New York, 1853.

Denig, John, *The Know Nothing Manual, or, Book for Americans No. 1, in which the Native American Platform and Principles as adopted by the Know Nothings are set forth and Defended . . . together with Dissertations on Romanism.* Harrisburg, Pennsylvania, 1855.

Derby, E. H., *The Catholic; Letters Addressed by a Jurist to a Young Kinsman Proposing to Join the Church of Rome.* Boston, 1856.

DeSanctis, L., *Rome, Christian and Papal: Sketches of its Religious Monuments and Ecclesiastical Hierarchy, with Notices of the Jesuits and the Inquisition.* New York, 1856.

Despotism; or, the Last Days of the American Republic. New York, 1856.

The Destruction of the Inquisition at Madrid. New York, 1844.

Dhu, Helen, *Stanhope Burleigh; the Jesuits in our Homes.* New York, 1855.

A Dialogue between Dominie and Patrick; or, the Bible vs. Papacy. Albany, 1860.

Dickinson, Austin, *Thoughts for Catholics and their Friends.* New York, 1844.

Dickinson, Mrs. Austin, *The Mother of St. Augustine.* New York, 1845.

Dill, Edward M., *The Mystery Solved, or Ireland's Miseries. The Grand Cause and Cure.* New York, 1852.

Doane, George W., *Puseyism, No Popery.* Boston, 1843.

Dowling, John, *The Burning of the Bibles.* Philadelphia, 1843.

Dowling, John, *The History of Romanism: from the Earliest Corruptions of Christianity to the Present Time.* 4th edition, New York, 1845.

Dowling, John, *The Life and Reign of Pope Pius the Ninth . . . together with a Biographical Sketch of his Predecessor, Gregory XVI.* New York, 1849.

Dowling, John, *Dr. Middleton's Letter from Rome.* New York, 1846.

Dreadful Scenes in the Awful Disclosures of Maria Monk. New York, 1836.

Dudley, Paul, *An Essay on the Merchandise of slaves and souls of Men; with an Application thereto to the Church of Rome.* Boston, 1731.

Dwight, Theodore, *Open Convents; or, Nunneries and Popish Seminaries Dangerous to the Morals and Degrading to the Character of a Republican Community.* New York, 1836.

Dwight, Theodore, *The Roman Republic of 1849; with Accounts of the Inquisition and the Siege of Rome.* New York, 1851.

Edgar, Samuel, *The Variations of Popery.* New York, 1849.

Education in Romish Seminaries. A Letter in Answer to Certain Inquiries respecting the Propriety of Selecting, as Places of Education, Seminaries Professedly under the Control of Religious Faculties of the Church of Rome. New York, 1845.

Elder, George A. M., *The Ursuline Convent: a Poem.* ——, 1835.

Elizabeth, Charlotte, *Alice Benden, or the Bowed Shilling: and Other Tales.* New York, 1841.

Elizabeth, C., *The Church Visible in All Ages.* New York, 1845.

Elizabeth, C., *Dangers and Duties.* New York, 1841.

Elizabeth, C., *The English Martyrology, abridged from Fox.* Philadelphia, 1843.

Elizabeth, C., *Falsehood and Truth.* 2nd edition, New York, 1842.

Elizabeth, C., *Glimpses of the Past; or, the Museum.* New York, 1841.

Elizabeth, C., *The Happy Mute.* Boston, 1842.

Elizabeth, C., *Letters from Ireland.* New York, 1843.

Elizabeth, C., *The Protestant Annual.* London, 1841.

Elizabeth C., *Ridley, Latimer, Cranmer and Other English Martyrs.* New York, 1844.

Elizabeth, C., *Second Causes; or, Up and Be Doing.* New York, 1843.

Elizabeth, C., *The Siege of Derry; or, Sufferings of the Protestants: a Tale of the Revolution.* New York, 1844.

Elizabeth, C., *War with the Saints; or, the Persecutions of the Vandals under Pope Innocent III.* New York, 1848.

Elliott, Charles, *Delineation of Roman Catholicism, drawn from the Authentic and Acknowledged Standards of the Church of Rome.* New York, 1851.

Ellis, B. F., *A History of the Romish Inquisition Compiled from Various Authors.* Hanover, Indiana, 1835.

Ellmer Castle. Boston, 1833.

Ely, Alfred B., *American Liberty, its Sources,—its Dangers,—and the Means of its Preservation.* New York, 1850.

Emerlina, G. D., *Frauds of Papal Ecclesiastics; to which are added Illustrative Notes from Letters by Gilbert Burnet and Gavin's Master Key to Popery.* New York, 1835.

The Encyclical Letter of Pope Gregory XVI., issued August 15, 1832. In which he Advocates Idolatry . . . a Union of Church and State . . . Exclusive Salvation . . . Condemns Liberty of Conscience . . . and Execrates the Liberty of the Press. Baltimore, 1836.

The Escaped Nun; or, Disclosures of Convent Life and the Confessions of a Sister of Charity. New York, 1855.

Evidence Demonstrating the Falsehoods of William L. Stone. New York, 1836.

An Exposition of the Principles of the Roman Catholic Religion, with Remarks on its Influence in the United States. Hartford, 1830.

Faber, George S., *The Difficulties of Romanism.* New York, 1840.

False Claims of the Pope. New York, 1842.

Familiar Letters to J. B. Fitzpatrick, Catholic Bishop of Boston, by an Independent Irishman. Boston, 1854.

Farrenc, Edmund, *Carlotina and the Sanfedesti; or, a Night with the Jesuits at Rome.* New York, 1853.

Feijo, Diego A., *Demonstration of the Necessity of Abolishing a Constrained Clerical Celibacy: Exhibiting the Evils of the Institution, and the Remedy.* Philadelphia, 1844.

F. H. B., *Historical Extracts: or, Facts Connected with the Years, A.D. 519, 1779, 1809*. Lowell, Massachusetts, 1853.

Field, Henry M., *The Good and the Bad in the Roman Catholic: Is that Church to be Destroyed or Reformed?* New York, 1849.

Finley, James B., *Evangelism, Catholicism, and Protestantism: Lectures on the Decline, Apostasy, and Reformation of the Christian Church*. New York, 1851.

The First Christian Martyr from Madeira, Rev. Arsenio Nicos de Silva. New York, 1849.

Fleming, Robert, *The Apocalyptical Key*. Philadelphia, 1850.

Fleming, Robert, *An Extraordinary Discourse on the Rise and Fall of Papacy; or, the Pouring out of the Vials in the Revelation of St. John*. New York, 1848.

Footprints of Popery; or, Places where Martyrs have Suffered. Boston, 1846.

Forbes, H., *A Few Words on Popery and Despotism, addressed to the Boston Young Men's Society in Aid of Italy, and Published for Distribution by that Association*. New York, 1850.

Fox, John, *A History of the Lives, Sufferings and Triumphant Deaths of the Primitive as well as the Protestant Martyrs from the Commencement of Christianity to the Latest Periods of Pagan and Popish Persecution*. Philadelphia, 1844.

Fox, T. B., *Sketches of the Reformation*. Boston, 1836.

Foxcroft, Thomas, *The Saints' United Confession, in Disparagement of their own Righteousness . . . In Opposition to Popish Abuse and Calumny*. Boston, 1750.

Frothingham, Charles W., *The Convent's Doom; a Tale of Charlestown in 1834*. 5th edition, Boston, 1854.

Frothingham, Charles W., *Six Hours in a Convent; or, the Stolen Nuns*. 8th edition, Boston, 1855.

Fulke, William, *Confutation of the Rhemish Testament with an Introductory Essay*. New York, 1834.

Fuller, Arthur B., *Liberty versus Romanism. Two Discourses Delivered in the New North Church*. Boston, 1859.

Fuller, Richard and John England, *Letters Concerning the Roman Chancery*. Baltimore, 1840.

Fysh, Frederic, *The Divine History of the Church; or, a Catechism of the Apocalypse, with a plan of the Apocalyptic Drama*. Philadelphia, 1845.

Gault, Robert, *Popery, the Man of Sin and the Son of Perdition.* New York, 1855.

Gaussen, S. R. L., *Geneva and Rome. Rome Papal as Portrayed by Prophecy and History.* New York, 1847.

Gavazzi, Alessandro, *The Lectures Complete of Father Gavazzi as Delivered in New York; as Reported by an Eminent Stenographer and Revised and Corrected by Gavazzi Himself; to which is Prefixed the Life of Gavazzi by G. N. Nicolini.* New York, 1853.

Gavazzi, Alessandro, *Lectures in New York, reported in full by T. C. Leland, Photographer; also the Life of Father Gavazzi, Corrected and Authorized by himself, together with reports of his Addresses in Italian to his Countrymen in New York, Translated and Revised by Madame Julie de Marguerittes.* New York, 1853.

Gavazzi, Alessandro, *The Life of Father Gavazzi.* London, 1851.

Gavazzi, Alessandro, *Orations.* London, 1851.

Gavin, Anthony, *The Great Red Dragon, or the Master Key to Popery.* Boston, 1854.

Gavin, Anthony, *The Master Key to Popery: Customs of Priests and Friars, and Rites and Ceremonies of the Popish Religion. Inquisition, etc.* Cincinnati, 1834.

Gavin, Anthony, *A Master Key to Popery, Giving a Full Account of All the Customs of the Priests and Friars and the Rites and Ceremonies of the Popish Religion.* ——, 1812.

Gavin, Antonio, *A History of Popery: giving a Full Account of all the Priests and Friars, and the Rites and Ceremonies of the Papal Church.* Hartford, 1845.

Gaylord, N. M., *Kossuth and the American Jesuits.* Lowell, Massachusetts, 1852.

Gibbings, R., *Roman Forgeries and Falsifications.* London, 1849.

Gilly, W. S., *Our Protestant Forefathers.* New York, 1836.

Giustiniani, L., *Intrigues of Jesuitism in the United States of America.* 7th edition, New York, 1846.

Giustiniani, L., *Papal Rome as it is, by a Roman.* 2nd edition, Baltimore, 1845. Another edition, Philadelphia, 1845.

Gonsalves, M. J., *Persecutions in Madeira in the Nineteenth Century.* New York, 1845.

Gonsalves, M. J., *The Testimony of a Convert from the Church of Rome: Narrative of the Religious Experience and Travels of the Reverend M. J. Gonsalves. Also a Narrative of Signorina Florencia D'Romani.* Boston, 1859.

Griffin, Edward D., *The Brazen Serpent.* New York, 1849.

Grimke, Thomas S., *Address on the Expediency and Duty of Adopting the Bible as a Class Book in every Scheme of Education from the Primary School to the University.* Charleston, 1830.

Griswold, Alexander, *The Reformation; a Brief Exposition of Some of the Errors and Corruptions of the Church of Rome.* Boston, 1843.

Grundy, Robert C., *The Temporal Powers of the Pope Dangerous to the Religious and Civil Liberties of the American Republic; a Review of the Speech of the Hon. Joseph R. Chandler delivered in the House of Representatives of the United States, January 10,* [sic] *1855.* Maysville, Kentucky, 1855.

Guicciardirri and the Popes; an Address delivered before the Adelphian Society of the Furman Institute at the Commencement, on Monday, June 16, 1851. Greenville, South Carolina, 1851.

Gurney, Joseph J., *The Papal and Hierarchical System Compared with the Religion of the New Testament.* 2nd edition, New York, 1843.

Hannah Corcoran, the Missing Girl of Charlestown. The Mysterious Disappearance Unraveled. The Convent and the Confessor. Attempt at Abduction Foiled! A Full and Complete Report of the Riot at Charlestown. Boston, 1853.

Hazel, Harry, *The Nun of St. Ursula; or, the Burning of the Convent; a Romance of Mt. Benedict.* Boston, 1845.

Headley, Joel T., *History of the Persecutions and Battles of the Waldenses.* New York, 1852.

Headley, Joel T., *Letters from Italy.* New York, 1845.

Helen Mulgrave; or, Jesuit Executorship: being Passages in the Life of a Seceder from Romanism. New York, 1852.

The History of Andrew Dunn. New York, 1835.

A History of Popery, including its Origin, Progress, Doctrines, Practice, Institutions and Fruits, to the Commencement of the Nineteenth Century. New York, 1834.

History of the Protestant Church in Hungary from the Beginning of the Reformation to 1850; with Special Reference to Transylvania. Boston, 1854.

Hobart, J. A., *Corruptions of the Church of Rome Contrasted with certain Protestant Errors—a Charge.* New York, 1818.

Hobart, John Henry, *The Principles of the Churchman Stated and Explained, in Distinction from the Corruptions of the Church of Rome, and from the Errors of Certain Protestant Sects.* New York, 1837.

Hogan, William, *Auricular Confession and Popish Nunneries.* Boston, 1845.

Hogan, William, *High and Low Mass in the Catholic Church; with Comments.* Boston, 1846.

Hogan, William, *Synopsis of Popery as it Was and as it Is.* Hartford, 1854.

Hook, Walter F., *The Novelties of Romanism, or Popery Refuted by Tradition.* New York, 1843.

Hopkins, John Henry, *The Church of Rome in her Primitive Purity Compared with the Church of Rome at the Present Day.* New York, 1835.

Hopkins, J. H., *The "End of Controversy" Controverted.* New York, 1845.

Hopkins, J. H., *The History of the Confessional.* New York, 1850.

Hopkins, J. H., *An Humble Address to the Bishops, Clergy and Laity of the Protestant Episcopal Church in the United States, on Tolerating Among Our Ministry of the Doctrines of the Church of Rome.* ——, ——.

Hopkins, J. H., *Lectures on the British Reformation.* Boston, 1844.

Hopkins, J. H., *The Novelties Which Disturb our Peace: Four Letters Addressed to the Bishops, Clergy and Laity of the Protestant Episcopal Church in the United States.* Philadelphia, 1844.

Hopkins, J. H., *A Second Letter to the Right Rev. Francis Patrick Kenrick.* Burlington, Vermont, 1843.

Hopkins, Samuel M., *Protestantism in the middle of the Nineteenth Century.* Auburn, New York, 1849.

Horne, Thomas H., *Mariolatry: or, Facts and Evidence Demonstrating the Worship of the Blessed Virgin Mary, by the Church of Rome.* Hartford, 1844.

Horne, Thomas H., *A Protestant Memorial.* New York, 1844.

Horne, Thomas H., *Romanism Contradictory to the Bible.* New York, 1833.

Horner, James M., *Popery Stripped of its Garb: or, the Work of Iniquity Checked in its Progress.* New York, 1836.

Howett, William, *History of Priestcraft in all Ages and Nations.* New York, 1833.

Hubbell, William L., *The Birth, Growth, Position and Perils of the American Republic; and the Duties of its Citizens; an Address delivered before Washington Chapter, No. 7, Order of United Americans, at South Norwalk, Connecticut, Dec. 28, 1855.* Waterbury, Connecticut, 1856.

Hughes, John and John Breckinridge, *Controversy between the Rev. Messrs. Hughes and Breckinridge on the Subject, "Is the Protestant Religion the Religion of Christ."* Philadelphia, 1833.

Hughes, John and John Breckinridge, *A Discussion on the Question, Is the Roman Catholic Religion, in any or in all of its Principles or Doctrines, Inimical to Civil or Religious Liberty? and the Question, Is the Presbyterian Religion, in any or in all of its Principles or Doctrines, Inimical to Civil or Religious Liberty?* Philadelphia, 1836.

Humphrey, Edward P., *A Discourse on the Spiritual Power of the Roman Catholic clergy. Delivered at Louisville before the Synod of Kentucky, October 13, 1849.* Louisville, 1850.

Hutchinson, E., *Young Sam: or, Native American's Own Book.* New York, 1855.

Illustrations of Popery. The Mystery of Iniquity Unveiled in its "Damnable Heresies, Lying Wonders, and Strong Delusion." New York, 1838.

The Important and Interesting Debate on the Claims of the Catholics to a Portion of the Common School Fund; with the Arguments of Counsel before the Board of Aldermen of the City of New York, on Thursday and Friday, the 29th and 30th of October, 1840. New York, 1840.

An Inquiry into the Fundamental Principles of the Roman Catholics, in Five Letters addressed to a Roman Catholic. By a Protestant. Washington, 1822.

Jackson, Luther, *Thoughts for Catholics and Their Friends.* New York, 1843.

Janeway, Jacob J., *Antidote to the Poison of Popery, in the Publications of Professor Schaff.* New Brunswick, New Jersey, 1854.

Janeway, Jacob J., *Antidote to the Poison of Popery in the Writings and Conduct of Professors Nevin and Schaff, professors in the German Reformed Church, in the U. S. of America.* New Brunswick, New Jersey, 1856.

Jarves, James J., *Italian Sights and Papal Principles, seen through American Spectacles.* New York, 1856.

Jarvis, Samuel F., *A Reply to Doctor Milner's "End of Religious Controversy," so far as the Churches of the English Communion are Concerned.* New York, 1847.

Jones, Charles P., *Roman Catholicism Spiritually Considered; or, the Church of Rome the Great Apostasy.* New York, ——.

Junkin, George, *The Great Apostasy: a Sermon on Romanism.* Philadelphia, ——.

Kalley, Robert R., *Persecutions in Madeira in the Nineteenth Century.* New York, 1845.

Kelly, J., and A. W. McClure, *The School Question; a Correspondence between Rev. J. Kelly . . . and Rev. A. W. McClure, Jersey City.* New York, 1853.

Kenneday, Grace, *Father Clement, a Roman Catholic Story.* Boston, 1827.

The Know Nothing. Boston, 1855.

The Know Nothing Almanac; or, True American's Manual for 1855. New York, 1855.

Know-Nothing: a Poem for Natives and Aliens. Boston, 1854.

Kurtz, B., and J. C. Morris, *The Year Book of the Reformation.* New York, 1844.

Laborde, Abbe, *Impossibility of the Immaculate Conception.* Philadelphia, 1855.

Landon, Walter S., *Popery: British and Foreign.* Boston, 1851.

Lathrop, John, *A Discourse on the Errors of Popery, Delivered in the Chapel of the University in Cambridge, September 4, 1793, at the Lecture founded by the Honorable Paul Dudley, esquire.* Boston, 1793.

Laurens, J. Wayne, *The Crisis; or, the Enemies of America Unmasked.* Philadelphia, 1855.

Leahey, Edward, *Narrative of the Conversion of the Writer from Romanism to the Christian Religion.* Philadelphia, 1846.

Lester, Charles E., *The Jesuits.* New York, 1845.

Letter to the Catholic Bishop of Boston. Proving that the Roman Catholic Religion is Opposed to a Republican Form of Government. Boston, ——.

A Letter from a Romish Priest in Canada to One who was taken Captive in her Infancy, and Instructed in the Romish Faith, but some time ago returned to this her Native Country, with an answer thereto, by a person to whom it was Communicated. Boston, 1729.

The Letters of the Madiai, and Visits to their Prisons. New York, 1854.

L'Hote, J. B., *An Appeal to Catholics.* New York, 1848.

Lipscomb, Andrew A., *Our Country; its Dangers and Duty.* New York, 1844. Other editions: New York, 1854, New York, 1857.

Litton, Edward A., *The Church of Christ, in its Idea, Attributes and Ministry; with particular reference to the Controversy on the Subject between Romanists and Protestants.* New York and Philadelphia, 1856.

The Lives of the Popes from A.D. 100 to A.D. 1853. New York, 1853.

Lorette. The History of Louise, Daughter of a Canadian Nun: Exhibiting the Interior of Female Convents. New York, 1833.

Lowell, Robert, *Five Letters against Certain Pretensions of the Papal Church.* Newark, 1853.

Luke, Jemima T., *The Female Jesuit; or, The Spy in the Family.* New York, 1851. Another edition: New York, 1860.

Luke, Jemima T., *A Sequel to the Female Jesuit; Containing her Previous History and Recent Discovery.* New York, 1852.

MacKenzie, W. B., *The Justified Believer; his Security, Conflicts and Triumphs.* Philadelphia, 1854.

MacKray, William, *Character and Prospects of the Church of Rome.* ——, 1837.

Maguire, Edward, *The New Romish Dogma of the Immaculate Conception; or, Trial of the Church of Rome before a Jury of Roman Catholics on a Charge of Imposing on the Consciences of Christian People a Yoke which neither We nor Our Forefathers were Able to Bear.* New York, 1855.

Mahoney, S. J., *Six Years in the Monasteries of Italy.* New York, 1836. Other editions: Boston, 1845, Hartford, 1851.

Major, Henry, *Mr. Major Refuted by himself; being an Answer to his "Reasons for Acknowledging the Holy Roman See," extracted from his own Writings.* Philadelphia, 1846.

Malan, Caesar, *Can I Join the Church of Rome while My Rule of Faith is in the Bible? An Inquiry Presented to the Conscience of the Christian Reader.* New York, 1844.

Marke, Richard, *Danger and Duty.* New York, 1844.

Marsh, George P., *The Papists and the Puritans; an address before the New England Society of the City of New York.* New York, 1845.

Martin, Joseph H., *The Influence, Bearing and Effects of Romanism on the Civil and Religious Liberties of our Country.* New York, 1844.

Marx, J., *History of the Robe of Jesus Christ, Preserved in the Cathedral at Treves.* New York, 1845.

Mason, Cyrus, *A History of the Holy Roman Inquisition.* Philadelphia, 1835.

Maurette, Jean J., *Der Papst und das Evangelium oder: Abschild von Rom.* New York, 1851.

Mayhew, Jonathan, *Popish Idolatry: a discourse . . . in the chapel of Harvard College.* Boston, 1765.

McClintock, John, *The Temporal Power of the Pope.* ——, 1855.

McCoan, J. C., *Protestant Endurance under Popish Cruelty: a Narrative of the Reformation in Spain.* London, 1853.

McCrindell, Rachel, *The Convent: a Narrative Founded on Fact.* New York, 1853.

McCrindell, Rachel, *The English Governess.* New York, 1844.

McCrindell, Rachel, *The School Girl in France; or, the Snares of Popery: a Warning to Protestants against Education in Catholic Seminaries.* 4th edition, New York, 1846.

McGavin, William, *The Protestant. Essays on the Principal Points of Controversy between the Church of Rome and the Reformed.* 2 v. 2nd edition, Hartford, 1833. Other editions: Hartford, 1834, Hartford, 1835, Middletown, 1833.

McGill, Alexander T., *Popery—the Punishment of Unbelief: a Sermon before the General Assembly of the Presbyterian Church at Baltimore, May 25, 1848.* Baltimore, 1848.

McGowan, John, *The French Convert: being a True Relation of the Happy Conversion of a Noble French Lady from the Error, and Superstition of Popery to the Reformed Religion, by means of a Protestant Gardener.* New York, 1724. Many other editions.

McKee, Joseph, *Popery Unmasked: being an Exposure of the False Translations of the Rhemish Testament, to which is added Differences between Two Popish Versions of the New Testament.* Baltimore, 1835.

McLeod, Donald, *The Bloodstone.* New York, 1853.

McLeod, John N., *Protestantism: the Parent and Guardian of Civil and Religious Liberty.* New York, 1843.

McMurray, A., *Awful Disclosures! Murders Exposed! Downfall of Popery! Death Bed Confession! Death Bed Confession and Renunciation of the Right Rev. Bishop McMurray, Bishop of the St. Mary's Roman Catholic Church, Montreal, Canada.* Buffalo, 1845.

Meeks, J. C., *Pierre and his Family; or, a Story of the Waldenses.* New York, 1841.

Mendham, Joseph, *The Literary Policy of the Church of Rome, exhibited in an Account of her Damnatory Catalogues, or Indexes, both Prohibitory and Expurgatory.* 2nd edition, New York, 1835.

Mendham, Joseph, *The Venal Indulgences and Pardons of the Church of Rome.* London, 1839.

Menno, S., *Departure from Popery.* Boston, 1825.

Meyrick, F., *Moral Theology of the Church of Rome.* Baltimore, 1856.

Michelet, M., *The Jesuits.* New York, 1845.

Michelet, M., *Spiritual Direction and Auricular Confession; their history, theory and consequences.* Philadelphia, 1845.

Middleton, Conyers, *A Letter from Rome, Showing the Exact Conformity of Popery and Paganism: or, the Religion of the Present Romans Derived from that of their Heathen Ancestors.* Baltimore, 1835.

Middleton, Conyers, *Dr. Middleton's Letter from Rome. Showing an Exact Conformity between Popery and Paganism.* New York, 1847.

Middleton, Conyers, *Pope and Pagan: or, Middleton's Letter from Rome, on the Similarity between Popery and Paganism.* Portland, Maine, 1846.

Monastier, Antoine, *A History of the Vaudois Church from its Origin, and of the Vaudois of Piedmont to the Present Day.* New York, 1849.

Monk, Maria, *Awful Disclosures of the Hotel Dieu Nunnery of Montreal.* New York, 1836.

Monk, Maria, *Further Disclosures of Maria Monk, Concerning the Hotel Dieu Nunnery of Montreal; and also her Visit to Nuns Island and Disclosures Concerning that Secret Retreat.* New York, 1837.

Monk, Maria, *Interview of Maria Monk with her Opponents, the Authors of the Reply to her Awful Disclosures, now in Press, Held in this City on Wednesday, August 17.* New York, 1836.

Moore, Charles K., *Book of Tracts on Romanism: Containing the Origin and Progress, Cruelties, Frauds, Superstitions, Miracles and Ceremonies of the Church of Rome.* New York, 1844.

Moore, T. V., *The Reformation the Tower of American Liberty.* New York, 1853.

Morris, Edward J., *Remarks of the Honorable E. Joy Morris, of Philadelphia, in the House of Representatives of Pennsylvania, February 12, 1856, Against the Introduction of the Monastic System and the Secret Religious Orders of the Church of Rome into that Commonwealth, Delivered on the Final Passage of the Bill to Incorporate the Third Order of Franciscans, in Cambria County, into a Body Politic.* Philadelphia, 1856.

Morse, Samuel F. B., *The Confessions of a French Priest, to Which are added Warnings to the People of the United States.* New York, 1837.

Morse, Samuel F. B., *Foreign Conspiracy Against the Liberties of the United States.* 5th edition, New York, 1841.

Morse, Samuel F. B., *Imminent Dangers to the Free Institutions of the United States through Foreign Immigration.* New York, 1835. Another edition: New York, 1854.

Morse, Samuel F. B., *The Proscribed German Student; being a Sketch of Some Interesting Incidents in the Life and Death of Lewis Clausing; to which is added; a Treatise on the Jesuits, a Posthumous Work of Lewis Clausing.* New York, 1836.

Murray, Nicholas, *Bishop Hughes Confuted. Reply to the Right Reverend John Hughes.* New York, 1848.

Murray, Nicholas, *The Decline of Popery and its Causes. An Address Delivered at the Broadway Tabernacle January 15, 1851.* New York, 1851.

Murray, Nicholas, *Letters to the Right Reverend John Hughes, First Series.* New York, 1847.

Murray, Nicholas, *Letters to the Right Reverend John Hughes, Second Series.* New York, 1847.

Murray, Nicholas, *Letters to the Right Rev. John Hughes, Roman Catholic Bishop of New York. Revised and Enlarged.* New York, 1855.

Murray, Nicholas, *Romanism at Home, Letters to the Hon. Roger B. Taney, Chief Justice of the United States.* New York, 1852.

A Narrative of Facts in the Recent Conversion of a Romanist. New York, 1844.

Narrative of Van Halen's Don Juan; Imprisonment in the Dungeons of the Inquisition at Madrid and his Escape in 1817 and 1818; to which are added his Journey to Russia, his Campaign under the Army of the Caucasus and his Return to Spain in 1821. New York, 1821.

Nevins, William, *Thoughts on Popery.* New York, 1836.

Norton, Herman, *The Life of the Rev. Herman Norton, to which are added Startling Facts, and Signs of Danger and of Promise.* New York, 1853.

Norton, Herman, *Record of Facts Concerning the Persecutions at Madeira in 1843 and 1846. The Flight of a Thousand Converts to the West Indies and also the Sufferings of Those who Arrived Safely in the United States.* New York, 1846.

Norton, Herman, *Signs of Danger and of Promise. Duties of American Protestants at the Present Crisis.* New York, 1844.

Norton, Herman, *Startling Facts for American Protestants! Progress of Romanism since the Revolutionary War. Its Present Position and Future Prospects.* New York, 1844.

Nuns and Nunneries: Sketches compiled Entirely from Romish Authorities. London, 1852.

Odel, Jeremiah, *Popery Unveiled; to which is Annexed a Short Recital of the Origin, Doctrines, Precepts and Examples of the Great Church Militant and Triumphant.* Bennington, Vermont, 1821.

Odenheimer, William H., *The True Catholic No Romanist.* New York, 1842.

On Purgatory and Infallibility. New York, 1839.

Orchard, Isaac, *Friendly Suggestions to an Emigrant, by an Emigrant.* New York, 1845.

Orr, Hector, *The Native American; a Gift for the People.* Philadelphia, 1845.

Our Country; its Dangers and its Duty. New York, 1844.

Our Liberties Defended; the Question Discussed: is the Protestant or Papal System most Favorable to Civil and Religious Liberty? By a Protestant, under the Signature of Obsta Principis and a Roman Catholic, under the Signature of Catholicus. New York, 1841.

Palmer, William, *Letter to N. Wiseman on the Errors of Romanism, In Respect to the Worship of Saints, Satisfactions, Purgatory, Indulgences, and the Worship of Images and Relics.* Baltimore, 1843. Another edition: Baltimore, 1849.

Palmer, William, *A Narrative of Events Connected with the Publication of the Tracts for the Times with Reflections on the Existing Tendencies to Romanism.* New York, 1843.

Papal Diplomacy and the Bull "In Coena Domini." London, 1848.

Parker, D. G., *A Compilation of Startling Facts; or, Romanism against Republicanism.* Chicago, 1856.

Parkinson, William, *The Romish Anti-Christ. A Sermon Delivered in the Meeting House of the First Baptist Church in the City of New York, Lord's Day, Nov. 28, 1830.* New York, 1831.

Party Spirit and Popery: or, the Beast and his Rider. New York, 1847.

Pepin, Francois, *A Narrative of the Life and Experiences of Francois Pepin who was for more than Forty Years a Member of the Papal Church, Embracing an Account of his Conversion, Trials and Persecutions in Turning to the True Religion of the Bible.* Detroit, 1854.

Percy, J. W., *Romanism as it Exists at Rome.* London, 1847.

Pierce, John, *The Right to Private Judgment in Religion, Vindicated against the Claims of the Romish Church, and all Kindred Usurpations, in a Dudleian lecture delivered before the University in Cambridge, 24 October, 1821.* Cambridge, 1821.

Pike, Richard, *Romanism, a Sermon.* Boston, 1854.

Pitrot, John C., *Americans Warned of Jesuitism; or, the Jesuits Unveiled.* New York, 1851.

Pitrot, John C., *Paul and Julia; or, the Political Mysteries, Hypocrisy, and Cruelty of the Church of Rome.* Boston, 1855.

Pitrot, John C., *Review of the Speech of Hon. J. R. Chandler of Pennsylvania on the Political Power of the Pope.* Boston, 1855.

Plumer, William S., *Rome against the Bible, and the Bible against Rome; or, Pharisaism, Jewish and Papal.* Philadelphia, 1854.

Political Popery; or, Bibles and Schools, with the Condition, Progress and Ulterior Objects of Romanists in the United States. New York, 1844.

Polk, Josiah F., *The Claim of the Church of Rome to the Exercise of Religious Toleration during the Proprietary Government of Maryland, examined.* Washington, 1846.

Pollock, Robert, *The Persecuted Family: a Narrative of the Sufferings of the Covenanters in the Reign of Charles II.* New York, 1841.

Pond, Enoch, *No Fellowship with Romanism.* Boston, 1843.

Pope Alexander VI and his Son Caesar Borgia. Philadelphia, 1844.

The Pope and the Presbyterians. A Review of the Warning of Jefferson Respecting the Dangers to be Apprehended to our Civil and Religious Liberty from Presbyterianism. By an "American Citizen." Philadelphia, 1844.

Pope or President? Startling Disclosures of Romanism as Revealed By its Own Writers. New York, 1859.

Popery Adjudged; or, the Roman Catholic Church Weighed in the Balance of God's Word and Found Wanting. Extracted from the Works of Emanuel Swedenborg. Boston, 1854.

Popery and Puseyism: being two Discourses Prepared agreeable to a Resolution of the Synod of Pittsburgh of 1843, and Preached before that Body, at Pittsburgh, September, 1844. By the Rev. Doctors Green and Magill. Pittsburgh, 1844.

Popery Exposed: or, the Secrets and Privacy of the Confessional Unmasked. New York, 1845.

Popery Unmasked. Notes of a Conference between two Missionaries of the Reformed Evangelical Church of Switzerland and Four Roman Catholic Priests. Boston, 1843.

Porter, N., *The Educational Systems of the Puritans and Jesuits Compared.* New York, 1851.

Potts, W. S., *Dangers of Jesuit Instruction.* New York, 1846.

Powell, Thomas, *An Essay on Apostolic Succession; being a Defense of a German Protestant Ministry against the Exclusive and Intolerant Schemes of Papists and High-Churchmen; and supplying a General Antidote to Popery.* New York, 1842.

Poynder, John, *Popery in Alliance with Heathenism; Letters Proving the Conformity which Subsists between the Romish Religion and the Religion of the Ancient Heathens.* London, 1835.

The Protestant Almanac for 1841. Baltimore, 1841.

The Protestant Annual; Exhibiting the Demoralizing Influence of Popery, and the Character of its Priesthood. New York, 1847.

The Protestant Catechism, Showing the Principal Errors of the Church of Rome. Charleston, 1828.

The Protestant Exiles of Zillerthal; their Persecutions and Expatriation on Separating from the Church of Rome and Embracing the Reformed Church. New York, 1844.

The Protestant Keepsake. London, 1840.

A Protestant's Resolution Shewing his Reasons why he will not be a Papist, Digested. 18th edition, Boston, 1746.

Quinet, Edgar, *The Roman Church and Modern Society.* New York, 1845.

Recantation; or, the Confessions of a Convert to Romanism: A Tale of Domestic and Religious Life in Italy. New York, 1846.

Red Cross of Catholicism in America; Startling Expose of an Infernal Catholic Plot. Know-Nothings Set at Defiance. Use of Fire Arms in Cathedrals. Confessions and Secret Correspondence. Boston, 1854.

Reed, Rebecca T., *Six Months in a Convent.* Boston, 1835.

Reeves, James, *Popery Renounced.* ———, 1829.

The Reformation in Europe. New York, 1845.

A Review of the Lady Superior's Reply to "Six Months in a Convent," being a Vindication of Miss Reed. Boston, 1835.

Ricci, Scipio de, *Female Convents. Secrets of Nunneries Disclosed.* New York, 1834.

Rice, N. L., *Romanism, the Enemy of Education, of Free Institutions and of Christianity.* Cincinnati, 1853.

Rice, N. L., *Romanism not Christianity: a Series of Lectures in which Popery and Protestantism are Contrasted, showing the Incompatibility of the Former with Freedom and Free Institutions.* Cincinnati, 1847.

Richardson, James, *The Roman Catholic Convicted upon his Own Evidence of Hostility to the Protestant Churches of Britain.* New York, 1823.

Richardson, N. S., *Reasons Why I am Not a Papist.* New Haven, 1847.

Robertson, D. F., *National Destiny and our Country, a Discourse.* New York, 1851.

Robins, S., *The Evidence of Scripture against the Claims of the Roman Church.* London, 1853.

Rogers, John, *Anti-Popery; or, Popery Unreasonable, Unscriptural and Novel.* 2nd edition, New York, 1843.

Roman Catholic Female Schools. New York, 1837.

Romanism Contradictory to the Bible. New York, 1832.

Romanism Incompatible with Republican Institutions. New York, 1844.

Romanists Disqualified for Civil Power; Proved from the Decrees of the Council of Trent, and other Authentic Documents of the Romish Church. New York, 1855.

Rome's Policy Toward the Bible, or Papal Efforts to Suppress the Scriptures in the Last Five Centuries exposed by an American Citizen. Philadelphia, 1844.

John Ronge, the Holy Coat of Treves, and the New German Church. New York, 1845.

Roussell, Napoleon, *Catholic and Protestant Nations Compared in their Threefold Relations to Wealth, Knowledge, and Morality.* Boston, 1855.

Ryder, William H., *Our Country; or, the American Parlor Keepsake.* Boston, 1854.

The Sanctity of the Church of Rome. New York, ——.

Sanderson, John P., *Republican Landmarks. The Views and Opinions of American Statesmen on Foreign Immigration.* Philadelphia, 1856.

Satanic Plot; or, Awful Crimes of Popery in High and Low Places, by a Know Nothing. Boston, 1855.

Saunders, Frederick and Thomas B. Thorpe, *A Voice to America; or, the Model Republic, its Glory and its Fall, with a Review of the Causes of the Decline and Failure of the Republics of South America, Mexico and of the Old World Applied to the Present Crisis in the United States.* 4th edition, New York, 1855.

Schaeffer, Frederick S., *The Blessed Reformation.* New York, 1817.

Schmucker, S. S., *Discourse in Commemoration of the Glorious Reformation of the Sixteenth Century.* 3rd edition, New York, 1838.

Schmucker, S. S., *The Papal Hierarchy.* ——, 1845.

Schmucker, S. S., *A Tract for the Times.* New York, 1853.

Seasonable Caveat against Popery. New York, 1844.

Secker, T., *Five Discourses against Popery.* Windsor, Vermont, 1827. Second edition: Columbus, Ohio, 1835.

Secker, T., *Five Sermons against Popery.* London, 1835.

The Secret Instructions to the Jesuits. 3rd edition, London, 1759.

Secret Instructions to the Jesuits. Princeton, New Jersey, 1831.

Secret Instructions to the Jesuits, with an Appendix Containing a Short Historical Account of the Society of Jesus, their Maxims, the Jesuit Oath, etc. Philadelphia, 1844.

Sherwood, Mary M., *The Nun.* Princeton, 1834.

Sherwood, Reuben, *The Reviewer Reviewed, or Doctor Brownlee versus the Bible, versus the Catholic Church, versus the Fathers, Ancient and Modern, versus his Own Creed, versus Himself.* Poughkeepsie, New York, 1840.

Sherwood, S., *Edwin and Alicia; or, the Infant Martyrs.* New York, 1835.

Shimeall, R. C., *End of Prelacy; or, a Treatise on Ministerial Parity and the Non-Efficacy of Sacramental Grace; versus the Romanism of the Prelatical Dogma of Unbroken Succession of its Cognate Sacramentarianism, Papal, Tractarian and High and Low Church.* New York, 1852.

Shobere, Frederic, *Persecutions of Popery: Historical Narratives of the Most Remarkable Persecutions Occasioned by the Intolerance of the Church of Rome.* New York, 1844.

Sinclair, Catherine, *Beatrice; or, the Unknown Relatives.* New York, 1853.

Sinclair, Catherine, *Modern Flirtations.* New York, 1853.

Sinclair, Catherine, *Modern Society.* New York, 1850.

Sinclair, Catherine, *Popish Legends; or Bible Truth.* London, 1852.

Sinclair, Catherine, *The Priest and the Curate; or, the Two Diaries.* London, 1853.

Sinclair, Catherine, *Shetland and the Shetlanders; or, the Northern Circuit.* New York, 1840.

Sister Agnes; or, the Captive Nun; a Picture of Convent Life. New York, 1854.

Slocum, J. J., *Reply to the Priest's Book, Denominated "Awful Exposure of an Atrocious Plot formed by Certain Individuals against the Clergy and Nuns of Lower Canada, through the Intervention of Maria Monk."* New York, 1837.

Smalnikar, A. B., *Important Discoveries: also, an Invitation to a Convention of the Republican Protestants against Papists and other Monarchists; or, of True Catholics against Pseudo-Catholics.* Pittsburgh, 1850.

Smith, B. M., *Popery Fulfilling Prophecy.* Philadelphia, 1851.

Smith, Samuel B., *Decisive Confirmation of the Awful Disclosures of Maria Monk, Proving her Residence in the Hotel Dieu Nunnery, and the Existence of the Subterranean Passages.* New York, 1836.

Smith, Samuel B., *The Escape of Sainte Frances Patrick, another Nun from the Hotel Dieu Nunnery of Montreal.* New York, 1836.

Smith, Samuel B., *The Flight of Popery from Rome to the West.* New York, 1836.

Smith, Samuel B., *Renunciation of Popery.* 6th edition, Philadelphia, 1823.

Smith, Samuel B., *Synopsis of the Moral Theology of the Church of Rome from the Works of St. Ligori.* New York, 1836.

Smith, Samuel B., *The Wonderful Adventures of a Lady of the French Nobility, and the Intrigues of a Romish Priest, her Confessor, to Seduce and Murder Her.* New York, 1836.

Smyth, Thomas, *Ecclesiastical Republicanism; or, the Republicanism, Liberality and Catholicity of Presbytery, in Contrast with Prelacy and Popery.* New York, 1843.

Smyth, Thomas, *The Prelatical Doctrine of Apostolic Succession Examined, and the Protestant Ministry Defended against the Assumptions of Popery and High Churchism.* Boston, 1841.

The Sons of the Sires; a History of the Rise, Progress and Destiny of the American Party, and its Probable Influence in the Next Presidential Election. Philadelphia, 1855.

Sopford, J., *Pagano-Papismus, or an Exact Parallel between Rome-Pagan and Rome-Christian.* London, 1844.

South End Forever. North End Forever. Extraordinary Verses on Pope Night, or, a Commemoration of the Fifth of November, giving a History of the Attempt, made by the Papishes, to blow up King and Parliament, A.D., 1588, together with some Account of the Pope himself and his wife, Joan. Boston, 17—.

Sparrow, William, *Romanism and Protestantism Compared as to their Temporal Influence. A Sermon Preached in the . . . Theological Seminary of the Protestant Episcopal Church in the Diocese of Virginia, November 23, 1851.* Alexandria, Virginia, 1852.

Sparry, C., *Extracts from the Theological Works of Peter Dens on the Nature of Confession and the Obligation of the Seal.* New York, 1843.

Sparry, C., *Popery in the Nineteenth Century; or, Popery, What it is, What it Aims at, and What it is Doing.* New York, 1846.

Speeches of Mr. Hopkins of Northampton on the Bill to Incorporate the College of the Holy Cross, in the City of Worcester, Delivered in the House of Representatives, April 24th and 25th, 1849, with an introductory letter to the members of the House. Northampton, 1849.

The Spirit of Popery: an Exposure of its Origin, Character and Results, in Letters from a Father to his Son. New York, 1844.

Spooner, John A., *The Catholic Saved from Popery.* New York, 1849.

Sprague, William B., *Contrast Between True and False Religions.* New York, 1837.

Spring, Gardiner, *A Dissertation on the Rule of Faith; delivered at Cincinnati, Ohio, at the Annual Meeting of the American Bible Society.* New York, 1844.

Stanley, J., *Dialogues on Popery.* New York, 1843.

A Startling Disclosure of the Secret Workings of the Jesuits; by a Former French Roman Catholic but now a Protestant and Colporteur, together with the Secret Seal of the Confessional, the Obligations of the Confessor and Confessed, the Creed and Oaths of Popery, the Secret Instructions of the Jesuits and much other Useful Information. ——, 1854.

Startling Facts for Native Americans. New York, 1855.

Steinmetz, Andrew, *History of the Jesuits.* 2 v. Philadelphia, 1848.

Steinmetz, Andrew, *The Novitiate, or a Year Among the English Jesuits.* New York, 1846.

Stevens, R. V. G., *An Alarm to American Patriots. A Sermon on the Political Tendencies of Popery, considered in Respect to the Institutions of the United States, in the Church of Church Street, Boston, November 27, 1834.* Boston, 1834.

The Story of the Inquisition. Boston, 184-.

Stratten, Thomas, *The Book of the Priesthood: An Argument in Three Parts.* New York, 1831.

Stuart, J. M., *America and the Americans versus the Papacy and the Catholics. A Lecture delivered in the New Jerusalem Temple.* Cincinnati, 1853.

A Supplement to "Six Months in a Convent," Confirming the Narrative of Rebecca Theresa Reed, by the Testimony of more than 100 Witnesses. Boston, 1835.

Taylor, C. B., *Memorials of the English Martyrs*. New York, 1853.

Taylor, Isaac, *Loyola: or Jesuitism in its Rudiments*. New York, 1849.

The Teachings of the Roman Catholic Church Compared with the Holy Scriptures. New York, 1852.

The Testimony of History against the Church of Rome. London, 1840.

Thacher, Thomas, *A Discourse on the Errors of Popery*. Cambridge, 1805.

Thayer, John, *Controversy. Between the Rev. John Thayer, Catholic Missionary, of Boston, and the Rev. George Lesslie, pastor of a Church in Washington, New Hampshire*. Boston, 1793.

Thomas, Abel C., *Triangle. The Catholic Question Considered. Both Disputants Answered*. Philadelphia, 1851.

Thornwell, James H., *Arguments of Romanists Discussed and Refuted*. Charleston, 1845.

Tisdale, W. S., *The Controversy between Senator Brooks, and John, Archbishop of New York, over the Church Property Bill*. New York, 1855.

Tisdale, W. S., *The Know Nothing Almanac and True American's Manual for 1856*. New York, 1856.

Tracts on Romanism. New York, 1836.

The Trial of the Pope of Rome, the Anti-Christ or Man of Sin Described in the Bible, for High Treason against the Son of God. Tried at the Sessions House of Truth before the Right Hon. Divine Revelation, the Hon. Justice Reason and the Hon. Justice History. Taken in Short Hand by a Friend to Saint Peter. 2nd edition, Boston, 1844.

The Trial of the Pope on the Testimony of the Sovereigns of the Old World, the Reformers and Martyrs, in which the President of the United States is Introduced as a New Witness. New York, 1846.

Turnley, Joseph, *Popery in Power; or, the Spirit of the Vatican*. London, 1850.

Turnley, Joseph, *Priestcraft; or, the Monarch of the Middle Ages*. London, 1850.

The Two Apocalyptic Beasts in St. John's Revelation Fully Explained and with an Accurate Engraving. New York, 1842.

Upham, C. W., *Principles of the Reformation: a Sermon*. Salem, 1826.

Vigil, Francis C., *Light in Darkness*. Boston, 1852.

A Voice from Rome Answered by an American Citizen; or, a Review of the Encyclical Letter of Pope Gregory XVI, A.D. 1842. Philadelphia, 1844.

Waddell, Thomas, *Letters to the Editors of the Catholic Miscellany: Illustrating the Papal Doctrine of Intention: the Opus Operatum, Romish Infallibility, and the Knavery of Popish Writers*. New York, 1830.

The Waldenses: Sketches of the Evangelical Christians of the Valley of the Piedmont. Philadelphia, 1854.

A Warning against Foreign Influence to the Patriotic Statesmen of the United States of America. ——, 184–.

Waterous, Timothy and Zachariah Waterous, *The Battle Axe and the Weapons of War, discovered by the Morning Light: Aimed at the Final Destruction of Priestcraft*. 2nd edition, New London, 1841.

Watson, H., *An Apology for the Bible*. New York, 1835.

Webber, C. W., *Sam: or, the History of a Mystery*. Cincinnati, 1857.

Weishampel, John F., *The Pope's Stratagem: "Rome to America!" An Address to the Protestants of the United States, against placing the Pope's block of Marble in the Washington Monument*. Philadelphia, 1852.

Weiss, M. Charles, *History of the French Protestant Refugees from the Revocation of the Edict of Nantes to our own Days*. New York, 1854.

West, Nathaniel, *The Ark of God—the Safe-Guard of the Nation. A Discourse in Defense of Protestantism*. Pittsburgh, 1852.

Wharton, C. H., *Concise View of the Principal Points of Controversy between the Protestant and Romish Churches*. New York, 1817.

What is Romanism? London, 1850.

Whatley, R., *The Errors of Romanism Traced to their Origin in Human Nature*. Philadelphia, 1843. Other editions: Philadelphia, 1844, London, 1837.

Whatley, R., *The Kingdom of Christ: and the Errors of Romanism*. New York, 1848.

White, J. Blanco, *Letters from Spain*. London, 1822.

White, J. Blanco, *The Poor Man's Preservative Against Popery*. New York, 1835.

White, J. Blanco, *Practical and Internal Evidence against Catholicism, with Occasional Strictures on Mr. Butler's Book of the Roman Catholic Church; in Six Letters Addressed to the Impartial among the Roman Catholics of Great Britain.* Boston, 1835. Another edition: Georgetown, 1826.

Whitley, T. W., *The Jesuit; a National Melodrama in Three Acts.* New York, 1850.

Whitney, Thomas R., *An Address on the Occasion of the Seventh Anniversary of the Alpha Chapter, Order of United Americans.* New York, 1852.

Whitney, Thomas R., *A Defense of American Policy.* New York, 1856.

Whittingham, William L., *A Letter to the Reverend Francis Patrick Kenrick.* New York, 1841.

The Wide Awake Gift and Know Nothing Token for 1855. New York, 1855.

Wigglesworth, Edward, *Some Thoughts upon the Spirit of Infallibility claimed by the Church of Rome . . . a Dudleian Lecture.* Boston, 1757.

Willis, M., *Popery, the Enemy of Public Morals.* Glasgow, 1836.

Wilson, Joseph S., *The Inquisition.* Milwaukee, 1853.

Winchester, Samuel G., *An Examination of the Romish Principle of Withholding the Scriptures from the Laity.* Philadelphia, 1831.

Wordsworth, Christopher D., *The Church of Rome or the Babylon of the Apocalypse.* Philadelphia, 1853.

Young, John, *Lectures on the Chief Points of Controversy between Protestants and Romanists.* London, 1845.

Young Sam. New York, 1855.

II. Other Sources

1. Public Records

(A) National

Elliot, Jonathan, *The Debates in the Several State Conventions on the Adoption of the Federal Constitution.* 4 v. Washington, 1836.

Journals of the Continental Congress. 34 v. Washington, 1904–1936.

Congressional Globe. Washington, 1833–1856.

House Documents. Washington, 1834–1847.

House Executive Documents. Washington, 1847–1857.

House Miscellaneous Documents. Washington, 1847–1857.

House Reports of Committees. Washington, 1834–1847.

Senate Documents. Washington, 1833–1847.

Senate Executive Documents. Washington, 1847–1857.

Senate Miscellaneous Documents. Washington, 1847–1857.

Senate Reports. Washington, 1847–1857.

(B) Colonies and States

Connecticut

Public Records of the Colony of Connecticut, 1636–1776. 5 v. Hartford, 1850–1890.

State Records. 2 v. Hartford, 1894–1895.

Delaware

Minutes of the Council of the State of Delaware, from 1776 to 1792. Historical Society of Delaware *Papers,* VI. Wilmington, 1887.

Georgia

Colonial Records of the State of Georgia (1732–1774). 26 v. Atlanta, 1904–1916.

Revolutionary Records of the State of Georgia (1769–1784). 3 v. Atlanta, 1908.

Maine

Documentary History of the State of Maine. 16 v. Portland, 1869–1910.

Maryland

Archives of Maryland. 51 v. Baltimore, 1883—in progress.

Massachusetts

Acts and Resolves, Public and Private, of the Province of the Massachusetts Bay. 21 v. Boston, 1869–1922.

Acts and Laws of the Commonwealth of Massachusetts. 9 v. Boston, 1890–1896.

Journals of the House of Representatives of Massachusetts. Boston, 1915—in progress.

Records of the Colony of New Plymouth in New England. 12 v. Boston, 1855–1861.

Records of the Governor and Company of the Massachusetts Bay in New England (1628–1686). 5 v. Boston, 1853–1854.

New Hampshire
> *Documents and Records Relating to the Province of New Hampshire.* 33 v. Concord, etc., 1867–1907.

New Jersey
> *Archives of the State of New Jersey.* 30 v. Newark, etc., 1880–1906.

New Haven
> *Records of the Colony and Plantation of New Haven (1638–1649).* Hartford, 1857.
>
> *Records of the Colony or Jurisdiction of New Haven (1653–1665).* Hartford, 1858.

New York
> *Colonial Laws of New York from the Year 1664 to the Revolution.* 5 v. Albany, 1894–1896.
>
> *Documents Relating to the Colonial History of the State of New York.* 15 v. Albany, 1856–1887.

North Carolina
> *Colonial Records of North Carolina.* 30 v. Raleigh, Winston, and Goldsboro, 1886–1914.

Pennsylvania
> *Colonial Records.* 16 v. Philadelphia, 1852–1853.
>
> *Pennsylvania Archives.* 91 v. Philadelphia and Harrisburg, 1852–1907.
>
> *Statutes at Large of Pennsylvania from 1682 to 1801.* 18 v. Harrisburg, 1896–1908.

Rhode Island
> *Records of the State of Rhode Island and Providence Plantations in New England.* 10 v. Providence, 1856–1865.

South Carolina
> *Statutes at Large of South Carolina.* 10 v. Columbia, 1836–1841.

Vermont
> *Records of the Council of Safety and Governor and Council of the State of Vermont.* 8 v. Montpelier, 1873–1880.

Virginia
> *Executive Journals of the Council of Colonial Virginia.* 4 v. Richmond, 1925–1930.
>
> Hening, William A. (editor), *The Statutes at Large, being a Collection of all the Laws of Virginia (1619–1792).* 13 v. Philadelphia and New York, 1823.

Journals of the House of Burgesses of Virginia (1727–1776). 12 v. Richmond, 1905–1915.

Journals of the House of Delegates of Virginia (1776–1790). 4 v. Richmond, 1828.

Legislative Journals of the Councils of Colonial Virginia. 3 v. Richmond, 1918–1919.

Minutes of the Council and General Court of Colonial Virginia 1622–1623, 1670–1676. Richmond, 1924.

2. Newspapers and Periodicals

(Dates indicate years actually consulted)

The American Union (Boston, Massachusetts). 1848–1856. Weekly.

The Boston Observer and Religious Intelligencer (Boston, Massachusetts). January 1, 1835–June 25, 1835. Weekly.

The Boston Recorder (Boston, Massachusetts). 1844–1850. Weekly.

Brownson's Quarterly Review (Boston, Massachusetts). 1844–1854. Quarterly Catholic journal.

The Christian Review (Boston, Massachusetts). 1836–1837. Quarterly.

The Christian Spectator (New York, New York). 1835. Quarterly.

The Christian Watchman (Boston, Massachusetts). 1819–1856. Weekly Baptist paper.

The Congregationalist (Boston, Massachusetts). 1849–1856. Weekly Congregational paper.

DeBow's Commercial Review of the South and West (New Orleans, Louisiana). 1846–1856.

The Episcopal Recorder (Philadelphia, Pennsylvania). 1831–1836. Weekly.

Freeman's Journal and Catholic Register (New York, New York). 1841–1854. Weekly Catholic paper.

The Home Missionary (New York, New York). 1828–1855. Monthly magazine. Organ of the American Home Missionary Society.

The Jesuit (Boston, Massachusetts). September, 1829–December, 1829. Weekly Catholic paper.

The Magazine of the Reformed Dutch Church (New Brunswick, New Jersey). 1826–1830. Monthly.

The Massachusetts Yeoman (Worcester, Massachusetts). 1824–1831.

The National Intelligencer (Washington, D. C.). 1849–1855. Daily.

The Native American and Yellow Blossom (Philadelphia, Pennsylvania). 1844. A daily published to ridicule the American Republican party.

The New Englander (Boston, Massachusetts). 1844–1856. Quarterly.

The New York Observer (New York, New York). 1823–1856. Weekly Presbyterian paper.

Niles' Weekly Register (Baltimore, Maryland). 1819–1849.

The Pilot (Boston, Massachusetts). 1841–1855. Weekly Catholic paper.

The Presbyterian Quarterly Review (Philadelphia, Pennsylvania). 1852–1855.

The Protestant Episcopalian and Church Register (Philadelphia, Pennsylvania). 1830–1838. Monthly.

The Southern Presbyterian Review (Columbia, South Carolina). 1847–1855. Quarterly.

United States Catholic Magazine (Baltimore, Maryland). 1843–1848. Monthly.

The Watchman of the South (Richmond, Virginia). 1837–1845. Weekly Presbyterian paper.

The Western Messenger: devoted to Religion and Literature (Louisville, Kentucky). 1835–1841. Semi-monthly.

3. Reports of Societies and Churches

American Baptist Home Mission Society, *Annual Reports of the Executive Committee.* New York, 1832–1844.

American Baptist Home Mission Society, *Proceedings of the Convention held in the City of New York, on the 27th of April, 1832, for the Formation of the American Baptist Home Mission Society, with the Constitution of the Society and a List of its Officers.* New York, 1832.

American Bible Society, *Annual Reports.* New York, 1816–1856.

American Education Society, *Annual Reports.* Andover and Boston, 1816–1856.

American Home Missionary Society, *Annual Reports . . . Presented by the Executive Committee.* New York, 1827–1856.

American Tract Society, *Annual Reports.* Boston, 1815–1856.

Annales de l'Association de la Propagation de la Foi, Recueil Periodique des Lettres des Évêques et des Missionaires des Deux Mondes, et de Tous les Documens Relatifs aux Missions et l'Association de la Propagation de la Foi. Lyons et Paris, 1823–1855.

Board of Domestic Missions of the Reformed Protestant Dutch Church, *Nineteenth Annual Report.* New York, 1851.

Board of Foreign Missions of the Presbyterian Church in the United States of America, *Annual Reports.* New York, 1838–1846.

Board of Missions of the General Assembly of the Presbyterian Church in the United States of America, *Annual Reports.* Philadelphia, 1840–1854.

Boston Ladies Society for Evangelizing the West, *Annual Reports.* Boston, 1843–1844.

Boston Society for the Prevention of Pauperism, *Annual Reports.* Boston, 1836–1854.

Dutch Reformed Church, *Acts and Proceedings of the General Synod of the Reformed Dutch Church in North America, at New York.* New York, 1837–1839.

Dutch Reformed Church, *Acts and Proceedings of the General Synod of the Reformed Protestant Dutch Church in North America convened at Kingston, New York, June, 1848.* New York, 1848.

Dutch Reformed Church, *A Digest of the Printed Minutes of the General Synod of the Reformed Dutch Church from the Year 1794 to June, 1848, Inclusive.* New York, 1848.

Ladies' Society for the Promotion of Education at the West, *Annual Reports.* Boston, 1847–1852.

Ladies' Society for the Promotion of Education at the West, *History of the Formation of the Ladies' Society for the Promotion of Education at the West; with two Addresses Delivered at its Organization by the Rev. Edward Beecher, D.D., and the Rev. E. N. Kirk.* Boston, 1846.

Methodist Episcopal Church, *Journals of the General Conference of the Methodist Episcopal Church, 1796–1856.* 3 v. New York, 1856.

Minutes of the General Association of Massachusetts. Boston, 1834–
    1855. Volumes published separately each year under identical
    titles.
Protestant Episcopal Church, *Journals of the General Conventions
    of the Protestant Episcopal Church in the United States, 1785–
    1835*. 3 v. Claremont, New Hampshire, 1874.
Society for the Promotion of Collegiate and Theological Education
    at the West, *Annual Reports*. New York, 1844–1855.
Society for the Promotion of Collegiate and Theological Education
    at the West, *Proceedings of the Public Meeting in behalf of
    the Society for the Promotion of Collegiate and Theological
    Education at the West, held in Park Street Church, Boston,
    May 28, 1845; including the Addresses of Rev. Drs. Hopkins,
    E. Beecher, Bacon and L. Beecher*. New York, 1845.
Western Baptist Educational Association, *Annual Reports of the
    Executive Committee*. Boston, 1834–1835.
Western Educational Society, *Annual Reports of the Directors*.
    Cincinnati, 1835–1837.
Western Foreign Missionary Society, *Annual Reports of the Board
    of Directors*. ——, 1834–1836.

4. Books and Pamphlets

Abbott, John S. C., *Sermon on the Duties and Dangers of the Clergy
    and the Church*. Boston, 1842.
*An Account of the Conflagration of the Ursuline Convent . . . by
    a Friend of Religious Toleration*. Boston, 1834. An attack on
    the convent burners.
*Address of the Catholic Lay Citizens of Philadelphia to their Fel-
    low Citizens in Reply to the Presentment of the Grand Jury in
    Regard to the Causes of the Late Riots in Philadelphia*. Phila-
    delphia, 1844.
Alger, William R., *An Oration Delivered before the Citizens of
    Boston, July 4, 1857*. Boston, 1857.
Austin, James T., *Argument of James T. Austin, Attorney General
    of the Commonwealth, before the Supreme Judicial Court in
    Middlesex on the Case of John R. Buzzell*. Boston, 1834.
Autodicus, *The Critique on the Vision of Rubeta: a Dramatic Sketch
    in One Act*. Philadelphia, 1838.
Awful Exposure of the Atrocious Plot formed by Certain Indi-

viduals against the Clergy and Nuns of Lower Canada through the Intervention of Maria Monk. New York, 1837.

Bacon, Leonard, *The American Church. A Discourse in behalf of the American Home Missionary Society.* New York, 1852.

Barber, Daniel, *The History of My Own Times.* Washington, 1827.

Barnes, Albert, *Home Missions.* New York, 1851.

Baxter, Roger, *The Most Important Tenets of the Roman Catholic Church Fairly Examined.* Washington, 1820. A theological defense of Catholicism.

Beecher, Lyman, *Autobiography and Correspondence.* 2 v. New York, 1865.

Beecher, Lyman, *The Works of the Rev. Lyman Beecher.* 3 v. Boston, 1852.

Bellows, Henry W., *Religious Liberty. The Alleged Failure of Protestantism; a Sermon Preached in the Unitarian Church, at Washington, on February 22, 1852.* Washington, 1852.

Bethune, George W., *The Relation of the Sunday School System to our Christian Patriotism. Annual Sermon in Behalf of the American Sunday School Union delivered at Philadelphia, May 16, 1847.* Philadelphia, 1847.

Bethune, George W., *The Strength of Christian Charity; a Sermon Preached before the Foreign Evangelical Society, New York, May 5, 1844.* Philadelphia, 1844.

Broom, Jacob, *An Address Delivered at Castle Garden, February 22, 1854, Before the Order of United Americans, on the Occasion of their Celebration of the 122 Anniversary of the Birthday of George Washington.* New York, 1854.

Brownell, Thomas C., *Errors of the Times; a Charge Delivered to the Clergy of the Diocese of Connecticut at the Annual Convention Holden in Christ Church, in the City of Hartford, June 13, 1843.* Hartford, 1843.

Brownlee, W. C., *Memorial of the Reverend W. C. Brownlee, D.D.* New York, 1860.

Brownson, Orestes A., *Works.* 20 v. Detroit, 1882–1887.

Buckingham, James S., *America: Historical, Statistical and Descriptive.* London, 1841.

Bushnell, Horace, *Barbarism the First Danger. A Discourse on Home Missions.* New York, 1847.

Carey, Mathew, *Reflections on the Subject of Emigration from*

Europe with a View to Settlement in the United States. 3rd edition, Philadelphia, 1826.

Catholicism Compatible with Republican Government, and in Full Accordance with Popular Institutions; or, Reflections upon a Premium Treatise issued by the American Protestant Society, under the Signature of "Civis." New York, 1844.

Chandler, Joseph R., *The Temporal Power of the Pope—a Full and Authentic Report of the Brilliant Speech of the Hon. Joseph R. Chandler of Pennsylvania in the House of Representatives of the United States, Jan. 11, 1855.* Philadelphia, 1855.

The Chronicles of Mount Benedict: a Tale of the Ursuline Convent, the Quasi Production of Mary Magdalen. Boston, 1837. Short novel attacking the convent burning.

Cobbett, William, *A History of the Protestant Reformation in England and Ireland; showing how that Event has Impoverished and Degraded the Main Body of the People in those Countries.* New York, 1832.

Colonel Fremont Not a Roman Catholic. ——, 1856. A Republican answer to Know-Nothing charges.

A Complete Exposure of the Order of "Know Nothings"; being a Revelation of all the Signs, Secrets, Peculiarities, Plans and Operations of that Mysterious Body. By one of the "Expelled." Philadelphia, 1854.

Cluskey, N. W., *Political Text Book and Encyclopaedia.* Washington, 1857.

Curtis, George Ticknor, *The Rights of Conscience and of Property; or, the True Issue of the Convent Question.* Boston, 1842. A plea for state compensation for the Ursuline order.

Davis, G. Lynn-Lachlan, *The Day Star of American Freedom.* New York, 1855. A book demonstrating Catholic contributions to religious liberty.

Davis, Henry Winter, *Speeches and Addresses Delivered in the Congress of the United States, and on Several Public Occasions.* New York, 1867.

DeBow, J. D. B., *Statistical View of the United States, Embracing its Territory, Population—White, Colored and Slave—Moral and Social Condition, Industry, Property and Revenue; the Detailed Statistics of Cities, Towns and Counties; being a Compendium of the Seventh Census.* Washington, 1854.

Documents Relating to the Ursuline Convent in Charlestown. Boston, 1842.

Dunne, Henry C., *Democracy versus Know-Nothingism and Republicanism.* Philadelphia, 1858.

Eckel, L. St. John, *Maria Monk's Daughter; an Autobiography.* New York, 1874.

Eliot, Andrew, *A Sermon Preached October 25th, 1759. Being a Day of Public Thanksgiving Appointed by Authority for the Success of the British Arms this year, especially in the Reduction of Quebec, the Capital of Canada.* Boston, 1759.

Elizabeth, Charlotte, *Personal Recollections.* New York, 1843.

England, John, *The Works of the Right Reverend John England, First Bishop of Charleston.* 7 v. Cleveland, 1908.

Exposition of the Mysteries and Secrets of the Order of "Know Nothings": with a Full and Authentic Account of their Origin and Progress; also their Forms of Initiation, Degrees, Passwords, Signs, Grips, Tokens, etc. By a late member of the Order. New York, 1854.

Facts for the People of the South. Abolition Intolerance and Religious Intolerance United. Know-Nothingism Exposed. Washington, 1855.

Fay, Richard S., *Argument before the Committee of the House of Representatives upon the Petition of Benedict Fenwick and others, with a portion of the Documentary Testimony.* Boston, 1835.

Fenwick, Benedict J., "The Destruction of Ursuline Convent at Charlestown, Mass.," United States Catholic Historical Society *Historical Records and Studies,* IX (New York, 1916), 187–190. A letter written by Bishop Fenwick in 1837 describing the convent burning.

A Few Words to the Thinking and Judicious Voters of Pennsylvania. ——, 1854. Campaign pamphlet directed at the Know-Nothing candidate for governor.

Fillmore, Millard, *Millard Fillmore Papers. Publications of the Buffalo Historical Society,* X and XI (Buffalo, 1907).

Finley, James B., *Autobiography.* Cincinnati, 1854.

Hale, Charles, *A Review of the Proceedings of the Nunnery Committee of the Massachusetts Legislature; and Especially their Conduct . . . on occasion of the Visit to the Catholic School in Roxbury, March 26, 1855.* Boston, 1855.

Hall, Edwin, *Colleges Essential to Home Missions; a Discourse delivered at the Ninth Anniversary of the Society for the Promotion of Collegiate and Theological Education at the West.* New York, 1853.

Hall, Newton, *The Land of the Forum and the Vatican; or, Thoughts and Sketches During an Easter Pilgrimage to Rome.* New York, 1853.

Hambleton, James P., *History of the Political Campaign in Virginia in 1855.* Richmond, 1856.

Harris, Benjamin G., *Speech of Benjamin G. Harris, esq., of St. Mary's County, upon the Report of the Committee on Secret Societies, in the House of Delegates of Maryland.* ——, ——.

Hibernicus, *"What Brings so Many Irish to America!"* A pamphlet Written by Hibernicus: one part of which Explains the Many Causes of Irish Emigration; the other the Consistency or Inconsistency of "Native Americanism" as it is. New York, 1845.

Hickok, Laurens P., *A Nation Saved from its Prosperity only by the Gospel. A Discourse in behalf of the American Home Missionary Society.* New York, 1853.

Hughes, John, *Brooksiana.* New York, 1855.

Hughes, John, *Complete Works of the Most Rev. John Hughes, D.D., Archbishop of New York.* 2 v. New York, 1866.

Hughes, John, *The Conversion and Edifying Death of Andrew Dunn.* Philadelphia, 1828.

Hughes, John, *The Decline of Protestantism and its Causes.* New York, 1850.

Hughes, John, *Kirwan Unmasked.* New York, 1848.

Hughes, John, *The Review of the Charge Delivered May 22nd, 1833 by the Right Reverend Onderdonk, on the Rule of Faith.* Philadelphia, 1833.

Ide, George B., *The Ministry Demanded by the Present Crisis.* Philadelphia, 1845.

Ives, I. M., *Two Lectures on the Inquisition, Delivered by Request before the Young Men's Association, Milwaukee, Wisconsin.* Milwaukee, 1853. A history and defense of the Inquisition.

Julian, George W., *Political Recollections, 1840–1872.* Chicago, 1884.

Julian, George W., *Speeches on Political Questions.* New York, 1872.

Kenrick, Francis Patrick, *A Vindication of the Catholic Church in a Series of Letters.* Baltimore, 1855.

Kirk, Edward N., *The Church and the College; a Discourse Delivered at the Thirteenth Anniversary of the Society for the Promotion of Collegiate and Theological Education at the West.* Boston, 1856.

Kirk, Edward N., *The Church Essential to the Republic.* New York, 1848.

Kirk, Edward N., *Sermons on Different Subjects.* 4th edition, New York, 1841.

The Know Nothings. An Exposure of the Secret Order of Know Nothings; the Most Ludicrous and Startling Yankee "Notion" Ever Conceived. New York, 1854.

Kossuth in New England: a full account of the Hungarian General's Visit to Massachusetts; with his Speeches and the Addresses which were made to him. Boston, 1852.

Kossuth, Louis, *Sketch of the Life of Louis Kossuth, Governor of Hungary; together with the Declaration of Hungarian Independence; Kossuth's Address to the People of the United States; all his great Speeches in England; and the Letter of Daniel Webster to Chevalier Hulseman.* New York, 1851.

Latrobe, C., *The Rambler in North America in 1832–1833.* 2 v. New York, 1835.

Letter of an Adopted Catholic Addressed to the President of the Kentucky Democratic Association of Washington City, on Temporal Allegiance to the Pope, and the Relation of the Catholic Church and Catholics, both Native and Adopted, to the System of Domestic Slavery and its Agitation in the United States. Washington, 1856.

The Life and Death of Sam in Virginia. Richmond, 1856. An anti-Know-Nothing novel.

Longstreet, Augustus A., *Know Nothingism Unveiled.* Washington, 1855.

Lyell, C., *A Second Visit to the United States of America.* 3 v. London, 1849.

Mahoney, Dorah, *Six Months in a House of Correction.* Boston, 1835. A burlesque of R. T. Reed's *Six Months in a Convent.*

Marryat, Frederick, *A Diary in America.* Philadelphia, 1839.

Marshall, Thomas F., *Speech of Hon. Thos. F. Marshall, in Oppo-*

sition to the Principles of the Know-Nothing Organization. Versailles, Kentucky, 1855.

Martineau, Harriet, *Society in America.* 3 v. London, 1837.

McGee, Thomas D., *The Catholic History of North America.* Boston, 1855.

McIlvaine, Charles P., *The Chief Dangers of the Church in these times: a Charge Delivered to the Clergy of the Diocese of Ohio at the Twenty Sixth Annual Convention of the Same. Gambier, September 8, 1843.* New York, 1843.

Memorial and Protest of the Trustees of the Public School Society of the City of New York to the Senate of the State of New York. Albany, 1841.

Moore, Justus E., *The Warning of Thomas Jefferson; or, a Brief Exposition of the Dangers to be Apprehended to our Civil and Religious Liberties from Presbyterianism.* Philadelphia, 1844.

Murray, Charles A., *Travels in North America.* London, 1854.

Murray, Nicholas, *American Principles on National Prosperity. A Thanksgiving Sermon Preached in the First Presbyterian Church, Elizabethtown, November 23, 1854.* New York, 1854.

Murray, Nicholas, *Memoirs.* New York, 1862.

Nichols, Thomas, *Forty Years of American Life.* 2 v. London, 1864.

O'Hanlon, John, *Life and Scenery in Missouri.* Dublin, 1890.

The Olive Branch; or, an Earnest Appeal in Behalf of Religion, the Supremacy of Law and Social Order, with Documents Relating to the Late Disturbances in Philadelphia. Philadelphia, 1844.

Peters, Absalom, *Collegiate Religious Institutions; a Discourse Delivered . . . before the Society for the Promotion of Collegiate and Theological Education at the West.* New York, 1851.

Philalethes, *An Exposition of the Principles of the Roman Catholic Religion with Remarks on its Influence in the United States.* Hartford, 1830.

Pike, John, *A Sermon Delivered before his Excellency Henry J. Gardner, Governor, his Honor H. W. Benchley, Lieutenant Governor, and the Hon. Council and the Legislature of Massachusetts at the Annual Election, Wednesday, January 7, 1857.* Boston, 1857.

Polk, James K., *The Diary of James K. Polk during his Presidency, 1845 to 1849.* 4 v. Chicago, 1910.

The Pope's Bull and the Words of Daniel O'Connell. New York, 1856. Republican campaign document.

Porter, N., *A Plea for Libraries. A Letter Addressed to a Friend in Behalf of the Society for the Promotion of Collegiate and Theological Education at the West.* New York, 1848.

Proceedings of the Democratic and Anti-Know-Nothing State Convention Held in the City of Montgomery, January 8th and 9th, 1856. Montgomery, Alabama, 1856.

Proselytizing; a Sketch of Know Nothing Times. Cincinnati, 1854. An anti-Know-Nothing novel.

Protestant Jesuitism. New York, 1836.

Reasons for Embracing the Catholic Religion: or Motives which Lately Influenced a Protestant Gentleman to Unite himself with the Catholic Church. Hartford, 1831.

Reception of Kossuth. New York, 1852.

Reed, Andrew and James Matherson, *A Narrative of the Visit to the American Churches by the Deputation from the Congregational Union of England and Wales.* London, 1835.

Reese, David M., *Humbugs of New York; being a Remonstrance Against Popular Delusion, whether in Science, Philosophy, or Religion.* New York, 1838.

Reflections on the Late Riots by Candid Writers in Poetry and Prose. Philadelphia, 1844.

Remarks on the Majority and Minority Reports of the Select Committee on Secret Societies of the House of Delegates of Maryland. New York, 1856. An attack on the Know-Nothing party.

Reply to the Address of the Native American Convention at Harrisburg, Pa., Feb. 1845, in a Series of Letters. Philadelphia, 1845.

Report of the Committee Relating to the Destruction of the Ursuline Convent. Boston, 1834.

Report of the Special Committee to Whom was Referred the Petition of the Catholics relative to the Distribution of the School Fund: together with the Remonstrances against the Same. New York, 1841.

A Review of Nicholas Murray's (Kirwan) "Decline of Popery" by a Protestant. New York, 1851.

A Review of Rev. Horace Bushnell's Sermon on "The Crisis of the Church," by a Yankee. Hartford, 1835.

Riddle, David N., *Our Country for the Sake of the World.* New York, 1851.

The Ritual and the Order of Know Nothings, with the Initiation Oaths taken by James Pollock, now Governor of Pennsylvania. ——, ——.

Saint George, Mary Edmund, *An Answer to Six Months in a Convent Exposing its Falsehoods and Manifold Absurdities.* Boston, 1835.

Saltmarsh, S., *The Signs of the Times. A Sermon.* Boston, 1854.

Scank, Philemon, *A Few Chapters to Brother Jonathan concerning Infallibility, etc.; or, Strictures on Nathan L. Rice's Defense of Protestantism.* Louisville, Kentucky, 1835.

Seward, William H., *Works.* 4 v. New York, 1853–1861.

Seymour, M. Hobart, *Mornings Among the Jesuits at Rome.* New York, 1849. Pro-Catholic propaganda.

Sibthorp, Richard W., *The True Path of the Christian Churchman wandering in the Mazes of Protestantism; Exemplified in Two Letters in Answer to the Inquiry Why have you become a Catholic.* New York, 1843.

Skinner, P. H., *The Welcome of Louis Kossuth, Governor of Hungary, to Philadelphia, by the Youth.* Philadelphia, 1852.

Sleigh, W. W., *An Exposure of Maria Monk's Pretended Abduction and Conveyance to the Catholic Asylum, Philadelphia.* Philadelphia, 1837.

Smith, H. B., *An Argument for Christian Colleges. An Address in behalf of the Society for the Promotion of Collegiate and Theological Education at the West.* New York, 1857.

Smith, Henry, *The Truly Christian Pulpit our Strongest National Defense. A Discourse in behalf of the American Home Missionary Society.* New York, 1854.

Smith, John C., *The Religion and Protestantism of '76. A Discourse delivered . . . Fourth of July, 1844.* Washington, 1844.

Smith, Samuel M., *To Every Sincere Inquirer after Truth with an Appendix containing the "Renunciation of Popery."* New York, 1834. Pro-Catholic propaganda.

Sons of St. Dominick, a Dialogue between a Protestant and a Catholic on the Defense of the Letter of the Presbyterian of Baltimore. Baltimore, 1812. A pro-Catholic argument.

Spaulding, M. J., *D'Aubigne's History of the Great Reformation in Germany and Switzerland Reviewed; or the Reformation in*

Germany Examined in its Instruments, Causes and Manner and in its Influence on Religion, Government, Literature and General Civilization. Baltimore, 1844.

Stetson, Caleb, *A Discourse on the Duty of Sustaining the Laws, Occasioned by the Burning of the Ursuline Convent.* Boston, 1834.

Stone, William L., *Maria Monk and the Nunnery of the Hotel Dieu; Being an Account of a Visit to the Convents of Montreal, and a Refutation of the "Awful Disclosures."* New York, 1836.

Swinson, William, *An Expose of the Know Nothings, their Degrees, Signs, Grips, Passwords, Charges, Oaths, Initiations.* Philadelphia, 1854.

Thacher, P. O., *Charge to the Grand Jury of the County of Suffolk . . . at the opening of the Municipal Court of Boston, Dec. 1, 1834.* Boston, 1834. Deals with the convent burning.

Thaxter, Lucy W., *An Account of Life in the Convent at Mount Benedict, Charlestown.* Manuscript written in 1843 by a former pupil. In Treasure Room, Harvard College Library.

Todd, John, *Colleges Essential to the Church of God; Plain Letters Addressed to a Parishioner in behalf of the Society for the Promotion of Collegiate and Theological Education at the West.* New York, 1848.

Towle, George M., *American Society.* 2 v. London, 1870.

The Trial of the Convent Rioters. Cambridge, 1834.

Trial of John R. Buzzell before the Supreme Judicial Court of Massachusetts for Arson and Burglary in the Ursuline Convent at Charlestown. Boston, 1834.

Trial of John R. Buzzell, the Leader of the Convent Rioters, for Arson and Burglary Committed on the Night of the 11th of August, 1834, By the Destruction of the Convent on Mount Benedict, in Charlestown, Massachusetts. Boston, 1834.

The Trial of Persons Charged with Burning the Convent in the Town of Charlestown (Mass.), before the Supreme Judicial Court Holden at East Cambridge on Tuesday, Dec. 2, 1834. Boston, 1834.

Trial of William Mason, Marvin Marcy, Jr. and Sargent Blaisdell, charged with Being Concerned in Burning the Ursuline Convent in Charlestown (Mass.), on the Night of the 11th of August, 1834. Boston, 1834.

The Truth Unveiled; or a Calm and Impartial Exposition of the

Origin and Immediate Cause of the Terrible Riots in Phila-delphia on May 6th, 7th and 8th A.D. 1844. By a Protestant and Native Philadelphian. Philadelphia, 1844.

Vale, G., *Review of the Awful Disclosures of Maria Monk.* New York, 1836.

The Vision of Rubeta; an Epic Story of the Island of Manhattan. Boston, 1838.

Washburn, Daniel, *The Man of God who was Disobedient unto the Word of the Lord. A Sermon Preached on the Occasion of Reading the Sentence of Deposition of L. Silliman Ives, to the Congregation of Trinity Church, Pottsville, Pa.* Philadelphia, 1854.

Wigglesworth, Edward, *The Authority of Tradition Considered at the Lecture Founded by the Hon. Judge Dudley in Harvard College, November 5, 1777.* Boston, 1778.

III. Secondary Accounts

1. Books

Augustina, Mary, *American Opinion of Roman Catholicism in the Eighteenth Century.* New York, 1936.

Baker, Thomas S., *Lenau and Young Germany in America.* Phila-delphia, 1897.

Bromwell, W. J., *History of Immigration to the United States.* New York, 1856.

Brownson, H. F., *The Life of O. A. Brownson.* 3 v. Detroit, 1898–1900.

The Charlestown Convent; its Destruction by a Mob on the Night of August 11, 1834; with a History of the Excitement before the Burning and the Strange and Exaggerated Reports Relat-ing Thereto, the Feeling of Regret and Indignation After-wards; the Proceedings of Meetings, and Expressions of the Contemporary Press. Boston, 1870.

Cobb, Sanford H., *The Rise of Religious Liberty in America.* New York, 1902.

Cornelison, Isaac A., *The Relation of Religion to Civil Government in the United States of America.* New York, 1895.

DeCosta, Benjamin F., *In Memoriam. Sister Sainte Claire, Order of St. Ursula.* Charlestown, 1876. An account of the convent burning.

DeCosta, Benjamin F., *The Story of Mount Benedict*. Somerville, 1893.

Desmond, Humphrey, *The Know Nothing Party*. Washington, 1904.

Dwight, Henry O., *The Centennial History of the American Bible Society*. 2 v. New York, 1916.

Evans, George H., *The Burning of the Mount Benedict Ursuline Convent*. Somerville, 1935.

Farley, John M., *The Life of John Cardinal McCloskey*. New York, 1918.

Flynn, Joseph M., *The Catholic Church in New Jersey*. Morristown, 1904.

Guilday, Peter, *A History of the Councils of Baltimore (1791–1884)*. New York, 1932.

Guilday, Peter, *The Life and Times of John England, First Bishop of Charlestown, 1786–1842*. 2 v. New York, 1927.

Hassard, J. R. G., *Life of the Most Reverend John Hughes*. New York, 1866.

Hay, M. V., *A Chain of Error in Scottish History*. New York, 1927. Useful for the European background of American anti-Catholicism.

Kapp, Friedrich, *Immigration and the Commissioners of Emigration of the State of New York*. New York, 1870.

Leahy, William, *The Catholic Church in New England*. 2 v. Boston, 1899.

Maury, Reuben, *The Wars of the Godly*. New York, 1928. Popular account of the anti-Catholic movement.

McMaster, John B., *With the Fathers*. New York, 1896. Contains an essay on "The Riotous Career of the Know Nothings."

Merriam, George A., *The Life and Times of Samuel Bowles*. 2 v. New York, 1885. Bowles, as editor of the Springfield *Republican*, was active in opposing the Know-Nothing party.

Monroe, James F., *The New England Conscience*. Boston, 1915. Contains an essay on the destruction of the Ursuline convent.

Morse, Edward L., *Samuel F. B. Morse, his Life and Journals*. 2 v. Boston, 1914.

Nason, Elias, *The Life and Public Services of Henry Wilson, Late Vice President of the United States*. Boston, 1876.

Noonan, Carroll John, *Nativism in Connecticut, 1829–1860*. Washington, 1938.

O'Daniel, V. F., *The Right Reverend Edward Dominic Fenwick, O.P., Founder of the Dominicans in the United States.* Washington, 1920.

O'Gorman, Thomas, *History of the Roman Catholic Church in the United States.* New York, 1895.

O'Malley, Thomas F., *New England's First Convent School.* ———, 1901. A brief account of the Ursuline convent.

Palmer, A. Emerson, *The New York Public School.* New York, 1905.

Schmeckebier, Laurence F., *History of the Know Nothing Party in Maryland. Johns Hopkins University Studies in History and Political Science,* XVII. Baltimore, 1899.

Scisco, L. D., *Political Nativism in New York State. Columbia University Studies in History, Economics and Public Law* (New York, 1893–) XIII (1901).

Shea, John Gilmary, *History of the Catholic Church in the United States.* 4 v. New York, 1886–1892.

Spafford, Harriet E. P., *New England Legends.* Boston, 1871. Contains an account of the burning of the Ursuline convent.

Steiner, Bernard C., *The Life of Henry W. Davis.* Baltimore, 1916.

Stickney, C., *Know Nothingism in Rhode Island. Brown University History Seminary Papers.* Providence, 1894.

Sweet, W. W., *The Story of Religions in America.* New York, 1930.

Thomas, M. Evangeline, *Nativism in the Old Northwest, 1850–1860.* Washington, 1936.

Thurston, Herbert, *No-Popery: Chapters on Anti-Papal Prejudice.* London, 1930.

Tusca, Benjamin, *Know Nothingism in Baltimore, 1854–1860.* New York, 1925.

Whitney, Louisa, *The Burning of the Convent; a Narrative of the Destruction, by a Mob, of the Ursuline School at Mount Benedict, Charlestown, as Remembered by one of the Pupils.* Boston, 1877.

Williams, Michael, *The Shadow of the Pope.* New York, 1932. A popular account of the anti-Catholic movement.

Wilson, Henry, *History of the Rise and Fall of the Slave Power in America.* 3 v. Boston, 1872–1877.

Wright, Richardson, *Forgotten Ladies.* Philadelphia, 1928. Contains a popular biography of Maria Monk.

2. Articles

"Anti-Catholic Movements in the United States," *Catholic World,* XXII (March, 1876), 810–822.

"The Anti-Catholic Riots of 1844 in Philadelphia," *American Catholic Historical Researches,* XIII (April, 1896), 50–64.

"The Anti-Catholic Spirit of the Revolution," *American Catholic Historical Researches,* VI (October, 1889), 146–178.

Bean, William G., "An Aspect of Know-Nothingism—the Immigrant and Slavery," *South Atlantic Quarterly,* XXIII (October, 1924), 319–334.

Billington, Ray A., "Anti-Catholic Propaganda and the Home Missionary Movement, 1800–1860," *Mississippi Valley Historical Review,* XXII (December, 1935), 361–384.

Billington, Ray A., "The Burning of the Charlestown Convent," *New England Quarterly,* X (June, 1937), 4–24.

Billington, Ray A., "Maria Monk and Her Influence," *Catholic Historical Review,* XXII (October, 1936), 283–296.

Billington, Ray A., "Tentative Bibliography of Anti-Catholic Propaganda in the United States (1800–1860)," *Catholic Historical Review,* XVIII (January, 1933), 492–513.

Boutwell, George S., "Kossuth in New England," *New England Magazine,* X (July, 1894), 525–543.

Brand, Carl F., "History of the Know Nothing Party in Indiana," *Indiana Magazine of History,* XVIII (1922), 47–81, 177–207, 266–280.

Caskey, W. M., "The Second Administration of Governor Andrew Johnson," *East Tennessee Historical Society Publications,* II (1930), 34–54. An account of the Know-Nothing campaign of 1855.

Cole, Arthur C., "Nativism in the Lower Mississippi Valley," *Mississippi Valley Historical Association Proceedings,* VI (1912–1913), 258–275.

Condon, Peter, "Constitutional Freedom of Religion and Revivals of Religious Intolerance," *United States Catholic Historical Society Records and Studies,* II–V (1901–1909), 401–431, 92–114, 145–217, 426–462.

Conners, Francis John, "Samuel Finley Breese Morse and the Anti-Catholic Political Movements in the United States," *Illinois Catholic Historical Review,* X (October, 1927), 83–122.

Cross, Ira, "The Origin, Principles and History of the American Party," *Iowa Journal of History and Politics,* IV (1906), 526–553.

Dohan, James H., "Our State Constitutions and Religious Liberty," *American Catholic Quarterly Review,* XL (April, 1915), 276–322.

Farrand, Max, "Immigration in the Light of History," *New Republic,* IX (December 23 and December 29, 1916).

"Fear of Catholicism in Colonial Pennsylvania," *American Catholic Historical Researches,* XVII (April, 1900), 74–77.

Foik, Paul J., "Anti-Catholic Parties in American Politics, 1776–1860," *Records of the American Catholic Historical Society of Philadelphia,* XXXVI (March, 1925), 41–69.

Fry, George T., "The Decline of Bigotry in America," *Current History,* XXVII (June, 1928), 396–402.

Gay, Constance M., "The Campaign of 1855 in Virginia and the Fall of the Know-Nothing Party," *Richmond College Historical Papers,* I (1916), 309–325.

Gladden, Washington, "The Anti-Catholic Crusade," *Century Magazine,* XLVII (March, 1894), 789–795.

Graham, J. E., "Anti-Catholic Prejudice, Ancient and Modern," *Ecclesiastical Review,* LIII (1915), 282–298.

Griffin, Martin I. J., "The Church of the Holy Trinity, Philadelphia . . . the First Opposition to Ecclesiastical Authority," *Records of the American Catholic Historical Society of Philadelphia,* XXI (March, 1910), 1–45.

Hansen, Marcus L., "The Second Colonization of New England," *New England Quarterly,* II (October, 1929), 539–560.

Hansen, Marcus L., "The Revolutions of 1848 and German Emigration," *Journal of Economic and Business History,* II (August, 1930), 630–655.

Haynes, George H., "The Causes of Know-Nothing Success in Massachusetts," *American Historical Review,* III (October, 1897), 67–82.

Haynes, George H., "A Chapter from the Local History of Know-Nothingism," *New England Magazine,* XV (September, 1896).

Haynes, George H., "A Know-Nothing Legislature," American Historical Association *Report* (1896), 175–187.

Hensel, W. V., "A Withered Twig; Dark Lantern Glimpses into

the Operation of Know Nothingism in Lancaster Sixty Years Ago," *Lancaster County Historical Society Papers,* XIX (June, 1915), 174–181.

Hewitt, Warren F., "The Know-Nothing Party in Pennsylvania," *Pennsylvania History,* II (April, 1935), 69–85.

Hughes, T., "An Alleged Popish Plot in Pennsylvania, 1756–1757," *Records of the American Catholic Historical Society of Philadelphia,* X (June, 1899), 208–221.

Hurt, Peyton, "The Rise and Fall of the 'Know-Nothings' in California," California Historical Society *Quarterly,* IX (March and June, 1930), 16–49, 99–128.

Jenkins, T. J., "Know-Nothingism in Kentucky and its Destroyer," *Catholic World,* LVII (July, 1893), 511–522.

Jones, Chester L., "The Legislative History of Exclusion Legislation," *Annals of the American Academy of Political Science,* XXXIV (September, 1909), 351–359.

Kealy, John, "A Catholic Pioneer in Maine," *America,* XL (October, 1928), 61–62. Deals with a conflict between the Reverend John Papst, S.J., and the Know-Nothings.

"Leisler's No-Popery Revolt in New York," *American Catholic Historical Researches,* XIV (July, 1897), 123–125.

O'Driscoll, Felicity, "Political Nativism in Buffalo," *Records of the American Catholic Historical Society,* September, 1937.

Oliver, John W., "Louis Kossuth's Appeal to the Middle West—1852," *Mississippi Valley Historical Review,* XIV (March, 1928), 481–495.

Overdyke, W. Darrell, "A History of the American Party in Louisiana," *Louisiana Historical Quarterly,* XV–XVI (October, 1932–July, 1933), 84–91, 256–277, 409–426, 581–588.

Page, Thomas W., "The Transportation of Immigrants and Reception Arrangements in the Nineteenth Century," *Journal of Political Economy,* XIX (November, 1911), 732–749.

Payne, Raymond, "Annals of the Leopoldine Association," *Catholic Historical Review,* I (1905), 51–63, 175–191.

"The Philadelphia Anti-Catholic Riots of 1844," *American Catholic Historical Researches,* N.S. VII (July, 1911), 231–233.

"Pope Day in the Colonies," *American Catholic Historical Researches,* N.S. III (April, 1907), 132–136.

Schafer, Joseph, "Know-Nothingism in Wisconsin," *Wisconsin Magazine of History,* VIII (September, 1924), 3–21.

Schneider, George, "Lincoln and the Anti-Know Nothing Resolutions," McLean County Historical Society *Transactions,* III (1900).

Senning, John P., "The Know-Nothing Movement in Illinois, 1854–1856," *Illinois Historical Society Journal,* VII (April, 1914), 7–33.

Shea, John G., "Pope Day in America," *United States Catholic Historical Magazine,* II (January, 1888), 1–7.

Steiner, Bernard C., "The Protestant Revolution in Maryland," American Historical Association *Report* (1907), 279–353.

Steiner, Bernard C., "The Restoration of the Proprietary of Maryland and the Legislation against the Roman Catholics during the Governorship of Capt. John Hart," American Historical Association *Report* (1899), 229–307.

Stephenson, George M., "Nativism in the Forties and Fifties with Special Reference to the Mississippi Valley," *Mississippi Valley Historical Review,* IX (December, 1922), 185–202.

Stritch, Alfred G., "Political Nativism in Cincinnati," *Records of the American Catholic Historical Society,* September, 1937.

Thompson, Mary P., "Anti-Catholic Laws in New Hampshire," *Catholic World,* LI (April–May, 1890), 22–30, 185–197.

Thompson, Ralph, "The Maria Monk Affair," *The Colophon,* Pt. 17 (1934).

"The Truth About Maria Monk," Catholic Truth Society *Publications,* XIX (1894).

Tucker, Ephraim, "The Burning of the Ursuline Convent," Worcester Society of Antiquity *Collections,* IX (1809), 40–61.

"The Very Reverend T. J. Donaghoe," *Records of the American Catholic Historical Society of Philadelphia,* XXIII (June, 1912), 69–90. Donaghoe was pastor of a church burned during the Philadelphia riots of 1844.

Walsh, J. J., "Keeping up the Protestant Tradition," *Catholic World,* CI (June, 1915), 321–331.

Watson, Thomas E., "The Truth About Maria Monk," *Watson's Magazine* (May, 1916), 3–26.

Zwierlein, F. J., "Know Nothingism in Rochester, New York," United States Catholic Historical Society *Records and Studies,* XIV (May, 1920), 20–69.

Index